PETER NORTON'S
INTRODUCTION
TO COMPUTERS
Essential Concepts
With
Microsoft Works
for Windows

GLENCOE

McGraw-Hill

New York, New York   Columbus, Ohio   Mission Hills, California   Peoria, Illinois

Library of Congress Cataloging-in-Publication Data

Norton, Peter, 1943-
    Peter Norton's introduction to computers :   Essential Concepts With Microsoft Works for Windows.
      p. cm.
      Includes index.
      ISBN 0-02-802896-1
      1. Microcomputers. 2. Microsoft Works for Windows. I. Title.
QA76.5.N6835   1995   94-25920
004--dc20   CIP

Peter Norton's Introduction to Computers :
Essential Concepts With Microsoft Works for Windows

Send all inquiries to:

Glencoe/McGraw-Hill
936 Eastwind Drive
Westerville, OH 43081

ISBN 0-02-802896-1

1 2 3 4 5 6 7 8 9   VH VH   99 98 97 96 95 94

Concept, development, and production provided by BMR, Corte Madera, California.
Development Management: Terrence P. O'Donnell
Interior Design and Art Direction: Juan Vargas, Vargas/Williams/Design
Production Supervision: Merrill Peterson, Matrix Productions
Photo Research: Monica Suder
Copyediting: Lyn Dupré
Artwork: Iikka Valli, Nadine Sokol
Electronic Composition: Edie Williams, Vargas/Williams/Design
Color Separation: Four Lakes Colorgraphics

CONTENTS

■ ■ ■ ■ ■ ■ ■ ■ ■ ■ ■ ■ ■ ■ ■ ■ ■

CHAPTER 3: USING MICROCOMPUTER SOFTWARE   69

PREFACE

■ ■ ■ ■ ■ ■ ■ ■ ■ ■ ■ ■ ■ ■ ■ ■ ■

You are entering a world where the skills you learn in this course will be fundamental to your success. Because computing has changed, the need for strong conceptual and practical computer skills has grown. The computer is not like any other appliance: You cannot treat it as you would the telephone—as a "black box."

Computers have gotten easier to use while they've become more powerful. The ways of using them either alone or in the networked environment you may find at work have grown into a large array of options for you, the end user.

This book should help you to become an intelligent end user of this important technology. Our goal is to turn a mysterious "black box" into a comprehensible "glass box," so that you can make more intelligent choices about everything that affects your information-technology needs: what computer, operating systems, and applications software do you need? How should you set up your file system to save space and still be accessible? What kinds of information and tools do you need on the computer's "desktop"? How can you customize the way you use your computer to increase your personal efficiency? How can you communicate effectively across a network with others in your organization and outside it?

Almost everything we do in our "information society" depends somewhat on information technology. No matter what you do, chances are that your personal and professional growth can be enhanced with the intelligent use of information technology. The challenge is to incorporate the basic concepts and skills of computing as appropriate into whatever your career and personal goals may be: a business career or a career of service as a health professional, teacher, or scholar. We hope that this book gives you the tools to reach your goals.

Peter Norton's Introduction to Computers: Essential Concepts With Microsoft Works for Windows combines the best of Peter Norton's complete computer concepts textbook with a tutorial on the leading integrated software program: Microsoft Works for Windows. This textbook contains all the information to empower you to become an intelligent user of computer software and technology. And in this single-volume format, you get all this information at a special low price.

This *Microsoft Works for Windows Tutorial* is only one of the instructional tools that complement *Peter Norton's Introduction to Computers*. Glencoe and Peter Norton have teamed up to provide a new approach to computer education, one not reflected in traditional computer textbooks. The text and its ancillary materials are grounded in the philosophy that it is knowledgeable and empowered end users who will provide the gains in productivity that both businesses and individuals need to achieve in the 1990s and beyond. Mere button pushing is not enough; in order to handle more and more complex computer tasks, both in the workplace and in the home, computer users must understand the concepts behind their computer hardware and software.

v

Reviewers

James Dailey, Rider College
Elizabeth Davis, Texas State Technical College
Pat Duffy, Trenton State College
Guy Giardine, Burlington County College
Lynn Groves, Mankato Technical College
Sallyann Hanson, Mercer County College
Dick Hol, Community Colleges of Spokane
David Letcher, Trenton State College
Perry Lund, William Penn College
Gary Margot, Ashland University
Len Parrino, Essex County College
Donald L. Phillips, University of North Florida
Sylvia Clark Pulliam, Western Kentucky University
John R. Ross, Fox Valley Technical College
Lorilee Sadler, Indiana University
Judy Scholl, Austin Community College
Devinder Sud, Devry Technical Institute
David Whitney, San Francisco State University
Maryanne Zlotow, College of DuPage

Photo Credits

Chapter 1   Figure 1-1: NYSE; Figure 1-2: General Electric; Figure 1-3: Jet Propulsion Lab; Figure 1-4: Dana L. Luke/Compaq; Figure 1-5: BCE; Figure 1-6: IBM; Figure 1-8: Intel; Figure 1-9: Seagate; Figure 1-10: Tandy/Radio Shack; Figure 1-14: Micrografx; Figure 1-16: Zeos; Figure 1-17: Apple Computer, Inc.; Figure 1-18: Zeos; Figure 1-19: Texas Instruments, Inc.; Page 20: Hewlett Packard; Figure 1-23: Kinesis Corporation; Figure 1-24: IBM.

Chapter 2   Figure 2-2: Intel; Figure 2-4, 2-5: IBM; Figure 2-6: Logitech; Figure 2-7: EO, Inc.; Figure 2-8: IBM; Figure 2-9: NCR; Figure 2-10: The Complete PC; Figure 2-11: Hewlett Packard; Figure 2-12: Apple Computer, Inc.; Figure 2-15: Texas Instruments; Figure 2-24: IBM; Figure 2-26: Tandy.

Chapter 3   Figure 3-10, 3-11: Microsoft; Figure 3-33: Q & E Software.

OUR TECHNOLOGICAL SOCIETY

OBJECTIVES

When you complete this chapter, you will be able to do the following:

- Discuss some of the many ways computers have an impact on our lives.
- Recognize four kinds of computer hardware.
- Explain the purpose of software.
- List the common types of computers available today and describe what kind of job each does best.
- Discuss the importance of ergonomics.

The computer is a truly amazing machine. Few tools let you do so many different tasks. Whether you want to track an investment, publish a newsletter, or design a building, you can do it with a computer.

In this chapter, we'll look at some of the many ways that computers affect us. We'll also take a peek under the hood of these magnificent machines to see what really makes them tick. We'll talk about the various types of computers and what tasks each does best. Finally, we'll address the issue of ergonomics, the physical relationship between the user and the computer, and how these machines can be used in a safe, comfortable working environment.

THE MULTIPURPOSE TOOL

Figure 1-1

At the New York Stock Exchange, traders use computers to buy and sell shares. Transactions that once took hours can now be completed in seconds, vastly increasing the volume of business.

Until the mid-1960s, computers were vastly expensive, special-purpose machines that only huge institutions such as governments and universities could afford. These early computers were used primarily to perform complex numerical tasks, such as calculating the precise orbit of Mars or recording statistics for the Bureau of the Census.

It wasn't until the mid-1960s that computers began to revolutionize the business world. IBM introduced its System/360 mainframe computer in April 1964, and ultimately sold some 33,000 of these machines. In the 1970s, Digital Equipment Corporation (DEC) took two more giant steps forward with the introduction of their PDP-11 and the VAX computer, which came in many sizes to meet different needs and budgets. Since then, computers have continued to shrink, and to provide more power for less money. The desktop computers that you see in homes and schools are now powerful enough for many business uses.

Along with computers' burgeoning role in business, other uses for these machines evolved rapidly. In this section, we'll explore some of the diverse ways that computers touch our lives.

Computers in Business

Computers are so fundamental to our modern society that, without them, our economy would grind to a halt. Every year, American businesses and governments process about 400 billion transactions, and the number is growing by 73 billion transactions annually (Figure 1-1). In the last few decades, computers have radically altered business practices, not just in this country, but also around the world.

Whether or not you work in an office, the way businesses use computers affects you every day. You're faced with computer-stored information about yourself every time you go to the bank, renew a subscription, or buy something by mail. From automatic tellers to credit cards, computers are part of the way we live.

Medicine and Health Care

In medicine today, computers are used for everything from diagnosing illnesses to monitoring patients during surgery and controlling permanent prostheses.

Several interesting medical applications use small, special-purpose computers that operate within the human body to help the body function better. Pacemakers are one example. Another is the cochlear implant, a special kind of hearing aid that allows profoundly deaf people to hear. Part of the device is a small computer that transforms sound into electrical impulses, which are then transmitted to the brain by a device implanted in the inner ear.

Another use of computers in the hospital is for automated imaging techniques, which produce a fully dimensional picture with much more detail and less risk than standard X-ray films. The first widespread type of imaging was computerized axial tomography (CAT) scans. More recent techniques include magnetic resonance imaging (MRI), shown in Figure 1-2, and positron emission tomography (PET). Using these techniques, doctors can look inside a person's body and study each organ in detail. As a result, conditions that might have been difficult to diagnose a few years ago can often be pinpointed at an early stage.

Education

In the last ten years, small computers have sparked a revolution in education. Everyone from preschool children to senior citizens can now put computers to work for their own intellectual benefit. You'll find computers in classrooms, museums, and libraries, and they're rapidly becoming as essential to the learning process as are books, paper, and pens.

Teachers are especially excited about the computer as an interactive learning tool. Unlike a recorded television show, computer-aided education (CAE) programs can prompt viewers for feedback and respond in appropriate ways. Similarly, interactive tutorials can teach, test for understanding, and reteach based on how much the student has learned. For example, a program called Calculus, published by Broderbund Software, covers an entire year of the subject. The program explains each major topic and then demonstrates it with solved examples and even short animated segments. If the testing feature of the program is turned on, it also presents the student with a few problems to solve. If the student solves the problems correctly, the program proceeds to the next topic. Otherwise, it reviews the area where the student is having trouble.

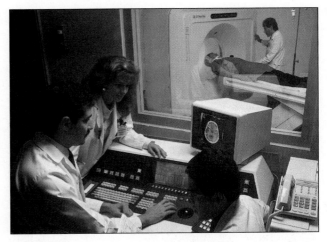

Figure 1-2

Magnetic resonance imaging (MRI) uses radio waves and a strong magnetic field to scan a patient's body.
A computer assembles this information into a picture that shows internal organs and certain types of diseased tissue.

Science

Scientists use computers to develop theories, to collect and test data, and to exchange information electronically with colleagues around the world. Researchers can access databases in distant locations—all without going any further than the closest computer.

It's also possible to simulate complex events with computers. Scientists can use powerful computers to generate detailed studies of how earthquakes affect buildings or pollution affects weather patterns. Sophisticated software allows intricate molecules to be designed, diagramed, and manipulated with a computer.

It would be impossible to explore outer space without computers. Satellites and space probes have beamed back to Earth a wealth of information concerning our solar system and the cosmos (Figure 1-3). Every second, giant satellite dishes receive thousands of signals, which are then transmitted to NASA's computers for detailed analysis. Researchers are even scanning the heavens with radio telescopes in an attempt to seek out signs of life elsewhere in the universe.

Figure 1-3

This close-up view of Jupiter's atmosphere is one of tens of thousands of pictures transmitted to the Earth by NASA's Voyager probes. Assembled and enhanced by computer, such images open up striking new vistas to Earthbound astronomers.

Archaeology

At one time, scientists used X rays to examine mummies, but the results were just that—X rays, without surface detail. Archaeologists can now use computers to peer through the wrappings of a mummy. Researchers at the University of Chicago's Oriental Institute used a CAT scanner to analyze a mummy's

Figure 1-4

An engineer inspects a prototype of an automobile engine fan that was designed and made entirely by computer. The computer-based design was used to guide a robot-controlled laser beam, which fabricated the fan from a vat of liquid plastic.

length and width in 3-millimeter visual segments. A computer then combined the segments into a detailed three-dimensional model of the person inside the wrappings.

Archaeologists also use computers to reconstruct information about past civilizations. For example, archaeologists studying a Mayan temple in the Guatemalan jungle used a computerized surveyor's transit to plot their precise location by reflecting a laser beam off a satellite fixed in orbit. Once they established their own position, they produced a highly accurate three-dimensional map of the temple by feeding their survey data into a computer.

Engineering and Architecture

Although drafting tables and T-squares are still around, their days may be numbered. An engineer or architect designing a product can be far more productive with a computer than with pencil and paper.

When you design an object with a computer, you create an electronic model by describing all three dimensions of the object. If you want to see the object from a different perspective, you can tell the computer to display another view. On paper, you have to produce a different drawing of each view, and, if you change the design, you have to redraw every affected view.

Designing objects with a computer this way is called computer-aided design (CAD). Specialized CAD systems are available for designing almost anything—from houses, cars, and buildings to molecules and spacecraft. Knowledge of CAD is now required for many engineering jobs. Figure 1-4 shows an engineer using CAD to design a mechanical part.

Manufacturing

In addition to product design, computers are playing an ever-increasing role in manufacturing. In some factories, computers control virtually everything. For example, take a power plant that generates steam. In this kind of factory, a computer monitors pressures and temperatures at hundreds of critical points throughout the plant. If the pressure or temperature in a pipe or tank exceeds a specified level, the computer can regulate the process directly by turning valves and adjusting burners.

Many factories use computerized robotic arms to position and weld components into place or to do repetitive or hazardous work. Automobile plants use robots to perform numerous tasks, including painting, welding, and cutting and bending sheet metal for body parts. Manufacturing with computers and robotics is called **computer-aided manufacturing (CAM)**. More recently, **computer-integrated manufacturing (CIM)** has given computers an additional role in designing the product, ordering parts, and planning production.

Legal Practice and Law Enforcement

The legal profession has begun to make extensive use of computers. Attorneys are now able to search quickly through huge collections of data, known as **data-**

bases, for precedents set by similar cases, documents, and depositions. With a computer, the time required to complete such a search can be reduced from hours to minutes or even seconds.

Police departments have been using **mobile data terminals (MDTs)** in squad cars for years (see Figure 1-5). When a police officer pulls over a car, the MDT, given just the vehicle license number for reference, can tell the officer who owns the car, whether it has been reported stolen, and other information. Using the driver's license number of the person behind the wheel, the officer can find out whether the license has expired, and whether there is a warrant for the driver's arrest.

Advanced techniques are used in other areas of law enforcement. In the courtroom, for example, a technique known as **DNA fingerprinting** can positively identify a person from traces of blood, skin, or hair left at the crime scene. Because the DNA in every person's body is unique, DNA fingerprinting can help to match the evidence to the suspect, confirming the guilt or innocence of the accused.

Government

There are well over 250 million people living in the United States. Three ways that the federal government uses computers to collect, process, and store the vast amount of information about its citizens are through the Social Security Administration, the Bureau of the Census, and the Internal Revenue Service.

Social Security numbers are issued to each U.S. citizen, and to other people who work or bank in the United States. Computers are used to correlate and update information about these people's earnings throughout their lives. Then, based on these tabulations, the government calculates what benefits should be paid to each person upon retirement.

The Bureau of the Census has counted people and surveyed their life conditions in the United States every ten years since 1790. In fact, it was the first civilian arm of government to use computers on a large scale. Today, much more powerful computers assemble census information. Government planners and social scientists use it to calculate the number of representatives each state sends to Congress, to keep tabs on the rise and fall of personal income, to track the housing and migration patterns of different groups, and for many other purposes.

The Internal Revenue Service uses its computers to record income-tax returns for millions of individuals and businesses every year. As you may suspect, the Internal Revenue Service doesn't just take your word for the amount you claim you owe when filing your taxes. It uses computers to check and cross-check returns with information received from many sources throughout the year.

The Military

Today, the military uses computers in a variety of ways aboard ships, submarines, and airplanes, as well as in certain weapons and satellites. Often, these computers are linked with land-based networks that tie together all the systems for optimum allocation of resources.

The military also uses computers in many of the same ways that businesses and other organizations do. In fact, military computers keep track of what may be the largest payrolls and human-resource management systems in the world.

Figure 1-5

Quebec patrol officers use a mobile telephone and terminal to tie into the main police computer. By checking central computer files, they can quickly fill in background about a crime and identify possible suspects.

Figure 1-6

A professional musician records a composition with a MIDI system. The digitally synthesized instrument parts are laid down individually, and can be played back together in any key. MIDI software can even transcribe the music as a printed score.

Entertainment

People in entertainment industries have found a wide range of uses for computers. Musicians use computers to create an amazing range of instruments and sounds simply by playing a keyboard. The Musical Instrument Digital Interface (MIDI) is a system that synchronizes hardware and software that produce electronic tones. Sound is a pattern of waves, and computers can bend and alter those waves into musical shapes. A musician can touch one synthesizer key to produce the sound of a violin, and another to clash a cymbal. By carefully mixing hundreds of thousands of sounds, a musician in a studio can record a pop song or a symphony (Figure 1-6). Computers also add exciting effects to live performances. Using a voice modulator, for example, a singer can hum notes to produce the sounds of various musical instruments.

In a drama theater, technicians can use coordinated computer-controlled lighting cues to brighten or dim the stage. The performing artists might even use computers to control the images and sounds of the performance itself.

Astounding computerized special effects have been achieved in the motion-picture industry. Movies now contain many visual tricks that could never be accomplished without the aid of computers. A number of ground-breaking films, including *Star Wars, Raiders of the Lost Ark, E.T., Terminator 2*, and *Jurassic Park*, have relied on firms such as Industrial Light and Magic (ILM), a company that has been at the forefront in pioneering cinemagraphic effects. At ILM, technicians can create the illusion of a locomotive flying through the air or a robot transforming into a human being through the use of computer graphics.

From *Tron* to *The Simpsons*, computerized animation and coloration have revitalized contemporary animated film. Elaborate scenes can now be animated that might once have been too costly to bring to life, such as the flying-carpet ride in Disney's *Aladdin*. Using computer programs based on the precise mathematical laws of physics, animators can create in a few hours what used to take days with hand-drawing techniques.

Computers at Home

You may be using computers in your home every day without realizing that you are. Most televisions contain small computers that automatically fine-tune the image, select the brightness, and correct the color tones. Many electrical appliances—such as washing machines, microwave ovens, dishwashers, and sewing machines—also use small computers to help them run more efficiently.

The environment of the home itself can be controlled and maintained by computers. A prototype intelligent house in Japan contains dozens of hidden sensors that feed information about temperature, humidity, airflow, human presence, and carbon dioxide levels to a central computer. The computer can monitor preset comfort levels and determine whether to turn on a heater or an air conditioner, or to open or close windows.

Although the Japanese intelligent house is at the cutting edge of computer-controlled comfort and convenience, American home designers are working toward features that are more immediately achievable. These features include a programmable electrical system that can control particular outlets and appliances. For example, when leaving for work, you might set the system for "At Work." The system would automatically turn off the lights, arm the security system, and let the temperature drop or rise to conserve energy. Just before your programmed return time, it would heat or cool the house in time for your arrival.

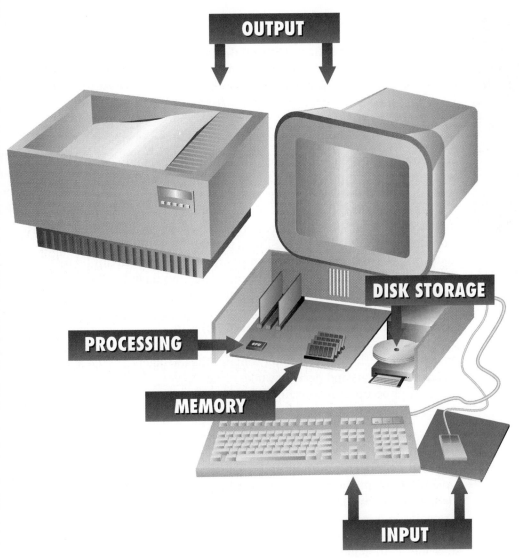

Figure 1-7

A computer system has four main hardware components: the processor; memory; input/output devices such as a keyboard, mouse, and monitor; and storage devices such as floppy- and hard-disk drives.

LOOKING INSIDE THE MACHINE

You may be wondering, how can a computer store and organize so much information, and do it so fast and accurately? These questions begin our adventure inside the computer. Like any machine, a computer has many parts. In this section, we'll look at the main components that make up a computer, so you will gain a basic understanding of how the parts come together to form a working computer.

Regardless of its shape or size, every computer that people use directly has five basic components:

1. A **processor**
2. **Memory**
3. **Input/output devices**
4. **Disk storage**
5. **Programs**

The first four items are the physical components of the machine, known collectively as **hardware** (see Figure 1-7). Item 5 consists of **software**—electronic

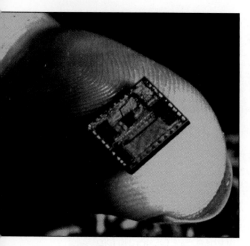

Figure 1-8

A CPU chip is tiny—typically, it is less than the width of a finger.

instructions that people write to tell the hardware what to do. Although the hardware of a computer is capable of performing marvelous tasks, it can't actually accomplish any of them without the vital instructions that software provides. In this section, we'll look at the physical components of the machine, the hardware. Then, we'll turn to the software that brings the physical parts to life.

The Processor

The complex procedure that transforms raw input data into useful information for output is called **processing**. To perform this transformation, the computer uses two components, the processor and memory.

The **processor** is the "brain" of the computer, the part that interprets and carries out instructions. In large computers, the processor often comprises a number of **chips**—slivers of silicon or other material that are etched with many tiny electronic circuits. The chips are plugged into **circuit boards**—rigid rectangular cards that contain the circuitry that ties them to other chips and to other circuit boards. In the small computers called **microcomputers** or **personal computers**, the processor is a single chip, called a **microprocessor**.

The term **central processing unit (CPU)** is used loosely to refer to a computer's processor, whether the latter is a set of circuit boards or a single microprocessor. The CPU of a computer contains the intelligence of the machine; it is where calculations and decisions take place. As you can see in Figure 1-8, this brainpower occupies an amazingly small space.

Memory

The CPU uses the computer's **memory** to hold pieces of information while it works with them and as a scratch pad for calculations. These pieces of information are represented electronically in the memory chip's circuitry, and while it remains in memory, the computer can access it directly. This built-in memory is called **random access memory (RAM)**. Unlike human memory, which can store information indefinitely, RAM holds information only while the computer is on. When you turn off or reset the computer, the information disappears unless you have saved it on a storage device.

The more RAM a computer has, the more it can do. Because the amount of memory in a computer affects the computer's capabilities, people often refer to that amount when describing the machine. The most common unit of measure for computer memory is the byte. A **byte** can be described as the amount of memory it takes to store a single character. Thus, each letter on this page would occupy a single byte of memory.

When we talk about memory, the numbers are often so large that we use a shorthand term to describe the values. **Kilobyte** and **megabyte** are the two most common terms used for this purpose. Although people often use them loosely to mean 1,000 bytes and 1 million bytes, in the context of computer memory these terms don't mean exactly that. A kilobyte is actually 1,024 bytes of memory, and a megabyte is 1,024 kilobytes—or 1,048,576 bytes. If you're wondering why these numbers aren't round, take a look at the Techview on page 9.

Kilobyte and *megabyte* are often abbreviated as *KB* and *MB*. So, a computer with 4 MB of memory actually has $4 \times 1,048,576 = 4,194,304$ bytes.

Why Isn't Memory Measured in Round Numbers?

At its lowest level, everything in a computer's memory is represented by numbers, whether the information consists of letters, numerals, punctuation marks, symbols, or computer commands. The computer represents these numbers with just two symbols—a 0 or a 1—rather than with the ten numeric symbols with which we're familiar from the base-10 number system. In other words, the computer uses *binary numbers* instead of decimal numbers.

In the decimal system, when you raise 10 to a power, the result is always a multiple of 10. For example, you always get a round number, as shown here:

$$10^1 = 10$$
$$10^2 = 100$$
$$10^3 = 1,000$$
$$10^6 = 1,000,000$$
$$10^9 = 1,000,000,000$$
$$10^{12} = 1,000,000,000,000$$

But when you raise 2 to a power in base 2, the result is a multiple of 2, as shown here:

$$2^1 = 2$$
$$2^2 = 4$$
$$2^3 = 8 \text{ byte}$$
$$2^8 = 256$$
$$2^9 = 512$$
$$2^{10} = 1,024 \text{ kilobyte (KB)}$$
$$2^{20} = 1,048,576 \text{ megabyte (MB)}$$
$$2^{30} = 1,073,741,824 \text{ gigabyte (GB)}$$

Because we are accustomed to describing quantities in powers of 10, we often use the terms kilobyte (1 thousand bytes), megabyte (1 million bytes), gigabyte (1 billion bytes), and terabyte (1 trillion bytes) to refer to these base-2 values. However, a true megabyte is 1,048,576—rather than exactly 1,000,000—bytes.

When the numbers are relatively small, the difference between a base-2 number and the base-10 approximation of it is also small; as numbers grow larger, however, the difference can become significant. A true gigabyte (1,073,741,824), for example, is about 70 megabytes more than 1 billion bytes.

Input/Output

Input/output (I/O) comprises all the ways a computer communicates with users and other machines or devices. **Input devices** accept data and instructions from the user. **Output devices** return processed data, that is, information, back to the user. Without I/O, a computer would be isolated. It couldn't receive instructions, and even if it had instructions permanently built in, it couldn't communicate the results of its work.

Over the years, input devices have been built in many forms for many special purposes. The most common input device is the **keyboard**, which accepts letters, numbers, and commands from the user. In addition, people often use a **mouse**, which lets them draw on the screen and give commands by pointing and clicking. Some other input devices are **trackballs**, **joysticks**, and **scanners**.

The mouse and trackball, as well as another instrument called a **digitizing tablet**, allow you to create images directly on screen. The joystick is especially well suited for quick-moving video games. A machine called a **scanner** can copy a printed page into the computer's memory, eliminating the time-consuming step of keying input manually.

The function of output is to present processed data—information—to the user. The most common output devices are the display screen, known as the **monitor**, and the **printer**. The computer sends output to the monitor when the

Figure 1-9

A hard-disk drive stores information on a stack of rigid platters that are normally sealed inside a dust-free chamber. As the platters spin, read/write heads dart across them to find or record data.

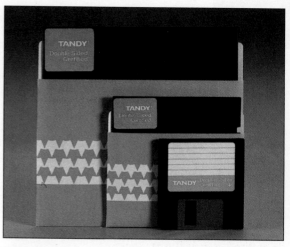

Figure 1-10

Over the years, floppy disks have shrunk while their capacity has greatly increased. The 3.5-inch disk at the right can hold more data than can either of the larger two disks.

user needs only to see the output. It sends output to the printer when the user needs a physical, or hard, copy. Multimedia systems can include stereo speakers as additional output devices.

So far, we've looked at the ways a computer communicates with people, but there's another important type of I/O. A computer also needs to communicate with other devices and machines. Although this process is usually hidden from the user, it's important to understand that the ability to communicate with other devices is a fundamental function of a computer.

Storage

A computer can function with just processing, memory, and I/O; but to be really useful, however, it also needs a place to keep data that it isn't processing currently. The purpose of **storage** is to hold data that the computer isn't using.

It's helpful to think of storage as an electronic file cabinet, and of memory as an electronic worktable. When you need to work with a set of data, the computer retrieves the data from the file cabinet and puts it on the table. When you no longer need the data, you put it back into the file cabinet. Although the processor can't work directly with data stored in the file cabinet, storage has three advantages over memory. First, there's a lot more room in storage than in memory. Second, storage retains its contents when the computer is turned off, whereas the data you put in memory disappears when you shut down the computer. Third, storage is much cheaper than memory.

The most common storage medium is the **magnetic disk**. As its name implies, a disk is a round, flat object that spins around its center. **Read/write heads**, which are similar to the heads of a tape recorder or VCR, float above and below the disk near its surface.

The device that holds a disk is called a **disk drive**. Some disks are built into their drive and aren't meant to be removed. Other kinds of drives allow you to remove and replace disks. Most personal computers have a nonremovable hard disk, as shown in Figure 1-9. In addition, there are usually one or two floppy-disk drives, which allow you to use removable floppy disks. Typically, a hard disk can store far more data than can a floppy, so the hard disk is used as the computer's primary filing cabinet. Floppy disks are used to load new programs or data onto the hard disk, to trade data with other users, or to make a second, backup copy of the data on the hard disk.

A computer can read and write information on a hard disk much faster than it can on a floppy disk. This speed differential occurs because a hard disk is built with heavier materials, spins much faster than a floppy disk, and is sealed inside a chamber where air or dust particles cannot get into the way of the heads. In fact, when a hard disk spins, the heads "fly" above the surface of the disk at a height of about fifteen-millionths (0.000015) of an inch, or about one-hundredth the diameter of a dust particle. Because you can remove floppy disks from a computer, they're encased in a plastic or vinyl cover to protect them from fingerprints and dust. Figure 1-10 shows the evolution of floppy disks from the old 8-inch disks, used in the late 1970s, to a common current form, the 3.5-inch floppy disk.

SOFTWARE BRINGS THE MACHINE TO LIFE

For the most part, computers are general-purpose machines: Many can be used just as effectively to work with numbers as they can to create documents or drawings, or to control other machines. The ingredient that sets up a computer to perform a certain task is **software**—electronic instructions that usually reside in storage. A specific set of these instructions is called a **program**. When a computer is using a particular program, we say it is **running** or **executing** that program. Because programs tell the machine's physical components what to do, without them a computer couldn't do anything. It would be just a box of metal and plastic.

Although the array of programs available is vast and varied, most software can be divided into two major categories: **system software** and **application software**. One major type of system software, called operating-system software, tells the computer how to use its own components. Application software tells the computer how to accomplish specific tasks for the user.

Operating Systems

When you turn on a computer, it goes through several steps to prepare itself for use. The first step is a self-test: The computer identifies the devices that are attached to it, counts the amount of memory available, and does a quick check to see whether the memory is functioning properly.

Next, the computer looks for a special program called an **operating system**. The operating system tells the computer how to interact with the user and how to use devices such as the disk drives, keyboard, and monitor. When it finds the operating system, the computer loads that program into memory. Because the operating system is needed to control many of the computer's most basic functions, it continues to run until the computer is turned off.

After the computer finds and runs the operating system, it's ready to accept commands from an input device—usually the keyboard or a mouse. At this point, the user can issue commands to the computer. A command might, for example, list the programs stored on the computer's disk or make the computer run one of those programs.

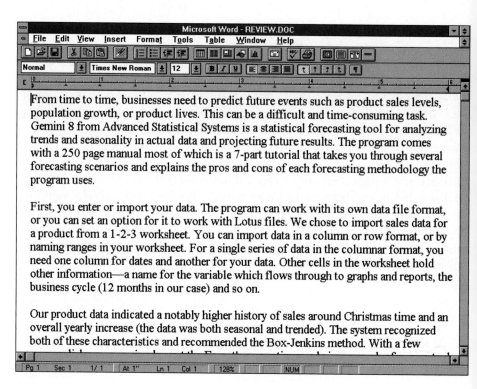

Figure 1-11

Microsoft Word for Windows is a full-featured word processor for the Windows environment that includes tools for checking spelling and grammar.

Companies that build computers don't necessarily develop their own operating systems. In fact, most IBM PCs and compatibles run one of four popular systems written by various software concerns: DOS, Unix, OS/2, or Microsoft Windows NT. One major hardware company that does create its own operating system is Apple Computer. Apple Macintosh computers will only run Apple's Macintosh operating system and Apple's version of Unix, A/UX.

Application Software

A computer that is running only an operating system isn't very useful. Because the operating system is mostly for the benefit of the computer, other programs are required to make the computer useful for people. The term *application software* describes programs that are for people. Application software has been written to do almost every task imaginable. There are literally thousands of these programs available for applications from doing word processing to selecting a college to attend.

There are several major categories of applications software. These categories are

- Business applications
- Utility applications
- Personal applications
- Entertainment applications

Business Applications. In spite of a growing trend toward use of computers in the home, the great majority of personal computers are still used in a business environment. (Of course, many of the applications that businesses need are also enormously valuable to individuals.) Business applications that

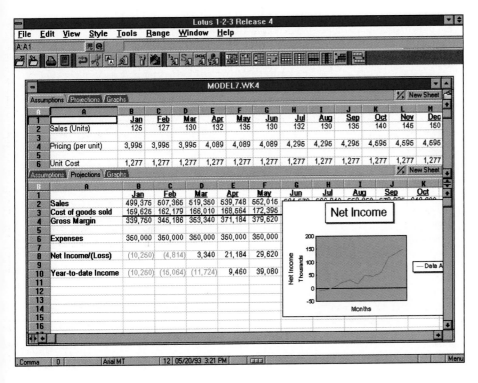

Figure 1-12

Lotus 1-2-3 is a popular spreadsheet program for analyzing numeric data and creating graphs and presentation-quality reports.

are widespread and most common are word processors, spreadsheets, and databases.

Although you can think of a **word processor** as a computerized version of a typewriter, these programs are actually far more capable than their mechanical predecessors. Most word processors not only allow you to make changes and corrections easily, but also let you check the spelling and even the grammar in your document, change the appearance of the type, add graphics, merge address lists with letters for group mailings, and generate indexes and tables of contents. You can use a word processor to create almost any kind of document: term papers, business letters, legal documents, newsletters, or even a book. Figure 1-11 shows a popular word processing program in action.

A useful companion for a word processor is software that handles **page layout** (or desktop publishing). Combining the functions of a traditional typesetter and a layout artist, a page-layout program merges the output of word processors and graphics programs to design professional-looking pages that are ready for the printer. Although many word processors can also do this, page-layout programs have more sophisticated features. Businesses use page-layout programs to create advertisements and sales catalogs. Publishers use them to lay out magazines and books.

Spreadsheet programs, such as the one shown in Figure 1-12, are number crunchers. The first popular spreadsheet program, developed for the Apple II computer, was called VisiCalc. The name was short for "Visible Calculator." A spreadsheet program displays a large grid of columns and rows that you can view one portion at a time. The areas where columns and rows meet are called **cells**. You can put text, numbers, or formulas into cells to create a worksheet, a kind of computerized ledger. Spreadsheets can also generate graphs and charts to show the relationships among numbers more vividly. Today, many spreadsheets are three-dimensional, allowing you to create not just a single worksheet,

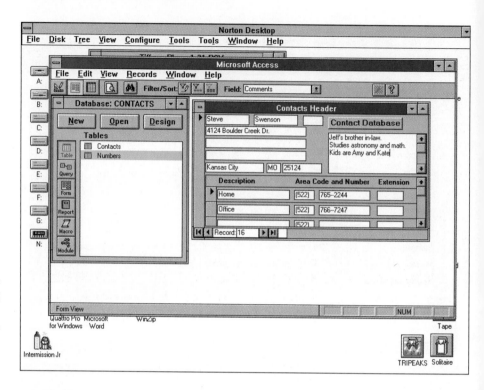

Figure 1-13

Microsoft Access is a database management system for storing and retrieving data. This database stores the addresses, phone numbers, and other information about friends and contacts.

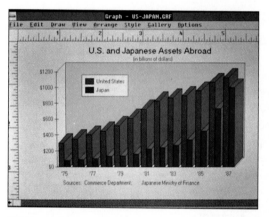

Figure 1-14

Presentation software such as Micrografx Graph can take information directly from electronic spreadsheets and databases to create high-impact graphs such as the one shown here.

but a stack of them that resembles an entire pad of ledger paper, with each sheet linked electronically to the others.

Database software (Figure 1-13) extends your ability to organize the data stored in your computer and provides many different means for searching out specific facts. When you put files into a filing cabinet, you generally arrange them in some logical order—often in alphabetical order by name. You can do this sorting with a database as well, but you're not limited to organizing just by name. You can file the same information by several categories, such as by company, geographical region, and birth date, or any way you want. Then, when you need to retrieve information from the database, you can look it up using any of the categories you've established. If you can't remember someone's name, but you know whom they work for, you can find him or her by entering his or her employer's name. You can also use the computer to select only those records that meet certain conditions. For example, a business could use a database program to list the names of all employees whose birthdays fall during the current month.

Graphics applications, a fourth type, come in several forms. Some are used to create illustrations from scratch; the user paints with electronic pointing devices instead of pencils or brushes. Such programs are referred to as either *paint* or *draw* programs, depending on how the software creates the image. Another type of business graphics software is **presentation graphics applications** (Figure 1-14). These programs create colorful, professional-quality graphs and charts based on numerical data that usually are imported from another program, such as a spreadsheet.

CAD software is yet another type of graphics software. CAD programs are most often used by architects and engineers to draw buildings or products before building or manufacturing gets underway.

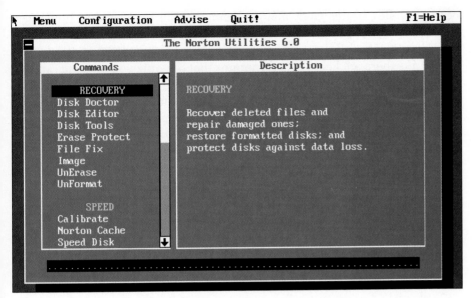

Figure 1-15

The Norton Utilities are a collection of useful programs for fixing damaged data files, preserving system security, and managing software and hardware devices on a computer.

Utilities. **Utilities**, which comprise the second category of application software, help you to manage and maintain your computer. This broad category of software includes many useful programs. There are so many tasks that you can't do, or can't do easily, with just the basic operating system and application software that many personal-computer users consider utilities a necessity.

Utility programs provide menus so you can easily choose programs to run, allow you to recover information that you accidentally delete from your computer, improve the speed or efficiency of your machine, and help you to organize the information on your system. Figure 1-15 shows the Norton Utilities, a collection of tools and programs for maintaining PC computer systems.

Personal Applications. As computers become more popular, software developers constantly come up with programs designed to take the drudgery out of personal chores and even to make those chores fun. For little more than the price of a hardcover book, you can buy a program that makes balancing your checkbook a breeze or helps you redesign the interior of your home. Programs such as these make up the third category of application software—personal applications. Other programs that fall into this category allow you to maintain a personal address book and appointment calendar, to do your banking without leaving home, to send electronic mail anywhere in the world, and even to connect to information services that provide large databases of valuable information. There's a program to do just about any job you can imagine, and the best thing about these applications is that most of them are inexpensive—in fact, some of them are free.

Entertainment Applications. Entertainment software is the fourth application software category. Arcade-style video games, flight simulators, interactive "whodunit" mysteries, and mind-bending puzzles are a few examples of the many entertainment programs that are available. Many educational programs can be considered entertainment software. For example, programs that teach children how to do mathematics, how to recognize the alphabet, or how to read whole words and sentences are almost always presented as games with rewards for correct answers. These programs can be superb educational tools because while children enjoy playing them, the children also learn fundamental skills.

Educational games aren't limited to the three Rs, though. For older children and adults there are geography programs that can quiz you on state capitals, state names, countries and their flags.

As you can see, the software industry is a fast-moving and innovative field. Every day, perceptive developers find new problems for software to solve, providing openings for new products. Competition constantly raises the stakes, fostering better and more imaginative software, at lower and lower prices.

THE SHAPES OF COMPUTERS TODAY

Computers come in many sizes and capabilities. The terms that describe the different types of computers have been around for some time, although the capabilities of each type have changed quickly. The terms are as follows:

- Supercomputer
- Mainframe
- Minicomputer
- Workstation
- Personal computer

All these types of computers can be connected together to form networks of computers, but each individual computer, whether or not it's on a network, falls into one of these categories. Many of today's microcomputers are as much as 50 times more powerful than their counterparts of a decade ago.

Supercomputers

A **supercomputer** is the most powerful computer available at a given time. These machines are built to process huge amounts of information and to do so very quickly. For example, scientists build models of complex processes and simulate the processes on a supercomputer. One such process is nuclear fission. A supercomputer is used to model the actions and reactions of literally millions of atoms as they interact, so scientists know exactly what will happen during every millisecond of a nuclear chain reaction.

Another complex study for which scientists used a supercomputer involved air pollution in Los Angeles. To create an accurate simulation of the Los Angeles basin and to predict the effects of various strategies for pollution control required a model that involved more than 500,000 variables, including geographic elevations, temperatures, and airborne chemicals. This simulation would have taken about 45 hours on a minicomputer. The supercomputer did it in ½ hour.

Because computer technology changes so quickly, the advanced capabilities of a supercomputer today may become the standard features next year, and next year's supercomputer will be vastly more powerful than today's. Supercomputers can cost from $10 million to $30 million, and consume enough electricity to power 100 homes.

Mainframe Computers

The largest type of computer in common use is the mainframe. **Mainframe computers** are designed to handle tremendous amounts of input, output, and storage. For example, consider the California Department of Motor Vehicles. This state agency maintains offices in every major city in California, each of which has many employees who work at computer terminals. A **terminal** is a special kind of computer that doesn't have its own CPU or storage; it's just an I/O device that acts as a window into another computer located somewhere else. The terminals at the California DMV offices are all connected to a common database in the state capital. The database is controlled by a mainframe computer that can handle the input and output needs of all the terminals connected to it. Each user has continuous access to the driving records and administrative information for every licensed driver and vehicle in the state—literally millions of records. Handling this volume of user access would be impossible on smaller systems.

Today's mainframe computers generally cost from $200,000 to several million dollars. It used to be common for mainframe computers to occupy entire rooms or even an entire floor of a high-rise building. They typically were placed inside sealed glass offices with special air conditioning to keep them cool, and raised floors for all the wiring needed to tie the machine together. This setup isn't used much anymore. Today, a typical mainframe computer looks like an unimposing row of large file cabinets, although it may still require a somewhat controlled environment.

Minicomputers

It's interesting to note that, at first, there were just computers. It wasn't until completely new kinds of computers came along that there had to be another term to distinguish the various types. When Digital Equipment Corporation (DEC) began shipping its PDP series computers in the early 1960s, the press dubbed these machines minicomputers, because of their small size compared to other computers of the day. Much to DEC's chagrin, the name stuck. (Later, when even smaller computers built around microprocessors came out, they were first called *microcomputers*, but eventually were named *personal computers*.)

The best way to explain the capabilities of a minicomputer is to say that they lie somewhere between those of mainframes and those of personal computers. Like mainframes, minicomputers can handle a great deal more input and output than personal computers can. Although some minis are designed for a single user, many can handle dozens or even hundreds of terminals.

Minicomputers cost anywhere from $20,000 to $250,000 and are ideal for many organizations and companies because they are relatively inexpensive, but have some of the desirable features of a mainframe.

Workstations

Between minicomputers and microcomputers—in terms of processing power—is a class of computers known as **workstations**. A workstation looks like a personal computer and is typically used by only one person, much as is a personal computer. Although workstations are still more powerful than the average personal computer, the differences in the capabilities of these types of machines are growing smaller.

Workstations differ significantly from microcomputers in two areas. Internally, workstations are constructed differently. They're generally based on another philosophy of CPU design called **reduced instruction set computing (RISC)**, which results in faster processing of instructions.

The other difference between workstations and microcomputers is that most microcomputers can run any of the four major operating systems—DOS, Unix, OS/2, and Microsoft Windows NT (and the Macintosh can run the Macintosh operating system as well as Apple's version of Unix, A/UX)—but workstations generally all run the Unix operating system or a variation of it.

Many people use the term workstation to refer to any computer or terminal that is connected to another computer. Although this usage was once a common meaning of the term, it has become outdated. These days, a workstation is a powerful RISC-based computer that runs the Unix operating system and is generally used by scientists and engineers.

Personal Computers

When people use the terms **personal computers** and **microcomputers**, they mean the small computers that are commonly found in offices, classrooms, and homes. Personal computers come in all shapes and sizes. Although most models reside on desktops, others stand on the floor, and some are even portable.

In 1981, IBM called its first microcomputer the IBM PC—which stands for personal computer. Within a few years, many companies were copying the IBM design, creating "clones" or "compatibles" that aimed at functioning just like the original. For this reason, the term *PC* has come to mean the family of computers that includes IBMs and compatibles. The vast majority of the microcomputers sold today are part of this family. The Apple Macintosh computer, however, is neither an IBM nor a compatible. It is another family of microcomputers made by Apple Computer. Thus, it is accurate to say that the Macintosh is a personal computer, but some people consider it misleading to refer to the Macintosh as a PC. However, we'll use the term "PC" as a simple abbreviation for "personal computer" referring to both IBM compatible models and Apple's Macintosh line.

Figure 1-16

In this IBM PC-compatible Zeos computer, the CPU, memory, and disk drives are housed together in a case (called the system unit), but the monitor and other components are separate.

Desktop Models.   The most common style of personal computer is also the one that was introduced first: the **desktop** model (Figure 1-16). Most of these computers are small enough to fit on a desk, but are a little too big to carry around with you. Some, like the Macintosh design shown in Figure 1-17, are quite compact. Today, many desktop models are being replaced by tower models. As you can see in Figure 1-18, the only difference between the desktop and tower models is that the main case, which is called the *system unit*, sits on end in the tower model. It is often placed on the floor to preserve desk space.

Today, PCs are seriously challenging mainframes and minicomputers in many areas. In fact, today's PCs are far more powerful than the mainframes of just a few years ago. Competition is producing smaller, faster models

Figure 1-17

The monitor, disk drives, CPU, and memory of this Macintosh computer are packaged together as a single compact unit.

Figure 1-18

Tower models have a system unit that stands on end, rather than lying horizontally. With these models, the system unit is often placed on the floor to free up desk space.

every year that generally cost from $500 to $7500, depending on their capabilities and capacity.

Notebook Computers.

Notebook computers, as their name implies, approximate the shape of an 8½-by-11-inch notebook and can easily fit inside a briefcase. Figure 1-19 shows a popular model. Laptops are the slightly larger predecessors of notebook computers. Also fully capable PCs, **laptops** typically have an almost full-sized keyboard. Because notebooks and laptops are fully functional microcomputers, they are used by people who need the power of a full computer wherever they go. Some models can plug into a "dock" on a desktop computer, to take advantage of the larger machine's big monitor and storage space.

Personal Digital Assistants.

Personal digital assistants (PDAs) are the smallest of portable computers. Often, they're no larger than a checkbook. PDAs, also sometimes called **palmtops**, are much less powerful than notebook or desktop models. Typically only about as powerful as the original IBM PC, they are usually used for special applications, such as creating small spreadsheets, displaying important telephone numbers and addresses, or keeping track of dates and agendas. Many can be connected to larger computers to exchange data.

This area of computing is evolving fast. Newer PDAs have **electronic pens** attached that let users write on or point at the screen directly. The latest generation of PDAs, called **personal intelligent communicators (PICs)**, can use infrared light to communicate with nearby computers and may have cellular telephone and fax capabilities built in.

Figure 1-19

Notebook computers can be just as powerful as desktop models; however, they are typically more expensive. Because they are often used without a desk, notebooks such as this Texas Instruments TravelMate come with a trackball, instead of a mouse.

WORKING SMART   **Buying Your First Computer**

If you haven't already faced the decision of what computer to purchase, you probably will soon enough. Buying your own computer isn't an easy process, considering the amount of money you're likely to spend. Should you buy a Macintosh, a PC, or some other machine? How much power do you need? Where should you put it? Here are a few tips for your first purchasing decision.

■ The most important factor affecting your purchase should be the tasks you want to do with your computer. Before talking to any salespeople, make a list of the kinds of tasks for which you will use your computer. After that, your first priority should be finding the best software for those purposes; then buy whatever machine it takes to run the applications that you've selected.

■ Talk to as many people as possible. Remember that emotions tend to run high when people talk about their allegiances to certain hardware or software, so take their biases with a grain of salt—but do pay special attention to any horror stories you hear. The most valuable information can be other people's bad experiences.

■ Before you give any company your money, find out about their customer service and support. A great deal on a computer is still a bad investment if you can't get help when you need it. And at some point, you probably will need a question answered about your hardware.

■ When deciding how much you can afford to spend, make sure to factor in the cost of software. Most computers are sold with the operating system loaded, but the machine isn't going to do you any good without the application software—word processor, spreadsheet, and so on—that you'll need.

■ If you don't have much computer experience, consider buying a Macintosh. Until recently, PCs delivered more power for your money, but that's changed rapidly as the Macintosh has become more competitive in price. Keep in mind that the software you want to use should be your most important consideration. Setting up your system and adding new equipment to it will be much easier with a Macintosh than with a PC, but if you need a machine that's compatible with computers you use at school or work, consider purchasing the same type of equipment that you use there.

Buying your first computer can be a challenging task. Before choosing a system, educate yourself by reading and by talking to knowledgeable users.

ERGONOMICS

Ergonomics, the study of the physical relationship between people and their tools—such as their computers—addresses how to make computers easier, safer, and more comfortable to use..

Any office worker will tell you that sitting at a desk all day can get very uncomfortable. Sitting all day and using a computer can be even worse. Not only does your body ache from being in a chair too long, but you can also injure your wrists by keyboarding all day or strain your eyes by staring at a monitor for hours on end. People are beginning to recognize the importance of good, ergonomically designed computer systems.

Figure 1-20

A good computer chair provides lower-back support and can be adjusted to different heights. Arm rests are also helpful.

Figure 1-21

People who spend long hours at a computer sometimes find that special "kneeling" chairs such as this one help them to maintain good posture.

Choosing the Right Chair

The first important element of an ergonomic computer system is a good, comfortable chair (Figure 1-20). There are three characteristics that you should look for in any office chair:

- Adjustable height: You should be able to adjust the chair so that your thighs are parallel to the floor and your feet are flat on the ground.

- Lower-back support: The chair should have an adjustable back that provides firm support when you sit in your normal position.

- Arm rests: Chairs with arm rests tend to cost a little more than do those without, but most people find that these chairs provide an extra degree of comfort when they are working at a keyboard for long periods, providing that the arm rests allow easy access to the desk.

Some people who spend a great deal of time at computers find special "kneeling" chairs beneficial (Figure 1-21). These chairs force you to maintain good posture; because they have no back rest and your knees are low, you have to sit up straight to keep your balance.

Preventing Repetitive Stress Injuries

Office workers have been demanding comfortable chairs for a long time, but the field of ergonomics is most often associated with computers. The reason is that ergonomics began getting a lot of attention when repetitive stress injuries started appearing among data-entry personnel who spend most of their working hours entering facts and figures into databases.

One injury that's especially well documented among office workers is **carpal tunnel syndrome**, a wrist or hand injury caused by extended periods of keyboarding. The carpal tunnel is a passageway in the wrist through which a bundle of nerves passes (Figure 1-22). In carpal tunnel syndrome, the tunnel becomes misshapen as a result of a person holding his or her wrist stiff for long periods, as people tend to do at a keyboard. When the tunnel becomes distorted, it can pinch the nerves that run through it and cause a great deal of pain and disability.

Carpal tunnel syndrome is the best known **repetitive stress injury**, a group of ailments caused by continually using the body in ways it wasn't designed to

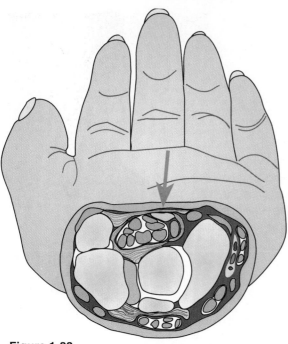

Figure 1-22

The carpal tunnel is a passage through the wrist that encases nerves and tendons (see arrow). Repetitive work at a computer keyboard can cause it to become deformed, resulting in painful pressure on the nerves.

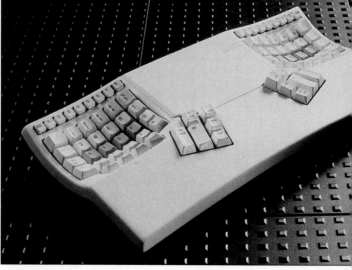

Figure 1-23

This ergonomic keyboard made by Kinesis Corporation is designed on the principle that a typist's left and right hands naturally point toward each other slightly, instead of facing straight ahead as they do when positioned on a standard keyboard. Separating the keys positions the typist's arms at shoulder width, whereas concave keypads elevate the thumbs, allowing the fingers to relax. Palm supports ease the strain on hands and wrists. Other manufacturers have developed different ergonomic designs to relieve the stress of working at a keyboard.

work. Carpal tunnel syndrome can become so debilitating that employees suffering from it have to take weeks or even months off work. It has even led to lawsuits against employers who fail to protect their employees against this type of injury by providing ergonomically designed workplaces.

Several solutions have been proposed to make working at a keyboard more comfortable and to help prevent carpal tunnel syndrome. The first is to set the keyboard at a proper height. When setting up their computer systems, most people just put their keyboards on their desks. The problem is, if your chair is positioned correctly, most desks are too high for good keyboard placement. Ideally, your hands should be at the same height as your elbows, or just slightly lower, when they hover above the keyboard. Many computer desks are slightly lower than traditional desks; others are equipped with retractable shelves that position the keyboard at the right height.

Another solution to wrist fatigue is a wrist support, which can be built onto the keyboard or just placed in front of it. A wrist support allows you to relax your arms and to use only your fingers to type.

Finally, one designer, Tony Hodges, realized that a flat keyboard is not well suited to the shape of our hands. After all, if you relax your arms, your thumbs tend to point up. Logically, then, keyboards should be designed with two sides, one for each hand. Hodges created just such a keyboard, called The Tony! Other manufacturers have followed his lead and designed ergonomic keyboards that allow people's hands to rest in a more natural position (Figure 1-23).

Protecting the Eyes

The last major area of concern for ergonomics is protecting people's vision. Staring at a computer screen for long periods can strain or even injure the eyes. Many users have found their vision deteriorating as a result of prolonged computer use. If looking at the screen for fewer hours isn't an option, here are some ways to reduce eye strain:

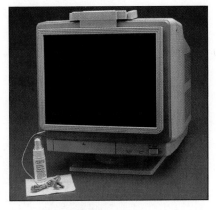

Figure 1-24

This specially coated glass screen cuts glare and improves character resolution. Screens such as this one come in several sizes, and are easy to mount on any monitor.

- Don't stare at the screen for long stretches. Maintaining your focus at the same distance for long periods tends to distort the shape of your eye's lens, so look away from your computer occasionally.

- Position your monitor between 2 and 2.5 feet from your eyes. This is close enough for you to see everything on the screen, but far enough away to let your eyes take in the whole screen at once.

- Try to position your monitor such that no bright lights, including sunlight, reflect off the screen. If you can't avoid reflections, get an antiglare screen (Figure 1-24).

- When you are shopping for a monitor, remember that most people prefer a relatively large screen (at least 13 inches, measured diagonally). A small screen encourages you to get too close.

- Look for a monitor that holds a steady image without appearing to pulsate or flicker.

SUMMARY

The Multipurpose Tool

- The first computers were used for complex numerical tasks.
- Computers began to revolutionize the business world in the 1960s.
- Modern medicine uses computers in many ways. One of the most interesting is computerized imaging techniques, such as MRI.
- Educators are interested in computers as tools for interactive learning.
- The scientific community uses computers to do research and to exchange information with colleagues around the world.
- Engineers and architects use computers to design objects and structures with the help of CAD techniques.
- Lawyers and law enforcement personnal use computers to access and create databases that contain records of court documents and criminal histories.
- Major governmental uses of computers include the Social Security system, the Bureau of the Census, the military, and the Internal Revenue Service.
- Musicians can use a MIDI system to combine or create sounds electronically, either in the recording studio or during live performances.
- Computers are used in theater and film to control stage lighting, to create special effects, and to streamline the animation process.

Looking Inside the Machine

- The hardware, or physical components, of a computer consist of a processor, memory, I/O devices, and storage.
- The processing function is divided between the processor and memory.
- The processor, or CPU, is the brains of the machine.
- Memory holds data as the computer works with them.
- The most common units of measure for memory are the byte, kilobyte, and megabyte (1KB = 1024 bytes and 1MB = 1024 KB).
- The role of input is to accept data from the user or other source.
- The role of output is to give the computer user audio and visual feedback, as well as to communicate with other computers and devices.
- Storage acts as the computer's file cabinet, holding data that are not currently being used by the CPU.

Software Brings the Machine To Life

- Programs are electronic instructions that tell the computer how to accomplish certain tasks.
- When a computer is using a particular program, we say that it is running or executing the program.
- The operating system tells the computer how to interact with the user and how to use the hardware devices attached to the computer.
- Application software tells the computer how to accomplish tasks required by the user.
- Four important kinds of application software are business applications, utilities, personal applications, and entertainment applications.
- The most common business applications are word processors, spreadsheet software, and database systems.
- Utilities help you to manage and maintain your computer.

The Shapes of Computers Today

- There are five types of computers: supercomputers, mainframes, minicomputers, workstations, and personal computers.
- Supercomputers are the most powerful computers in terms of processing; they are used for problems requiring complex calculations.
- Mainframe computers, which generally have many terminals connected to them, are used to handle massive amounts of input, output, and storage.
- Minicomputers are smaller than mainframes, but larger than microcomputers. They usually have multiple terminals.
- Workstations look like microcomputers, but are more powerful and are based on RISC processors.
- Personal computers are also called microcomputers. The term *PC* is used to denote microcomputers that are either IBM PC compatibles or Macintosh computers.

- Desktop computers and tower models are the most common type of personal computer.
- Laptops, notebooks, and PDAs are used by people who need computing power outside the office.

Ergonomics

- Ergonomics is the study of the physical relationships between humans and their tools, such as computers.
- Office chairs should be adjustable in height, have lower-back support, and have arm rests.
- Desks that allow proper keyboard height and special ergonomic keyboards have been developed to prevent carpal tunnel syndrome, a type of repetitive stress injury.
- To avoid damaging your eyes, avoid staring at the screen for long periods, position your monitor between 2 and 2.5 feet from your eyes, make sure no bright lights reflect off your screen, and use a monitor that has a relatively large screen without noticeable flicker.

REVIEW QUESTIONS

1. Imagine what your future career will be, and decide whether you'll need to use a computer. If you will, describe three ways in which a computer will assist you in your work. If you will not, explain why a computer won't be necessary.
2. Think of three situations in which you might encounter computers outside of school or work.
3. Choose one type of work discussed in this chapter, and describe briefly how it has changed because of computers.
4. List three ways computers are used in government.
5. In one or two sentences, define the following terms and give an example of an object or device that is associated with each term:
   a. Processing
   b. Input
   c. Output
   d. Storage
6. What are the main units of measure for computer memory, and what does each of them mean?
7. Describe the difference between an operating system and application software.
8. Give examples of how a car-rental agency might make use of word processors, spreadsheets, and database applications.
9. List the five main types of computers discussed in this chapter, and describe how each one is used.
10. Why is it bad for you to stare at a screen for long periods?

DISCUSSION QUESTIONS

1. What do you think are some of the reasons that the computer revolution has progressed so far in such a short time?

2. Assume that you have the use of a supercomputer for one day. Describe the kind of work you do with it.

3. Where do you think the future of computers is heading? What forces will make this so? Can you imagine possible alternatives?

HOW COMPUTERS WORK

OBJECTIVES

When you complete this chapter, you will be able to do the following:

- Explain why computers use the binary number system.
- Describe the two main parts of the CPU and how they work together to process data.
- Differentiate between RAM and ROM.
- Understand how a video monitor displays images.
- Discuss the advantages and disadvantages of different types of printers.
- Explain how input and output devices communicate with the rest of the computer.
- Understand how data are organized on a disk drive.
- Describe various optical storage devices.
- Understand the importance of organizing and backing up files.

Even people who have been using computers for years still marvel at what these machines can do: how at lightning speed and with amazing accuracy they can sort a mailing list, balance a ledger, typeset a book, or create lifelike models of objects that have never existed.

Just how a computer does all this may seem magical, but in fact it is a process based on simple, if clever, concepts. All the words, numbers, and images you put into and get out of the computer are manipulated in relatively simple ways by the computer's processing components.

In this chapter, we will take an odyssey inside the computer. We will begin with a look at data: what they are, how they differ from information, and what form they take in the computer. We'll continue by looking at the variety of input/output devices that are used to get data into and out of a computer. Then we'll explore storage media and devices. We'll conclude our journey by looking at data storage alternatives and methods for backing up data.

TRANSFORMING DATA INTO INFORMATION

Even though most computers can't respond to human speech, people talk to them all the time. It often seems like computers can understand us, because they produce information that we understand. In fact, though, computers can't understand anything. All they can do is recognize two distinct physical states produced either by electricity, magnetic polarity, or reflected light—essentially, they can tell when a switch is either on or off.

Although each tiny signal a computer identifies in this way is meaningless, the computer contains so many switches, called transistors, and operates at such phenomenal speeds that we can use it to assemble these individual signals into complex patterns that are meaningful to us. But the computer accomplishes all this without understanding; the ideas, vision, and conclusions have to come from people.

The term we use to describe the signals with which computers work is **data**. Although the words *data* and *information* are often used interchangeably, there's an important distinction between them. In the strictest sense, *data* are the raw and individually meaningless signals computers manipulate to produce information.

Because converting data to information and back is such a fundamental part of what computers do, you have to know how the conversion works to understand how a computer works.

Number Systems

To a computer, everything is a number. Numbers are numbers, letters are numbers, and punctuation marks, symbols, and even the computer's own instructions are numbers. Take, for example, this sentence:

```
Here are some words.
```

It looks like a string of alphabetic characters to you and me, but to a computer it looks like this:

72 101 114 101 32 97 114 101 32 115 111 109 101 32 119 111 114 100 115 46

In fact, even this sequence of numbers is sort of a shorthand representation of how the computer really sees the sentence. The computer actually sees our sentence as a string of 160 ones and zeros (Figure 2-1). Understanding how the CPU can represent numbers in different ways, and why it has to, is fundamental to understanding how a computer converts data into information.

Unfortunately, computers don't use the same number system as the one we use. In fact, people who program computers use several number systems, in addition to the familiar base 10 (or decimal) scheme that we use all the time. The most important of these are the binary, or base 2, system and the hexadecimal, or base 16, system.

The essential thing to recognize and understand about the different number systems is that each one is just a different method for representing quantities. The quantities themselves don't change; it's just that the symbols used to represent them are different. When you use a term such as *base 10* to describe a number system, the second part of the term (the number) describes the number of symbols that number system uses. For example, the base 10 number system has ten symbols, and the base 16 system has 16.

```
0100  1000  0110  0101  0111  0010  0110  0101
0010  0000  0110  0001  0111  0010  0110  0101
0010  0000  0111  0011  0110  1111  0110  1101
0110  0101  0010  0000  0111  0111  0110  1111
0111  0010  0110  0100  0111  0011  0010  1110
```

Figure 2-1

In this binary version of the sentence "Here are some words," each pair of four digits represents the numerical code for one character. For example, 0100 1000 is the base-2 representation of 72, an ASCII H.

The Decimal Number System.

Most cultures use the decimal or base 10 number system. It is generally believed that we use this number system because we have ten fingers on our hands.

The symbols we use to represent numbers when we write them are the numerals 0 through 9. Although most of us aren't taught to start counting from zero, zero is really the first symbol of the sequence as well as the first symbol in every number system. But what do we do when we're writing numbers and we get to ten? Although ten is just one more than nine, the problem is that we've run out of symbols, so we have to start using two numerals, instead of only one, to represent numbers at that point.

The logical way to represent these larger numbers is to start the sequence over again, and to include another numeral that represents how many times we've completed a full sequence. The "1" in the number "10" indicates that the sequence has been completed once, and the "0" indicates that we are on the first number of this new sequence.

This concept of using the available symbols, in order, until we've used them all, and then adding another digit is the basis of all number systems.

The Binary Number System.

When computers were being developed, the problem of storing data was one of the most difficult to overcome. Think about it—if you wanted to build a machine that could add two numbers together, say, 1 + 1, you would have to give the machine the capability to hold those numbers in some way before you even began to approach the problem of how to make it add them.

To build a device that could store data with the mechanical technology available at the time, the data itself had to be reduced to its most fundamental state, which is the state where there are only two conditions—on or off. You could also describe them as true or false, yes or no, open or closed, and so on.

A mechanical device available at the time, the relay, was essentially a switch that would go on when a voltage was applied to it, and off when the voltage was removed. The on or off condition of relays could be used to describe the two fundamental states of data.

Now you're probably wondering what good this does, because the machine can represent only two numbers, but if you use more relays, you can represent larger and larger numbers.

For example, suppose you connect each relay to a light bulb, and you decide that a light bulb that is off is a 0 and one that is on is a 1. As you can see in

Relay 1	Relay 2	Relay 3	Pattern
🔆	🔆	🔆	1
🔆	🔆	🔆	2
🔆	🔆	🔆	3
🔆	🔆	🔆	4
🔆	🔆	🔆	5
🔆	🔆	🔆	6
🔆	🔆	🔆	7
🔆	🔆	🔆	8

Relay 1	Relay 2	Pattern
🔆	🔆	1
🔆	🔆	2
🔆	🔆	3
🔆	🔆	4

Decimal (base 10)	Binary (base 2)
0	0
1	1
2	10
3	11
4	100
5	101
6	110
7	111

the table above on the left, two relays give you four patterns: both lights off, one or the other light on, or both lights on. In the table above on the right, three relays can display eight combinations.

Note that the patterns in the lightbulb tables aren't in random order. They're arranged logically—following the same method used to count with any number system. Compare them with those in the table to the left, which show how to count to seven in the binary (base 2) number system.

So, if you replace each unlit light bulb with a zero and each lit bulb with a one, you can begin to count using binary numbers. Just three relays will let you represent eight distinct quantities (zero through seven in decimal).

Because it's so much simpler to develop hardware that can distinguish between two distinct conditions (on or off) than among any greater number, hardware still stores data in these two fundamental states. A computer's CPU is made up of small switches called **transistors**. They're similar in principle to relays, but far more sophisticated. Transistors can now be made so small that some CPUs have over a million of them. Like its predecessor, though, a transistor can hold only a single piece of data; it's either on or off, open or closed. These individual pieces of data are called **bits**, a contraction of the longer term

Table 2-1
Decimal, Binary, and Hex Numbers

Decimal	Binary	Hex
0	0000	0
1	0001	1
2	0010	2
3	0011	3
4	0100	4
5	0101	5
6	0110	6
7	0111	7
8	1000	8
9	1001	9
10	1010	A
11	1011	B
12	1100	C
13	1101	D
14	1110	E
15	1111	F

binary digits. To the computer, a closed transistor represents a binary one; an open transistor represents a zero.

The Hexadecimal Number System.

Because binary numbers would make encoding instructions and decoding output so time consuming, it made sense to devise a method to represent all the ones and zeros that make up binary numbers in a form that's easier to read, write, and understand.

A larger unit of measure for data is a group of eight bits, called a **byte**. This unit is the most important way of grouping bits together.

The base 16 number system, which is also called *hexadecimal* or *hex*, uses 16 symbols to represent numbers. Since there are only nine numerals in the English alphanumeric system (0 through 9), hex uses letters instead of numerals to stand for values greater than nine. Table 2-1 shows the decimal, binary, and hex representations for the values 0 through 15.

Notice that the largest hex digit, F, corresponds to a binary 1111. Another way to say this is that a single hex digit can represent any possible combination of four bits. Therefore, since a byte is made up of eight bits, any byte can be represented by exactly two hex digits. Take, for example, the binary number

01110101

When you split this number into two groups of four bits, it becomes

> 0111   0101

Now, from Table 2-1, you can see that

> 0111 (binary) = 7 (base 16)
> 0101 (binary) = 5 (base 16)

When you write numbers in a number system other than base 10, it's customary to follow the number with another subscript number to show which number system you're using. For example, when we combine these two hexadecimal digits to form one number, the number is followed by a subscript 16 to show that the number is a hex representation. This number is 75_{16} or 75 hex.

Another method for indicating that a number is represented in hex digits is to follow the last digit with the character "h" or "H," or, less commonly, "X." This method is actually more common in the computer world than is the subscript method. The "h" or "X" is not part of the number (hex digits go up to F); it just shows that the number is represented with hex digits (for example, 75H or 75h).

You may remember from elementary math that an ordinary base 10 number such as 123 can be split up and recombined like this:

$$
\begin{aligned}
1 \times 10^2 &= 100 \\
2 \times 10^1 &= 20 \\
3 \times 10^0 &= \underline{3} \\
& 123
\end{aligned}
$$

The 1 in 123 represents 100, which is 10^2. The 2 is really 20, which is 2×10, and the 3 is just 3. You can do the same computation with hexadecimal numbers with the added benefit of finding out what the base 10 equivalent of the number is. All you have to do differently is to substitute 16 for the 10s:

$$
\begin{aligned}
7 \times 16^1 &= 112 \\
5 \times 16^0 &= \underline{5} \\
& 117
\end{aligned}
$$

Representing Data

Because a bit can represent only two unique symbols, a zero or a one, there has to be a larger unit of data made up of a collection of bits to represent numbers and other symbols, such as the characters and punctuation marks that we use in written languages.

This larger unit, or group of bits, has to have enough bits to represent all the symbols that might be used, including numeric digits, the uppercase and lowercase characters of the alphabet, punctuation marks, mathematical symbols, and so on. In addition to these common symbols, there needs to be some extra room for commands to control devices. For example, if you're typing a sentence into a computer, when you press the return key, or the tab key, you want those keys to have a special effect on your text: both on the display you look at as you type in the text, and on a piece of paper you print out with a printer.

To have this effect, these special keys must produce special invisible characters that your display and printer can interpret, but that don't show up in your text. These characters are called **control characters** or **control codes**. We'll go into more detail about control codes later; for now, you should know that they exist, and that there are more than two dozen of them.

Let's make a list of the characters and symbols we've identified that we know we want to be able to represent.

Uppercase alphabetic characters	26
Lowercase alphabetic characters	26
Numerals	10
Punctuation and other symbols	32
Control characters	24
Total	118

So far, our list adds up to 118. Now look at this table, which shows the number of symbols that can be represented by an increasing number of bits.

Bits	Symbols
2	4
3	8
4	16
5	32
6	64
7	128
8	256
9	512
10	1024

As you can see, we could represent all of our symbols using a unit of seven bits, but that would leave us only ten to spare. Seven bits just aren't enough; however, eight bits double the capacity. With eight bits, we can represent all 118 symbols we've defined and have 138 symbols left. A unit with more than eight bits would provide too many extra symbols and would waste space. Thus, the most logical number of bits for the larger unit is eight. As you may recall, a group of eight bits is called a byte.

Now let's take a look at the two most important systems that have been developed for representing symbols with binary numbers or bits, EBCDIC and ASCII, and a newer standard, Unicode.

EBCDIC. Among the first complete systems for representing symbols with bits was the BCD (Binary Coded Decimal) system. IBM defined BCD for one of its early computers. BCD codes consisted of six-bit words, which allowed a maximum of 64 possible symbols. BCD computers could work with only uppercase letters and very few other symbols. This system wasn't adequate for long.

The need to represent lowercase in addition to uppercase alphabetic characters required 52 codes for a complete alphabet alone and led to IBM's development of the EBCDIC system. **EBCDIC**, pronounced "EB-si-dic," is an acronym for Extended Binary Coded Decimal Interchange Code.

EBCDIC is an eight-bit code that defines 256 symbols. EBCDIC is still commonly used in IBM mainframe and mid-range systems, but is rarely encountered in personal computers.

ASCII. Today, the ASCII character set is by far the most common. Initially ASCII, which stands for American Standard Code for Information Interchange, was an eight-bit code, but the eighth bit served a special purpose and was called the **parity bit**. So, effectively, the original ASCII was a seven-bit code that defined 128 symbols.

Later, parity bits became unimportant, so IBM took charge again and developed an enhanced version of ASCII that made use of the eighth bit, allowing ASCII to describe 256 symbols. When IBM did this, they didn't change any of the original 128 codes, which allowed programs and software designed to work with the original ASCII to continue to work with data in the new character set.

One way to look at ASCII codes is to realize that the symbol associated with the code is yet another way to describe eight binary digits. For example, the binary number we worked with earlier,

$$01101111$$

which is 111 decimal (and 6F hex), is represented in the ASCII character set by the lowercase letter o. Table 2-2 shows portions of the ASCII character set, with the decimal, hexadecimal, and binary equivalents.

Unicode. A new standard for data representation, called **Unicode**, will provide two bytes for representing symbols. With two bytes, a Unicode character could be any one of more than 65,000 different characters or symbols—enough for every character and symbol in the world, including the vast Chinese, Korean, and Japanese character sets. If a single character set were available to cover all the languages in the entire world, computer programs and data would be interchangeable.

HOW A COMPUTER PROCESSES DATA

Two components handle processing in a computer: the central processing unit and the memory. Both are located on the computer's main system board, or **motherboard**.

The Central Processing Unit

The **central processing unit (CPU)** is where data are manipulated. You can think of it as the computer's brain. In a microcomputer, the entire CPU is contained on a tiny chip called a *microprocessor*, which is no larger than your smallest fingernail. The chip is mounted on a piece of plastic with metal leads attached to it (Figure 2-2). Every CPU has at least two basic parts, the *control unit* and the *arithmetic logic unit*.

The Control Unit. All the computer's resources are managed from the **control unit**, whose function is to coordinate all the computer's activities. You can

Table 2-2
Portions of the ASCII Character Set

Character	Decimal	Hex	Binary	
♂	011	0B	0000 1011	(home)
♀	012	0C	0000 1100	(form feed)
♪	013	0D	0000 1101	(carriage return)
♪	014	0E	0000 1110	
→	026	1A	0001 1010	
←	027	1B	0001 1011	
:	058	3A	0011 1010	(colon)
;	059	3B	0011 1011	(semicolon)
<	060	3C	0011 1100	(less than)
=	061	3D	0011 1101	
>	062	3E	0011 1110	(greater than)
?	063	3F	0011 1111	
A	065	41	0100 0001	
B	066	42	0100 0010	
C	067	43	0100 0011	
D	068	44	0100 0100	
E	069	45	0100 0101	
a	097	61	0110 0001	
b	098	62	0110 0010	
c	099	63	0110 0011	
d	100	64	0110 0100	
e	101	65	0110 0101	
ü	129	81	1000 0001	
é	130	82	1000 0010	
â	131	83	1000 0011	
½	171	AB	1010 1011	
¼	172	AC	1010 1100	
╚	200	C8	1100 1000	
╔	201	C9	1100 1001	
╩	202	CA	1100 1010	
╦	203	CB	1100 1011	
╠	204	CC	1100 1100	
═	205	CD	1100 1101	

Figure 2-2

The Intel Pentium CPU chip at the center of the mounting is surrounded by gold leads that connect it to the rest of the computer.

think of the control unit as a traffic cop, directing the flow of data around the CPU and around the computer.

The control unit contains the CPU's instructions for carrying out commands. The **instruction set**, which is built into the circuitry of the control unit, is a list of all the operations that the CPU can perform. Each instruction in the instruction set is accompanied by **microcode**—very basic directions that tell the CPU how to execute the instruction. When the computer runs a program, it looks up the commands contained in the program in the CPU's instruction set and executes them in order.

The Arithmetic Logic Unit. When the control unit encounters an instruction that involves arithmetic or logic, it passes control to the second component of the CPU, the **arithmetic logic unit (ALU)**. The ALU includes a group of registers—memory locations built directly into the CPU that are used to hold data that are being processed by the current instruction. For example, the control unit might load two numbers from memory into the registers in the ALU. Then, it might tell the ALU to divide the two numbers (an arithmetic operation), or to see whether the numbers are equal (a logical operation).

Memory

The CPU contains the logic and the circuitry to run the computer, but one thing it doesn't have built into it is room to store programs and data. The CPU does contain registers for data and instructions, but these are small areas that can hold only a few bytes at a time. In addition to the registers, the CPU needs to have thousands—or, more often, millions—of bytes of space where it can hold whole programs and the data being manipulated by those programs.

The memory to which we're referring here is a short-term holding area that is built into the computer's hardware. Physically, this memory consists of some chips either on the motherboard or on a small circuit board attached to the motherboard. This built-in memory allows the CPU to store and retrieve data very quickly.

There are two types of built-in memory, and there's more than one way to categorize them. One way of categorizing memory is by how permanent it is. Some memory chips always retain the data they hold even when the computer is turned off. This memory is called **nonvolatile**. Other chips—most of the memory in a microcomputer—do lose their contents when the computer's power is shut off. The memory of these chips is **volatile**.

ROM. Another way of categorizing memory is by how you can use it. Some memory chips always hold the same data. They're nonvolatile, and, in addition, the data in them can't be changed. In fact, putting data permanently into this kind of memory is called "burning in the data." The data in these chips can only be read and used—it can't be changed, so the memory is called **read-only memory (ROM)**.

One of the main reasons that a computer needs ROM is so that it knows what to do when the power is first turned on. Among other things, ROM contains a set of start-up instructions that check to see that the rest of memory is functioning properly, look for hardware devices, and look for an operating system.

RAM. Memory that can be changed is called **random-access memory (RAM)**. When people talk about computer *memory* in connection with microcomputers, they usually mean the volatile RAM memory. The purpose of RAM is to hold programs and data. Physically, it consists of some chips on a small circuit board.

We use the term *random access* because the CPU accesses its memory using a **memory address**, which is a number that indicates a location in the memory chip, much as a post office box number indicates in which slot mail should be placed. So the computer doesn't have to search its entire memory to find the data it needs; it can look up the address and go directly to it. Memory addresses start at zero and go up to however many bytes of memory there are in the computer.

FACTORS AFFECTING PROCESSING SPEED

Over the past 15 years, the power of microcomputers has increased dramatically. When people talk about computing power, they usually mean the speed with which the computer processes data. Therefore, more power really means faster processing.

The circuitry design of a CPU determines its basic speed, but several additional factors can make chips already designed for speed work even faster. You've already been introduced to some of these, such as the CPU's registers and the memory. In this section, we'll see how these two components, as well as a few others such as the cache, clock speed, data bus, and math coprocessor, affect a computer's speed. Figure 2-3 shows how these components might be arranged on the computer's motherboard.

How Registers Affect Speed

The registers in the first PCs could hold two bytes—16 bits—each. Most CPUs sold today, for both PCs and Macintosh computers, have 32-bit registers. The size of the registers, which is sometimes called the **word size**, indicates the amount of data with which the computer can work at any given time. The bigger the word size, the faster the computer can process a set of data. If all other factors are kept equal, a CPU with 32-bit registers can process data twice as fast as one with 16-bit registers.

Memory and Computing Power

The amount of RAM in a computer can have a profound effect on the computer's power. More RAM means the computer can use bigger, more powerful programs, and those programs can access bigger data files.

More RAM also can make the computer run faster. The computer doesn't necessarily have to load an entire program into memory to run it, but the more of the program it can fit into memory, the faster the program will run. For example, a PC with 2 MB of RAM is capable of running Microsoft Windows, even

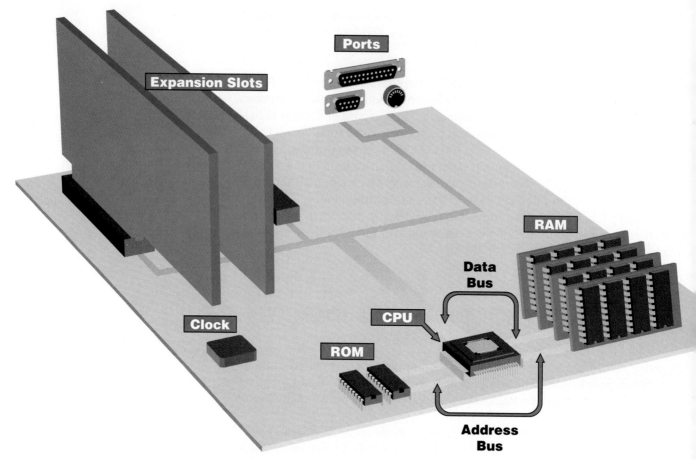

Figure 2-3

This simplified drawing shows
how the major components are
arranged on the motherboard
of a personal computer. A
computer's speed is governed
by how well these components
work individually and as a
group.

though the program actually occupies about 10 MB of disk storage space. When
you execute Microsoft Windows, the program doesn't need to load all its files
into memory to run properly. The computer loads only the most essential parts
into memory. When it needs access to other parts of the program on the disk, it
can unload, or **swap out**, nonessential parts, and **swap in** the program code or
data it needs. On the other hand, if your PC has 4 MB of RAM or more, you'll
notice a dramatic difference in how fast Microsoft Windows loads.

The Computer's Internal Clock

Every microcomputer has a **system clock**, but the clock's primary purpose is
not to keep the time of day. Like modern wristwatches, the clock is driven by a
piece of quartz crystal. The molecules in the quartz crystal vibrate millions of
times per second, at a rate that never changes. The computer uses the vibra-
tions of the quartz in the system clock to time its processing operations.

Over the years, clock speeds have increased steadily. For example, the first
PC operated at 4.77 megahertz. *Hertz* is a measure of clock cycles per second.
One cycle is the time it takes to perform one operation, such as moving a byte
from one memory location to another. *Megahertz* (MHz) means "millions of cy-
cles per second." Today, the fastest PCs are approaching speeds of 100 MHz.
All other factors being equal (although they never are), a CPU operating at 66
MHz can process data 14 times as fast as one operating at 4.77 MHz.

The Bus

In microcomputers, the term **bus** refers to the paths between the components of a computer. There are two main buses in a computer, the data bus and the address bus. The one that you hear the most about is the data bus, so when people just say "the bus," they usually mean the data bus.

The Data Bus.

The **data bus** is an electrical path that connects the CPU, memory, and the other hardware devices on the motherboard. Actually, the bus is a group of parallel lines. The number of lines in the bus affects the speed at which data can travel between hardware components, just as the number of lanes on the highway affects how long it takes people to get to their destinations. Since each wire can transfer one bit at a time, an eight-wire bus can move eight bits at a time, which is a full byte. A 16-bit bus can transfer two bytes, and a 32-bit bus can transfer four bytes at a time.

PC buses are designed to match the capabilities of the devices attached to them. So when CPUs could send and receive only one byte of data at a time, there wasn't any point in connecting them to a bus that could move more data than that. As microprocessor technology improved, chips were built that could send and receive more data at once, and bus designs allowed a wider path through which the data could flow.

The Address Bus.

The second bus that is found in every microcomputer is the address bus. The **address bus** is a set of wires similar to the data bus, but it connects only the CPU and memory, and all it carries are memory addresses.

The reason that the address bus is important is that the number of lines in it determines the maximum number of memory addresses. For example, recall that one byte of data is enough to represent 256 different values. If the address bus could carry only eight bits at a time, the CPU could address only 256 bytes of memory. Actually, most of the early PCs had 20-bit address buses, so the CPU could address 2^{20} bytes, or 1 MB, of data. Today, most CPUs have 32-bit address buses that can address 4 GB (over 4 billion bytes) of memory.

One of the biggest hurdles in the evolution of PCs is that DOS, the operating system used on the vast majority of them, was designed for machines that could address only 1 MB of memory. When PCs began including more memory, special software methods had to be devised to address it. The two methods are called **expanded memory** and **extended memory**. Extended memory is a faster method, but it is still slower than direct memory addressing.

Cache Memory

Among the most time-consuming operations a CPU must perform is moving data back and forth between memory and the CPU's registers. The problem is simply that the CPU is faster than RAM. One partial solution to this problem is to include a memory cache in the CPU. A **cache** is similar to RAM, except that it is extremely fast compared to normal memory, and it is used in a different way.

When a program is running and the CPU needs to read data or instructions from regular memory, the CPU first checks to see whether the data are in the cache. If the data that it needs aren't there, it goes ahead and reads the data from the regular memory into its registers, but it also loads the data into the cache at the same time. The next time that the CPU needs that same data, it finds them in the cache and saves the time needed to load the data from regular memory.

Now let's turn to the devices we use to get data to a computer's processor.

INTERACTING WITH THE COMPUTER

Like computers themselves, **input/output (I/O)** devices have come a long way; today, keyboards, mouse and pen devices, scanners, and high-resolution monitors and printers are the norm. Here now, or just around the corner, are a range of other fascinating devices and technology, including voice recognition and digital photography.

In this section, we'll look at the variety of I/O devices, starting with the most common: the keyboard, mouse, and trackball. Then we'll discuss a few other ways of getting data into a computer. Next we'll move on to the most important output devices: the monitor and the printer, and we'll explain how I/O devices are connected to the rest of the computer through ports, expansion boards, and expansion slots.

THE KEYBOARD

A computer **keyboard** is still just a collection of switches, albeit neatly hidden beneath keycaps. Similarly, a mouse is just a clever package of buttons, switches, and other simple electronic devices. What's changed since the days of toggle switches are the form and arrangement of these devices, how we use them, and how the computer reacts to them.

The Standard Keyboard Layout

Keyboards for personal computers come in a number of styles. The various models may differ in size, shape, and "touch," but except for a few special-purpose keys, most keyboards are laid out almost identically. The most common keyboard layout used today was established by IBM's enhanced keyboard, shown in Figure 2-4. It has 101 keys arranged in four groups. The first

Figure 2-4

The most popular keyboard for IBM PC-compatibles has 101 keys, arranged in groups. Across the top are an escape key and 12 function keys; below these are alphanumeric keys for entering data. The middle group consists of cursor-movement keys and other keys that control the display and printing. At the far right is a numeric keypad.

Alphanumeric Layouts: QWERTY vs. Dvorak

The QWERTY layout of the alphanumeric keys on a keyboard has been with us a long time. It was originally developed for manual typewriters, in which each letter was attached to an arm that sprang up and pressed an inked ribbon against paper. Early typewriters had a tendency to jam: if you pressed two keys in rapid succession, the arms connected to them got stuck together. The QWERTY layout was designed to prevent such tangles. Locating keys in somewhat awkward positions made typists slow down, so keys didn't get stuck.

Obviously, a computer keyboard can accept characters a lot faster than a manual typewriter. Recognizing the awkwardness of the QWERTY

keyboard, some people have recommended that we change the layout. One solution, the **Dvorak keyboard**, uses a more logical design that places the most commonly used keys close together. The Dvorak design is supposed to be much easier to use and much faster than the QWERTY layout. People with limited dexterity sometimes use the Dvorak layout to maximize their output, but it has never caught on with the general public. Why? It's probably because there's a catch-22 involved in making the transition: You learn to type on QWERTY keyboards because QWERTY is the standard, and, once you've mastered that layout, it becomes second nature, so you aren't likely to choose to make a switch.

two, the alphanumeric keys and the numeric keypad, are used to get text and numbers into the computer.

The **alphanumeric keys**—the part of the keyboard that looks like a typewriter—are arranged the same way on virtually every keyboard. This common arrangement is sometimes called the **QWERTY** layout because the first six keys on the top row of letters are Q, W, E, R, T, and Y. The **numeric keypad**, which is usually located on the right side of the keyboard, is the part that looks like an adding machine, with its ten digits and mathematical operators (+, -, *, and /).

The other two parts of the keyboard are the function keys and the cursor-movement keys. The **function keys** (F1, F2, and so on), which are usually arranged in a row along the top of the keyboard, allow you to give the computer commands without typing long strings of characters. What each function key does depends on the program you're using. For example, in most programs, F1 is commonly the help key. When you press it, a screen displays information about using the program.

The fourth part of the keyboard is the set of **cursor-movement keys**, which let you change the position of the cursor on the screen. When you use a word-processing program, there's a mark on the screen where the characters you type will be entered. This spot, called the **cursor**, can appear on-screen as a box, a line, an arrow, or a symbol that looks like a capital I, known as an **I-beam pointer**. To edit text, you move the cursor around the displayed document.

THE MOUSE AND OTHER INPUT DEVICES

If you'd bought a personal computer in the early 1980s, a keyboard would probably have been the only input device that came with it. Today, however,

Figure 2-5

A mouse converts movements the user makes on a flat surface into movements the cursor makes on the screen. Moving the arrow cursor to a different position on the screen is called "pointing."

the vast majority of microcomputers also come with a **mouse**, a pointing device that lets you move a cursor or pointer on the screen just by moving the mouse around on a flat surface (Figure 2-5).

A mouse lets you position the cursor anywhere on the screen quickly and easily, without using the cursor-movement keys. A mouse also allows you to create graphic elements on the screen, such as lines, curves, and freehand shapes, and makes using menus and message boxes easier.

Other input devices that have established the computer as a versatile tool for many users are the trackball, pen, touch screen, bar-code reader, and scanning devices.

Using the Mouse

You use a mouse by pointing. Since the mouse controls the cursor's position, you can move the cursor by moving the mouse. Push the mouse forward, and the cursor goes up; move the mouse to the left, and the cursor goes to the left. To point to an object or location on the screen, you simply use the mouse to place the cursor on top of the object or position.

Everything you do with a mouse you accomplish by combining pointing with three simple techniques: clicking, double-clicking, and dragging. To **click** on something with the mouse means to move the pointer or cursor to the item on the screen and to press and release the mouse button once. To **double-click** on an item means to point to it with the cursor and to press and release the mouse button twice in rapid succession. Finally, to **drag** an item, you position the mouse cursor over the item, then depress the button and hold it down as you move the mouse.

Mouse Devices

Although most mouse devices work similarly, many kinds are available. A mouse can have one, two, or three buttons. It usually isn't a problem to have only one button, because many programs use only one. Programs that do make use of a second or third button provide you with another way to indicate a click of these buttons—such as by pressing the shift key on the keyboard while you click the mouse button. With a two- or three-button mouse, the primary or main button is the one on the left, because most people are right-handed and use their right index finger to click the main button. As with a keyboard, however, you can reconfigure most mouse devices to make another button primary. Left-handers often do this so they can use a mouse with the same ease as right-handed people.

Another way to categorize mouse devices is by the way they connect to the computer. Ultimately, every mouse is connected to the computer's **bus**, which is the backbone through which all the components of the computer communicate. Some mouse devices are connected to the computer's bus through a special electronic card, and others tie into the bus indirectly by way of another device called a serial port. A **serial port** is a socket to which you can connect external devices such as a mouse or modem. Since many computers come with built-in serial ports but no special socket for a mouse, some mouse devices are designed to plug into a serial port. Such a mouse is called a **serial mouse**. The other option for computers without a built-in mouse port is a mouse that comes with a special card that slides into one of the expansion slots inside the com-

Figure 2-6
A trackball works like an upside-down mouse. To use it, you rotate the ball while the rest of the device remains stationary.

puter. One edge of these cards attaches to the back of the computer, providing a special port just for the mouse. This kind of mouse is called a **bus mouse**.

Although most mouse devices are connected directly to computers with a cord, some are not. A cordless mouse communicates with a special controller in or near the computer by transmitting a low-intensity radio or infrared signal. Although cordless mouse devices are more expensive than their tailed cousins, many people like the freedom of movement they allow without the restriction of a cord.

The Trackball

A **trackball** (Figure 2-6) is a pointing device that works like an upside-down mouse. You rest your thumb on the exposed ball and your fingers on the buttons. To move the cursor around the screen, you roll the ball with your thumb. Because you don't move the whole device, a trackball requires less space than a mouse. Trackballs are particularly popular among users of notebook computers, for example, and are built into some, such as Apple Computer's Power-Book.

Functionally, there's nothing more to a trackball than to a mouse; the two work in much the same way. Nonetheless, a great deal of engineering has been invested in trackballs, and they now come in all shapes and sizes. IBM actually makes a device that you can use as either a trackball or a mouse.

Pens

Pen-based systems use an electronic **pen** as their primary input device. You hold the pen in your hand and write or print on a special pad or directly on the screen (Figure 2-7). You can also use the pen as a pointing device, like a mouse, to select commands.

Although pen-based systems would seem like a handy way to get text into the computer for word processing, perfecting the technology to decipher people's handwriting reliably is so complex that pens aren't generally used to enter large amounts of text. They're more commonly used for signatures or messages that are stored and transmitted as a graphic image, like a FAX. The computer may not be able to decipher your scrawled note, but if it appears on your coworker's screen and he can, that's all that's required. As handwriting-recognition technology becomes more reliable, pens will undoubtedly be increasingly important input devices.

Touch Screens

Touch screens like the one pictured in Figure 2-8 work by presenting the user with a menu of choices from which to select. When the user makes up her mind, she touches the menu choice, or button, displayed on the computer's screen. Most touch-screen computers use sensors in, or near, the computer's screen that can detect the touch of a finger, but another technology uses pressure detected on a pad beneath a regular monitor. In this kind of device, sensors in a flat pad or box beneath the base of the monitor measure the monitor's weight at many points. When someone touches the screen, the changing weights and forces transferred down to the sensors allow the device to calculate the location of the touch.

Touch screens are appropriate in environments where dirt or weather would render keyboards and pointing devices useless, and where a simple, intuitive interface is important. With a touch-screen interface, there's only one device with which to contend, so these systems are easy to use. Touch-screen computers are best suited for simple applications such as automated teller machines or public information kiosks.

Bar-Code Readers

The most widely used input device after the keyboard and mouse is the flat-bed or hand-held **bar-code reader** commonly found in supermarkets and department stores. These devices convert a pattern of printed bars on products into a

Figure 2-7

An electronic stylus lets users write directly on the screen of this pen-based computer, which also incorporates a FAX and a cellular telephone. Although some pen-based systems can recognize hand-printed characters, they don't always interpret the characters accurately.

Figure 2-8

A touch screen helps this French-speaking traveler to ask the computer to display information about Ontario. Hardware senses the location of her finger on the screen.

product number by emitting a beam of light—frequently from a laser—that reflects off the bar code image (Figure 2-9). A light-sensitive detector identifies the bar-code image by the special bars at both ends of the image. Once it has identified the bar code, it converts the individual bar patterns into numeric digits. The special bars at each end of the image are different, so that the reader can tell whether the bar code has been read right side up or upside down.

After the bar-code reader has converted a bar-code image into a number, it feeds that number to the computer, just as though the number had been typed on a keyboard.

Imaging Scanners and Optical Character Recognition

The bar-code reader is actually just a special type of image scanner. **Image scanners** convert any image into electronic form by shining light onto the image and sensing the intensity of the reflection at every point (Figure 2-10). Color scanners use filters to separate the components of color into the primary additive colors (red, green, and blue) at each point (Figure 2-11).

The beauty of the image scanner is that it translates printed images into an electronic format that can be stored in a computer's memory, and with the right kind of software, you can alter a stored image in interesting ways. In fact, an entire family of application software, called **image-processing software**, deals with manipulating scanned images.

Another type of software used with image scanners is software for optical character recognition. **Optical character recognition (OCR)**, which is commonly used by banks, converts the scanned image of a typed or printed page into text that can be edited on the computer. When a scanner first creates an image from a page, the image is stored in the computer's memory as a **bitmap**,

Figure 2-9

As the checker passes a can over this flatbed bar-code reader, the device reads the bar code and relays the code to a computer that dentifies the product, displays its price, and adds the amount to the total.

Figure 2-10

When you move a hand-held scanner across a printed image, it shines light on the image and measures the intensity of the reflection. Software then digitizes this information and displays the information on screen.

Figure 2-11

A color flatbed scanner filters reflected light from an image to separate the light into its component colors, which are then reassembled on the display.

which is a grid of dots, each dot represented by one or more bits. The job of OCR software is to translate that array of dots into text that the computer can interpret as letters and numbers.

Despite the complexity of the task, OCR software has become quite advanced. Today, for example, many programs can decipher a page of text received by a FAX machine. In fact, computers with FAX modems can use OCR software to convert FAXes they receive directly into text that can be edited with a word processor.

THE MONITOR

Although there are many kinds of input devices, there are currently just three common types of output devices: monitors, printers, and sound systems. Of the three, monitors are perhaps the most important because they are the output devices that people interact with most intensively.

Two basic types of monitors are used with microcomputers. The first is the typical monitor that you see on a desktop computer; it looks a lot like a television screen, and works the same way. This type uses a large vacuum tube, called a **cathode ray tube (CRT)**. The second type, known as a **flat panel monitor**, is commonly used with notebook computers. Most of these employ **liquid crystal displays (LCDs)** to render images. Either of these types can be **monochrome**, displaying only one color against a contrasting background (often black), or **color**.

How a CRT Monitor Displays an Image

A CRT monitor is a high-precision piece of equipment. What it actually does, however, is relatively simple. Near the back of a monochrome monitor housing is an electron gun. The gun shoots a beam of electrons through a magnetic coil, which aims the beam at the front of the monitor. The back of the monitor's screen is coated with phosphor, a chemical that glows when it's exposed to the beam. The screen's phosphor coating is organized into a grid of dots called **pixels** (a contraction of *picture elements*).

Actually, the electron gun doesn't just focus on a spot and shoot electrons there. It systematically aims at every dot of phosphor on the screen, starting at the top-left corner and scanning to the right edge, then dropping down a tiny distance and scanning another line. Like eyes reading the letters on a page, the electron beam follows each line of pixels from left to right until it reaches the bottom of the screen. Then it starts over. As the electron gun scans, the circuitry driving the monitor adjusts the intensity of each beam to determine how brightly each pixel glows.

A color monitor works just like a monochrome one, except that there are three electron beams instead of just one. The three guns represent the primary additive colors (red, green, and blue). Each dot on the screen is actually made up of three tiny red, green, and blue phosphors arranged in the shape of a triangle. When the beams of each of these guns are combined and focused on a point on the screen, the phosphors at that point light up to form a tiny spot of white light. Different colors can be displayed by combining various intensities of the three beams.

The speed at which a monitor scans the screen is an important factor. A monitor that scans too slowly can produce an annoying side effect known as **flicker**. A flickering screen appears to pulsate rapidly. Besides being annoying, flicker can cause eye strain.

Although the elements composing the tiny points on monitor screens are called phosphors, they're really more fluorescent than phosphorescent. Something that is *phosphorescent* can be charged by light, and will give off that light after the source is removed. Something that is *fluorescent* gives off light only while it's being subjected to energy. The pixels on a display screen light up when the electron guns target them, and immediately lose their light when the electron beam passes by.

For this reason, the more times the monitor paints the screen during a period of time, the less flicker there will be. The number of times a monitor scans the entire screen each second is called the **refresh rate**. Most monitors operate at at least 60 Hz, meaning they refresh the screen 60 times per second, and the better monitors operate at 70 to 90 Hz, refreshing the screen 70 to 90 times per second.

The Video Controller

The quality of the images that a monitor can display is defined more by the capabilities of another device, called the **video controller**, than by those of the monitor itself. The video controller is an intermediary device between the CPU and the monitor. The controller contains the memory and other circuitry necessary to send information to the monitor for display on the screen.

The video controller uses its own special memory to maintain the image that it receives from the CPU and sends to the monitor. In fact, the memory on a video controller is designed to be shared by the CPU and the controller; for this reason, it's called **dual-port memory**.

You could say that dual-port memory actually has two doors into each byte. The CPU goes through the front doors to set each byte; then the video controller comes along and opens all the back doors at once to let the bytes flow out to the monitor.

All microcomputers have a video controller, so what we've said so far applies to whatever monitor you're using or plan to use. If you use a Macintosh, this is generally everything you need to know unless you are working with high-quality graphics. However, several types of video controllers are available for the PC world.

The most important thing to know about PC video controllers is that most of them can operate in several modes. Some modes take advantage of the monitor's maximum resolution, whereas others don't even approach the maximum. More important, some modes can display only text, whereas others can display graphics.

Unlike the Macintosh, which has always been able to display graphics, many early PCs could display only text. Generally, people didn't mind the limitation, because at the time, most software was text based. People used microcomputers primarily for word processing and creating spreadsheets, both of which worked well in text mode. Even today, many popular DOS-based programs are designed to operate in text mode.

In text mode, the video controller divides the screen into a number of columns and rows for displaying whole characters. Although there are several text modes, the most common one displays 80 columns of characters on 25 rows. An 80- by 25-character (not pixel) screen can display up to 2000 characters at a time (80 × 25). Text modes can only display the alphabetic characters, numbers, and other symbols that appear on a standard keyboard—plus a range of graphic characters that are part of the PC character set.

In graphics mode, the controller can direct the monitor's phosphor guns to shoot beams at any point on the screen; there's much more information with which to contend than in text mode: There are 2000 character positions on the screen in a text mode; in a 640- by 480-pixel graphics mode, the same screen has 307,200 pixel positions.

Some video modes require more memory than many PCs have. That's another reason video controllers come with their own dedicated memory.

Over the years, the PC's graphics capabilities have improved tremendously. The first video controller available with the PC was the Color Graphics Adapter (CGA). By modern standards, CGA resolution was rough. Demand for increased resolution led IBM to develop the Enhanced Graphics Adapter (EGA), and later the Video Graphics Array (VGA). Today, CGA and EGA are standards of the past. Almost every PC sold comes with at least VGA output. Many are packaged with another adapter, the Super VGA (SVGA). IBM computers come with that company's Extended Graphics Array (XGA), which is similar to SVGA.

Flat Panel Monitors

Because CRT monitors are big and require a lot of power, they aren't practical for notebook computers, which are small enough to fit in a briefcase and have to run off a small battery built into the computer. Instead, notebooks use flat panel monitors that are only about one inch thick.

There are several types of flat panel monitors, but the most common is the **liquid crystal display (LCD) monitor** (Figure 2-12). The LCD monitor creates images with a special kind of liquid crystal that is normally transparent, but becomes opaque when charged with electricity. If you have a hand-held calculator, it probably uses liquid crystal. One disadvantage of LCD monitors is that, unlike phosphor, the liquid crystal does not emit light, so there is not enough contrast between the images and their background to make them legible under all conditions. One common way to address this problem is to backlight the screen. Although this makes the screen easier to read, it requires additional power, which can be a problem for portables.

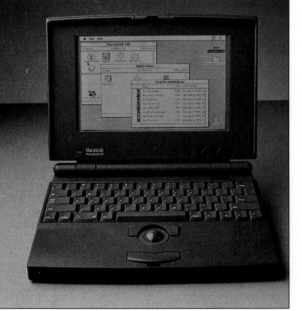

Figure 2-12

This LCD monitor uses liquid crystals to create the equivalent of a monochrome CRT display. Although LCDs have improved greatly since they were first introduced, they can still be hard to read under certain lighting conditions.

PRINTERS

Besides the monitor, the other important output device is the printer. It might seem that printing would be a one-way operation, with data moving from the computer to the printer. Although by far the greater volume of data does travel from the computer to the printer, communication must also go the other way. Before it can send data for printing, the computer must check the printer's status—whether the printer is turned on and ready to accept commands, turned on but off-line or out of paper, or not working because of some other error. Only when it has determined that the printer is on-line and ready to accept commands can the computer send information to be printed.

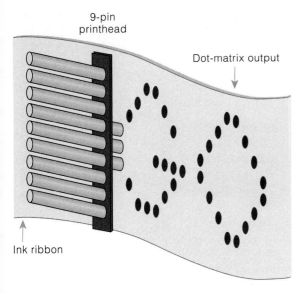

9-pin printhead

Dot-matrix output

Ink ribbon

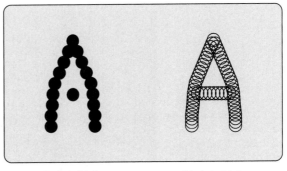

9 dots high; dots overlap only slightly

24 dots high; dots overlap substantially

Figure 2-14

Newer dot-matrix printers use a larger number of overlapping pins to create a smoother image. The dot pattern of the 9-pin printer at the left looks jagged beside the 24-pin output to the right.

Figure 2-13

The pins of a dot-matrix printer are arranged in a column on the print head. As the print head moves back and forth across the page, different arrays of pins pop out and press against an inked ribbon.

Three principal types of black-and-white printers are used with microcomputers: dot-matrix printers, laser printers, and ink-jet printers. In evaluating these types, four criteria are most important: image quality, speed, noise level, and cost of operation.

Dot-Matrix Printers

Dot-matrix printers were the first type of printer commonly used with personal computers. Dot-matrix printers have a print head that travels back and forth on a bar from the left edge of the paper to the right. Inside the print head are a number of pins that can extend from the head to strike the paper through an inked ribbon, as shown in Figure 2-13. As the print head moves from left to right, different combinations of pins pop out and strike the paper.

Most early dot-matrix printers had nine pins, so the characters that they printed had a maximum vertical resolution of nine dots. Now many dot-matrix printers have 24 pins, which produce a very high-quality character image. Figure 2-14 shows the difference in quality between the use of nine pins and 24 pins to form the letter *A*.

Like monitors, most dot-matrix printers have text modes and graphics modes. The clarity of each character can also depend on the mode in which the printer is set. In text mode, the PC sends character codes to the printer. The printer looks up a dot pattern for each character and adjusts the pins in the head to create an image of the letter or symbol the code represents. In graphics modes, the computer sends data for every possible dot on a line, and the printer responds by either striking a pin at that point, or not striking one.

Compared to laser and ink-jet printers, dot-matrix printers are noisy. They also generally produce the lowest print quality. On the other hand, they're by far the least expensive, in terms of both initial cost and cost of operation.

Figure 2-15

A laser printer produces its high-resolution output quickly and quietly. Because they are generally more expensive than other types of printers, laser printers are often shared by several computers in an office.

Besides low cost, dot-matrix printers remain popular because they're perfectly suited for some jobs. They create images by striking the paper, so they can be used for multicopy forms such as checks, shipping forms, and invoices, which rely on impact to transfer printed characters from one copy to the next.

Laser Printers

Although **laser printers** like the one shown in Figure 2-15 are more expensive than the other types of printers, their print quality is higher. They're also much faster and are very quiet. As the name implies, a laser is at the heart of these printers. A separate computer is built into the printer to interpret the data that it receives from the computer, and to control the laser. The result is a highly complicated piece of equipment.

Just as the electron gun in a graphics monitor can target any pixel, the laser in a laser printer can aim at any point on a drum, creating an electrical charge. **Toner**, which is composed of tiny particles of oppositely charged ink, sticks to the drum in the places the laser has charged. Then, with pressure and heat, the toner is transferred off the drum to paper. Also like a monitor and its video controller, laser printers contain special memory to store the images they print.

Laser printers can typically produce between 4 and 12 pages of text a minute; if you're printing graphics, the output can be a great deal slower. The resolution of laser printers is measured in **dots per inch (DPI)**. The most common laser printers have resolutions of 600 DPI, both horizontally and vertically; some high-end models have resolutions of 1200 DPI. The printing industry stipulates a resolution of at least 1200 DPI for top-quality professional printing.

The quality and speed of laser printers make them ideal for office environments where several users can easily share the same printer. Another advantage of laser printers is convenience. Most can use standard, inexpensive copy paper, which is loaded into a paper tray. In contrast, most dot-matrix printers use continuous perforated paper. After the paper is taken off the printer, the perforations must be removed and the pages separated from each other. The final advantage of laser printers is that they are quiet.

Ink-Jet Printers

Ink-jet printers create an image directly on paper by spraying ink through as many as 64 tiny nozzles (Figure 2-16). Although the image they produce isn't generally quite as sharp as the output of a laser printer, the quality of ink-jet

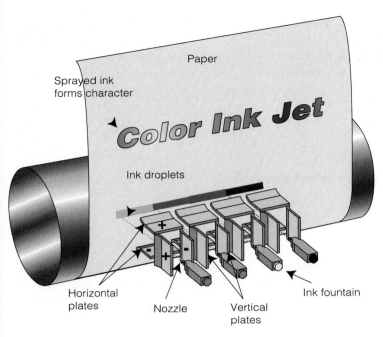

Horizontal plates
Nozzle
Vertical plates
Ink fountain

Electrically charged plates control direction of ink jet spray.

Figure 2-16

The print head of an ink-jet printer contains up to 64 tiny nozzles like the one shown. As the print head travels across the page, each nozzle ejects fine bursts of fast-drying ink.

images is still high. In fact, some of the best color printers available today are ink-jet printers.

In general, ink-jet printers offer an excellent middle ground between dot-matrix and laser printers, providing print resolution of around 360 dots per inch. Like laser printers, ink-jet printers are quiet and convenient, but they're not particularly fast. Typically, an ink-jet printer is more expensive than a dot-matrix printer, but costs only about half as much as a laser printer.

Plotters

A **plotter** is a special kind of output device. It's like a printer in that it produces images on paper, but it does so in a different way. Plotters are designed to produce large drawings or images, such as construction plans for buildings or blueprints for mechanical objects.

A plotter uses a robotic arm to draw with colored pens on a sheet of paper. The instructions that a plotter receives from a computer consist of a color, and beginning and ending coordinates for a line. With that information, the plotter picks up the appropriate pen, positions it at the beginning coordinates, drops the pen down to the surface of the paper and draws to the ending coordinates. Plotters draw curves by creating a sequence of very short, straight lines.

STORING INFORMATION IN A COMPUTER

Among the most important parts of a computer system are the devices that allow you to save the products of your labor. The physical components, or materials, on which data are stored are called **storage media**. Storage media have evolved dramatically since computers were in their infancy, and this pace has quickened since the introduction of PCs.

Two main technologies are used to store data today: magnetic and optical storage. Although devices that store data typically employ one or the other, some combine both technologies. The primary types of **magnetic storage** are

- Floppy disks
- Hard disks
- Magnetic tape

The primary types of **optical storage** are

- CD-ROM
- WORM
- Magneto-optical media

The most common storage devices use magnetic technology. Floppy disks are removable from the floppy-disk drive, the device that reads from them and writes to them. Hard disks are not removable from the hard-disk drive. They are permanently built-in disks that are much faster, and can store much more information, than floppy disks. Some storage manufacturers provide another type of device that combines some of the benefits of floppy disks and hard disks—the removable hard disk. Almost all microcomputers sold today come with a hard disk and at least one floppy-disk drive. A magnetic-tape drive is an add-on peripheral that is often used to create a backup copy of a hard disk, preserving the latter's contents in case the hard disk is damaged.

Optical devices are gaining rapidly in popularity. The best-known optical device is **CD-ROM**, the drive that uses the same technology as audio CD players which attach to stereos. Other optical device drivers include **write once, read many (WORM)** drives, **magneto-optical** drives, and **recordable CD-ROM** drives.

In this section, we'll look at the important storage media and devices, find out for what each is best suited, and get into the nuts and bolts of how these devices work.

MAGNETIC STORAGE

The actual data that computers store on tape and disks are the same as the data in internal memory—they are just collections of bits and bytes. The difference lies in the methods that storage devices use to preserve the data.

How Magnetic Media Work

The three most common storage devices—floppy-disk drives, hard-disk drives, and tape drives—all use similar techniques for reading and writing data, because all use the same medium (the material on which the data are stored). The surfaces of floppy disks, hard disks, and magnetic tape are all coated with a magnetically sensitive material (usually iron oxide), which reacts to a magnetic field.

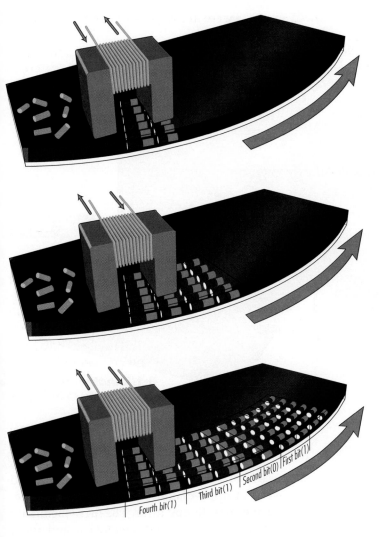

Figure 2-17

As the read/write head passes over the disk's surface, the direction of current in its electromagnet aligns iron particles on the disk in one of two polarities.

Just as a transistor can represent binary data as "on" or "off," the strength of a magnetic field can be used to represent data. But a magnet has one important advantage over a transistor: It retains its polarity without a continual source of electricity.

So that data can be stored, the surfaces of disks and magnetic tapes are coated with millions of tiny iron particles. Each of these particles can act as a magnet, taking on a magnetic field when subjected to an electromagnet. So that they can write data to the medium, the **read/write heads** of a disk drive or tape drive contain electromagnets that charge the particles of iron on the storage medium as the latter pass by the head (Figure 2-17). The read/write heads record strings of 1s and 0s by alternating the direction of the current in the electromagnets.

To read data from a magnetic surface, the process is reversed. The read/write head passes over the disk or tape while no current is flowing through the electromagnet. Since the storage medium has a magnetic charge but the head does not, the storage medium charges the magnet in the head, which causes a small current to flow through the coil in one direction or the other, depending on the polarity of the particles. The disk or tape drive senses the direction of the flow as the storage medium passes by the head.

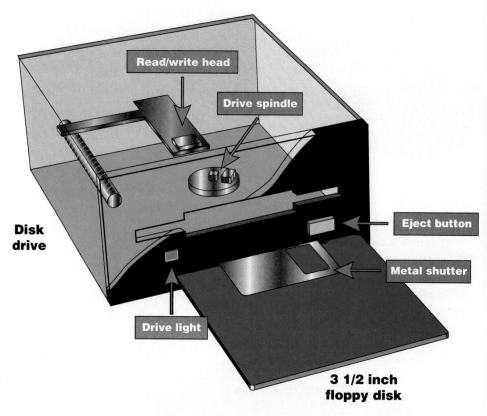

Figure 2-18

This floppy-disk drive takes a
3½-inch disk, which rotates
rapidly on the spindle as the
read/write head moves across
the disk's surface.

Floppy-Disk Drives

A **floppy disk** is a round, flat piece of plastic that is coated with iron oxide and
encased in a plastic or vinyl cover. A **floppy-disk drive** (Figure 2-18) is a device that reads and writes data to and from floppy disks. The drive includes a
spindle that rotates the disk, and read/write heads that can move in and out as
the disk spins to position themselves at any spot on the disk's surface. This
flexibility is important, because it allows the heads to access data **randomly**,
rather than **sequentially**. In other words, the heads can skip from one spot to
another without having to scan through data that are stored between the old
and new locations.

Floppy disks, which are sometimes called **diskettes**, spin at around 300
revolutions per minute (RPM), so the longest it can take to position a desired
point under the read/write heads is the amount of time required for one revolution—about ⅕ second. The farthest the heads would ever have to move is
from the center of the disk to the outside edge (or vice versa).

The most common uses of floppy disks are the following:

■ *Moving files between computers that are not connected through communications
   hardware*: One of the easiest ways to move data between computers is to
   copy the data to a floppy disk, to remove the floppy disk from the drive,
   and to insert it in the drive of another computer.

■ *Loading new programs onto a system*: Although extremely large programs are
   available on CD-ROM or tape, most programs are sold on floppy disks.
   When you buy a program from a software retailer, you **install** it by copying the contents of the floppy disks onto your hard disk, or by running
   a small program on the floppy disks that installs them on your hard disk
   automatically.

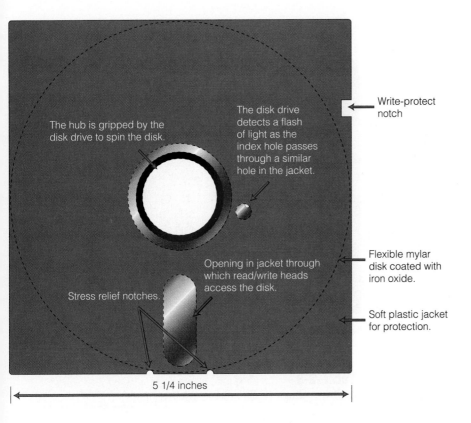

The hub is gripped by the disk drive to spin the disk.

The disk drive detects a flash of light as the index hole passes through a similar hole in the jacket.

Write-protect notch

Opening in jacket through which read/write heads access the disk.

Stress relief notches.

Flexible mylar disk coated with iron oxide.

Soft plastic jacket for protection.

5 1/4 inches

Figure 2-19

A 5¼-inch disk spins inside a flexible plastic jacket that has cutouts that provide access to the disk's surface.

- *Backing up data or programs, the primary copy of which is stored on a hard disk*: **Backing up** is the process of creating a duplicate set of the hard disk's programs and data for safekeeping. Most people rely on a hard disk for the bulk of their storage needs. But what if the hard disk malfunctions or is damaged? So that you protect against data loss, it's always wise to back up a hard disk. One common way of doing so is to copy files onto floppy disks.

Types of Floppy Disks

Floppies come in two physical sizes: 5¼ inch and 3½ inch. The size refers to the diameter of the disk, not to the capacity. The 5¼-inch type, shown in Figure 2-19, is encased in a flexible vinyl envelope with an oval cutout that allows the read/write head to access the disk. The 3½-inch type, shown in Figure 2-20, is encased in a hard plastic shell with a sliding metal cover. When the disk is inserted into the drive, the cover slides back to expose the disk to the read/write head. It's important to realize that both these types are floppy disks. The term *floppy disk* refers to the disk inside, not to the square plastic protector.

The 5½-inch floppy disks come in two capacities: *double density* and *high density*. The 3½-inch size come in three capacities: *double density, high density,* and *very high density*. The **density** of the disk is a measure of the quality of the disk surface: the higher the density, the more closely the iron-oxide particles are packed, and the more data the disk can store. Table 2-3 shows the capacity, in bytes, of each kind of disk.

As noted, the sizes given in the table are for DOS-based machines. The Macintosh does not use 5¼-inch disks. A double-density Macintosh floppy

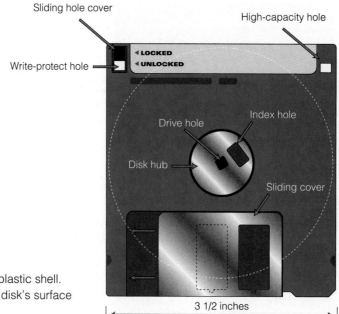

Sliding hole cover

High-capacity hole

Write-protect hole

◄ LOCKED
◄ UNLOCKED

Drive hole

Index hole

Disk hub

Sliding cover

3 1/2 inches

Figure 2-20

A 3½-inch floppy disk has a hard plastic shell.
A sliding metal cover protects the disk's surface
while the disk is out of the drive.

Table 2-3
Floppy-Disk Dimensions and Capacities (DOS-Based Machines)

Diameter (inches)	Sides	Tracks	Sector/ Track	Sectors	Bytes/ Sector	Bytes	KB	MB
5¼	2	40	9	720	512	368,640	360	.36
3½	2	80	15	2400	512	1,228,800	1,200	.7
5¼	2	40	18	1440	512	737,280	720	1.2
3½	2	80	18	2880	512	1,474,560	1,440	1.44
3½	2	80	36	5760	512	2,949,150	2,880	2.88

disk holds 800 KB, not 720 KB—a result of the different ways the two machines use the disks. A Macintosh high-density disk holds 1.4 MB, just like a DOS disk.

How Data Are Organized on a Floppy Disk

When you buy new floppy disks, they're nothing more than we've described here: simple, coated disks encased in plastic. Before the computer can use them to store data, they must be magnetically mapped so that the computer can go directly to a specific point on the disk without searching through data. The process of mapping a disk is called **formatting** or **initializing** the disk. Every new floppy disk must be formatted.

The first thing a floppy drive does when formatting a disk is to create a set of magnetic concentric circles called *tracks*. The number of tracks on a floppy disk varies with the type of disk; most high-density disks have 80. The tracks

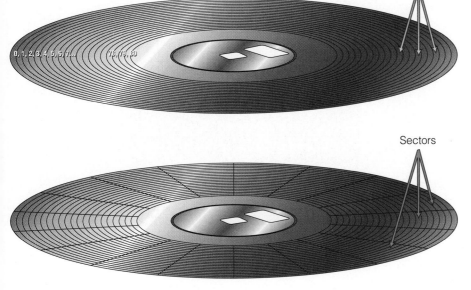

Tracks

0, 1, 2, 3, 4, 5, 6, 7...   78, 79, 80

Figure 2-21

The tracks on a disk are arranged in concentric circles, which are usually numbered in sequence from the outside in.

Sectors

Figure 2-22

Sectors are the short segments that result when a disk's tracks are divided into pie-shaped wedges.

on a disk do not form a continuous spiral like those on a phonograph record; each one is a separate circle. Most are numbered from outermost to innermost starting from zero, as shown in Figure 2-21.

Each track on a disk is split into smaller parts called **sectors** (Figure 2-22). All the sectors on the disk are numbered in one long sequence, so the computer can access each small area on the disk with a unique number.

When people refer to the number of sectors a disk has, the unit they use is **sectors per track**. If a disk has 80 tracks and 18 sectors per track, it has 1440 sectors (80 × 18)—not 18 sectors.

Like any flat object, a floppy disk has two sides. Some early drives could read data on only one side of a disk, but today, all floppy-disk drives can read and write data on both sides of a floppy disk. To the computer, the second side is just a continuation of the sequence of sectors. The 3½-inch, 1.44-MB floppy disk has a total of 2880 sectors (80 tracks per side × 2 sides × 18 sectors per track).

On most disks, a sector contains 512 bytes, or ½ KB. The different capacities of disks are generally a function of the number of sides, tracks, and sectors per track. Table 2-3 shows how the capacities of disks relate to the dimensions.

As you may recall from our discussion of memory, 1 MB of memory is 1024 KB, or 1,048,576 bytes. With disk storage, these values are different. More often, 1 MB means 1 million bytes; 1 KB, however, still means 1024 bytes.

The sector is the smallest unit with which any disk can work. Each bit and byte within a sector can have different values, but the drive can read or write only whole sectors at a time. Even if the computer needs to change just one byte out of 512, it rewrites the entire sector.

Since files usually are not a size that is an even multiple of 512 bytes, some sectors contain unused space after the end of the file. Further, the DOS operating system allocates groups of sectors, called **clusters**, to files. Cluster sizes vary, depending on the size and type of the disk, but they can range from 4 to 64 sectors for a hard disk. A small file that contains only 50 bytes will use only a portion of the first sector of a cluster assigned to it, leaving the remainder of the first sector, and the remainder of the cluster, allocated but unused.

```
AUTOEXEC 000          785 06-19-93   4:39p
CHKLIST  MS           162 06-25-93   5:34p
        41 file(s)       497281 bytes
                       35553280 bytes free

E:\>dir

 Volume in drive E is DEV_SYSTEMS
 Volume Serial Number is 1DE7-222A
 Directory of E:\

BC            <DIR>       04-27-93   10:39p
GFC320        <DIR>       04-27-93   10:39p
GLTC          <DIR>       04-27-93   10:39p
GRNLEAF       <DIR>       04-27-93   10:39p
MSVC          <DIR>       04-27-93   11:10p
PROC          <DIR>       04-27-93   10:39p
TMP           <DIR>       04-27-93   10:39p
PROC     ENV    2048     04-25-93    3:27p
TREEINFO DT     8786     06-22-93   11:02p
TREEINFO NCD    3899     06-22-93   11:02p
        10 file(s)       14733 bytes
                       47505408 bytes free

E:\>
```

Figure 2-23

A typical DOS directory listing.

How the Operating System Finds Data on a Disk

A computer's operating system is able to locate data on a disk because each track and sector is labeled, and the location of all data is kept in a special log on the disk. Labeling tracks and sectors is called performing a **logical** or **soft format**. A commonly used logical format performed by the MS-DOS operating system for PCs creates these four disk areas:

> The boot record
>
> The file-allocation table (FAT)
>
> The root directory
>
> The data area

The **boot record** is a small program that runs when you first start the computer. This program determines whether the disk has the basic components of the DOS operating system that are necessary to run DOS successfully. If it determines that the required files are present and the disk has a valid format, it hands off control to one of the DOS programs that continues the process of starting up. This process is called **booting**—because the boot program makes the computer "pull itself up by its bootstraps."

The boot record also describes other disk characteristics, such as the number of bytes per sector and the number of sectors per track—information that the operating system needs to access the data area of the disk.

The **file allocation table (FAT)** is a log that records the location of each file and the status of each sector. When you write a file to a disk, the operating system checks the FAT for an open area, stores the file, and identifies the file and its location in the FAT.

Users don't normally need to see the information in the FAT, but they do often use the **directory** information. The directory on a disk lists specific information about each file, such as the file's name, its size, the time and date that it was created or last modified, and so on. Figure 2-23 shows a typical DOS directory listing.

The part of the disk that remains free after the boot sector, FAT, and directory have been created is the **data area**.

Figure 2-24

A hard-disk drive consists of multiple rigid platters on a shared spindle. The assembly is sealed inside an airtight vacuum chamber.

Hard Disks

Today, the hard disk is the primary storage device for all computers. Since a hard disk stores so much data, it's sometimes called a **mass-storage device**—along with tape, optical disks, and other media that can store a great deal of data. Much of what you've learned about floppy disks and drives applies to hard disks as well. Like floppy disks, hard disks store data in tracks that are divided into sectors. Physically, however, hard disks look quite different from floppy disks.

A **hard disk** is a stack of metal platters that spin on one spindle, like a stack of rigid floppy disks (Figure 2-24). Each platter is coated with iron oxide, and the entire unit is encased in a sealed chamber. Unlike floppy disks, where the disk and drive are separate, the hard-disk drive, or hard drive, is the whole unit. It includes the hard disk, the motor that spins the platters, and a set of read/write heads. You generally can't remove the hard disk from its drive; the two terms are used interchangeably to mean the whole unit, both disk and drive. However, some manufacturers make removable hard disks that plug into a separate drive unit.

Hard disks have become the primary storage device for microcomputers because they're incredibly convenient. In both speed and capacity, they outperform floppy disks at every turn. A high-density 3½-inch floppy can store 1.44 MB of data. Today, hard disks range in capacity from 80 MB on up. One-GB disks and larger are no longer uncommon. With a hard disk, most people can store all their programs and files in one location.

Hard disks are sealed inside an airtight vacuum chamber. This allows the heads of a hard disk to fly much closer to the surface of the disk, also allowing much greater precision. In fact, the heads of hard disks fly so close to the surface of the disk that if a dust particle, a human hair, or even a fingerprint were placed on the disk it would bridge the gap between the head and the disk, causing the heads to crash. A **head crash**, in which the head touches the disk, destroys the data stored in the area of the crash, and can destroy a read/write head as well.

Remember that hard disks consist of several platters stacked one atop another. To the disk-drive controller, this configuration just means that the disk has more than two sides; in addition to a side 0 and side 1, there are sides 2, 3, 4, and so on. Some hard-disk drives hold as many as 12 disks, but both sides of disks are not always used.

With hard disks, the number of sides that the disk uses is specified by the number of heads. For example, a particular hard-disk drive might have six disk platters (that is, 12 sides), but only ten heads, indicating that two sides are not used to store data. Often, these are the top side of the top disk and the bottom side of the bottom disk.

Because hard disks are actually a stack of platters, we use a new term, **cylinder**, to refer to the same track across all the disk sides. For example, track 0 (the outermost track) on every disk is cylinder 0.

Like floppy disks, hard disks generally store 512 bytes of data in a sector, but, because of their higher tolerances, hard disks can have more sectors per track—54, 63, or even more sectors per track are not uncommon.

Tape Drives

Tape drives read and write data to the surface of a tape the same way an audio cassette recorder does. The difference is that a computer tape drive writes digital data instead of analog data—discrete "ones" and "zeros" instead of the finely graduated signals created by sounds.

The best use of tape storage is for data that you don't use very often. Because a tape is a long strip of magnetic material, the tape drive has to write data to it sequentially—one byte after another. Sequential access is inherently slower than is the direct access afforded by media such as disks. When you want to access a specific set of data on a tape, the drive has to skip over all the data you don't need to get to the data you want. The result is a long access time. In fact, the access time varies depending on the speed of the drive, the length of the tape, and the position on the tape to which the head wrote the data in the first place.

Although the sequential access of a tape drive makes it an impractical storage medium for data you need often, it is well suited for other purposes, such as backing up your system's entire hard disk. Because hard disks usually have capacities much greater than floppy disks, backing up or restoring a system with floppies can be a long and tedious process requiring dozens or even hundreds of floppy disks. Tapes have much larger capacities than do floppy disks, and backup software can usually perform a backup unattended.

Today, most tapes are housed in cassettes that contain both reels of the tape. They come in several sizes, ranging from large cassettes that are approximately 8 by 5 inches down to microcassettes no more than 2 inches long.

OPTICAL STORAGE DEVICES

Today, **optical storage** is the main alternative to magnetic storage. Optical storage techniques make use of the pinpoint precision possible with laser beams. A laser uses a concentrated and narrow beam of light. The only difference between laser light and regular light is that, in the laser's beam, the light is **coher-**

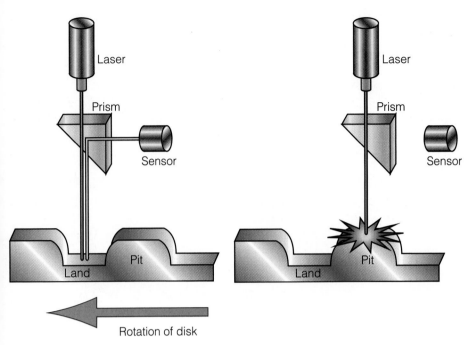

Figure 2-25

The surface of an optical disk is etched with tiny lands and pits that are the equivalent of binary 1s and 0s. Lands reflect light to a sensor; pits scatter light.

ent—all the light energy is perfectly aligned in the same direction, allowing it to be focused with tremendous precision on an extremely tiny area.

Optical storage devices focus a laser beam on the recording medium, which is a spinning disk. Some areas of the medium reflect the laser light into a sensor, whereas others scatter the light. As the disk rotates past the laser and sensor, a spot that reflects the laser beam into the sensor is interpreted as a one, and the absence of a reflection is interpreted as a zero.

Data are laid out on an optical disk more like they are on a phonograph record than on a magnetic disk. Like a phonograph record, an optical disk has one long track that starts at the outer edge and spirals inward to the center. Also like a phonograph record, the data on an optical disk are permanently stamped into the surface of the disk. A spot that reflects the laser light into the sensor is called a **land**, and one that scatters the light is called a **pit** (Figure 2-25).

Like a track on a magnetic disk, the track of an optical disk is split up into sectors, but with optical disks each sector has the same length. Thus, the drive must slow the disk's rotation to allow the heads to read the data stored in sectors near the disk's center.

Although reading data from an optical medium is a relatively simple undertaking, writing data is another matter. The problem is that it's difficult to modify the surface of an optical medium. Unlike magnetic media where any spot on the surface is physically just like any other spot—even when there's data on it—with optical media, the surface is physically pitted to reflect or scatter the laser's light.

CD-ROM

The familiar compact disk is a popular medium for storing music. In the computer world, however, the medium is called **compact disc, read-only memory (CD-ROM**; Figure 2-26). CD-ROM uses the same technology that is used in

Figure 2-26

A CD-ROM drive such as this one can actually play music CDs on a computer that has a sound board and speakers installed.

music CDs. In fact, if you have a sound board and speakers connected to your computer, you can play CDs with your PC.

The fact that you can't write data to a CD-ROM doesn't mean that this storage medium isn't useful. In fact, many applications rely on huge volumes of data that rarely change. For example, dictionaries; encyclopedias; medical, legal, or other professional reference libraries; music; and video all require tremendous amounts of data that you wouldn't normally want to alter—even if you could.

In addition to these uses, software companies can distribute their products on CD-ROM. Because of the high precision and data density possible with CD-ROM, a single CD can typically hold up to 600 MB of data. Because of CDs' high capacities and the fact that no one can change the data on CDs, some companies regard CDs as the distribution medium of choice.

Another exciting application of CD-ROM technology is **CD-Interactive (CD-I)**. CD-I stores digital audio, full-motion video and graphics, animation, text, and data on a CD. What's exciting about this idea is not so much what CD-I stores on a CD, but rather how it allows you to access the data. With CD-I, you choose what you want to see and hear in an interactive environment. For example, with a CD-I system, you can tour the Smithsonian Museum and view only the items in which you are interested, or learn about a subject by going through a predefined curriculum that tailors itself to your knowledge level.

Write Once, Read Many (WORM)

The tremendous capacities of CDs have lured engineers and hardware manufacturers to work hard to develop writable optical devices. The first ventures into developing a writable optical technology resulted in the **write once, read many (WORM)** drive. As with the CD, once data have been etched into the surface of a WORM disk, they cannot be changed.

WORM is an ideal medium for making a permanent record of data. For example, many banks use WORM disks to store a record of each day's transactions. The transactions are written to an optical disk and become a permanent record that can be read but never altered.

Magneto-Optical

Magneto-optical (MO) disks combine some of the best features of both magnetic and optical recording technologies. An MO disk has the capacity of an optical disk, but can be rewritten with the ease of a magnetic disk.

The medium that MO disks use is unlike that of either an optical or a magnetic disk. The disk is covered with magnetically sensitive metallic crystals sandwiched inside a thin layer of plastic. In its normal state, the plastic surrounding the crystals is solid, preventing them from moving. To write data to the disk, an intense laser beam is focused on the surface of the medium, which very briefly melts the plastic coating enough to allow a magnet to change the orientation of the crystals. The magnet has an effect at only the precise focal point of the laser, because only there is the plastic coating fluid enough to allow the crystals to be reoriented.

MO disks are available today in various sizes and capacities. Some of them look identical to 3½-inch floppy disks, but have capacities of more than 1 GB. Although MO drives aren't quite as fast as hard drives, their performance is impressive, and MO disks are portable.

ORGANIZING AND PROTECTING STORED DATA

Since the hard disk is most people's primary storage device, it's important to know how to organize and protect the data stored on it. If you work at your computer every day, it doesn't take long to amass hundreds, or even thousands, of data files. Fortunately, operating systems include some valuable tools for keeping track of your work.

Organizing Your Files

The most important organizational tool for hard disks is the **directory** or **folder**, which is a listing of other files and directories. If you have 500 files to keep track of, you can organize them by creating any number of different directories. And since a directory can contain other directories, you can create a hierarchical structure with major categories and multiple levels of subgroupings. The term *directory* is used more often on DOS-based machines, because you use the DIR command to list the contents of a directory. *Folder* is the preferred term on the Macintosh, because each directory is represented graphically by a folder icon. A similar icon represents directories in Microsoft Windows.

Organizing by Application.

There are two common strategies for setting up hierarchical file systems on a hard disk. The first is to organize by application. Say that you typically create the vast majority of your data files with three programs—a word processor, a spreadsheet, and a draw program. The program files for these applications could be located in three directories called WP, SS, and DRAW. Then, your data files could be stored in subdirectories within these three main directories. A **subdirectory** is a directory that exists within another directory. Your word-processing documents would go in sub-directories of the WP directory, your spreadsheets would go in subdirectories of the SS directory, and so on. Then, when you needed to find a text document, you would know to look in the WP directory.

Organizing by Client or Project. A more effective way to organize your files is to create directories for each major client or project. An attorney who works on three or four cases at a time could create a directory for each case and keep all the related files within that directory. Appropriate subdirectories would help her to customize each directory and to organize its contents further.

Protecting Your Data with Regular Backups

No matter how well you organize the files on your hard disk, you still need to back up the data stored there. Data on hard disks can be damaged or lost in a number of ways: a disk crash, a virus, a hardware malfunction, or simply an accidental erasure. One way or another, everyone who uses computers eventually loses some data, so it's important to keep backups.

There are two basic back-up strategies: incremental and full backup. To perform an **incremental backup**, you back up just the files that you've created or changed since the last backup. The problem, of course, is remembering which files these are. Fortunately, back-up utilities solve this problem for you by keeping track of your files and maintaining records of the backups you perform. Every stored file contains the date when it was created or last changed, so the back-up software can simply compare these dates to those in its log. DOS's own backup program does this, and it also allows you to define **backup sets**—groups of files that you want to back up routinely.

Incremental backup is fast because you back up only what's been changed; however, a full backup is simpler and a little safer. It's simpler because you don't have to go through the process of selecting files or directory trees to back up—you just indicate that you want to back up the entire disk. It's a little safer because you create a mirror image of your entire disk that can be easily restored to a new disk in the event of a hard-disk crash.

To perform a **full backup**, you create a copy of every file, whether the file had been changed or not. Depending on the volume of data you're backing up and the storage medium you use, full backups can take anywhere from a few minutes to a few hours to complete. Time isn't really an issue, however, because you can buy software that performs backups automatically; you don't even have to be present.

In addition to choosing a back-up strategy, it's important to consider what storage medium to use and how often to back up. If backing up your files on floppy disks takes more than 20 minutes, a tape might be a better choice. You're not likely to back up your data very often if it's too big a chore.

Finally, there's the question of how often to back up. A useful back-up plan complements the way you work. For someone who creates only a few letters or memos a day, an incremental backup performed at the end of each day or even once a week may be sufficient. For people who generate large amounts of data, weekly full backups are safer.

As a last thought, keep in mind that a real disaster like a flood or fire can destroy your backup data along with your regular data. It's a good idea to guard against such catastrophes by keeping backup data in a separate location.

SUMMARY

Transforming Data into Information

- The binary numbering system works the same way as the decimal and hexadecimal numbering systems, except it has only two available symbols instead of 10 or 16.
- Hex provides a convenient way to summarize binary code, because one hex digit can represent four binary digits.
- In the two most common character-code sets, EBCDIC and ASCII, characters consist of one byte—eight bits—of data.

How a Computer Processes Data

- A microcomputer's processing takes place in the CPU, the two main parts of which are the control unit and the ALU.
- Within the CPU, program instructions are retrieved and translated with the help of an internal instruction set and the accompanying microcode.
- The actual manipulation of data takes place in the ALU, which is connected to registers that hold data.
- A portion of memory called ROM is nonvolatile (or permanent): it is used to hold instructions that run the computer when the power is first turned on.
- The biggest part of memory, called RAM, is volatile (or temporary): programs and data can be written to and erased from it as needed.
- The CPU accesses each location in memory with a unique number, called the memory address.

Factors Affecting Processing Speed

- The size of the registers, also called word size, determines the amount of data with which the computer can work at a given instant.
- The amount of RAM can also affect speed, because the CPU can keep more of the active program and data in memory, rather than in storage.
- The computer's system clock sets the pace for the central processing unit.
- There are two kinds of buses, the data bus and the address bus, both of which are located on the motherboard.
- The size (or width) of the address bus determines the number of bytes of memory the CPU can access.
- The cache is a type of high-speed memory that contains the most recent data and instructions that have been loaded by the CPU.

The Keyboard

- There are four parts to the standard keyboard: the alphanumeric keys, the numeric keypad, the function keys, and the cursor-movement keys.

The Mouse and Other Input Devices

- The mouse is a pointing device that lets you control the position of the cursor on the screen without using the keyboard.

- Using the mouse involves four techniques: pointing, clicking, double-clicking, and dragging.

- In many systems, the mouse is used to manipulate icons on the screen.

- A trackball provides the functionality of a mouse, but requires less space on the desktop.

- With pen-based systems, you use an electronic pen to write on a special pad or directly on the screen.

- Touch-screen computers accept input directly through the monitor. Users touch electronic buttons that are displayed on the screen.

- Bar-code readers, such as those used in grocery stores, can read bar codes, translate them into numbers, and input the numbers.

- Image scanners convert printed images into digitized formats that can be stored and manipulated in computers.

- An image scanner equipped with OCR software can translate a page of text into a string of character codes in the computer's memory.

The Monitor

- Computer monitors are roughly divided into CRT and flat panel monitors, and into monochrome and color monitors.

- A CRT monitor works with an electron gun that systematically aims a beam of electrons at every pixel on the screen.

- The vertical resolution of the screen is the number of rows of pixels; the horizontal resolution is the number of pixels in each row.

- Monitor manufacturers try to ensure that the scan rate of the monitor is high enough to eliminate flicker (at least 60 Hz).

- The video controller is an interface between the monitor and the CPU.

- The video controller contains dual-port memory that receives data from the CPU and gives them to the monitor.

Printers

- The three most common types of printers are dot-matrix, laser, and ink-jet printers.

- Dot-matrix printers are inferior to laser and ink-jet printers in most respects, but they are far less expensive.

- Laser printers produce the highest-quality print and are quiet, fast, and convenient to use, but they are also the most expensive type of printer.

- Ink-jet printers offer a middle ground between dot-matrix printers and laser printers.

- Plotters create images with a robotic arm that picks up pens and draws lines on a large sheet of paper.

Storing Information in a Computer

- Storage devices can be classified as magnetic or optical.
- The most common magnetic storage devices are floppy disks, hard disks, and magnetic tape.
- The most common optical devices are CD-ROM, WORM, and magneto-optical disks.

Magnetic Storage

- Magnetic storage devices work by polarizing tiny pieces of iron on the magnetic medium.
- The read/write head contains an electromagnet that creates the magnetic charge in the medium.
- Floppy-disk drives read and write to floppy disks, a direct-access medium.
- Floppy disks are most often used to transfer files between computers, as a means for selling new programs that are then installed to a hard disk, and as a back-up medium.
- Floppy disks come in two sizes: 3½ inch, and 5¼ inch.
- Before a disk can be used, it must be formatted, or initialized—a process in which the read/write heads record tracks and sectors on the disk.
- At the same time as the physical formatting is taking place, the computer's operating system establishes the disk's logical formatting by creating the boot sector, the FAT, the root directory, and the data area.
- A hard disk, which has much greater storage capacity than a floppy disk, is accessed with a hard-disk drive.
- Hard disks can store more data than floppy disks because the medium, precision, and the speed at which the disks rotate permit densely packed data and rapid access.
- Because data stored on magnetic tape take longer to access, it is best to use tape to store data that will not be needed frequently.

Optical Storage Devices

- CD-ROM uses the same technology as does a music CD; a laser reads lands and pits from the surface of the disk.
- CD-ROM disks can store up to 600 MB, but they cannot be written to.
- WORM drives also use a laser to read data that are etched on the surface of a disk, but the user is able to write data once onto a new disk; after the data are written, however, they cannot be changed.
- Magneto-optical drives write data with a high-powered laser capable of melting the plastic on the disk covering, and a magnet that aligns the crystals under the melted area. A less powerful laser reads the alignment of the crystals.

Organizing and Protecting Stored Data

- Most people organize the files on their hard disk by creating a hierarchical directory structure, with file directories and subdirectories.

- The two most common strategies for organization are by application and by client or project.
- The two main backup strategies are incremental backup and full backup.

REVIEW QUESTIONS

1. List three reasons why computers use the binary number system, rather than the decimal system.
2. List the two main components of a CPU, and explain what each one does.
3. What are the two most common input devices used with personal computers? For what is each of them used?
4. How is a trackball different from a mouse?
5. Identify the four major types of printers, and give a brief description of each.
6. List the three most common types of magnetic storage device.
7. Why is a magnetic medium more appropriate as a storage medium than an array of transistors?
8. What advantage do direct-access storage media have over sequential media?
9. Which optical medium matches the following descriptions?
   a. Does not allow you to write data.
   b. Allows you to write data once.
   c. Allows you to read and write data at will.
10. Describe how magneto-optical drives use both magnetic and optical technology.

DISCUSSION QUESTIONS

1. For each of the following examples, briefly explain what data might make up the information you need to perform each task:
   a. Reading a newspaper
   b. Deciding what to wear on a given day
   c. Filling out an income-tax form
   d. Determining what kind of car to buy
2. Explain how a laser printer creates text and graphic images on a piece of paper. Find out how a photocopier works, and compare these two technologies.

USING
MICROCOMPUTER SOFTWARE

OBJECTIVES

When you complete this chapter, you will be able to do the following:

- Define *operating system.*
- Discuss the major functions of an operating system.
- List the most important PC operating systems.
- Explain the purpose of word-processing software.
- Discuss the features of word processors.
- Describe the usual applications of a word processor.
- Describe some common applications of spreadsheet software.
- Discuss the features of spreadsheets.
- List and describe the types of cell entries.
- Understand how spreadsheets and graphics work together.
- Explain what is meant by the term *spreadsheet model.*
- Discuss some common applications of database-management system (DBMS) software.
- Describe some of the features of a DBMS.
- List and describe the types of data that a database can hold.
- Explain how a DBMS can quickly retrieve data.
- Understand how to use tables, fields, records, forms, and queries.

Every computer has, at its lowest software level, a layer of intelligence that breathes life into the machine. When you turn on a computer, built-in instructions direct it to find and run its operating system, which continues to operate for the entire time the computer is on. This special program supervises the operation of the computer's hardware devices and coordinates the flow of control and data.

In this chapter, we'll explore the operating system—what it does and how it functions. We'll also discuss graphical environments and command-line interfaces and see how they're integrated with the operating system. After that, we'll take a closer look at the most popular microcomputer operating systems: DOS, OS/2, Windows NT, Unix, and the Macintosh operating system. Finally, we'll look at three types of applications software used commonly in business.

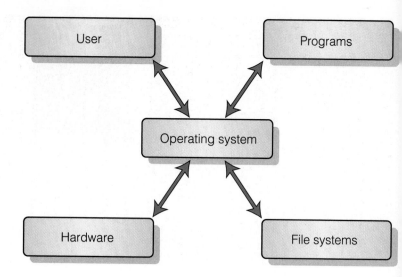

Figure 3-1

The OS is the core of what makes a computer work. It works behind the scenes as an intermediator for requests from users and programs; it manages and drives the computer's hardware, and reads and writes data to and from the disk drives.

WHAT IS AN OPERATING SYSTEM?

An **operating system (OS)** is itself a computer program. However, it's a very special program—perhaps the most complex and important one on a computer. The OS wakes up the computer and makes the computer recognize the CPU, memory, keyboard, video display system, and disk drives. In addition, it provides the facility for users to communicate with the computer, and it serves as a platform from which to run application programs.

Certainly, you can use a computer every day without knowing what type of OS it uses, but people who buy software and maintain their systems themselves have to be better informed. For example, whenever you purchase a new software product, you have to know whether that product will work with your particular computer and OS. Some software companies support their products for only certain OSs or only particular versions of an OS.

When you turn on a computer, the first thing it does is to perform a self-diagnosis called a **power on self test (POST)**. During the POST, the computer identifies its memory, disks, keyboard, display system, and any other devices attached to it. The next thing the computer does is to look for an OS to boot. The term *boot* comes from the early days of computing; it's short for "bootstrap." When you turn on a computer, it uses the first program that runs to "pull itself up by its bootstraps." A PC looks for the OS on the primary floppy-disk drive first; if it finds a bootable OS there, it uses that OS; otherwise, it looks on the primary hard disk.

Once the computer boots its OS, it keeps at least part of it in memory at all times. As long as the computer is on, the OS has four primary jobs (Figure 3-1):

- Providing either a command-line interface or a graphical user interface for the user to communicate with the computer
- Managing the hardware devices on the computer
- Managing and maintaining the disk file systems
- Supporting other programs

The first OS function we'll look at is providing a user interface. There are two broad categories of OS interfaces: command-line interfaces and graphical

```
C>
C>prompt $p$g

C:\WINDOWS>
```

Figure 3-2

The standard user prompt in MS-DOS consists of a letter representing the current disk drive and a greater-than sign meant to look like the tip of an arrow. The "prompt" command allows you to change the prompt to anything you want. Here, the user has changed from the standard prompt to one that displays not only the current drive letter, but the current directory as well.

user interfaces. To use an OS with a **command-line interface**, you type words and symbols on the computer's keyboard. With a **graphical user interface** (**GUI,** pronounced "goo-ee"), you select actions by using a mouse or similar pointing device to click on pictures called **icons**, or to pick options from menus. Every OS provides a user interface, whether it's made up of text or is graphical in nature.

The Command-Line Interface

DOS, the most widely used OS in the world, has a command-line interface, which means that the user controls the program by typing commands at a **prompt**. In DOS, the default prompt is the letter of the current disk drive followed by a greater-than symbol (C>) (Figure 3-2). Most DOS users, however, change their prompt to reflect not only the current drive, but the current directory as well. The prompt indicates that the OS is ready to accept a command. To enter a command, you use the keyboard to type words and symbols. If you type a command incorrectly, the OS responds with a message indicating that it did not understand your command. This happens often, even for users who are well versed in the command language. Simply misspelling a command will generate an error message. When this happens, you just retype the command correctly.

You can issue a command that tells the computer to display the names of the files on the computer's disk drive or the name of a program you want to run. This process of typing characters and pressing the Enter key is how you issue (or enter) commands with a command-line interface.

The Kernel and the Shell.   The central functions of an OS are controlled by the **kernel**, whereas the user interface is controlled by the **shell**. For example, the most important part of DOS is a program with the file name "COM-MAND.COM." This program has two parts. The kernel, which remains in memory at all times, contains the low-level machine code for handling the management of the hardware for other programs that need these services and for the second part of COMMAND.COM—the shell. The shell, which in DOS is also called the **command interpreter**, takes control of the computer's screen, gets user input from the keyboard, interprets that input, and acts on it. The command interpreter is the part of the program that establishes the command-line interface.

On DOS systems, at least part of the COMMAND.COM program is always in memory, providing the low-level services of hardware and disk management to programs. However, the low-level functions of the OS and the command-interpreting functions are separate, so it is possible to replace the standard MS-DOS command interpreter with a different one. In other words, you can keep the DOS kernel running, but use a different user interface. This is exactly what happens when you load Microsoft Windows. When you type "WIN" at the DOS prompt, the Windows program takes over as the shell, replacing the command-line interface with a graphical user interface.

The Shell Game. Many different shells can use the DOS kernel. For example, NDOS (Norton DOS) is a command-line shell that offers improvements over the command interpreter that is built into COMMAND.COM. There's even a graphical user interface that comes with DOS: It's called the *DOS Shell*.

In certain situations, it can be useful to go one step further by temporarily replacing the alternative shell with the original DOS command line. For example, some applications programs offer a feature that lets the user temporarily return to the OS command line. Often, you invoke this feature by choosing a menu option such as "Shell" or "DOS Shell." This provides a convenient way to leave a program temporarily so that you can copy a file or perform some other task, and then quickly return to the application program without unloading and reloading the program and data files. What this feature actually does is to execute another copy of COMMAND.COM. When the second copy of the OS runs, the command interpreter takes control of the computer's screen and keyboard and awaits user input in the same way as the first copy does. The only difference is that the application program remains in memory. To return to the application program, you type "exit" at the DOS prompt. This terminates the program (the second copy of COMMAND.COM) and returns control of the computer to the application program.

The Graphical User Interface

Many people think that the most significant development in the computer world since manufacturers began building computers around microprocessors was the development of the **graphical user interface (GUI)**. At last, computers could work the way people work—visually.

The Macintosh, which offered the first commercially successful graphical OS, was the brainchild of Steve Jobs, one of the co-founders of Apple Computer. Apple announced the Macintosh to the world with a ground-breaking one-minute commercial that ran during the 1984 Superbowl. The ad featured a muscular runner bursting into a movie theater full of faceless figures in pin-striped suits and hurling a sledgehammer through the screen they were watching. The commercial ran only once, and nobody anticipated the excitement that this single showing would generate.

Working in a Windowed Environment. Since the advent of the Macintosh, something all GUIs have in common is the concept of **windows**. A window can contain a project you're working on, a panel for entering information, or information that a command or program has generated. Some windows have

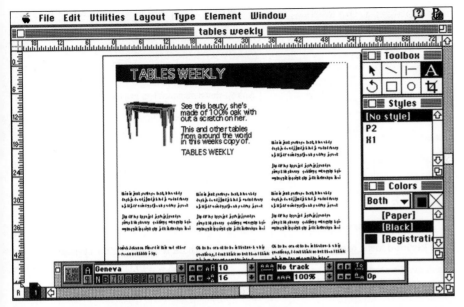

Figure 3-3

Note the graphic representations in Aldus PageMaker's Toolbox.

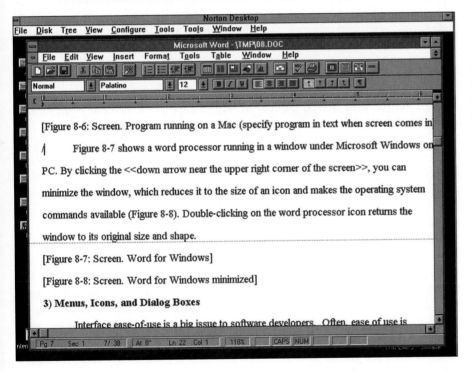

Figure 3-4

With environments that offer a GUI, programs run in a window, or a rectangular box, on the screen. Windows in most of these environments have a border area with scroll bars and buttons to control the display of the window. The upper-right corner of the word-processor window has two buttons—one with an arrow pointing up, the other with one pointing down. By clicking the up arrow, you can expand the window to occupy the entire screen. By clicking the down arrow, you can minimize the window, or reduce it to an icon on the desktop.

controls on them that you can use to change the size or shape of the window or to pan the information in the window. Figure 3-3 shows Aldus Pagemaker running in a window on a Macintosh. You can change the shape of the window by using the mouse to drag the edges or corners of the window to a new location.

Figure 3-4 shows a word processor running in a window under Microsoft Windows on a PC. By clicking the down arrow near the upper-right corner of the screen, you can minimize the window, which reduces the window to the size of an icon and makes the OS commands available. Double-clicking on the word-processor icon returns the window to its original size and shape.

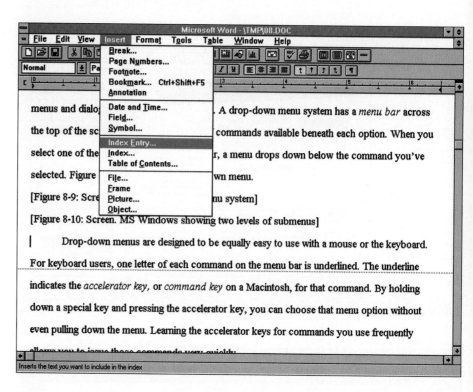

Figure 3-5

Today's programs, especially those written for GUIs, sport menu bars across the top of the screen. Users can make selections either with the keyboard or with a mouse; with many programs, the user can always see the menu.

Menus, Icons, and Dialog Boxes. Interface ease of use is a big issue to software developers. Often, ease of use is measured by how **intuitive** the interface is. With an intuitive interface, you should be able to use a system effectively even if you've never seen it before. How the interface works should be obvious. Such an interface is called **user friendly**. Designing a good interface is especially difficult, because it has to be simple enough for inexperienced users to understand, but sophisticated enough that it doesn't slow down experienced users.

One of the most important components in the development of GUIs has been the evolution of menu systems as a means of offering command options to users. A **menu** is a list of commands that the user can issue in a given context. For example, the initial menu of an accounting program might prompt the user to choose the general accounting area that she wants to work in (e.g., Accounts Payable, Accounts Receivable, or General Ledger). After the user chooses "Accounts Receivable," another menu may appear that prompts the user for what she wants to do in the accounts-receivable area: enter invoices or update the customer file.

Menus have evolved over the years from numbered or lettered lists of commands to the GUIs we have today. The sophisticated menu systems found in GUIs use drop-down menus and dialog boxes (or pop-up menus). A drop-down menu system has a **menu bar** across the top of the screen displaying the types of commands available beneath each option. When you select one of the commands on the menu bar, a menu drops down below the command you've selected. Figure 3-5 shows such a drop-down menu.

Drop-down menus are designed to be equally easy to use with a mouse or the keyboard. For keyboard users, one letter of each command on the menu bar is underlined. The underline indicates the **accelerator key**, or **command key** on a Macintosh, for that command. By holding down a special key and

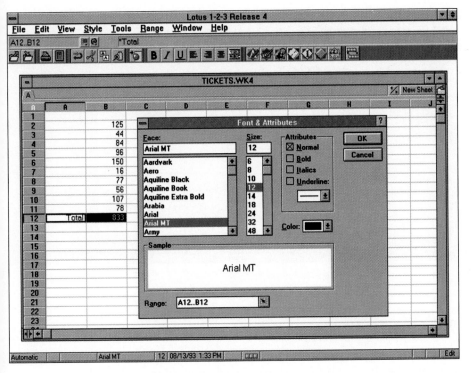

Figure 3-6

Programs get input from a user through pop-up panels, or dialog boxes. This dialog box allows the user to set the attributes of the text in a selected area of the screen. You can change the font, face, and color of the text, in addition to checking boxes for special attributes such as bold, italics, and underline.

pressing the accelerator key, you can choose that menu option without even pulling down the menu. Learning the accelerator keys for commands that you use frequently allows you to issue those commands very quickly.

Dialog boxes (which are also called *panels* or *pop-up menus*, depending on the particular environment) are special-purpose menus that are sensitive to the context in which they're used. For example, in some programs, you can select some text and click a mouse button, and a special menu pops up allowing you to set attributes of the text such as the typeface, font, or color (Figure 3-6).

The most intuitive interfaces use objects and symbols called **icons** that everyone is already familiar with, including people who have never used a computer before. For example, it's fairly obvious what an icon representing a trash can on a computer screen is for: throwing things away. You discard something by dragging its icon to the trash can. When you release the mouse button, the object disappears into the bulging trash can.

The Digital Desktop.

Apple's Macintosh computer introduced the metaphor of the computerized desktop—an environment familiar to everyone. The Macintosh OS includes tools and objects common to any real-life desk or office—from word processor to calculator and notepads, to files, folders, and trash cans. The notepads, reports, and projects appear in windows that you can arrange to overlap, just as you can arrange pieces of paper on a physical desktop. To focus on a particular project, you can arrange the window so that it overlays all the others, or you can maximize it to occupy the entire screen. Now that GUIs have become available on almost every type of computer, the desktop metaphor has followed. For example, the Norton Desktop and the Norton Desktop for Windows create a computerized desktop on DOS-based PCs. X.desktop does the same for Unix-based computers. For PCs running OS/2, it's the Workplace Shell.

Figure 3-7

Even programs that provide an elegant user interface for selecting files have to use the OS to get a list of files on the disk. When the user issues a command to open a file, the program "contacts" the OS. This contact is called a *system call*. There are many types of system calls; in this case, the program asks the OS for a list of all the files in the current directory. When the program receives the list of files, it displays them neatly in a scrollable window where the user can choose one with the keyboard or mouse.

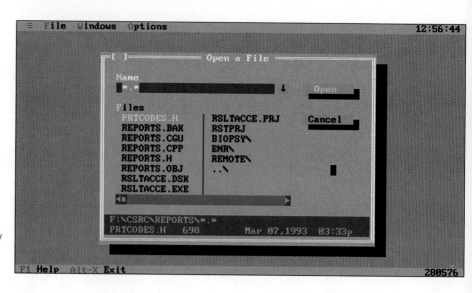

Managing the Hardware

Although the user interface is the most visible function of the OS, the OS has several other important functions. One is managing how hardware is used. When programs run, they need to use the computer's memory, monitor, disk drives, and occasionally other devices as well, such as I/O ports. The OS serves as the intermediary between programs and the hardware.

Regardless of the type of user interface your computer has (command-line or graphical), the OS intercepts commands to use memory and other devices, keeps track of what programs have access to what devices, and so on. For example, when you enter the directory command at an OS prompt or click on a folder in a GUI, the OS interprets the action as a command to list the files in that directory or folder. The program logic in the kernel responds to the command by interrupting the CPU and instructing the CPU to go to the disk drive and retrieve the names of the files it finds in the directory or folder. The OS intercepts the data stream (the file names) returning from the disk drive and displays it on the screen (Figure 3-7). This is one reason the kernel must always remain in memory—it has to be there to tell the CPU how to use the other hardware devices.

Managing the File System

In Chapter 2, we looked at how the disk controller and disk drive work together to store bits and bytes of data on a disk, but we did not consider the data that the OS tells the computer to read and store. OSs group data together into logical compartments for storage on disk. These groups of data are called *files*. Computers store information in files. Files may contain program instructions or data created or used by a program.

Most programs you purchase come with numerous files—some may even include hundreds. These programs also let you create your own sets of data and store them as files with names that you assign.

The OS maintains the list of files on a disk. On IBM and compatible computers, each disk drive has its own directory, identified by the letter assigned

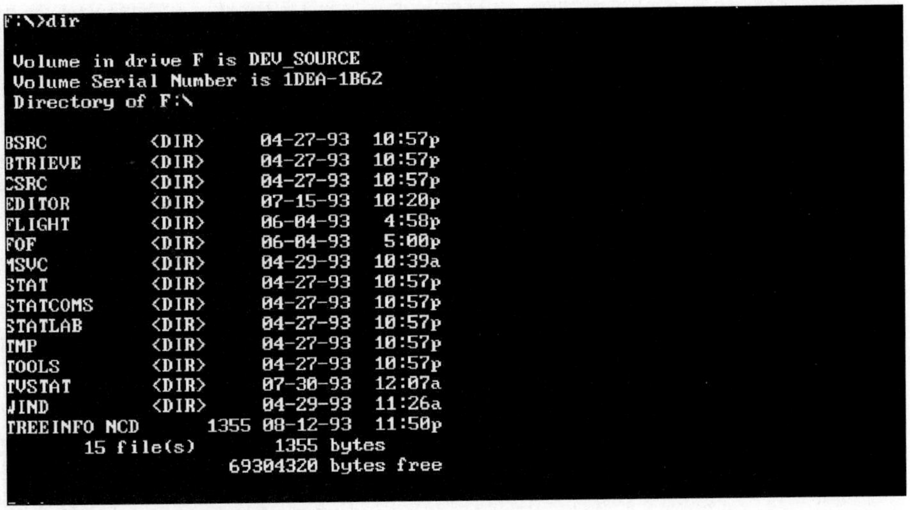

```
F:\>dir

 Volume in drive F is DEV_SOURCE
 Volume Serial Number is 1DEA-1B62
 Directory of F:\

BSRC         <DIR>      04-27-93   10:57p
BTRIEVE      <DIR>      04-27-93   10:57p
CSRC         <DIR>      04-27-93   10:57p
EDITOR       <DIR>      07-15-93   10:20p
FLIGHT       <DIR>      06-04-93    4:58p
FOF          <DIR>      06-04-93    5:00p
MSVC         <DIR>      04-29-93   10:39a
STAT         <DIR>      04-27-93   10:57p
STATCOMS     <DIR>      04-27-93   10:57p
STATLAB      <DIR>      04-27-93   10:57p
TMP          <DIR>      04-27-93   10:57p
TOOLS        <DIR>      04-27-93   10:57p
TVSTAT       <DIR>      07-30-93   12:07a
WIND         <DIR>      04-29-93   11:26a
TREEINFO NCD       1355 08-12-93   11:50p
        15 file(s)          1355 bytes
                        69304320 bytes free
```

Figure 3-8

The DOS DIR command displays the names of and other information about files and subdirectories on a disk. Displayed here is the root, or top, directory of a hard disk (the F: drive). It shows the names of 14 subdirectories and one file. Notice in the summary following the directory listing that the DIR command counts subdirectories and files together.

to the drive. Floppy-disk drives are usually assigned the letters A and B, whereas hard-disk drives are lettered beginning with C. To use the DIR command to view the directory of a drive other than the one you're currently using, you include the drive letter followed by a colon after the DIR command:

DIR A:

This command displays the files on the floppy disk in the A drive. In a graphical environment, you click on the icon that represents your computer's floppy-disk drive (usually a small picture of a floppy disk), and a window appears with the list of files.

As you begin to use a computer, you will find that you accumulate a large number of word-processing, spreadsheet, database, and other types of files very quickly. This creates a problem. When there are hundreds of files on a disk, finding the one you want can be time consuming. To avoid this, you need to use another means provided by the OS to organize files into smaller, more logical groups. The facility OSs provide to do this is subdirectories, or folders within folders.

A **subdirectory** is an additional directory that you can create. When you list a disk's main directory, called its **root directory**, subdirectory names appear in the listing similar to the way that file names appear. The only difference is that next to the name of the subdirectory, the DIR command displays <DIR>, indicating that this is the name of a subdirectory. Figure 3-8 shows a directory listing of the root directory of a hard disk. The files are shown with their size in bytes and the date and time when they were last modified. You can also see several subdirectories in the list that display <DIR> instead of a file size.

The equivalent of a subdirectory on a Macintosh computer is the folder, which is represented by an icon that looks like a manila file folder (Figure 3-9). In Microsoft Windows, subdirectories are also represented graphically by a file-folder icon, but they're still called directories and subdirectories, rather than folders. With a Macintosh or a PC using Norton Desktop for Windows, you access a disk's root directory or folder by clicking the disk drive's icon on the desktop. However, with a Macintosh, it's not usually called the root directory; more often, it's called the root folder or just the drive folder.

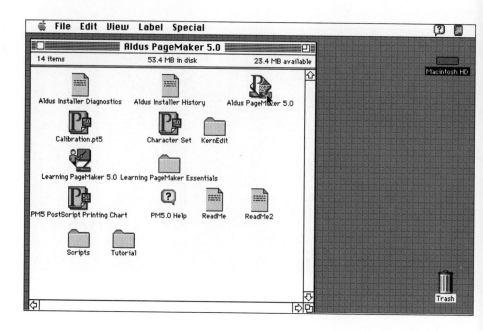

Figure 3-9

On a Macintosh the file folders represent subdirectories.

To organize your disk logically, you should store related files together in subdirectories or folders that have meaningful names. Subdirectories and folders can contain other subdirectories and folders, so you can create a hierarchy (or tree) of them that branches off the root directory.

Supporting Programs

Another major function of an OS is to provide services to other programs. Often, these services are similar to those that the OS provides directly to users. For example, when you want your word-processing program to retrieve a document you've been working with, the word processor will list the files in the directory that you specify.

To do this, the program calls on the OS to list the files. The OS goes through the same process to build a list of files whether it receives its instructions directly from a user or from an application program. But when the request comes from an application, the OS sends the results of its work to the application program instead of directly to the computer screen.

Some of the other services that an OS provides to programs are saving files to disk, reading them from disk into memory, checking available disk or memory space, allocating memory to hold data for a program, reading keystrokes from the keyboard and displaying characters or graphics on the screen.

POPULAR PERSONAL COMPUTER OPERATING SYSTEMS

In this section, we'll take a closer look at each of the important personal computer OSs; we'll discuss some of their benefits and drawbacks, as well as some of their characteristics and most interesting aspects.

DOS

MS-DOS (Figure 3-10) is the most common and popular of all the PC OSs. The reasons for its popularity continue to be the overwhelming volume of available software and the large installed base of Intel-based PCs. By the time Intel released the 80286, DOS had become so popular and entrenched in the marketplace that DOS and DOS applications represented the majority of the PC software market. At that time, IBM compatibility was a necessity for successful products, and "IBM compatibility" meant computers that run DOS as well as IBM's computers that run DOS.

Figure 3-10

Microsoft DOS is the most prevalent OS for personal computers today.

Using DOS Commands.

Because DOS is the biggest-selling program of all time, thousands of applications have been developed to run on DOS-based machines, and millions of users have learned to use the DOS command-line interface. Although DOS is not exactly user friendly, most people find they can use it with practice. That's primarily because you need to know only a handful of commands to be a proficient DOS user, and most of them are easy to remember. For example, here are a few of the most common DOS commands:

Command	Purpose
DIR	Displays a directory listing
COPY	Copies a file
RENAME or REN	Renames a file
DEL or ERASE	Erases a file
CHDIR or CD	Changes the current directory
MKDIR or MD	Makes a new directory
FORMAT	Formats a disk

Most of these commands require **arguments**, which are specific pieces of information required to complete the command. For example, the COPY command requires the name of the file you want to copy and the directory you want to copy it to. The command

COPY LETTER01.DOC C:\MEMOS

tells DOS to copy the file named LETTER01.DOC into the MEMOS directory of the C: drive, which is generally the computer's internal hard disk.

Internal and External Commands.

Overall, DOS has about 70 commands. About 25 of them are built into the DOS command interpreter. Because the program code for them remains resident in memory most of the time, these built-in commands are called **internal commands**. There isn't enough memory for all the DOS commands to reside in RAM, so the remaining commands are **external commands**—separate programs included with DOS.

Because they are memory resident, internal commands can be carried out very quickly at any time. On the other hand, external commands remain in disk storage, usually in the DOS directory. When these commands are issued, DOS has to find them on disk, read the instructions, and then carry out the command. As a result, external commands are executed much more slowly than internal ones.

Microsoft Windows.

In spite of all the upgrades and improvements that have been made over the years, the biggest thing that ever happened to DOS was

Figure 3-11

Microsoft Windows provides a
GUI for DOS-based personal
computers.

Microsoft Windows (Figure 3-11). The first version of Windows was released in 1987. Microsoft had come to accept the popularity of the Mac and users' desire for a GUI. Windows was the PC answer. However, it wasn't until Microsoft released Windows 3.0 in 1990 that the program really took off. Suddenly, home users and businesspeople alike began converting en masse from pure command-line DOS to Windows.

Microsoft Windows can run standard DOS programs, either in a window within the GUI or full-screen. To take full advantage of the Microsoft Windows environment, though, you need programs written specifically for Windows. Microsoft itself is a major developer of programs written for Microsoft Windows. However, many other software developers also produce versions of their programs for DOS, Microsoft Windows, and the Macintosh.

As is true of any GUI, the benefits of Microsoft Windows are several. First, it's easier for new computer users to learn to use a mouse, icons, and drop-down menus than it is to learn to use a command-line OS. It's just more intuitive than typing commands at the keyboard. In addition, Microsoft Windows programs conform to a standard way of working. A Microsoft Windows word processor works similarly to the way a Microsoft Windows spreadsheet (or any other type of Windows program) works. This means that experience you gain by learning one Windows program is applicable to every other Microsoft Windows program. Finally, Microsoft Windows allows users to switch between running programs quickly and easily.

Microsoft Windows does require a fairly fast and capable computer—and, to realize the most benefit from the graphical environment, the computer should also have a fast, high-resolution monitor. Whereas basic DOS needs less than 3 MB of disk space, Microsoft Windows can consume up to 10 MB. In addition, Microsoft Windows needs a minimum of 2 MB of RAM, with at least 4 MB recommended for running most Windows applications.

OS/2

After the introduction of the Intel 80286 processor, both IBM and Microsoft recognized the need to take advantage of the multitasking capabilities of this CPU. They teamed up to develop OS/2, a modern multitasking OS for Intel microprocessors. The partnership did not last long, though. Technical differences of opinion and IBM's perception of Microsoft Windows as a threat to OS/2 (which proved to be accurate) caused a rift between the companies that ultimately led to the dissolution of the partnership.

IBM continued the development and promotion of OS/2 as a strategic cornerstone of its System Application Architecture (SAA). OS/2 is IBM's OS for the small computers in the mosaic of its hardware offerings. Microsoft decided to use its own experience with OS/2 and to improve on OS/2 with Windows NT. Like Windows NT, OS/2 is a single-user multitasking OS.

OS/2, like DOS, has a character-based command-line mode, but unlike DOS, the command interpreter is a separate program from the OS kernel, and it is invoked only when you click one of the "OS/2 Prompt" icons within the Workplace Shell. Its command syntax and file system are similar to those of DOS (Figure 3-12); however, OS/2 is a true multitasking OS. OS/2 computers

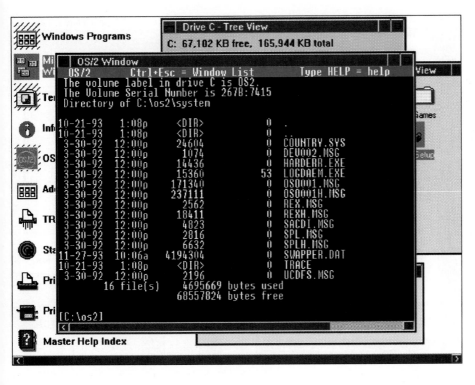

```
Windows Programs
                    Drive C - Tree View
                    C: 67,102 KB free, 165,944 KB total

        OS/2 Window
    OS/2        Ctrl+Esc = Window List        Type HELP = help        View
    The volume label in drive C is OS2.
    The Volume Serial Number is 267B:7415
    Directory of C:\os2\system

    10-21-93    1:08p    <DIR>            0    .
    10-21-93    1:08p    <DIR>            0    ..
    3-30-92    12:00p    24604            0    COUNTRY.SYS
    3-30-92    12:00p     1074            0    DEU002.MSG
    3-30-92    12:00p    14436            0    HARDERR.EXE
    3-30-92    12:00p    15360           53    LOGDAEM.EXE
    3-30-92    12:00p   171340            0    OSO001.MSG
    3-30-92    12:00p   237111            0    OSO001H.MSG
    3-30-92    12:00p     2562            0    REX.MSG
    3-30-92    12:00p    18411            0    REXH.MSG
    3-30-92    12:00p     4823            0    SACDI.MSG
    3-30-92    12:00p     2816            0    SPL.MSG
    3-30-92    12:00p     6632            0    SPLH.MSG
    11-27-93   10:06a   4194304           0    SWAPPER.DAT
    10-21-93    1:08p    <DIR>            0    TRACE
    3-30-92    12:00p     2196            0    UCDFS.MSG
               16 file(s)    4695669 bytes used
                            68557824 bytes free

    [C:\os2]
```

Figure 3-12

OS/2, like DOS, has a character-based command-line mode.

and DOS computers format and use floppy disks in nearly the same way, so they can read and write each other's disks with ease.

OS/2 commands are similar to those in DOS. Many commands are, in fact, identical to their DOS counterparts. Others differ only slightly, and, of course, OS/2 has more commands because OS/2 is larger, more comprehensive, and more modern.

Presentation Manager (PM) is the graphical environment for OS/2. The Workplace Shell is the equivalent of a desktop manager for PM. In OS/2, you specify the name of the shell you want in the system start-up files.

The Macintosh OS

The Macintosh is a purely graphical machine. In fact, there is no equivalent of a command-line interface available for it. Its tight integration of OS, GUI, and desktop makes it a favorite for people who do not want to deal with a comand-line interface.

The Macintosh's graphical capabilities made that machine the early forerunner in computerized graphics fields such as desktop publishing. In fact, publishing and drawing software for the Macintosh is of such a professional quality that many large publishing companies use it exclusively.

The Macintosh desktop sports a menu bar across the top of the screen with pull-down menu options, as well as icons for disk drives, printers, programs, and folders that can contain programs, files, or other folders (Figure 3-13). When you click on a folder, it opens into a window to display its contents.

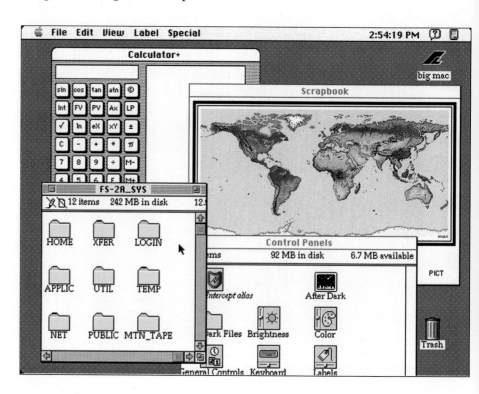

Figure 3-13

Macintosh desktop.

Microsoft Windows NT

With Microsoft Windows NT, Microsoft has expressed its commitment to writing software, not just for desktop PCs, but also for powerful workstations and network and database servers. Microsoft Windows NT is neither necessarily a replacement for DOS, nor a new version of DOS—it's an altogether new OS, designed from scratch for the most modern and capable machines available.

Microsoft Windows NT offers built-in features that no other PC OS has—with the possible exception of Unix. In addition to the traditional Unix features of strict system security, built-in networking, built-in communications and electronic-mail services, development and system-administration tools, and a GUI, Microsoft Windows NT can run Microsoft Windows applications and many Unix applications directly.

Microsoft Windows NT departs from the DOS tradition and joins Unix and OS/2 in a true multitasking environment. Microsoft Windows NT is based on a microkernel (a relatively small main control program that stays in the computer's memory), like DOS, Unix, and OS/2. In addition to being multitasking, Microsoft Windows NT is designed to take advantage of symmetric multiprocessing.

Built-in Features. Microsoft Windows NT is a purely graphical OS; its native interface is a GUI (Figure 3-14). The look and feel of Microsoft Windows NT's GUI is similar to that of Microsoft Windows for DOS systems. The major difference is that, unlike Microsoft Windows, the GUI not only comes with the OS—it *is* the OS. However, unlike the Macintosh, Windows NT allows you access to command-line DOS. Microsoft Windows NT can support multiple simultaneous DOS sessions by simply running the DOS command interpreter as a program under Windows NT (either in a window or full screen).

Now let's look at one of the most universal types of applications software.

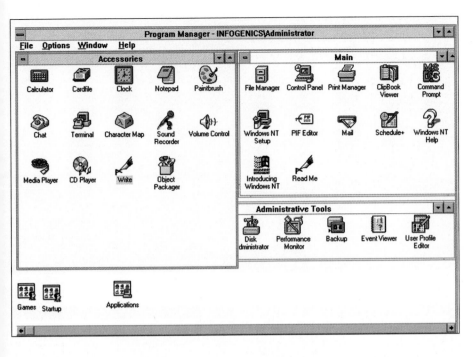

Figure 3-14
Windows NT.

USING A WORD PROCESSOR

At work, at school, or at home, we all need to capture our thoughts, plans, and ideas in writing. For most people, writing is an everyday occurrence. One of the most pervasive uses of computers is for creating and managing documents. The need to create documents is so common that almost every computer user owns some form of word-processing software.

As in most competitive industries, software companies strive to produce products better than those of their competitors, to gain a larger share of the marketplace. Word-processing software and its users benefit from this competition. Developers invest considerable amounts of time and money in thinking up ways to make writing—and word processing in general—easier.

In this section, we'll look at some features that have found their way into the standard equipment lists of most high-quality word-processing packages. We'll start with the basics—what a word-processor screen looks like, and how to enter text and to get around. Then, we'll take a look at some of the more powerful aspects of word processors.

Your Window into the Document

When you first start a word processor, you find yourself in an editing screen. Of course, every word processor looks different and works a little differently. Some take over a computer's entire screen, converting it into an electronic blank sheet of paper. Figure 3-15 shows WordPerfect 6.0 for DOS running in text mode. WordPerfect is a popular word processor that's available for almost every kind of computer.

Many word processors, especially those designed for graphical environments, open a window that you can arrange to suit you. On a computer with a

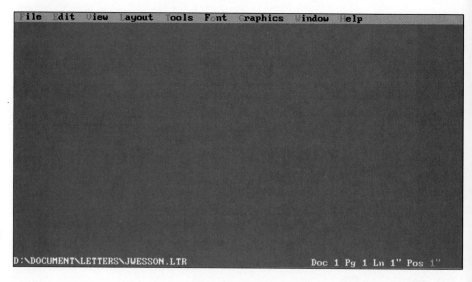

Figure 3-15

WordPerfect 6.0 for DOS
provides a menu bar across the
top of the screen for issuing
commands. The bottom line
indicates the current file, and the
cursor position and page within
the file. The area between the
menu on the top line of the
screen and the status information
on the bottom line of the screen
is the editing area.

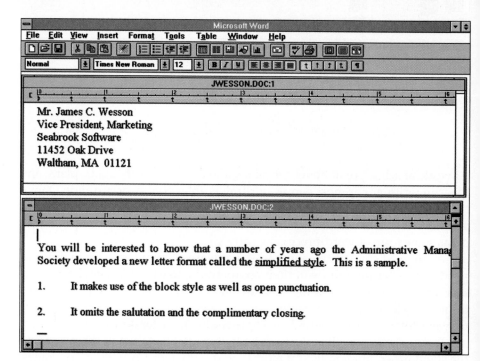

Figure 3-16

In windowed environments, you
can create multiple windows—
each containing a different
document, or different views
of the same document.

sufficiently large monitor, you can open several windows, each with a different document or with different views of the same document, and can arrange
them such that you can quickly change from window to window simply by
clicking in the one you want. For example, if you want to see text on page 1
and on page 25 of a document at the same time, you can open a new window
and arrange the two windows such that you can see both (Figure 3-16). Most of
the time, though, you'll want to open up the window such that it uses the entire screen.

　　Word processors that are designed for graphical environments display on-
screen text that closely resembles what the printed document will look like
(Figure 3-17). This feature is called **WYSIWYG** (pronounced "wiz-ee-wig"),
which is an acronym for "**What You See Is What You Get.**" When the Macintosh was introduced in 1984, it was the first computer with the graphic power

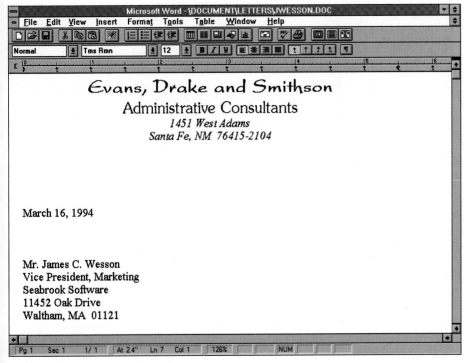

Figure 3-17
Today, most word processors, especially those designed for graphical environments (i.e., the Macintosh, Windows, and Windows NT), display on the screen text and graphics that closely resemble what the printed document will look like.

to be WYSIWYG, and the term was coined to distinguish it and other early graphical word processors from the common systems of the day, which didn't have the same capability. Today, the most powerful and popular word processors are all written for graphical environments (the Macintosh and Microsoft Windows) and, as such, are WYSIWYG.

Entering Text

You create a document by typing text with the computer's keyboard. In a new document, the word processor will place a cursor in the upper-left corner of the window. In nongraphical word processors, the cursor is likely to be a flashing horizontal bar or block. In graphical ones, the cursor may be a flashing vertical bar. As you type characters, the cursor advances across the screen, showing you where the next character will be placed.

Correcting a Typing Mistake.

If you make a mistake as you type, there are several ways you can fix the error using special keys such as those shown in Figure 3-18. If the mistake was in the last word you typed (just to the left of the cursor), you can use the backspace key on an IBM-compatible keyboard to move back to the point where the mistake began. Use the delete key on the main keypad for a Macintosh keyboard. The backspace key or delete key on a Macintosh moves the cursor to the left and at the same time, removes the characters it moves over.

On IBM compatible keyboards you can use the delete key to remove letters at the cursor position. Each time you press the delete key, the character beneath the cursor (or to the right of the cursor, if the cursor is displayed as a vertical line) is removed, and the characters that follow shift to the left to compensate. As you type the replacement characters, they are inserted into the text at the cursor position and the characters following shift back to the right.

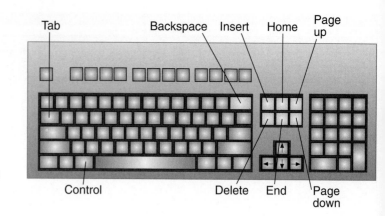

Figure 3-18

You can use the backspace, insert, or delete keys such as those shown on this IBM compatible keyboard to edit quickly.

Most word processors also have a feature that lets you move the cursor from word to word, rather than just moving by one character at a time. To do this in Microsoft Word (for Windows), for example, you hold down the control key and press the left or right arrow key. The cursor jumps to the first character of the word on the left or right. Learning all your word processor's cursor movement keys from the outset can quickly pay off in time savings by reducing keystrokes.

You can also use a mouse to help make corrections. By moving the mouse cursor over a letter and clicking the mouse button, you can move the cursor directly to the letter. (The mouse has its own cursor that is separate from the keyboard—or text— cursor.) This method takes only a few keystrokes to replace the letter. As you gain experience with a word processor, you'll gradually develop a sense of the way that's easiest for you to correct errors.

Word Wrap. With a word processor, you don't have to worry about moving the cursor down to the next line as your text nears the right edge of the screen— the cursor will automatically drop down to the next line. If you begin to type a word that won't fit near the edge of the screen, the program will move the whole word to the next line. This feature is called **word wrap**.

Since the program automatically wraps text, the only time you have to press the enter or return key is at the end of a paragraph. The word-wrap feature maintains the format of the lines of a paragraph continuously and automatically. For example, if you add or delete a word from the middle of a paragraph, every line from that point to the end of the paragraph will be reformatted so the text flows smoothly from line to line.

Scrolling and Getting Around. When you get near the bottom of your word processor's screen or window, you don't have to be concerned about running out of room to type. When you reach the right edge of the bottom line, the top line on screen will move out of view and the rest of the lines will move up to make room for a new line at the bottom. This is called **scrolling**.

When your document is larger than a full screen's height, the screen is like a window that you move up and down to see different parts of the document. Pressing the down arrow key when the cursor is at the bottom of the screen causes the text of the document to scroll up as you move down through the document. Conversely, pressing the up arrow key while the cursor is at the top of the screen makes the text scroll downward as you move up through the document (Figure 3-19).

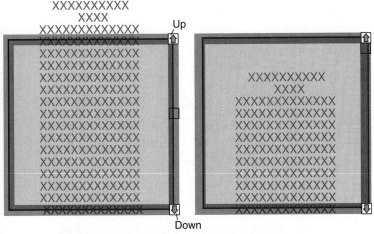

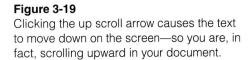

Scrolling the text downward with the up arrow

Figure 3-19
Clicking the up scroll arrow causes the text to move down on the screen—so you are, in fact, scrolling upward in your document.

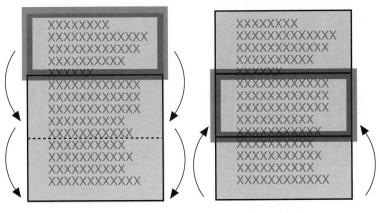

Page up and page down scrolls one page's worth of text.

Figure 3-20
Press the page up and page down keys to move the window one screen's depth.

You can move your view of the document more quickly by pressing the page up and page down keys. These keys move the window up or down one full screen (Figure 3-20). With some word processors, however, these keys reposition your window to the top of the previous or next *printed page*—which may be several screen pages away.

Another way to move up and down is by using the mouse and **scroll bar**. On the right edge of the screen (Figure 3-21) is a vertical bar with an arrow button at the top pointing upward, and one at the bottom pointing down. These buttons are called **scroll arrows.** By clicking the mouse cursor on these buttons, you can scroll the window up and down one line at a time, regardless of where the text cursor is on the screen.

Also located on the vertical scroll bar is a **scroll box**. In a large document, you can move quickly through it by dragging the scroll box up or down along the scroll bar to the relative position you want to go to. For example, to move quickly to the middle of a document, you can drag the scroll box to the middle of the scroll bar. Then, to position your text cursor precisely, just click the spot where you want it with the mouse.

The arrow keys are probably the only cursor-movement keys that universally work the same way from one word processor to another. There are, however, some widely accepted norms for the way the rest of the cursor-control

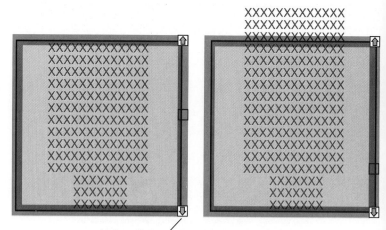

Figure 3-21

Clicking the down scroll arrow moves the text up one line at a time, which means you are scrolling down through your document.

Using the mouse to hold down the down arrow to scroll up, one line at a time

and positioning keys should work. For example, with most word processors, the home key positions the cursor at the beginning of the current line and the end key (as mentioned before) positions it at the end of the line.

By holding down the control key and pressing the home key, you can quickly go to the top of a document. Similarly, control down arrow takes you to the bottom of the document. Most word processors also provide a way to move the text cursor quickly to the top and bottom of the current window without scrolling the window. Commonly, control page up positions the text cursor at the top of the window and control page down places it at the bottom.

Tabs and Indentation. The keyboard's tab key moves the text cursor forward (to the right) until it encounters a tab stop. A **tab stop** is a point on the screen measured from the left edge (or margin) of the document. When you create a new document, tab stops are typically defined at every fourth or fifth character, or at every ½-inch mark. Most word processors allow you to change or remove the tab stops by displaying a ruler across the top or bottom of the screen that shows where tabs are defined. In some word processors, the ruler and tab stops are visible at all times. Tabs are a great deal more useful than just to indent the first line of a paragraph. Tabs can be invaluable aids for aligning columns of text accurately.

Making the Change

The freedom to modify existing documents is one of the simplest yet most powerful aspects of a word processor. You can easily make changes to text by positioning the cursor with the arrow keys or mouse, then using the delete key to remove unwanted characters and simply typing the replacement text. For bigger changes, there are better tools.

Selecting Text and Blocks. A **block** is a contiguous group of words, sentences, or paragraphs in your document that you earmark for one of several purposes (which we'll look at shortly). Most graphical word processors allow you to mark text easily by positioning the mouse cursor at the beginning of the block, then pressing and holding down the mouse button while you move the mouse cursor to the end of the block, called **dragging**. As you hold down the

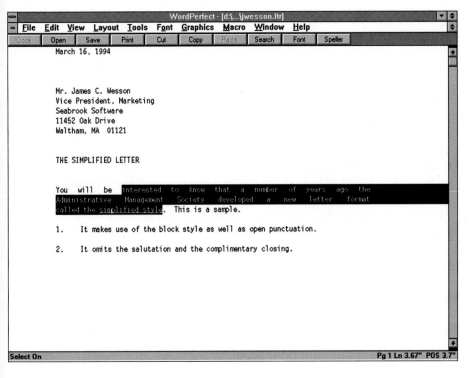

Figure 3-22

To select text with a mouse, hold the mouse button down while you move the mouse over the text—the text will be highlighted as it is selected.

mouse button and move the mouse cursor over the text, the text will change color to indicate that the text is **selected** (Figure 3-22).

You can select text with the keyboard as well. In some word processors, you select text with the keyboard by holding down one of the shift keys and moving the cursor with the arrow keys. In WordPerfect for DOS (one of the most popular word processors), you select text with the keyboard by first issuing the Block command (by holding down the alt key and pressing F4); then, you move the cursor with the arrow keys to select the block.

To deselect a block with a mouse, click the mouse anywhere on the screen. The block will disappear. To deselect using the keyboard, press one of the cursor movement keys such as an arrow key.

Inserting and Deleting Text.
In the section "Entering Text," you learned how to move the cursor to a mistake, delete the offending characters, and make a correction by typing the correct characters. Inserting the correct characters in the middle of a line results in the characters to the right of the cursor moving over to allow room for the new characters.

Another way to make a correction like this is to use the word processor's **overtype mode**. In overtype mode, you need only to position the cursor at the beginning of the text you want to replace, and to type the replacement text. As you type characters, they will replace the existing text, rather than moving it to the right. In some word processors, overtype mode is called **typeover mode**.

Most word processors default to **insert mode** (where characters are inserted into a line), rather than to overtype mode. You switch between insert and overtype mode by pressing the keyboard's insert key, which acts like a toggle switch.

Some word processors have special key combinations for deleting a word, sentence, line, or an entire paragraph or page. The quickest way to delete a block of text is to select it using one of the methods described in the previous section, and then to press the delete key. Most word processors provide an Undo command that allows you to retrieve deleted text if you make a mistake (although, if you do make a mistake, you have to issue the Undo command immediately after the deletion).

Moving, or Cutting and Pasting, Blocks of Text.

With some word processors, moving text is as easy as selecting it with a mouse, then dragging it to a new location and dropping it. In other systems, the same edit might involve selecting the text, moving the cursor to the position you want the text to occupy, and then pressing another key combination.

Sometimes, you may want to move some text that you can't easily move by dragging (like moving a paragraph from page 25 to page 2). Almost every word processor provides an invisible holding area or buffer, often called a **clipboard**, for cutting and pasting text. You can select sections of text and then issue a **Cut command** (often shift + delete) to remove the text from your document to the clipboard. Then, you position your cursor where you want the text to be located and issue the **Paste command** (often control + insert). The word processor will insert the text from the clipboard starting at the cursor position.

Search and Replace.

One exceptionally handy feature found in every word processor is **search and replace** or **find and change**. With search and replace, you can make the program look for every occurrence of a sequence of characters, word, name, or phrase, and replace each one with new text. For example, say that you create a 10-page document, then realize that you misspelled a person's name in dozens of places throughout the document. Instead of spelling the name "Stevens," you spelled it "Stephans."

By choosing "Search and Replace" from a menu, you can easily replace the name with the proper spelling everywhere it occurs. When you select the menu option you enter the text to search for, and the text to replace it with. To complete the command you step through the document, replacing each occurrence one at a time, or you can have the program replace them all automatically.

Formatting Text

Now that you know how to enter text into a document and to edit it, let's take a closer look at making the text look good.

Typeface Families and Fonts.

The term **typeface** refers to the style of the letters, symbols, and punctuation marks in your document. Typefaces have names such as Times, Helvetica, and Palatino. In addition to the basic style, a typeface also has variations. Bold and italic are two variations a typeface may have.

A **typeface family** includes all the bold, italic, and bold-italic variations that go along with a particular typeface. Thus, Times Roman and Times Italic are two different typefaces that belong to the same typeface family—the Times family.

In word processing, size and distance are measured in units of **points** and **picas**. Typically, points are used for vertical measurements such as the height of characters or the space between lines, whereas picas are used for larger horizontal measurements such as the width of a column or page. In basic word processing, you won't run into picas very often. You will, however, need to use point measurements to specify the size of your type.

This is 8 point Times Roman

This is 9 point Times Roman

This is 12 point Times Roman

This is 24 point Times Roman

Figure 3-23

Point size affects both the horizontal and vertical size and spacing of characters.

There are 72 points to an inch—so an 8-point font will yield nine lines of text in 1 inch of vertical space with no space between the lines. A 9-point font results in eight lines per inch, and a 12-point font in six lines per inch. The important thing to remember is the larger the point size is, the larger the characters are (Figure 3-23).

A **font** is the complete set of type (including bold, italic, and bold-italic, and all sizes) for a given typeface in a specific size. Most word processors come with at least a handful of fonts built in. In graphical environments such as the Macintosh and Microsoft Windows, you also have access to any additional fonts on the system. You can also purchase additional fonts for use with any program on the computer including your word processor.

There are two general categories of fonts. Every character of a **monospace font** takes up exactly the same amount of horizontal space. Monospace fonts resemble the output of a typewriter because every character aligns perfectly with the characters above and below it. Courier is the most common monospace font.

Most fonts, however, are not monospace fonts. They are **proportional** or **kerned** fonts. With a proportional font, each character may have a slightly different width. An example is the letters *M* and *I*. The letter M is much wider than the letter I. In a proportional font, the I will take up less horizontal space than the M. In a monospace font, the letters take up the same amount of space regardless of their width.

Typefaces also fall into two additional broad categories—**serif** and **sans serif**. Serif type has fancy curls and decorative adornments. Sans serif type does not (sans means "without" in French). Some people think that sans serif fonts have a more modern look, but serif fonts exude elegance and are said to hold a body of text together better.

Applying Fonts to Your Document.

There are two ways you might apply a font to your text. In an empty document, or at any point within an existing document, you can select a font so that every character you type from that point on will be in the new font. The second way you might apply a font is to change the font of text you've already entered. In practice, you use both methods.

Printing Your Documents

The purpose of creating documents is, of course, to print and use them. In this section, we'll cover the important highlights of printing your documents.

Printers.

Most word processors support almost all of the most popular printers sold today, in addition to many older printers that are no longer available. Supporting a printer means knowing how to use the features of a printer such as setting bold, italic, and underlined characteristics, and how to use the printer's graphic modes.

Most printers can print many typefaces and sizes, and a good word proces-sor relieves you of most of the details about printer compatibility. In fact, you have to be concerned with your type of printer only once—when you initially install your word-processing software and tell it what type of printer you have.

Print Preview. A feature many word processors provide is the ability to pre-view pages before you print them. This capability is called **print preview**. Print preview shrinks the pages of your document down so you can see an entire page at once or even to view facing pages at the same time. Sometimes there is a feature that allows you to magnify the page. You usually can't edit your text in print preview, but it is especially helpful for seeing how margin settings and headers and footers will affect your document before you waste paper to find out.

Printing the Document. Since your word-processing system is already aware of the type of printer you have, printing is usually as simple as picking Print from a menu or clicking a printer button on a tool bar. Most word processors allow you to print either the entire document, a single page, a range of pages, or selected text.

ADVANCED WORD-PROCESSOR FEATURES

In this section, we'll look at some of the more advanced features that many word processors offer. We'll investigate how these tools can make word pro-cessing faster and easier.

Checking Your Spelling

Every serious word processor has a **spell checker**. The ability to check your spelling can go a long way toward providing you with an added sense of con-fidence that a document will be professional in every sense—with no mis-spelled words.

Spell checkers work by looking up every word in a document in an inter-nal dictionary. These dictionaries typically contain thousands of words and will find and verify just about every common word in a document. There are, however, many words that spell checkers will question because they don't find them in their dictionaries—for example, the names of people and companies, and many abbreviations and acronyms. For this reason, good spell checkers allow you to create your own custom dictionaries that the spell checkers will use for reference in addition to their standard dictionaries.

Unfortunately, spell checkers are not yet smart enough to check for the context of a word. Some words will be considered correct even if the usage is wrong. For example, consider the sentence

It was a pleasant seen.

Clearly, "seen" should be "scene"—but the spell checker will go right by it because "seen" is a correctly spelled word. Because spell checkers can check only for spelling, and not for usage, new products called **grammar checkers** have emerged on the market. These packages check for word usage, correct grammar, and sometimes even things like writing style. They are usually sold separately, although the trend is to integrate them into word processors.

Using a Thesaurus

A feature that's becoming standard in word processors is an on-line thesaurus. A **thesaurus** provides a list of alternative words with similar meanings. When you compose a document and think that a word just isn't quite right, you can highlight the word and bring up the thesaurus for a list of viable alternatives.

Using an Outliner

An **outliner**, or **outline view**, is a powerful tool for planning and rearranging large documents. An outline is a plan, or a map, of a document. Most documents that are more than several pages in length can and should be broken up into logical sections or groups—like the sections of this chapter. Preparing an outline in advance of composing the text of your document can help you plan its content and ensure that you cover each topic in a logical order.

Some word processors have a separate view for displaying the outline of a document—a kind of switch between displaying the normal text and displaying just the outline of the document. Outlines are made up of heading levels, possibly with text written underneath. A word processor typically numbers headings according to their levels—starting with 1 (the most prominent heads) to 2, 3, or as many subheading levels as you want. You can assign a special look to each heading, so that the headings are easily distinguishable.

Outliners let you promote and demote heading levels. You can also move headings around in the outline—and all the text associated with a heading moves with it automatically!

Styles and Style Sheets

A **style sheet** is a collection of your favorite or most-used text and formatting elements. For documents that require a great deal of formatting with different pieces having different fonts, sizes, or margins, a style sheet can save a great deal of time in the long run.

You create style sheets in some very different ways from one word processor to the next. The basic idea, though, is that you create a collection of individual styles once, then save them as a style sheet. In some word processors, when you create a new document, you choose a style sheet from a list. The new document is preloaded with all your defined styles for that type of document. You can modify the styles that already exist or you can create new ones.

Using style sheets can be a tremendous time saver when you want to make universal changes. Let's say you are using a style sheet and decide that the level 1 heads should really be set in Palatino instead of Times New Roman. All you have to do is to change the definition of that style, and every level 1 head in the document changes to Palatino. In addition, every document using that style sheet will change.

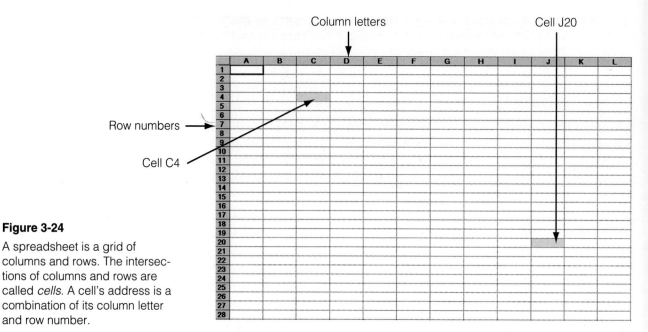

Figure 3-24

A spreadsheet is a grid of columns and rows. The intersections of columns and rows are called *cells*. A cell's address is a combination of its column letter and row number.

SPREADSHEETS

A **spreadsheet** is a tool for calculating and evaluating numbers. It also offers capabilities for creating reports and presentations to communicate what analysis reveals. Spreadsheet software makes these tasks easy by providing a visual framework to work within, and providing the tools that you need to make number crunching a breeze.

Not so long ago, worksheets were multicolumn paper grids that came in pads. Accountants used the oversized pages to prepare financial statements by hand, penciling numbers in the rows and columns and using adding machines to make calculations.

The electronic spreadsheet offers a huge improvement over its paper predecessor. The computer takes care of arithmetic, mistakes are much easier to correct, and powerful features let you automate and illustrate your work. Whereas paper spreadsheets were the tools of accountants, spreadsheet programs are tools for anyone who needs to record, organize, or analyze numbers.

The basic idea of a spreadsheet program is fairly simple—give each intersection of columns and rows an address and allow the user to enter information there. These intersections of rows and columns are called **cells.** Most spreadsheets number rows from the top of the spreadsheet to the bottom. Some also number columns from left to right, but most of them letter the columns from left to right, starting with the letter *A*.

You identify a cell in a spreadsheet by its address, which is a combination of its column letter and row number. For example, C4 is the address of the cell at the intersection of the third column (column C) and the fourth row (row 4). A1 is the top left cell of a spreadsheet and J20 is the cell at the intersection of the J column (the tenth column) and row 20 (Figure 3-24).

In addition to allowing you to enter information into cells, spreadsheet programs calculate mathematical formulas that you put in cells, print your spreadsheets, and also allow you to save them to disk. Like a word processor,

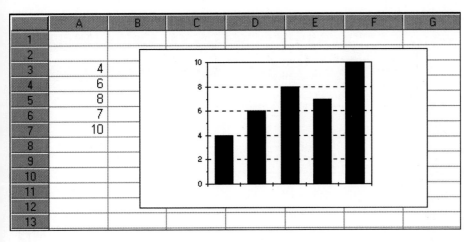

Figure 3-25

In most spreadsheets, creating a graph is as simple as selecting a range of cells and clicking a graph button.

a spreadsheet program is a framework in which you create data files, save them, and retrieve them later.

The word *spreadsheet* is sometimes used to refer to spreadsheet data files that have been created in a spreadsheet program and saved. More often, and for the rest of this chapter, we'll call the data files **worksheets.** That way, it will be clear whether we're talking about a spreadsheet program or a data file.

The uses for spreadsheets are tremendously diverse. You can use a spreadsheet for spur-of-the-moment numeric calculations that you don't need to save, for long-term projects that accumulate monthly or yearly data, and for myriad other applications, from producing billing invoices to preparing financial statements and tax worksheets. In general, you use a spreadsheet to deal with numeric data and especially to perform any kind of analysis on those data.

Graphics and Presentations

Spreadsheets are excellent tools for creating graphs and presentation materials, because these capabilities are built right into them. With many spreadsheet programs, creating a graph is as simple as using the mouse to select a block of cells, and clicking a Graph button. Figure 3-25 shows such a graph created in exactly this way. For fancier graphs, you just need to open a menu and choose the type of graph you want.

In addition to giving you the ability to create graphs and images, some spreadsheets allow you to create a slide show of graphs you've created. You define the order in which you want the graphics presented, and can specify either that there be a time interval for the program to display each one or that it should display the next graph when a key is pressed. Spreadsheet slide shows are an excellent medium for technical presentations as well as demonstrations.

CREATING A WORKSHEET

A typical opening screen for a spreadsheet might look something like Figure 3-26. There is often a row of letters or numbers across the top of the window (the column headings) and a row of numbers down the left edge of the window (the row numbers). With some spreadsheets, visible lines separate the

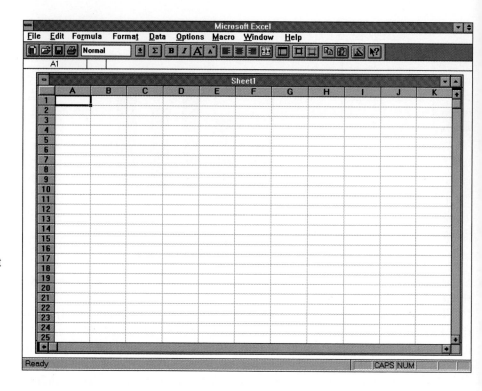

Figure 3-26

The work area in a spreadsheet is a grid of rows and columns. Visible near the top of the screen is the menu from which users can select actions such as loading previously saved worksheets or formatting cell entries.

columns and rows, creating a grid effect so you can easily see the column and row of a cell. With others, there are no lines—there is just an invisible grid ready to accept data.

There are a few common ways to move around a worksheet. The page up and page down keys move you up and down one screen's depth as you look at different areas of the worksheet. Sometimes the tab and shift-tab keys move your window right and left one screen's width.

In a worksheet, the cursor is usually a large block that covers an entire cell. The cursor in a worksheet indicates which cell is the current cell. In a worksheet, you first move the cursor to select a cell—then you begin to type information.

Some spreadsheets have a menu across the top of the screen from which you choose operations such as loading or saving a spreadsheet file and printing it. Others do not always have a menu. In some, such as Lotus 1-2-3 for DOS, you have to press a special key to activate the menu. For example, in Lotus 1-2-3, you use the forward slash (/) key. Like other types of applications, though, spreadsheets are migrating into graphical environments and the standards there dictate that menus are always visible.

Entering Information

The whole point of a spreadsheet program is to give you flexibility for presenting any collection of textual or numeric data in a logical and attractive way. You can put numbers, single characters, sentences, dates, symbols, and anything else you can think of into a cell. The spreadsheet program, however, treats your entry as one of several distinct types of data. Generally, there are four types of cell data:

Labels (text—words or phrases)

Numbers

Dates and/or times

Formulas

Labels.

A **label** is text that you type into a cell—any word or sequence of characters that has any meaning to you or to someone else. They're called *labels* instead of *text* because it's assumed that most text in a worksheet is for the purpose of labeling columns or rows of numbers.

With most spreadsheets, you do not have to do anything special to enter a label—just position the cursor on the cell you want to put a label into, and begin typing. For example, if you want to put the word *Sales* into cell B2 in Lotus 1-2-3 for Windows, you would use your keyboard's arrow keys to position the cell cursor on cell B2 (or click cell B2 with your mouse). Then, you type the word *Sales*, and press the enter key. The cell will display the word ("Sales").

There is an area on the screen that displays the actual contents of the cell. The word *Sales* is the **display value** of the cell—not the cell's actual content. With most spreadsheets, the area that displays the contents of a cell is called the *input line* or *input box*. When you begin typing an entry into a cell, the input line (or box) becomes active and the letters or numbers you type display there as you type them. In fact, as you type characters, they may not display in the actual cell until you press the enter key.

Numbers.

When you begin a cell entry by typing numbers, spreadsheet programs assume that you're entering a number. A cell with a number in it displays the number it contains. In other words, if you enter the number 125 into cell C2, it will display 125, and its content displayed in the input box will also be 125.

The main difference between labels and numbers is that the computer can calculate numbers. It cannot calculate labels. There may be some confusion if you want to enter a label that displays the text *1st Quarter*. As soon as you type the first character (the numeral *1*), the spreadsheet assumes you're entering a number. There is no problem with the alphabetic characters following the number 1 until you press the enter key—then the computer can't recognize the string of characters following the numeral as numbers. In this case, you have to tell the spreadsheet up front that you're entering a label by beginning your entry with the code it will understand as a label. For example, in Lotus 1-2-3 for DOS, to enter *1st Quarter* as a label, you actually type *'1st Quarter*.

One thing to keep in mind about entering numbers into a worksheet—you do not have to type in any kind of formatting or numeric punctuation, except for a decimal point. You do not even have to type a decimal point if the number does not have precision to the right of the decimal point.

Also, worksheets will not accept numbers with commas in them. To enter the number *5,280*, just type in "5280" without the comma—even if you really want the number to be displayed with a comma. If you do type a comma, the spreadsheet program will reject the number. There's a better way to format the display of numbers for both comma separators and trailing decimal places (we'll look at this in the section "Setting the Display and Print Formats").

Dates and Times.

Of course, you can enter the text *January 31, 1994* and *11:24AM* into a worksheet cell. Sometimes, entering dates and times as text this way is OK—but there is a better way. What if you wanted the spreadsheet to display the actual date and time, and be updated every time you opened the spreadsheet? Or what if you want to have the spreadsheet actually calculate using the date or time?

▭						NOTEBK1.WB1
	A	B	C	D	E	F
1		January	February	March	Qtr 1	
2	Sales	22,500	24,750	25,250	72,500	
3	Cost of Goods	18,600	19,500	19,800	57,900	
4	Gross Margin	3,900	5,250	5,450	14,600	
5						
6	Expenses	4,500	5,100	5,200	14,800	
7	Net Income	(600)	150	250	(200)	
8						
9						

Figure 3-27

A simple worksheet.

Dates and times that you want to use for calculations have to be a special kind of cell entry. Most spreadsheets allow you to enter dates in a convenient way, like "10/09/95," but internally, they treat the dates as consecutive numbers starting with day zero as January 1, 1900. Using this methodology, January 1, 1995 is actually day 34,700; January 2, 1995 is day 34,701; and so on. Dates prior to January 1, 1900 use negative numbers.

Time values also work in a special way. Different programs store time entries in different ways, but a common way is as a fractional number representing the percentage of the day that has elapsed. With this method, a single cell can contain both a date and a time. For example, at 8 o'clock in the morning, 8 of the 24 hours of the day have elapsed, so 8 AM can be represented by the fraction 8/24 or 1/3 or .333333. Similarly, at 2:24 in the afternoon, 864 of the 1,440 minutes in a day have elapsed, so 2:24 PM is represented as 0.6. Three AM January 2, 1995 is represented as 64,701.125.

Formulas. The final type of cell entry is a calculation or **formula.** A formula can be a simple mathematical equation, or as complex as you can make it. It can calculate numbers, dates, or times. Spreadsheet programs recognize all the usual arithmetic operators. The plus (+) operator adds values, a minus sign (-) subtracts, the asterisk (*) denotes multiplication, and a forward slash (/) signifies division.

Formulas that perform arithmetic operations with numbers work just as you would expect. Entering "4+2" into a cell causes the cell to display "6", although its content remains the formula. (This is another example of the difference between the display value of a cell and its actual contents.)

Most of the time, it's more useful to **reference** other cells in a formula, rather than **hard-coding** the parts of a formula. For example, Figure 3-27 shows a small worksheet. Cells B2 and B3 contain numbers (and display the numbers they contain). Cell B4 contains the formula +B2–B3 but *displays* the result of the subtraction—the value in B2 minus the value in B3. (Note that there is a plus [+] at the beginning of a formula so the program can use a cell address that starts with a letter as a number value and not a label.) Building formulas that are generalized (not hard-coded) this way allows you to easily substitute any different values in cells B2 and B3 without need to change the formula in B4. Moving the cell cursor up to cell B2 and entering a new number causes cell B4 to recalculate immediately and to display the new answer.

You can also mix and match cell references and numbers for the parts of equations—for example, +C5-C4*12/365. This example brings up an interest-

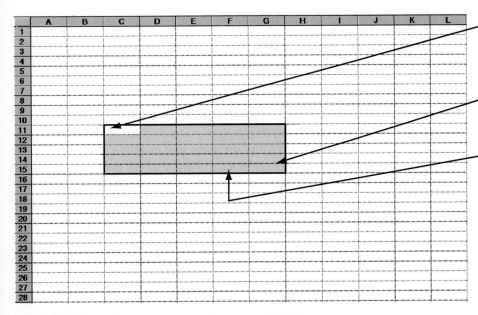

1 First, put the mouse cursor on one corner of the block that you want to select; press and hold down the mouse button.

2 While holding down the mouse button, move the cursor to the opposite corner of the block.

3 While you drag the mouse, the color of the cells underneath will change. Release the button and the block will remain highlighted.

4 With the block selected, you can use the mouse to open menus and select commands to perform operations on the selected block.

Figure 3-28
It is easy to select a block of cells with the mouse.

ing point. Sometimes it's not immediately apparent in what order the spreadsheet will perform a calculation. For example, will

$$6 + 4 * 2$$

yield 20—or 14? The answer is 14, and the reason is that spreadsheets (and most programs that allow you to do mathematical operations) do multiplication and division before addition and subtraction. This is called the **order of precedence.** Sometimes, though, you want to force a formula to do calculations in a certain order. You can override the default precedence by enclosing parts of a formula in parentheses. Entering

$$(6 + 4) * 2$$

will give a result of 20, because the parentheses force the formula to add the 6 and 4 before performing the multiplication by 2.

So far, we've looked at three items that allow you to create formulas in cells: numbers (as in "6 + 4"), operators (+,-,*,/), and cell references (C2 or A1). In addition to these, there are two more very important items that can be used as formula values—block references (or ranges) and functions.

Block References or Ranges. A **block reference** is an address of not just a single cell, but a rectangular block that may contain many different cells. For example, C11 refers to the single cell at the intersection of the third column and eleventh row. C11..G15 is a reference to the block of cells that span from cell C11 (the upper left corner of the block) to cell G15 (the lower right corner of the block).

In Figure 3-28, a spreadsheet user selects this block of cells by placing the cursor on cell C11, then pressing the mouse button and dragging the cursor to the lower right corner of the block (cell G15). When a block is selected, the program displays the cells within the block in a different color.

The reason that you might want to select a block of cells will become clear in a moment—for now, though, keep in mind that the notation of a block of cells is the addresses of the upper-left and lower-right cells, separated by two periods (C11..G15). Also keep in mind that you can easily select a block of cells with the mouse or keyboard.

Functions.

A **function** is a tool that's built into a spreadsheet program that you can use in cell formulas to perform special operations. Since functions are actually part of the spreadsheet program itself, you usually can't change them or create your own; you can only use the functions that are provided with your spreadsheet software. Let's look at an example.

Earlier, we saw an example of a formula that added the contents of two cells. We put the formula

+B2+B3

into cell B4 to add the values in B2 and B3 and to display the result in B4. Another way to do this same addition is with a special function. In Lotus 1-2-3, the special function is called @SUM. The @ symbol tells the spreadsheet that a function is to follow, instead of text characters, so every function is preceded with this symbol. Other programs use other symbols—for example, Excel uses the equal-to (=) sign. Just remember that these are functions.

You identify the cells you want to sum by enclosing references to them in parentheses following the function name, like this:

@SUM(B2, B3)

If you want to add a whole column or block of numbers, it's much easier with @SUM. Instead of writing a formula with each individual cell address, you can give it a single block reference.

The items, or list of items separated by commas, enclosed in the parentheses following function names are called **arguments.** As you just saw, the @SUM function can take as its arguments either a list of cell addresses, or a single block reference. In fact, it can even take a combination of cell addresses and block references. Some functions take a fixed number of arguments, whereas others can accept a variable number of them (like the SUM function); still others require no arguments at all.

Relative and Absolute Addresses.

As mentioned before, a cell address is the combination of a cell's column letter and row number. When a cell reference is included in a formula, by default, the reference is relative to the cell with the formula in it. For example, suppose cell D4 contains a formula that adds the contents of cells B4 and C4. Because the formula is relative, though, a more accurate translation of the formula would be "add the values of the two cells to the left of the current cell." Thus, you could copy this cell to any other location, and it would still add the values of the two cells to its immediate left (not B4 and C4).

Relative cell references make it easy to create a worksheet quickly by entering formulas once and copying them to other locations. Sometimes, though, you want a formula that isn't relative. For example, each cell formula in the column takes the value of the cell above it (a relative reference) and multiplies it by a number in cell B1 (cell B1 for every formula—an absolute reference). Merely entering the formula

+B1 * B5

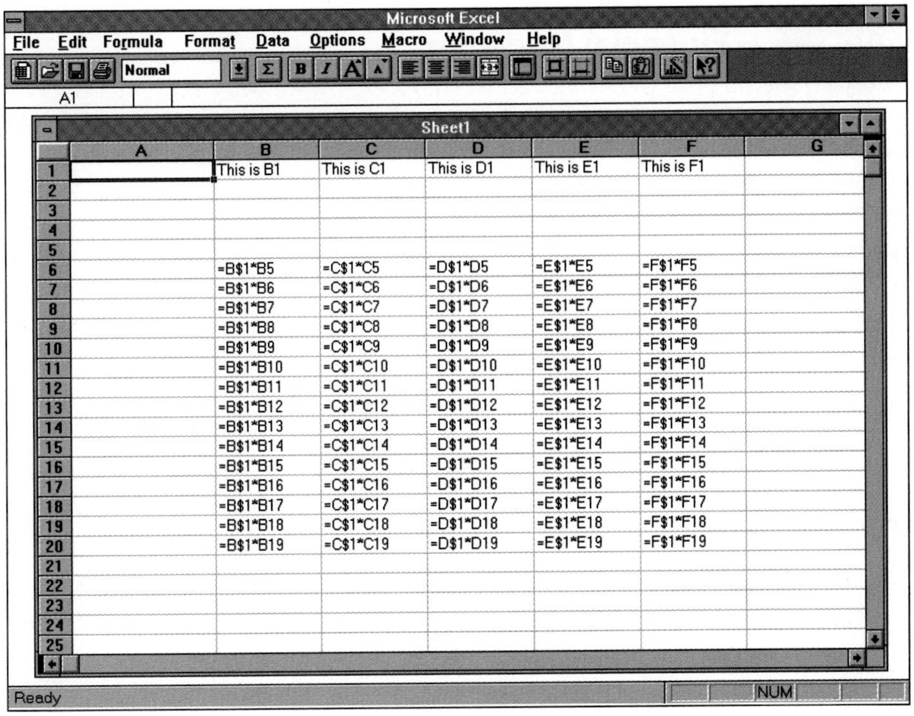

Figure 3-29

The formula in cell B6 refers to cell B$1. The dollar sign before the 1 indicates that wherever this formula is copied, it will always refer to row 1. When this formula is copied down through row 20, every resulting formula refers to cell B1. When this column of formulas is copied to the right, the column reference changes to refer to the current column, but the row reference is always the same.

in cell B6 will work fine. But when you copy this formula down through row 20, each succeeding cell will reference a lower cell (B2 * B6, B3 * B7, and so on). You have to make the reference to cell B1 absolute in the formula, so that it doesn't change when you copy it.

To make a reference absolute, you precede either the column letter or row number (or both) with a dollar sign ($). B1 is a reference to cell B1 that is absolute as to both row and column. In this example, though, we need an absolute reference for only the row number, so the correct formula is

+B$1 * B5

This fixes the row portion of the address, so that anywhere you copy the formula, it will reference the cell on row 1 of the current column. Copying this formula down the length of the column produces subsequent formulas that all reference cell B1 (B$1 * B6, B$1 * B7, and so on).

Since the formulas in this example are not absolute with respect to column (we entered B$1, not B1), we could replicate this entire column in columns to the right. The formulas in each column would correctly reference the top cell in their respective columns (C1, D1, and so on), as shown by the real cell contents displayed in Figure 3-29.

The Power of "What-If" Analysis.

The real power and beauty of the electronic spreadsheet lies in its ability to explore how some numbers affect others.

Say you're running a local courier service that features same-day delivery in your metropolitan area. You've just finished setting up the budget for the upcoming year on your favorite spreadsheet program. The worksheet includes not only data, but also formulas and built-in functions that compute totals, averages, and so on.

NORTON NOTEBOOK

Financial Modeling

Financial modeling is the process of simulating the financial performance of a company using a spreadsheet. The purpose of a financial model is to project the future financial performance of the company. Spreadsheet software makes this projection possible because it lets you see the effect of plugging different numbers into the formulas that make up the model.

Here's a highly simplified example of a financial model. Say you run a bicycle messenger service. The messengers are paid 50 percent of the price of each delivery. Other than the salaries of the messengers, your only operating expenses are your office rent, utilities (electricity, telephone, and garbage), a computer system, and the two-

way radio system that you use to communicate with your messengers.

You can plug in different sales volumes and determine the profit you would make. The information might be vital if you were planning to move offices or buy a new two-way radio system.

Naturally, financial models for larger companies can be far more complicated. The most common type of model has areas in the spreadsheet for each of the primary financial statements—balance sheet, income statement, and cash flow statements. Each of these financial statements might be linked to other spreadsheets, so the data can be imported automatically and analyzed here.

Small businesses use spreadsheets to track sales and expenses.

	JAN	FEB	MAR	APR	MAY	JUN	JUL	AUG	SEP
DELIVERIES	$14,024.50	$12,565.00	$13,100.00	$10,989.75	$11,654.00	$19,800.00	$10,750.25	$7,564.00	$10,955
INCOME	$7,012.25	$6,282.50	$6,550.00	$5,494.88	$5,827.00	$9,900.00	$5,375.13	$3,782.00	$5,477
RENT	$450.00	$450.00	$450.00	$450.00	$450.00	$500.00	$500.00	$500.00	$500
UTILITIES	$45.67	$65.45	$54.40	$50.73	$48.67	$48.30	$65.40	$52.18	$45
COMPUTER	$1,500.00	$0.00	$50.00	$25.00	$0.00	$1,000.00	$25.00	$0.00	$0
RADIO	$150.00	$5.00	$5.00	$5.00	$25.00	$5.00	$5.00	$150.00	$5
WAGES	$2,500.00	$2,500.00	$2,500.00	$3,000.00	$3,000.00	$3,000.00	$2,000.00	$2,000.00	$2,000
TOTAL EXPENSE	$4,645.67	$3,020.45	$3,059.40	$3,530.73	$3,523.67	$4,553.30	$2,595.40	$2,702.18	$2,550
PROFIT	$2,366.58	$3,262.05	$3,490.60	$1,964.15	$2,303.33	$5,346.70	$2,779.73	$1,079.82	$2,926
NET PROFIT	25519.75								

The budget looks good, but it's based on uncertain data. For example, the annual cost of fuel is calculated on current gasoline prices. If the price of gas goes up by 20 cents per gallon, how would that affect your budget? With your spreadsheet, you can find out in seconds. Just enter a new number into the cell labeled "Avg. Fuel Cost," and let the formulas and functions do the rest.

This ability to experiment with different numbers is known as *modeling*, or *what-if analysis*. Nobody can predict the future, but with what-if analysis, you can be ready for it when it arrives.

The whole model can get immensely complicated, but the goal is still the same. You still want to see how different data affect the profitability of the company. The results of the financial model help you to make basic business decisions, such as

- How much inventory can the company afford to keep on hand?

- How big a bonus should employees receive?

- Is it better to find less expensive parts or to raise your prices?

In the old days, the financial models used to answer these kinds of questions were created by accountants or the financial manager of a company, such as the chief financial officer. But with the ever-widening use of computers, all kinds of business people are now creating and gaining from financial models. Large businesses assume that their new employees are sufficiently adept with a spreadsheet to create financial models. Owners and managers of small businesses are equally likely to use such models to help them make decisions. Given the great value that a financial model can have when you are making business decisions, and the ease with which these models can be made with modern spreadsheet software, the ability to create financial models has become an essential—and basic—business skill.

MODEL.WB1:1

	A	B	C	D	E	F	G	H	I	
5		Jan	Feb	Mar	Apr	May	Jun	Jul	Aug	
6	**REVENUE**									
7	Product sales	$77,903	$75,905	$73,908	$71,910	$69,913	$67,915	$69,913	$71,910	$
8	less returns and allowances	(3,116)	(3,036)	(2,956)	(2,876)	(2,797)	(2,717)	(2,797)	(2,876)	
9	Net Sales	74,786	72,869	70,951	69,034	67,116	65,198	67,116	69,034	
10										
11	**COST OF GOODS SOLD**									
12	Product costs	45,201	44,042	42,883	41,724	41,090	39,916	41,090	42,264	
13										

MODEL.WB1:2

	A	B	C	D	E	F	G	H	I	J	K	L	
1	**INCOME STATEMENT ASSUMPTIONS**												
2													
3		Jan	Feb	Mar	Apr	May	Jun	Jul	Aug	Sep	Oct	Nov	
4													
5	*Product pricing and costs*												
6	Unit sales	1,950	1,900	1,850	1,800	1,750	1,700	1,750	1,800	1,850	1,900	1,950	
7	Unit price	39.95	39.95	39.95	39.95	39.95	39.95	39.95	39.95	39.95	39.95	39.95	
8	Unit materials cost	14.45	14.45	14.45	14.45	14.75	14.75	14.75	14.75	15.25	15.25	15.25	
9	Unit labor cost	6.17	6.17	6.17	6.17	6.17	6.17	6.17	6.17	6.17	6.17	6.17	
10	Unit overhead allocation	2.56	2.56	2.56	2.56	2.56	2.56	2.56	2.56	2.56	2.56	2.56	
11	Return percentage	4%											
12													

CashFlow / Beginning / BS_Assump \ IS_Assump / Inventory / I / J /

Large corporations use spreadsheets to prepare financial statements.

Setting the Display and Print Formats

You've seen that the content of a worksheet cell is separate from that cell's display value. There's also a third attribute of cells, the **display format.** Changing display values doesn't change the real contents of a cell in any way—it simply alters the way the cell shows its value. For example, you may want a number to display as a percentage, rather than as a decimal value.

Although, most often, the display format is used in connection with cells that display number values, display formats also apply to cells that simply contain text. And remember that number values can be plain numbers, times, dates, or formulas.

Numeric Cells.

The reason you don't have to worry about the format of numbers as you enter them into a cell is that the cell will display its value in the way that is specified by its current display format anyway. Numeric formats apply both to cells that contain numbers and calculation cells that display a numeric result of a formula.

Numeric-format attributes that specify the number of decimal places to display to the right of a decimal point are the most common. For example, if you build a worksheet that has cell values which represent money, you may want these dollar amounts to display a dollar sign, a trailing decimal point, and zeros, even if the values of the cells are round numbers.

Formatting numbers is a simple procedure. With most programs, you select the range to be formatted, pull down a menu, and select Format, then choose the format you want. You can format individual cells independently or select large blocks of cells (or even entire columns and rows) to format them all at once.

Date and Time Cells.

As you saw earlier, when you enter a date or time into a worksheet cell, the program converts your entry into a number, then applies a special date or time display format to the cell. The content of the cell, though, is just a number (usually the number of days since the beginning of the twentieth century, or since the beginning of 1980).

To prove this, you can enter a date into a cell, and reformat it using one of the standard numeric formats such as General. The date will be transformed into a number. Since dates are just a special type of numeric format, you can open the format menu and select Date to transform the number back into a date. Usually, when you select Date from a format menu, you're presented with several options for date formats.

Text Cells.

Whereas numeric and date formats apply to only those cells with numeric values, other types of attributes apply to any kind of cell, including those which contain labels or text. These attributes are similar to the type of text attributes you might apply to text in a word-processor document: different typefaces, point sizes, bold, italics, and underline. Some spreadsheet programs even allow you to use color to embellish your worksheets and to provide presentation results.

Printing Your Worksheet

In early spreadsheet programs, it was sometimes a real challenge to produce exactly the output you wanted. Today, printing features are much more powerful, especially in graphical environments like the Macintosh and Microsoft Windows.

Printing is basically a two-step process:

1. Select the range or block of cells to print.
2. Issue the print command.

Unfortunately, the ranges you might want to print are not always conveniently shaped like a sheet of paper—a situation that sometimes requires you to resort to some gymnastics to get exactly what you want. For greater control over the paging, you can insert page breaks directly into the worksheet, or specify the ranges and print each page independently.

Two features that most graphical spreadsheets offer are *print to fit* and *scaling*. Scaling allows you to shrink or enlarge a worksheet by specifying a per-

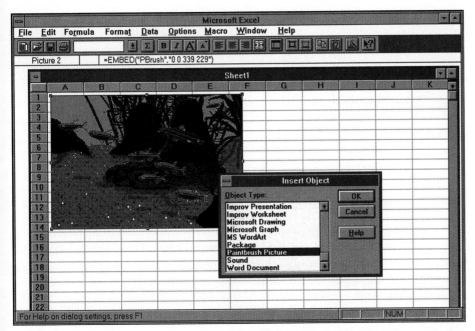

Figure 3-30
You import graphic images into a spreadsheet by choosing them from a dialog box. You can resize and even change them within some spreadsheet programs.

centage of its normal size. For example, a scaling factor of 90 percent will shrink the worksheet text to 90 percent of its normal size. Print to fit essentially calculates a scaling factor that will make your worksheet fit on a page. Another tactic that you can use to squeeze a worksheet onto a printed page is to turn it sideways. This is called *landscape orientation*. Printing in landscape can be especially helpful with wide worksheets.

Some spreadsheets provide a print-preview mode similar to the print-preview modes of word processors. Print preview allows you to see how the spreadsheet will break up your worksheet, and how margins, headers, and footers will affect the printed document as well.

EXTENDING THE SPREADSHEET

In this section, we'll look at some features that are standard equipment on most spreadsheets and others that are only available with some specific products.

Integrating Graphics

Most of the newer spreadsheet programs, especially the graphical ones, allow you to integrate graphics directly into a worksheet. Most systems allow you to import all the standard and common graphics file formats, and some even let you create and modify existing graphic images from within the spreadsheet program.

With most systems, importing a graphic image is a straightforward procedure. You open a menu, select a command to import a graphic file, and choose the file to import—it appears in a box on the face of the worksheet (Figure 3-30). Then, you can move the graphic by dragging it with the mouse, and can change its shape and size by dragging the corners of the box.

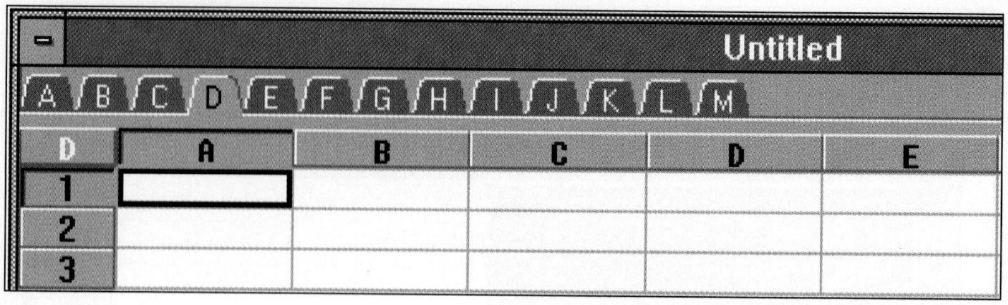

Figure 3-31

Three-dimensional (3-D) spreadsheets have tab icons along the top or bottom edge of the worksheet window. You can quickly go to a page by clicking its icon with the mouse. Each page is a full-size worksheet, and formulas can refer to cells on other pages.

Three-Dimensional (3-D) Spreadsheets

Some of the newer spreadsheets provide a third dimension in addition to the classical two-dimensional array of columns and rows. These spreadsheet programs carry the worksheet metaphor from a sheet of columnar paper to the entire pad. In them, the third dimension represents pages of a notebook (Figure 3-31). At the top or bottom of the worksheet window is a row of tabs like those you would find in a real notebook. To turn to another page, you click the tab of the page you want to go to.

In a three-dimensional worksheet, commands and cell formulas can access cells and blocks on any other page. The page is simply a third component of a cell's address. For example, the full address of cell C4 on the first (A) page is A:C4. Cell D20 on the E page is E:D20. To add these cells, the formula would be

+A:C4 + E:D20

Page references are necessary, though, only for accessing another page. You can omit them to reference cells on the current page.

Just as cell references on a single page are relative, allowing you to insert rows and columns, page references are also relative. You can insert new pages and delete pages, and cell formulas will remain relative to the page they're on. With a three-dimensional spreadsheet, you can use pages to hold the detail of computations that feed into another page, or entire worksheets.

HOW DBMSs ARE USED

DBMSs are some of the most pervasive applications for which computers are used. Since the first commercial computers became available, DBMSs have been a primary use of computers in the business world. Companies in every industry rely heavily on their DBMSs. The thousands of national and local banks that tie into worldwide banking networks, manufacturing companies, and companies and institutions in health-care fields, to name just a few, store untold volumes of transactions and information every day.

A **database-management system** (DBMS) is the tool computers use to achieve the processing and orderly storage of data. A **database** is a repository for related collections of data. For example, an address book can be a database where the names, addresses, and telephone numbers of friends and business contacts are stored. A company database might contain information about customers, vendors, employees, sales, and inventory. Each piece of information can be added to a database and extracted later in meaningful ways. The DBMS is the program (or collection of programs) that allows users (and other programs) to access and work with a database.

Personal computers have brought database management to the desktops of individuals both in business and at home. Although the average individual doesn't usually need an inventory tracking system at home, there are numerous personal uses for DBMSs. Many people with computers at home use commercial software products for managing household purchases, keeping track of friends and business contacts, and even for preparing menus and shopping lists and categorizing and sorting grocery-store coupons.

The DBMS

A DBMS is a program, or collection of programs, that stores data in a way that allows the DBMS to access those data at any time. Because database files can grow extremely large—perhaps even many gigabytes on large systems—recalling data quickly is not a trivial matter. A database can provide quick access, especially when it is running on powerful hardware.

In fact, one of the best reasons to use a database is not just the speed of retrieval of data, but also easy and quick manipulation of data. Today, even on home systems, the ability to change the organization of the data or to edit individual data is what makes using an electronic DBMS so appealing.

In addition to providing quick access and data manipulation, a DBMS also provides a means to join (or relate) data in separate databases. For example, you can quickly analyze the types of products a customer purchases most often by relating customer information and orders information. We'll look more at these features in the section "Linking Database Tables."

Programs and the DBMS

Like an operating system, a DBMS can provide services both to users and to other programs. Often, when users think they're using a DBMS directly, they're really using a program, which provides a user interface, that works with the DBMS to give them direct access to databases.

At the heart of a DBMS is a program called the **database engine.** The database engine is akin to the operating system's kernel in that they can both access and manipulate at a low level: hardware in the case of an operating system, and files containing data in the case of a database engine. The database engine receives its instructions from other programs. Instructions the engine receives might include "open a file," "go to customer X," "add a new customer," and so on.

Interactive Databases

Most PC-based DBMSs include powerful programs for accessing data in databases. With some of them, the program simply is the DBMS, and you may not even be aware of the distinction between the database engine and the interface. In Microsoft Access, for example, you're presented with a standard Windows interface that includes a File menu option. Using the File menu, you can open databases and change, delete, or add new information.

Figure 3-32

A database may contain many tables like the one pictured here. A table is a collection of similar data. This table contains customer information, with each customer's data on a separate row. The columns distinguish a certain type of data for each customer, such as names, addresses, and so on. With some systems, rows are called records and columns are called fields; some of these systems also refer to a table as a database.

Customer ID	Company Name	Contact Name	Contact Title	Address
ALWAO	Always Open Quick Mart	Melissa Adams	Sales Representative	77 Overpass Ave.
ANDRC	Andre's Continental Food Market	Heeneth Ghandi	Sales Representative	P.O. Box 209
ANTHB	Anthony's Beer and Ale	Mary Throneberry	Assistant Sales Agent	33 Neptune Circle
AROUT	Around the Horn	Thomas Hardy	Sales Representative	Brook Farm
BABUJ	Babu Ji's Exports	G.K.Chatterjee	Owner	Box 29938
BERGS	Bergstad's Scandinavian Grocery	Tammy Wong	Order Administrator	41 S. Marlon St.
BLUEL	Blue Lake Deli & Grocery	Hanna Moore	Owner	210 Main St.
BLUMG	Blum's Goods	Pat Parkes	Marketing Manager	The Blum Building
BOBCM	Bobcat Mesa Western Gifts	Gladys Lindsay	Marketing Manager	213 E. Roy St.
BOTTM	Bottom-Dollar Markets	Elizabeth Lincoln	Accounting Manager	23 Tsawassen Blvd.
BSBEV	B's Beverages	Victoria Ashworth	Sales Representative	Fauntleroy Circus
CACTP	Cactus Pete's Family Market	Murray Soderholm	Sales Agent	87 Yuca Dr.
CAESM	Caesar's Mediterranean Imports	Olivia LaMont	Marketing Manager	9308 Dartridge Ave.
CHEAC	Cheap Chow Markets	Louisa Scarpaczyk	Sales Representative	1225 Zephyrus Rd.
COMME	Commoner's Exchange	Terry Hargreaves	Sales Associate	Exchange House
CONSH	Consolidated Holdings	Elizabeth Brown	Sales Representative	Berkeley Gardens
DOLLC	Dollarwise Convenience Store	Sean O'Brien	Assistant Sales Agent	98 N. Hyde Dr.
DUNNH	Dunn's Holdings	Sylvia Dunn	Owner	The Dunn Building
EASTC	Eastern Connection	Ann Devon	Sales Agent	35 King George
EMPIT	Empire Trading	Ronald Merrick	Sales Representative	7 Baxter Hill
FAMIC	Family Corner Market	April Cienkewicz	Marketing Assistant	4242 Maple Blvd.
FITZD	Fitzgerald's Deli and Video	Shannon MacArthur	Marketing Assistant	Eastgate Center
FOODI	Foodmongers, Inc.	Grover Smith	Owner	418 - 6th Ave.
FRASD	Fraser Distributors	Peter Fraser	Marketing Manager	Rosewood
FREDE	Fred's Edibles, Etc.	Paula Anchor	Sales Associate	1522 College Blvd.
FRUGF	Frugal Feast Comestibles	Rona Rumalski	Marketing Manager	Evans Plaza
FRUGP	Frugal Purse Strings	Bill Lee	Assistant Sales Representative	418 Datablitz Ave.
FUJIA	Fujiwara Asian Specialties	Hugo Zajac	Sales Manager	72 Dowlin Pkwy.
GARCA	Garcia's All-Day Food Mart	Adele Williams	Marketing Manager	401 Rodeo Dr.

DATABASE BASICS

In this section, we'll jump right into the nuts and bolts of DBMSs, to see what makes them work. We'll start by looking at the structure of database tables, including fields for holding different types of data, then we'll discuss keys and indexes—the tools the DBMS uses to sort data and to retrieve them quickly. Finally, we'll look at forms—our window into a database—and discuss some of the techniques and methods for creating relationships between tables.

The Database Structure

Figure 3-32 shows a table composed of columns and rows. It's a database of customer information. A particular set of data such as this is called a **table:** It is an arrangement of columns and rows. Each customer in the table appears on a separate row of the table. The columns of the table are called **fields,** and the rows are called **records.** When you add a customer to a customer database, you add a new row that contains a space for each field for the new record. Likewise, when you process a sale and generate an invoice, a record is added to an invoice database.

Fields.
The fields of a table separate the types of information contained in that table. For example, each record in the customer table has a name, address, and phone number, and each field exists in every record. The sequence of fields in a database table is strictly defined for every record. The phone number field, for example, must contain a phone number for every record—it cannot contain a phone number on some rows and a social security number on others.

The fields of a database table are defined by the person who creates the table. Different DBMS products offer a variety of field types. The most commonly used field types are text fields, date fields, and numeric fields, but other specialized types are necessary in some situations.

Text Fields.

A **text field** holds a string of alphanumeric characters. A text field might contain a person's name, a company name, an address, or any other meaningful textual information. A text field can also be used for numbers, but it treats them as just a string of digits, rather than a number. For numeric data that you will not need to use for calculations, a text field is fine—for example, a zip code. You would not want to use a zip code for calculations. As a text field, it would accommodate foreign addresses that sometimes contain letters; and U.S. zip codes, such as 07760, would keep the leading zero in place. A numeric field would automatically drop the leading zero.

Numeric and Currency Fields.

Number fields hold numbers. With most programs, you can select a display format for numbers. The actual number in the field does not contain any formatting, but when the program displays the number, it can add a comma separator between thousands and millions, display or not display precision to the right of the decimal point, and include other special characters such as a dollar sign.

Some database programs provide more than one type of number field. A number field may be limited in the range of values it can contain. If you know your database will use this field for only whole numbers in that range, you can save storage space and a small amount of processing time by using a short number field. For larger numbers and numbers that need a floating decimal point, you would use a regular number field, which uses more bytes of storage space.

A **currency field** is a number field with the display format set up by the software to represent money. A currency field displays its values with comma separators, two decimal places of precision for cents, and sometimes a dollar sign. Internally, DBMS programs treat data in currency fields as a special kind of number. Often, the actual number stored in the field is not a floating-point number (one with a decimal point). Floating-point numbers take up more storage space than is needed for numbers that will never have more than two decimal points of precision. Typically, the DBMS converts dollars and cents to cents by multiplying the value by 100. It takes less space to store a whole number that is 100 times larger than to store numbers that have a floating decimal point.

Date and Time Fields.

Date fields and **time fields** are specialized fields. Like dates and times stored in cells in a spreadsheet, dates and times in a database are stored internally as a number, but are displayed as either a date or a time. When you enter a date or time into a date/time field, the DBMS accepts your input in the format of a date or time, but converts it to a number before storing it in the database. This way, the data take less disk space, and you can easily use dates and times in calculations.

In addition to converting dates to numbers for storage and computational ease, most DBMS products provide automatic error checking for dates and times. For example, when you enter a date into a date field, the DBMS program will check it to ensure that the date is a valid one. Most systems are aware of leap years, ensuring that every date entered is valid.

Logical Fields.

A **logical field** (sometimes called a **yes/no field**) is a field that can hold one of only two values. Logical fields can be used for any type of data where there are only two possible values, although the descriptions you give for the choices are unlimited (yes or no, true or false, on or off, retail or wholesale, etc.). Because a logical field can contain only two possible values, it takes only a single bit (⅛ byte) to store a logical value.

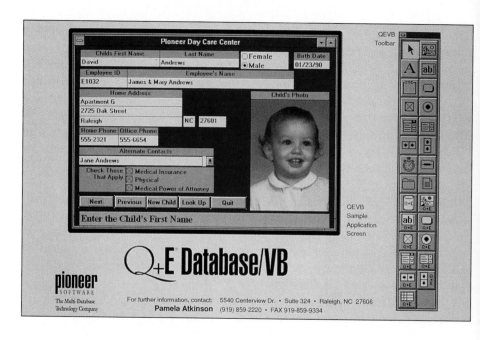

Figure 3-33

Databases can contain graphic
images, such as photographs,
in binary fields.

Memo Fields. A **memo field** is a special field that can contain information of
variable length. For example, in an address book, you would use text fields for
people's names, addresses, and phone numbers. Text fields normally have a
fixed maximum length, and, most of the time, a maximum length does not present a problem. However, say you want to add a field for comments or notes.
It's impossible to know in advance how large to make a text field for this type
of data. In many records, you may not enter any notes, but in others, you may
want to save a few words or a short sentence. In still others, you may want significantly more notes and comments. A memo field solves this problem.

Binary Fields. A **binary field** is a special field for storing binary objects, or
BLOBs (Binary Large OBject). A BLOB might be a graphic image file such as
clip art, a photograph, a screen image, or other graphic art or formatted text. A
BLOB can also be sound tracks and video files, objects such as graphs or worksheets created with a spreadsheet or word processor, or even external binary
files such as a spreadsheet or word-processor document.

   The information database used by a child-care center shown in Figure 3-33
contains a binary field that includes a scanned photograph of a child.

Calculated Fields. Some DBMSs allow you to create special fields that perform calculations. A calculation might be the sum of other numeric fields, or a
formula that calculates the tax on a subtotal. Calculations are associated with
the screen, or **form,** that a program displays, rather than with the database
table itself.

   Not every DBMS provides calculated fields. In those that do not, calculations are performed by the program that creates and updates the screen or generates a report.

Counter Fields. A **counter field** contains a unique numeric value that the
DBMS assigns for every record. When you enter a record into a new, empty
table with a counter field, the counter field for that record will be set to 1. The

second record gets a 2, and so on. A counter field in a table ensures that every record will have a completely unique value in that field.

A counter field can be used to sort records for a report. Sorting on the counter field will arrange the records in the order in which they were originally entered. Counter fields may also be used for creating records that must be numbered sequentially. For example, using a counter field for invoice numbers will ensure that each new invoice is given a sequential number.

Sorting the Data

One of the most powerful features of DBMSs is their ability to sort the information they contain either for a printed report or for you to browse through on the computer's screen. DBMSs use keys or indexes to produce sorted data. Let's see how that works.

The Primary Key.
A **primary key** defines a default sort order for a table. This is the order in which the records of a table are displayed on the screen or printed in a report if no alternate order is specified. A primary key is usually associated with a single field in a table (such as a customer ID number), and values that you enter into that field must be unique—different for every record in the table. Defining a customer-number field as the primary key will prevent users from inadvertently entering duplicate entries (two customers with the same ID).

The primary key of a table can also be made up of more than a single field. This type of primary key is called a **segmented key.** For example, the primary key can contain three segments—last name, first name, and middle initial. With this arrangement, the default sort order of the table will be primarily by last name, and, for each identical last name, records will be sorted by first name, and so on. You wouldn't want to define a primary key for only a last name or for a last name–first name combination, because doing so would prevent you from entering two records with the same name.

With most databases, when you enter a new record, it's appended to the end of the file that contains the table data. Any amount of sorting or changing keys will never affect the physical order of records in this file, because the database keeps the key information separate from the data. The key is itself a miniature representation of the data table, but it contains only the key field and a number that corresponds to the physical record number in the data table. However, the key table is sorted. To find a record by a specific key value, the DBMS can quickly find the required information in the key table (because it is sorted) make a note of the physical record number, and then return to the data file and move directly to the record's data by using the record number.

Indexes.
An index is essentially the same as a key. In Microsoft Access, the primary key is special. One is required for every table to ensure that records are unique, and it specifies the default order of records. But you can also add other keys, called **indexes,** for other sort orders you want for reports, or to speed up searches.

Defining indexes also has another benefit. It can make searching the database for specific records much quicker. For example, if you often search a certain field for values (such as searching for a surname in the "Last Name" field), if the field is not defined as an index, locating records can take anywhere from a few seconds to several minutes, depending on the size of the table and the number of records in it. Searching for a specific value in a keyed (or indexed)

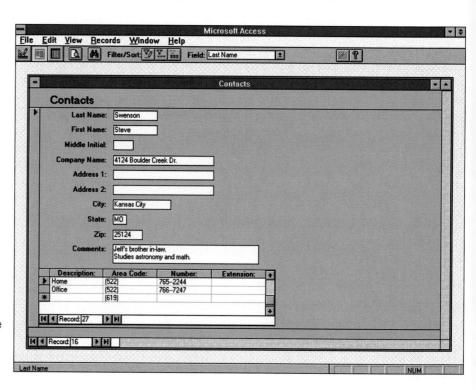

Figure 3-34

Many database systems provide a way to create forms for tables quickly. This figure shows the form Microsoft Access created automatically for the contacts database. Note that the form contains both the header and detail tables. The easiest way to create a custom form is to create a default form, like the one shown here, then to customize it by moving the fields around and adding any embellishments.

field is much quicker—in fact, it is almost immediate, because the DBMS uses the presorted key information to find key values quickly and to determine the physical location of the key's data in the data file.

Forms

Although earlier you saw a database table that looked similar to a spreadsheet, most of the time, it's not convenient to work with a database that way. Database programs provide you with tools to build **forms**—custom screens for displaying and entering data. A form can be linked to a single table, or to multiple tables with relationships that you define.

The Default Form. Most database programs provide a quick way to create a rudimentary form for data entry automatically. Figure 3-34 shows a form created this way by Microsoft Access for an address-book table. These "default" forms are not very flashy, but creating them is quick and easy. You can also create forms from scratch yourself, but it's easier to create a default form and then to customize it to your liking.

Fields and Control Tools. With graphical databases, when you place a field onto a form, you select a data-entry tool that is appropriate for the field. A **data-entry tool** is the mechanism the user will use to enter data into the field. For example, in an invoicing form, the fields for a customer's name and address should be text boxes. No fancy controls are needed here because each new customer's information must be entered manually. With other fields, though, controls may be appropriate. The "Terms" field will receive a value that indicates the number of days the customer may take to pay the invoice. This company's terms policy here includes 10-day, 20-day, or 30-day terms. A **list box** is a field control that lists several options on it from which the user can select a choice.

By creating the Terms field with a list box and loading it with the values "10 days," "20 days," and "30 days," the user will be able to click the appropriate selection for the customer (Figure 3-35).

Figure 3-36 shows several more types of field controls. One of these is the check box, which is appropriate for logical fields. A **check box** displays a check mark when it's clicked. **Radio buttons** are convenient when only one option among several choices is possible. A **drop-down box** looks like an edit field but has a down arrow at its right edge. Clicking the arrow causes a box with choices to drop down below the field. Selecting an option closes the box and brings the choice into the field. A **combination box** combines an edit field and a drop-down box. With a combination box, you can either click the arrow to display a list of common values for the field, or type a new value into the edit box.

Figure 3-35

This tool shows a set of "radio buttons." As on old-fashioned car radios, you make a selection, but only one button can be depressed at any time. This tool is here attached to a field that can have one of three possible values.

Verifying an Entry with a Mask.

In addition to selecting a control for a field to ease data entry, you can make a form perform validations or conversions on data entered with a **mask** specification. With some systems, masks are associated with data-entry forms, and you specify them while creating the form; on others, masks are associated with table fields, and you specify them while you define the field during table creation.

A mask can have a simple function such as converting typed characters to upper- or lowercase. The "State" field in the customer table has such a mask. If the user types "ny," "Ny," or "nY," the mask will convert the entry to "NY." If the user types "NY" to begin with, the mask does nothing. Using a mask to manage conversions between upper- and lowercase can greatly ease data entry and ensure that data are entered uniformly (which becomes critical later on, when you search for specific data).

A mask can also display a field's contents in a certain format. For example, the "Phone" field in the customer table is a text field with the mask

(###) ###-####

The form interprets the literal characters in the mask (the parentheses, space, and hyphen) as characters it is supposed to display at each position in the string of numbers that make up the phone number. With this mask, a user needs to type only the digits of the phone number into the field. The mask will display the number with the literal characters inserted. For example, to enter the phone number "(605) 555-1234," the user only needs to type

6055551234

The mask will cause the form to display

(605) 555-1234

Figure 3-36

An edit box is for typing information; check boxes are appropriate for a logical or yes/no field; radio buttons are good for making a selection among several possible values. When you click on a pick list, a menu of choices pops up, from which you make a selection. A spin control is for numeric values, and a combination box combines an edit field and a drop-down menu.

Embellishing a Form.

Most database programs for graphical environments allow you to customize forms as much as you like. In addition to associating controls with fields, you can specify text and background colors or text fonts and faces, and even include graphic images such as logos or designs on a form.

INTERACTING WITH THE DATABASE

The majority of the time you spend using a database program, you work interactively with the database forms to update existing records and to create new

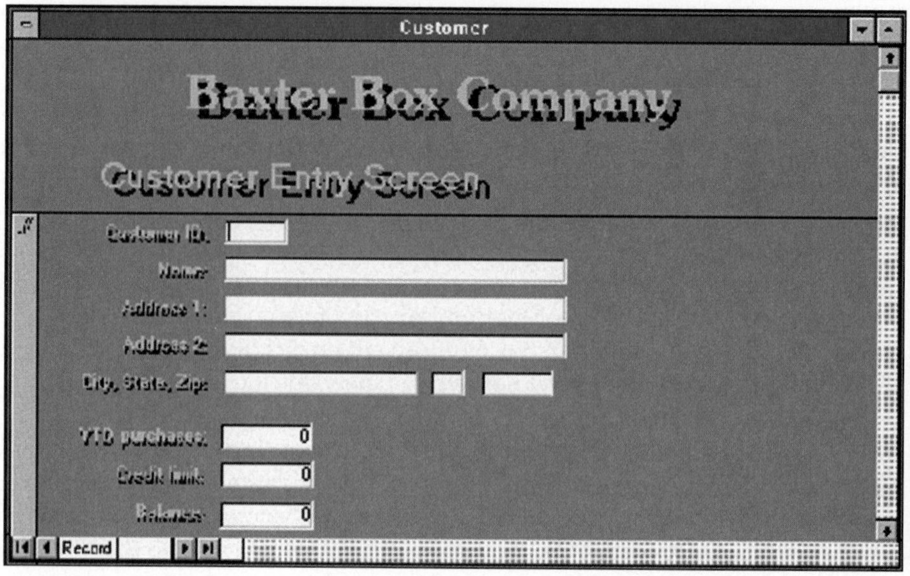

Figure 3-37

To move between records in
Microsoft Access, the user
presses the arrow buttons in the
lower-left corner of the form.

ones. In this section, we'll describe some of the procedures a database user performs during a typical session.

Navigating, Viewing, and Editing Records

In this section, we'll look at the simplest movement commands—going directly to the first or last records in a table, and browsing through them one record
at a time. We will also investigate the mechanics of using a form for adding
new records and updating existing ones.

Moving Between Records. Once you've loaded a table or run a form, the
database program gives you ways to move around in the table. Microsoft Access uses the button bar, shown in the lower-left corner of the form in Figure
3-37. The buttons on the bar represent the commands for moving between
records. From left to right, they mean

- Go to the first record in the table.
- Go to the previous record.
- Go to the next record.
- Go to the last record.

To add a new record, you go to the last record in the table by clicking the
last-record button, and then click the next-record button. A blank form will appear that you can fill out by typing the information on the keyboard.

Adding a Record. To add a record with some systems, you move to the last
record in the table, then click the button that moves to the next record, or press
the down arrow key. Because, when you're on the last record, there is no next
record, this action indicates that you want to add a new record—so the DBMS
appends a new blank record and places a cursor in the first field of the form.
Some systems have a menu option to add a new record. When you choose it,
the system places you in a blank form.

When you design a form, you determine the order in which field data will
be entered. This order is called the **tab order,** because, on some older systems

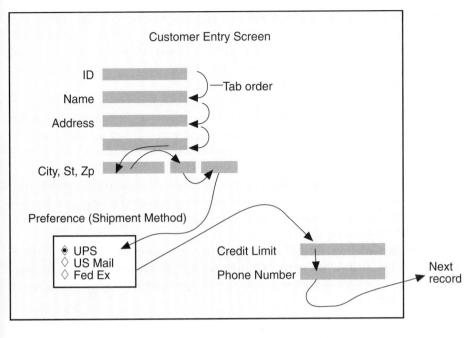

Figure 3-38

When you enter a form for data entry, most often the cursor goes to the first field in the table. Pressing the enter or tab key moves the cursor to the next field. Often, pressing shift+tab moves the cursor back up through the fields.

using the tab key was the only way to proceed through the fields of a database form. In the contacts form, the "First Name" field is the first tab stop, and, as such, when you click the Next Record button to add a new record, a cursor appears in this field on a blank form.

You begin entering the new record by typing a name into the field. When you've finished typing the name, you can press the tab key or enter key to move to the next field (Figure 3-38). To go backward (move to a prior field), hold down the shift key and press the tab key (shift+tab).

In forms with only a single table, pressing enter or tab in the last field on the form saves the record and moves to a new, blank form. In forms that include fields from more than one table (such as the contacts form), when you complete the last field on the main form, the cursor moves to the first field of the subform (in this case, the phone numbers form) so you can enter phone numbers for this contact. When you complete the last field of a row in the subform, the cursor creates a new, blank row in the subform for another phone number. To clear the form and enter another contact, click the next record button at the bottom of the form.

In addition to using tab (or enter) to move forward through fields, or shift+tab to move backward, you can go directly to any field at any time by clicking on it with the mouse.

Modifying and Deleting Records.

Changing an existing record is easy. Of course, you first have to display the record you want to change. In graphical databases such as Paradox for Windows and Access, a single click of the mouse on a field will "select" the field. When a field is selected, its color may change and a cursor will appear in the field at the point where you clicked the mouse. You can use the mouse again to position the cursor where you want to make a change, or you can use the keyboard's arrow keys if you prefer. Then, just type your change into the field.

After you have made the change, you can move on. With some systems, you may have to press the enter key for your changes to take effect; others will prompt you to confirm your changes before allowing you to move to another record.

To delete a record, you also have to display it first. Then you select the Delete command from the menu, and the record is deleted. With your form design, you specify whether or not cross-reference records in a subform should be deleted with the record in the main form. Again, some systems will prompt you to confirm before proceeding with the deletion.

Using a Filter. Setting a **filter** allows you to browse through only those records that meet some criterion. For example, if you want to see only contacts in the city of Dallas, you can set a filter for the "City" field and only the records that contain "Dallas" in that field will be displayed.

While a filter is set, you cannot access any records that do not meet your filter criteria. On some systems, filters are saved as a part of a form or table definition. With others, filters are completely independent of the forms or tables, and you set them up on the fly.

Filters provide a quick and convenient way to narrow down the number of records you have to work with, but they are not meant for elaborate criteria. For more complex sets of criteria, you should use queries, which we'll look at in the next section.

Searching a Database

Looking through a database one record at a time is not an efficient way to find data that you need to locate. Databases contain hundreds (if not thousands) of records, so finding a certain record this way can be time consuming and tedious. Fortunately, there are tools that allow you to find a specific record quickly and easily.

Most database programs provide two basic ways to find records—with a Find command and with queries. The Find command provides a quick way to search out a record without going through a complex procedure. Queries provide more versatile methods for locating records, but they're a little more complex to design, so once you've gone to the trouble of defining them, you can save them for future use.

Using the Find Command. The Find command is a commonly used command in most database systems. The Find command opens the Find pop-up menu or dialog box, where you specify your search criteria.

To use Find, you type the text you want to search for into a text box, and then indicate which field to search in. You can specify either a single field or all fields. In addition, you can specify whether the Find operation should proceed from the current record to the end of the file (forward or down), or from the current record to the beginning of the file (backward or up). The default search direction is from the current record to the end of the file.

The Find command is convenient for quick searches for a name or word, but you can't create an elaborate set of criteria for Find. It searches for a single string, either in one field or in all the fields. Also, the Find command can operate on only one table at a time, and you can't save the criteria you specify for future use.

SQL. At the heart of every DBMS is a language that is similar to a programming language, but different in that it's designed specifically for communicating with a database. Early on, there were no standard languages. Each DBMS developer created methods to allow users to search for and select records and fields from tables.

However, eventually one language did emerge as a standard. This language (like so many other things in the computer world), was developed originally by IBM. The language is called **SQL** (pronounced "S-Q-L"). IBM developed SQL in the late 1970s and early 1980s as a way to standardize query languages across the many mainframe and minicomputer platforms that company produced.

SQL differs significantly from programming languages. First, most programming languages are still procedural. A **procedural** language consists of commands that tell the computer what to do—instruction by instruction, step by step. An SQL statement isn't really a command to the computer. Rather, it is a description of some of the data contained in a database. SQL is **nonprocedural** because it does not give step-by-step commands to the computer or database—it just describes data, and *sometimes* instructs the database to do something with the data.

The simplest way to explain how you use a query language is to say that you draw terms and phrase structures from the language to ask, or **query,** the database about information it contains. If you formulated a question to a database in English, it might look like this:

> Do you have any records in the "contacts" database where the "City" field contains "Kansas City" and the name in the "First Name" field starts with "R"?

Just formulating a question like this in English goes a long way toward helping to create a query in a query language such as SQL. The first step required to translate this question into SQL is to recognize that SQL statements are not really questions—they're statements (the answer to the preceding question might be "Yes"—which probably would not help a great deal). In SQL, you tell the database

- Which fields you want it to work with.
- The table (or tables) with which it will be working.
- The criteria for selecting records.

Rewriting the statement might produce:

> Show me the "First Name," "Last Name," and "Company Name" fields from the "contacts" table where the "City" field contains "Kansas City" and the "First Name" field starts with "R."

Translating the statement into SQL from this point is a simple matter.

> SELECT [First Name], [Last Name], [Company Name]
> FROM Contacts
> WHERE ((City="Kansas City") AND ([First Name]="R."))

The keywords "SELECT," "FROM," and "WHERE" tell the SQL engine how to interpret each part of the statement. In this example, the brackets around the field names are needed only because the field names contain spaces, and the brackets help the database to interpret each field name correctly.

SQL has only a few dozen or so basic keywords. The SELECT keyword tells SQL to display the records that match the criteria. SELECT can be replaced with UPDATE and used with the SET keyword to alter the contents of a field in a table.

Although SQL is a widely accepted standard, not every DBMS supports it. But SQL has been around for quite a while, and each year it finds its way into another database product—a recent example is Microsoft Access.

Creating Reports

Just as a form can be based on a query, reports are based on queries. A report can use a single table, or multiple tables that are linked with one-to-many relationships. Other tables can also be included in a report as another source for data similar to a lookup field on a form.

Let's use an invoice as an example. A printed invoice is a type of report like many others. The invoice table is the main (or driving) table for this report. Invoice line items are brought into the report with a link between the invoice table and the line-items table. Other information comes from other tables as well. The details of a customer's company name and address might come from a separate table, as well as the descriptions associated with term codes and product codes.

Designing a report is similar in many ways to designing a form. There are, however, several additional criteria you have to consider. First, the order in which records appear in a report is more critical than it is with a form. For reports that will perform numeric computations, the order can be especially critical.

A number of variations could be useful. For example, sorting by invoice number provides a chronological sequence of invoices. Applying this sort and setting a selection criterion for the "Invoice Date" field to be equal to a single day will produce a sales report for the specified day. The report can also be sorted by customer or by customer number, and can span a greater period of time (such as a month) to show a periodic (say, monthly) summary of each customer's purchases.

Calculated fields can be included in a report with DBMSs that support them. On other systems, calculations are built directly into the report definition.

SUMMARY

What Is an Operating System?

- An OS serves four functions:
    - Providing a user interface
    - Managing hardware devices
    - Managing and maintaining the disk file systems
    - Supporting other programs
- A command-line interface requires the user to type in commands at the keyboard, whereas a graphical user interface (GUI) is controlled with a mouse.
- Most OSs have a kernel that remains in memory at all times and a shell that controls the user interface.
- DOS is most often used with a command-line shell, but other shells are available, including the DOS Shell, The Norton Desktop, and Microsoft Windows.
- The GUI, which is controlled through drop-down menus and dialog boxes, was first popularized by the Macintosh.

- One common feature of GUIs is the ability to set up different working areas, called windows, on a computerized desktop.

Popular Personal Computer Operating Systems

- DOS is the most widely used OS.
- The most popular shell for DOS is Microsoft Windows, a program that sets up a windowing GUI.
- IBM's OS is OS/2, a single-user, multitasking system for Intel-based machines.
- The Macintosh's OS is unlike DOS, OS/2, and Unix in that the GUI is an integral part of the system; there is no command-line interface on the Macintosh.

Using a Word Processor

- Word processors are designed for entering and manipulating text.
- The editing screen in a word processor is designed to look like a page.
- You can correct typing mistakes easily by using backspace, delete, insert, or typeover.
- Word wrap moves the cursor to the beginning of the next line when the text reaches the end of the previous line.
- There are always many ways to move around in a document using either a mouse or the keyboard.
- Tabs and indentations are simple formatting tools for offsetting paragraphs.
- Cut, move, and paste expedite relocating of blocks of text.
- Search and replace finds or consistently modifies one phrase throughout a document.
- Formatting means changing typefaces, fonts, and justification of margins.
- Word-processing packages generally support all of the most popular printers.
- Print preview saves time and paper by allowing you to see the output before you actually print the document.
- Organizing the storage structure well and choosing meaningful names for each file make electronic-document storage work to your advantage.

Advanced Word-Processor Features

- Spell checking makes sure every word matches an entry in the dictionary, but it is no substitute for proofreading because it cannot check to make sure the context is correct.
- Grammar checkers look for usage, correct grammar, and writing style.
- An on-line thesaurus offers alternate words that may be more accurate or interesting than the original choice.
- Many people use the outlining feature in word processors to organize their ideas before they start writing.
- Style sheets are a collection of text and formatting elements that you use most frequently.

Spreadsheets

- A spreadsheet is used primarily as a tool for calculating and analyzing numbers.
- Spreadsheets are designed to emulate multicolumn worksheets comprised of columns and rows.
- The smallest portion of a spreadsheet is called a cell.
- Each cell has a unique address.
- The three basic entries into a cell are labels, numbers, and formulas.
- Formulas contain raw numbers, references to other cells, and functions the application provides such as the @ function.
- References to other cells can be relative or absolute.
- What-if analysis is a powerful tool for making an educated guess about the future.
- Choosing the best format for presentation of labels, numbers, dates, time, and formulas is key for clear understanding of what the spreadsheet represents.
- You can print a whole spreadsheet or a block, but it is important to plan page breaks carefully so the final product is readable.
- Most spreadsheets have print-to-fit, scaling, and landscaping to help you with readability.

Extending the Spreadsheet

- Macros are an executable combination of commands or keystrokes.
- Most spreadsheets have mathematical tools for difficult operations.
- Integrating graphics or scanned images into a spreadsheet can make all the difference in the clarity of a presentation.
- Three-dimensional spreadsheets have a multiple page metaphor using the additional pages to hold the detail of computations that feed into other pages.

How DBMS Are Used

- Database applications are used to store and manipulate data.
- A database application can be used in many business functions including sales and inventory tracking, accounting, employee benefits, payroll, production, and more.
- A DBMS is a program or collection of programs that store data and allow access to that data.
- A DBMS provides services both to users and to other programs.
- The heart of a DBMS is a database engine.

Database Basics

- A set of data arranged in columns and rows in a database is called a table.
- The columns are fields which combine to make rows of records.
- Fields can contain text, numeric, or logical information.

- By using keys and indexes, you can sort information in many ways.
- Forms are custom screens for displaying and entering data.
- When designing a form, you must first consider the type of data to be entered and which data entry tool would be most suitable: typing text; marking a check box; clicking a radio button; or choosing from a list box, drop-down box, or combination box.
- Masks perform validations or conversions on data entered into a field.

Interacting with the Database

- Each database interface offers various ways to navigate through and edit records.
- Common editing operations are adding, modifying, and deleting.
- Filters let you browse through records that meet a set of criteria.
- Searches provide a way to set up complex criteria and look at very specific records.
- SQL is a non-procedural query language for communicating with a database.
- SQL describes data and sometimes instructs the database to do something with the data.
- OBE is a front end for a query language that collects the facts about a query and composes the query statement by itself.
- Forms for entering data can be designed using queries.
- Reports for presenting data after they have been processed are also designed using queries.

REVIEW QUESTIONS

1. List three functions of an OS.
2. Identify and describe the major OSs found on small computers.
3. Briefly explain what a GUI is and why some people prefer this type of interface.
4. Explain the comparison of a word processor to a blank piece of paper. List five of the advantages that word processors provide over other methods of creating documents.
5. Describe the benefits of using a word processor in a graphical environment versus using a text-mode word processor.
6. Give short definitions of each of the following terms:
   a. Typeface
   b. Typeface family
   c. Font
7. What are some of the benefits that spreadsheets offer over other types of programs?
8. Explain how the display format of a cell alters the contents of the cell.
9. Define the terms *database, table, record, row,* and *field.*
10. What is a table *key*? How does it differ from an *index* and a *primary key*?

DISCUSSION QUESTIONS

1. Compare and contrast the features of OS/2, Unix, and Microsoft Windows NT.

2. Give an example of a process or system (other than the ones described in the chapter) that could be modeled with a spreadsheet. What would be some of the benefits of creating such a model?

3. Try to translate the following query into SQL: Show the "City," "State," and "Zip" fields of records from the "Customer" table where the "Last Name" starts with the letters *Smi*.

GLOSSARY

■ ■ ■ ■ ■ ■ ■ ■ ■ ■ ■ ■ ■ ■ ■ ■ ■ ■ ■

10Base-T: an Ethernet network standard that makes use of centralized panels, or concentrators, and provides the convenience of the star topology to Ethernet's linear bus.

80286: an Intel processor released in 1982; has a 16-bit data bus and is faster and more efficient than the 8086 or 8088 Intel processor.

80386: an Intel processor released in 1985; a 32-bit processor that can access approximately 4 GB of memory and features virtual 86 mode; *see also* **80386 DX**, **80386 SX**.

80386 DX: the name for the 386 since the introduction of the 386 SX in 1988.

80386 SX: a lower-cost 386 with a 16-bit data bus; released in 1988.

80486: an Intel processor introduced in 1989; combines a 386 DX processor, an 80387 math coprocessor, and a cache memory controller on a single chip, making it faster than the 386; *see also* **80486 DX**, **80486 SX**.

80486 DX: the name for the 486 since the introduction of the 486 SX in 1990.

80486 SX: a lower-cost 486 with a disabled math coprocessor; released in 1990.

8086: the first member of the 80×86 family of processors, introduced by Intel in 1978; has a 16-bit data bus.

A

accelerator key: the key indicated by an underlined letter of a command on a drop-down menu; allows a user to choose a menu option by pressing that key, without pulling down a menu; called a **command key** equivalent on the Macintosh.

access time: the time it takes a read/write head to move from one place on a recording medium to another; *see also* **average access time**, **maximum access time**.

accounts-payable module: software that keeps track of transactions representing purchases from suppliers, liabilities incurred to employees and creditors, and payments on those liabilities; generally a subset of a complete set of accounting software modules.

accounts-receivable module: software that processes cash sales, credit sales, and subsequent cash receipts on credit sales and that maintains databases that reflect customer accounts and account status; generally a subset of a complete set of accounting software modules.

adapter card: a circuit board that plugs into a computer's expansion slot and that may serve various purposes; also called a **board**, a **card**, or an **expansion board**.

adding value: processing input data so that the information output is in a useful form.

address bus: an electronic pathway that carries data between a computer's CPU and its memory.

algorithm: a set of ordered steps, or procedures, to solve a problem.

all points addressable (APA): refers to graphics modes which allow a user to change the color of any pixel on the screen through a computer program.

alphanumeric keys: the part of a keyboard that looks like a typewriter, usually arranged in a standard QWERTY keyboard layout.

alternation: a way of altering program flow in which a program makes the computer test for a condition, then alternately executes one set of instructions or another; generally implemented with the "if-then-else" or "if" construct; more commonly called **conditional branching**.

ALU: *see* **arithmetic and logic unit**.

American Standard Code for Information Interchange: *see* **ASCII**.

analog signal: a signal with finely graduated changes over time—for example, the signal of a sound wave.

antivirus software: a program that scans disks and memory for viruses, detects them, and eradicates them.

APA: *see* **all points addressable**.

application software: programs that computer users work with most often—especially for mainstream purposes such as creating documents, spreadsheets, graphics, and so on; *see also* **database**, **desktop publishing software**, **graphics application**, **spreadsheet**, **word processor**.

ARCNET (Attached Resource Computer NETwork): a common network protocol (but one that is fading in popularity) based on the star topology; inexpensive and easy to set up and expand but slow and awkward to troubleshoot and maintain.

argument: (1) in command-line DOS, a specific piece of information required to complete a command; (2) in a spreadsheet, an item of information needed to perform a function; (3) in programming, an item of information needed by a function, or subroutine, to carry out its instructions.

arithmetic and logic unit (ALU): one of two basic parts (together with the control unit) of a CPU; handles arithmetic operations, such as adding numbers, and logical operations, such as comparing numbers.

ASCII (American Standard Code for Information Interchange): pronounced "ask-ee"; initially a seven-bit code (with the eighth bit known as the parity bit) used to represent 128 symbols, including all basic alphanumerics, with bits of data; formalized by the American National Standards Institute but later enhanced by IBM; now an eight-bit system that describes 256 symbols.

assembler: a computer program that takes assembly language instructions that are meaningful to people and converts them into machine language.

assembly language: a low-level programming language that uses programming codes in place of the 0s and 1s of machine language.

asymmetrical multiprocessing: a multiprocessing system in which one main CPU retains control over the computer, as well as over other processors.

audit: a procedure of reviewing and validating a company's record-keeping, accounting, or general business practices to determine the level of reliability, accuracy, and appropriateness of the business's functions.

average access time: the average time it takes a read/write head to move from any one place on a storage medium to any other.

B

backup copy: a copy of a program or datafile, usually on diskettes or magnetic tape, which is kept in reserve in case the original becomes damaged; *see also* **full backup, incremental backup**.

backup set: a group of program files or datafiles that the user wants to backup routinely.

bar-code reader: an input device used to read bar codes, translate them into numbers, and input the numbers; often used in retail stores.

BASIC (Beginners All-purpose Symbolic Instruction Code): a programming language that is popular and easy for beginners to use; developed in 1964.

batch mode: a method of processing information in which transactions are saved and processed in groups called batches.

baud rate: a measure of modulation rate used in serial communications; the number of discrete signaling events per second.

BBS: *see* **bulletin-board service**.

binary digit: *see* **bit**.

binary field: in a database, a special field for storing a binary large object.

binary large object (BLOB): a graphic image file, such as clip art, a photograph, a screen image, or other graphic art; a sound track or video file; an OLE object such as a graph or worksheet created with a spreadsheet or word processor; or an external binary file, such as a spreadsheet or word-processor document.

bit (BInary digiT): an individual piece of data; either a 0 or a 1.

bitmap: a method of displaying graphic images on a monitor by altering the color of individual dots on a coordinate system.

BLOB: *see* **Binary Large OBject**.

block: a contiguous group of letters, words, sentences, or paragraphs selected in a document or spreadsheet for one of several purposes, such as moving or cutting and pasting.

block reference: in a spreadsheet, an address of a block of data that may contain many different cells; also called a **range**.

board: *see* **adapter card**.

boot: the process of starting a computer.

boot record: part of a disk's logical formatting system; contains a program that runs when a user first starts a computer and that determines whether the disk has the basic instruction sets necessary to run the computer's operating system; also called a **boot sector**.

bug: an error in a program; *see also* **logic error**.

bulletin-board service (BBS): an on-line information service that can be accessed via modem or over a network

bus: the electronic pathway in the motherboard that allows communication between components of a computer; *see also* **address bus, data bus**.

bus mouse: a mouse connected to a computer by an adapter card, or a card, that plugs into an available expansion slot.

byte: eight bits; the amount of memory required to store a single character; a unit of data capable of storing 256 unique values.

C

C: a programming language developed in the early 1970s; currently the language of choice among many software-development companies; *see also* **C++, portable language**.

C++: an extremely powerful and efficient programming language developed in the early 1980s; a superset of the C language with object-oriented extensions.

cache: a type of high-speed memory that contains the most recent data and instructions accessed by the CPU.

CAM: *see* **computer-aided manufacturing**.

card: *see* **adapter card**.

card reader: a device attached to computers up to the 1970s to hold, read, and interpret stacks of keypunched paper cards representing programs and data; often the main input device for computers equipped with them.

carpal tunnel syndrome: an injury of the wrist or hand commonly caused by extended periods of keyboarding; the best known of the repetitive stress injury group of ailments.

CASE: *see* **Computer-Aided Software Engineering**.

cathode ray tube (CRT): a bell-shaped glass housing that uses an electron gun to create a bright, clear image on the face of a monitor; used with the most common computer monitors.

CD-I: *see* **Compact Disk-Interactive**.

CD-ROM (compact disk, read-only memory): the most common type of optical storage, in which a laser reads lands and pits from the surface of a disk (as on a music CD); can store up to 600 MB but cannot be written to; *see also* **optical storage**.

cell: an area of a spreadsheet where a column and a row intersect to form a box in which a user enters formulas, text, or numbers.

central processing unit (CPU): the processing component (generally referred to as the **chip**) located on the motherboard that interprets and executes program instructions and communicates with input, output, and storage devices.

Centronics interface: a special cable connector at the printer end of a parallel printer cable; prevents users from plugging the wrong end of the cable into the printer.

CFC: *see* **chlorofluorocarbon**.

change agent: anyone in an organization—such as a systems analyst—who effects some new procedure or way of doing business.

char: *see* **character**.

character: (1) a number, letter, symbol, or punctuation mark; (2) a single, eight-bit variable; also called a **char**.

check box: a software tool that displays a check mark or "x" on the screen when clicked; used for entering data in logical fields where only two values are possible—yes or no, on or off, and so on.

chip: a sliver of silicon or other material etched with the electronic circuits that perform the operations of a computer; *see also* **microprocessor**.

chlorofluorocarbon (CFC): a compound used to clean computer chips and known to destroy ozone.

CIM: *see* **computer integrated manufacturing**.

circuit board: a rigid, rectangular card consisting of chips and electronic circuitry connected to a motherboard or to other circuit boards.

CISC: *see* **complex instruction set computing processor**.

class: in the source code for an object-oriented program, a sequence of statements that defines an object.

click: to press and release a mouse button once with the cursor over an item or selection on the screen.

client-server computing: a network of computers that consists of a file server and individual nodes that may share programs and data from the server; the server commonly runs a database-management program, and clients request and process specific data as required.

clip art: pre-made creative artwork supplied commercially in electronic form; used in DTP.

clipboard: a holding area maintained in memory and used for storing text, graphics, sound, or video that has been copied or cut.

cluster: in DOS, a group of disk sectors.

CMYK separations: *see* **process color separations**.

coax: *see* **coaxial cable**.

coaxial cable: a cable made up of a single wire in the center of an insulator wrapped in mesh; also called **coax**.

COBOL (COmmon Business Oriented Language): a high-level programming language used to develop business data-processing applications; developed by a government-appointed committee in 1960 to solve the problem of incompatibility among computer manufacturers; easy to read but tedious to use.

code generator: a program that looks at design specifications and actually generates, or produces, program source code.

coherent: perfectly aligned in the same direction (referring to a laser light); able to be focused precisely on a tiny area.

color monitor: a monitor with a multicolor display.

color separations: separate pages prepared for printing each color used on each page of a document; *see also* **process color separations**, **spot color separation**.

combination box: a data entry tool that combines an edit field and a drop-down list box.

command interpreter: a program that accepts commands from a user, interprets them, and acts on them.

command key equivalent: *see* **accelerator key**.

command-line interface: a user interface based on words and symbols typed at a prompt using the computer's keyboard.

Compact Disk-Interactive (CD-I): an application of CD-ROM technology that stores digital audio, full-motion video and graphics, animation, text, and data on a CD, allowing users to interact with a program that uses a tremendous volume of data.

compact disk, read-only memory: *see* **CD-ROM**.

compiler: a program that translates a file of program source code into object code.

compiling: the first step in the process of converting program source-code files into an executable program.

complex instruction set computing (CISC) processor: one of the methodologies under which microcomputer CPUs are designed; the most common type of microprocessor found in small computers; contains large instruction sets with hundreds of instructions.

computer-aided manufacturing (CAM): a term applied to the use of computer and robotics technology to automate manufacturing functions in industry.

Computer-Aided Software Engineering (CASE): software that helps programmers to design computer programs.

computer integrated manufacturing (CIM): a manufacturing process coordinated by a computer, which designs a product, orders parts, and plans production.

computer program: *see* **software**.

concentrator: a centralized panel used in a 10Base-T Ethernet network.

conditional branching: *see* **alternation**.

configure: to adapt a computer to the particular needs of a user.

construct: a framework for a particular type of manipulation of control flow.

control character: an invisible character that a computer display and printer can interpret; also called a **control code**.

control code: *see* **control character**.

control flow: the order in which program statements are executed.

control unit: one of two basic parts (together with the ALU) of a CPU; contains instructions for carrying out activities of the computer.

cooperative multitasking: a multitasking system in which programs periodically check with the operating system to see if other programs need the CPU and, if so, relinquish control of the CPU to the next program.

copy protection: a set of techniques that prevent the illegal copying of software.

counter field: in a database, a field that contains a unique, incrementing numeric value (such as an invoice number) that the DBMS automatically assigns for every new record.

CPU: *see* **central processing unit**.

credit history: information about a person's accounts and debts.

crop mark: a mark showing precisely where the corners of a page are; used for aligning pages properly for a press.

CRT: *see* **cathode ray tube**.

currency field: in a database or spreadsheet, a number field with the display format set up by the software to represent money.

cursor: a highlight on the screen of a monitor that shows where the characters to be typed will be entered; can appear as a box, line, arrow, or I-beam pointer or, in a spreadsheet, as a large block covering an entire cell.

cursor-movement keys: the keys on the keyboard that allow the user to change the position of the cursor on the screen.

Cut command: a feature that allows a user to remove text or data from a document or spreadsheet and place it on a clipboard.

cyberspace: the electronic network now available to computer users.

cylinder: a term used to refer to the same track across all the disk sides of a hard disk.

D

DAT: *see* **digital audio tape drive**.

data: facts, numbers, letters, or symbols that become usable information when processed.

data area: part of a disk's logical formatting system; the part of the disk that remains free to store data after the boot sector, file-allocation table, and root directory have been created.

database: (1) an integrated collection of data stored on a direct access storage device; a set of related information; (2) application software that allows a user to enter, update, and retrieve data and to organize and search that data in multiple ways.

database client: a program running on a networked computer that receives data by accessing a database server.

database engine: the program within a DBMS that can access and manipulate files containing data; receives its instructions from other programs.

database management system (DBMS): the software tool computers use to achieve the processing and orderly storage of data; a program or programs that store an integrated collection of data and provide easy access to it.

database server: the primary computer within a network; stores and processes software applications and data for use by other computers or nodes within the network.

data bus: an electronic pathway connecting the CPU, memory, and other hardware devices of a motherboard; sometimes referred to simply as the **bus**; *see also* **Extended Industry Standard Architecture bus**, **Industry Standard Architecture bus**, **Microchannel Architecture bus**.

data communications: the electronic transfer of information between computers.

data compression: a reduction in the volume of data achieved by an algorithm that encodes repeating sequences of data; reduces the amount of time necessary to transfer data.

data-encoding scheme: a method that a disk drive uses to translate bits of data into a sequence of flux reversals, or changes in magnetic polarity, on the surface of a disk.

data-entry tool: in application software, a mechanism used to enter data; *see also* **check box**, **combination box**, **drop-down box**, **list box**, **radio button**.

datafile: a collection of stored user data.

datafile object: an object within a datafile.

data processing (DP): *see* **information systems**.

data-transfer rate: the number of bytes that a data storage device can transfer per second.

date field: in a database, a special field that stores the date.

DBMS: *see* **DataBase Management System**.

debugger: a program that executes each command in a program one step at a time so that a programmer can walk through the source code on-screen and track down hard-to-find logic errors.

decision-support system: software that helps a user make decisions—for example, by querying and manipulating data to create an annual budget for an organization.

declare: to create a variable within a program; the same as to **define**.

define: *see* **declare**.

demodulation: the process of converting an electric computer signal that has traversed a telephone line back into sound or other data.

density: a measure of the quality of a disk's surface; the higher the density, the more closely the iron-oxide particles are packed and the more data the disk can store.

desktop model: a PC designed to sit on a desk.

desktop publishing (DTP) software: software that allows a user to perform design, typesetting, and pasteup functions with a single application program and to produce high-quality, camera-ready printed pages; also called a **page layout program**.

dialog box: a special-purpose menu that gives or requests information from the user and that is sensitive to the context in which it is used; also called a **panel** or a **pop-up menu**.

digital audio tape (DAT) drive: a tape drive that typically has two read heads and two write heads and that has a very high data storage capacity.

digital signal: a signal that a computer sends; made up only of 0s and 1s and transmitted by telephone line.

directory: the most important organizational tool for a hard disk; a listing of other files and directories (term used mostly for DOS-based machines); same as a **folder** on a Macintosh.

disk drive: a device that holds a removable floppy disk or a nonremovable hard disk to store data.

diskette: *see* **floppy disk**.

display format: in a spreadsheet, the way in which values appear within a cell—for example, as a percentage or a dollar amount.

display value: in a spreadsheet, the text or data that appears in a cell.

distributed computing: a system that allows users to draw on the processing power of other computers in a network.

distributed database: a system that integrates databases located on different computers within a network.

distributed processing: a system configuration in which two or more geographically dispersed computers in a network accommodate or share applications.

DNA fingerprinting: a technique used to positively identify a person with the help of a computer by matching a trace of blood, skin, or hair left at a crime scene to a suspect.

document-oriented computing: computing organized around the goal of producing a corporate document.

dot-matrix printer: the first type of printer commonly used with PCs; operates by wires striking paper through an inked ribbon to create an image; noisy and lower quality in printing than other types of printer, but also less expensive.

dot prompt: a period character, or "dot," at which a user types commands (especially dBASE).

dots per inch (DPI): a measurement of the print resolution of laser printers; commonly 600, both vertically and horizontally, but can be up to 1800.

double-click: to press and release a mouse button twice in rapid succession over an item on the screen.

download: to retrieve a file from a remote computer.

DP: *see* **data processing**.

DPI: *see* **dots per inch**.

drag: to depress the button of a mouse over an item on the screen, hold it down, and move the mouse; can be used to define blocks or to move objects, among other things.

driver: a program that accepts requests from an application program and causes a device, such as a sound or video card, to execute those requests.

drop cap: an enlarged capital letter that occupies two or more lines of type at the beginning of a paragraph.

drop-down box: a box used in application programs as a data-entry tool; displays choices from which a user may make a selection.

DTP: *see* **desktop publishing**.

dual-port memory: the part of the video controller that receives data from the CPU and gives it to the monitor; memory shared by the CPU and the controller.

Dvorak keyboard: a keyboard layout that uses a more logical design than QWERTY, with the most commonly used keys positioned close together; supposed to be easier and faster than QWERTY.

dynamic data exchange (DDE): a technique for linking applications that allows a user to move data from one application into another or others, such as from a spreadsheet into a word-processor document; changes made within one application are automatically reflected in linked applications.

E

EBCDIC: pronounced "eb-si-dick"; *see* **Extended Binary Coded Decimal Interchange Code**.

editor: in programming, a simple word-processor-like program into which a programmer or computer user types statements.

EISA bus: *see* **Extended Industry Standard Architecture bus**.

electromagnet: a magnet made by wrapping a wire coil around an iron bar and sending an electric current through the coil; reversing the direction of the current's flow reverses the polarity of the magnetic field; similar to the way in which magnetic storage devices store data.

electronic mail (e-mail): a system for exchanging written messages between networked users.

electronic pen: *see* **pen**.

e-mail: *see* **electronic mail**.

EMS: *see* **Lotus, Intel, Microsoft Expanded Memory Specification**.

encapsulate: to include within one object.

encryption: a form of security in which data is encoded to prevent use by unauthorized individuals; users must decode data.

enhanced small device interface (ESDI): a common interface standard that incorporates much of the intelligence of the hard-disk controller into the drive.

ergonomics: the study of the physical relationship between people and their tools, such as computers.

error-correction protocol: a standard for correcting errors via modems that occur when static interferes with computer communication through a telephone line.

ESDI: pronounced "ee-es-di-eye"; *see* **enhanced small device interface**.

Ethernet: the most common network protocol; based on linear-bus topology; inexpensive and simple.

executable: able to be executed.

execute: to make a computer load and carry out a program, or a specific set of instructions; same as **run**.

expanded memory: a separate section of memory from 0 KB to 32 MB in size accessed through a memory page frame in upper memory; together with extended memory, allows PCs to address increased amounts of data in memory.

Expanded Memory Specification (EMS): *see* **Lotus, Intel, Microsoft Expanded Memory Specification**.

expert system: a knowledge-based computer system that makes decisions according to a list of rules compiled by experts in a given field; the closest thing to artificial intelligence available today; *see also* **knowledge base**.

Extended Binary Coded Decimal Interchange Code (EBCDIC): an eight-bit code developed by IBM to define 256 symbols; commonly used in IBM mainframe and mid-range systems.

Extended Industry Standard Architecture (EISA) bus: a 32-bit data bus developed by hardware manufacturers other than IBM; faster than the ISA bus but compatible with models that used that bus.

extended memory: memory in addition to conventional memory used to run and manage applications; together with expanded memory, helps PCs to address increased amounts of data in memory.

eXtended Memory Specification (XMS): memory built into a computer in excess of the 1 MB that DOS can address; allows programs to access extended memory directly through the XMS driver.

external command: one of about 45 DOS commands that are separate programs included with DOS and do not reside in memory.

external modem: an external communications device that contains the circuitry and logic to modulate data signals; connected to a computer via a serial port and to a telephone system via a standard telephone jack.

F

FAT: *see* **file-allocation table**.

fiber-optic cable: a thin strand of glass wrapped in protective coatings; transfers data by means of pulsating beams of light rather than electric frequencies; efficient, fast, and precise, but less flexible than wire cables.

field: one or more data categories in a database; a column in a table; *see also* **counter field, currency field, date field, logical field, lookup field, memo field, number field, text field, time field**.

file-allocation table (FAT): part of a disk's logical formatting system; a table log maintained by DOS that records the location of each file and the status of each sector.

file server: a computer node that consists of a shared disk-storage device on a LAN; stores software applications and the users' remotely accessed datafiles; also called a **network server** or a **server**.

file transfer: the sending of a file from one computer to another, as by modem.

file-transfer protocol: a set of rules or guidelines that dictates the format in which data will be sent from one computer to another.

find and change: *see* **search and replace**.

flash memory: a type of storage that can store several megabytes of information on a card the shape of a credit card; widely available but not yet commonly used; data on the card are usually retained even if the power fails or the card is removed from the system.

flat-file database: a nonrelational database; data are not connected or linked to other related databases.

flat-panel monitor: a monitor commonly used with notebook computers, generally using an LCD to render images; *see also* **liquid crystal display monitor**.

flicker: the apparent rapid pulsating of a screen of a monitor that scans too slowly.

float: a variable that can store numbers with decimal points.

floating-point arithmetic: a computer technique that the math coprocessor uses to translate numbers into scientific notation.

floppy disk: a removable magnetic disk made of a thin, flexible piece of plastic coated with iron oxide and enclosed in a plastic case or protective jacket; comes in 2-inch, 3½-inch, and 5¼-inch sizes; typically used to load new programs or data onto a hard disk, trade data with other users, or make a backup copy of data on a hard disk; also called a **diskette**; *see also* **magnetic storage**.

floppy-disk drive: a device that reads and writes data to and from a floppy disk.

flowchart: a graphical representation using lines and geometric symbols of a procedure or computer program.

folder: *see* **directory, subdirectory**.

font: a specific typeface and style (such as bold or italic) displayed in a particular point size; *see also* **monospace font, proportional font, sans serif font, serif font**.

for loop: a loop in which a programmer begins with a known value and that value changes by a known amount until it reaches a known limit and then stops; *see also* **nested for loop**.

form: in a database, a custom screen used for displaying and entering data.

format: (1) a DOS function that prepares a disk to store data; in the process, read/write heads record tracks and sectors on the disk; same as to **initialize**; (2) *see* **mask**.

formula: in a spreadsheet, a mathematical equation within a cell.

FORTRAN (FORmula TRANslator): the first high-level programming language, introduced in 1957; specifically designed for mathematical and engineering programs.

fragmented: the condition of a file that DOS has split up and filed in separate areas of a disk.

freeware: software available for use at no cost; may or may not be copyrighted; *see also* **public-domain software**.

Front end: the part of a program with which a user interacts directly.

full backup: a copy of every file on a disk transferred to and stored on backup media for safekeeping; *see also* **backup copy**.

full-duplex communication: simultaneous communication, or transmission, between a sending and a receiving computer across a common data path or communications link.

function: (1) in a spreadsheet, a tool that can be used in cell formulas to perform special operations, such as adding the values in several cells; (2) in programming, a block of statements, or subprograms, designed to perform specific functions or tasks; also called a **paragraph**, **procedure**, **routine**, or **subroutine**.

functional specifications: detailed information needed to design and develop a computer program.

function keys: the keys on a keyboard that allow a user to give computer commands without typing long strings of characters; usually arranged in a row along the top of the keyboard and designated as F1, F2, and so on.

G

grammar checker: a word-processor feature that checks for word usage, correct grammar, reading level, and sometimes even things like writing style.

graphical user interface (GUI): a user interface that works visually and is based on the selection of actions using a mouse or a similar pointing device to click on icons or to pick options from menus.

graphics application: software that allows a user to create illustrations from scratch or from information from another program; *see also* **presentation graphics application**.

groupware: application software that takes advantage of the concept of workgroup computing.

GUI: pronounced "goo-ee"; *see* **graphical user interface**.

H

hard-code: in a spreadsheet, a specific value used as part of a formula.

hard disk: a nonremovable enclosed magnetic disk included in most PCs; a stack of metal platters, each coated with iron oxide, that spin on a spindle and are encased in a sealed chamber; holds much more information than a floppy disk and is used to store relatively large amounts of data; *see also* **magnetic storage**, **mass-storage device**.

hardware: the physical components of a computer, including a processor, memory, I/O devices, and disks.

Hayes AT command set: the command set that has set the standard for modem communications between computers; AT stands for "attention" and precedes every command; also called the **AT command set**.

head crash: a touching of the head and the disk; destroys all data stored in the area and can destroy a read/write head.

header/detail relationship: *see* **one-to-many relationship**

high-level language: (1) originally, any language easier to understand than machine language; (2) currently, a language further removed from machine code than assembly language; uses more meaningful words and phrases and provides facilities for altering program flow.

holographic memory: a storage medium currently being developed; a three-dimensional optical medium capable of storing 6.5 terabytes (more than 1 million MB) of data in a small cube.

horizontal resolution: the number of pixels in each row on a monitor.

hybrid network: a combination of linear bus, star, and ring topologies; often used in wide-area networks.

hypermedia: a programming environment that allows non-programmers to create custom applications; an extension of hypertext that brings together the multimedia facilities of graphics, video, and sound, as well as a programming language based on objects, icons, and metaphors; *see also* **stack**.

hypertext: a flexible software technology used to create electronic books; provides fast and flexible access to search criteria and provides quick access to information in large documents.

I

I-beam pointer: a type of cursor that looks like a capital I, usually used for the entering or editing of text in a graphical environment.

icon: a graphical screen element that executes one or more commands when selected with a mouse or other pointing device.

IDE: *see* **integrated drive electronics**.

image-processing software: a program used to manipulate scanned images.

image scanner: an input device that converts printed images into digitized formats that can be stored and manipulated in a computer with the appropriate software program; frequently just called **scanner**.

incremental backup: a copy of only the files that have been created or changed since the last backup; *see also* **backup copy**.

index: in a database, a key other than the primary key; used for sorting and to speed up searches.

Industry Standard Architecture (ISA) bus: a 16-bit data bus developed by IBM; has become an industry standard.

information: (1) data that have been entered into and processed by a computer; (2) any nontangible item that affects business.

information systems (IS): (1) the systems, or rules and procedures, that businesses use to accumulate, organize, and dispense information; (2) the division or department within a large company that is responsible for developing, installing, and maintaining computer systems; also called **data processing** or **management information systems**.

initialize: *see* **format**.

ink-jet printer: a printer that creates an image directly on paper by spraying ink; has a quality and speed higher than a dot-matrix printer, but lower than a laser printer.

input: raw data, assumptions, and formulas entered into a computer.

input device: computer hardware that accepts data and instructions from a user; *see also* **bar-code reader**, **image scanner**, **joystick**, **keyboard**, **mouse**, **pen**, **scanner**, **touch screen**, **trackball**.

input/output (I/O) card: an adapter that provides general-purpose ports to connect various peripheral devices (such as printers, a mouse, and so on) on the back of a computer; *see also* **parallel port**, **serial port**.

input/output (I/O) device: hardware that enables a computer to communicate with a user and with other machines or devices; *see also* **input device**, **output device**.

insert mode: a mode in which characters typed are inserted into a line rather than replacing existing type.

install: to copy a program from diskettes to a computer's hard disk.

instruction set: a list of all operations, or a set of instructions, that the CPU can perform; built into the circuitry.

integrated drive electronics (IDE): one of the common hard-disk interface standards; places most of the controller's circuitry on the drive itself rather than on a separate controller board.

interlacing: a method of displaying higher resolution on a monitor screen, but with increased flickering; the electron gun paints, or scans, every other line instead of each line in order.

internal command: one of about 25 DOS commands whose program code is built into the DOS command interpreter; remains resident in memory after booting.

internal modem: an internal communications device, or a circuit board that plugs into one of the computer's expansion slots.

Internet: the huge network that links many of the world's scientific, research, and educational computers, as well as some commercial networks; also called **the Net**.

interrupt request: a signal that the keyboard controller sends to the CPU when it has received a complete keystroke.

intuitive interface: a program interface system that can be used effectively even by someone who has never seen it before; also called a **user-friendly interface**.

I/O: *see* **input/output**.

IS: *see* **information systems**.

ISA bus: *see* **Industry Standard Architecture bus**.

J

joystick: an input device that controls cursor movement for computer games and for some professional applications; often used by individuals with disabilities.

justify: to align both the left and right margins; accomplished in word processing by the insertion of spaces between words and sometimes between characters.

K

KB: *see* **kilobyte**.

kern: to make fine adjustments in the space between adjacent letters in a document.

kerned font: *see* **proportional font**.

kernel: the part of an operating system that controls a computer's central functions, such as the management of hardware and internal memory.

keyboard: the most common input device; allows a user to enter letters, numbers, symbols, punctuation marks, and commands into a computer; *see also* **alphanumeric keys, cursor-movement keys, function keys, numeric keypad**.

keyboard buffer: the part of a computer's memory that receives a scan code from the keyboard controller when a key has been pressed.

keyboard controller: the tiny computer chip—inside either a computer or a keyboard—that notes that a key has been pressed and places a scan code into the keyboard buffer.

keypunch: a machine used to punch holes in a card to represent data that was fed into early computers.

kilobyte (KB): 1,024 bytes of memory.

knowledge base: a large, highly detailed database; sometimes used with an expert system.

L

label: in a spreadsheet, text typed into a cell to label a column or a row; may be any word or sequence of characters.

LAN: *see* **local-area network**.

land: a spot that reflects laser light into the sensor of an optical disk drive.

laptop computer: a portable computer small enough to be held on a lap but slightly larger than a notebook computer.

laser printer: a printer that operates by focusing a laser beam on a photostatic drum; produces the highest-quality print of all PC printers, and is quiet, fast, and convenient to use, but is also more expensive than other types of printers; *see also* **dots per inch, toner**.

LCD: *see* **liquid crystal display monitor**.

library: a collection of functions that have been compiled to object code.

LIM: Lotus, Intel, Microsoft; *see* **Lotus, Intel, Microsoft Expanded Memory Specification**

linear bus network: a computer topology in which all network nodes and peripheral devices are attached to a single conduit.

linker: a program that combines object modules produced by the compiler and converts them into a final executable program, or load module.

linking: in programming, assembling object-code modules into an executable program file.

liquid crystal display (LCD) monitor: the most common type of flat-panel monitor, generally used in portable computers; creates images with a special kind of liquid crystal.

list box: in a database, a field control that lists several options from which a user may select for data entry.

load module: an executable program.

local-area network (LAN): a system of PCs that are located relatively near to each other and connected by wire so that individual users can cooperatively process information and share resources.

local-area network administrator: a person in charge of setting up, operating, and maintaining a LAN.

logical field: in a database, a field that can hold one of only two values—yes or no, true or false, on or off, retail or wholesale, and so on; also called a **yes/no field**.

logical format: an operating system function in which each track and sector is labeled and the locations of all data are kept in a special log on the disk; also called a **soft format**; *see also* **boot record, data area, file-allocation table, root directory**.

logic error: a bug in which the code is syntactically correct but tells the computer to do the wrong thing.

log on: to access a computer system.

long integer: a four-byte variable for large whole numbers.

lookup field: in a database, a field that contains some identifying factor that can be used to validate entries and simplify data entry.

loop: *see* **repetition construct**.

Lotus, Intel, Microsoft Expanded Memory Specification (EMS): a specification that allows programs to use more than the standard 640K of conventional memory in DOS.

M

machine code: the code that the CPU recognizes as its instructions in executable program files.

machine language: a low level of programming consisting of a set of coded instructions that can be directly executed by the CPU.

Macintosh: the line of PCs produced by Apple Computer; uses a Motorola microprocessor and Apple Computer's own operating system.

macro: a feature that allows a user to store and then automatically issue a sequence of commands or keystrokes.

magnetic disk: the type of magnetic storage that is the most common storage medium; a round, flat computer component that spins around its center; *see also* **floppy disk, hard disk, read/write head**.

magnetic storage: a type of data-storage technology that works by polarizing tiny pieces of iron on the magnetic medium; *see also* **magnetic disk, magnetic tape**.

magnetic tape: a type of magnetic storage that has much more capacity than a floppy disk but that requires significant time to access data; best used to store data that will not be needed frequently, such as to backup an entire hard disk.

mailing list: a database consisting of people's addresses and other relevant information.

mainframe computer: a large multiuser computer system designed to handle tremendous amounts of input, output, and storage; generally used to perform business applications and contain large and commonly accessed databases; the largest type of computer in common use.

management information systems (MIS): *see* **information systems**.

mask: in a database, a specification for validating or converting data entered, such as converting all typed characters to upper or lowercase; called a field **format** in Microsoft Access.

massively parallel processors: up to thousands of processors that work together within a single computer, thereby increasing the computer's speed; most machines using this technology are still in the research and development phase.

mass-storage device: a device such as a hard disk, tape, optical disk, or other type of medium that can store a great deal of data.

master pages: in DTP, special pages within a document set aside for elements common to all pages in the document, such as page numbers, headers and footers, ruling lines, margin features, special graphics, and layout guides.

materials-requirement planning (MRP): a computer program that plans and controls the flow of materials needed to produce products in the manufacturing process.

math coprocessor: a chip or part of a chip that speeds up math-intensive processing by using floating-point arithmetic to perform calculations for the CPU.

maximum access time: the largest possible access time for a disk.

MB: *see* **megabyte**.

MCA bus: *see* **Microchannel Architecture bus**.

MDT: *see* **mobile data terminal**.

megabyte (MB): 1,024 kilobytes (1,048,576 bytes) of memory.

member function: a function defined in a given class

memo field: in a database, a special field that can contain text information of variable length, such as comments or notes

memory: one of two processing components (along with the CPU) of a computer; a short-term holding area built into the computer's hardware; the location where instructions and data are stored while they are being manipulated; *see also* **random-access memory, read-only memory**.

memory address: a number that indicates a location in the memory chips so that the computer can find data quickly without searching its entire memory sequentially.

menu: a list of program commands displayed on-screen for selection by the user.

menu bar: a bar across the top of an application program screen of a drop-down menu system; displays the types of commands available to a user.

Microchannel Architecture (MCA) bus: a 32-bit data bus developed by IBM; much faster than the ISA bus, but not compatible with early models of Intel CPUs.

microcode: basic directions that tell the CPU how to execute an instruction; located in the control unit.

microcomputer: *see* **personal computer**.

microprocessor: an integrated circuit on a single chip that is the CPU or brain of a computer.

millisecond: 0.001 second; the unit used to measure access time in computers.

minicomputer: a computer smaller than a mainframe but larger than a PC and able to handle much more input and output than a PC; most can have multiple users, although fewer than a mainframe.

MIS: *see* **information systems**.

mission-critical application: *see* **vertical application**.

mobile data terminal (MDT): a display terminal used by a police officer in a squad car to access information about a vehicle or an individual from a central computer.

modem: a device that allows computers to communicate through telephone lines; the modulation and demodulation of electronic signals that can be processed by computers; *see also* **demodulation, modulation**.

modulation: the process of converting data from a computer into a signal that can traverse a telephone line.

monitor: an output device that has a screen like that of a television on which the user may see displayed information; *see also* **cathode ray tube, color monitor, flat-panel monitor, liquid crystal display monitor, monochrome monitor, video controller**.

monochrome monitor: a monitor that displays only one color against a contrasting background.

monospace font: a font in which each character takes up exactly the same amount of horizontal space.

motherboard: the computer's main system board, where the CPU and the memory are located; most also have connectors for cards that can be added through expansion slots.

mouse: an input device that allows a user to draw on a screen and to control the cursor by pointing and clicking while moving it around on a flat surface; the user clicks, double-clicks, drags, or points the mouse to make it work; *see also* **bus mouse, optical mouse, serial mouse**.

MRP: *see* **materials-requirement planning**.

multimedia: a computer system that combines text, graphics, animation, music, voice, and video media; may include stereo speakers as an output device.

multiprocessor operating system: an operating system that can take advantage of more than one CPU.

multitasking: an operating system that can execute more than one program at a time; *see also* **cooperative multitasking, preemptive multitasking**.

multiuser operating system: an operating system that allows more than one user to use the computer at one time.

N

nanotechnology: a science based on the creation of molecules that can be used to hold data or to perform tasks.

nested for loop: a for loop inside another for loop.

network: a system of interconnected computers that can communicate with each other and share applications and data.

network-interface card (NIC): a device through which computers in a network transmit and receive data.

network protocol: a set of standards used for network communications.

network server: *see* **file server**.

network version: a version of software that a company can purchase and legally load onto a network so that some or all company employees can use the same software.

NIC: *see* **network-interface card**.

node: an individual computer on a network.

nonprocedural language: a language that does not give step-by-step commands to a computer or database but rather sends instructions to the computer in English-like statements.

nonvolatile memory: memory that retains data even when the computer is turned off.

notebook computer: a portable computer, approximately 8½ by 11 inches, that fits inside a briefcase.

number field: in a database, a field that holds numbers; also called a **numeric field**.

numeric keypad: the part of a keyboard that looks like an adding machine, with 10 digits and mathematical operators; usually located on the right side of the keyboard.

O

object: a self-contained unit defined within an object-oriented programming statement; contains both data and functions.

object code: the code used to generate a machine language program; the translation of a source-code file.

object-code file: a disk file that stores object code; also called an object module.

object embedding: the process of integrating a copy of data from one application into another, as from a worksheet into a word-processor file.

Object Linking and Embedding (OLE): a broad term that refers to application integration and that encompasses both dynamic data exchange and object embedding.

object module: *see* **object-code file**.

object-oriented programming (OOP): a program assembly using pieces, or objects, that encapsulate information with instructions and combine complex steps into a single procedure; *see also* **object**.

OCR: *see* **optical character recognition software**.

one-to-many relationship: the most common type of relationship between database tables, in which a header table and detail tables are linked by a common field; also called a **header/detail relationship**.

OOP: pronounced "oop"; *see* **object-oriented programming**.

operating system (OS): system software that provides an interface for a user to communicate with the computer, manages hardware devices (disk drives, a keyboard, a monitor, and so on), manages and maintains disk file systems, and supports application programs.

optical character recognition (OCR) software: a program that allows a scanner to translate typed or printed text into strings of character codes in the computer's memory for processing.

optical mouse: a mouse that has no moving parts but has a built-in photodetector that senses the mouse's movement over a special pad with gridlines printed on it.

optical storage: the main alternative to magnetic storage; uses a laser beam to read, write, and/or transfer data to the appropriate medium; *see also* **compact disk, read-only memory; write once, read many drive**.

order of precedence: in a spreadsheet, the order in which mathematical operations are performed, with multiplication and division before addition and subtraction.

OS: *see* **operating system**.

outliner: in word processing, a map or method for planning, developing, and rearranging information in large documents; also called an **outline view**.

outline view: *see* **outliner**.

output: information generated through the processing of input data.

output device: computer hardware that returns processed data, or information, to a user; *see also* **monitor, plotter, printer**.

outsource: to use the services of consultants or system vendors to manage information.

overtype mode: a mode in which characters typed replace existing text; also called **typeover mode**.

P

page layout program: *see* **desktop publishing software**.

paragraph: (1) in word processing, a division of parts in a document; numbered consecutively; (2) in programming, another name for a **function** (definition 2).

parallel interface: *see* **parallel port**.

parallel port: a communication port through which bits representing data can flow simultaneously at a high speed; also called a **parallel interface**.

parity bit: an extra bit in a byte used to detect errors; used in the original version of ASCII.

part: in word processing, a division of sections within a document; lettered in order; sometimes split into paragraphs.

Pascal: a programming language developed in 1971; highly structured and popular for its implementation of object-oriented extension but used largely for educational purposes.

password: a secret code that verifies a person's identity and is often required before a person can log on to a company's computer system.

Paste command: a feature that allows a user to remove text from a clipboard and place it in a document at the cursor position.

PC: (1) an IBM personal computer or any of its compatibles; (2) as used in this book, any personal computer.

PDA: *see* **personal digital assistant**.

peer-to-peer computing: a network arrangement in which each computer has access to all or some of the resources on other nodes.

pen: an input device that allows a user to write on or point at a special pad or the screen of a pen-based computer, such as a PDA.

Pentium: the fastest and most powerful member of the Intel family of microprocessors; introduced in 1993.

personal computer: a small computer commonly found in an office, classroom, or home; also called a microcomputer; *see also* **PC**.

personal digital assistant (PDA): the smallest of portable computers, about the size of a checkbook; much less powerful than a notebook or a laptop; *see also* **personal intelligent communicator**.

personal intelligent communicator (PIC): the latest type of PDA; can use infrared light to communicate with nearby computers and may have cellular phone and fax capabilities.

personal-productivity application: a program that focuses on a task performed by an individual and involves a lot of user interface—for example, a word processor, electronic spreadsheet, or database.

PIC: *see* **personal intelligent communicator**.

pica: a unit of measurement used for horizontal distances, such as the width of a column or a page; 1 pica equals 12 points.

pit: a spot in an optical disk that scatters the light of a laser.

pixel: the dots, or picture elements, in the grid of a monitor screen.

plotter: an output device that creates images with a robotic arm by using pens to draw lines on a large sheet of paper; commonly used for computer-aided design and presentation graphics.

point: (1) to place a cursor over an item or position on the screen with a mouse; (2) a measurement used for vertical distances such as the height of characters or the space between lines; 72 points are approximately equal to 1 inch, and 12 points equal 1 pica.

point-of-sale (POS) terminal: a computerized cash register commonly used in retail stores to record and monitor sales transactions; often tied directly into a company's accounting system.

polarized: the condition of a magnetic bar with ends having opposite magnetic polarity.

port: a socket into which external devices, such as I/O devices, are connected on the back of a computer; also called an **interface**.

portable computer: a computer that can easily be carried around; *see also* **laptop computer**, **notebook computer**, **personal digital assistant**.

portable language: a language, such as C, with which written programs can easily be "ported" to other computers equipped with the same compiler.

ported: (1) an application that has been translated from one machine to another; (2) to be connected to a computer through a port.

POS: *see* **point-of-sale terminal**.

POST: *see* **power on self test**.

power on self test (POST): a self-diagnosis test performed when a computer is first turned on; identifies the computer's memory, disks, keyboard, display system, and other attached devices.

preemptive multitasking: a multitasking system in which the operating system maintains a list of processes that are running and the priority of each process; at any time, it can preempt the process that is running and reassign the time to a higher-priority task.

presentation: the manner in which information appears (as when data is presented in a chart).

presentation graphics application: software that allows a user to create colorful, professional-quality graphs and charts based on numerical data imported from another program, such as a spreadsheet.

primary key: in a database table, the element that determines a default or primary sort; usually a single field; *see also* **index**.

printer: an output device that produces a hard copy on paper; *see also* **dot-matrix printer**, **ink-jet printer**, **laser printer**.

print preview: the ability of a word processor or a spreadsheet to shrink the pages of a document so that an entire page or even facing pages can be seen on-screen in their completed format, before the document is printed.

private: in programming, refers to data and functions that are shielded from access by any program statement other than those initiated by the class containing the object itself.

procedural language: a high-level programming language consisting of commands that tell a computer what to do—instruction by instruction, step by step.

procedure: (1) another name for a **function** (definition 2); (2) the course of action taken to solve a problem.

process color separations: separations printed for each page for each of the three printing primary colors (cyan, magenta, and yellow), as well as for black; also called **CMYK separations**.

processing: transforming raw input data into useful information for output; also called **adding value**.

processor: computer hardware that interprets and carries out instructions for such tasks as performing calculations or sorting data; the "brain" of the computer; *see also* **microprocessor**.

profiler: a software-development tool that collects statistics about a program and helps programmers to make the system run more efficiently.

program: *see* **software**.

prompt: a symbol displayed on-screen that tells a user where to type a command in a command-line interface.

proportional font: a font in which each character may have a slightly different width; that is, the letter M takes up more space than the letter I; also called a **kerned font**.

prototype: (1) a model that embodies the concepts, look, and feel of an eventual software system; (2) in object-oriented programming, a description within the datafile of functions that a datafile object can perform, such as changing the current key, searching for a record, and so on.

pseudocode: a code that is between English and actual programming code and that some programmers use to get ideas down on paper without worrying about actual programming-language syntax and rules.

public-domain software: software that is not copyrighted and is therefore available for use without cost or restriction; *see also* **freeware**.

Q

QBE: *see* **query by example**.

QBE form: a form in which a user types values or symbols into fields to specify search criteria; *see also* **query by example**.

query: in a database, a search question that instructs the program to locate records that meet specific requirements; *see also* **query by example**.

query by example (QBE): in a database, a feature that allows a user to enter facts about a query into a form, from which the application program composes a query statement for processing.

QWERTY: the arrangement of keys on a standard keyboard; the first six letters on the top row of keys are Q, W, E, R, T, and Y.

R

radio button: in a database, a convenient data-entry tool used when only one option among several choices is possible.

ragged right: text aligned only on the left margin so that the right margin is uneven.

RAID: *see* **redundant array of inexpensive disks**.

RAM: *see* **random-access memory**.

random access: a method used to access a record of a file directly by its address rather than sequentially.

random-access memory (RAM): a computer's volatile, temporary, memory built into its CPU; stores information while the information is being worked on but holds the information only until the computer is turned off or reset.

RDBMS: *see* **relational database**.

read-only memory (ROM): nonvolatile, or permanent, memory in the computer's CPU; includes the computer's start-up instructions, which cannot be changed.

read/write head: a magnetic device that floats closely above or below the surface of a magnetic disk and that reads, records, and erases information; contains an electromagnet that creates magnetic charge in a medium.

real time: a method of processing information as it is received.

record: in a database, a row in a table; a collection of data items that may be fixed or variable in length; one or more records usually make up a datafile.

reduced instruction set computing (RISC) processor: a microprocessor used by some personal and mid-size computers, including workstations; contains only a handful of instructions and therefore works more quickly than the CISC processor.

redundant array of inexpensive disks (RAID): a set of hard disks, all of which work together, with a file spread across them; also called a **disk array.**

reference: in a spreadsheet, the address of a cell used as part of a formula.

refresh rate: the number of times a monitor scans the entire screen each second.

register: a memory location in the ALU; temporarily stores data during processing; *see also* **word size.**

registration mark: a mark allowing for precise alignment of color separations and multiple-page layout used on the press.

relational database: a database capable of linking tables; a collection of related files that share at least one common field; also called a **Relational DataBase Management System.**

Relational DataBase Management System (RDBMS): *see* relational database.

repetition construct: a program that executes repeatedly a set of instructions until, or while, a condition is true; also called a **loop;** *see also* **for loop, nested for loop.**

repetitive stress injury: an ailment caused by continual use of the body over a long period of time in a way in which it was not designed to work; *see also* **carpal tunnel syndrome.**

requirement: a detailed plan developed by a systems analyst that explains to programmers the goals of a system and what information is to be managed.

requirements analysis: the process of defining users' needs as a basis for systems development; department managers and system users tell IS what they need to perform a particular business function that is planned for automation.

ring topology: a computer topology in which network nodes connect in a circular chain.

RISC: *see* **reduced instruction set computing processor.**

ROM: *see* **read-only memory.**

root directory: part of a disk's logical formatting system; the disk's main directory, which lists specific information about each file, such as its name and size, the time and date it was created or last modified, and so on; called a drive folder or a root folder on a Macintosh.

routine: another name for a **function** (definition 2).

RS-232: the current standard for serial communications for input and output communication with peripherals.

run: *see* **execute.**

S

sans serif font: a typeface without serifs (fancy curls and decorative adornments).

scan code: the code that tells the keyboard buffer what key has been pressed on the keyboard; *see also* **keyboard controller.**

scanner: an input device used to copy a printed page into a computer's memory without requiring manual keying; *see also* **image scanner, optical character recognition software.**

scroll arrow: an arrow at the top, bottom, right, or left of a scroll bar that allows a user to scroll the window up or down one line at a time or to the right or left by clicking the mouse cursor on the arrow.

scroll bar: a vertical or horizontal bar on the right edge or bottom of a screen that allows a user to move a display, thus bringing formerly hidden parts of a document onto a screen; *see also* **scroll arrow, scroll box.**

scroll box: a box located on the scroll bar; allows a user to move quickly through a large document to the relative position desired by dragging the box along the scroll bar.

scrolling: the movement of an entire document in relation to the window view; moving text or graphics up or down, or left or right, in order to see parts of the file that cannot fit on the screen; *see also* **scroll arrow, scroll bar, scroll box.**

SCSI: pronounced "scuzzy"; *see* **small computer system interface port.**

SDLC: *see* **Systems-development lifecycle.**

search and replace: a feature that allows a user to tell a program to look for a sequence of characters and replace each occurrence with new text; also called **find and change.**

section: in word processing, the largest division of a document; numbered consecutively and sometimes split into lettered parts.

sector: a segment or division of a track on a disk; *see also* **sectors per track.**

sectors per track: the number of sectors in each track of a disk.

segmented key: in a database, a primary key made up of more than one field.

selected: chosen for some purpose, as a block of text; indicated by a change in color.

sequential access: a method used to access data by moving through the data in the order they were stored; the method used on a tape drive.

serial mouse: a mouse device designed to plug into a serial port.

serial port: a general-purpose socket or port through which external devices such as a mouse or modem can be connected to a computer; data transmission occurs one bit after another in series; optional for IBM PCs but built into Macintosh computers and many Unix workstations.

serif font: type with curls and decorative ornaments; most long texts are set in serifed type because it is thought easier for such reading.

server: *see* **file server.**

shareware: software distributed free on a trial basis but requiring a fee for long-term use.

shell: a part of an operating system that controls the user interface; also called the **command interpreter.**

short number: a whole number between -32,767 and +32,767.

signature: a multiple-page layout.

SIMM: *see* **single in-line memory module.**

single in-line memory module (SIMM): a memory board with memory chips on it; can be added to a computer to increase its memory.

site license: an agreement that allows a company to purchase a program and to use the program on a given number of computers; generally less expensive than separate copies of the program for each computer.

small computer system interface (SCSI) port: a device that extends the bus outside the computer by way of a cable, which allows devices such as hard disks or CD-ROM drives to be connected to one another in a daisy chain.

soft format: *see* **logical format.**

software: a collection of electronic instructions that programmers write using a programming language, and that a computer's CPU can interpret to carry out a specific task; usually resides in storage; also called a **computer program** or a **program.**

software piracy: the illegal copying or use of software; now a felony.

sound board: a device that produces audio sounds and usually provides ports in the back of a computer for external speakers.

source code: the program statements that programmers create when they write a program; *see also* **source file**.

source-code analyzer: a software-development tool that examines a program and generates a report on many aspects of that program.

source file: the file that the program code is stored in; also called a **source code** or a **source-code file**.

spell checker: a word-processing feature that checks spelling.

spot color separation: a separation representing items in a particular color.

spreadsheet: application software that displays a large grid of columns and rows into which a user enters text, numbers, and/or formulas for calculations; a computerized ledger, or worksheet, used for calculating and evaluating numbers; can create reports and presentations to communicate information; used for such things as financial analysis, record keeping, and data entry and management; *see also* **worksheet**.

SQL: pronounced "see-Q-uel"; the standard query language used for searching and selecting records and fields from a database table.

stack: a program of Hypercard (also called **Hypercards** and **stacks** on the Macintosh) based on the metaphor of a stack of cards on which users can program instructions to call dialog boxes and sound or video clips and to define buttons and procedures.

star network: a computer topology in which network nodes connect to a center hub through which data packets are routed.

statement: a line of text that a programmer types into an editor to represent a command.

storage: the holding of data not currently being used by the computer; *see also* **magnetic storage**, **optical storage**, **storage media**.

storage media: the physical components, or materials, on which data are stored.

string: a sequence of characters, usually used to store text.

style sheet: in word processing, a collection of favorite or most-used text and formatting elements.

subdirectory: a directory within another directory; called a **folder** on a Macintosh.

subform: in a relational database, the design form used to create database tables and associated with detail.

subroutine: in BASIC, another name for a **function** (definition 2); designed to perform a set of operations.

supercomputer: the most powerful computer available at a given time; often used for scientific applications.

swap in: the loading into a computer's RAM of the program code or data essential to the computer's current activity.

swap out: the unloading from a computer's RAM of any program code or data not essential to the computer's current activity.

symmetrical multiprocessing: a multiprocessing system in which no single CPU controls all others; each processor added to the system provides a linear increase in system capacity.

syntax: precise and accurate grammar; used in object-oriented programming.

system administrator: a person who is responsible for managing and supporting a computer system.

system call: instructions written into a computer program to request services, such as saving a file to disk, from the operating system.

system clock: the internal clock of a microcomputer; maintains the time for the CPU.

system integrator: a person who designs, develops, or implements computer systems and networks.

systems analyst: an individual who analyzes and designs software systems and provides maintenance and support functions for the users.

systems-development lifecycle (SDLC): a formal methodology and process for the analysis, design, development, and maintenance of computer systems.

system software: a program that performs specific functions on a computer and its components; *see also* **operating system**.

T

table: in a database, a set of data arranged in columns and rows.

tab order: in a database, the order in which field data are entered.

tab stop: a point on a screen measured from the left edge (or margin) of the document.

tape drive: a device that reads and writes data to the surface of a magnetic tape; generally used for backing up or restoring the data of an entire hard disk; *see also* **digital audio tape drive**, **sequential access**.

tax-return preparation: the processing of tax returns, often with the help of computers.

technical documentation: detailed documents that describe program or database structures, menu systems, screen layouts, data, and processing flow and that are compiled for the benefit of all people involved with a system-development project.

telecommute: to work at home part-time but have access to a computer system at work via modem.

terminal: an I/O device connected to a multiuser computer and consisting of a monitor and keyboard.

terminal-based application: an application where input and output occur at a terminal while processing occurs on a mainframe computer, often in another geographical location.

text field: in a database, a field that stores the time.

thesaurus: a list of alternative words with similar meanings provided on-line by a word processor.

time field: in a database, a special field that stores the time.

token ring: a common LAN protocol, based on ring topology, where linked computers share an electronic token to facilitate the passing of data.

toner: a composition of tiny particles of oppositely charged ink that sticks to the drum of a laser printer and then is transferred to paper to create an image.

topology: the physical layout of wires that connect computers in a network; *see also* **hybrid network**, **linear bus network**, **ring topology**, **star network**.

touch screen: a computer screen that accepts input directly through the monitor; users touch electronic buttons displayed on the screen.

track: to adjust letter spacing by squeezing an entire block of text so that all of the letters are closer together.

trackball: an input device that functions like an upside-down mouse but is located in a keyboard or in a case next to a keyboard; requires less desktop space than a mouse.

transaction-oriented system: a business system with a goal of completing a specific transaction, such as selling a product or making a delivery.

transistor: a small switch that has replaced the larger relay in a computer's CPU; holds a single bit of data.

trapping: in DTP, the process of adding a tiny overlap to adjacent color elements on a page to account for possible misalignment in the press.

twisted-pair wire: wire made up of two copper strands individually shrouded in plastic, twisted around each other, and bound in more plastic; commonly used for data and voice communications and used to connect computers in a LAN; also called **unshielded twisted-pair wire**.

type checking: a process used in compiling programs to recognize errors and display messages for programmer reference; the ability to declare a named variable in a program and check for consistency to that value.

typeface: the style of the letters, symbols, and punctuation marks in a document (Times, Helvetica, Palatino, and so on); *see also* **typeface family**.

typeface family: all the variations (bold, italic, bold-italic, and so on) that go along with a particular typeface.

typeover mode: *see* **overtype mode**.

U

UART: a chip on the computer's I/O card on the motherboard that converts parallel data from the bus into serial data that can flow through a serial cable or telephone wire.

Unicode: a code currently being developed to represent data; will provide two bytes to represent more than 65,000 characters or symbols; will cover all languages of the world and make computer programs and data internationally interchangeable.

upload: to send a file to a remote computer.

upward compatibility: the ability of hardware or software to interact with all of the same equipment and software with which its predecessors could interact.

user documentation: instructions, or manuals, that tell end users how to use a system.

user-friendly interface: *see* **intuitive interface**.

user identification code: a code that identifies a person to a computer system before the person can log on.

user interface: the part of a program that interacts with a person using the program; *see also* **command-line interface**, **graphical user interface**.

utilities: software that enhances the capabilities of an operating system for managing and maintaining a computer and makes the computer easier to use.

V

value-added reseller (VAR): a software retailer who may perform as consultant, system integrator, technician, and trainer in the use of special-purpose software.

VAR: *see* **value-added reseller**.

variable: a part of a computer's memory that a program reserves for its own use; a number of bytes of memory that can hold a value that might change; *see also* **character, float, long integer, string**.

vertical application: a program that performs every phase of a critical business function and is usually custom developed; focuses on data processing; also called a **mission-critical application**.

vertical resolution: the number of rows of pixels on a monitor.

video board: a board that processes video images and provides ports for access to or from a VCR or video camera.

video controller: an interface device that connects the monitor and the CPU and that contains the memory and other circuitry necessary to send information to the monitor for display on the screen; *see also* **dual-port memory**.

virtual 86 mode: the ability of an Intel processor 386 and above to run several DOS programs at the same time; allows software to simulate multitasking using DOS, which cannot perform true multitasking.

virtual memory: a CPU's simulation of memory by accessing a disk drive and using it as internal memory.

virus: a parasitic program—designed as a prank or as sabotage and usually damaging—that is buried within a legitimate program or stored in the boot sector of a disk.

volatile memory: memory that retains data only until the computer is turned off; *see also* **random-access memory**.

W

WAN: *see* **wide-area network**.

what you see is what you get (WYSIWYG): a display mode that shows a document as it will appear when printed.

wide-area network (WAN): two or more LANs connected together, generally across a wide geographical area.

window: an area on a computer screen in which an application or document is viewed and accessed.

wireless communication link: a medium such as a radio antenna or communications satellite that connects computers over long distances.

word processor: application software used to create and modify a document.

word size: the size of a register (usually 32 bits in current microcomputers); determines the amount of data with which the computer can work at a given time.

word wrap: in word processing, a feature that determines when a word extends beyond the right margin and automatically shifts it to the next line.

workgroup computing: a business application that combines personal-productivity and vertical applications to create programs that let groups of users share applications and datafiles in a network.

worksheet: a spreadsheet datafile that has been created in a spreadsheet program and saved; sometimes called a **spreadsheet**.

workstation: (1) a computer smaller than a minicomputer but faster and more powerful than a PC; usually has a single user; generally based on RISC and operated by Unix or one of its variations; (2) a term used in the past, but now obsolete, to refer to any computer or terminal connected to another computer

WORM: *see* **write once, read many drive**.

write once, read many (WORM) drive: a type of permanent optical storage that uses a laser to read data from the surface of a disk; data cannot be changed after written.

write protection: a process that prevents the contents of a disk from being changed.

WYSIWYG: pronounced "wiz-ee-wig"; *see* **what you see is what you get**.

X

XMS: *see* **eXtended Memory Specification**.

Y

yes/no field: *see* **logical field**.

Z

'zine: a publication geared to a specific and often small audience, often produced by a small staff (sometimes as small as one).

INDEX

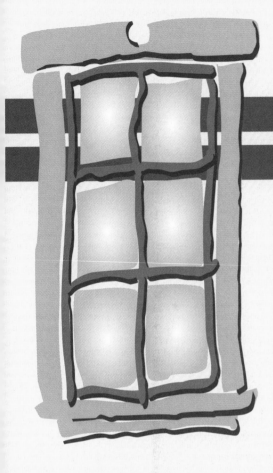

MICROSOFT WORKS FOR WINDOWS

A TUTORIAL TO ACCOMPANY PETER NORTON'S INTRODUCTION TO COMPUTERS

NED RACINE

CAROLYN TAYLOR

GLENCOE
McGraw-Hill

New York, New York   Columbus, Ohio   Mission Hills, California   Peoria, Illinois

Microsoft Works for Windows:
A Tutorial to Accompany
Peter Norton's Introduction to Computers

Send all inquiries to:
Glencoe/McGraw-Hill
936 Eastwind Drive
Westerville, OH 43081

MS-Works is a registered trademark of
Microsoft Corporation

ISBN: 0-02-802884-8

1 2 3 4 5 6 7 8 9 VH VH 99 98 97 96 95 94

ONTENTS

CHAPTER 3   USING STANDARD WORD-PROCESSING FEATURES

CHAPTER 4   FORMATTING TEXT

CHAPTER 7   **CREATING AND EDITING**
                  A DATABASE

CHAPTER 8   MANIPULATING AND REPORTING DATABASE INFORMATION

**CHAPTER 11   CHARTING SPREADSHEET
INFORMATION**

This *Microsoft Works for Windows Tutorial* is only one of the instructional tools that complement *Peter Norton's Introduction to Computers*. Glencoe and Peter Norton have teamed up to provide a new approach to computer education, one not reflected in traditional computer textbooks. The text and its ancillary materials are grounded in the philosophy that it is knowledgeable and empowered end users who will provide the gains in productivity that both businesses and individuals need to achieve in the 1990s and beyond. Mere button pushing is not enough; in order to handle more and more complex computer tasks, both in the workplace and in the home, computer users must understand the concepts behind their computer hardware and software.

INTEGRATION SOFTWARE: MORE FUNCTIONS IN ONE PROGRAM

Microsoft Works for Windows incorporates word processor, spreadsheet, database, and communications applications into one program. Each application is powerful, offering many of the most useful functions found in stand-alone applications.

Because *Works* applications share the same menu structure and many of the same document navigation tools, moving and transferring information from application to application is easy. For example, sales figures and a chart from a *Works* spreadsheet can be dropped into an annual report created by the *Works* word processor and sent over modem to another location. This concept of integration of software tools is reshaping personal computing.

STRUCTURE AND FORMAT OF THE MICROSOFT WORKS FOR WINDOWS TUTORIAL

This book exposes you to a range of functions and techniques. You will be given the opportunity to perform these functions several different ways. You will see that *Works for Windows* can adapt to the way you want to work, rather than your adapting to it. Because *Works for Windows* is such a rich program, practicing new functions and techniques is an important part of your work. To help you practice, each lesson includes the following:

- *Guided Practice.* Step-by-step instructions on using the functions and techniques introduced in each lesson.

- *Practice Applications.* Opportunities to practice solving problems with *Works.*

- *Lesson Applications.* This section lets you apply the functions and techniques you have learned in each lesson.

In addition, each chapter offers a *Chapter Review*—a brief summary of the chapter's most important points—and *Chapter Applications*—an opportunity to integrate all the functions and techniques you have learned in a chapter while practicing *Works* problem-solving skills. Finally, each chapter presents *Challenge Applications,* rigorous problems that challenge you to polish and expand your new *Works* skills.

An important part of studying computing is learning computer terminology. To make learning this terminology easier, commands and key words are highlighted as they are introduced in context, allowing you to see immediately what each key word means and what each command does. In addition, both mouse techniques and time-saving keyboard command shortcuts are provided. Also many frequently used *Works* commands are accessed via the toolbar, thus Toolbar options are also given when a command is introduced.

Illustration of *Works* screens show each command's place in the *Works* overall menu structure. Frequent illustrations of document screens allow you to compare your work with practice exercises. Exercises interspersed throughout the book review *Works* Help features and encourage you to expand your use of them.

Practice documents on the Student Data Disk are combined with plentiful exercises to emphasize the most commonly used word processor, spreadsheet, database, and communications functions and techniques. You practice by creating the same kinds of documents you will be creating in your office or home, from simple memos to reports.

After you complete this book, you will have been exposed to the skills necessary to create, process, and present information in a variety of ways using *Microsoft Works for Windows.*

ABOUT PETER NORTON

Peter Norton is a pioneering software developer and author. Norton's *Desktop for Windows, Utilities, Backup, AntiVirus,* and other utility programs are installed on millions of PCs worldwide. His *Inside the IBM PC* and *DOS Guide* have helped millions of people understand computers from the inside out. Glencoe has teamed with this most trusted name in computing to help you better understand the role computers will play in your life. You may use this resource as a textbook now and a reference later as you begin your productive use of computers in your chosen profession.

REVIEWERS

Jan Haslan, Santa Rosa Junior College

Lyndon Hebenstreit

MICROSOFT WORKS

FOR WINDOWS

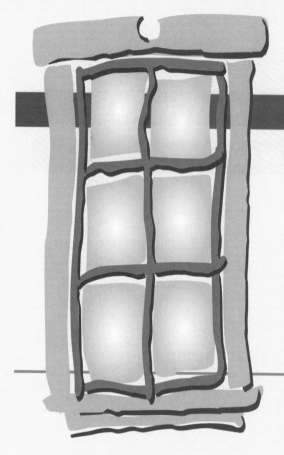

CHAPTER 1

APPLICATION

SOFTWARE

OVERVIEW

This chapter introduces you to application software. A personal computer loaded with Windows system software is almost ready for use, but does not yet have any instructions telling it how to accomplish the types of tasks people usually want to do. Application software is what directs the computer in completing specific, user-defined tasks. Two philosophies govern what type of application software to buy. One is to purchase a different program for every type of job that needs to be done: one for writing letters or other text documents, one for preparing financial reports, one for analyzing data, and so on. Another is to buy a package that combines several types of application software into one package. The result of this combination is called "integrated software." This chapter introduces such an integrated software package, known as Microsoft Works.

CONTENTS

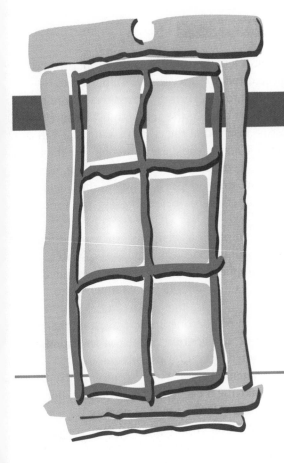

AN OVERVIEW OF

APPLICATION

SOFTWARE

OBJECTIVES

After completing this lesson you will be able to do the following:

- *Describe the need for application software.*
- *Identify some basic kinds of business and personal applications for which application software has been developed.*
- *Explain the difference between specific and integrated application packages.*

KEY WORDS

In this lesson you will learn the meaning of the following terms:

application	*integrated software*
application hardware	*operating system*
application software	

THE NEED FOR APPLICATION PROGRAMS

Think of a car without a driver. It sits there ready to do a job: transporting people. To perform its expected function, a car needs a person to operate it. The person, in turn, must follow certain procedures before the car can be operated properly. To start the car, the person must be sure the car is not in gear. The key must be inserted in the ignition and turned to operate the starter. When the engine starts, the driver must be sure the brake is released. The transmission is engaged and, once the car is rolling, it must be steered and braked at appropriate times. A car is a system that includes equipment, supplies (gas and oil), a person to operate the car, and procedures that must be followed.

The same is true for a computer. In previous chapters you learned that computer equipment includes a coordinated group of devices or parts, called **hardware**. The computer's supplies consist of electricity obtained from a wall socket. And, just like a car, a computer needs a person to operate it.

To prepare a computer for use, the person operating it turns on the power and loads a program, or set of instructions, called the **operating system,** which controls the coordinated operation of the equipment. Loading the Windows operating system into a personal computer can be compared to turning the key and starting a car. The car is running, but unless the person knows how to operate it, the car is of no use.

Similarly, a computer is not ready to do anything useful until it has loaded a set of procedures that tells it how to do specific tasks. An **application** is the name given to a job that is to be performed by a computer. **Application software** is the set of instructions that directs the computer in performing an application. Sometimes an application is referred to as a **tool,** indicating its usefulness.

Through the years, developers of application software have identified a number of specific areas that present common computer-processing needs. The most popular applications for personal computers fall into five broad categories:

Word processing

Database management

Spreadsheets

Data communications

Graphics

One way to provide application software is to create a separate software package to handle each type of job. Many hundreds of specialized software packages are available, each of which sets up a computer to do one type of job.

Another approach is to combine several applications in one package. This results in **integrated software** that allows the computer to switch among several applications. This method gives the computer user the flexibility to go from one kind of job to another without having to exit one application and load a new one each time a switch is made. Integrated software also has the advantage of allowing the user to transfer data from one type of application to another. For example, you can take a chart you created with spreadsheet software and use it in a word-processing file.

The application software that you will learn about and use in this book, Microsoft Works, is an integrated package. The next lesson identifies and describes the purpose and capabilities of each of the applications available in Works and also discusses the advantages of integrating them.

LESSON REVIEW QUESTIONS

Write a brief answer to these questions on a sheet of paper.

1. What is application software and what does it do?

2. What role does application software play in preparing a computer for use?

3. How do computer equipment, operating system software, and application software work together in a computer system?

4. What is an integrated software package?

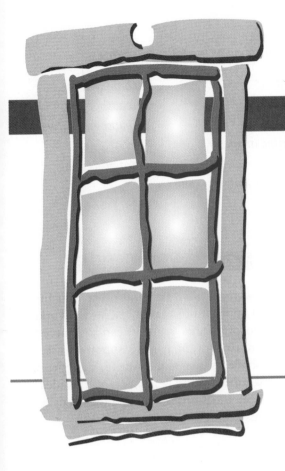

LESSON 2

INTEGRATING APPLICATION SOFTWARE WITH MICROSOFT WORKS

After completing this lesson you will be able to do the following:

- *Describe the advantage of computerized word processing over traditional typing.*

- *Define the term "database" and explain the value and use of database software.*

- *Describe the appearance and value of spreadsheet reports for business and other uses.*

- *Describe the basic use for and features of a draw program.*

- *Explain why communications software is necessary to use telephone lines to exchange information between computers.*

- *Explain the principles behind and value of integrated software application packages.*

KEY WORDS

In this lesson you will learn the meaning of the following terms:

bitmapped graphics	draft	record
data	edit	spreadsheet
cell	field	spreadsheet software
data communications	graphic images	text
data compatibility	modem	word processing
database	object-oriented graphics	
database file	pixels	

USING THE MICROSOFT WORKS APPLICATION TOOLS

Microsoft Works puts four applications (and a draw tool) at your fingertips. The convenience of integrated applications makes Microsoft Works ideal for use in schools. With Microsoft Works, students can have access to all four software programs (and a draw tool) in a single, simple-to-use package. (The draw tool does not have its own icon; instead, it is part of the word-processor and database programs.) Figure 2-1 illustrates this idea.

The following sections describe the functions served and the needs fulfilled by the four software programs built into Microsoft Works.

WORD PROCESSING

Written communication is essential to modern society. To illustrate, the U.S. Postal Service processes and delivers some 150 billion letters every year. Business and government organizations generate most of these documents, though individuals also contribute to this volume. Billions of other written documents are never handled by the mail service because they are used internally, within the organizations in which they originate. Courts, attorneys, and law enforcement agencies generate untold billions of additional documents.

Computerized methods for generating letters and other text documents were introduced in the 1970s and grew rapidly during the 1980s. To appreciate the extent to which computers have streamlined the preparation of business correspondence, consider the work traditionally performed in preparing a typewritten letter. The words originated either in handwritten form or by dictation. Regardless of the method used, the result was a **draft** or preliminary copy of a document intended for review by its originator. Changes were made either to reflect new ideas or to correct errors in typing.

FIGURE 2-1
Microsoft Works encompasses four different kinds of programs in a single software package.

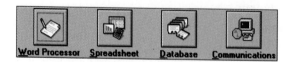

Then the entire document was retyped and read again. This procedure was sometimes repeated several times in the course of getting a single letter ready to mail. Office workers spent more time correcting and retyping documents than in any other kind of work.

More than 100 million personal computers and computer workstations are now installed in business offices. Most of these are used, at least in part, to prepare text documents. The word **text** refers to a document that is made up mostly of words. The term **word processing** describes the special way in which text documents are handled on computers. With a typewriter or handwriting, a document is created directly by the machine or writing instrument. When you press a key on a typewriter, an image appears on paper. When you press a key on the computer keyboard, the entry is recorded in an area of the computer's memory reserved for your document. At the same time, the entry appears on the computer screen. At this point, no printing takes place. Your document exists only temporarily in computer memory.

When you finish a draft of the document, you can save it on a disk file for permanent storage. You can also print the document. The difference between typing and word processing is that in word processing the text is saved in an electronic file. The document can be brought back and printed at any time. Capturing a document and printing it are two separate acts. Capturing occurs when you type the document and save it. Printing takes place at any time and as a separate operation. With a typewriter, creating and printing are the same thing.

The advantage of word processing over typing is that, by storing a document in a computer file, you eliminate the need to retype the whole thing every time you make a change. Instead, you can retrieve the file and edit or modify the text as necessary. The corrected text can be saved as another file, and as many drafts as necessary can be printed and revised to develop a final document. A modern desktop computer is shown in Figure 2-2.

DATABASE

Data consist of raw, unprocessed facts that are captured in a computer system. A data item is an individual piece of information that conveys meaning. For example, look at the information provided on the driver's license shown in Figure 2–3. Spaces are provided for the name, address, city, state, and ZIP code. Each of these spaces contains a single data item. Together, these data items provide a set of information about a person.

Imagine the amount of data that is required for all of the drivers' licenses in a single state. At one time, all of this information was kept on paper in endless file folders and file cabinets. Today, because of the capability that computers have for storing and processing data, most large collections of data are kept in computerized database files. A **database file** is a collection of **records**, each of which contains data about a specific person, place, or thing. Each **record** in the database contains the same types of data. For example, each driver's license in a file of drivers' licenses contains one person's name, address, height, weight, date of birth, and other information.

FIGURE 2-2
*Desktop computers have
become standard office
tools. Courtesy of NEC
Computer, Inc.*

Each of these types of data is called a **field**. An example of a Works database file that lists driver's license information is shown in Figure 2-4.

A collection of records organized and stored for computer processing, usually in multiple files, is known as a **database**. Thus, for example, records for all drivers' licenses in an entire state would form a database. Microsoft Works includes database capabilities. A typical computer like the one you use in school does not have the capacity to handle massive files like those for drivers' licenses. However, in many situations a desktop computer can be valuable for database applications—for example, for keeping student records. A database in your school's administrative office would probably include the names of all the students in the school, their class schedules, their grades, their birthdays, and other student-related information.

The advantage of a computerized database over a database kept on paper lies in the computer's ability to sort quickly through large numbers of fields and records. For example, even with a student body of several thousand, a computer could alphabetize the entire set of records in a matter of seconds.

FIGURE 2-3
*A driver's license is a
collection of data items
about a person.*

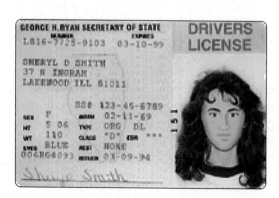

	Field1	Field2	Field3	Field4	Field5	Field6	Fi
1	LAST NAME	FIRST NAME	STREET	CITY	ST	SEX	
2	CLOSE	ROSANNE M.	1214 CENTER	SANTA ROSA	CA	F	
3	MILLER	JONATHAN E.	84 W. BINDER	SANTA ROSA	CA	M	
4	BONEUS	WALTER S.	800 HAMWAY	SANTA ROSA	CA	M	
5	SILVERSMITH	ANN T.	11 E. PINERIDGE	SANTA ROSA	CA	F	
6	BALLSTER	CYNTHIA E.	19875 ORANGE RD	SANTA ROSA	CA	F	
7	ROLLEY	WILLIAM W.	8999 PILOT	SANTA ROSA	CA	M	
8	GOULDEN	RAY B.	55 MAIN ST.	SANTA ROSA	CA	M	
9	JOHNSEN	NORMAL L.	1221 E. BASELINE	SANTA ROSA	CA	M	
10	FRECKMAN	ANNA MARIE	909 MARTINILLE WY.	SANTA ROSA	CA	F	
11	KERNSEY	MARY LOU	10 VISTA CIRCLE	SANTA ROSA	CA	F	
12	WILLIAMS	EDWARD T.	5454 121ST ST	SANTA ROSA	CA	M	

Alternatively, the computer could be used to identify students born on a certain day or students who have at least three classes together.

The database tools in Microsoft Works are designed to guide you in creating a database, retrieving information, analyzing data, and preparing reports derived from records in the database.

SPREADSHEETS

In addition to creating text documents and managing large amounts of data, one of the most critical needs of every business operation is the ability to calculate budgets and financial reports. Before the advent of computers, accountants and bookkeepers spent much of their time writing budgets and financial statements by hand on large paper grids, called **spreadsheets,** which are divided into columns and rows. Each square in the spreadsheet— the intersection of one column and one row—is called a **cell.**

The problem with handwritten spreadsheets is that many of the numbers in the spreadsheet are related mathematically through formulas. For example, one entire column of numbers may be the sum of numbers in several other columns, or one column may be the product of another column and some constant. One column of a spreadsheet, for example, might list the budget for new office equipment for the current year. The next column might be the budget for the next year, and this second column is calculated by multiplying every figure in the first column by the estimated rate of inflation, say 1.065. If the estimated rate of inflation changes (which it tends to do every month), the second column would have to be recalculated. In a handwritten spreadsheet, every time one number changes, all of the related numbers must be recalculated manually. With a large spreadsheet, this process can be extremely time consuming.

With spreadsheet software, the formulas used to calculate related values can be entered into the spreadsheet. Once the formulas are inserted, the process of updating mathematically related values becomes automated. In the previous example, the figures in the second column could be entered as the first column times a constant, and the result held in a cell given the name INFLATION. At first the inflation rate was entered as 1.065 and the computer calculated the second column automatically. If the inflation rate changed to 1.07, you could change the value in the INFLATION cell to 1.07 and the computer would recalculate the second column immediately. An example of a budget created in the Works spreadsheet tool is shown in Figure 2-5.

Because of the time and tedium they save, spreadsheet application programs, such as the spreadsheet tool in Microsoft Works, have revolutionized the bookkeeping and accounting professions. But spreadsheet software can be used for many more purposes than just financial calculations. Any task that requires a large number of numerical calculations is made much simpler with spreadsheet software.

DATA COMMUNICATIONS

Recall that a personal computer can transmit data to or receive data from another computer over telephone lines. This is done by equipping computers with special sending and receiving devices called **modems**. Procedures for transmitting data between computers, usually through telephone lines or other cables, are called **data communications**. Your computer can communicate and receive data if it is equipped with a modem

FIGURE 2-5

This budget was created using the Works spreadsheet tool.

	A	B	C	D	E	F	G
1			Two Year Budget				
2							
3	INCOME		Year 1	Year 2	Inflation		
4	Food Products		$122,000.00	$128,100.00	1.05		
5	Paper Products		$24,500.00	$25,725.00	1.05		
6	Pet Food & Supplies		$12,800.00	$13,440.00	1.05		
7	Sundries		$48,000.00	$50,400.00	1.05		
8							
9	TOTAL INCOME		$207,300.00	$217,665.00			
10							
11	EXPENSES						
12	Cost of Goods Sold		$98,000.00	$102,900.00	1.05		
13	Rent		$28,000.00	$29,400.00	1.05		
14							
15							
16							
17							
18							
19							
20							

Microsoft Works - [2YRBUDG.WKS]

File Edit View Insert Format Tools Window Help

Arial   10

B1

Press ALT to choose commands, or F2 to edit.

along with communications software that controls the operations of the modem.

A modem is needed because of the special way in which computers communicate. Computers are binary devices—they operate with a series of electrical signals, or pulses, each of which is either on or off. Because there are only two possibilities, these signals can be represented using binary code, which uses just two numeric values, 0 and 1. This binary code, which consists of electrical signals, is different from normal telephone signals, since telephones were developed initially to carry human voices. To transmit binary code, modems generate special signals that translate binary code into changing tones that can be handled by telephone lines. When signals are received, the modem converts them back to binary code that the receiving computer can use.

COMPUTER GRAPHICS

Text documents, financial reports, and data reports use letters and numbers to convey information. Sometimes, though, it is important to spice up the document or report to grab the attention of the person reading it. **Graphic images,** such as pictures, graphs, drawings, and borders, are often included in documents and reports to attract the reader's attention and to help convey a message.

Computer graphics come in several formats. In general, these formats can be classified as either bitmapped or object-oriented graphics. A computer screen is composed of thousands of tiny dots called **pixels**. On a black-and-white screen, each pixel is controlled by one bit. **Bitmapped graphics** are displayed on a computer screen by turning the pixels that make up the image from white to black. A bitmapped graphic is a map that tells each bit whether or not to turn its pixel black. Software packages that are referred to as "paint" programs allow the user to create bitmapped graphic images. **Object-oriented graphics,** on the other hand, are displayed on a computer screen as a mathematical description of a path that is drawn on the screen. For example, if you draw a square, the information about this square indicates that you have drawn a square of a certain size at a certain location on the screen. Software packages that are referred to as "draw" programs allow the user to create object-oriented graphics.

A draw application makes it possible to work with images created in another program or by someone else. These graphic images can be printed as separate documents, but they are usually imported into a document created by another application, such as a word processor, database, or spreadsheet. For example, after a report is created on the word processor, you can use a draw program to make a box around a paragraph of important information, or you can use a graphic already created in a draw program to call attention to some part of the report. The graphic image shown in Figure 2-6 was created with the Works spreadsheet tool.

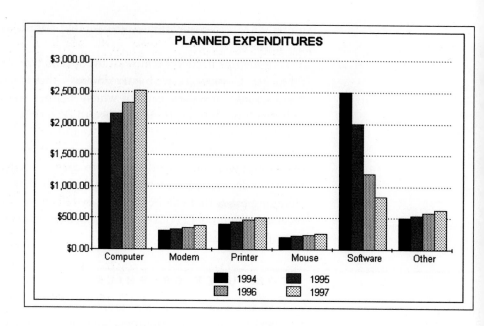

SOFTWARE INTEGRATION

At this point, you might wonder what advantages an integrated software package has over separate application programs. After all, you could simply install a word-processing package, a spreadsheet package, a database package, a communications package, and a draw package separately on your computer's hard disk.

One benefit of software integration is the ability to switch between applications quickly without having to exit the program. For instance, after you finish creating a letter with the Microsoft Works word processor, you can save your letter and then quickly switch to the spreadsheet package to work on this month's budget. But this is just a time-saving feature.

The more important feature of a good integrated software package is **data compatibility**. This term means that the information you create and save in one application—for instance, the word processor—can be understood by all the other applications that are included with the integrated software package. For example, suppose a friend of yours has moved to a new city and has misplaced her address book. She has written to you asking for the addresses and phone numbers of several friends. Fortunately, you keep these addresses in a database file created in Microsoft Works. In a letter to your friend that you write with the Works word processor, you report on current events in your city. Near the end of the letter, you want to enter the addresses and phone numbers that your friend has requested. You simply search the database file for the records you need and then copy these records directly into your letter. Figure 2-7 shows an example of this kind of operation. Spreadsheet data related to computer costs have been imported into a word-processing file named Purchase Projections.

FIGURE 2-7

Microsoft Works makes it possible for you to import data from one application into another.

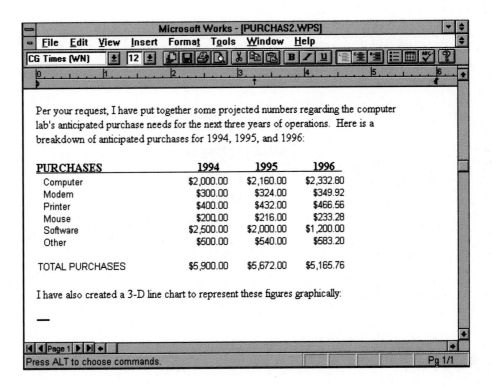

THE GUIDED PRACTICE WORK SETTING

In the remaining chapters of this book, you will use Microsoft Works as you learn. To help you gain confidence with the features of Microsoft Works, you will complete guided practice sections that simulate a realistic work setting. To enhance the value of your learning, assume that you are a new employee in your school's computer laboratory. The manager of the computer lab expects you to learn and perform many of the tasks involved in running the lab.

The computer lab provides a range of services to students and teachers. Students use the computer systems to complete class assignments and teachers use the lab to keep track of student attendance and grades. The manager for whom you work is responsible for all of the resources in the lab. An important part of the management function involves using Microsoft Works to create text documents, budgets, and other school-management documents, as well as information reports for school and district administrators.

Your job is to assist the manager in collecting, managing, and reporting on information about the operations of the computer lab. Each tutorial in the remaining chapters guides you through the steps you need to perform your job.

LESSON REVIEW QUESTIONS

Write a brief answer to these questions on a sheet of paper.

1. What are some advantages of integrated software packages over individual software application programs?

2. What are some benefits of word processors over typewriters?

3. What are spreadsheets? Describe one general use of computerized spreadsheets in business.

4. What is a database? In what situations are computers valuable for database management?

5. What piece of equipment must be connected to a computer to prepare it for telecommunications?

CHAPTER REVIEW

■ An integrated software package combines several application programs that can be used to create, manage, report on, and integrate data. Microsoft Works includes a word processor, a spreadsheet program, a database program, a communications program, and a draw (computer graphics) tool.

■ A word processor is used to create, edit, and print text documents. A spreadsheet program is used to manage numeric data. A database program stores data in an organized format. One important feature of a database program is the ability to locate and display (or print) selected information stored in the database.

■ A communications program allows two or more computers to exchange data through the use of modems. With a communications program, a modem, and telephone lines, a computer user can access information stored in a computer that is located hundreds, even thousands, of miles away. A draw tool is used to create or display object-oriented graphics that can be placed in word-processing, spreadsheet, or database documents.

■ The biggest advantage of an integrated package, such as Microsoft Works, is data compatibility. Works allows the user to create a document with one of the Works tools and then imports all or part of that document into another Works tool.

REVIEW QUESTIONS

TRUE-FALSE

Write your answers on a sheet of paper.

1. System software is an example of an application program.

2. Application programs are stored on disks and brought into memory for use.

3. There is no connection between application programs and system software; you can use application programs without system software.

4. An application program directs a computer to perform a job needed by a human user.

5. An integrated software package is designed to do one type of job and to handle it completely.

6. An advantage of computerized word processing is that it eliminates the need to retype documents completely each time a new draft is needed.

7. Spreadsheet software is valuable for recording and printing information, but users are still required to handle computations manually.

8. A computer set up to communicate with other computers over the telephone lines does not require a modem.

9. A text file is a file that contains a series of data items that describe people, places, things, or events in a standard, fixed format.

MULTIPLE CHOICE

Write your answers on a sheet of paper.

1. To be complete, a computer requires equipment that can _____.

   a. input, process, output, and store

   b. keyboard, display, and print

   c. process, store, and print

   d. use disk files, memory, and a processor

2. A startup disk is any disk that has _____.

   a. storage

   b. an electronic file

   c. system software

   d. RAM

3. Before you can use a personal computer, _____ must be loaded into RAM.

   a. application programs

   b. system software

   c. document files

   d. utility software

4. An application is _____.

   a. a special unit of computer storage equipment

   b. a job performed at a computer keyboard

   c. any job for which there is a printed output

   d. a job that is to be performed by a computer

5. Application software programs _____.

   a. operate in coordination with operating system software

   b. eliminate the need for operating system software

   c. are stored on disk and do not have to be brought into memory to be used

   d. are part of the operating system software

6. If you want to write a letter, you would use the _____ in the Microsoft Works program.

   a. word processor

   b. database

   c. spreadsheet

   d. data communications programs

7. A group of data items, or fields, makes up a _____.

   a. byte

   b. record

   c. bit

   d. file

8. To support communication between your computer and others over telephone lines, you need a device called a _____.

   a. disk file

   b. disk drive

   c. modem

   d. communications connector

9. Business budgets are usually presented in documents called _____.

   a. expense reports

   b. spreadsheets

   c. financial statements

   d. operating statistics

10. Your computer system needs a modem if you are using a _____ application.

   a. spreadsheet preparation

   b. legal documents

   c. database management

   d. data communications

SHORT-ANSWER QUESTIONS

In one or two complete sentences, write definitions for the following terms:

1. application

2. integrated software

3. database

4. spreadsheet

5. file

6. application software

7. word processing

8. data compatibility

9. record

HAPTER APPLICATIONS

Assume that you have the following tasks to complete this week. For each task, identify the Works tool you would use and explain your selections. Could the data integration features of Microsoft Works be used to help complete these tasks? If so, how? If not, explain why not.

1. You want to record and classify information about your compact discs and cassette tapes.

2. You need to complete an economics term paper on automobile purchasing.

3. You are considering buying a car, and you will need to borrow money from a bank to pay for it. The interest rate that you expect to pay on the loan is 9 ½ percent. However, the total amount of interest you will pay and the amount of your monthly payments will depend on whether you apply for an 18-month loan, a 24-month loan, or a 36-month loan. You want to calculate the interest and monthly payment amounts for all three loan periods.

HALLENGE EXERCISES

These assignments call for outside work to develop information not presented in this chapter.

1. Visit a library and look at a copy of an annual report of a business, or get copies of business financial statements from an accounting text. Copy or create graphs or charts that interpret the numeric information visually.

2. Visit the computer lab in your school or get information from your instructor on the equipment and software you will use to complete this course. Go to a computer store and get prices on comparable equipment and software packages. What does this information tell you about the need for care in using computer facilities at school?

3. At a computer store, get information on an on-line data service such as Prodigy. Find out what the service costs and what benefits are offered. Also find out what equipment and software are needed to connect a personal computer to this service. Make a brief presentation or write a brief report about the potential value of database information services for computer users.

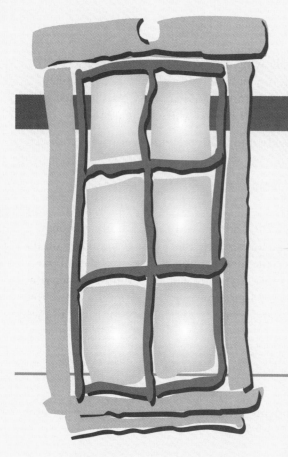

CHAPTER 2

INTRODUCTION TO
MICROSOFT WORKS

OVERVIEW

This chapter provides an introduction to the Microsoft Works program, including hands-on guided practices in which you follow detailed instructions as you start to use this software package. The chapter includes a discussion of dialog boxes and menus used in the Works package. You will also have an opportunity to start the Works word-processor, spreadsheet, and database programs and to use on-screen help features.

CONTENTS

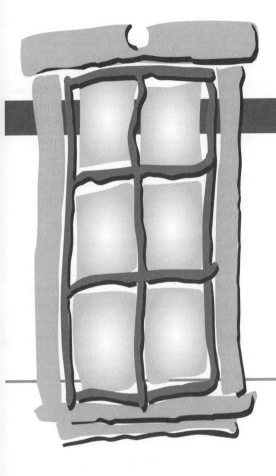

USING DIALOG BOXES AND MENUS IN MICROSOFT WORKS

OBJECTIVES

After completing this lesson you will be able to do the following:

- *Explain how menu selection is different when using the keyboard instead of the mouse.*
- *Describe the basic components of a Works screen.*
- *Describe the kinds of buttons and boxes used in a dialog box.*
- *Explain how text is entered in a text box.*
- *Open new document windows for the word-processor, database, and spreadsheet applications.*
- *Quit Works without saving a document.*

KEY WORDS

In this lesson you will learn the meaning of the following terms:

check box	*icon*	*radio button*
dialog box	*keyboard shortcut*	*text box*
dimmed	*list box*	*text button*
ellipsis	*message box*	

STARTING WORKS

There are several ways to start the Microsoft Works program. If the computer you are using is part of a network of computers, you will need special instructions for starting the program. The following two-step procedure is appropriate for most nonnetworked computers where the Microsoft Works program files are in the Works directory that was created when the program was installed.

1. After entering Windows, you will first see the Program Manager screen. Figure 3-1 shows a typical Program Manager screen. Your screen may have different icons, but opening Microsoft Works is the same.

2. Locate and double-click the Microsoft Works 3.0 application **icon** (a symbol of a function, program, or tool).

While the program is being loaded into the computer's memory, a copyright message is displayed. Then the Startup window or dialog box shown in Figure 3-2 appears. By making choices in this window or dialog box, you can tell Works such things as which application you want to use and whether you want to create a new document or reopen an existing document. Works includes four applications—word-processing, database, spreadsheet, and communications programs—and a draw tool.

USING DIALOG BOXES

A **dialog box** lets you tell Works exactly how you want a command carried out. The dialog box is the program's way of asking you to provide additional information that Works needs to execute the command you

FIGURE 3-1
A typical Program Manager screen.

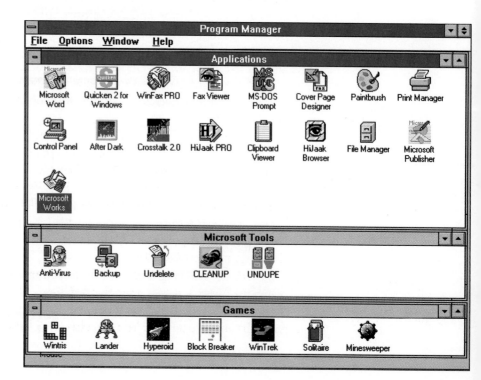

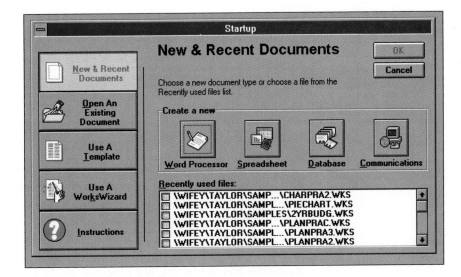

chose. You respond by using the buttons, boxes, and submenus in the dialog box to tell Works exactly what you want done. To make the names of dialog box buttons, boxes, and submenus stand out from the rest of the text in this book, each word in those names has been capitalized—even if not capitalized on screen. For example, the Recently used files list box has been capitalized to read Recently Used Files. Window or screen names will also be capitalized, for example, the Step-By-Step Help windows. The Startup dialog box offers two ways to make choices: text buttons and a list box.

TEXT BUTTONS

Text buttons are squares or rectangles. They are called text buttons because the text you see on a button indicates the action that takes place when you click it. For instance, a text button with OK on it provides a way for you to tell Works that it's OK to close the dialog box because you have made all the selections you want. When you click a Cancel button, you are telling Works to close the dialog box and cancel any selections you have made. The Startup dialog box has four text buttons with icons instead of text. For example, when you click on the Word Processor button, Works will take you to the word-processor application. If a text button is shaded gray or **dimmed**, the button cannot be selected at the moment. For example, when the Startup dialog box is displayed, the OK text button is dimmed. Normally one text button in a dialog box has a thick black border; often this button is the OK button. Pressing the Enter key is the equivalent of clicking on whichever button has a thick black border.

You select a text button by clicking it with a mouse pointer. A text button with a thick border, such as an OK button, can be selected either by clicking or by pressing the Enter key.

The Startup dialog box has one button depressed: the New & Recent Documents button. If you press the Enter key, Works will assume you want to work with a new or recent document, just as if you clicked on the New & Recent Documents button. You can also use a list box to execute a command.

FIGURE 3-3

The Recently used files list box from the Startup window.

LIST BOXES

A **list box** is a special scrolling box that is found in several Works dialog boxes. A list box contains a list of words or file names from which to select. For example, the list box displayed in the Startup dialog box provides a way for you to select and open a recently used file. The list box in Figure 3-3 contains the names of Works files. You can select a file by double-clicking on its name. This will not only open the file, but also the application used to create the file. When you use other list boxes in Works, be sure you have finished selecting all other options in the dialog box before you double-click on a file name.

There are other ways to choose commands in Works. For example, click on the Word Processor text button, one of four text buttons indicated under Create A New in the Startup dialog box.

The menu bar for the Works applications is the same as the menu bar in other Windows applications. You will learn about the word-processor application later. For now, move your mouse pointer to the Format menu name and click once to open the menu (or press Alt+T). The Format menu is shown in Figure 3-4. Some menus and dialog boxes offer several levels of commands. The first command on the Format menu, for example, is Font And Style...; when you click on a command followed by an ellipsis (...) a dialog box will open. Click on Font And Style to see the dialog box in Figure 3-5. In addition to text buttons and list boxes, the Font And Style dialog box offers other ways to make choices.

RADIO BUTTONS

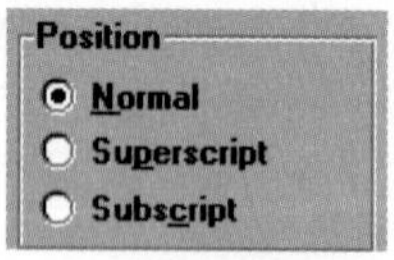

Position
- ● **N**ormal
- ○ Su**p**erscript
- ○ Sub**s**cript

Radio buttons are small, round buttons that are either on or off. A radio button is on when a black dot appears in the center of the button. If several radio buttons are grouped together, only one button in the group can be selected at a time.

A radio button is selected by clicking inside the button. A radio button is automatically deselected when another button in the group is selected.

FIGURE 3-4

The Format menu.

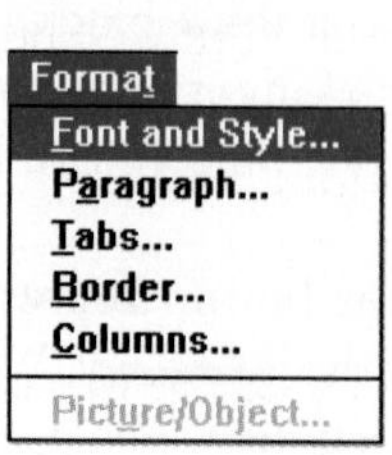

Format
Font and Style...
Paragraph...
Tabs...
Border...
Columns...
Pic**t**ure/Object...

FIGURE 3-5

The Font and Style dialog box offers several ways to make choices.

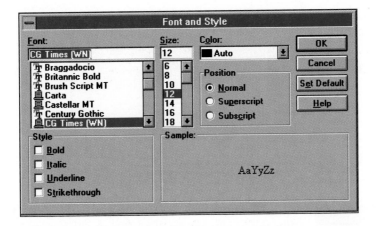

CHECK BOXES

Check boxes are small squares that provide you with specific choices. When there are several check boxes in a group, you can select one or more in the group. For instance, in the Format Font And Style dialog box, you can select all or any one of four check boxes.

A check box is selected when you click it to place an **X** inside the box. A check box that is currently selected can be deselected by clicking the box to remove the X. Close the Font And Style dialog box by clicking Cancel. Click on the Edit menu name (Alt +E). Click on the Find command. This dialog box has a long, open rectangle called a *text box*.

TEXT BOXES

A **text box** is a rectangular area in which you type text that the program needs to carry out an operation. For instance, the Find dialog box has a Find What text box in which you type the text you want to search for in a document.

You can type text by clicking an insertion point inside the text box. If you want to return to a text box, type the underlined letter in the text box name. For instance, click the Match Case check box. To return to Find What, type **N**. Your insertion point is again in the Find What box. When a text box is highlighted, you can delete existing text by typing other text or by pressing the Delete key.

You can move from one text box to the next either by clicking the mouse or by pressing the Tab key. The Tab key can also move you from the current text box to any other dialog box element. If you press the Tab key to move to a text button, that button appears with a thick black border. If you move to a check box or radio button, the name of the box or button is surrounded by a dotted box. For example, if you press the Tab key. Works uses a dotted box to show that you have moved to the Match Whole Word Only check box. Click on Find Next without entering text in the Find What text box. You will see the message box shown in Figure 3-6.

FIGURE 3-6

*This message box appears
when you try to find text
without telling Works what
text to find.*

MESSAGE BOXES

A **message box** is another kind of dialog box that appears from time to time when you are working in an application. Some messages alert you when you have made an error; others provide instructions on what to do next. The No Match Found message box in Figure 3-6 does both. Normally a message box has only text buttons, and you must select one of them to make the message box disappear.

USING KEYBOARD SHORTCUTS

You have been introduced to the mouse as a hand-held device used for opening menus and making selections. Some items, or commands, on a menu can be chosen by typing a combination of keys shown next to the command name. The combination generally uses the [Ctrl] or [Shift] key and a letter. This method can be a time-saver because you do not have to take your hands off the keyboard, as you do when using the mouse to make a menu choice. These key combinations are called **keyboard shortcuts**.

In the guided practice exercises in this textbook, you are given a choice of using the mouse to select from the menu or using a keyboard shortcut. For instance, you will see an instruction to choose Save from the File menu written as follows:

Choose Save ([Ctrl]+S) from the File menu.

You can use the mouse to make the selection from the menu, or you can press the [Ctrl] and S keys simultaneously, as shown in parentheses. Either method chooses the command. You can also open a menu and choose a command by typing the underlined letter in the command name. For example, to open the File menu and choose the Save command, you can press [Alt]+F followed by S.

GUIDED PRACTICE

STARTING WORKS AND OPENING NEW DOCUMENT WINDOWS

Today is your first day on the job in your school's computer lab. The lab director wants you to spend the day becoming familiar with Microsoft Works, the application software package you will be using. In this practice exercise, you will learn how to start Works and open new document windows using the word-processor, database, and spreadsheet applications.

1. Turn on the computer and start Windows. (If special procedures are needed to start Windows on your computer, your instructor will provide them.) Wait for the Program Manager window to appear, and then locate the Microsoft Works 3.0 application icon. Double-click the icon to start the program.

2. In the Startup window or dialog box, click on the Word Processor icon.

3. A window appears that is similar to the one shown in Figure 3-7. Don't be concerned if the ruler or toolbar is not displayed in your window; you will learn how to show or hide them in the next guided practice. Notice the name Works gives to this document: Word1.

4. Click on the File menu ([Alt]+F). Click on Close (or type **C**) to return to the Startup window.

5. Click the Database icon in the Startup dialog box. Click on the View menu ([Alt]+V). Click on List (or type **L**). Works changes the Data1 document screen from a blank area into a spreadsheet pattern, as shown in Figure 3-8. Notice that the rectangle to the right of 1 is highlighted.

6. Type **Last Name.** This is how you enter information into the database using List view. Notice also that Last Name appears in the text box above the database.

7. Press the [Tab] key. Type **First Name.** Press the [↓] arrow on your keyboard. Type **Nancy.** Use the mouse pointer (a cross rather than an arrow now) to click on Last Name. These are three ways of moving within the database in List view: with the [Tab] key, the arrow keys, and with a mouse.

FIGURE 3-7

A new word-processing document window.

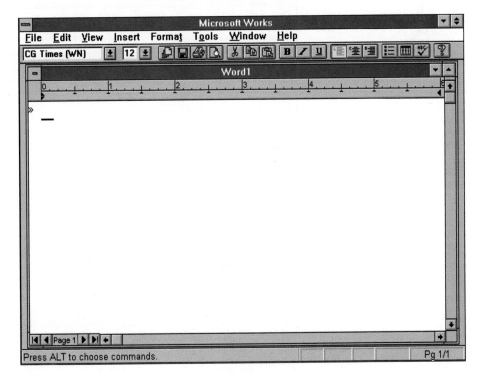

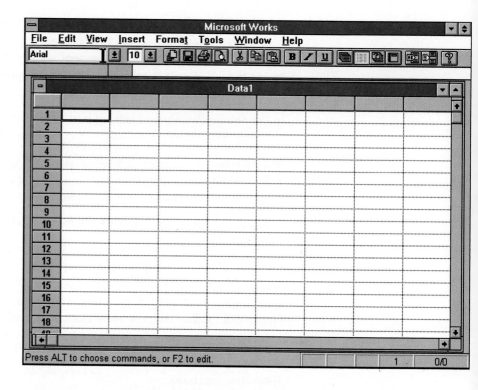

8. Notice the name of this file: DATA1. Click on the File menu. Click on Close. At the Save Changes to DATA1? message box, click on No.

9. Click on the Spreadsheet icon in the Startup dialog box.

BE IV CELL A1

10. Type 7777. Just as with the database, numbers appear to the right of the 1 and in the text box. Press Tab and type 8888. Press the ↓ arrow and type 9999. Click on the rectangle holding the 7777. You can move in a spreadsheet the same way you moved in the database. Notice that Works has temporarily named this spreadsheet Sheet1.

   Now you have worked with the word processor, spreadsheet, and database in Works. Not only does Works give temporary names to these documents (Word1, Sheet1, and Data1), but it also gives each type of document a different extension: .WPS (for word processing), .WKS (for spreadsheet), .WDB (for database), and .WCM (for communication files). Later you will have several documents open at once, and you will be able to switch quickly among them.

REMEMBER TO ENTER

11. Click on the File menu (Alt+F). Click on Save (or type S)

12. Later you will learn more about the Save As dialog box. For now notice that Works highlights Sheet1 as its suggested title for the document.

CLICK OK

13. Type **Practice**. Works deletes Sheet1 and replaces it with your suggested title. At the bottom of the window, in the Save File As Type text box, Works knows that this file was created by the spreadsheet application. If you saved the file now, Works would add the .WKS extension to the file name. Click Cancel.

14. Pull down the File menu and click on Close. Click on No. At the Startup window click on Cancel. The Startup window disappears.

15. Pull down the Works File menu and click on Exit Works (or type **X**). Works returns you to Program Manager.

FIGURE 3-10

The Save As dialog box.

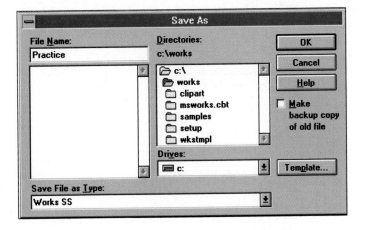

LESSON REVIEW QUESTIONS

Write a brief answer to these questions on a sheet of paper.

1. What is the difference between a text button and a text box?

2. Why does Works dim some text buttons and commands?

3. Why do you think Works gives a different extension to each type of document?

4. What is the difference between a dialog box and a message box?

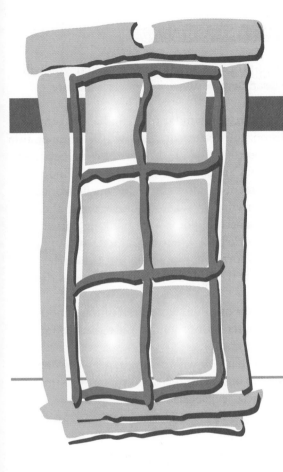

LESSON 4

EXAMINING A DOCUMENT WINDOW AND USING ON-SCREEN HELP

OBJECTIVES

After completing this lesson you will be able to

- *Turn the ruler and the tool palette display on and off.*
- *Explain the purpose of the status bar, ruler, and tool palette.*
- *Open and close the Microsoft Works Help program.*
- *Open an existing Works document.*

KEY WORDS

In this lesson you will learn the meaning of the following terms:

cursor	*on-screen Help*	*work area*
insertion point	*status bar*	
menu bar	*toolbar*	

THE WORD PROCESSOR'S DOCUMENT WINDOW

Let's look again at a new word-processor document. This time you will explore elements found in the document window. These elements are labeled in Figure 4-1.

The **menu bar** at the top of the screen is similar to menu bars in other Windows applications. In addition, the document window has the ruler, title bar, work area, status bar, sizing buttons, end mark, control-menu icon, window borders, and scroll bars that are common to Microsoft Windows. The large, blank space in the document window is the document **work area**. This is the part of a word-processor window where you insert text and graphics into your document. The **insertion point**—the blinking **cursor**—shows the place in the document workspace where a character will appear the next time you press a key. The short, horizontal line just below the cursor in a new document window is the **end mark**, which identifies the end of the document.

When you move the mouse pointer onto the work area of the window, the arrow turns into an I-beam. In later lessons you will use the I-beam to click an insertion point in existing text.

There are two window elements that you will not see in all Works application windows: the ruler (available only with the word processor) and the page arrows (not available with the spreadsheet).

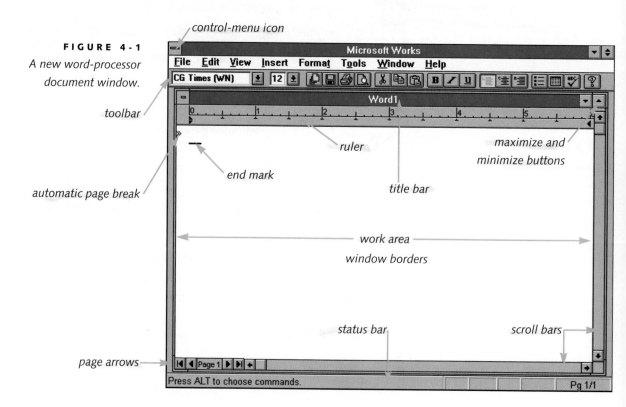

FIGURE 4-1
A new word-processor document window.

TOOLBAR

The **toolbar** is at the top of the Works window, between the menu bar and the title bar. The toolbar is a group of icons, each offering a shortcut for an action in Works. The toolbar also includes two list boxes at the left of the tool bar. Each Works application has a different toolbar, although some elements of the toolbar remain the same. Notice that when you point to an icon on the toolbar, its name appears momentarily.

RULER

The **ruler** is the area at the top of the document window between the title bar and the work area. The ruler lets you set tab stops and indent paragraphs. In a later lesson you will learn how to use these ruler controls to format parts of a document. You hide or show the ruler in the Works window by choosing the ruler option on the View menu. If the ruler is displayed, a checkmark will show beside the Ruler command.

STATUS BAR

Works displays the current page number, based on where your cursor is, at the lower left of the window. The **status bar** has a special set of scroll arrows to help you move through your document. Click on the far left arrow, and it will take you to the first page of your document. Click on the next arrow, and it will take you to the previous page. Similarly, the arrows to the right of the page window will take you to the following page or the last page in your document. The page number on the status bar will change if clicking the scroll arrows changes the page number.

ON-SCREEN HELP

The Microsoft Works package comes with an **on-screen Help** program that is installed on your computer's hard disk along with the four application programs and draw tool. The Help program provides information to help you use the applications. For example, if you want more information about the word-processor document window, you can pull down the Help menu and click on Contents to display the Works For Windows Help Contents window, shown in Figure 4-2. You can then click on the Word Processor application button to read more information about that application. Works also provides other help tools. In the next guided practice, you will learn how to use both the Works Help program and the Help On Help program.

FIGURE 4-2

*The Microsoft Works Help
Contents window.*

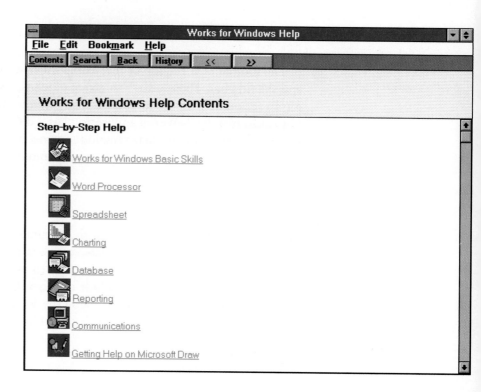

FIGURE 4-2

*The Microsoft Works Help
Contents window.*

GUIDED PRACTICE

EXAMINING A DOCUMENT WINDOW AND USING ON-SCREEN HELP

In this exercise you will start Works and examine the elements of a word-processor document window by first opening a new document. Then you will use Microsoft Works to learn more about document windows, as well as to search for other topics.

1. If necessary, start the Works program.

2. Start the word processor.

3. If the ruler is not displayed, choose Ruler from the View menu.

4. The first list box on the toolbar displays the fonts available for your document. Point to and press on the arrowhead (⬇) to the right of the first list box. This opens a list of fonts, as shown in Figure 4-3 (your list may be different). Examine the names of the fonts available on your system. Click on the same arrowhead to close the Font Menu list box.

5. Repeat the procedure described in step 4 to open and examine the Font Size list box. Close the Font Size list box.

6. Select Contents from the Help menu to display the Works For Windows Help Contents window.

7. If necessary, scroll to the bottom of the window to see all of the icons.

FIGURE 4-3
*The Font Name list box
with a list of the fonts
available on your system.*

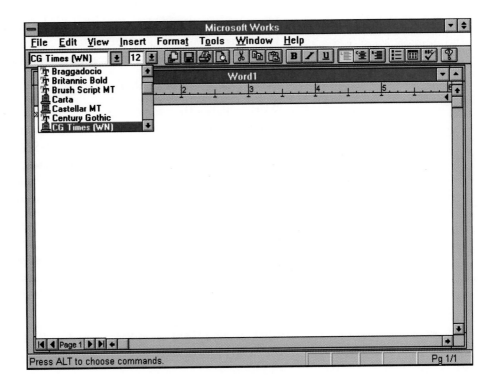

8. Click on the Word Processor icon to see the list of Step-By-Step Help topics available, as shown in Figure 4-4. You can also click on the text, Word Processor, beside the icon to open the Step-By-Step Help topics window. If you pass your mouse pointer over the text, your pointer becomes a pointing hand.

FIGURE 4-4
*The topics listed here are
available in the Help
system when you need
step-by-step information
about the word-processor
tool.*

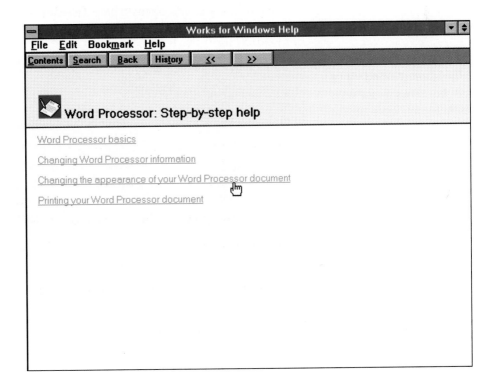

9. Notice the four underlined phrases on the Word Processor: Step-By-Step Help screen. As with any help screen, clicking on an underlined phrase will take you to another, more specific screen.

10. Double-click on the control-menu icon to close the help screen.

11. Works offers other ways to open the Help program. Click on the ? toolbar button at the far right of the toolbar. Works opens the Learning Works dialog box, as shown in Figure 4-5. Notice that the ? Instructions button is depressed. This is the default when the Learning Works screen appears. Instructions for using the other four text buttons are contained in the box at the center of the screen.

12. Clicking on the Cue Cards button opens the Cue Cards window. If you do this, then click on the Show Cue Cards button, and Cue Cards will remain on the document screen to prompt you as you use a Works function. Click on the OK button and Works switches back to the word-processor document screen, this time with the Cue Cards displayed, as shown in Figure 4-6.

13. Click on ▷ I Want Help From Cue Cards. The Cue Card will display the Word Processor Menu and ask what it can help you with, as shown in Figure 4-7.

14. Click on Close to close the Cue Card. Works gives you a choice of whether to continue working with Cue Cards or to close them. For now click on Close Cue Cards.

15. Click on the ? toolbar button to reopen the Learning Works dialog box. Click on Access The Help Library dialog box, shown in Figure 4-8. Works has filled the list box with five help topics. Double-clicking on one of these topics opens a help screen devoted to the topic.

FIGURE 4-5
The Learning Works dialog box offers several ways to become more familiar with Works.

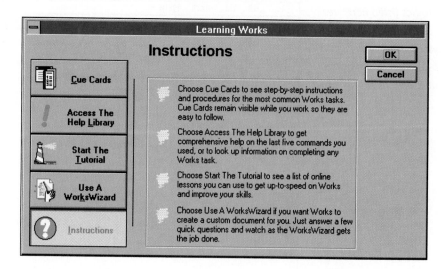

FIGURE 4-6
A Cue Card appears to help guide you through a Works function.

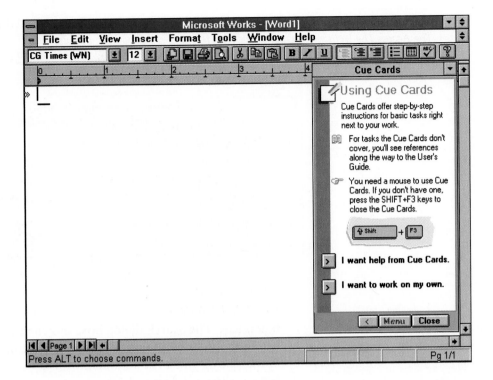

FIGURE 4-7
A Works Cue Card knows what application you are using and asks what help you need.

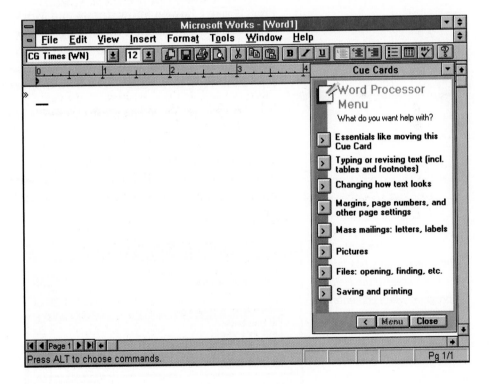

FIGURE 4-8

*The Access The Help
Library dialog box.*

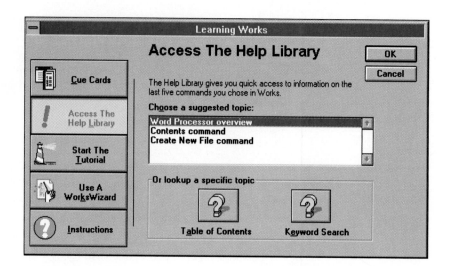

16. Clicking on the Table Of Contents button opens the screen shown in Figure 4-2. Click on the Keyword Search button and the Search dialog box opens. The Search dialog box, shown in Figure 4-9, allows you to search the Help program for dozens of topics. Type **New**. Works shows you a list box filled with topics beginning with the word new, as shown in Figure 4-10.

17. Press ⟨Enter⟩. Click on Show Topics and Works will show you help lesson topics (or double-click on the highlighted topic in the list box). If you click on the Go To button, Works will take you to the topic highlighted in the Go To list box at the bottom of the screen, in this case the Changing Chart Type help screen, as shown in Figure 4-11.

18. Select Exit from the help screen File menu to close the help screen. Click on the ? toolbar button to return to the Learning Works dialog box. By clicking on the Start The Tutorial button, the tutorial screen appears, as shown in Figure 4-12. The Works tutorial is a series of brief lessons, a way to learn new Works functions or review functions you have not used for a while. Click on the Exit Tutorial: X button to exit the tutorial.

FIGURE 4-9

*The Search dialog box lets
you search the Help
program when you enter
the topic.*

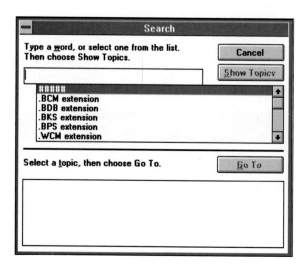

FIGURE 4-10

*Typing **new** tells Works to display a list of topics beginning with the word new.*

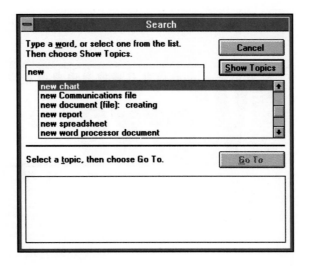

FIGURE 4-11

The Changing Chart Type help screen.

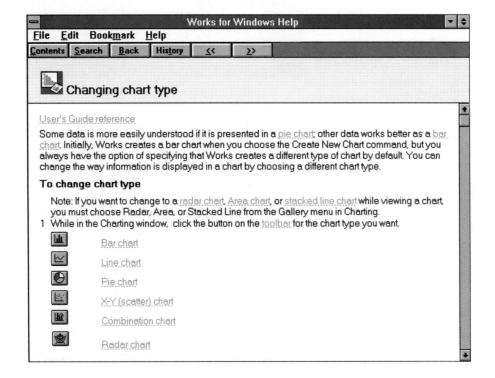

19. Click on the ? toolbar button to return to the Learning Works screen, then click on the Use A WorksWizard button. This opens the Use A WorksWizard dialog box, shown in 4-13.

20. By double-clicking a topic in the Choose A WorksWizard list box (or selecting the OK button once you have highlighted a topic), you open a step-by-step tutorial shaped by your answers to simple questions. Double-click on Address Book. The Address Book WorksWizard screen, as shown in Figure 4-14, appears.

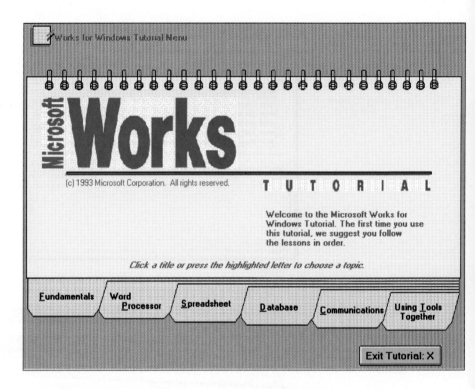

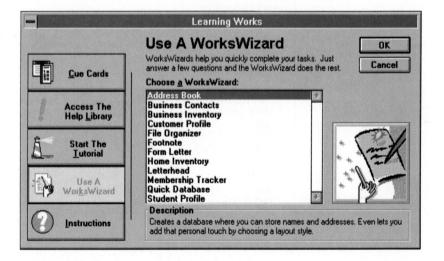

21. Click on Next and the WorksWizard takes you through the creation of an address book. Click on Cancel any time to cancel the WorksWizard. Click Cancel now.

FIGURE 4-14

*The first screen of the
Address Book
WorksWizard.*

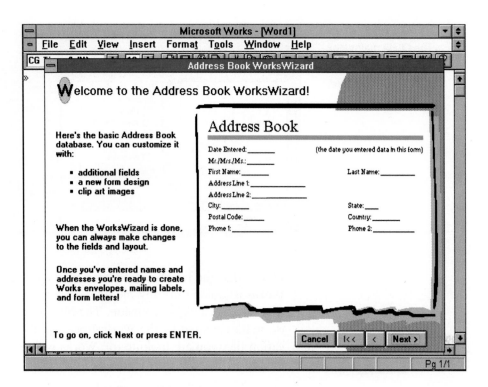

FIGURE 4-14

*The first screen of the
Address Book
WorksWizard.*

GUIDED PRACTICE

OPENING AN EXISTING DOCUMENT

Now that you know how to start Works, open a new document window, and use the Help system, the lab manager wants you to explore some other items on the word-processor menus and dialog boxes. In this exercise, you will learn more about Works by selecting and opening a file stored on your Student Data Disk.

1. Start Works and insert your Student Data Disk in the floppy-disk drive. Click on the Open An Existing Document text button. In the Open dialog box select the floppy drive holding your Student Data Disk by clicking on the letter for that drive in the Drives list box. The Open dialog box on your screen should be similar to the one shown in Figure 4-15, depending on which drive holds your Student Data Disk.

2. Click on the ⊞ arrow of the File Name list box to scroll through the Works files on the Student Data Disk.

3. In the List Files Of Type list box, click on the ⊞ arrow to reveal other file display options. Select Works WP (*.wps) by clicking on it.

FIGURE 4-15
*The Open dialog box
displays files from any
drive.*

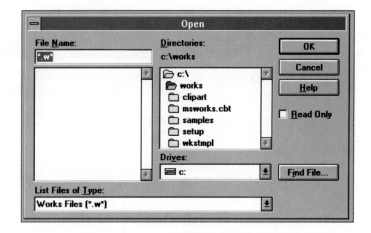

4. Notice that the File Name list box now contains *.wps. This means that Works is looking for any file (the asterisk tells Works to look for any file) that has a .wps extension. The file-name list shrinks to reveal only those files created by the Word Processor. By telling Works which application files you are looking for, Works will reduce the number of file names you need to sort through.

5. Open the List Files Of Type list box again, and this time select Works DB (*.wdb).

6. Works now only selects file names ending with .wdb, the Works extension for database files. This screen is shown in Figure 4-16.

7. Double-click the file name EQUIPME1.WDB to open the file. The document appears on your screen, as shown in Figure 4-17. You will have a chance to correct this document later.

8. Click the Close command on the file menu. If the Save Changes To EQUIPME1.WDB ? message box appears, click the No button. Works returns you to the Startup dialog box.

9. Quit Works and remove your data disk from the floppy-disk drive.

FIGURE 4-16
*By using the List Files Of
Type list box, Works will
select only the files created
by a single application.*

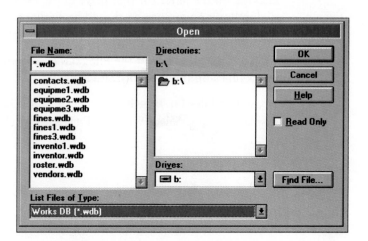

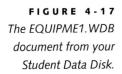

FIGURE 4-17
The EQUIPME1.WDB document from your Student Data Disk.

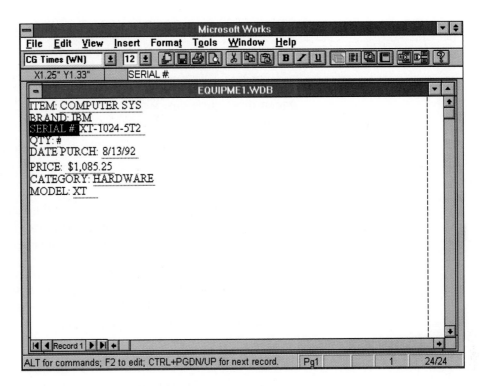

LESSON REVIEW QUESTIONS

Write a brief answer to these questions on a sheet of paper.

1. List the steps you should follow to turn on your computer and load Microsoft Works.

2. How many list boxes are on the toolbar and what information do they display?

3. How can you hide or display the ruler?

4. The Microsoft Works Help program for the word processor includes the topic Word Processor basics. Explain how you reach the help screen displayed for Word Processor basics.

5. What additional steps must you take when you open an existing document instead of a new document?

PRACTICE APPLICATIONS

Complete the following exercises. Some exercises ask you to answer one or more questions. Write a brief answer to these questions on a sheet of paper.

1. Start Works. Select each of the Works applications. Briefly describe the changes you see in the document window when you choose each application.

2. Close the last application and return to the Startup window. Which Works tool does not have its own text button? Click the Open An Existing Document button. Why does the File Name text box contain *.w*? What does * mean?

3. Click the Help button. Read the information displayed on the screen. What happens when you click on the underlined word directory? Quit Works.

CHAPTER REVIEW

- Works has four applications (word processor, database, spreadsheet, and communications) and a draw tool.

- Many features on Works menus and in dialog boxes are familiar to Windows users because they are similar to those used in other Windows software.

- A dialog box contains buttons and boxes that you use to tell Works exactly how you want a command carried out.

- Many Works menu items can be chosen by typing a combination of keys known as a keyboard shortcut.

- Works provides an on-screen Help system that enables you to find information on how to use Works while you are creating documents.

- The Help system also includes Cue Cards and WorksWizards to offer step-by-step tutorials for learning new Works functions.

- To open an existing document, you double-click the name of the file in the File Name list box of the Open dialog box.

REVIEW QUESTIONS

TRUE-FALSE

Write your answers on a sheet of paper.

1. The status bar provides information about the currently selected menu and dialog box options.

2. To access an existing file, you choose New from the File menu.

3. Instead of using a mouse, you can use the first two letters in the name of a menu item as a shortcut key combination to select the item.

4. If a Works menu option is dimmed, it is not available for selection.

5. Some menu items in Works cannot be chosen by using keyboard shortcuts.

6. If a text button has a thick black border, it can be selected by pressing the Enter key.

7. In a menu item, the ellipsis (...) indicates that that item is not available at the moment.

8. In Works, the word-processor program and the spreadsheet program are both called tools.

9. If changes to a document window have not been saved when you close a document, Works displays a message that lets you save the changes, close the document without saving the changes, or cancel the Close command.

10. In a dialog box, you can move from one text box to the next using either the [Tab] key or the mouse.

SHORT-ANSWER QUESTIONS

1. What steps would you take to get on-screen help about using the Open option on the File menu?

2. What is the difference between a menu and a dialog box?

3. In a dialog box, what is the difference between a text box and a list box?

4. In a dialog box, what is the difference between a text button and a radio button?

5. In a dialog box, how do you select the OK command button using the keyboard?

LESSON APPLICATIONS

1. If necessary, start Works. Open a new word-processor document. Use the following keyboard commands. When a dialog box appears, click the Cancel button.

   [Alt] F+A

   [Alt] H+[Shift]+[F1]

   [Alt] T+C+[Tab]

2. With a new word-processor document open, choose Page Setup from the File menu. Notice the sample page displayed. Click the Margins tab and select the Landscape radio button. Click the Margins tab and note the measurements for the margins. Then click the Source, Size, And Orientation tab again. Click the Portrait radio button. Select the Margins tab again and note the measurements for the margins. How does the Margins dialog box sample page change when the page orientation is changed in the Source, Size, And Orientation dialog box? When you are finished, choose Cancel.

HAPTER APPLICATIONS

1. If necessary, start Works and open a new word-processor document. Open the Font And Style dialog box from the Format menu. Write a brief answer to these questions on a sheet of paper:

   a. What does the Font Name list box do?

   b. Identify any text boxes that appear in the dialog box. How can you identify a text box?

   c. Identify any buttons that appear in the dialog box. Are they radio buttons or text buttons?

   d. How many check boxes are there in the dialog box?

   e. Click on the Courier font. Click on another font. How does the Sample box change when you select different fonts?

2. Close the dialog box and then quit Works. Describe the procedure you used to return to the Program Manager.

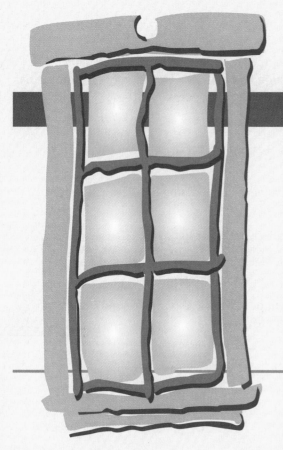

CHAPTER 3

USING STANDARD WORD-PROCESSING FEATURES

OVERVIEW

This chapter introduces many of the features of the Works word-processing tool. In this chapter you will have a chance to work with existing documents and to create new documents. First you will practice navigating through a document. Then you will learn how to create, print, and edit a new document. You will learn how to use the Works Print dialog box to establish print settings. In doing so, you will also learn how to highlight, copy, and move sections of a document. And you will learn how to use the Save As dialog box to name a document and store its file on a disk.

CONTENTS

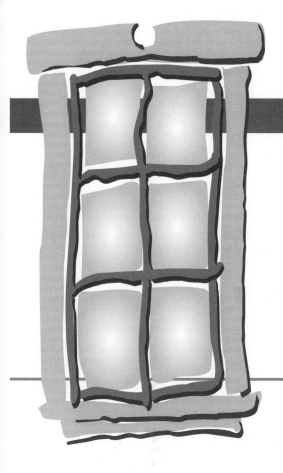

LESSON 5

GETTING STARTED WITH THE WORD PROCESSOR

OBJECTIVES

After completing this lesson you will be able to do the following:

- *Explain the basic purpose of selecting; formatting; cutting, copying and pasting; and finding and replacing text.*

- *Explain the benefits of printing different versions of a document.*

- *Navigate through a text document.*

KEY WORDS

In this lesson you will learn the meaning of the following terms:

boldface	*highlighting*	*scrolling*
Clipboard	*italics*	*search*
copy	*paste*	*word wrap*
cut	*preview*	
format	*replace*	

ORD-PROCESSING TASKS

Four basic tasks are involved in creating a document with a word processor:

Entering text.

Editing text.

Printing text.

Saving text to a file.

A word processor has many special features that make entering, editing, printing, and saving text easy. These special features of a word processor are described in this chapter and in Chapters 7 and 8.

ORD-PROCESSING FEATURES

You have already learned about the need for word processing and some standard capabilities of computer-based word processing. Word processing is the creation of text documents—such as letters, term papers, and business reports—through the use of a computer. You can prepare text documents using other techniques. For instance, when you write a grocery list on paper by hand, you are creating a text document, that is, you are organizing written words to convey meaning. You can also use a typewriter to prepare text documents, such as essays and other reports. However, a computer provides many document-creation capabilities that a pencil and paper or a typewriter just can't give you.

Consider this example: Suppose you want to insert a new sentence in the middle of a letter you have just created. If you created the letter on a typewriter, you might have to retype the entire letter to include the new sentence. If you created the letter with word processing on a computer, however, you would insert text without having to retype your existing work. The word-processing program (also known simply as the word processor, although this term can be confusing, because the person who uses the word-processing program is also called the word processor) determines how to adjust the existing text to make room for the new text. This capability is part of a feature called **word wrap**. This name describes the feature that pushes, or wraps, text onto new lines to make room for inserted text. The program can also wrap text backward: Text can be pushed backward and upward to fill empty space that is created when a section of text is deleted. When you type text for a new letter into a computer, the word-wrap feature automatically moves your entries to a new line as you come to the end of each line you are entering. The only time you press the (Enter) key when typing text is when you want to force the text to the next line, usually when you want to start a new paragraph.

Word wrap illustrates one of the basic benefits of using a computer to work with text: You can edit a document as often as you need to without having to retype the entire document each time you make changes. The following sections describe some other features that are available with word-processing programs.

SELECTING TEXT

You have already learned that when you want to do something to a file, you first select it, then tell the computer what you want to do. Similarly, when you want to perform some action on a certain piece of text, you first select the text you want to work with, then tell the word processor what you want to do. Text is selected by **highlighting** it. Highlighting reverses the normal text display. The selected text appears as white characters on a black background, as shown in Figure 5-1. A word can be highlighted, or selected, by double-clicking; a line of text can be highlighted by clicking to the left of the line; a paragraph can be highlighted by double-clicking to the left of the paragraph. Part of a word, sentence, or paragraph can be selected by dragging the I-beam over the portion you want to highlight while holding down the left mouse button. An entire document is highlighted by selecting Select All from the Edit menu.

FORMATTING TEXT

Word-processing programs allow you to **format** (change the appearance of) characters in a document. This is done by first selecting the characters, then specifying the format you want applied. For example, after you have

FIGURE 5-1

The highlighted text in this display appears as white characters on a black background.

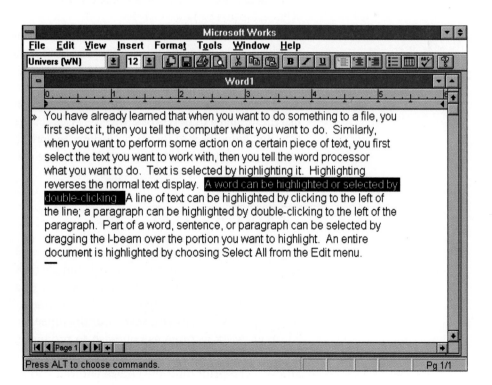

highlighted text, you can instruct the word processor to change the characters in the selected text to **boldface** (like this) or *italics* (like this). Other character formats are discussed in a later chapter.

Word-processing programs also allow you to change the way paragraphs appear. As with character formatting, you must first select the paragraphs, then specify the format. Examples of paragraph formatting include changing margins (the space between the left or right margin and the left or right edge of your paper), adjusting tab settings (indentions), and adjusting the space between lines (single spacing, $1\frac{1}{2}$ spacing, or double spacing).

CUTTING, COPYING, AND PASTING

Word processors offer other ways of changing text that involve cutting or copying selected text. When you **cut** text using a Windows application, the text is deleted from the document and placed in the **Clipboard**. When you **copy** text, it is not deleted from the document, but a copy is placed in the Clipboard. You can **paste** text from the Clipboard to anywhere in a displayed document. The same text can be pasted again and again in as many places as you choose. Text that you cut or copy stays in the Clipboard until you use the Cut or Copy command the next time or until the computer is turned off. You can cut or copy from a single character to a whole document. The Clipboard is available in all the Works tools (and in other Windows applications), making it easy to exchange information from one application to another.

FINDING AND REPLACING TEXT

You can use a word processor to search through a document for one or more characters (including two special characters that represent tabs and paragraphs) or words. The Find dialog box shown in Figure 5-2(a) is used to perform a **search**. If you want to perform a search and also instruct Works to **replace** all or selected occurrences of the text that it finds, you can use the Replace dialog box shown in Figure 5-2(b). For instance, you would use this dialog box to instruct Works to search for all occurrences of the phrase word-processing program and replace it with the phrase word processor.

PRINTING TEXT

You can print a document as often as you wish. You may want to print several different versions so that you can check how each one appears on paper. Also, you can **preview** the appearance of a document on your screen. Keep in mind that a printed copy of a document does not have to be the final copy. As long as you save your documents on disk, you can review and edit your work as often as you wish to produce a new version of the document. With Works, you can print the entire document or just selected pages, and you can print multiple copies without choosing the Print command more than once.

FIGURE 5-2

(a) The Find dialog box is used to search for text or special characters.

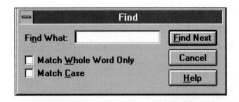

(b) The Replace dialog box is used to perform a search when you want to replace text by clicking either the Replace or Replace All button.

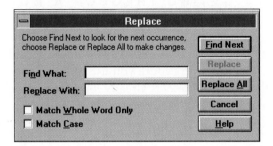

NAVIGATING THROUGH A WORD-PROCESSING DOCUMENT

A multipage word-processing document is displayed on your screen as one continuous document. Works uses chevrons (>>) to indicate where one page ends and the next one begins, a page break you add manually appears as a dotted line. If a word-processing document is longer than one window, you will need to use the keyboard or the mouse to scroll through it.

Scrolling is the action of moving into view parts of a document that are not currently displayed in the window. The scroll bars, scroll arrows, and scroll boxes are the standard window elements that you use to move different parts of the document into view. The vertical scroll bar, shown in Figure 5-3, is used to move through a document one window at a time. After clicking on a scroll arrow, you can move one line up or down with each click of the mouse button; or you can press on a scroll arrow for continuous scrolling. Also, you can drag a scroll box to move through large sections of a document at a time. For instance, you can move to the end or beginning of a document by dragging the scroll box to the bottom or top of the scroll bar.

FIGURE 5-3

The vertical scroll bar is used to move to other pages of a multipage document.

The insertion point, or cursor, does not move when you scroll through a document using the vertical scroll bar. Instead, it remains where you last used it. To move the insertion point to a new location, click the I-beam where you want to begin inserting text or editing. You can also move the insertion point with the arrow keys. The right (→) and left (←) arrow keys move the insertion point to the right and to the left one character at a time. The up (↑) and down (↓) arrow keys move the insertion point up or down one line at a time.

If you know the specific page you want to go to in a word-processing document, you can move the insertion point and the window display to the top of that page using the Go To dialog box. To display this dialog box, choose Go To from the Edit menu.

The scroll bars, arrow keys, and Go To dialog box are the basic ways of navigating through a word-processing document in Works. The Works on-screen Help program describes additional keyboard controls you can use.

GUIDED PRACTICE

NAVIGATING THROUGH A DOCUMENT

In this exercise you will practice using the mouse and the keyboard to move through the RULES.WPS document stored on your Student Data Disk. The exact procedure you use to begin this guided practice depends on whether or not Works is already loaded into your computer's memory. In either case, be sure your Student Data Disk is in the floppy drive.

1. Display the Open dialog box by selecting the Open An Existing Document button in the Startup dialog box or by choosing Open from the File menu.

2. If necessary, make the drive with your Student Data Disk the current drive. Click on the ⬇ arrow beside the Drives list box if the drive with your Student Data Disk is not displayed. Once the correct drive is displayed, click it. The File Name list box displays the files on your Student Data Disk.

3. Locate the file name RULES.WPS in the list box by using the ⬇ arrow to scroll the list box.

4. Double-click on the file name to open the RULES.WPS document. (The four capital letters at the top left corner of the document signify header and footer paragraphs. You will learn about these in a later lesson.)

5. When the document window is displayed, click on the maximize button (▲) to enlarge the RULES.WPS document window to fill the Works window. Click several times in the gray area of the vertical scroll bar below the scroll box to display the end of the RULES.WPS document, as shown in Figure 5-4.

6. Click several times in the gray area of the vertical scroll bar above the scroll box to display the beginning of the RULES.WPS document.

7. Click once or twice on the down scroll arrow (⬇), then press on the down scroll arrow and hold down the left mouse button.

8. Click once or twice on the up scroll arrow (⬆), then press on the up scroll arrow.

9. Drag the scroll box to the bottom of the scroll bar. If the end mark of the document text (a short horizontal line) is not displayed, click the up scroll arrow to bring it into view.

10. Click an insertion point by positioning the I-beam and clicking in the blank area below the last line of text in the document.

11. Drag the scroll box to the top of the scroll bar, and click an insertion point at the beginning of the document.

FIGURE 5-4

After clicking several times in the scroll bar below the scroll box, the end of the RULES.WPS document is displayed. The maximized document fills the Works window.

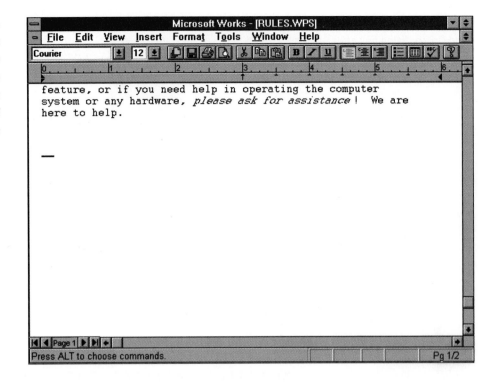

12. Use the keyboard arrow keys to move the insertion point down several lines, then to the right and left several spaces.

13. Use the ⬆ arrow key to move the insertion point back to the beginning of the document.

14. Choose the Go To command from the Edit menu to display the Go To dialog box.

15. Type **2** in the text box (as shown in Figure 5-5) and click OK or press the Enter key to close the dialog box and go to page 2 of the document. Notice that the insertion point now appears at the top of the window. Look at the lower right corner of the status bar and you will see 2/2. This means that your insertion point is now in the second page of a two-page document. Continue practicing these navigating techniques as time permits.

16. When you have finished practicing, choose Close from the File menu (or type Alt +F to open the File menu and then type **C**).

17. If the message box in Figure 5-6 is displayed, click on the No button to tell Works that you do not want to save changes to the RULES.WPS document. (Note: This message box may appear even though you have made no changes to text in a document. For instance, the message box will appear if you pressed the Enter key and added a blank line or if you pressed the spacebar and added a blank space to the document.)

18. If you are not continuing on to the Practice Applications, choose Exit Works from the File menu to exit the Works program.

19. Eject your Student Data Disk from its drive.

FIGURE 5-5

*The Go To dialog box after typing **2** in the text box.*

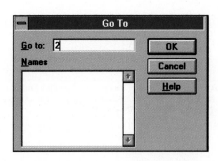

FIGURE 5-6

This message box appears if you have made changes to a document that has not been saved.

PRACTICE APPLICATIONS

Complete the following exercises. Some exercises ask you to answer one or more questions. Write a brief answer to these questions on a sheet of paper.

1. Open the RULES.WPS document. Click an insertion point in front of the title Computer Lab Rules. What is the quickest way to move the cursor to the end of the first line of item 2? *POINT MOUSE POINTER + CL*

2. Display the last item in the document. What would happen if you typed the words **The End** without first clicking an insertion point at the end of the document? Where would the text that you type appear? *WHERE INSERTION POINT IS*

3. When the last line of the document is displayed in the document window, what is the quickest way to view item 5 in the RULES.WPS document? *USE SCROLL BAR + THEN POINT MOUSE*

4. Click an insertion point at the beginning of the RULES.WPS document, then close the document without saving any changes you have made.

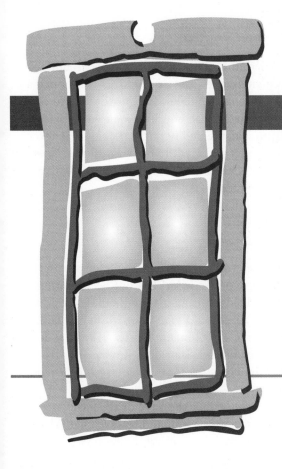

LESSON 6

CREATING A DOCUMENT

OBJECTIVES

After completing this lesson you will be able to do the following:

- *Create a new word-processing document.*

- *Name a document and save it on your Student Data Disk.*

- *Explain when it is appropriate to use the Save and Save As commands.*

KEY WORDS

In this lesson you will learn the meaning of the following terms:

existing document
file format
save

CREATING A NEW DOCUMENT IN WORKS

The RULES.WPS file you opened in Lesson 5 is called an **existing document** because it has already been created and saved. Typically, you open an existing document to review its contents, to make changes to it, or to print it. If you want to create a new document, first check to make sure that the New & Recent Documents button is depressed (it is the default whenever you start Works). Then you tell Works which tool you want to use. Click on the Word Processor button, and a document window will appear with a blank work space, allowing you to enter text.

SAVING A DOCUMENT

The text you type and the changes you make to a document exist in temporary RAM only. If a copy of your work in RAM has not been written to a disk for permanent storage, it will be lost during a system failure or power outage. To prevent the loss of text, you should save your work frequently— every 5 to 10 minutes. When you **save** a document, Works writes the document in RAM to a file either on your hard disk or on a floppy disk. By saving your work, you create a magnetic copy that can be stored for reuse at a later session.

In Works you save a file by choosing either the Save or the Save As command from the File menu. Use the Save command to save changes that you have made to an existing document. The Save As dialog box does not appear and the file is saved under the same name. Use Save As to give a name to a new document you have created or to give a new name to the changes you have made to an existing document.

SAVING A DOCUMENT FOR THE FIRST TIME

Use Save As when you are naming a document for the first time. A Save As dialog box, similar to the one shown in Figure 6-1, appears, and you type the name of the document and select the directory and drive where the file should be stored. A file name can be up to eight characters long (uppercase, lowercase, or a combination), not including the three-letter extension (such as .WPS or .WSS) at the end of the file name. Because a period must always begin a file extension, Windows will not allow you to use a period as part of the file name.

SAVING AN EXISTING DOCUMENT UNDER A DIFFERENT NAME

Use Save As when you want to save two versions of a document. When you give the document a different name, the original version remains unchanged; the changes you make appear only in the file with the new name.

FIGURE 6-1

The Save As dialog box is used to give an untitled document a file name so that it can be stored on a disk. In this illustration the B drive holds the Student Data Disk.

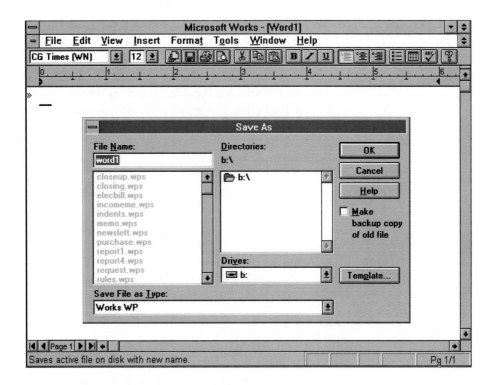

SAVING A DOCUMENT IN OTHER FILE FORMATS

Use Save As when you want to save the file in a format other than the format in which it was created. The Save File As Type list box lets you choose various formats for your documents. When you save a document using a different **file format,** the Works formatting code converts to the formatting code used by the other application. For example, if you save a document with Word for Windows 2.0 selected on the Save File As Type list box, the Works document will be converted to a Word for Windows document that can be opened on a personal computer using Microsoft Word 2.0. Figure 6-2 shows a list of formats available on the Save File as Type list

FIGURE 6-2

A Microsoft Works 3.0 document can be converted to another file format selected from the Save File As Type list box.

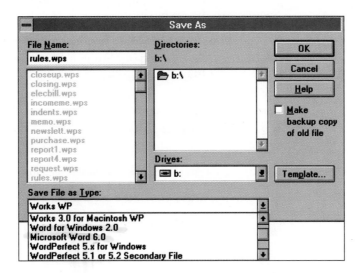

box. The list you see on the submenu depends on which file conversion programs were selected for installation on your system when Works was installed.

In addition to being able to save a Works file in a format like WordPerfect, Works for the Macintosh, and so on, you can also choose to save the text of your document without formatting. This means that your text can be used in almost any word-processor application.   (TEXT)

GUIDED PRACTICE

CREATING AND SAVING A DOCUMENT

In this exercise you will open a new word-processing document window, enter text, and save the document on your Student Data Disk.

You have been assigned to create a document that explains briefly how to turn on each computer system in the lab. A copy of this document will be mounted on a card placed next to each computer system. Students who are new to the lab can refer to this card to start their systems with a minimum of help from the lab staff.

The exact procedure you use to begin this guided practice depends on whether or not Works is already loaded into your computer's memory. In either case, be sure your Student Data Disk is in the floppy drive.

1. Display the Startup window by starting Works. If Works is already loaded into memory, make sure the New & Recent Documents button is depressed.

2. Click on the Word Processor button to open an untitled document window. Now you are ready to enter the text for computer start-up instructions. Don't be concerned about correcting any errors you make as you type. You will have an opportunity to correct them later.

3. Type the following paragraphs. As you type, glance at your screen periodically to observe how words are wrapped whenever you fill an existing line with text. Press the [Enter] key two times to start a new paragraph.

   To start this PC, locate the power switch on the side of the computer. Switch it to the on position.

   When the Program Manager window appears, click on the Microsoft Works icon, and insert your Student Data Disk in the floppy disk drive. Click on the Open An Existing Document button to open a file. Find the drive that holds your Student Data Disk, and click on it to display your student data files. If you see the file name in the Recently Used Files list box, double-click on the name to open the file. If you are creating a new file, click on the tool you want to use, for example, the spreadsheet.

4. Choose Save As from the File menu to display the Save As dialog box.

5. If necessary, make your Student Data Disk current by clicking the [↓] arrow beside the Drives list box. Double-click on the correct floppy drive. A list of files will appear in the large File Name list box.

6. If necessary, highlight the text in the File Name text box by double-clicking.

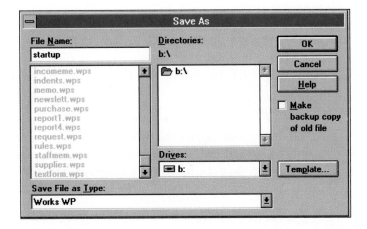

7. Type **STARTUP**. When you begin typing, the letters you type will replace Word1. Your screen should be similar to the one shown in Figure 6-3.

8. Click on the **OK** button or press the [Enter] key to store the document in the file named STARTUP on your Student Data Disk and to return to the document window.

   Notice that the name STARTUP.WPS now appears in the title bar of the document window. Depending on the printer you use and the fonts you have available, your screen display and print-outs may vary. However, your document window should be similar to the one shown in Figure 6-4.

9. Unless you are continuing with the following practice applications, quit Works and remove your data disk from the floppy-disk drive.

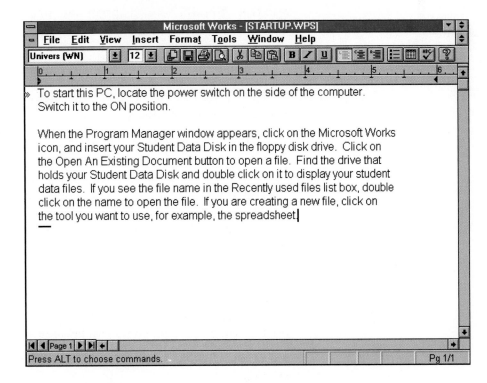

PRACTICE APPLICATIONS

Complete the following exercises. Some exercises ask you to answer one or more questions. Write a brief answer to these questions on a sheet of paper.

1. If necessary, open the STARTUP.WPS document. Position the cursor at the end of the last line of the document and press the [Enter] key two times. Add the following paragraph: Use the Save As dialog box to save your new document.

2. Try to close the document. Describe what happens. Why was a message displayed? *ASKS — SAVE CHANGES*

3. Click on the Cancel button in the message box. What happens when you do this? *RETURNS TO DOCUMENT WINDOW*

4. Try to close the document again. This time click on the No button. Describe what happens when you do this. Do you think the text you added in step 1 was saved? How can you determine whether or not it was saved?
EXITS OLD FILE + GOES BACK TO WORD WINDOW

CHANGES NOT SAVED
OPEN EXISTING

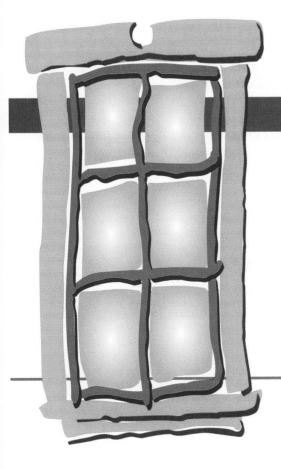

OBJECTIVES

After completing this lesson you will be able to do the following:

- *Use several basic techniques for highlighting text.*

- *Edit selected text.*

- *Change settings in the Print dialog box.*

- *Print a document.*

KEY WORDS

In this lesson you will learn the meaning of the following terms:

hard copy
print preview
selection bar

A PROCESS FOR EDITING A DOCUMENT

When you enter text in a document, you are creating a draft version of the document. Remember that a draft is a preliminary version of a file. Before you print a final version, you will need to locate and correct errors or make changes to the content and appearance of the document.

As you may recall, the process of locating and correcting errors and making changes to a document is called editing. If you prefer to edit a printed copy (**hard copy**) of the draft version of a document, use the following process:

1. Print a draft of the document.

2. Proofread the document (check it for errors).

3. Mark corrections and changes on the printed draft.

4. Make corrections and changes to the document in Works (or other word processor).

5. Print a final version of the document.

Another approach to editing involves proofreading the document and examining its overall appearance in Works before printing a hard copy of the first draft version. Works provides a **print preview** feature that allows you to see how a document will appear on a page before it is actually printed.

REVIEWING A DOCUMENT BEFORE PRINTING

In Works, you can choose Print Preview from the File menu (or click on the Print Preview button on the toolbar) to make sure that your document's overall appearance is the way you want it to look when printed. For instance, in the first Print Preview window (shown in Figure 7-1) you see an entire document page in a reduced size. Viewing the document page in this first Print Preview window allows you to see the margins that are currently set and to make decisions about any changes you may want to make before printing the document.

When you move the pointer onto the document page in this Print Preview window, the pointer changes into a magnifying glass. When you click with the magnifying glass once, the Print Preview window changes from standard view to half-zoom display, showing a larger image of the page. Click on the page again and Works changes to full-zoom view and an actual-size view of a document page. Click on the page again and you return to standard view.

Of course, switching to the full-zoom view leaves only a portion of the page visible. Therefore, you should position the magnifying glass on the portion of the page you want to examine before you click the mouse button.

This actual-size view of a document page allows you to read the document to make sure that none of the text is missing on the right edge of the text lines. For example, under certain circumstances, text lines that appear in your document window are cut off in a printed copy of the document.

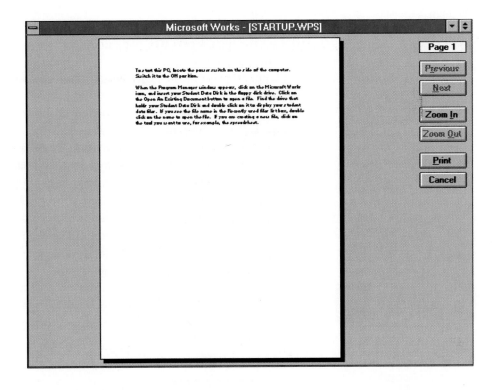

FIGURE 7-1
This reduced-size Print Preview window is displaying the STARTUP.WPS document.

With print preview you are able to use the scroll bars to see how the top, bottom, left, and right edges of your document will appear when printed.

Print Preview windows are used only for viewing a document. To make document changes, you must return to the Document window. No matter what view you are in, you can click on the Cancel box to return to the Document window.

ZOOM

PRINTING A DOCUMENT

When you are ready to print a document in Works, choose Print from the File menu to open a Print dialog box similar to the one shown in Figure 7-2. The name of the printer currently installed appears at the top of the box.

All Works Print dialog boxes provide two radio buttons for selecting a range of pages. If you choose not to print all pages in a document, click on the button before the word Pages and then type in the page numbers of the

FIGURE 7-2

The Print dialog box.

range in the From and To text boxes. For example, if you want to print pages 2 through 4 of a five-page document, you would type **2** in the From text box and type **4** in the To text box. You specify the number of copies you want to print in the Number Of Copies text box. One copy is the default number.

The What To Print box offers two radio buttons. The first button, Main Document, is the default. The second button allows you to print envelopes.

Below the What To Print area are two check boxes. Draft Quality Printing prints fastest, but this selection may not be suitable for the final version of a document. Draft quality means that Works will print characters without the bold, italic, underline, or color accents you may have added. Works will use only its default font, usually Courier, when printing in draft quality. Works will also not print charts, drawings, or other objects in draft quality. Draft Quality does print faster than Works' usual printing speed. You will be introduced how to print merge in another lesson.

If you want to print one copy of the entire document in the active document window, save time by clicking on the Print button on the toolbar. Clicking on the Print button, however, will not allow you to choose the options in the Print dialog box.

GUIDED PRACTICE

PREVIEWING AND PRINTING A DOCUMENT

Your supervisor wants you to print two draft copies of the STARTUP.WPS document. In this practice exercise, you will use the Print Preview windows to examine the STARTUP.WPS document before printing draft copies.

1. If necessary, open the STARTUP.WPS document.

2. Choose Print Preview or press V from the File menu.

3. In print preview, move the pointer over the page to change the pointer to a magnifying glass.

4. Move the magnifying glass over the text of the STARTUP.WPS document, then click once to change from standard view to half-zoom view. Click again to see an actual-size view of text in the document.

5. Click on the scroll bars to see the top, bottom, left, and right boundaries of your document.

6. Click again to return to the standard view. Click on the Cancel button to return to the document window.

7. Choose Print (Ctrl+P) from the File menu.

8. Click the Draft Quality Printing check box.

9. If necessary, double-click the Number Of Copies text box to highlight it, then type **2**. Other settings should remain the same as those shown in Figure 7-2.

10. Click OK to start the printing process.

11. Proofread one of the printed copies. Mark any errors that you find.

12. If you have finished work for the day, quit Works and remove your Student Data Disk from the floppy-disk drive.

CORRECTING AND HIGHLIGHTING TEXT

In Works, you use special editing keys and commands to make corrections and changes to a document. The editing key you will use most is the Del key. When you press the Del key, the character to the right of the cursor is erased. As discussed in the previous chapter, when you want to apply formatting changes to text, Works needs to know exactly which text you want to work with. Highlighting, or selecting, is the technique you use to tell Works where to apply the changes you make. You can highlight a character, word, phrase, sentence, paragraph, page, or longer section. There are several ways to highlight text; the technique you use depends on the amount of text you want to select.

If you have used other Windows applications, you are already familiar with techniques for highlighting text. The Works document window has a special invisible column in the left margin called a **selection bar**. As shown in Figure 7-3, when you position the pointer in the selection bar, the shape

FIGURE 7-3

Notice the shape of the mouse pointer when it is positioned in the selection bar. Use the selection bar when you want to highlight lines of text in a document.

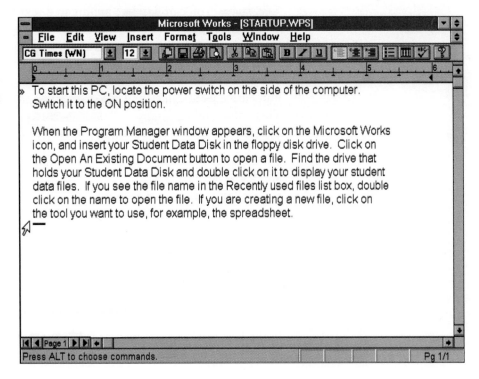

of the mouse pointer changes from an I-beam to an arrow, as shown in Figure 7-3. Here are the basic techniques for using the selection bar, as well as standard highlighting techniques:

■ *Highlighting any amount of text.* You can highlight any amount of text by clicking the I-beam (the text pointer) and dragging it over the text while holding down the left mouse button. You can also use the shift-clicking technique to highlight text by clicking an insertion point at the beginning of the text you want to highlight, holding down the (Shift) key, and then clicking an insertion point at the end of the text you want to highlight.

■ *Highlighting a word.* Move the insertion point onto a word and double-click to highlight the word.

■ *Highlighting more than one word.* First double-click a single word. Then hold down the (Shift) key and drag the I-beam to the right or left of the highlighted word to select as many other words as you want.

■ *Highlighting a line of text.* Position the pointer in the invisible selection bar—the first column on the left edge of the document window. Click on the selection bar next to the line you want highlighted.

■ *Highlighting more than one line of text.* Position the pointer in the selection bar, then drag the pointer up or down next to the lines you want to highlight.

■ *Highlighting a paragraph.* Position the pointer in the selection bar next to the paragraph you want to highlight, then double-click.

■ *Highlighting an entire document.* Choose Select All or press A on the Edit menu. You can deselect highlighted text by clicking anywhere in the document window. To avoid deleting or changing text unintentionally, always deselect highlighted text as soon as you have finished making your changes. If you delete highlighted text by mistake, or if you make unintended changes, you may be able to undo the deletion or change by immediately choosing the Undo command ((Ctrl)+Z) from the Edit menu. This command undoes your last action only, so it is important to use it before you make any additional changes to the document.

GUIDED PRACTICE

EDITING A DOCUMENT

The lab director has reviewed the STARTUP.WPS document and has marked a few changes on the printout. Follow these steps to update the draft version with the changes and to save the new version under the name STARTUP2.WPS:

1. If necessary, open the STARTUP.WPS document.

2. In the first line, change the word **this** to **the**. First, click an insertion point immediately to the right of the letter **h** in this.

3. Press the ⌴Del⌴ key two times to delete the letters i and s.

4. Type the letter **e.**

5. In the same line, highlight the word locate by double-clicking the word. Your document should look like the one in Figure 7-4.

6. Type **find** and press the spacebar to replace the word **locate** with the word **find.**

7. In the first line of the document, double-click the word **the** in the phrase **the power switch.** Do not release the mouse button.

8. When the word the is highlighted, drag across the next three words, **the power switch,** to highlight them. Release the mouse button. In the next steps you will copy the highlighted phrase **the power switch** and paste a copy of it in the next sentence, replacing the word **it.**

9. Choose Copy (⌴Ctrl⌴+C) from the Edit menu.

10. Double-click the word **it** (after **Switch** in the next sentence) to highlight the word.

11. Choose Paste (⌴Ctrl⌴+V) from the Edit menu to paste a copy of the phrase **the power switch,** replacing the word **it.** Figure 7-5 shows the document window after **it** in the second sentence is replaced with **the power switch.**

IN LAST SENTENCE

12. Click an insertion point in front of the letter **I** in **If.** Hold down the ⌴Shift⌴ key and click an insertion point after the period that ends the sentence. When the entire sentence—**If you are creating a new file, click on the tool you want to use, for example, the spreadsheet**—is highlighted, release the ⌴Shift⌴ key. This highlight is shown in Figure 7-6.

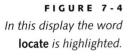

FIGURE 7-4

In this display the word **locate** *is highlighted.*

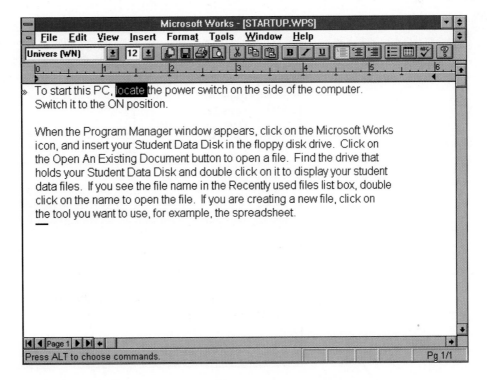

FIGURE 7-5

After you replace **it** *in
the second sentence with*
the power switch, *your
document should be similar
to the one shown here.
In the next steps you
will cut the last sentence
and move it.*

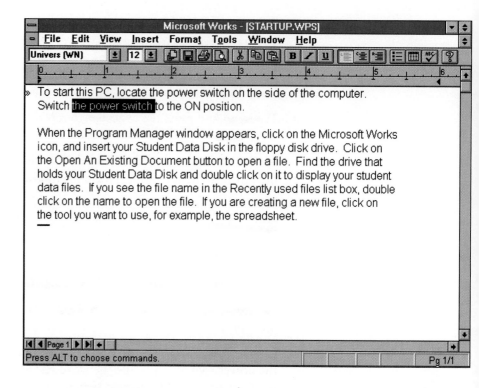

13. To remove the sentence, choose Cut ([Ctrl]+X) from the Edit menu, as
    shown in Figure 7-6.

    ESC

    When the menu closes, the highlighted sentence will be deleted from
    the document. If you open the Clipboard (use [Alt]+[Tab] to return to
    Program Manager and double-click on the Clipboard viewer icon—
    usually located in the Main Program Group window), you will see the

FIGURE 7-6

*This illustration shows the
Cut command chosen on
the Edit menu.*

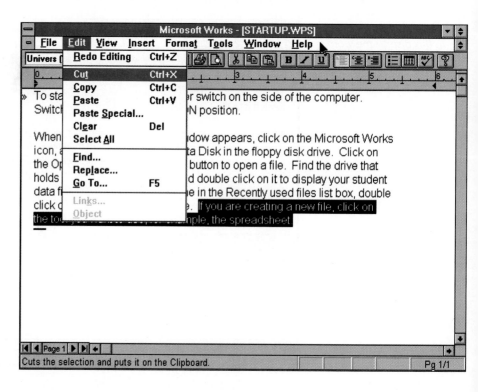

sentence If you are creating a new file, click on the tool you want to use, for example, the spreadsheet. Use Alt + Tab to return to your document.

2 Dı৯৯ড়
R৯৯৯৯)

14. Click an insertion point to the left of the first word in what is now the last sentence in the document.

15. Choose Paste (Ctrl+V) from the Edit menu to insert the sentence at the current insertion point.

16. Add two spaces at the end of the sentence you have just moved to separate it from the sentence that follows.

17. Correct any other errors you may have identified when you proofread your copy of the draft. You have completed the editing tasks for your supervisor. You can now save the new version of the file under a different name.

18. Choose Save As from the File menu to display the Save As dialog box. Because the file name STARTUP.WPS appears in the Save Document As text box, click to the right of the P in STARTUP.WPS and type **2**.

19. Click on the OK button or press the Enter key to save the new version under the file name STARTUP2.WPS. Now you have one version of the document named STARTUP.WPS and another version named STARTUP2.WPS. The STARTUP2.WPS document window is shown in Figure 7-7.

FIGURE 7-7
The STARTUP2.WPS version of the STARTUP.WPS document.

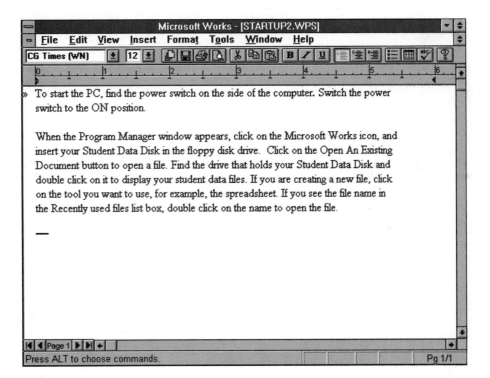

20. You should close a file whenever you have finished working on a document. Closing a file removes its window from the screen and clears the file from memory. If you do not close a file, it remains on your screen in memory until you exit Works. Close the STARTUP2.WPS document by clicking on the Close command. This takes you back to the Startup window.

PRACTICE APPLICATIONS

1. Open the file MEMO.WPS, stored on the Student Data Disk. Read the contents of this file. If you have a printer attached to your computer system, print a copy of this file. Proofread the text for errors, marking corrections on the printed copy. If you do not have a printer, read the screen version of the document and note any errors on a sheet of paper.

2. Click an insertion point after DATE in the first line and type the current date.

3. Reverse the order of the first and second paragraphs of the MEMO.WPS document.   ✓ *BEFORE SWITCH*

4. In the second line of the third paragraph, delete the first use of the word **however**.

5. Correct any spelling and punctuation errors that you have found, and then save the edited version of the document as MEMO2.WPS.

6. Print a copy of MEMO2.WPS.

CHAPTER REVIEW

■ A computer-based word-processing program provides features for editing and formatting text; copying, cutting, and moving text; finding and replacing text; printing text; and saving text to a file. There are several ways to navigate through a document quickly using window scrolling features. When you know the page number you want to jump to, you can use the Go To Page dialog box.

■ Before you can make a formatting change to text in a document, you must select the text you want to change. Characters are selected by high-lighting. You can highlight text by dragging, double-clicking, or shift-clicking. In addition to these usual ways to highlight text, the Works word-processing document window has a selection bar in which the mouse pointer changes to an arrow that can be clicked or dragged to select one or more lines of text.

■ Works allows you to revise a document as often as necessary, creating several drafts that eventually result in a final version. The Works Print dialog box allows you to specify the pages of the document that you want to print, the number of copies that you want to print, and the print quality.

REVIEW QUESTIONS

TRUE-FALSE

Write your answers on a sheet of paper.

1. The word-wrap feature in a word-processing program can wrap text either forward or backward.

2. Highlighting is selecting text in preparation for formatting or changing it in some way.

3. When you use the Copy command to move (paste) text to a new location, the text is deleted from its original location.

4. A word-processing program typically provides the capability to locate a particular word or phrase in a document.

5. In a word processor, the Enter key is used when you want to force the beginning of a new line before you have reached the end of a line.

6. When you use the scroll bar to go to the end of a document, the cursor moves to the end of the document.

7. When you use the Cut command to cut highlighted text from a document, the text cannot be retrieved.

8. The last document to be saved and stored on a hard disk or floppy disk is called a new document.

9. In Works, Save and Save As are interchangeable commands that perform the same task.

10. In Works, you can save a document in file formats that allow it to be opened using other word-processing application software.

SHORT-ANSWER QUESTIONS

1. Is it possible to perform word processing without a computer? Explain your answer.

2. When you use a word-processing program, what is the purpose of highlighting text?

3. What is the difference between searching for text and replacing text?

4. Briefly explain the purpose of the Clipboard in using the Cut, Copy, and Paste commands in the Works word processor.

5. Explain why it is important to save a new document that you have created before you quit Works.

LESSON APPLICATIONS

1. Open the REPORT1.WPS file, which is located on your Student Data Disk. Use the techniques you learned in this chapter to perform the following steps:

   a. Click an insertion point at the beginning of the document.

   b. Scroll to the end of the document by clicking in the vertical scroll bar.

   c. Scroll to the beginning of the document using the scroll arrow.

   d. Use the Go To Page command to go to page 2 of the document.

   e. Move the cursor to the beginning of the document.

   f. Close the REPORT1.WPS document without saving any changes that may have been made.

2. Create a new document and enter the following text. Save the document on your Student Data Disk, using the file name MYTEXT.WPS.

   A word-processing program can save you time in creating and editing text documents. For example, you can use the Works word processor to create and edit letters, memos, notes, and reports for school or work.

You can create all of these kinds of documents using a type-writer, of course. However, if you use a typewriter, it will be more difficult to correct any errors that you make. In fact, you might even have to retype all or part of a document if major errors need to be corrected. Creating documents with a word processor can be enjoyable.

3. Correct any errors that you may have made while entering the MYTEXT.WPS document. Move the last sentence in the document to the start of the first paragraph. Then print the document. Save the revised document on your Student Data Disk under the name MYTEXT2.WPS.

CHAPTER APPLICATIONS

1. Open the REPORT1.WPS document on your Student Data Disk. Scroll down to the paragraph that begins **The excessive wait times** . . . . This paragraph contains two numbered items. Reverse the order of these items; then delete the word **second** that appears in the first numbered item. Perform any other corrections necessary to make the new order of items read correctly. Explain the procedures you followed to complete this exercise.

2. Save the revised version of the report as NEWREPOR.WPS. Print the entire document, but print two copies of page 3 only. Explain what steps you followed to perform this print operation. After the document pages are printed, close the document and quit Works.

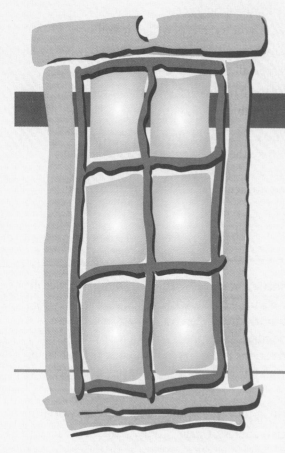

CHAPTER 4

FORMATTING TEXT

OVERVIEW

In this chapter, you will begin using formatting features that show the power of the word-processing program in Microsoft Works. The Works word processor provides numerous features for changing fonts, type styles, margins, line spacing, and page size, and for setting tabs.

As you work through the guided practices in this chapter, you will learn how to change the way characters and paragraphs appear in print and you will learn how to apply settings that affect an entire document.

CONTENTS

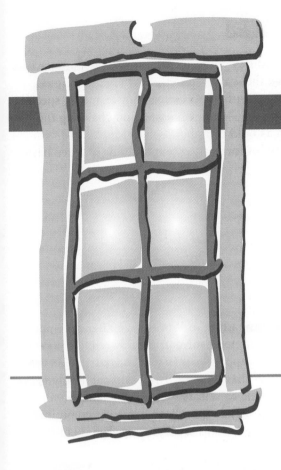

LESSON 8

UNDERSTANDING WORKS' FORMATTING CAPABILITIES

OBJECTIVES

After completing this lesson you will be able to do the following:

- *Define the term "formatting" as it applies to word-processing techniques.*

- *Explain the differences between character, paragraph, and document formatting.*

- *Describe some basic character, paragraph, and document-formatting features.*

KEY WORDS

In this lesson you will learn the meaning of the following terms:

alignment	*justified*	*portrait*
character	*landscape*	*subscript*
formatting	*line spacing*	*superscript*
document	*margins*	*type size*
formatting	*paragraph*	*type style*
font	*formatting*	
indents	*point*	

ASIC FORMATTING PROCEDURES

Formatting refers to the procedures you use to set up the appearance of a document or to alter or enhance the way text appears when it is printed. Examples of formatting include selecting line spacing (for example, specifying single spacing or double spacing), setting margins, and changing the appearance of characters (such as bold or italic).

In Works, it is helpful to think of formatting text in terms of three basic levels:

Character formatting

Paragraph formatting

Document formatting

HARACTER FORMATTING

When you perform **character formatting** in Works, you alter the appearance of one or more characters. Character formats usually apply to one or more words. For example, you can apply italic (*italic*) to a particular word or phrase in a sentence or to the entire sentence. Also, you can apply more than one formatting option at a time to selected text. For example, you can apply both bold and italic (***bold italic***) to text. Both options remain in effect as you type the text of the sentence and until you deselect them (turn them off).

You can also change the appearance of text after it has been typed. For example, you can highlight existing text and then select character formats such as bold and italics. These formats will be applied to the highlighted text only. When you format highlighted text within other existing text, you do not need to deselect the formatting options after they have been applied.

You can change the appearance of text by applying a different font, type style, or type size. In Works (and most other applications), **font** refers to a type design such as Geneva, Helvetica, or Times. These font names are actually the names of typefaces created and named by typeface designers. In traditional typesetting, a font is all of the characters in a specific size and style of type, for example, 12-point Helvetica bold.

The font names you see on your toolbar and menus are fonts that are available in Windows. A **type style** is a variation within a font. Plain, bold, italic, underline, outline, and shadow are font attributes (or type styles) available in Works. **Type size** refers to the measure of a character's height in **points**. There are 72 points in an inch; therefore, a character that has a type size of 12 points is one-sixth of an inch tall.

In Works, you can select different fonts, type styles, and type sizes using Bold, Italic, and Underline buttons on the toolbar and the commands on the Format menu. The Font And Style dialog box (Figure 8-1), which you discovered in Chapter 5, is displayed when you choose the Font And Style command from the Format menu. The Font And Style dialog box can be used to select a font name, style or attribute, and type size, as well as a type

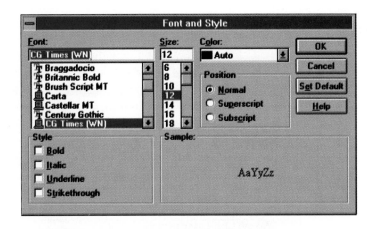

color, without having to reopen a menu for each format. (If you have a color monitor, you can display text in color. However, you cannot print the text in color unless you have a color printer.)

The Font and Style dialog box is also used when you want selected text to print as superscript or subscript. When you click on the **Superscript** button, ← CTRL + selected text is positioned a little above the normal line of text (for example, the 2 in X^2). When you click on the **Subscript** button, selected text is positioned a little below the normal line of text (for example, the 2 in H_2).

CTRL =

PARAGRAPH FORMATTING

In Works, you create a new paragraph every time you press the [Enter] key. A paragraph can be as short as a single character or as long as an entire document. In Works, even a blank line space is counted as a paragraph. Before you can change the appearance of a paragraph, you must select it. A single paragraph can be selected either by clicking an insertion point anywhere in the paragraph or by highlighting part or all of the paragraph. Several paragraphs can be selected by highlighting at least a part of each one. After selecting one or more paragraphs, you can use **paragraph formatting** to change paragraph alignment, line spacing, and indents.

Some Works dialog boxes use tabs to divide information into sections. The Paragraph dialog box is one of these. Click on the Indents And Alignment tab to display the information shown in Figure 8-2.

Works offers four choices for the alignment of text between the margins of a page. Figure 8-3 shows paragraphs formatted for left, center, right, and justified alignment. When a new document is opened, Works automatically aligns text to the left. When you apply **justified** alignment, text in all but the last line of the paragraph runs to the edge of the right margin. For left, center, or right paragraph alignment, you can click one of the three alignment buttons on the toolbar shown in the document windows in Figure 8-3.

Line spacing refers to the amount of space between lines of type in a paragraph. Figure 8-4 shows paragraphs in single-line spacing, 1½ line spacing, and double-line spacing. You can choose Line Spacing from the

FIGURE 8-3

The paragraphs in these document windows illustrate how the alignment buttons on the toolbar can be used to format paragraphs: (a) left alignment, (b) centered alignment, (c) right alignment, and (d) justified alignment (formatted by using the Paragraph dialog box).

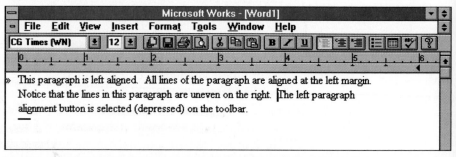

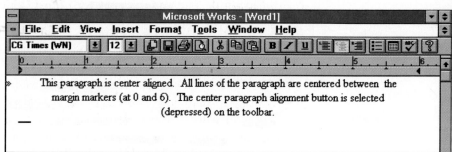

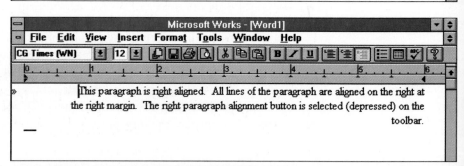

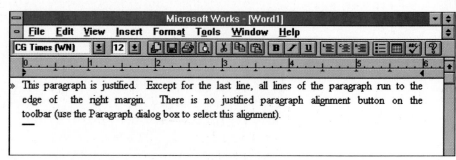

FIGURE 8-4

The paragraphs in these document windows illustrate different types of spacing: (a) single spacing, (b) 1½ spacing, and (c) double spacing.

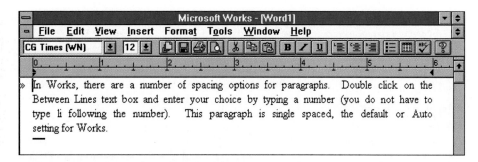

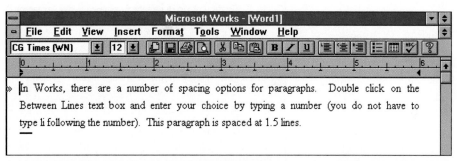

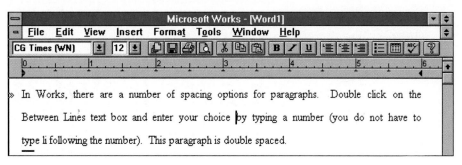

Breaks And Spacing tab in the Paragraph dialog box. Change paragraph spacing by replacing the setting in the Between Lines text box. The default setting is Auto, which adjusts for the height of the type font you have selected. This setting results in a single-spaced paragraph. Entering **1.5** results in 1½-line spacing, entering **2** results in a double-spaced paragraph.

Notice that Works offers you the chance to preview your selection before you leave the dialog box. After you make your selection in one of the text boxes, click on another text box. The sample page will adjust to show your changes.

Works also offers keyboard shortcuts to format paragraph spacing. Press Ctrl +1 for single spacing, Ctrl +5 for 1½-line spacing, and Ctrl +2 for double spacing.

Indents refer to the way the lines of a paragraph are set off from surrounding text. In Works, you can set left, right, or first-line indents by adjusting the margin markers on the ruler or by using the text boxes in the Indents And Alignment tab from the Paragraph dialog box. Left or right indents are used when you want all lines of a paragraph to be indented. First-line indents are used when you want only the first line of a paragraph to be indented. The second paragraph in Figure 8-5(a) is formatted with left

FIGURE 8-5

(a) The second paragraph in this document window is formatted for left and right paragraph indents. (b) The paragraph in this document window is formatted with a first-line indent.

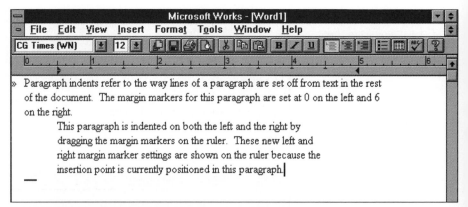

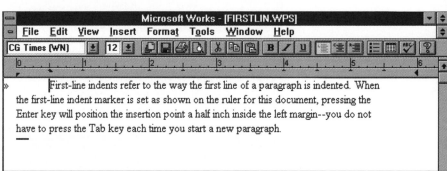

and right paragraph indents. The paragraph in Figure 8-5(b) is formatted with a first-line indent. You will learn how to set paragraph indents in Chapter 8.

DOCUMENT FORMATTING

In Works, **document formatting** is used to set margins, page size, and other specifications that apply to an entire document. When you set document formats, they apply only to the document that is currently open.

In Works, most of the document formatting options are available in the Page Setup dialog box. When you choose Page Setup from the File menu, a Page Setup tab dialog box similar to the one shown in Figure 8-6 is displayed.

The Margins tab (Figure 8-6) allows you to set the margins of your document and preview those changes before you leave the dialog box. **Margins** refer to the white space that surrounds the text on a printed page. Left and right margin settings determine the amount of white space in the left and right margins. Top and bottom margin settings determine the amount of white space in the top and bottom margins. White space reserved for margins does not appear in the document window, but you can see it when you choose Print Preview from the File menu. The default setting for top and bottom margins is 1 inch. The default setting for left and right margins is 1.25 inch. Header and footer margins will be discussed in Chapter 8.

The options available under Source, Size And Orientation depend on the printer you are using. The default selection for all printers is letter-size ($8\frac{1}{2}$ x 11in.) paper in **portrait** or tall orientation. When you select the Portrait

FIGURE 8-6

*A Page Setup dialog box
with the Margins tab
selected.*

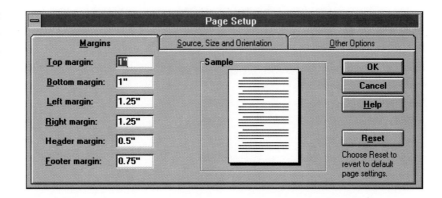

radio button (the default choice), the short edges of the paper are at the top
and bottom of the page. Select the Landscape button when you want to
print in **landscape** or wide orientation. When you select the Landscape
button, the long edges of the paper are at the top and bottom of the page.
Notice that when you switch between the Portrait and Landscape buttons,
the width and height values change places. The page sample also changes to
reflect your choices. The Paper Source text box offers several options,
depending on your printer, as does the Paper Size box.

*MANUAL FEED
ENVELOPE A*

Other document settings that affect the entire document include page
breaks, headers, footers, and beginning page numbers. These settings are
discussed in Chapter 8.

*LEGAL 8"x14
ENVELOPE!*

FIGURE 8-7

*The Source, Size And
Orientation dialog box is
displayed when you click
on the Source, Size And
Orientation tab in the Page
Setup dialog box.*

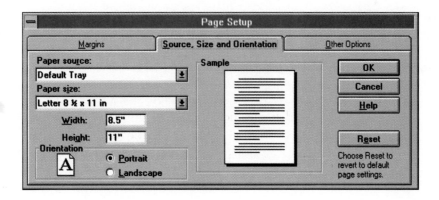

LESSON REVIEW QUESTIONS

Write a brief answer to these questions on a sheet of paper.

1. In Works, what is the difference between character and paragraph
   formatting?

2. In general, how do character and paragraph formats differ when applied
   to new text and existing text?

3. Identify the menus and dialog boxes used to select character, paragraph,
   and document format options.

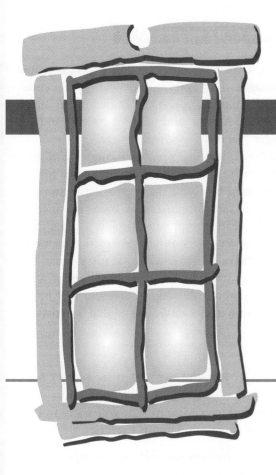

LESSON 9

FORMATTING

NEW TEXT

OBJECTIVES

After completing this lesson you will be able to do the following:

- *Specify that new text will be formatted in italic.*
- *Specify that new text will be formatted as underlined characters.*
- *Specify that new text will be formatted in bold.*
- *Deselect character format.*
- *Specify that lines of a paragraph will be centered.*
- *Deselect paragraph format options.*
- *Set and delete tab settings.*

KEY WORDS

In this lesson you will learn the meaning of the following terms:

heading lines	*memo*	*tab*
interoffice memo	*memorandum*	*tab stop*

SETTING FORMATS BEFORE ENTERING NEW TEXT

As the previous lesson explained, the techniques for formatting new text and existing text are slightly different. To specify formats before you enter text, you first select one or more formatting options from the menus and the dialog boxes; then you enter the text. As you enter text, characters and paragraphs conform to the format you have specified.

In the Guided Practice that follows, you will practice formatting new text for a memorandum that you will create. A **memorandum**, or **memo** for short, is an informal written document from one member of an organization to one or more other members of the same organization. Because a memo is not intended to be read by people outside the organization, it is often called an **interoffice memo**. If the organization does not have interoffice memo stationery with the heading lines **Date, To, From**, and **Re** already printed, these words are typed in when the memo is written. These **heading lines** provide identifying and tracking information about the memo. You will type in heading lines when you create a memo in the following guided practice.

GUIDED PRACTICE

APPLYING CHARACTER FORMATS TO NEW TEXT

In this exercise you will specify character formats that will apply to the text you enter for a memo. The text is included in this exercise.

1. Double-click on the Works icon in the Program Manager window and click on the Word Processor button in the Startup window.

2. Click on the Open Existing File command on the File menu to open the Open dialog box. If necessary, make the floppy drive with the Student Data Disk the current drive.

3. Locate and double-click ELECBILL.WPS in the File Name list box. The document shown in Figure 9-1 will be displayed on your screen.

Your first task is to add a second paragraph to the memo. You will format the first sentence of this second paragraph in italic to emphasize its importance.

4. Click an insertion point after the paragraph. If necessary, press the Enter key twice to leave a blank line between the first paragraph and the second paragraph you are about to type.

5. Click on the Italic button on the toolbar (or press Ctrl+I).

6. Type the sentence that follows, putting two blank spaces after the period that ends the sentence. Press the Tab key to indent the first line.

Per your request, I will be implementing special energy-saving procedures beginning this month.

After you have finished typing the first sentence, you must deselect the italic type style so that the next sentence will appear in plain text style.

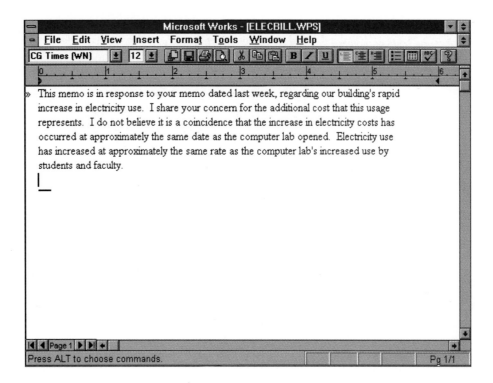

7. To deselect the Italic type style, click the Italic button on the toolbar (or press Ctrl + Spacebar).

8. Type the following text, which is the beginning of the second sentence of the second paragraph. Press the Spacebar once to leave a blank space after you type the last word, **sure**.

   For example, the lab staff will be checking computer systems
   to make sure

Next you will underline the word **all** as you type it.

9. Click on the Underline button on the toolbar (or press Ctrl +U).

10. Type **all** to enter the underlined word **all**. Do not press the Spacebar after typing the word.

11. Deselect the underline type style by repeating step 9 (or press Ctrl + Spacebar).

12. Press the Spacebar once and type the following text. Be sure to press the Spacebar twice after typing each period.

   computer devices are turned off after each use by a lab visitor.
   To demonstrate our seriousness, we are planning to fine lab
   visitors $5.00 for failing to turn off equipment after they have
   completed their use of the equipment.

13. Compare your screen display of the document with the one shown in Figure 9-2. If the text differs, make any necessary corrections. Again, your choice of font may affect the look of your document.

   For extra emphasis, you are going to apply both bold and italic type styles to the final sentence you will be writing in the second paragraph.

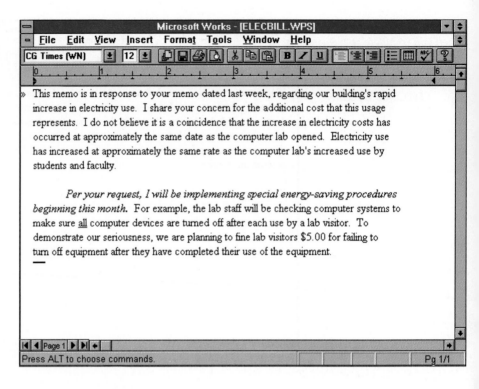

To do this, select the Italic and Bold buttons on the toolbar. You can also use the Font And Style dialog box, but clicking toolbar buttons is faster.

14. Select an insertion point after the last paragraph. Type two spaces.

15. Click the Bold and Italic toolbar buttons to select both type styles. The next text you type will be formatted in bold and italic type styles. Type the following text as the final sentence of the second paragraph.

    Three fines or failure to pay a fine within 30 days will result in the revocation of lab privileges for one semester.

16. When you have finished entering the sentence, click on the Bold and Italic buttons to return to plain text (or press Ctrl+Spacebar). Figure 9-3 shows the ELECBILL.WPS document before the changes are saved under a new name.

17. Save the document as ELECBIL2.WPS.

The previous exercise guided you through completion of the body, or message portion, of the memo on the electricity usage situation. In the guided practice that follows, you will type heading lines for the memo.

GUIDED PRACTICE

APPLYING PARAGRAPH FORMATS TO NEW TEXT

In this exercise you will complete the memo you created in the previous guided practice. You will also enter and format the title (**Memo**).

1. If necessary, open ELECBIL2.WPS.

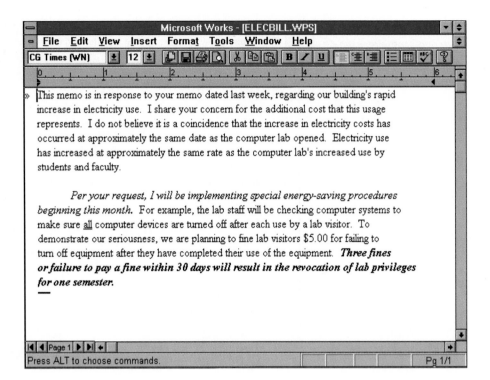

2. Click an insertion point in the blank line just above the first line of text in the document. If there is not already a blank line, click an insertion point at the beginning of the first line of text and press the (Enter) key once. Move your insertion point to this blank line.

3. Open the Paragraph dialog box from the Format menu. Click on the Indents And Alignment tab. Click on the Center button. Notice that the highlighted paragraph in the sample has changed to a centered paragraph. Click the OK button or press (Enter). Notice that the insertion point has jumped to the center of the blank line at the top of the document.

4. Turn on uppercase mode by pressing the (Caps Lock) key, then type **MEMO**.

5. Press the (Caps Lock) key again to turn off uppercase mode, then press the (Enter) key. The cursor is centered on the new blank line you created when you pressed the (Enter) key.

In the next step you will change the blank-line paragraph alignment from center to left.

6. Open the Paragraph dialog box from the Format menu. If necessary, click on the Indents And Alignment tab. Click on the Left button and press (Enter) (you can also use the Left Align paragraph button on the toolbar). The paragraph will jump to the left margin, taking the cursor with it. Compare your document window with the one shown in Figure 9-4.

7. Choose Save from the File menu to save the new version of the document using the current name, ELECBIL2.WPS.

FIGURE 9-4

After you complete step 6, your document should look like this.

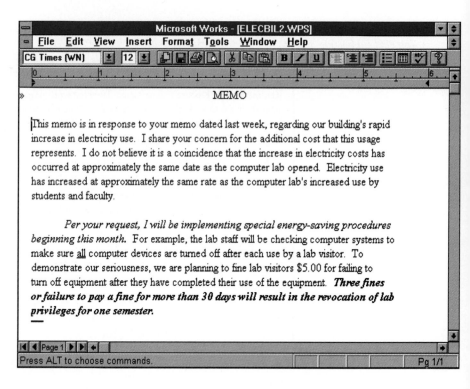

SING TABS

Now you will set a new tab to improve the appearance of the heading lines of your ELECBIL2.WPS memo. A **tab** is a setting that determines how far the cursor skips when you press the [Tab] key. The character position where text begins is called the **tab stop**.

By default, Works positions a tab every half inch (0.5"). To reduce the separation between the label for a memo heading and the text of the heading, you can change the default tab settings. For example, the default tabs of 0.5" and 1" produce this separation in the heading lines:

DATE: October 22, 1993
FROM: Sue Dilenko, Computer Lab
TO: Patricia Vincent
RE: Electricity usage

The amount of space between the heading labels (DATE, FROM, TO, and RE) and the heading text is wider than necessary. You can improve the appearance of the heading lines by changing the tab setting to 0.75". When you make this change, the space between the heading entry and the heading text is decreased (closed up). With a new tab set at 0.75", the separation in the heading lines looks like this:

DATE: October 22, 1993
FROM: Sue Dilenko, Computer Lab
TO: Patricia Vincent
RE: Electricity usage

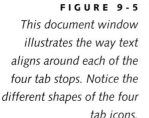

USING THE RULER TO SET TAB STOPS

With the Works word processor, you use the ruler to create, delete, or change tabs. When you set a new tab stop on the ruler, the default tab stops to the left of the new stop are automatically removed. For example, if you set a tab stop at the 0.75" tick mark on the ruler, the 0.5" default tab stop is automatically removed.

Tab stops are also set by using the Tabs dialog box from the Format menu. The four tab alignment radio buttons determine how text will align around the tab stop when you begin typing.

The Left Tab Alignment button is the default. When you tab (press the Tab key to move the insertion point) to a Left tab stop (**↑**), the left edge of the text you enter (that is, the first character you type) is aligned on the tab stop. When you tab to the Right tab stop (**↑**), the last character you enter is aligned on the tab stop. The Center tab stop (**↑**) is used to center text on either side of the tab stop. The Decimal tab stop (**↑**) is used to align decimal numbers on the decimal point. Figure 9-5 illustrates how text aligns around the four different tab stops.

To position a tab stop, simply move the mouse pointer on the ruler to where you want the tab stop to appear, then click the mouse button twice. This opens the Tabs dialog box, shown in Figure 9-6. You can select a different tab alignment by clicking one of the other tab buttons. Also, you can change a tab stop that is already set on the ruler to a different alignment by clicking on its position and double-clicking on a different alignment button. Works will change the tab, close the Tabs dialog box, and return you to

FIGURE 9-5

This document window illustrates the way text aligns around each of the four tab stops. Notice the different shapes of the four tab icons.

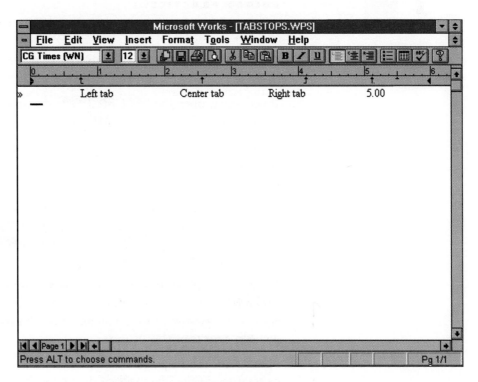

FIGURE 9-6

The Tabs dialog box is used to insert, delete, or change tabs.

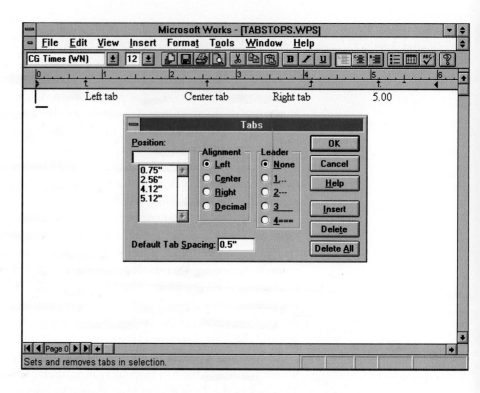

your document. You can move a tab stop by dragging it along the ruler. You can delete a tab stop you have added by pointing to it and dragging it off the ruler.

GUIDED PRACTICE

ADDING AND DELETING TAB STOPS

In this exercise you will set a tab stop to prevent excess space in the heading lines of the memo, and then type the heading lines.

1. If necessary, open the ELECBIL2.WPS document. Place your insertion point on the blank line after **MEMO**.

2. If the ruler is not already displayed in the document window, choose Ruler from the View menu.

3. Open the Tabs dialog box by double-clicking on the top half of the ruler. Notice that the insertion point is in the Position text box and that the Left Alignment button is selected. Type **.75** (Works assumes the measurement is in inches). Click OK. Notice that a left tab icon appears on the ruler to represent the new tab stop position.

5. For practice, set another tab stop at 1.5" on the ruler by pointing and clicking twice on the 1.5" tick mark. When the Tabs dialog box opens, click on the Center button. Change this tab to right and decimal alignment by repeating this process.

6. Point to the tab stop at the 1.5" tick mark and drag the tab icon below or above the ruler, then release the mouse button. The practice tab stop no longer appears on the ruler.

FIGURE 9-7

The left-align tab stop set at the 0.75" tick mark.

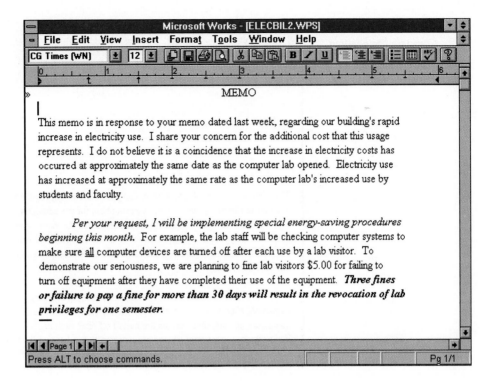

You are now ready to enter the heading lines for the memo using the tab stop you set at the 0.75" tick mark on the ruler.

7. If necessary, position the cursor at the left margin on the line below the centered title, **MEMO**.

8. Type **DATE:** and then press the [Tab] key once. The cursor moves to the tab stop set at 0.75" from the left margin.

9. Type today's date (for example, **October 22, 1994**), and then press the [Enter] key.

10. Type the remaining three heading lines for the memo:

    FROM: Sue Dilenko, Computer Lab
    TO: Patricia Vincent
    RE: Electricity utilization

Be sure to create a blank line between the final heading line and the first paragraph of text in the body of the memo. When you are finished, your screen should appear similar to the one shown in Figure 9-8.

You should now remove your new tab setting in case later on you want to insert text between the headings and the first paragraph. In other words, you do not want the 0.75" tab stop to apply to any new paragraphs you insert after the heading.

11. If necessary, position the cursor in the blank line between the heading and the body of the memo.

12. Point to the tab stop at 0.75", drag it off of the ruler, and release the mouse button.

FIGURE 9-8

*Compare the heading
entries for your memo with
the ones shown here.*

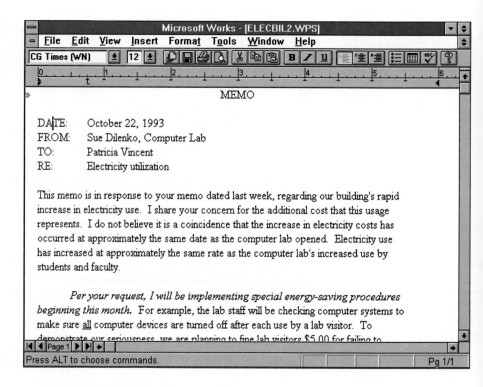

13. Click an insertion point in one of the heading lines. Notice that the tab stop reappears on the ruler when the insertion point is positioned in one of the heading-line paragraphs.

14. Save this version of the memo as ELECBIL3.WPS.

15. Preview the memo before printing it by choosing Print Preview from the File menu. Your screen should look like the one shown in Figure 9-9.

FIGURE 9-9

*After step 15, your Print
Preview window should
look like the one in
this display.*

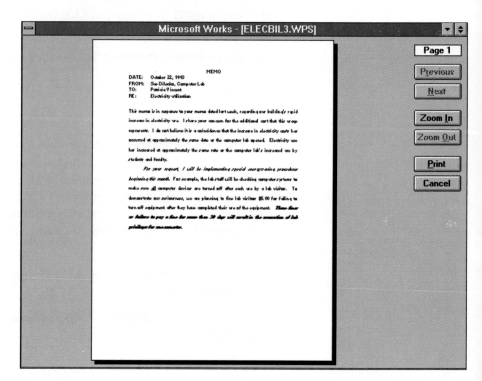

16. Click the preview page twice with the magnifying glass to change to full-zoom view. Read the contents of the page. When you are satisfied with the document, click the page again to return to standard view.

17. In Print Preview, click on the Print button to print a copy of the memo.

18. Close the ELECBIL3.WPS document window, saving any changes you have made since the last time you saved.

PRACTICE APPLICATIONS

1. Start a new document. Type the following paragraph, specifying these formats:

 a. Format the word **boldface** in bold.

 b. Format the word *italicize* in italic.

 c. Format the word underline in underlined text.

 As you create a typed document, you will often find it necessary to enhance some text for emphasis or to make it stand out from the rest of the text. The techniques you can use to enhance the printed page depend partly on the printer you're using. Virtually all impact and laser printers can bold-face, italicize, and underline text.

2. Add two heading lines to the paragraph you typed in Exercise 1. The first heading line should read **WORD PROCESSORS:** and the second line should read **Character Formatting Techniques**. Both lines should be centered and formatted for bold print.

3. Name the document FORMATS.WPS, and save it on your Student Data Disk. Print two copies of the document.

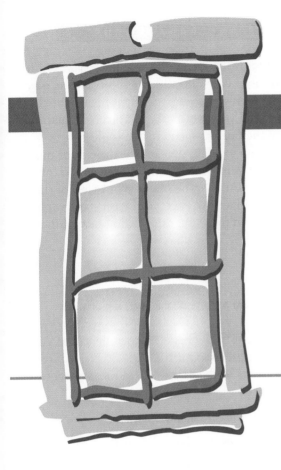

FORMATTING
EXISTING TEXT

OBJECTIVES

After completing this lesson you will be able to do the following:

- *Change the type style of existing text.*
- *Change the type size of existing text.*
- *Change the line spacing of existing paragraphs.*
- *Justify text in existing paragraphs.*
- *Open two documents and switch between the two open document windows.*
- *Split a document window.*

KEY WORD

pane

FORMATTING EXISTING CHARACTERS AND PARAGRAPHS

The procedures for formatting existing characters and paragraphs of text are similar, but not identical, to those you followed when formatting new text. To apply character formats to existing text, you must first highlight the section of text to be formatted. Then you specify the character-formatting commands that are available on the Format menu or the toolbar.

To apply paragraph formats to an existing paragraph, the cursor must be positioned in the paragraph you want to format. If you want to format two or more paragraphs at a time, you must highlight part or all of the paragraphs to which the formats will apply. Then you select paragraph format options from the toolbar or from the Paragraph dialog box of the Format menu.

GUIDED PRACTICE

APPLYING CHARACTER FORMATS TO EXISTING TEXT

In this exercise you will open the STARTUP2.WPS document that you created earlier. You need to create a title line for the start-up procedures, then you will apply character formats to the title line and the first sentence of the first paragraph.

1. Choose Open Existing Files from the File menu.

2. Locate the file name STARTUP2.WPS on your Student Data Disk. Double-click the file name to open the document.

3. If necessary, click an insertion point in front of the first word in the body of the STARTUP2.WPS document, then type **STARTUP PROCEDURES.** Press the Enter key twice to create a title line and a blank line space between the title and the body of the document.

4. Highlight the title by clicking the pointer in the selection bar next to the title line.

   The character formats you select next will be applied to all the characters that are highlighted.

5. Choose Font And Style from the Format menu. The Font And Style dialog box opens.

6. Select 14 on the Font Size list box.

7. Click the Bold check box to select the bold type style. Notice how the sample changes to reflect your choices. The Font And Style dialog box should look like the one shown in Figure 10-1.

8. Click on the OK button or press the Enter key to return to the document window. The characters in the title have increased in size to 14 points and now appear in bold type style.

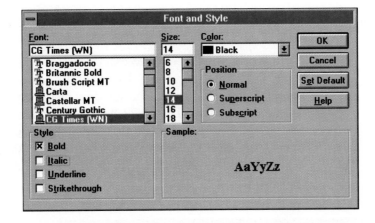

9. Click an insertion point to the left of the first character in the first sentence of the first paragraph. Use the shift-click method to highlight the sentence. Then do the following.

   a. Click an insertion point in front of the **T** in **To.**

   b. Hold down the (Shift) key.

   c. Click an insertion point after the period at the end of the sentence.

   d. Release the (Shift) key.

10. Click the Italic button on the toolbar (or press (Ctrl)+I) to format the characters in the highlighted sentence in italic type style. Click an insertion point in the title line. Compare your document with the one shown in Figure 10-2.

11. Save the document under the current name STARTUP2.WPS, and close the document.

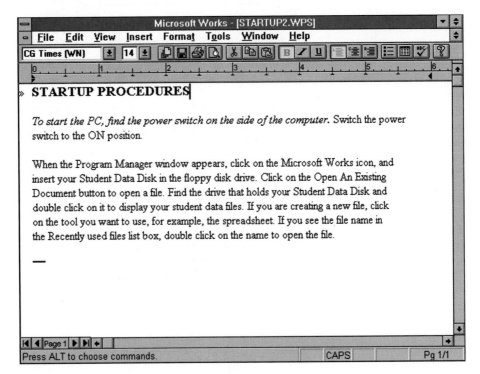

SWITCHING BETWEEN OPEN DOCUMENTS

In Works you can have several document windows open at the same time. Each time you open a document, its name is listed on the Window menu. Figure 10-3 shows the Window menu with both the ELECBIL3.WPS document and the STARTUP2.WPS document open. The document opened last is displayed foremost on the screen. To switch to another open document, you select the document name from the Window menu. Works places a checkmark beside the name on the menu and displays the document on your screen.

SPLITTING THE DOCUMENT WINDOW

The Window menu offers another valuable tool. By selecting the Split command, a shaded line appears across the document screen and your mouse pointer changes to the ADJUST pointer. When you have moved the ADJUST pointer to wherever you want the document window to be split, click the mouse button or press the (Enter) key. The document window will have two panes, as shown in Figure 10-4. When you want to close the panes, move your mouse pointer to the top of the ruler over the second pane. The ADJUST pointer will return. Drag the ADJUST pointer onto the first ruler (or just double-click with the ADJUST pointer), and the document window will no longer be split.

FIGURE 10-3
All open documents are listed on the Window menu.

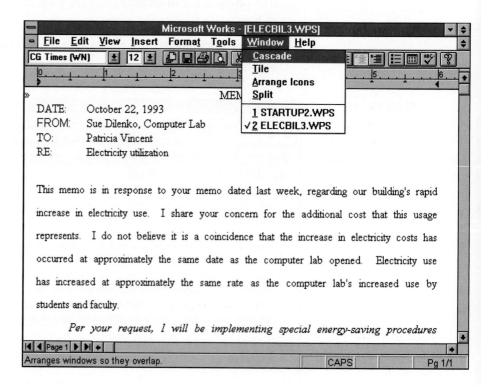

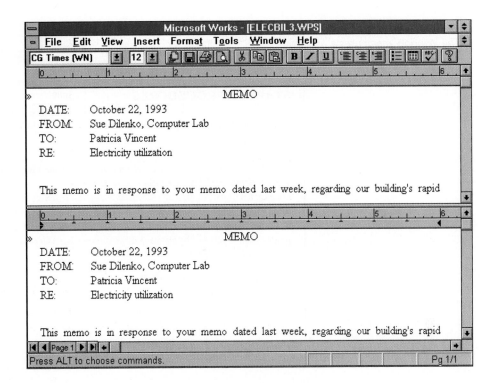

FIGURE 10-4

By using the ADJUST pointer, you can display two parts of your document at once.

Splitting the document into panes allows you to see two parts of your document at one time. Notice that each pane has its own scroll bar and arrows. If you are copying text from the end of your document to the beginning, for example, you can fill one pane with the beginning of your document and the other with the end. This will make your copying easier.

GUIDED PRACTICE

APPLYING PARAGRAPH FORMATS TO EXISTING TEXT

In this exercise you will change paragraph formatting in the STARTUP2.WPS and the ELECBIL3.WPS documents. You will also practice using the Window menu to switch between two open documents.

1. If necessary, close any document window that is open.

2. Choose Open Existing File from the File menu to display the Open dialog box.

3. Locate and open the ELECBIL3.WPS document.

4. Repeat step 2.

5. Locate and open the STARTUP2.WPS document. Even though you cannot see the ELECBIL3.WPS document, it is in RAM and its name is listed on the Window menu.

Because you opened STARTUP2.WPS last, this document window is displayed on your screen. In the following steps you will practice switching from one document to the other.

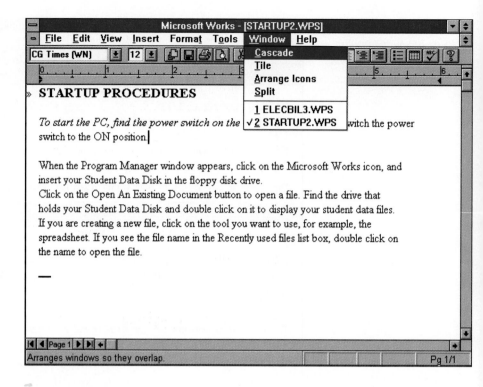

6. Open the Window menu. Both document file names are listed in the bottom section of the menu. The file name of the current document (STARTUP2.WPS) is checked, as shown in Figure 10-5.

7. Click the file name ELECBIL3.WPS and release the mouse button. The document ELECBIL3.WPS is now displayed on your screen. If you open the Window menu now, you will see that ELECBIL3.WPS is now checked and STARTUP2.WPS is no longer checked.

8. Click an insertion point anywhere in the first paragraph of the ELECBIL3.WPS document, press the mouse button, and drag to the second paragraph to highlight a part of both paragraphs. It is not necessary for both paragraphs to be highlighted completely. If any part of a paragraph is highlighted, Works will apply the paragraph formats you select.

9. Select the Paragraph dialog box from the Format menu and click on the Breaks And Spacing tab—because you have highlighted more than one paragraph, the Line Spacing boxes are empty. Type **2**. Click on another text box and the sample changes to show a double-spaced paragraph. Click on OK.

10. Return to the Paragraph dialog box. Click on the Indents And Alignment tab. Click the Justified button twice to return to the document window or click on OK. (Depending on the font you are using, the paragraph may not look justified on screen. It will look justified, however, in Print Preview.)

11. Click anywhere in the document to deselect the highlighted text.

In the next step you will scroll through the ELECBIL3.WPS document to see the format changes. You will notice that, since you formatted for double spacing, there is too much space between the paragraphs.

12. Scroll through the document to review the format changes you have just made to the ELECBIL3.WPS document. Click an insertion point in the blank space between paragraphs, then press the Del key once.

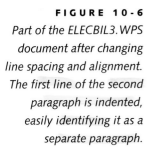

13. Click an insertion point at the beginning of the second paragraph. Part of the ELECBIL3.WPS text is shown in Figure 10-6.

14. Save the changes to ELECBIL3.WPS, using the keyboard shortcut Ctrl+S.

15. Select STARTUP2.WPS from the Window menu.

16. Select the title (which Works identifies as a paragraph) **STARTUP PROCEDURES** by clicking an insertion point anywhere in the paragraph.

17. Click the Center A Paragraph button on the toolbar. The title is now centered.

18. Use the keyboard command Ctrl+S to save the changes to STARTUP2.WPS.

19. Close both document windows.

FIGURE 10-6

Part of the ELECBIL3.WPS document after changing line spacing and alignment. The first line of the second paragraph is indented, easily identifying it as a separate paragraph.

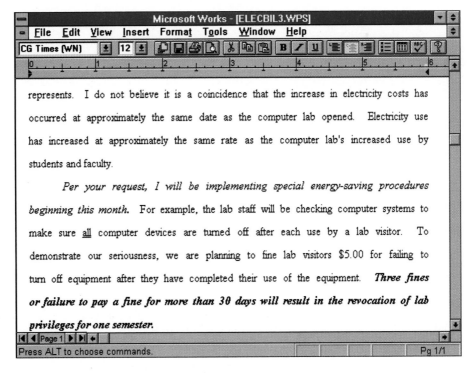

PRACTICE APPLICATIONS

1. Open the CLOSEUP.WPS document on your Student Data Disk.

2. Format the title MEMORANDUM in bold and in 14-point type size.

3. Set a tab stop so that all the heading entries (the date, Sue Dilenko, and so on) begin at 0.75" from the left margin. Use the Backspace key to delete any extra tabs.

4. Justify the three paragraphs in the body of the memo. (Again depending on the font you are using, the text may not appear justified on the screen. Print preview, however, would show the text justified.)

5. In the third paragraph of the memo, apply bold type style to the phrase **please be conscientious.**

6. Save the document as CLOSEUP2.WPS.

7. Close the document window.

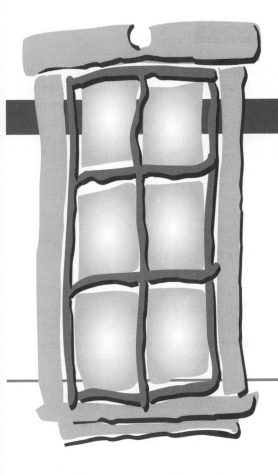

LESSON 11

USING DOCUMENT FORMATS

After completing this lesson you will be able to do the following:

- *Explain how document formatting differs from character and paragraph formatting.*
- *Change the top, bottom, left, and right margins in a document.*
- *Change the paper size used for printing a document.*

FORMATTING A DOCUMENT IN WORKS

In Works, document formatting options apply to all paragraphs and all pages within a document file. The procedures used to format a new and an existing document are the same. You select format options for an entire document in the Page Setup dialog box, which is displayed when you choose Page Setup from the File menu. You set margins in the Margins tab dialog box, the default tab when you open the Page Setup dialog box. Figures 11-1a and b show two of the Page Setup tab dialog boxes.

GUIDED PRACTICE

APPLYING DOCUMENT FORMATS

In this exercise you will change the top margin of the ELECBIL3.WPS memo to 2 inches and the right and left margins to 1 inch. Then you will change the STARTUP2.WPS document. This text is to be printed several times and pasted onto 3- by 5-inch cards that will be placed next to each computer system station in the lab. Therefore, you need to change the document margins to conform to the width of the cards.

1. If necessary, open STARTUP2.WPS and ELECBIL3.WPS. Make sure that ELECBIL3.WPS is the currently displayed document.

FIGURE 11-1

(a) The Margins tab dialog box and (b) the Source, Size And Orientation tab dialog box apply document formatting.

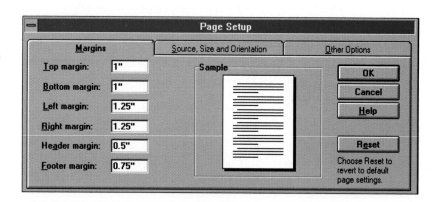

2. Choose Page Setup from the File menu to display the Page Setup dialog box. Some selections in the Page Setup dialog box depend on the printer selected in the Printer Setup command.

3. If necessary, click on the Source, Size And Orientation tab. Select 8½ x 11 in. from the Paper Size list box, and Portrait from the Orientation area, as shown in Figure 11-1b.

4. Click the Margins tab.

5. If necessary, double-click in the Left Margin text box to highlight it; then type **1** to specify a 1-inch left margin (the " measurement is optional).

6. Select the Right Margin text box; then type **1** to specify a 1-inch right margin.

7. Select the Top Margin text box; then type **2** to specify a 2-inch top margin.

8. Compare your Document dialog box with the one shown in Figure 11-2.

9. Press the [Enter] key once to close the Page Setup dialog box and return to the document window. Notice that the right-margin marker has moved to the 6.5" position on the ruler, as shown in Figure 11-3.

10. Save the completed document as ELECBIL4.WPS.

11. Select STARTUP2.WPS from the Window menu.

12. Choose Page Setup from the File menu to display the Page Setup dialog box.

13. If necessary, click the Margins tab to open the Margins tab dialog box.

14. Change the left margin to 0.5" by highlighting the Left Margin text box and typing **0.5**.

15. Change the top margin to 0.5", the right margin to 4", and the bottom margin to 0.5". Notice how the sample page has changed.

16. Click OK to close the Page Setup dialog box.

FIGURE 11-2
The Document dialog box after setting 1-inch left and right margins and a 2-inch top margin.

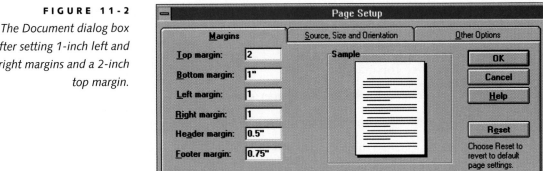

FIGURE 11-3

The document window after changing the margin settings. Notice the Right-Margin marker at the 6.5" tick mark on the ruler.

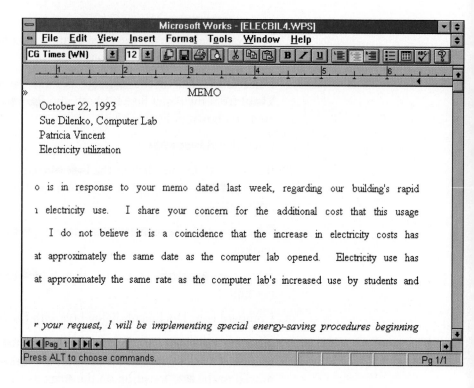

17. Choose Print Preview from the File menu to see how the document would print. Click the Cancel button to return to the document window.

18. Save the document as STARTUP3.WPS, then print the document.

19. Close the STARTUP3.WPS document.

20. Print ELECBIL4.WPS, then close the document.

PRACTICE APPLICATIONS

1. Open the document CLOSING.WPS, stored on your Student Data Disk.

2. Set new margins as follows:

   a. Left margin: 1.5"

   b. Right margin: 0.75"

   c. Top margin: 1.5"

3. Select the 8½ x 14 in. paper size (legal size).

4. Preview the document displayed on legal-size paper.

6. Change the page size to 8½ x 11 in.

7. Save the document as CLOSING2.WPS, then print the document.

CHAPTER REVIEW

Procedures differ for formatting new and existing text. Character and paragraph formatting are applied to existing text by first selecting the text and then specifying the formatting. To format new text, the formatting options are specified first, then the text is entered.

The Font And Style dialog box and toolbar are used to specify character formats. The Paragraph dialog box, toolbar, and ruler are used to specify paragraph formats. The Page Setup dialog box is used to specify formats for the entire document.

The Window menu offers a quick way to switch between open documents and to split a document window into panes.

REVIEW QUESTIONS

TRUE-FALSE

Write your answers on a sheet of paper.

1. In Works, you alter the appearance of characters by selecting paragraph formatting options.

2. To format existing characters, you must first highlight the characters, then select the formatting options that you want to apply.

3. Character formats apply to selected characters in a document, whereas paragraph formats apply to an entire document.

4. You specify character formats by selecting options from the File menu.

5. You specify paragraph formats by selecting options from the Window menu.

6. You select paragraph and document formatting options from the same menu.

7. You can use the File menu to specify formats that apply to an entire document, such margin settings.

8. To apply the underline type style to an existing word in a paragraph, you first highlight the word and then choose Underline from the Font And Style dialog box.

9. You can change document margins by using text boxes displayed in the Page Setup dialog box.

10. To center an existing paragraph, you must first delete the text of the paragraph, then select the Center Align button from the toolbar, and finally center the paragraph.

SHORT-ANSWER QUESTIONS

1. Consider that a word appears both in an existing document and in a document that you are about to type. In both documents, you want to apply the bold type style to the word. Describe the different procedures you would follow to format the word in bold in each of the documents.

2. From a procedural standpoint, how are character formatting and paragraph formatting similar? How are they different?

3. What is the difference between justified text and left-aligned text?

4. If the page size of a document is 8½- by 11 inches and you want text lines that are 5½ inches wide with equal left and right margins, how would you calculate the left and right margin settings?

5. If you want to print text on 8½- by 14-inch paper so that all text starts 1½ inches from the top of each page and appears 2 inches from the left and right edges of the paper, how should you specify page size and top, left, and right margins?

LESSON APPLICATIONS

1. Open a new word-processing document, then open the Format menu. Examine each item on the menu, and determine whether the menu item performs character or paragraph formatting. If a menu item applies character formatting, explain why this is so. In other words, why doesn't the item apply paragraph formatting? If the menu item applies paragraph formatting, explain why this is so.

2. Open the MYTEXT2.WPS document that you created in Chapter 6, Lesson Applications, step 2. At the end of the existing text, enter the following paragraph. Before you begin entering the new text, specify that the text will be justified and double spaced. As you enter text, format the phrase **as many times as you wish** in italic. Also underline the last sentence.

   Another advantage of a word processor is the capability of printing a document as many times as you want to. When a document has been stored on a disk, you can recall and print it at any time. You can also print multiple copies of a document or print selected pages of a document.

   After you have entered this paragraph, preview the document, then save it as MYTEXT3.WPS.

3. In MYTEXT3.WPS, format the phrase **at any time** in bold type. Then change the format of all paragraphs to single spacing.

4. Change the top margin of MYTEXT3.WPS to 0.5" and the left and right margins to 2.5". Preview the document, then print it. Save the newly formatted document as MYTEXT 4.WPS.

5. Using your mouse pointer, hold the arrow over the first icon on the toolbar. After a moment the name of the icon will appear. Continue the process until you have displayed the names for all the icons.

6. Split the document window into panes. Use each pane's scroll bars to arrange the text so that the first paragraph is in the top pane, and the last paragraph is in the bottom pane. Close the document.

CHAPTER APPLICATIONS

1. Find a page in a news magazine, journal, or book that you believe is attractively formatted. The contents of the page you choose should be in a single-column format. Using Works, enter the contents of the page and duplicate the format as closely as possible. Save the document under a name of your choice. Print the document and compare it with the original.

2. Use Works to enter two or three paragraphs of a term paper that you have already completed using a typewriter. Format the document more attractively than was possible when you typed the document originally. Attempt to use the footnoting features in Works to create any footnotes that appear in your original term paper. (The Works Help system provides step-by-step instructions for creating and formatting footnotes.)

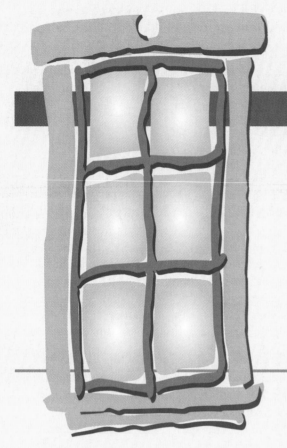

CHAPTER 5

PRODUCING DOCUMENTS

OVERVIEW

The word-processing features you studied in the previous chapters are useful in preparing simple documents that require only basic formatting. However, Works provides many other capabilities to enhance the usefulness and appearance of your documents.

In this chapter you will learn to use advanced formatting capabilities, including the creation of headers, footers, and page numbers for documents. You will also learn how to use the spell-checking feature of Works.

CONTENTS

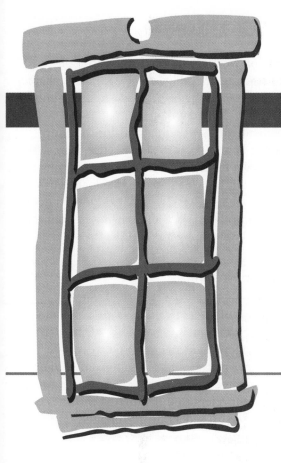

PARAGRAPH INDENTS

OBJECTIVES

After completing this lesson you will be able to do the following:

- *Explain the difference between paragraph indents and margins.*

- *Explain the differences between an indent, a first-line indent, a right indent, and a hanging indent.*

- *Use margin markers to set left, right, and first-line indents.*

KEY WORDS

In this lesson you will learn the meaning of the following terms:

bullets	*left indent*	*right indent*
first-line indent	*margin marker*	
hanging indent	*paragraph indent*	

SING FIRST-LINE AND HANGING INDENTS

You have already used several of Works' paragraph formatting features by setting tab stops, paragraph alignment, and line spacing. In this chapter you will learn how to use the margin markers on the ruler to apply another kind of paragraph formatting known as indents.

When you begin a new document, you set the margins for the entire document in the Page Setup dialog box. (Default margin settings are 1 inch for top and bottom margins and 1.25 inches for left and right margins.) The left ▶ and right ◀ **margin markers** on the ruler indicate the document's left and right margin settings. This white space does not appear in a document window, but you can see it in print preview and when you print the document.

PARAGRAPH INDENTS

Paragraph indents are the amount of space by which text is indented from the left or right inside edge of a document's margins. All lines of these paragraphs are indented. Paragraph indents are used to set one or more paragraphs apart from other paragraphs in the document. For example, a paragraph might be indented on both the left and right to indicate that it is a quotation. **Left indent** refers to indenting all the lines of text on the left side; **right indent** refers to indenting all the lines on the right side. Left and right margin markers can also be dragged along the ruler to create indents for selected paragraphs.

You set a **first-line indent** to indent only the first line of each selected paragraph (or paragraphs that will be typed after you make the setting). When a first-line indent is set, you do not have to use the Tab key to indent the first line of each new paragraph as you type—the insertion point automatically positions itself each time you create a new paragraph by pressing the Enter key. The left margin marker is made up of two small triangles that can be dragged independently. The position of the top triangle determines where the first line of a paragraph begins. The position of the bottom triangle determines where all the other lines of the paragraph begin. If you want the first line to be indented (as this paragraph is indented), drag the top triangle along the ruler to the right of the bottom triangle, as shown in Figure 12-1.

HANGING INDENTS

A **hanging indent** is another kind of first-line indent that is useful when you are typing itemized or numbered lists. When you use a hanging indent, the first line of a paragraph starts to the left of the rest of the lines of text in the paragraph. A hanging indent format makes it easier for the reader to locate the beginning of each item in a list of items, especially when numbers or **bullets** (special characters such as *, •, •, and ■) are used. To set a hanging indent, first drag both triangles of the left margin marker to the

FIGURE 12-1

The ruler is set for a first-line indent. Notice that the top triangle of the margin marker is on the 0.5" tick mark, and the bottom triangle of the margin marker is on the 0" tick mark. (The Quick Formats tab dialog box in the Paragraph dialog box can also be used to create a first-line indent of 0.5".)

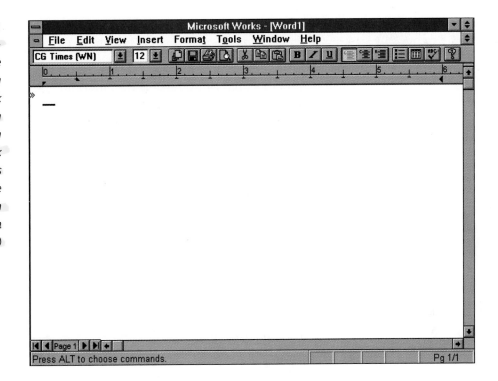

position on the ruler where you want all lines except the first line of the paragraph to begin. Then drag the top triangle of the margin marker to the left of the bottom triangle, as shown in Figure 12-2. If you do not want the first line of a paragraph to start to the left of the other lines in a paragraph that are set for a hanging indent, you can use the Tab key to start the first line where the bottom triangle is positioned.

FIGURE 12-2

This ruler is set to format paragraphs with hanging indents. Notice that the top triangle of the left margin marker is on the 0" tick mark and the bottom triangle is on the 0.5" tick mark.

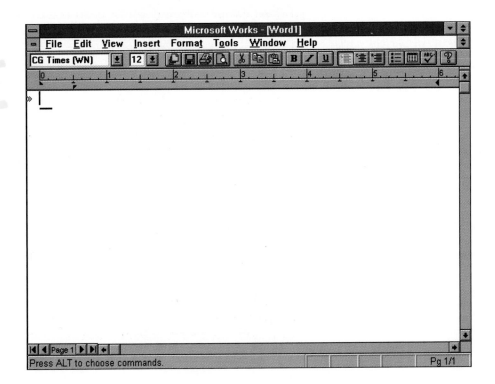

In this exercise you will apply additional formats to paragraphs in a report that has already been saved. This report provides details about the use of lab resources for the first six months of the lab's operations. Although the body of the report has been entered and saved to a file named REPORT1.WPS, the report still needs additional formatting.

1. If necessary, start Works, then open the file REPORT1.WPS on your Student Data Disk.

2. Take a few moments to scroll through this document and note its formatting.

3. Return to the top of the document.

4. Click an insertion point anywhere in the paragraph that begins with **1. To determine hardware utilization.**

5. Drag to highlight part of the text in this paragraph, all of the next paragraph, and part of the paragraph that begins with **3. To provide additional material.**

6. Drag the left margin marker (composed of two triangles) to the 0.5" tick mark on the ruler. At this point, your document window should look similar to the one shown in Figure 12-3.

7. Point to the top triangle of the left margin marker and drag it to the 0" tick mark on the ruler. Click anywhere in the document to deselect the

FIGURE 12-3

After step 6, your document window should look similar to the one shown here.

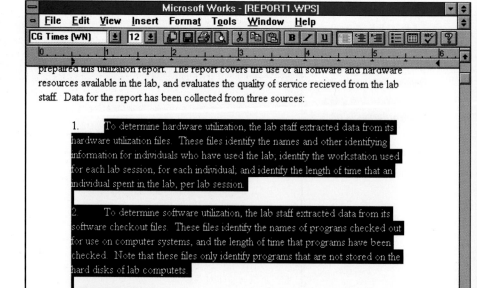

highlighted text. Your document window should look similar to the one shown in Figure 12-4 (when the insertion point is in one of these three paragraphs formatted for hanging indents).

8. Click an insertion point in the line that begins * **Of the 320 question-naires** and drag to highlight this paragraph and the next six (all begin with an asterisk). The last paragraph you are to select begins with * **The Computer Tutor.**

9. Drag the left margin marker to the 0.75" tick mark on the ruler to indent the selected paragraphs ¾ inch from the left margin.

10. Drag the top triangle of the left margin marker to the 0.5" tick mark, so that the first line of each selected paragraph starts at this point. Do not deselect the highlighted paragraphs.

11. Drag the right margin marker to the 5.25" tick mark to set a right indent of ¾ inch.

12. Click to deselect the highlighted text, then review the appearance of the new format settings.

13. Scroll to the paragraph that begins * **Forty-three percent.**

14. Format the three remaining paragraphs that begin with an asterisk. Use the skills you have learned to duplicate the settings you created in the previous paragraphs. Your screen display of these paragraphs should look similar to the one shown in Figure 12-5.

15. Save the document as REPORT2.WPS.

16. Close the document window.

FIGURE 12-4

After step 7, your document window should look similar to the one shown here.

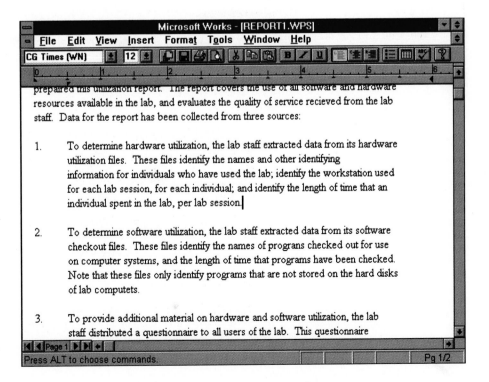

FIGURE 12-5

After completing step 14, your screen display of the last three paragraphs with hanging indents should look similar to the one shown here.

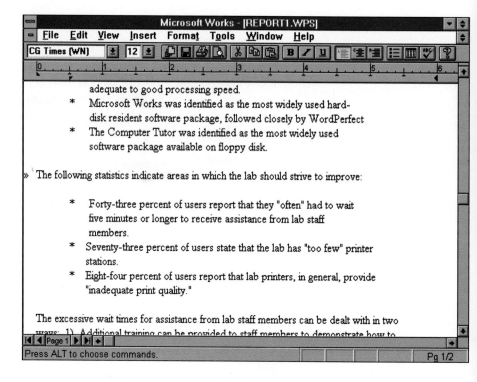

PRACTICE APPLICATIONS

1. Open the RULES.WPS document and format all of the numbered paragraphs for hanging indents, so that the numbers in the first line of each paragraph begin at the 0" tick mark and the lines of text begin at the 0.5" tick mark.

2. Preview the changes. Save the changes as NEWRULES.WPS, then close the document.

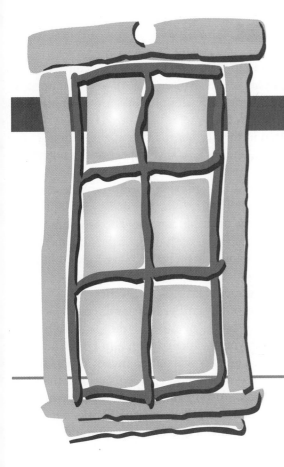

LESSON 13

HEADERS, FOOTERS, AND PAGE BREAKS

OBJECTIVES

After completing this lesson you will be able to do the following:

- *Format a document with headers and footers.*
- *Eliminate headers and footers from the first page of a document.*
- *Identify and delete automatic page breaks and insert manual page breaks.*

KEY WORDS

In this lesson you will learn the meaning of the following terms:

automatic page break   *header*
footer   *manual page break*

USING HEADERS AND FOOTERS

Formal documents that print on more than one page may include a header and page numbers. A **header** is one or more lines of text that appear at the top of every page of a document. A header provides a way of identifying all pages that belong to a single document.

A page number can be inserted in the header of a document or in a separate footer. A **footer** is one or more lines of text that appear at the bottom of each page of a document.

Most word processors have options that allow you to specify the contents of a header and footer one time. Then the word processor will print the header and/or footer on each page of the document. The program will also automatically print the page number on each page of the document. In Works you specify standard headers and footers in the Headers And Footers dialog box, shown in Figure 13-1, which is displayed when you choose Headers And Footers from the View menu.

You can quickly add information to standard headers and footers by using header and footer codes. For instance, enter **&d** in the Header Or Footer dialog box to add the date to your header or footer. In Figure 13-1, this date code is added to the header. (Works will automatically center the date.) Since the date code is linked to your computer system's clock, the date in the header is automatically updated. Also in Figure 13-1, the page-number code **&p** is entered in the footer. When this code is entered, Works automatically numbers the pages of the document and makes page-numbering changes.

If you do not want a header or footer to print on the first page (the title page) of a document, you can select the No Header On 1st Page or No Footer On 1st Page check boxes, shown in Figure 13-1. When these boxes are checked, the page number 1 also does not print on the first page of your document (but the page number 2 does print on the second page).

Works also offers another way to add headers and footers to your document. By selecting the Use Header And Footer Paragraphs option from the Headers And Footers dialog box, Works creates header and footer paragraphs, as shown in Figure 13-2. Notice that Works has added a new kind of page-number code to the footer paragraph. Creating header and footer paragraphs offers the opportunity of adding text to your headers and footers, as well as a drawing or other object.

Another advantage of header and footer paragraphs is that they can be formatted like any text would be. As with standard headers and footers,

FIGURE 13-1

Use the Headers And Footers dialog box to enter text that is to appear at the top of all pages or at the bottom of all pages of the document named in the title bar.

Headers and Footers	
Header: &d	**OK**
Footer: &p	**Cancel**
☐ No header on 1st page ☐ Use header and	**Help**
☐ No footer on 1st page footer paragraphs	

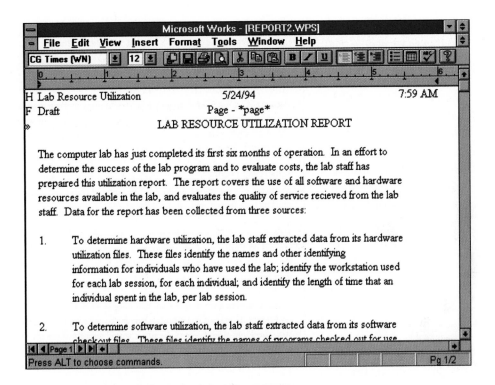

you can use header and footer paragraphs separately. If you do not want a header, do not type any text in the header paragraph and remove the date symbol. If you do not want a footer, do not type in any text and remove the page-number symbol from the footer paragraph (or paste it to the header—you can cut and paste between header and footer paragraphs just like you would with any paragraph).

SETTING AUTOMATIC AND MANUAL PAGE BREAKS

Works automatically determines where a new page begins based on the settings you specify for top and bottom margins in the Page Setup dialog box. When all the lines that can fit on one page of a document have been typed, Works inserts an **automatic page break**, indicated by a chevron (»), as shown in Figure 13-3a. Occasionally you may find it necessary to change the position of an automatic page break in a document. For example, you would not want to print a document with a paragraph heading at the bottom of a page (as shown in Figure 13-3a), separated from its related paragraph.

You cannot delete an automatic page break, although by clicking an insertion point before the paragraph heading and pressing the Enter key to enter blank lines you can push the paragraph heading to the top of the next page. A better method, however, is to force the paragraph heading to the next page by inserting a **manual page break**. Insert a manual page break by moving the insertion point to the beginning of the line where you want the new page to begin, then choosing Page Break from the Insert menu (or press Ctrl+Enter). Works displays a manual page-break marker, shown in Figure 13-3b, by creating a dotted line across the page.

FIGURE 13-3

(a) If the document in this window is printed with an automatic page break, the heading MEETING TIMES will print on one page and the related paragraph that follows will print on the next page. (b) If a manual page break is inserted, the heading MEETING TIMES will be forced to print on the same page with its related paragraph.

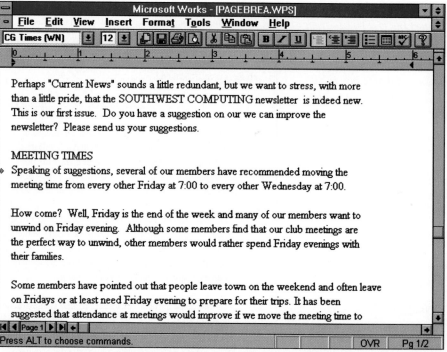

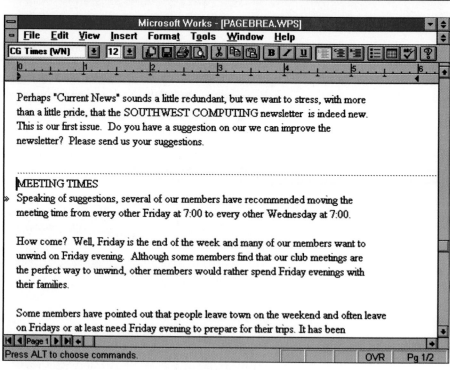

SETTING HEADERS AND FOOTERS

In this exercise you will practice specifying headers and footers for an existing document. You will also look for automatic page breaks in the document window, as well as in print preview, and practice inserting manual page breaks.

1. Open the REPORT2.WPS document, if necessary.

2. Choose Headers And Footers from the View menu. Select Use Header And Footer Paragraphs, if necessary, and press Enter to exit the Headers And Footers dialog box. Click the insertion point in the header paragraph. Notice that in the header paragraph the insertion point is positioned at the left margin, a center-aligned tab stop is set at the center point between the margin markers, and a right-aligned tab stop is set at the right margin. These are the default settings.

3. Type **Lab Resource Utilization**, press the Tab key, and press Ctrl+; (semicolon) to insert today's date. Press Tab again and press Ctrl+Shift+; (semicolon) to insert the current time at the right tab symbol. Your header paragraph should resemble the one in Figure 13-2.

4. Click your insertion point in the footer paragraph to the right of the **F**.

5. Type **Draft**. Your footer should resemble the one in Figure 13-2.

6. Print the current version of REPORT2.WPS. Notice that the information you typed in the header and footer paragraphs appears on each page.

7. Open the Headers And Footers dialog box. Select No Header On 1st Page and No Footer On 1st Page. Print the current version of REPORT2.WPS.

8. Scroll through the document window to identify automatic page breaks. Find the list item that begins ***Sixty-nine percent of users**. Click an insertion point in front of the asterisk. You want to force this line to the top of the next page. Choose Page Break from the View menu (or press Ctrl+Enter). Again the text in your document may break differently depending on the font you are using.

9. Choose Print Preview to preview the pages of the document. Notice that in print preview there is no header or footer on the first page. However, when you click the Next button, you will see header and footer information in the top and bottom margins of page 2, as you specified. Click the magnifying glass to make sure that the second page is numbered correctly with the number 2.

10. If necessary, double-click the magnifying glass to return to the initial preview window. Click on the Cancel button to return to the document window.

11. Save the document as REPORT3.WPS.

12. Print one copy of the document and review the printed report.

13. Close the REPORT3.WPS document.

PRACTICE APPLICATIONS

Complete the following exercises. Some exercises ask you to answer one or more questions. Write a brief answer to these questions on a sheet of paper.

1. Open the NEWRULES.WPS document stored on your Student Data Disk. Explain how the current header and footer will appear when printed. Will the header and footer print on the first page (title page) of the document? What are two different ways of determining this?

2. Click on the Use Header And Footer paragraphs check box in the Headers And Footers dialog box. Click on OK. How did the header and footer change? Create a new header and footer for the document by opening the Headers And Footers dialog box. Type **&p** in the Header box and **&d** in the footer box. Press (Enter). Click on Print Preview to examine the new header and footer. Where does the date appear on the previewed page?

3. Scroll through the NEWRULES.WPS document. To prevent the last paragraph from appearing on a page by itself, insert a manual page break before the second-to-last paragraph in the document. Save the changes to NEWRULES.WPS and close the document.

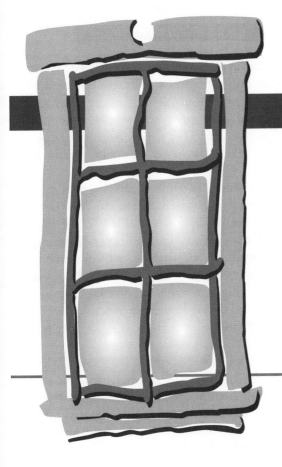

FINDING AND
REPLACING TEXT

OBJECTIVES

After completing this lesson you will be able to do the following:

- *Use the Find dialog box to search for a specified text string within a document.*

- *Explain the difference between the Match Whole Word Only and Match Case check boxes that are available in the Find dialog box.*

- *Use the Replace dialog box to locate a specified text string and replace the string, either selectively or globally.*

- *Explain the difference between a selective replacement and a global replacement.*

KEY WORDS

In this lesson you will learn the meaning of the following terms:

global replacement   *text string*
selective replacement

USING THE FIND DIALOG BOX TO SEARCH FOR TEXT

When editing or formatting a document, you might occasionally want to jump to a particular word or phrase within the document. For instance, suppose you want to review the first list of asterisked items in the lab resource utilization report. You could scroll down until you find the first paragraph that begins with an asterisk. However, with long documents, scrolling through multiple pages of text can be time consuming and is unnecessary.

Most word processors, including Works, provide a search capability that you can use to locate a **text string**—a particular character, word, or phrase within a document. When you instruct Works to search for a text string, the search begins at the position of the cursor and continues through the entire document. When a text string is found, it is highlighted and the search is discontinued until you give instructions either to continue or end the search.

In Works you specify a search by choosing Find from the Edit menu. When you choose this option, the Find dialog box, as shown in Figure 14-1, appears. You use the Find What text box to enter the text string that you want to find.

The Find dialog box has two check boxes: Match Whole Word Only and Match Case. Use the Match Whole Word Only check box when you want Works to ignore partial matches. For example, when this check box is not selected, a search for the text string **report** would also find other words that contain this string, such as **reported** and **reporting**. On the other hand, when you select the Match Whole Word Only check box, a search for the word **report** ignores longer words that contain this text string.

If you want to limit a search for a text string with specific upper- or lowercase letters, you can turn on the Match Case check box. For example, if Match Case is turned on when you begin a search for the word **report**, Works ignores words like **Report** and **REPORT** that do not match the specified text string. When Match Case is turned off, **Report** and **REPORT**, as well as **report**, are found.

GUIDED PRACTICE

USING THE FIND DIALOG BOX

In this exercise you will search for the text string **percentage of** in the REPORT3.WPS document. Then you will insert a missing value to complete one of the sentences in the document.

1. Open the REPORT3.WPS document.

FIGURE 14-1

Use the Find dialog box to search a document for a text string.

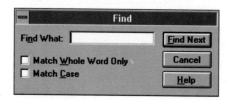

2. If necessary, position the cursor at the top of the document.

3. Choose Find from the Edit menu to display the Find dialog box. If the Find dialog box covers up a part of the screen you want to see during a search, click on the title bar and drag the box to another location.

4. In the Find What text box, type **percentage of** to indicate the text string to be located. You do not need to select either of the check boxes for this search.

5. Click on the Find Next button or press the [Enter] key to start the search. Works highlights the words **percentage of** and waits for you to continue the search or to close the Find dialog box.

6. Click the Cancel button to return to the document.

7. Click an insertion point after the highlighted words **percentage of** and type a space and **78 percent.** to complete the sentence. Your screen should look similar to the one shown in Figure 14-2.

8. Save the document under the current name REPORT3.WPS.

9. Close the document if you are not going to the next section.

USING THE REPLACE DIALOG BOX

In Works you can instruct the program to replace all or selected occurrences of a particular text string by choosing Replace from the Edit menu. Replacing all occurrences of a text string is called a **global replacement**. When you choose this option, the Replace dialog box, as shown in Figure

FIGURE 14-2

After you have completed step 7, your document should look similar to the one shown here.

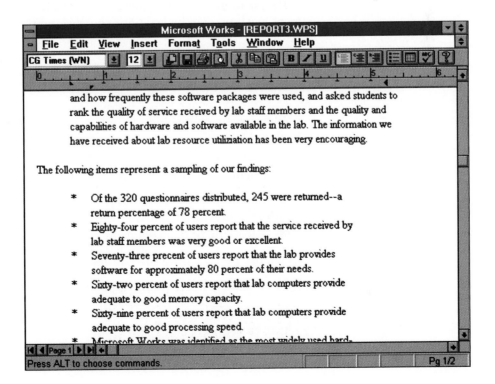

FIGURE 14-3

The Replace dialog box is used to specify both selective and global replacements.

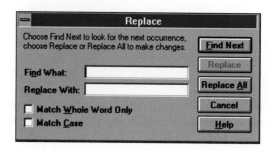

14-3, appears. The Replace dialog box is similar to the Find dialog box shown in Figure 14-1.

When you use the Find dialog box, Works searches a document until it finds the text string in the Find What text box. If you want to replace the found text, you type the replacement text directly into the document. When you use the Replace dialog box, you can type the replacement text in the Replace With text box. If you want to replace the found text with the replacement text, all you have to do is click the Replace button.

Use the Replace button when you want to perform a **selective replacement**. In this case you can examine each text string that is found to determine whether it should remain the same or be replaced with the text you typed in the Replace With text box. Use the Replace All button when you want to perform a global replacement. In this case, Works replaces all occurrences of the text string with the text you typed in the Replace With text box automatically, without asking you to verify each change.

The Match Whole Word Only and Match Case check boxes in the Replace dialog box are used in the same way they are used in the Find dialog box. When you click the Find Next button, Works begins the search at the position of the insertion point and continues until the entire document has been searched or until you click on the Cancel button.

GUIDED PRACTICE

REPLACING TEXT

In this exercise you will perform two replace operations in the text REPORT3.WPS document. First you will do a global replacement of the text string **rank** with the text string **rate**. Then you will do a selective replacement of the text string **users** with the text string **respondents**.

1. If necessary, open the REPORT3.WPS document. If you are continuing from the previous Guided Practice, make sure the insertion point is at the beginning of the document.

2. Choose Replace from the Edit menu to display the Replace dialog box.

3. In the Find What text box, type **rank**.

4. Press the [Tab] key once to position the cursor in the Replace With text box.

5. Type **rate** (the word that will replace the word **rank**).

6. Click on the Replace All button. Works finds and replaces all occurrences. Click Replace All again. Works displays the message box shown in Figure 14-4, meaning that the only occurrence of the word has been replaced.

7. Click on the Close button to close the message box, and then click on the Cancel button to close the Replace dialog box.

To make selective changes in the following steps, it is important that your search begin at the location described in the instructions. The first occurrence your search finds should be the same one described in the instructions.

8. Position the cursor at the beginning of the REPORT3.WPS document.

9. Choose Replace from the Edit menu.

10. In the Find What text box, type **users**.

11. Press the ⌐Tab⌐ key once to position the cursor in the Replace With text box.

12. Type **respondents** (the word that will replace some occurrences of the word **users**).

13. Click on the Find Next button. Your screen display should look similar to the one shown in Figure 14-5.

If you do not see the word **users** highlighted, you may need to drag the dialog box out of the way. After seeing how the word **users** is used in the document, you decide to leave it unchanged and continue the search.

14. Click on the Find Next button to continue the search without making a change.

15. Replace the next six occurrences of the word **users** with the word **respondents**. Each time you click the Replace button, Works will highlight the next occurence of the word **users**.

16. Leave the rest of the occurrences unchanged.

17. When Works returns you to the top of your document, where you began your search, click on the Cancel button to return to your document window.

18. Save the document under the current name REPORT3.WPS and close the document.

FIGURE 14-4

This message box is displayed after you click on the Replace All button after rank has been replaced in step 6.

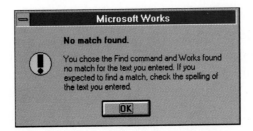

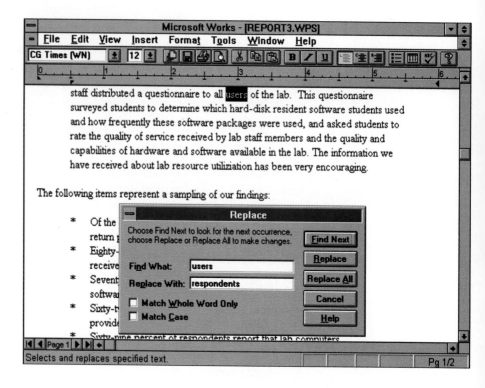

PRACTICE APPLICATIONS

Complete the following exercises. Some exercises ask you to answer one or more questions. Write a brief answer to these questions on a sheet of paper.

1. Open the RULES.WPS document. Search for the text string **1.50**. When the text string is found, click an insertion point after it and type (**or $2.00 for a 3.5" disk**). Save the document as RULESCHA.WPS.

2. Position the cursor in item 8 in the RULESCHA.WPS document. Search for the word **software**. Explain how Works searches through the document. How do you know when Works has found all occurrences of a text string? Close the RULESCHA.WPS document window.

3. Open the STARTUP.WPS document located on your Student Data Disk. Replace all occurrences of the word **ON** (in capital letters only) with the lowercase word **on**. Save the document as REVSTART.WPS, then close the document.

4. Open the REPORT4.WPS document, and replace all occurrences of the word **extracted** with the word **processed**.

5. In the REPORT4.WPS document, find and replace the word **identify** with the word **contain**. Save the document as ALTREPOR.WPS, then close the document.

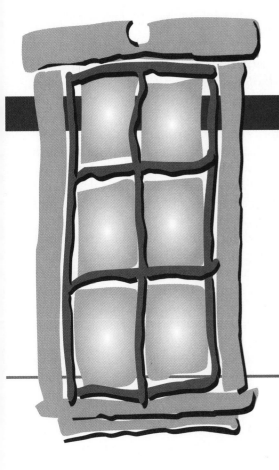

LESSON 15

CHECKING SPELLING AND WORD USAGE

OBJECTIVES

After completing this lesson you will be able to do the following:

- *Use the Works spelling checker to identify and correct spelling, capitalization, and repeated word errors.*
- *Use the Change To text box in the Spelling dialog box.*
- *Explain the differences between and uses for the buttons in the Spelling dialog box.*
- *Explain the limitations of the word processor's spelling checker.*

KEY WORDS

In this lesson you will learn the meaning of the following terms:

custom dictionary
spelling checker

S PELLING-CHECKER FEATURES

Most word processors include a **spelling checker** that helps to identify words that are misspelled. In addition to incorrectly spelled words, the Works spelling checker identifies repeated words, such as the the. It's always a good idea to spell-check a new document; however, keep in mind that spell-checking is not a replacement for careful proofreading. A spelling checker cannot identify a word that is spelled correctly but used incorrectly (such as the word **their** used in place of the word **there** or **too** used in place of **two**).

In Works you can check the spelling of words in an entire document by choosing Spelling from the Tools menu or by clicking the Spelling Checker button on the toolbar. To spell-check only a part of a document (even a single word), you highlight the text you want to check and then choose the Spelling command. When searching an entire document, Works begins its search at the position of the insertion point and continues searching to the end of the document. When Works identifies a possible error, the dialog box shown in Figure 15-1 is displayed. If no errors are identified, the Spelling dialog box is not displayed. Instead, Works displays a message box stating "Spelling finished."

The Spelling dialog box shown in Figure 15-1 allows you to customize the way documents are checked for spelling errors. Select Skip Capitalized Words and words containing capital letters are ignored. When the Always Suggest check box is turned on, Works suggests alternate spellings for a word it does not recognize during a spell-check.

If you use many technical words and proper nouns that are not in the Works dictionary, you can create a customized dictionary by adding these words to your own **custom dictionary**. The custom dictionary is automatically opened and used along with the Works dictionary when you perform a spell-check. You can add words to the custom dictionary during a spell-check by clicking the Add button in the Spelling dialog box.

The contents and use of the Spelling dialog box shown in Figure 15-1 are explained in the following paragraphs.

NOT IN DICTIONARY, REPEATED WORD, IRREGULAR CAPITALIZATION

When Works finds a questionable word, it indicates (in the first line of the dialog box) the kind of problem it has found. In Figure 15-1, Not In Dictionary is identified as a problem with the word **speling**. Works is

FIGURE 15-1

*The Spelling dialog box with **speling** identified as a word that could not be found in the Works dictionary.*

Spelling
Not in Dictionary: speling
Change To: spelling
Suggestions: spelling / spellings / spewing / spieling / spilling
Ignore / Ignore All
Change / Change All
Add / Cancel
Suggest / Help
Skip capitalized words
Always Suggest

suggesting that the word may be misspelled, but it is up to you to decide. Other kinds of problems that may be identified include repeated words and failure to capitalize normally capitalized words.

CHANGE TO

When the Always Suggest check box is selected in the Spelling dialog box, Works suggests a spelling in the Change To text box. This is where you type in a correction if there is no suggestion or if none of the suggestions is right.

SUGGESTIONS

When the Always Suggest check box is selected in the Spelling dialog box, Works suggests other possible spellings for the misspelled word in the list box.

IGNORE

Click the Ignore button to tell Works you do not want to change the spelling of the highlighted word.

IGNORE ALL

Click the Ignore All button to tell Works that you want all occurrences of the highlighted word left unchanged. The spelling checker will ignore all other occurrences of this word in the document.

CHANGE

When the Change button is displayed, you click on it to change the spelling of a word to the way it is spelled in the Change To text box. When repeated words are found (such as **the the**), clicking on the Change button will remove one of the repeated words. Works will display the repeated word in the first line of the dialog box.

CHANGE ALL

Click on the All button to tell Works to change all occurrences of the word identified.

ADD

Click on the Add button to add the highlighted word to the custom dictionary.

SUGGEST

If the Always Suggest check box has been turned off, you can click on the Suggest button to turn it on for a particular highlighted word.

CANCEL

Click on the Cancel button to close the Spelling dialog box before Works has finished a spell-check.

SPELL-CHECKING A DOCUMENT

In this exercise you will use the Works spelling checker to identify and correct misspelled words in the REPORT3.WPS document. For practice only, you will create a custom dictionary, then remove the word you added to the dictionary.

1. Open the REPORT3.WPS document. If necessary, click an insertion point at the beginning of the document so that your spell-check follows the same sequence as the one described in this exercise. (Pressing Ctrl+Home will place the cursor at the top of the document. Pressing Ctrl+End will place the cursor at the end of the document.)

2. Choose Spelling from the Tools menu. As shown in Figure 15-2, Works identifies **prepaired** as a word not in the dictionary and suggests **premiered** as an alternate spelling. Since you want to change the word to **prepared**, you can either type the correct spelling in the Change To text box or double-click on the suggested word. (If necessary, click the Always Suggest box.)

3. Double-click on the word **prepared** in the Suggestions list box. Works replaces **prepaired** with **prepared** and continues with the spell-check.

4. When Works highlights the word **recieved**, type **received** in the text box. Then click on the Change button or press the Enter key to change the spelling in the document and to continue spell-checking.

5. When Works highlights the word **programs** in the text box and suggests the word **programs** as a replacement, click on the Change button or press the Enter key to change **programs** to **programs**.

FIGURE 15-2

Works has highlighted the word **prepaired** *and suggests the word* **premiered** *as a replacement.*

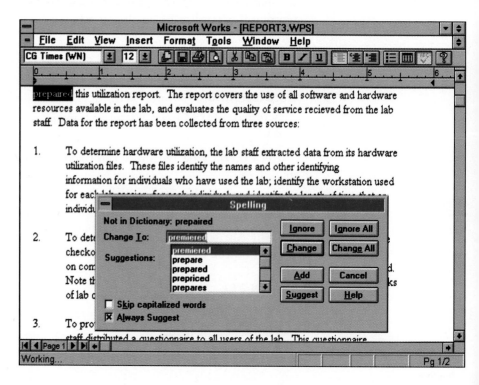

6. Continue spell-checking and making the necessary changes. When the word **matrix** is displayed, click on the Add button to add it to the custom dictionary. Until the word is removed from the custom dictionary, Works will recognize **matrix** as a correctly spelled word in all documents you create in Works.

If you are using a computer in a school lab, remove the word **matrix** from the custom dictionary so that the next student who uses the computer can practice adding it to the dictionary. Directions for removing the word **matrix** from the dictionary are given in the next step.

* CHECK IF AVAILABLE

7. Select Open Existing File from the File menu. In the Directories box of the Open dialog box, select the C:\WINDOWS\MSAPPS\PROOF directory. In the File Name box type CUSTOM.DIC. Press [Enter]. When Works displays the Open File As dialog box, click on the Word Processor button. Works will open CUSTOM.DIC, which is really a list of words. Delete **matrix**. Although you can delete or correct words in CUSTOM.DIC, never add words or change the order of words this way. If you do, Works will be unable to recognize the words.

8. Select Close from the File menu. Works will ask if you want to save your changes to CUSTOM.DIC. Select Yes.

9. Save the document as REPORT5.WPS.

10. Print the document, then close REPORT5.WPS.

PRACTICE APPLICATIONS

1. Open the TEXTFORM.WPS document and spell-check it. Use your judgment about which words to ignore and which words to replace. Do not add any words to the custom dictionary. Save the document as NEWTEXT.WPS, then close it.

2. On a new screen, enter a half page of text from any page in this chapter, then spell-check the document. Use your judgment about which words to ignore and which words to replace. Do not add any words to the custom dictionary. Save the document as PRACSPEL.WPS.

3. If necessary, open the PRACSPEL.WPS document. Choose Help from the menu bar to look up information about using the Works thesaurus. After reading the on-screen Help information, return to the PRACSPEL.WPS document. Highlight a word in the document that you would like to look up in the Works thesaurus. Choose Thesaurus from the Tools menu. Close the PRACSPEL.WPS document without saving any changes.

CHAPTER REVIEW

Professional-looking documents often require extensive formatting, including the specification of additional indents and spacing for selected paragraphs and the creation of headers and footers. Works provides features for specifying these formats.

Most word-processing packages, including the Works word processor, include features to search for and replace text strings in a document. The Find command is used to search for a text string in a document. The Replace command is used to automate the replacement of a text string that occurs several times in a document.

The spelling checker lets you identify repeated words, words with capitalization errors, and misspelled words. Although a spelling checker can suggest alternate spellings, it is up to you to specify the correct spelling.

REVIEW QUESTIONS

TRUE-FALSE

Write your answers on a sheet of paper.

1. You can select paragraph line spacing from the toolbar or from the Format menu.

2. The term **hanging indent** refers to the first line of a paragraph that starts to the right of the rest of the lines of a paragraph.

3. Paragraph indents are set on the ruler with tab stops.

4. A header appears in the top margin of the pages of a document.

5. A page number can be located either in a header or in a footer.

6. You can use the date and time codes to display the current date and time in a header or footer.

7. Text in header and footer paragraphs cannot be formatted like other text is formatted.

8. To specify a selective replacement operation, click on the Replace All button in the Replace dialog box.

9. Clicking on the Add button in the Spelling dialog box adds words to the custom dictionary that are not found in the Works dictionary.

10. All words the spelling checker identifies in the Not In Dictionary line at the top of the Spelling dialog box are misspelled words.

SHORT-ANSWER QUESTIONS

Write a brief answer to these questions on a sheet of paper.

1. What are the two ways you can use to instruct Works to format a paragraph with 1-inch left and right paragraph indents?

2. Without using dialog boxes, how do you instruct Works to indent the first line of a paragraph ½ inch?

3. How do you add the current date to a standard header or footer?

4. What procedures do you use to create a footer that looks like this?

   REPORT 2

   Page 2

5. Consider that you are spell-checking a document and the Works spelling checker identifies the word PageMaker as Not In Dictionary. This word appears several times in the document, and you want to keep the spelling just as it is. What are two ways to prevent the spelling checker from identifying other occurrences of this word?

LESSON APPLICATIONS

1. Open the INDENTS.WPS document on your Student Data Disk. Indent the second, third, and fourth paragraphs 1 inch from the left and right margins. Then create hanging indents for these three numbered paragraphs so that the first line of each paragraph begins at the 0.5" tick mark. Save the document changes under the existing name, then close the document.

2. Open REPORT1.WPS on your Student Data Disk. Type a centered header that reads **Utilization Report**. Include a date at the header's right margin.

3. Spell-check REPORT1.WPS, then find all occurrences of the word **percent**, but don't replace them.

4. In REPORT1.WPS, replace all occurrences of the word Utilization with the word **use**. Save the document as NEWREPOR.WPS, then close the document.

5. Spell-check the document MYTEXT4.WPS, which you created in the Lesson Application for Chapter 7. Save the document as MYTEXT5.WPS.

CHAPTER APPLICATIONS

Complete the following exercises. Some exercises ask you to answer one or more questions. Write a brief answer to these questions on a sheet of paper.

1. Open the document STAFFMEM.WPS on your Student Data Disk. Select the first three paragraphs and apply a ½-inch right indent to these paragraphs. Apply a hanging-indent format to the first line of each numbered paragraph. The first line should start at the left margin and the other lines should start at the 0.5" tick mark. Apply 1½ line spacing to all numbered paragraphs. Make sure the document does not contain a page break in the middle of a numbered paragraph. Save the document as STAFMEM2.WPS.

2. If necessary, open the document STAFMEM2. Spell-check the document, making any corrections and changes you consider necessary. Use the Replace All button to replace the word **file** with the word **database**. Save the document under the current name, then print and proofread the document. Do you find any typographical or spelling errors? If so, explain why the spell-checking operation failed to locate these errors. Also explain whether, in general, you believe it is more efficient to spell check a document before or after you perform a Replace All operation.

CHALLENGE EXERCISES

1. For this exercise you will use the document NEWSLETT.WPS on your Student Data Disk. Eventually, the text in this document will be pasted onto an 8½ by 11-inch sheet of paper that is folded in the middle. The result is a four-page newsletter in which each page is 8½ inches in height and 5½ inches in width. Your job in this exercise is to size the document to create four 5½ by 8½-inch newsletter pages. You will also need to complete the following tasks:

   a. Save the document as NEWSLREV.WPS.

   b. The interview, which appears at the end of the document, must be placed on the second page of the newsletter. The interview must take up the entire second page—no more and no less. You will have to use your judgment and word-processing skills to make this interview fit. You may delete information from the interview if necessary, but first try to use other techniques to make the interview fit.

   c. If the "Current News" article does not fit entirely on the page, move any text that does not fit either to the third or the fourth page of the newsletter. Use your judgment to determine how to do this. Do not delete any material from the "Current News" article.

   d. When you have finished editing the document, spell-check it and create a footer that contains the name of the newsletter and the page number. This footer should appear on each page.

   e. Change the current font (Courier) to CGTimes for the body of the newsletter and use Universe (or another sans serif font available to you) for article headings and subheadings. Format the headings and subheadings in bold and italic. You may want to apply other formats to the document, such as a larger type size for the newsletter title or for headings and subheadings. However, keep in mind that these changes will affect the way the text fits on the page.

   f. Most Works dialog boxes have a Help text button, a quick way to get directions for the specific function you are using. Perform another spelling check on REPORT3.WPS. Before you finish the spell check, click on the Help text button. Read about counting words in Works. How many words are in the Works dictionary?

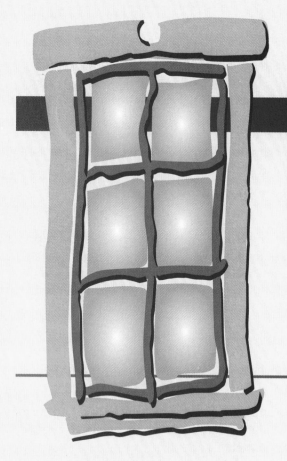

CHAPTER 6

USING STANDARD

DATABASE FEATURES

OVERVIEW

This chapter provides an introduction to a number of the basic features of the Works database program. The chapter begins with a discussion of the structure of a database and explains some of the techniques for managing a database. You will learn how to open a database and identify its components. You will also practice navigating through a database, changing database views, and printing all or selected records in a database.

CONTENTS

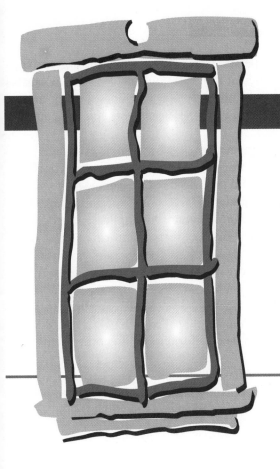

LESSON 16

GETTING STARTED WITH THE DATABASE PROGRAM

OBJECTIVES

After completing this lesson you will be able to do the following:

- *Define the term database management.*
- *Describe the differences between fields, records, and files.*
- *Describe each of the three major functions of a database.*
- *Explain the purpose of sorting records in a database.*
- *Describe the difference between a query and a report.*
- *Name three different ways in which you can view a database.*
- *Navigate through a database in list view.*

KEY WORDS

In this lesson you will learn the meaning of the following terms:

append	*query*
ascending order	*record-selection rules*
database management	*scroll box*
descending order	*sorting*
navigation buttons	

WHAT IS DATABASE MANAGEMENT?

In a company, a manager is a person who is responsible for organizing, keeping track of, and making efficient use of resources. Company resources generally include employees, computers and other machines, money, and even time. When you practice effective time management, you use your time wisely.

Computers can be used as a management tool by helping a manager organize and keep track of stored information. An organized collection of information that can be managed and processed in different ways is called a database. So **database management** refers to techniques for collecting, organizing, processing, and reporting on information. An application program, such as the Works database program, assists users in performing these database management functions.

As you may recall, a database is organized into fields and records. A field is the smallest unit in a database; it contains a piece of information about a person, place, event, or business transaction. The characters XT-1024-5T2 might be an example of information in a field called SERIAL NUMBER. The date 8/13/92 might be an example of information in another field called DATE.

By itself, each field in a database has little meaning. For example, what could the characters XT-1024-5T2 possibly mean if no other related information exists? For fields to have meaning, they must be organized in some way. Consider the following information:

FIELD NAME	FIELD CONTENT (Value or field entry)
ITEM:	COMPUTER SYS
BRAND:	IBM
SERIAL #:	XT-1024-5T2
PURCHASE QUANTITY:	1
DATE:	8/13/92
PURCHASE PRICE:	$1085.25

When the contents of these fields are organized and viewed together, they form a meaningful record. A record, then, is a collection of information that relates to a specific person, thing, or event. Figure 16-1 shows how the information in the previous table looks in the Works form view of one record in a database. The record shown in Figure 16-1 includes fields (brand, serial number, and so on) that describe one item that is owned by an organization.

All of the records for equipment owned by an organization could be contained in an equipment or inventory file. A file is a collection of related records. Some database management programs also use the term database file to refer to a collection of related records. In Works, the terms file, database, and database file mean the same thing.

FIGURE 16-1

A form view of record 1 of the EQUIPME1.WBD database.

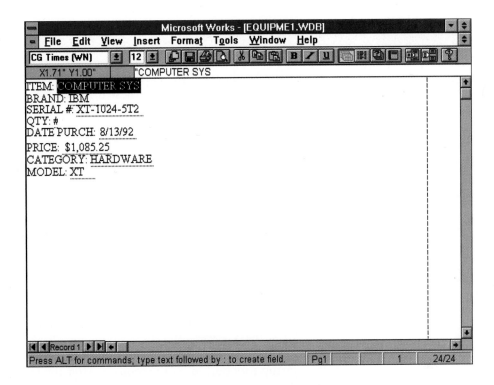

Figure 16-2 shows part of a database file named EQUIPME1.WDB. Each row of information in the list contains one record. The field names are represented in the list as column headings: ITEM, BRAND, SERIAL #, QTY, DATE PURCH, PRICE, CATEGORY, and (if you use your scroll bars) MODEL.

FIGURE 16-2

A list view of some of the records in a database file named EQUIPME1.WDB. Each column heading represents a field name and each row contains one record.

	ITEM	BRAND	SERIAL #	QTY	DATE PURCH	PRICE	CATEG
1	COMPUTER SYS	IBM	XT-1024-5T2	1	8/13/92	$1,085.25	HARDW
2	COMPUTER SYS	IBM	XT-1206-5T3	1	8/13/92	$1,085.25	HARDW
3	MODEM	HAYES	H4775-84S	1	8/13/92	$129.00	HARDW
4	COMPUTER SYS	COMPAQ	C9664-Q54	1	8/13/92	$1,795.28	HARDW
5	COMPUTER SYS	COMPAQ	C9675-Q4	1	8/13/92	$1,795.28	HARDW
6	COMPUTER SYS	COMPAQ	C9676-Q9	1	8/17/92	$1,795.28	HARDW
7	MOUSE	MICROSOFT	C3K699926PN682	1	8/23/92	$68.50	HARDW
8	MOUSE	MICROSOFT	C3K9626PN9261	1	8/23/92	$68.50	HARDW
9	COMPUTER SYS	IBM	XT-1047-5T2	1	8/23/92	$1,012.45	HARDW
10	COMPUTER SYS	BELL	B67269UT09	1	8/26/92	$1,695.25	HARDW
11	COMPUTER SYS	BELL	B67269UT911	1	8/26/92	$1,695.25	HARDW
12	MS-WORKS	MICROSOFT	M69266-86-26	1	8/27/92	$178.25	SOFTW.
13	MS-WORKS	MICROSOFT	M69266-92-45	1	8/27/92	$178.25	SOFTW.
14	MS-WORKS	MICROSOFT	M69266-62-83	1	8/27/92	$178.25	SOFTW.
15	MS-WORKS	MICROSOFT	M69266-92-47	1	8/27/92	$178.25	SOFTW.
16	MS-WORKS	MICROSOFT	M69266-26-46	1	8/27/92	$178.25	SOFTW.
17	PRINTER	EPSON	E9260?T843	1	8/29/92	$329.85	HARDW
18	PRINTER	EPSON	E92702T844	1	8/29/92	$329.85	HARDW
19	WORDPERFECT	WORDPERF	J-6926-2025	1	8/30/92	$385.50	SOFTW.
20	WORDPERFECT	WORDPERF	J-6926-2028	1	8/30/92	$385.50	SOFTW.

DATABASE FUNCTIONS

The Works database program provides many techniques for managing your data. In general, all of these techniques are designed to perform three major functions:

1. Creating and modifying a database.

2. Reorganizing or reordering (changing the appearance of) data in a database.

3. Reporting on the contents of a database.

The following sections explain the database management tasks you can perform with the Works database program.

CREATING AND MODIFYING A DATABASE

You create a new database file by selecting the Database button from the Works Startup box. To return to the Startup box, you can either select Create New File from the File menu in the database program or click on the Startup tool button on the toolbar. After the Database button is selected, Works responds by opening, in form view, a database document window (Data1). To add a field, type the name of the field (up to 15 characters) followed by a colon (:), and then press (Enter). Works displays a Field Size dialog box, as shown in Figure 16-3.

This dialog box is used to specify a width and height for the field you have just named (a field can hold up to 254 characters). If you want a multiline field, enter a number larger than 1 in the Height text box. When you click on the OK button in the Field Size dialog box, the new field name appears, followed by a dotted underline. This is your new field. Continue these steps until you have defined all your database fields. After you have defined the database fields, you can give the new database file a name and save it on a disk.

If you would like to insert a field and format its size in one step, select the Field command from the Insert menu. This command displays the Insert Field dialog box, shown in Figure 16-4.

After defining fields, it is a good idea to give the new database file a name and save it on a disk. You can begin entering information into the fields

FIGURE 16-3

The Field Size dialog box appears after you have entered a new field name.

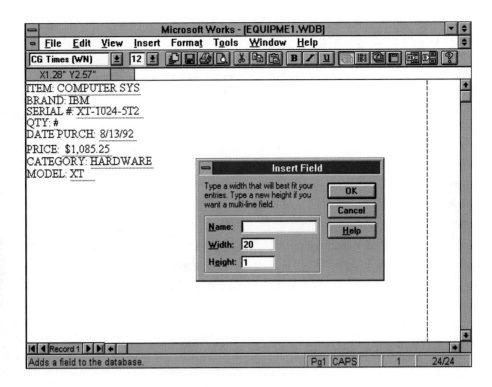

immediately or you can close the database file and reopen and work on it later. When you are ready to create records for your database, you enter information into the fields you defined when you created the database. When you have finished entering information into the fields of the first record, press Tab. Works provides you with empty fields for the second record and all the records that follow, until you have finished entering information.

From time to time you will find it necessary to modify (edit) information in a database. You can delete, insert, or **append** (add to the end of the database) records, and you can change the contents of any record to make it correct. As explained later in this chapter, you can also change the arrangement of fields to make data entry more convenient.

REORGANIZING A DATABASE

You can reorganize a database by changing the order of the records or by using special features for selecting and displaying specified records. **Sorting** is the process used to reorder records according to the contents of a particular field. For instance, in a database that contains inventory items, you can sort records in **alphabetic order** by item name or in numeric order by price. You can also sort records in **ascending** or **descending order**. An alphabetic ascending order sort organizes records from A to Z, while an alphabetic descending order sort organizes records from Z to A. A numeric ascending sort organizes records from lowest to highest number. A numeric descending sort organizes records from highest to lowest number. Sorting can make it easier to locate and edit records and helps to present information in an organized manner.

QUERYING A DATABASE

You can perform a simple search of any database to display records that contain a specified text string in one or more fields. A more sophisticated search involves the use of a query. A **query** is created when you want to specify a set of conditions—called **record-selection rules**—that Works uses to determine which records to display or print. For example, Figure 16-5 shows records from the EQUIPME1.WDB database file. These records conform to the record-selection rule in which the ITEM field contains the text COMPUTER SYS. Chapter 11 discusses in detail these special features for manipulating a database.

PRINTING A DATABASE

As is true with the Works word processor, you can print database records by specifying the number of copies, the range of pages, and the page orientation in the Print dialog box. Works allows you to print all or selected records in a database. If your records are displayed in form view, Works will print the records as forms. If the records are displayed in list view, the records will be printed in the rows and columns shown in list view. These and other Works database views are described in the next section.

VIEWING DATABASE CONTENTS

In Works you can view the contents of a database in different ways:

1. In a record-by-record form (form view)
2. In a list of records (list view)

FIGURE 16-5
The EQUIPME1.WDB database after applying record-selection rules.

Microsoft Works - [EQUIPME1.WDB]

File   Edit   View   Insert   Format   Tools   Window   Help

"COMPUTER SYS

	ITEM	BRAND	SERIAL #	QTY	DATE PURCH	PRICE	CATEG
1	COMPUTER SYS	IBM	XT-1024-5T2	1	8/13/92	$1,085.25	HARDW
2	COMPUTER SYS	IBM	XT-1206-5T3	1	8/13/92	$1,085.25	HARDW
4	COMPUTER SYS	COMPAQ	C9664-Q54	1	8/13/92	$1,795.28	HARDW
5	COMPUTER SYS	COMPAQ	C9675-Q4	1	8/13/92	$1,795.28	HARDW
6	COMPUTER SYS	COMPAQ	C9676-Q9	1	8/17/92	$1,795.28	HARDW
9	COMPUTER SYS	IBM	XT-1047-5T2	1	8/23/92	$1,012.45	HARDW
10	COMPUTER SYS	BELL	B67269UT09	1	8/26/92	$1,695.25	HARDW
11	COMPUTER SYS	BELL	B67269UT911	1	8/26/92	$1,695.25	HARDW
25							
26							
27							
28							
29							
30							
31							
32							
33							
34							
35							
36							

Press ALT to choose commands, or F2 to edit.   1   8/24

FIGURE 16-6

A report view of the same database information shown in list view in Figure 16-2.

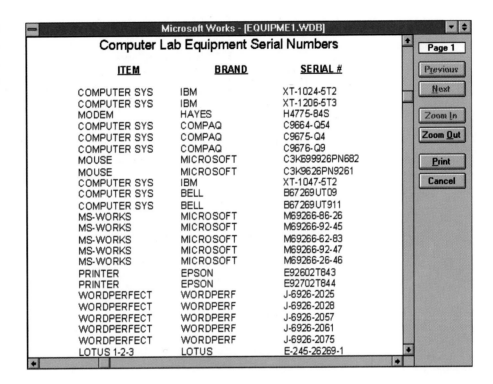

3. In a list of records resulting from your query (query view)

4. In a table-formatted report (report view)

The Works database program differs from other Works programs in that you can look at information in several different ways. When you want to concentrate on one record at a time, you can use the form view as shown in Figure 16-1. By switching to the list view, shown in Figure 16-2, you can view a list of records.

You can also view records in a table format as shown in Figure 16-6, by creating a report to display the information you want to see in the way that you want to see it. Figure 16-6 shows the information in the EQUIPME1.WDB database displayed in report view. As noted in the previous section, the principal reason for creating a report is to print all of, or a part of, database records in a list format. However, you can also use a report simply to view the database. You will learn more about data view, list view, query view, and report view in the next lesson.

AVIGATING IN LIST VIEW

Although form view is often used to enter new data in a database, list view is most often used for navigating through a database. You can use the scroll bars in the same way you used them in the word-processor window to display additional information in the list view window. Dragging the **scroll box** on the vertical and horizontal scroll bars moves the highlight through the database proportionately to the scroll box's position on the scroll bar. After scrolling to bring other records or fields into view, you can click a field in the new display to highlight it. In list view a highlighted, or active, field is surrounded by a border, as shown in Figure 16-7.

FIGURE 16-7

In list view a border around a field in a record indicates that it is the highlighted, or active, field.

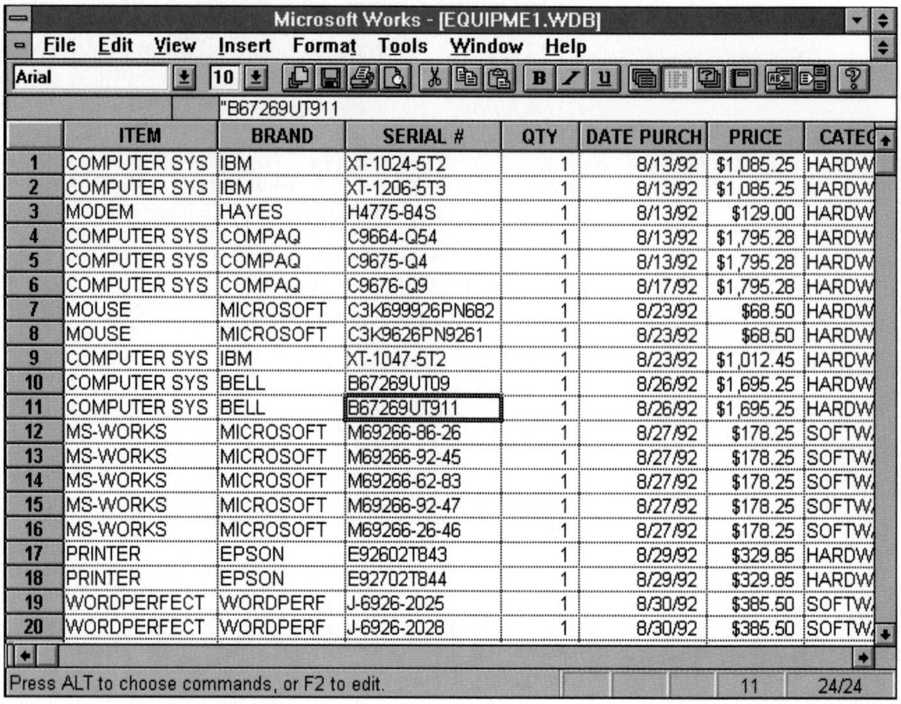

SPLIT WINDOWS

When you want to compare information in records that are in different parts of a large database, you can use the ADJUST pointer, shown in Figure 16-8, to split a database document window into panes, just as you did with a word-processor document in Chapter 7. By leaving one window stationary, you can compare a record in that pane with any other records

FIGURE 16-8

A list view window that has been split into two separate windows.

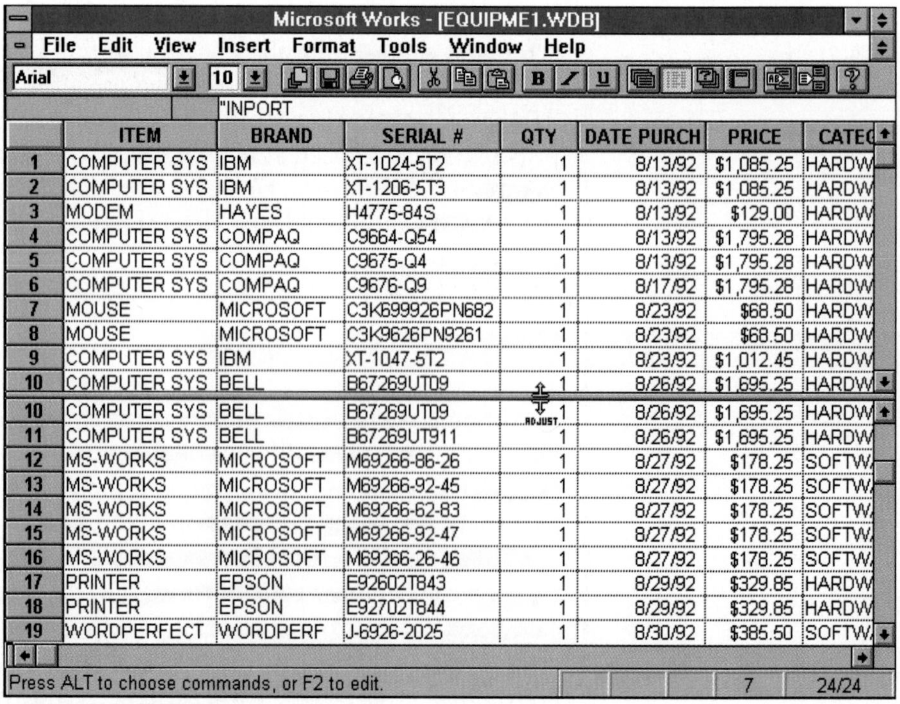

in the database by using the second pane's vertical scroll bar to scroll through the database. By moving your mouse pointer to the left of the left horizontal scroll arrow or to the left of the first column label, you can also turn on the vertical ADJUST pointer (you can also select Split from the Window menu). Using the vertical or horizontal split bars, you can split a window into upper and lower panes or side-by-side panes. If you use both the vertical and the horizontal ADJUST pointer, you can divide a window into four panes. Figure 16-8 shows a window that is split into upper and lower panes.

The special scroll arrows, called **navigation buttons**, shown in Figure 16-9, are also valuable in working with database files in form view. Clicking on these arrows moves you to the first or last record or the previous or following record. The number in the record-number indicator is the number of the record viewed on screen.

NAVIGATION KEYS

In addition to using the scroll bars and the navigation buttons to navigate through a database, you can move the highlight one record or one field at a time, using the keys listed here. In the next chapter, you will use these same keys when you enter information into the fields of a new database.

KEY	MOVES THE HIGHLIGHTED
Tab or →	Right one field
Shift + Tab or ←	Left one field
↓ (This works best in list view)	Down one record
↑ (This works best in list view)	Up one record
Ctrl + Page Up	Previous record
Ctrl + Page Down	Next record
Click on record number (list view)	Select entire record

navigation buttons →

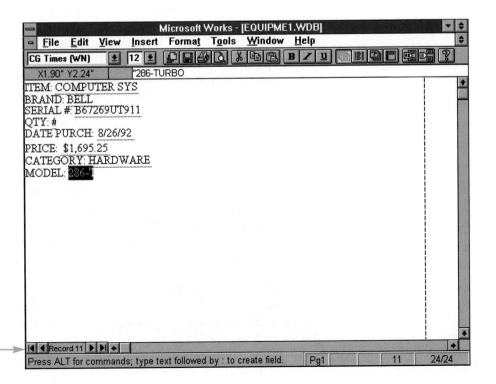

FIGURE 16-9
The navigation buttons in form view.

NAVIGATING A DATABASE IN LIST AND FORM VIEW

In this exercise you will display records in the EQUIPME1.WDB database file in list view and practice moving about in list view. The EQUIPME1.WDB file, which is stored on your Student Data Disk, contains a list of all equipment and supplies for the computer lab.

1. If necessary, start the computer, insert your Student Data Disk in the floppy-disk drive, and start Works.

2. Select the database tool in the Startup dialog box.

3. If necessary, make the Student Data Disk current to display the list of database files on this disk.

4. Locate and double-click the file EQUIPME1.WDB.

Figure 16-2 shows the database in list view as it was originally saved. If your display is different, follow the directions in step 5 to change to list view.

5. If the EQUIPME1.WDB file is not displayed in list view, as shown in Figure 16-2, choose List from the View menu.

6. If the first field in record 1 is not already active, click it. Then press the ↓ three times to move to the first field in record 4.

7. Press the Tab key twice to move to the SERIAL # field for record 4.

8. Click the → in the horizontal scroll bar to display the rest of the fields in record 4, if they are not already visible.

9. Make the PRICE field for record 4 active by clicking it.

10. Click the ↓ in the vertical scroll bar to display the last record in the database.

11. Use the horizontal scroll bar to bring the ITEM field into view, if necessary. Make the ITEM field in record 21 (WORDPERFECT) active.

In the next steps you will split the window into two panes.

12. Scroll to the top of the database and click the BRAND field for record 4.

13. Turn on the ADJUST pointer by clicking below the maximize and minimize buttons. Drag the ADJUST pointer on the vertical scroll bar to just below record 4, as shown in Figure 16-10. Scroll the lower window pane to compare the prices of other computer systems with the price of the Compaq model in record 4.

14. Click the ADJUST pointer on the shaded line dividing the panes, and drag it on the vertical scroll bar to just above the up scroll arrow. Release the mouse button. The list view is now displayed in a single window.

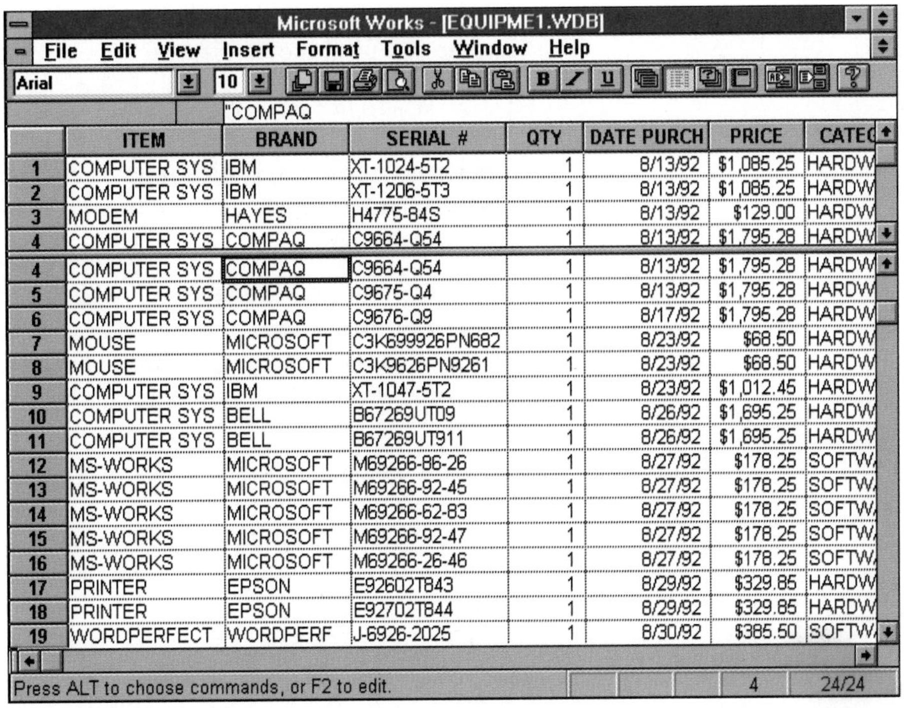

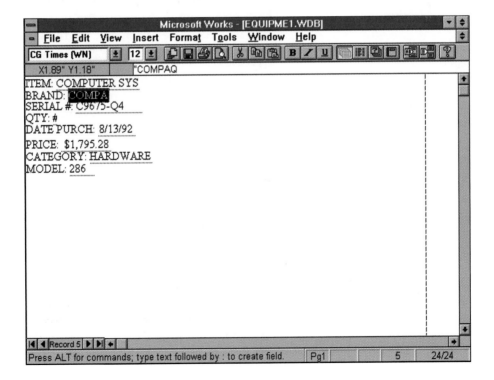

FIGURE 16-10

After step 13, your screen display should look similar to the one shown here.

15. Select Form view from the View menu.

16. Record 4 appears in the record-number indicator box. Click the far left navigation button ◄. The record-number indicator now shows record 1. Click the first right navigation button four times. Your document window should resemble the screen shown in Figure 16-11.

FIGURE 16-11

After step 16, your screen display should look similar to the one shown here.

Microsoft Works - [EQUIPME1.WDB]

ITEM: COMPUTER SYS
BRAND: COMPA
SERIAL #: C9675-Q4
QTY: #
DATE PURCH: 8/13/92
PRICE: $1,795.28
CATEGORY: HARDWARE
MODEL: 286

17. Select the SERIAL # field in record 5, then move to record 12 by clicking the until the number 12 appears in the record-number indicator box. Notice how the highlight remains in the SERIAL # field.

18. Move about in the database using the scroll bars, navigation buttons, and keys. Are the navigation keys as effective in form view as in list view? What happens when you use the scroll bars in Form view?

19. Return to List view. Drag the adjust pointer to divide the window into panes; then use the scroll bars in each pane to compare records and fields in different parts of the database. When you have finished practicing these techniques, drag the split bars to their original positions. If necessary, click an insertion point in the first field of record 1.

20. Close the EQUIPME1.WDB file without saving any of the changes you made while practicing navigation techniques.

21. If you are not continuing with the Practice Applications at this time, quit Works and remove the Student Data Disk from the floppy-disk drive.

PRACTICE APPLICATIONS

Complete the following exercises. Some exercises ask you to answer one or more questions. Write a brief answer to these questions on a sheet of paper.

1. If necessary, start Works and insert your Student Data Disk in the floppy-disk drive. Open the file EQUIPME3.WDB. Use the navigation techniques from the guided practice to display other fields in the file. In record 8, make the last field, MODEL, active. Display and make the ITEM field active in the last record that contains information in the database (record 24). Then move to the first field in the first record and make it active.

2. Which navigation techniques did you use to perform Exercise 1? Do you believe you could have performed the exercise more efficiently by using different techniques? If so, explain what you could have done differently. When you have finished these two exercises, close the EQUIPME3.WDB file without saving any changes you have made. Then quit Works if you are not going on to the next section.

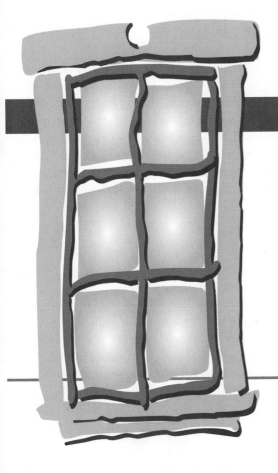

LESSON 17

USING THE FOUR DATABASE VIEWS

After completing this lesson you will be able to do the following:

- *Switch window displays among form, list, query, and report views.*

- *Compare the form and list view displays and explain the advantages and disadvantages of each.*

- *Explain how a form is used to display database records.*

- *Explain how a report is created.*

- *Explain how a query is created and used to display selected database records.*

DATABASE VIEWS

In the previous lesson, you examined database files in the row-and-column format that is displayed when you choose List from the View menu. To view a database in a record-by-record format, choose Form from the View menu. In addition to these two ways of displaying database records, Works provides two other view commands: Query, when you want Works to display only those records that match your query, and Report, which is used to view and print records in a table format. The following sections describe each view in more detail and suggest views to use for various database management tasks.

LIST VIEW

When you choose List from the View menu, Works displays records in a row-and-column format. The size of your screen determines the number of records and fields you can view at one time in a window display. However, as you learned in the previous lesson, you can use navigation techniques to bring additional records or fields into view.

List view can be used for entering, finding, and sorting information. If you delete a field in list view, it is deleted from all forms and reports in the database.

FORM VIEW

When you choose Form from the View menu to display a database, Works displays all the fields for one record. An advantage to this approach is that you can see all the fields for a record at one time—a capability that is not always possible with list view because all fields may not fit on one screen. A disadvantage to this approach is that you can view only one record at a time. You can, however, use the navigation tools to scroll through the database. Figure 17-1 shows a record displayed in the standard form that Works uses when you create a new database.

Form view can be used to enter and edit information in a record or to search a database to find specific information. This is an appropriate view to use when you want to concentrate on one record at a time or when you want to enter new records. You can add, delete, or change records and fields in this view.

If you want to accent your form, form view offers the ability to add rectangles, borders, graphics, colors, and shadings. You can add shading in list and report views as well, but form view allows you more flexibility in accenting your database (see Figures 17-1a and b).

FIGURE 17-1

(a) The standard form that is automatically displayed in form view when you create a new database. (b) Some of the accents that Works can add to a form.

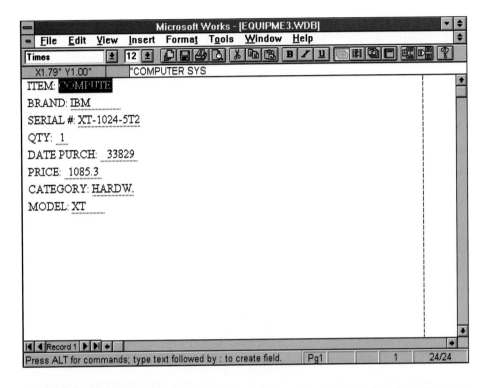

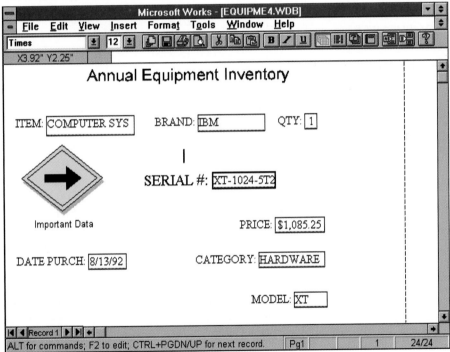

REPORT VIEW

In Form or List view, your printout must reflect the layout on your screen. In Report view, however, you can choose which fields to print and how you want them displayed on the page. For example, if you want to build a report based on the information in EQUIPME1.WDB, you choose which fields you want to print in your report. Later you can create another report based on this database but with different fields selected. Figure 17-2 shows a report generated by selecting the first three fields of EQUIPME1.WDB.

When you select Report from the View menu, Works displays the Reports dialog box, allowing you to choose among the reports you have created for a database. For example, the Reports dialog box in Figure 17-3 shows that two reports, Report1 and Report2, have been created for the EQUIPME1.WDB database (Works highlights the last report created). When you select one of these reports, Works lists records in report view according to the format specified in the report.

FIGURE 17-2

By selecting only the first three fields of EQUIPME1.WDB, you can generate a report displaying only that information.

ITEM	BRAND	SERIAL #
COMPUTER SYS	IBM	XT-1024-5T2
COMPUTER SYS	IBM	XT-1206-5T3
MODEM	HAYES	H4775-84S
COMPUTER SYS	COMPAQ	C9664-Q54
COMPUTER SYS	COMPAQ	C9675-Q4
COMPUTER SYS	COMPAQ	C9676-Q9
MOUSE	MICROSOFT	C3K699926PN682
MOUSE	MICROSOFT	C3K9626PN9261
COMPUTER SYS	IBM	XT-1047-5T2
COMPUTER SYS	BELL	B67269UT09
COMPUTER SYS	BELL	B67269UT911
MS-WORKS	MICROSOFT	M69266-86-26
MS-WORKS	MICROSOFT	M69266-92-45
MS-WORKS	MICROSOFT	M69266-62-83
MS-WORKS	MICROSOFT	M69266-92-47
MS-WORKS	MICROSOFT	M69266-26-46
PRINTER	EPSON	E92602T843
PRINTER	EPSON	E92702T844
WORDPERFECT	WORDPERF	J-6926-2025
WORDPERFECT	WORDPERF	J-6926-2028
WORDPERFECT	WORDPERF	J-6926-2057
WORDPERFECT	WORDPERF	J-6926-2061
WORDPERFECT	WORDPERF	J-6926-2075
LOTUS 1-2-3	LOTUS	E-245-26269-1

Microsoft Works - [EQUIPME1.WDB]

Computer Lab Equipment Serial Numbers

Page 1 / Previous / Next / Zoom In / Zoom Out / Print / Cancel

FIGURE 17-3

This Reports dialog box lists Report1 and Report2, which were created to display and print database information in table format.

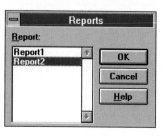

Reports

Report:
Report1
Report2

OK / Cancel / Help

UERY VIEW

Query view is used when you want to select only those records that match one or more record-selection rules. As with report view, query view will generate a report of selected fields that can be examined and printed. Query view, however, offers more flexibility in selecting those fields. The Works database query function will search in a variety of ways, including looking for exact matches to your query, partial matches, greater-than or less-than comparisons, and information that falls within a certain range. For example, if you want to print a report listing information for computer lab equipment with purchase prices more than $1000, query view will generate a report such as the one shown in Figure 17-4.

In the same way that Works attaches reports to a database, Works can also attach queries. Previously defined queries can be selected by using the Queries dialog box, as shown in Figure 17-5.

FIGURE 17-4

This report was created by using the Works database query function.

	ITEM	BRAND	SERIAL #	QTY	DATE PURCH	PRICE	CATEG
1	COMPUTER SYS	IBM	XT-1024-5T2	1	8/13/92	$1,085.25	HARDW
2	COMPUTER SYS	IBM	XT-1206-5T3	1	8/13/92	$1,085.25	HARDW
4	COMPUTER SYS	COMPAQ	C9664-Q54	1	8/13/92	$1,795.28	HARDW
5	COMPUTER SYS	COMPAQ	C9675-Q4	1	8/13/92	$1,795.28	HARDW
6	COMPUTER SYS	COMPAQ	C9676-Q9	1	8/17/92	$1,795.28	HARDW
9	COMPUTER SYS	IBM	XT-1047-5T2	1	8/23/92	$1,012.45	HARDW
10	COMPUTER SYS	BELL	B67269UT09	1	8/26/92	$1,695.25	HARDW
11	COMPUTER SYS	BELL	B67269UT911	1	8/26/92	$1,695.25	HARDW
25							
26							
27							
28							
29							
30							
31							
32							
33							
34							
35							
36							

Microsoft Works - [EQUIPME1.WDB]

File Edit View Insert Format Tools Window Help

Arial   10

"COMPUTER SYS

Press ALT to choose commands, or F2 to edit.   1   8/24

FIGURE 17-5

The Queries dialog box, similar to the Reports dialog box.

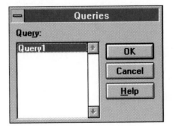

SWITCHING FROM ONE VIEW TO ANOTHER

Here are several techniques for switching between different views in a Works database:

FIGURE 17-6

Use the toolbar buttons to switch among Form, List, Query, and Report views.

Switch to Form, List, Query, or Report view by choosing the appropriate command from the View menu.

Switch to Report view by choosing a report name from the Reports dialog box.

Switch between Form, List, Query, and Report views by clicking the tool buttons on the toolbar, as shown in Figure 17-6.

Press F9 to switch between Form and List views.

NAVIGATING IN FORM VIEW

In form view, when you click a field the field becomes highlighted to show that it is the active field. In this view, as in list view, you can use either the Tab key or the arrow keys to move the highlight to the next field in the form. Pressing Ctrl+↑ takes you to the previous record. Ctrl+↓ takes you to the next record. When the last field in a record is highlighted in form view, pressing the Tab key advances the highlight to the first field. You can also use the navigation buttons at the bottom left of the document window.

GUIDED PRACTICE

SWITCHING VIEWS AND NAVIGATING IN DATA VIEW

In this practice exercise you will switch between list view and form view in the EQUIPME1.WDB database. You will also practice using several techniques for navigating through a database in form view.

1. If necessary, start Works and insert your Student Data Disk in the floppy-disk drive. Open the EQUIPME1.WDB database file. The database opens in form view.

2. Choose List from the View menu to display the database in list view. The first field in record 1 should be active.

3. Choose Form from the View menu to display record 1 with the ITEM field selected. Your screen should look similar to the one in Figure 17-7.

4. Press the Tab key three times to move the highlight to the value in the QTY field. (If your field contains a # instead of a value, the field is not wide enough to display the value. You will learn how to adjust field size later.)

5. Highlight the value in the BRAND field.

FIGURE 17-7

After step 3, your screen display should look similar to this one.

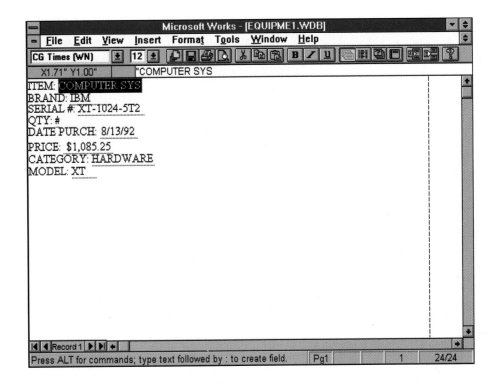

6. Click on the List view toolbar button to switch to list view. (If necessary, display the toolbar by clicking on the Toolbar command on the View menu.) Notice that the same field (BRAND) in record 1 is highlighted when the list view window is displayed.

7. Click to make the SERIAL # field in record 3 active in list view.

8. Click the Form view toolbar button to switch to form view.

9. Press Ctrl + ↓ four times to move to the SERIAL # field of record 7.

10. Press Shift + Tab to move up one field from the SERIAL # field to the BRAND field.

11. Click the Query view toolbar button to switch to query view.

12. Click the Cancel button to return to form view.

13. Click the Last navigation button (the far right button) to move quickly to the last record in the database (record 25).

14. Display record 20 by clicking the Previous button (the left arrow) five times.

15. Click on the Report command on the View menu. Select Report2 from the Reports dialog box to switch from form view to report view.

16. Your screen display of Report2 should look similar to the one shown in Figure 17-8. Notice that the top left field is selected.

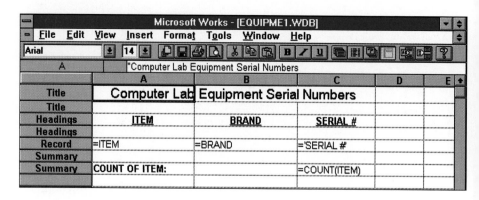

	A	B	C	D	E
Title	Computer Lab	Equipment Serial Numbers			
Title					
Headings	ITEM	BRAND	SERIAL #		
Headings					
Record	=ITEM	=BRAND	='SERIAL #		
Summary					
Summary	COUNT OF ITEM:		=COUNT(ITEM)		

18. Click on the List view toolbar button. Select Report from the View menu, and then select Report1.

20. Use the toolbar button to switch to Query view.

21. As time permits, continue practicing switching among the views and navigating through the database.

22. Close EQUIPME1.WDB without saving any changes you have made to the database.

PRACTICE APPLICATIONS

Complete the following exercises. Some exercises ask you to answer one or more questions. Write a brief answer to these questions on a sheet of paper.

1. If necessary, start Works. Open the EQUIPME3.WDB database. Display record 8 in form view. While you are in form view, display the last record in the file that contains data, then display the first record in the file.

2. Describe two ways to a) go to first record, b) go to last record, c) show Form view, d) show List view.

3. Use the keyboard command to switch from form view to list view. Switch back to form view using one of the toolbar buttons. Switch to query view.

4. Switch back to list view and close EQUIPME3.WDB without saving any changes you have made. Quit Works and eject your Student Data Disk from the floppy-disk drive.

5. The content portion of a field can be referred to by several terms. Click on the Help toolbar icon to open the Learning Works screen. Click on the Access The Help Library text button. Select the Table of Contents button. Click on the Database. On the Database: Step-By-Step help screen, select Database Basics. When the Database Basics screen is displayed, click on Database Overview. Open the File menu and select the Print Topic command. What terms does Works use?

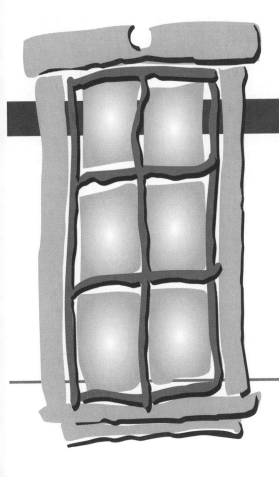

PRINTING A

DATABASE

OBJECTIVES

After completing this lesson you will be able to do the
following:

- Print a report that includes all records in a database .
- Print a single record.

PRINTING REPORTS AND QUERIES

In Works you can print reports or queries that include all or part of the information in a database. After selecting a report or query, you can preview it before printing by choosing Print Preview from the File menu. When you are ready to print the report or query, you can select the Print button in print preview, or you can choose Print from the File menu to open the Print dialog box. The Print dialog box is used to specify the number of copies and range of pages you want to print. Select All to print a single copy of every page of the report or query.

PRINTING FORMS

In addition to being able to preview and print a database in report or query view, it is also possible to preview and print individual records that are displayed in form view. In print preview you can examine the way a record appears on a sheet of paper when it is printed. When you are ready to print one or more records, choose Print from the File menu. The Print dialog box is used to specify the number of copies and the range of records (pages) you want to print. For example, you can print the entire database, one record per page, by clicking on the All records button; or you can print the current record by clicking on the Current record only. These options are shown in Figure 18-1.

GUIDED PRACTICE

PRINTING RECORDS

In this exercise you will produce three printouts using information in the EQUIPME1.WDB file: (1) a report of all records in the file, using Report1; (2) a report of records using Report2; and (3) a copy of record 7 using form view.

1. Click on the Report command on the View menu. If necessary, start Works and open the EQUIPME1.WDB file in list view.

2. Select Report1 from the Reports dialog box to display the database in report view.

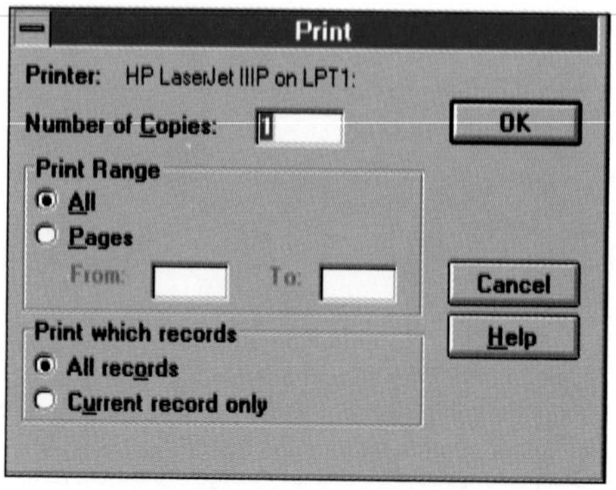

FIGURE 18-1
With the database displayed in form view, the Print dialog box offers options for printing records.

Print
Printer: HP LaserJet IIIP on LPT1:
Number of Copies: [1]   [OK]
Print Range
⦿ **A**ll
○ **P**ages
From: [ ]   To: [ ]   [Cancel]
Print which records   [Help]
⦿ All records
○ Current record only

FIGURE 18-2

*After you choose Print
Preview, your screen
display of Report1 of the
EQUIPME1.WDB file
should look similar to the
one shown here.*

AFTER
TWO
ZOOMS

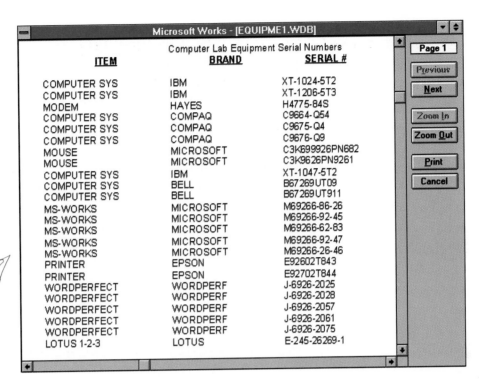

3. Preview the report by choosing Print Preview from the File menu.

   Use the magnifying glass icon to enlarge the document until it looks similar to the one in Figure 18-2.

4. Close the preview window to return to report view.

5. Choose Print ([Ctrl]+P) from the File menu. Make sure that 1 is displayed in the Number of Copies text box, as shown in Figure 18-3, then click on the OK button or press the [Enter] key to print a copy of Report1.

   In the following steps you will print one record in form view:

7. Select Form view from the View menu and display record 12.

8. Preview the record in print preview, then close the print preview window.

9. Choose Print ([Ctrl]+P) from the File menu to display the Print dialog box.

10. Make sure 1 is displayed in the Number of Copies text box.

11. Select Current record only.

12. Click on the OK button, or press the [Enter] key to print one copy of record 12.

13. Close the EQUIPME1.WDB database file without saving any changes.

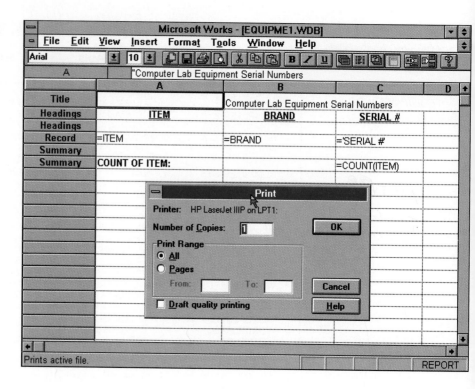

PRACTICE APPLICATIONS

1. Start Works, then open EQUIPME1.WDB. Print all the records in the database using list view. Print the last record in the database. After the database has been printed, close EQUIPME1.WDB without quitting Works.

2. Open EQUIPME3.WDB and print the database using Report1. Switch to form view and print the first record in the database.

CHAPTER REVIEW

A database is a file of related records. A record, which is made up of a set of fields, contains information about a specific person, thing, or event. The database, then, is an organized collection of information that can be managed and processed in different ways. Procedures for database management include entering, organizing, editing, and reporting data in a database. Queries and reports are created by using filters to select only certain fields.

The Works database program provides capabilities for displaying records in form, list, query, and report views. Form view offers the opportunity to accent forms with borders, shading, icons, and color. Database information can be printed in all four views. Form view offers the option of printing one record at a time.

REVIEW QUESTIONS

TRUE-FALSE

Write your answers on a sheet of paper.

1. A record is a single item of data that describes a person, object, event, or transaction.

2. An appended record is one that is added to the end of an existing database.

3. A descending sort organizes alphabetic information from A to Z.

4. A standard form is automatically created when you create a new database.

5. In the Works database program, the terms file and database generally mean the same thing.

6. Form view displays one record per screen.

7. List view is used to print a database in a table format.

8. If a report contains a heading, you can see the heading at the top of the report in report view.

9. The toolbar can be used to switch between report view and form view.

10. In Works you cannot print in query view.

SHORT-ANSWER QUESTIONS

Write a brief answer to these questions on a sheet of paper.

1. In a database, what is the difference between a field and a record?

2. How do you know if one or more reports have been created for a database?

3. Not including print preview, what are the ways of viewing records in a database?

4. What view is used to change the standard form that is created automatically when you create a new database?

5. Explain when you would use scroll bars, split windows, and the navigation buttons.

LESSON APPLICATIONS

Complete the following exercises. Some exercises ask you to answer one or more questions. Write a brief answer to these questions on a sheet of paper.

1. Open the database file INVENTOR.WDB, which is stored on your Student Data Disk. If necessary, choose List view from the View menu. Perform the following steps:

   a. Make the last field in the first record active.

   b. Make the first field in record 12 active.

   c. Select the last record in the database.

   d. Select the first record in the database.

2. Once again display the INVENTOR.WDB file in list view. Switch to record 4 in form view by clicking the navigation arrow buttons. In form view, perform the following steps:

   a. Go to record 5 using the scroll box; then go to record 3 using the navigation buttons.

   b. Use the arrow keys to move through the fields of record 3.

   c. Use the Tab key to move through the fields, then use Shift + Tab to move in reverse order through the fields.

   d. Click on the ITEM field to select it. Use the Tab key to move through the fields of record 3. What happens when you press the Tab key after highlighting the last field in the record?

   e. Return to list view using the keyboard command.

CHAPTER APPLICATIONS

1. Open the ROSTER.WDB file stored on your Student Data Disk. Switch to list view. How many records are stored in this database?

2. Display record 1 in form view. What steps did you take to display this record? Display record 13 in form view. Is this form a standard form? How can you tell?

3. Return to list view. Are any reports attached to this database? Are there any queries attached?

4. Print ROSTER.WDB in list view. Switch to form view and print record 4 of the database.

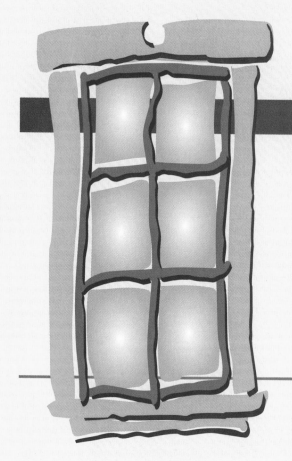

CHAPTER 7

CREATING AND

EDITING A DATABASE

OVERVIEW

A Works database consists of fields, records, layouts designed for screen display, printed forms, queries, and reports. In Chapter 9 you examined features in existing database files. In this chapter you will learn how to create a new database file by defining fields and entering information into records. You will also learn how to make changes to a database by adding, deleting, and rearranging fields as well as by adding, deleting, and editing records.

CONTENTS

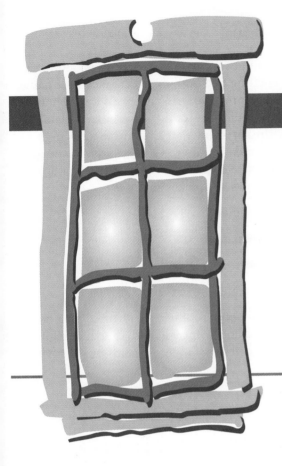

LESSON 19

CREATING A DATABASE

OBJECTIVES

After completing this lesson you will be able to do the following:

Define the structure of a database by specifying field names, types, and formats.

Name and save a new database file.

Enter information into the records of a new database.

KEY WORDS

In this lesson you will learn the meaning of the following terms:

formula bar

THE DATABASE CREATION PROCESS

With a word processor you can open a new file, begin typing, and save the file at any time. Simply by entering text and saving it under a file name, you have essentially created a word-processing document. With a database, however, you must perform a few additional steps to organize the database file before you enter data. You already know that a database file is organized into fields and records. However, it is up to you, the user, to specify how these fields and records should be organized within the database.

In Works, database creation follows a four-step process:

1. Open a new database document window.

2. Define field names, sizes, and formats.

3. Name and save the new database file.

4. Enter information into fields to create records.

To start the process, select the database tool in the Startup dialog box. Works displays an untitled database document window, shown in Figure 19-1. The following sections describe how you define fields by specifying names, sizes, and formats.

DEFINING FIELDS

The next step in creating a database involves defining the fields you want to use in the records of your database. You define a field by giving it a name and size. You can further define the field by telling Works how the information in the field should be formatted.

FIGURE 19-1
This window is displayed when you select the database tool from the Startup dialog box.

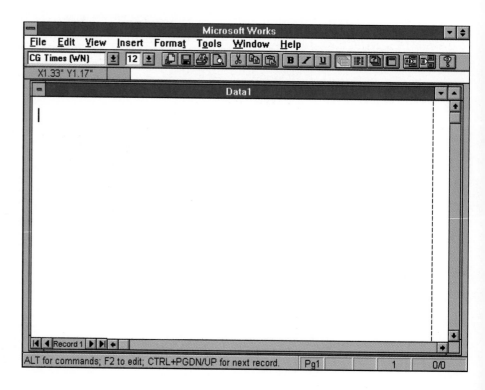

NAMING A FIELD

As you learned in Lesson 16, the easiest way to begin naming fields is to begin typing. For example, if your new database file will have Last Name as its first field, type **Last Name**. Then type a colon (:) and press the [Enter] key—you can name up to 256 fields in a database. Works opens the Field Size dialog box, as shown in Figure 19-2. As its name implies, the Field Size dialog box is used to size fields. A field may be 254 characters wide. A field name cannot begin with a single quotation mark ('), but can be up to 15 characters wide. Normally you will want to use just enough characters in a field name to make the field easy to identify when you need to find information in a database.

The Field Size dialog box suggests that your field have a width of 20 characters and a height of 1 character (it can have a height of up to 325). Click OK to accept the default field size. To create the second field, click an insertion point where you want to add the new field on the form. Then select Field from the Insert menu. Works displays the Insert Field dialog box, a way to name and size your field in one step. Type **First Name:** in the Name Text box, as shown in Figure 19-3. Accept the field size defaults and click OK. You now have two fields named and sized, as shown in Figure 19-4.

You use the Show Field Name command on the Format menu to tell Works to show or hide the field name in the standard form displayed in form view. Unless you deselect the option by clicking to remove the checkmark, the field name is displayed. Select each field name and then deselect the Show Field Name to hide the field name, as shown in Figure 19-5. To show the field names again, select the field and reselect the Show Field Name option. The Show Field Name option does not affect the database display in list view—field names are always displayed at the top of a list view column.

FIGURE 19-2

The Field Size dialog box sets the size of your fields.

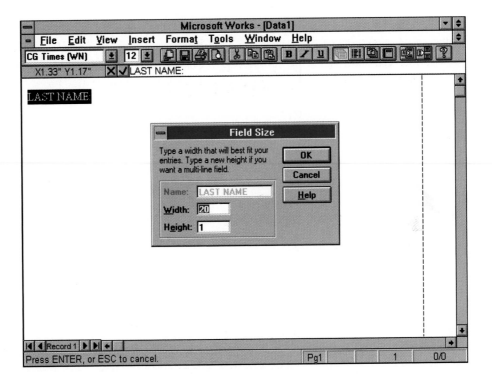

FIGURE 19-3

*The Insert Field dialog box
allows you to name and
size a field.*

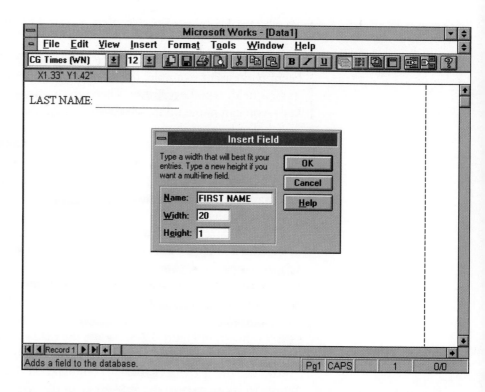

FIGURE 19-4

*With two fields named and
sized, your form should
resemble this one.*

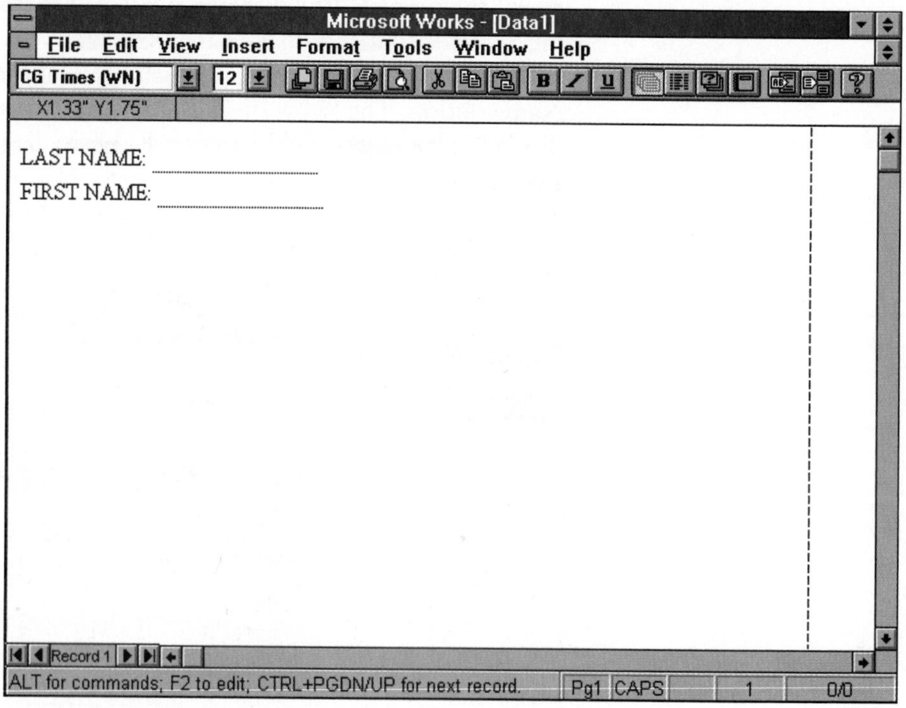

FIGURE 19-5

The database from Figure 19-4 with the Show Field Name command deselected

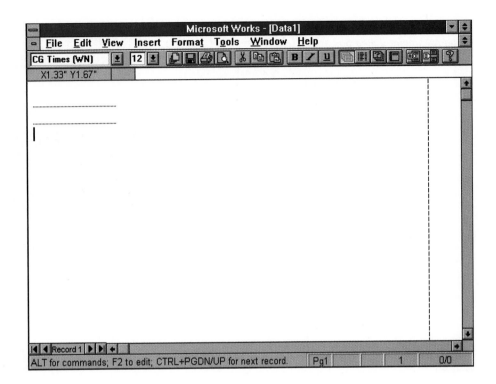

FIGURE 19-5

The database from Figure 19-4 with the Show Field Name command deselected

SELECTING A FIELD FORMAT

You can format the appearance of data in a selected field by clicking on the Format menu's Alignment command. Works displays the Alignment dialog box. The appearance of the Alignment dialog box depends on whether you are in form view or list view. Figure 19-6a shows the Alignment dialog box and its default selection for form view. Figure 19-6b shows the Alignment dialog box and its default selections for list view.

In form view, clicking the General radio button aligns text from the left and numbers from the right of the field. The Left, Right, and Center buttons produce the effect you would expect.

In list view (and query and report views, as well) you have the option of aligning text both vertically and horizontally. When you select the Wrap Text check box, data that are too long for the width of the field will wrap to other lines within that field. The Vertical radio buttons determine how Works aligns data in a field, whether at the top, center, or bottom of a list view field. The vertical alignment options only affect fields that are formatted for a height greater than one character or a field in which text is wrapping. Figure 19-7 shows these vertical alignments.

After you format a field using the Alignment command, Works automatically aligns the data that you enter in that field. Fields aligned in one view are not affected in another view. A field may have a center alignment in list view, for example, but a left alignment in form view.

FIGURE 19-6

The Alignment dialog box and its default settings for (a) form view and (b) list view.

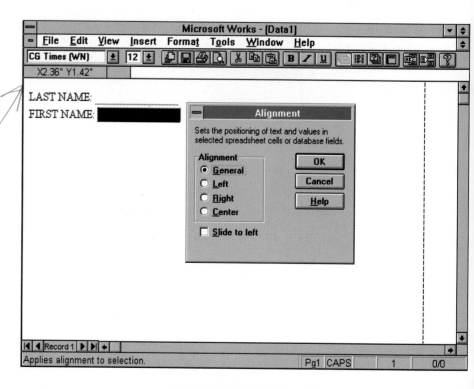

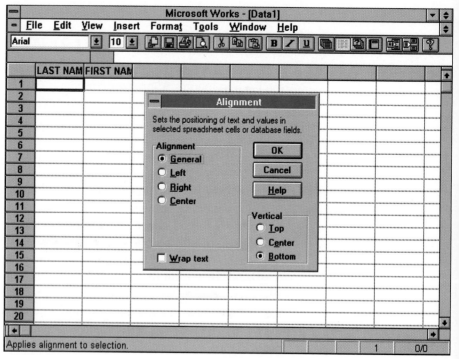

FIGURE 19-7

The three vertical alignments available from the Alignment dialog box in list view.

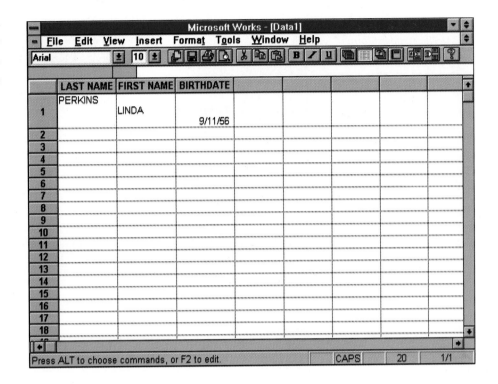

 AMING AND SAVING A DATABASE FILE

After naming and formatting fields for the new database, you need to name the file and save it to a disk. Name a new database file in the same way you name a new word-processing document: by choosing either the Save or the Save As command from the File menu to open the Save As dialog box. A database file name can contain up to eight characters. You do not need to add the database extension .WDB to the document name. Works will do that automatically.

ENTERING INFORMATION INTO FIELDS

After you have defined the fields of the database, you can begin entering information in either form view or list view. Form view displays the fields in a standard form layout, as shown in Figure 19-8a. When you switch to list view, you see the same field names used as column headings, as shown in Figure 19-8b.

When you type information into a field in either view, the information is displayed first in the **formula bar** at the top of the screen, as shown in Figures 19-8a and b. It is a good idea to proofread the information in the formula bar carefully before entering it into the field. You can correct typing errors in the formula bar by clicking an insertion point on the bar and using the Delete or Backspace key to delete characters. You can also highlight the field and delete everything there by pressing the Delete key. Or you

FIGURE 19-8

(a) The standard form in form view. Information has already been entered into the ITEM field of record 1. Information for the BRAND field has been typed in the formula bar but has not been entered into the BRAND field. (b) The list view of the same information. Notice that the bar just below the menu bar is the same in both views.

CANCEL
BUTTON

can click the **Cancel button** to cancel everything in the formula bar before it is placed in a field. Clicking the **Enter button** or pressing the ⟨Enter⟩ key enters and highlights the information in the active field. To enter information and at the same time advance to the next field, press the ⟨Tab⟩ or ⟨→⟩ key. Notice the two numbers at the bottom right of the document window. The first number indicates what record the highlighted field belongs to.

To prevent accidental loss of information while you are creating a database, choose the Save command (⟨Ctrl⟩+S) from the File menu every 5 or 10 minutes to save the data you have entered. Remember that you can select the Undo command from the Edit menu to cancel a deletion, if you select the Undo command immediately after making the deletion.

GUIDED PRACTICE

DEFINING FIELDS AND ENTERING INFORMATION

The lab manager has asked you to create a database that can be used to record and process fines that students and faculty have been assessed for failing to follow lab rules about conserving energy. In this practice exercise, you will create six fields for a new database. After defining the fields, you will save the database file with the name FINES.WDB and then enter the information shown below.

LAST NAME	FIRST NAME	ID #	FINE	DATE	DATE PD
TOLLERUDE	MICHAEL	415-92-2506	$5.00	9/24/94	9/25/94
LEIFETZ	JOHN	815-92-5925	$5.00	9/24/94	
MEINEKE	SANDRA	591-69-9262	$1.50	9/25/94	
MOSCONI	SALVATORE	692-92-9221	$1.50	9/25/94	
PERKINS	MARTIN	159-88-2692	$1.50	9/25/94	9/28/94
RANDALL	ALLEN	691-60-0027	$5.00	9/25/94	9/27/94

1. Start Works and insert your Student Data Disk in the floppy-disk drive.

2. In the Startup dialog box, select the database tool to open a new document window.

3. Press the [Caps Lock] key so that all field names will be typed in uppercase characters.

4. Type **LAST NAME:** to specify the name for the first field in the database. Press [Enter] twice to accept the default field size in the Field Size dialog box.

5. Highlight the blank field after the field name you have just created. Click on the Alignment command on the Format menu to open the Alignment dialog box. Notice that the General radio button is selected by default. Click **OK** or press the [Enter] key to close the Alignment dialog box, and return to the document window.

6. Click an insertion point on the next line under the first letter of the first field name. Type **FIRST NAME:** to specify the second field name.

7. Press the [Enter] key twice to accept the default field size settings. The FIRST NAME field is added to the database file and is automatically formatted with General alignment.

8. Type **ID #:** and press [Enter] to specify the third field name. Press the [Enter] key to accept the default size settings.

9. Type **FINE:** and press [Enter] to specify the fourth field name. Type **8** as the width and press [Enter].

10. Name the fifth field **DATE:**, and type **10** as the width. Press [Enter].

11. Name the sixth and last field **DATE PD:**, and type **10** as the width. Press [Enter].

12. Choose Save As from the File menu. Make sure the Student Data Disk directory is currently displayed in the list box, then type **FINES** to name the database file. Click on the OK button to save the database file to disk.

THE ENTER AREA

13. Highlight the first field (named LAST NAME) in the first record.

14. Type **TOLLERUDE**. Check the formula bar to make sure the spelling is correct, then press the [Tab] key to enter the information in the first field and advance the highlight to the FIRST NAME field.

15. Type **MICHAEL**. Check the formula bar, then press the [Tab] key.

16. Type the following information in the next four fields. Press the [Tab] key after you have verified each entry in the entry bar.

    ID #:   415-92-2506

    FINE: $5.00

    DATE: 9/24/94

    DATE PD: 9/25/94

17. Continue entering information for all six records, shown at the beginning of this guided practice.

18. Switch to list view and move your highlight to the first field of the first record.

19. Click on the Alignment command from the Format menu, and then format the field to be center-aligned. Notice that aligning one field in a column aligns the entire column.

20. Move your highlight to the first field of the last record. Open the Alignment dialog box. Click on the General radio button. The entire column returns to general alignment.

21. Save the information you have entered in the FINES.WDB database file by selecting Save ([Ctrl] +S) from the File menu.

PRACTICE APPLICATIONS

Complete the following exercises. Some exercises ask you to answer one or more questions. Write a brief answer to these questions on a sheet of paper.

1. Create a database named VENDORS.WDB. Use the following table to create fields and records. Remember to type a colon after each field name.

2. What field width did you select in the Field Size dialog box for ID # and PHONE? What happens if you press the (Tab) key, instead of the (Enter) key, after entering information in the PHONE field?

VENDOR	ID #	ADDRESS	CITY	PHONE
AZ COMPUTERS	83-425	892 Black Canyon Hwy.	Glendale	555-9520
COMPUWORLD	83-952	9105 Thomas Rd.	Scottsdale	555-0259
SOFTWARE CITY	84-931	4267 Old School Rd.	Phoenix	555-9252

3. In list view, highlight the second record in the PHONE field. Click on the Number command on the Format menu. In the Number dialog box, click on the Help button. Read the explanation of the Number command and its formats. What is the advantage of having a color printer when using the Comma format?

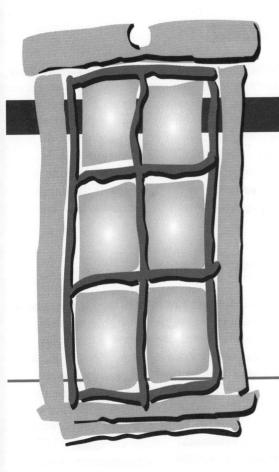

LESSON 20

EDITING A DATABASE

OBJECTIVES

After completing this lesson you will be able to do the following:

- *Insert records and fields into a database.*

- *Delete records and fields from a database.*

- *Edit the content of existing records.*

KEY WORDS

In this lesson you will learn the meaning of the following terms:

calculating field
handle

CHANGING AN EXISTING DATABASE

A database is said to be dynamic because its contents change continually to keep up with new data. For example, in a customer database that a store might use to keep track of clients and business transactions, new records are added to reflect new customers and new business transactions. Records are deleted to reflect customers who have moved or who no longer do business with the store. From time to time information in existing records needs to be corrected to reflect changes in customer addresses, phone numbers, and other information. Sometimes even the structure of the database may need to be changed by adding new fields or by deleting fields that are no longer needed.

INSERTING FIELDS AND RECORDS

You can insert a new field in either form or list view. In list view you highlight the field in any record to the right of where you want the new field, then choose the Record/Field command from the Insert menu to display the Insert dialog box. You use this dialog box, shown in Figure 20-1, to insert both fields and records. Select Field and then OK, and a new field appears in the column before the field that is currently selected. You can also use the Insert Field toolbar button, shown in Figure 20-2a. (The Insert Record button is pictured in Figure 20-2b.) In Figure 20-3, the new field has been inserted in the column to the left of the FINE field, which was active when the new field was created. A field created in list view is not automatically inserted in its proper place in a form, but you can move it. Select Field Name

FIGURE 20-4

The Insert dialog box inserts both fields and records.

	LAST NAME	FIRST NAME	ID #	FINE	DATE	DATE PD	
1	TOLLERUDE	MICHAEL	415-92-2506	$5.00	9/24/94	9/25/94	
2	LEIFETZ	JOHN	815-92-5925	$5.00	9/24/94		
3	MEINEKE	SANDRA	591-69-9626	$1.50	9/25/94		
4	MOSCONI	SALVATORE	692-92-9221	$1.50	9/25/94		
5	PERKINS	MARTIN	15		9/28/94		
6	RANDALL	ALLEN	69		9/27/94		

Inserts records or fields.   CAPS   2   6/6

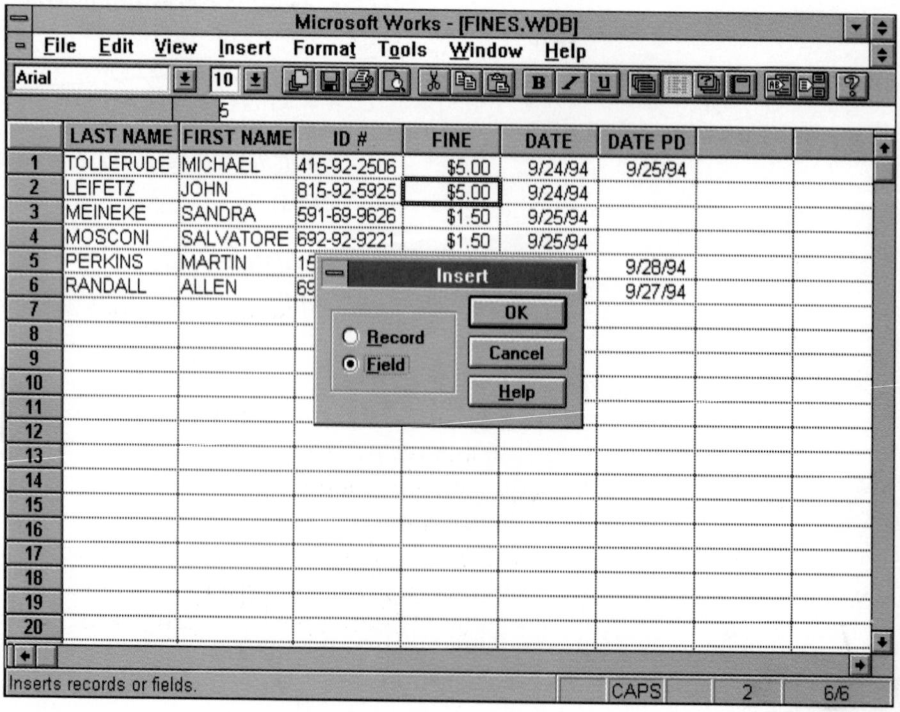

FIGURE 20-2

(a) The Insert A Field button. (b) The Insert A Record button.

FIGURE 20-3

A new field has been inserted in the FINES.WDB database. The Field Name dialog box is used to name a new field created in list view.

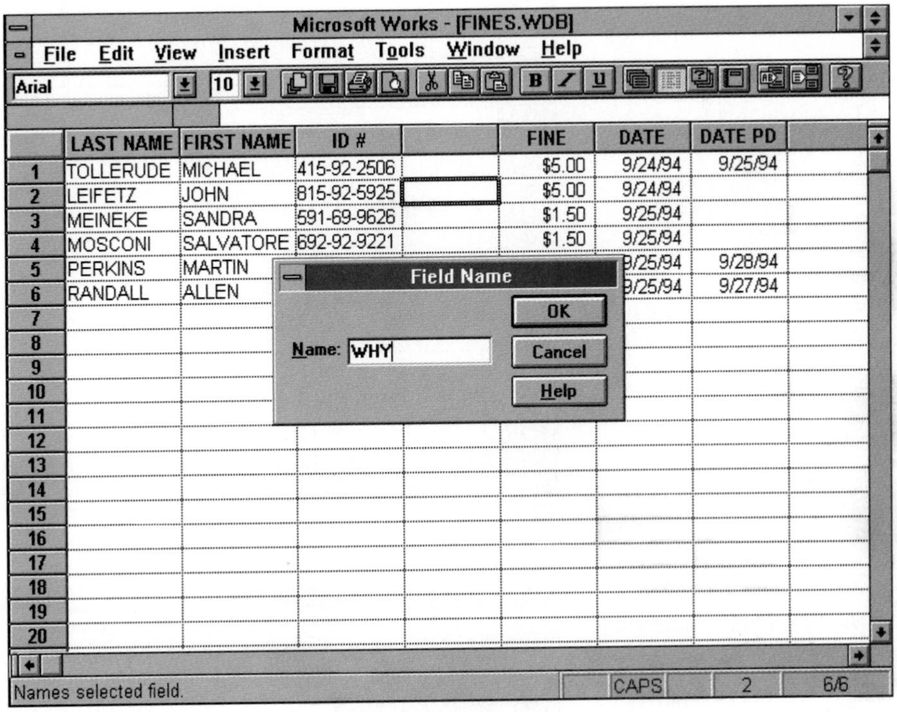

	LAST NAME	FIRST NAME	ID #		FINE	DATE	DATE PD	
1	TOLLERUDE	MICHAEL	415-92-2506		$5.00	9/24/94	9/25/94	
2	LEIFETZ	JOHN	815-92-5925		$5.00	9/24/94		
3	MEINEKE	SANDRA	591-69-9626		$1.50	9/25/94		
4	MOSCONI	SALVATORE	692-92-9221		$1.50	9/25/94		
5	PERKINS	MARTIN				9/25/94	9/28/94	
6	RANDALL	ALLEN				9/25/94	9/27/94	
7								
8								
9								
10								
11								
12								
13								
14								
15								
16								
17								
18								
19								
20								

Microsoft Works - [FINES.WDB]

File Edit View Insert Format Tools Window Help

Arial   10

Field Name

Name: WHY

OK

Cancel

Help

Names selected field.   CAPS   2   6/6

[handwritten margin note: SEE FORM VIEW AFTER NAMING FIELD ?]

from the Edit menu to name the field. The Field Name dialog box is shown in Figure 20-3. Name the field **WHY** and press Enter. The FINES.WDB now has a new, named field, as shown in Figure 20-4.

To insert a new field directly into a database in form view, click an insertion point where you want the new field inserted. Then you can either insert the field using the Insert A Field button on the toolbar or select the Field command from the Insert menu. Either way, Works opens the Insert Field dialog box, which you used in the last lesson. After naming the field WHY and accepting the other defaults, the FINES.WDB will have a new named field, as shown in Figure 20-5.

In Works you can insert a new record at any location in an existing database in either form view or list view. In form view, for example, if you want to insert a record before record 2, you first need to select record 2. Then you select the Record command from the Insert menu. Works will insert a new blank record before record 2, label the record as record 2, and renumber the records following the new record.

To insert a new record before record 2 in list view, you highlight all of record 2 by clicking on the record number to the left of the record's first field. Then select the Record/Field command from the Insert menu. Works will insert a record above the record you highlighted and renumber all

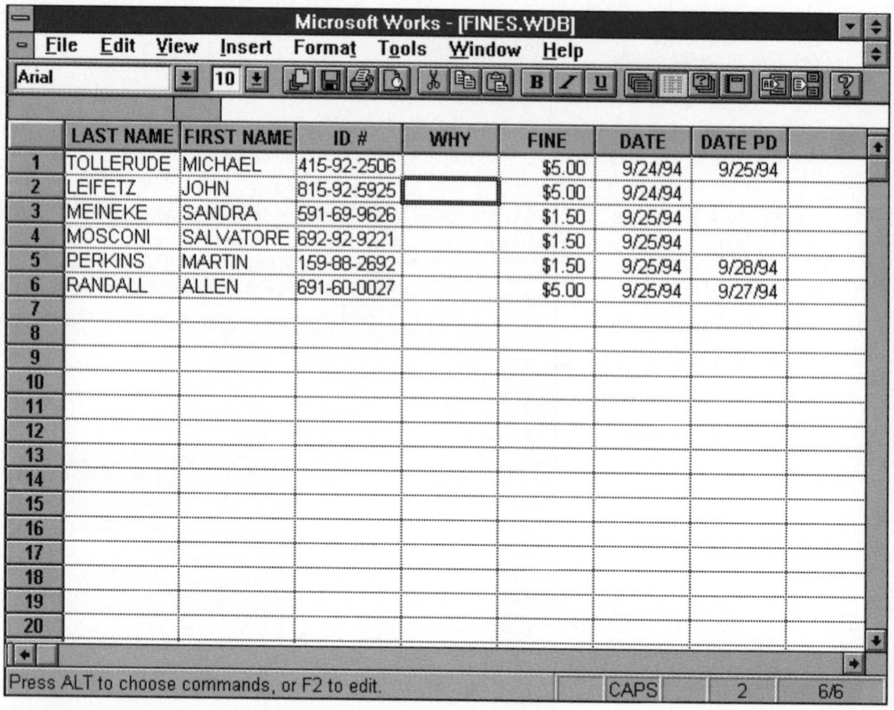

FIGURE 20-4

The FINES.WDB database in list view after the WHY field is inserted in the column to the left of the FINE field.

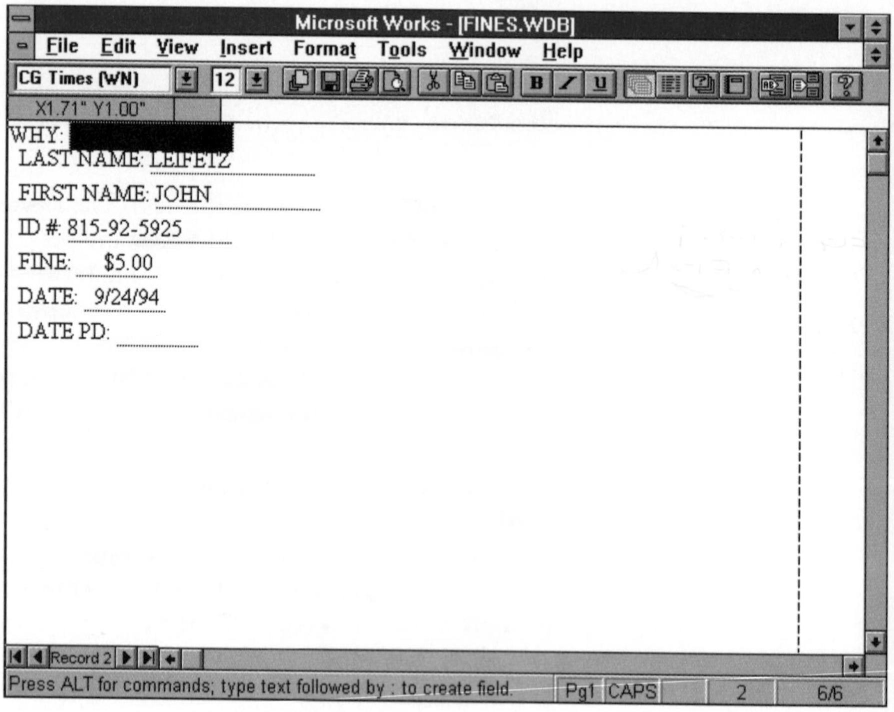

FIGURE 20-5

The FINES.WDB database in form view after the WHY field is inserted.

FIGURE 20-6
*The FINES.WDB file just
after a blank record is
inserted.*

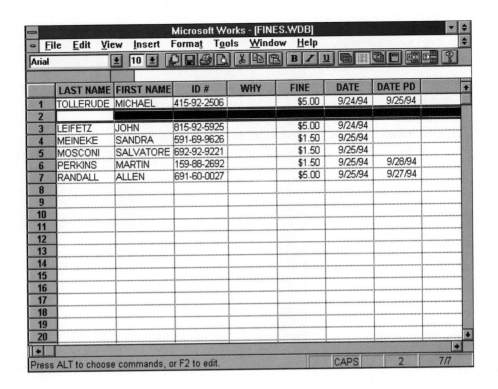

records following the new record. Figure 20-6 shows the same database after the new record has been inserted.

Works offers two shortcuts for adding records and fields. Selecting the Insert Record button or the Insert Field button from the toolbar will also insert a record or field in form or list view.

DELETING FIELDS AND RECORDS

To delete a field in list view, highlight the field you want to delete, then choose Delete Record/Field from the Insert menu—you can delete more than one field by highlighting the fields you want to delete. The Delete dialog box, shown in Figure 20-7, appears, asking whether you want to delete a record or a field (Record is the default). When you delete a field, Works removes all information from the fields and closes the space. If you decide to undo your deletion, the Undo Delete Field command on the Edit menu ([Ctrl] +Z) will return the field to your database with all its information. If you have made other changes since you deleted a field and Undo Delete Field is not available, you can close the database without saving your changes and return to your database without the field deleted. This means that you will lose other changes you have made to the database, as well. Figure 20-8 shows the FINES.WDB after the FIRST NAME field has been removed.

Deleting fields from a database in form view is slightly different. First highlight the field you want to delete. Then select Delete Selection from the Insert menu. Works displays a warning, shown in Figure 20-9, advising you that you cannot undo this operation. Press [Enter] and the FINES.WDB file, shown in Figure 20-10, will change to reflect your deletion.

FIGURE 20-7

*The Delete dialog box
appears when you choose
Delete Record/Field from
the Insert menu and you are
in list view. The default
setting, Record, has been
changed to Field.*

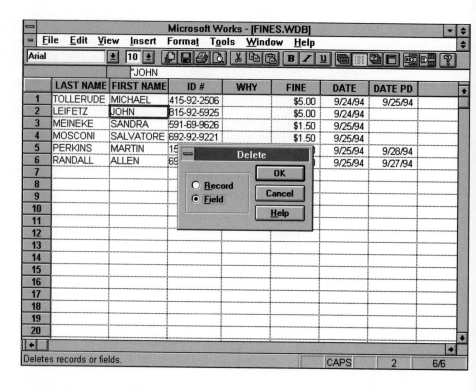

FIGURE 20-7

*The Delete dialog box
appears when you choose
Delete Record/Field from
the Insert menu and you are
in list view. The default
setting, Record, has been
changed to Field.*

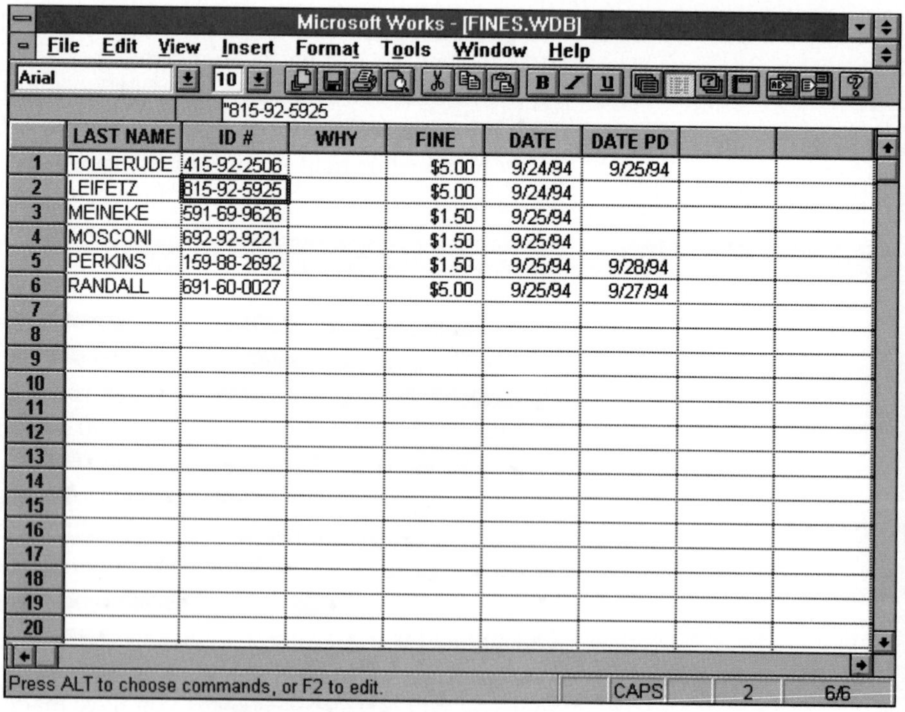

FIGURE 20-8

*The FINES.WDB file in list
view after the FIRST NAME
field has been removed.*

If you want to delete data in a field but not delete the field itself, high-light the field and select Clear Field Entry from the Edit menu (or press the Delete key). If you want to delete the data in several fields, highlight those fields and follow the same steps. Use the Undo Clear command from the Edit menu to reverse the last Clear command.

FIGURE 20-9

This warning appears when you try to delete a field in form view.

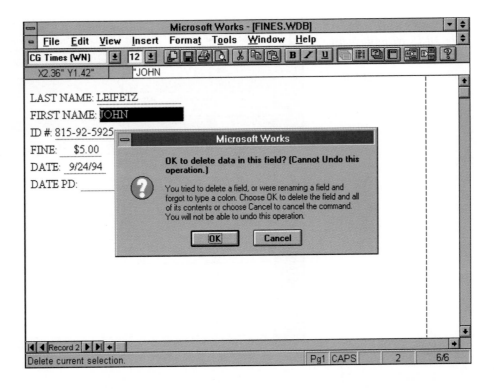

FIGURE 20-10

The FINES.WDB file in form view after the FIRST NAME field has been removed.

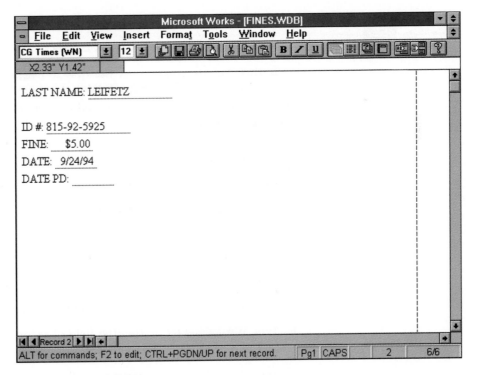

Deleting a record is similar to deleting fields. In list view, highlight a field in the record you want to delete. Select the Delete Record/Field command from the Insert menu, keeping the default Record setting. Figure 20-11 shows the FINES.WDB file after record 3 has been deleted. To delete a record in Form view, scroll to the record you want to delete. Select Delete Record from the Insert menu. Works will delete the record and renumber the following records.

FIGURE 20-11
*The FINES.WDB file in list
view after record 3 has
been deleted.*

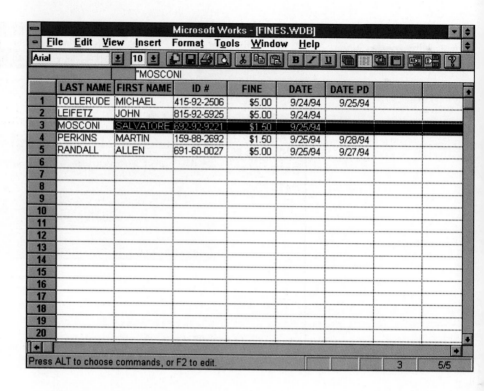

GUIDED PRACTICE

INSERTING AND DELETING RECORDS

In this exercise you will use list view to insert a new record and remove an existing record in the FINES.WDB database you created in the last lesson. The records you have entered into the FINES.WDB database are in order by the date when a fine was assessed. However, you accidentally overlooked one record for September 24. You will insert this record before the current record 3.

1. Open and display the FINES.WDB database in list view.

2. Make any field in record 3 active. The first field in record 3 contains the name **MEINEKE**.

3. Choose Record/Field from the Insert menu to create a blank record before the row containing the name MEINEKE. Select OK or press the (Enter) key when the Insert dialog box appears. The inserted record becomes record 3, as shown in Figure 20-12.

4. Type **WOLOFSON,** in the first field of record 3, then press the (Tab) key and type **Jennifer** in the second field.

5. Type the following information in the remaining fields:

ID#:   216-42-9255

FINE: $1.50

DATE: 9/24/94

DATE PD: 9/25/94

FIGURE 20-12
The FINES.WDB with the new, empty record 3 inserted.

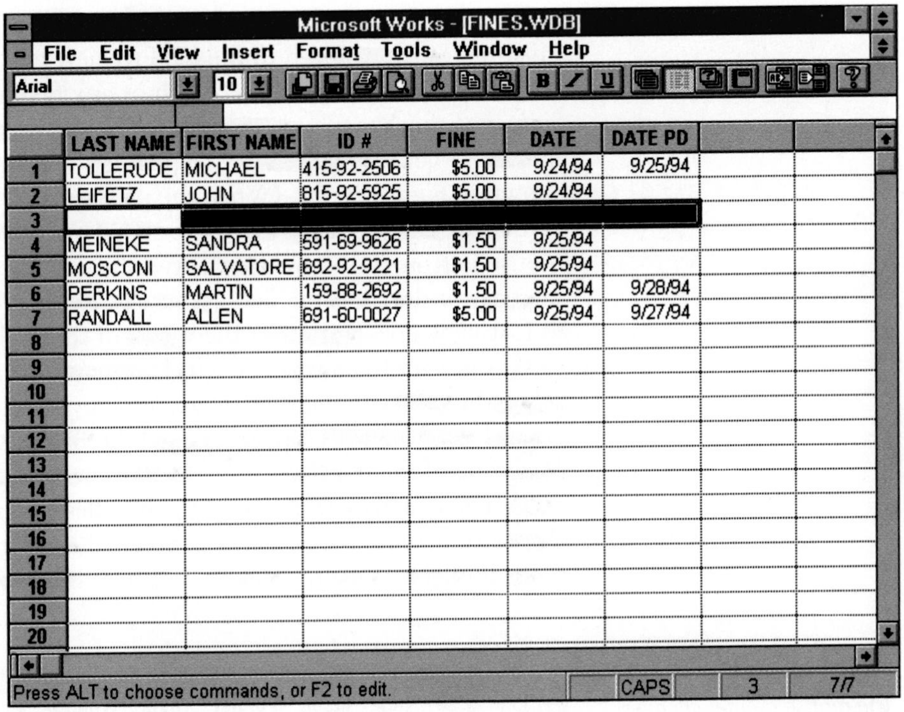
Microsoft Works - [FINES.WDB]
File Edit View Insert Format Tools Window Help
Arial
10
LAST NAME FIRST NAME ID # FINE DATE DATE PD
1 TOLLERUDE MICHAEL 415-92-2506 $5.00 9/24/94 9/25/94
2 LEIFETZ JOHN 815-92-5925 $5.00 9/24/94
3
4 MEINEKE SANDRA 591-69-9626 $1.50 9/25/94
5 MOSCONI SALVATORE 692-92-9221 $1.50 9/25/94
6 PERKINS MARTIN 159-88-2692 $1.50 9/25/94 9/28/94
7 RANDALL ALLEN 691-60-0027 $5.00 9/25/94 9/27/94
8
9
10
11
12
13
14
15
16
17
18
19
20
Press ALT to choose commands, or F2 to edit.
CAPS
3
7/7

6. Choose Save (Ctrl+S) from the File menu to save the information you just entered to the FINES.WDB database.

In the next steps you will remove a record from the FINES.WDB database for a student, Salvatore Mosconi, who has moved from the district.

7. Position the highlight on any field in record 5 (the LAST NAME field contains the name MOSCONI).
8. Choose Delete Record/Field from the Insert menu. Press Enter to accept the Delete dialog box default setting. The record for Salvatore Mosconi is now permanently removed from the database, as shown in Figure 20-13.
9. Save the database under the current name FINES.WDB.

CHANGING THE NAME AND SIZE OF A FIELD

You can change the name of a field at any time without changing the information in the field. In list view begin changing a field name by highlighting a field and choosing Field Name from the Edit menu. When the Field Name dialog box appears, type the new name in the Name text box and click OK. In form view, highlight the field name you want to change and begin typing, ending the name with a colon(:). Press Enter and the form displays the new field name. Changing a field name in one view automatically changes the field name in the other view.

So far you have not had to increase the width of a field for information that is longer than the width Works provides by default. If Works cannot fit an entire value in the space provided in a number field, number symbols

(###) are substituted for the value. The value remains in the field, but you must increase the width of the field to view it.

You can easily change the width of any field to display more data. In list view, position the mouse pointer on the vertical line that separates two field names in the column heading to produce the two-headed arrow pointer shown in Figure 20-13. (When the pointer is positioned anywhere else in the column heading, it appears in the shape of a cross.) When you press the mouse button, you can drag the two-headed arrow to the left or right to increase or decrease the field (column) width. Changing the width of a field in List view does not affect the width of that field in form view.

If you want to change the width or height of a field in form view, first select the field you want to resize. When you select a field in form view, small square **handles** appear around the field, as shown in Figure 20-14. Drag one of the handles on the right to increase or decrease the width of the field. You can also drag one of the handles on the bottom of the field up or down to increase the height of a field. Changing the size of a field in form view does not affect the size of that field in list view.

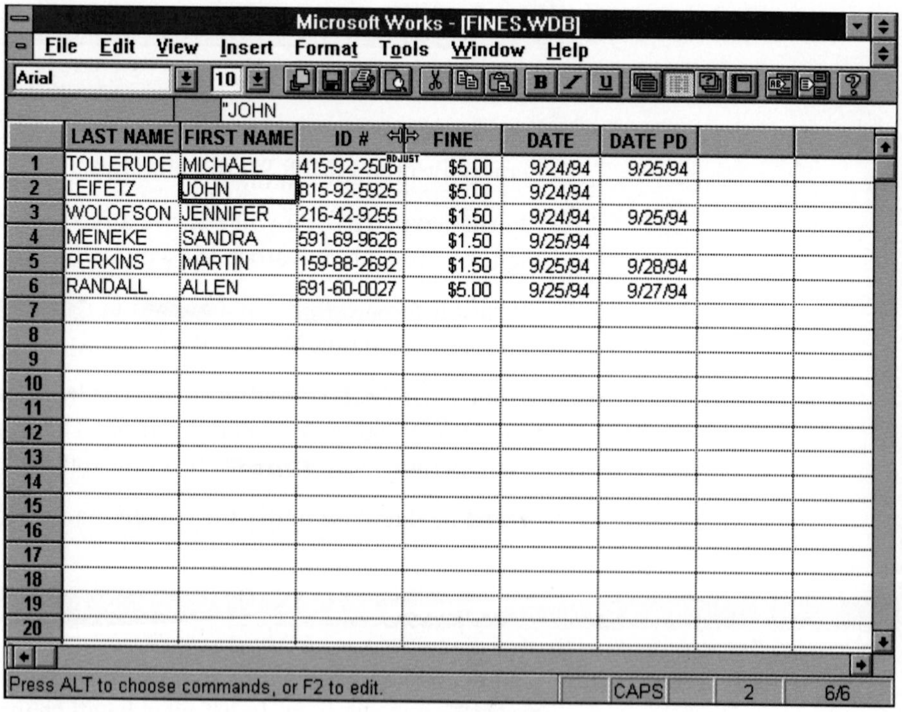

FIGURE 20-13

The mouse pointer changes to a two-headed arrow pointer when it is positioned on the vertical line between field names in list view.

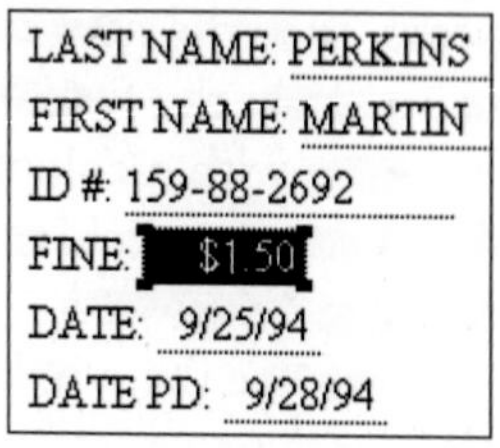

FIGURE 20-14

The small square handles around the FINE field's data indicate that the field is selected. The width of the FINE field was decreased by pointing to the top handle on the right and dragging it to the left.

GUIDED PRACTICE

INSERTING, DELETING, AND CHANGING FIELD NAMES

In this exercise you will use list view to insert and then delete a field. Your lab manager wants you to add a WHY field to the FINES database. This field will be defined to contain a code number to indicate the reason the lab user was fined. For instance, a code number 1 in the WHY field could mean that the student left a software disk at a computer station instead of returning it to the checkout desk; a code number 2 could mean that the student failed to turn off the power switch on a monitor; and so on.

1. Start Works and display the FINES.WDB database in list view, if necessary.

2. Click on any record in the DATE field column, so that the new WHY field column will be inserted to the left of the DATE field column.

3. Choose Record/Field from the Insert menu to display the Insert dialog box.

4. Click on the Field radio button.

5. Chose OK or press ⟨Enter⟩. The new field is now inserted.

6. Click on the Field Name command from the Edit menu.

7. Type WHY in the Name text box. Press ⟨Enter⟩. Notice that the field name WHY appears at the top of the column to the left of the DATE field.

8. Highlight any field in the WHY column.

9. Choose the Alignment command from the Format menu. Select the Center radio button from the Alignment section of the dialog box and click OK. The code numbers you enter in the WHY field will now be centered.

   The WHY field is just as wide as all the other fields, even though you need only enough space for a one- or two-digit code. In the next step you will drag the WHY field column to decrease its width.

10. Position the mouse pointer directly over the vertical line that separates the WHY and the DATE fields names, then drag it to the left until the WHY field is approximately the size of the word WHY. Release the mouse button. Your WHY field should be about the size of the one shown in Figure 20-15.

    When you create a new field, you need to enter information for existing records in that field. In the next steps you will enter information in the WHY field for records 1 and 2.

11. Click an insertion point in the WHY field for record 1, if necessary, and type the code number 2. Press the ⟨↓⟩ key to advance to the same field in the next record. Then type the code number 1.

    After considering the usefulness of the information in the WHY field, your lab manager asks you to delete the field from the FINES.WDB database.

FIGURE 20-15
The WHY field after it has been resized.

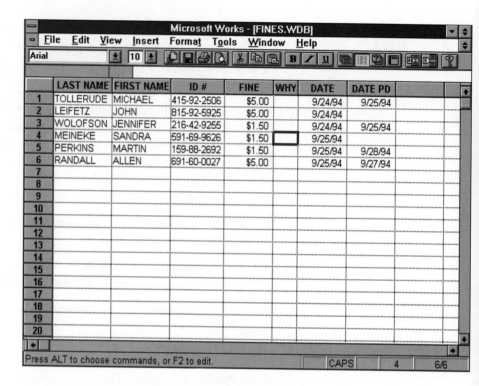

12. In list view, click on the WHY field for any record to make it active.

13. Choose Delete Record/Field from the Insert menu. Select the Field radio button. Click OK to delete the WHY field.

In the next steps you will change the field name DATE to DOF.

14. Click in a DATE field to make it active, then choose Field Name from the Edit menu to display the Field Name dialog box.

15. Type **DOF** in the Name text box and press the Enter key.

16. Save the database under the current name, FINES.WDB.

EDITING RECORDS

Occasionally you will need to correct errors in the database. To make a correction, you must change an existing field's content to reflect the change in a record. For instance, a customer might move and thus require a change in his or her address and phone number fields.

In Works editing records is easy. In either list view or form view, you can highlight the field you want to change. The information in the highlighted field appears on the formula bar. Delete the information on the formula bar by highlighting it and pressing the Delete key, or click an insertion point within the formula bar information and delete some or all of the information using the Delete or Backspace key. The new information you type in the formula bar can then be entered in the field by clicking in the formula box or pressing the Tab or Enter key.

GUIDED PRACTICE

CHANGING FIELD CONTENT

In this exercise you will enter changes in the FINES.WDB file. You may need to resize some of the fields with the mouse pointer in order to better read the information in the fields. An error in the last name of record 1 needs to be corrected by changing the name TOLLERUDE to TOLLEREW. Also, change the ID # in record 4 from 591-69-9262 to 591-69-9626.

1. Start Works and open the FINES.WDB database in list view, if necessary.

2. Click in the LAST NAME field for record 1 to place the field information TOLLERUDE in the formula bar.

3. Click an insertion point in the space after the second E in TOLLERUDE, then press the [Backspace] key three times to delete the last three letters of the name.

4. Type **EW** to change the entry to TOLLEREW, then press the [Tab] key or the [Enter] key.

5. Click in the ID # field for Sandra Meineke's record (record 4) to place the field information in the entry bar.

6. Click an insertion point at the end of the ID number in the entry bar, and press the Backspace key four times to delete the last four characters of the number.

7. Type **9626** and then press the [Tab] key or the [Enter] key to complete the change. Your screen should look similar to the one shown in Figure 20-16.

8. Save the revised database using the name FINES1.WDB.

FIGURE 20-16
The FINES.WDB database after changes are made to records 1 and 4.

	LAST NAME	FIRST NAME	ID NUMBER	FINE	DOF	DATE PD		
1	TOLLEREW	MICHAEL	415-92-2506	$5.00	9/24/94	9/25/94		
2	LEIFETZ	JOHN	815-92-5925	$5.00	9/24/94			
3	WOLOFSON	JENNIFER	216-42-9255	$1.50	9/24/94	9/25/94		
4	MEINEKE	SANDRA	591-69-9626	$1.50	9/25/94			
5	PERKINS	MARTIN	159-88-2692	$1.50	9/25/94	9/28/94		
6	RANDALL	ALLEN	691-60-0027	$5.00	9/25/94	9/27/94		
7								
8								
9								
10								
11								
12								
13								
14								
15								
16								
17								
18								
19								
20								

Microsoft Works - [FINES1.WDB]

File   Edit   View   Insert   Format   Tools   Window   Help

Arial   10   1.5

Press ALT to choose commands, or F2 to edit.   4   6/6

CALCULATING FIELDS IN A DATABASE

You can have Works calculate information in a database by creating a **calculating field.** For instance, a database record can include a calculating field to store values that result from multiplying unit prices of items in the PRICE field by the numbers of items in the QTY field. A calculating field can be created and formatted when you set up a new database, or it can be added at any time to an existing database.

To create a calculating field for an existing database, add a formula to a field—this will add the same formula to the same field in each record. Works offers five ways to create calculating fields:

Mathematical operators, for example, +, –, *, /, and , (comma)

Numbers, such as 1, 19, 412, and 14.7

Field references, for example, B3, D16, and B2:D2

Field names, such as PRICE, QTY, and COST

Functions, the built-in equations included with Works, including addition (SUM), average (AVG), and rounding (ROUND).

These calculating tools can be used in combinations, but a field can have only one formula. Your Microsoft Works *User's Guide* offers suggested formulas, as well as descriptions of the 76 functions available for databases and spreadsheets.

In Figure 20-17, for example, the VALUE field will calculate its field by multiplying the QTY field by the PRICE field. The numbers were automatically formatted as currency by selecting the Number command from the

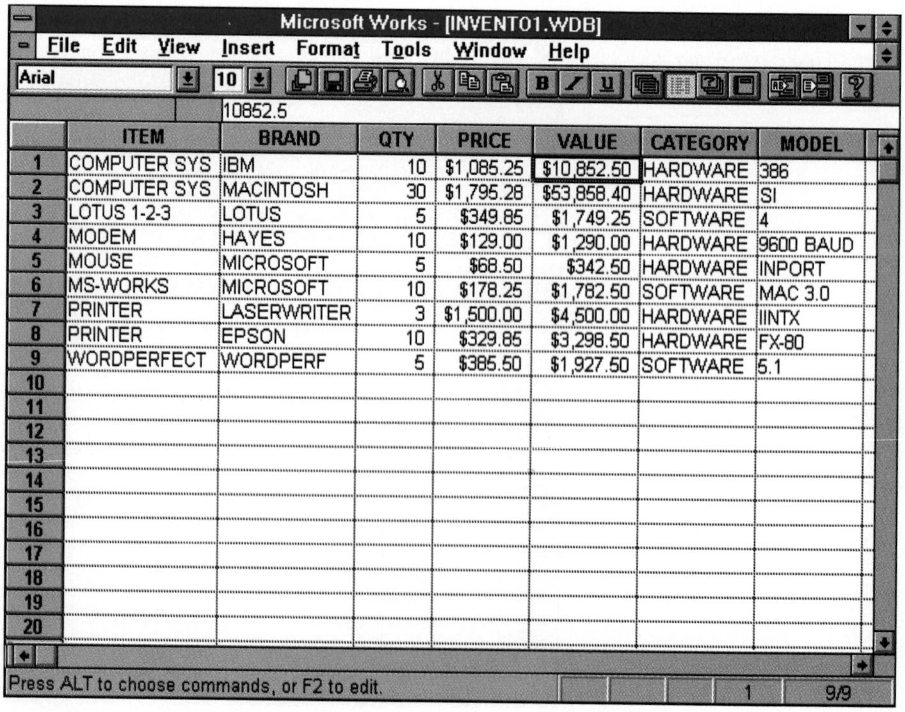

FIGURE 20-17

The VALUE field in this illustration was calculated by using a formula.

	ITEM	BRAND	QTY	PRICE	VALUE	CATEGORY	MODEL
1	COMPUTER SYS	IBM	10	$1,085.25	$10,852.50	HARDWARE	386
2	COMPUTER SYS	MACINTOSH	30	$1,795.28	$53,858.40	HARDWARE	SI
3	LOTUS 1-2-3	LOTUS	5	$349.85	$1,749.25	SOFTWARE	4
4	MODEM	HAYES	10	$129.00	$1,290.00	HARDWARE	9600 BAUD
5	MOUSE	MICROSOFT	5	$68.50	$342.50	HARDWARE	INPORT
6	MS-WORKS	MICROSOFT	10	$178.25	$1,782.50	SOFTWARE	MAC 3.0
7	PRINTER	LASERWRITER	3	$1,500.00	$4,500.00	HARDWARE	IINTX
8	PRINTER	EPSON	10	$329.85	$3,298.50	HARDWARE	FX-80
9	WORDPERFECT	WORDPERF	5	$385.50	$1,927.50	SOFTWARE	5.1

Microsoft Works - [INVENTO1.WDB]

File Edit View Insert Format Tools Window Help

Arial   10   10852.5

Press ALT to choose commands, or F2 to edit.   1   9/9

FIGURE 20-18

The Number dialog box offers a variety of ways to format numbers.

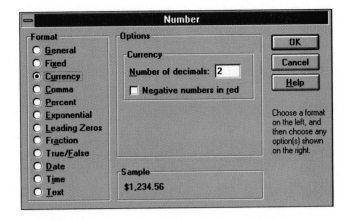

Format menu. This displayed the Number dialog box, as shown in Figure 20-18. By selecting currency, the numbers were given dollar signs and formatted with two decimal places, the default when selecting Currency.

PRACTICE APPLICATIONS

1. Open the EQUIPME1.WDB database file on your Student Data Disk.

2. Change the purchase date for records 7 and 8 to 8/24/1992.

3. Change the name of the purchase date field from DATE PURCH to DATE PURCHASED.

4. Widen the DATE PURCHASED column until the field name is visible.

5. Before record 12, add a record containing the following information:

ITEM:	COMPUTER SYS
BRAND:	MAC
SERIAL #:	SI-935934
QTY:	1
DATE PURCH:	8/23/92
PRICE:	1,289.50

6. How is the information in the PRICE field of the new record different from what you typed? Why do you think it is different?

7. Save the file under the name EQUIPPRA.WDB and close the database.

CHAPTER REVIEW

You create a new database by defining fields. You then enter information into the fields to create a record.

In list view and form view, you can enter information in records, insert or append records, and delete records. You can also add or delete a field, change a field name, or change the size of a field.

REVIEW QUESTIONS

TRUE-FALSE

Write your answers on a sheet of paper.

1. In creating a database, you must specify field names before you can enter field information.

2. In form view or list view, you can change a field name at any time.

3. Once you have inserted a field in form view, you cannot change the width of the field.

4. Either letters or numbers can be entered into fields.

5. Field information is first typed in the formula bar then entered into the field.

6. Entering = at the beginning of a field entry tells Works that the number is currency.

7. You can insert a record in either form view or list view.

8. When you insert a record in form view, it is not automatically inserted in list view.

9. When you delete a record in list view, it is not automatically deleted in form view.

10. You can rename a field in form view by choosing Field Name from the Edit menu.

SHORT-ANSWER QUESTIONS

Write a brief answer to these questions on a sheet of paper.

1. What is the difference between a field name and field information?

2. Which character cannot be used as the initial character in a field name?

3. Suppose a new field you have created for a database requires more space for entering information in the field. Describe how you can increase the default width of a field in list view.

4. Describe how you can specify the appearance of field information when you name the field. How can an existing field be reformatted to change the way information appears?

5. In form view, where in the document window would you find the number of the current record?

LESSON APPLICATIONS

1. Create a database that contains the names, phone numbers, and addresses of at least five of your friends. Save the database file using the name FRIENDS.WDB.

2. Add two records to your FRIENDS.WDB database, then insert a date field called BIRTHDAY. Save the database under the current name.

3. Print one copy of the database.

CHAPTER APPLICATIONS

1. Use Figure 20-19 as a guide to create a database called PRACTICE.WDB. Enter all of the data for the five records shown in the figure.

2. Delete record 3 from the PRACTICE.WDB database, then insert a record for yourself (your name, phone number, and so on) at the top of the database so that the inserted record becomes record 1. Finally, insert a field between the LAST NAME and the FIRST NAME fields. Call this field MI (for middle initial) and change the field width to an appropriate size. Save the revised database as PRACTIC2.WDB.

3. Open the FINES1.WDB database and change the name of the ID # field to ID NUMBER. Save the file under the current name.

FIGURE 20-19

Use this illustration as a guide for creating your PRACTICE.WDB database.

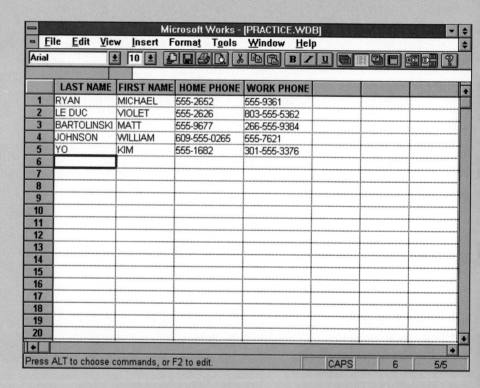

CHALLENGE EXERCISE

Open the database INVENTO1.WDB on your Student Data Disk. Insert a new computing field named VALUE between the PRICE and CATEGORY fields. Highlight a field in the VALUE column and enter –QTY * PRICE on the formula bar. Press the [Enter] or [Tab] key.

Open the Number dialog box and format the numbers in the VALUE field for currency. Compare your screen with the one shown in Figure 20-17. Save the database under the name COMPINVE.WDB.

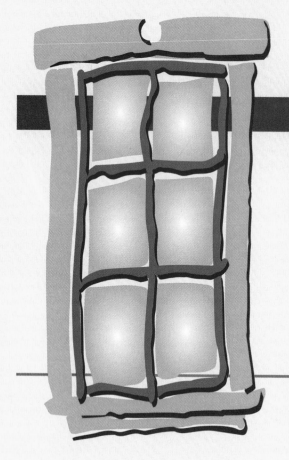

CHAPTER 8

MANIPULATING AND REPORTING DATABASE INFORMATION

OVERVIEW

In Chapter 9 you learned some basic principles about database information and in Chapter 10 you learned how to create and edit a database using the Works database application. In this chapter you will learn even more about the power of the database application. You will learn how to sort and search a database; how to set up record selection rules in a query that can be used for displaying specified records; and finally, how to create, format, and print a database report.

CONTENTS

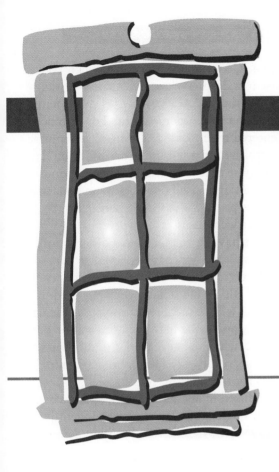

LESSON 21

SORTING AND SEARCHING A DATABASE

As you remember from Chapter 9, sorting is a process in which you arrange the records in a database in a desired order. By default, Works places database records in the order they are created. This is called **natural order,** or **serial order.** In some cases natural order is useful. For instance, if the records for a database are entered by the date and time of the transaction, then the database will be organized in a natural order based on date and time. In the FINES.WDB database that you created in the previous chapter, records were entered sequentially based on the date on which fines were incurred. When the database is printed, this natural order can be useful in identifying how many fines were assessed on a given day.

Often, however, database records have to be placed in a different order to meet the needs of managers. For instance, suppose the computer lab manager wants to print a report to determine those lab users who have been assessed two or more fines. If the FINES.WDB database is organized by the dates of the fines, the names of users will be scattered throughout the database. In other words, as Figure 21-l shows, the first fine assessed for JOHN LEIFETZ would appear as record 2, while the next record of a fine assessed for this same person would appear as record 11. This approach makes it difficult to locate multiple records for the same person.

However, if the database is organized in last-name order, as shown in Figure 21-2, multiple records for a single lab user are easier to identify. So sorting provides a way to meaningfully organize records within a database.

FIGURE 21-1

In this display of the FINES3.WDB database, records are in natural order.

	LAST NAME	FIRST NAME	ID #	FINE	DOF	DATE PD		
1	TOLLEREW	MICHAEL	415-92-2506	$5.00	9/24/94	9/25/94		
2	LEIFETZ	JOHN	815-92-5925	$5.00	9/24/94			
3	WOLOFSON	JENNIFER	216-42-9255	$1.50	9/24/94	9/25/94		
4	MEINEKE	SANDRA	591-69-9628	$1.50	9/25/94			
5	JOHNSON	WILLIAM	262-62-9254	$5.00	9/25/94	9/26/94		
6	PERKINS	MARTIN	159-88-2692	$1.50	9/25/94	9/28/94		
7	RANDALL	ALLEN	691-60-0027	$5.00	9/25/94	9/27/94		
8	ASHLEY	ROBIN	229-02-9151	$1.50	9/26/94			
9	HARDING	ELLEN	159-26-9277	$5.00	9/27/94			
10	FERNANDEZ	PAUL	692-11-2998	$5.00	9/27/94	10/1/94		
11	LEIFETZ	JOHN	815-92-5925	$1.50	9/27/94			
12	ASHLEY	ROBIN	229-02-9151	$1.50	9/28/94			
13	RANDALL	ALLEN	691-60-0027	$1.50	9/28/94	10/3/94		
14	JOHNSON	WILLIAM	577-59-1169	$1.50	9/28/94			
15	PAPILLON	RONALD	620-44-9151	$5.00	10/1/94			
16	RICHARDS	DENISE	792-06-0206	$1.50	10/1/94	10/5/94		
17	PARRISH	MAXINE	629-22-2691	$1.50	10/2/94	10/4/94		
18	LEIFETZ	JANINE	602-93-2698	$5.00	10/3/94	10/5/94		
19	PERKINS	MARTIN	159-88-2691	$1.50	10/4/94	10/5/94		
20	LING	JANETTE	692-66-9217	$5.00	10/5/94	10/5/94		

Microsoft Works - [FINES3.WDB]

File   Edit   View   Insert   Format   Tools   Window   Help

Arial   10   "TOLLEREW

Press ALT to choose commands, or F2 to edit.   1   22/22

FIGURE 21-2

In this display of the FINES3.WDB database, records have been sorted into alphabetic order, based on the contents of the LAST NAME field.

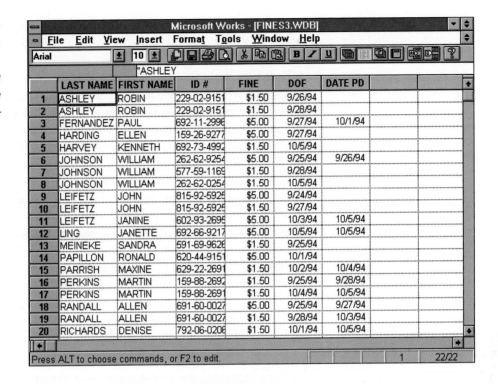

THE SORT RECORDS DIALOG BOX

In Works you use the Sort Records dialog box to specify the way in which you want records to be sorted. This dialog box, shown in Figure 21-3, appears when you choose Sort Records from the Tools menu.

You can sort on one or more sort fields. A **sort field** tells Works to group records in order, based on the content of the sort field. For example, the database in Figure 21-2 was sorted on the LAST NAME field, which is selected in the Sort Records dialog box shown in Figure 21-3.

It is often necessary to identify more than one sort field. For example, by sorting on both LAST NAME and FIRST NAME, you ensure that records for different individuals who have the same last name but different first names will not be mixed in the list. Multiple records for JOHN LEIFETZ will appear together, as will multiple records for JANINE LEIFETZ. By adding the ID # field to the sort, you ensure that records for individuals who have the same last and first names (such as two WILLIAM JOHN-SONs) will not be mixed in the list. Two people may have the same first and last names, but they will have different identification numbers. To sort on

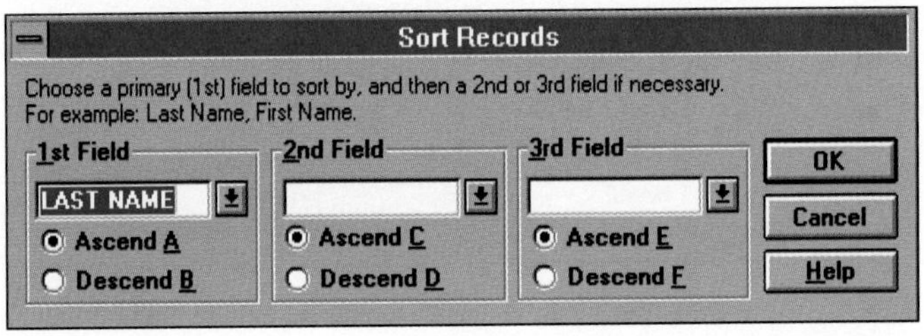

FIGURE 21-3

The Sort Records dialog box is used to select a sort field.

more than one field, you select the most significant field or **key field**, to sort first in the Sort Records dialog box; then you select the least important field, to sort last.

Figure 21-4 shows the result of a three-field sort in which LAST NAME was selected first because it is the most important sort field, FIRST NAME was selected second, and ID # was selected last because it is the least important sort field. Notice that records 6, 7, and 8 are all for WILLIAM JOHNSON, but that the ID # sort ensures that the records for each individual named WILLIAM JOHNSON will appear together. The 1st Field list box shown in Figure 21-3 contains the field name LAST NAME. When you press on the down arrow beside this list box, a list of all the fields in the FINES3.WDB database appears, as shown in Figure 21-5. This is the submenu you use to select one or more sort fields.

Look again at the dialog box shown in Figure 21-3. Note that Ascend or Descend is available for each field. Unless the Descend radio button is turned on, Works sorts a field in ascending order. An **ascending sort** organizes text records from A to Z. This means that records with names in the LAST NAME field that begin with the letter A will appear before records with last names that begin with B, and so on through the alphabet. Numeric

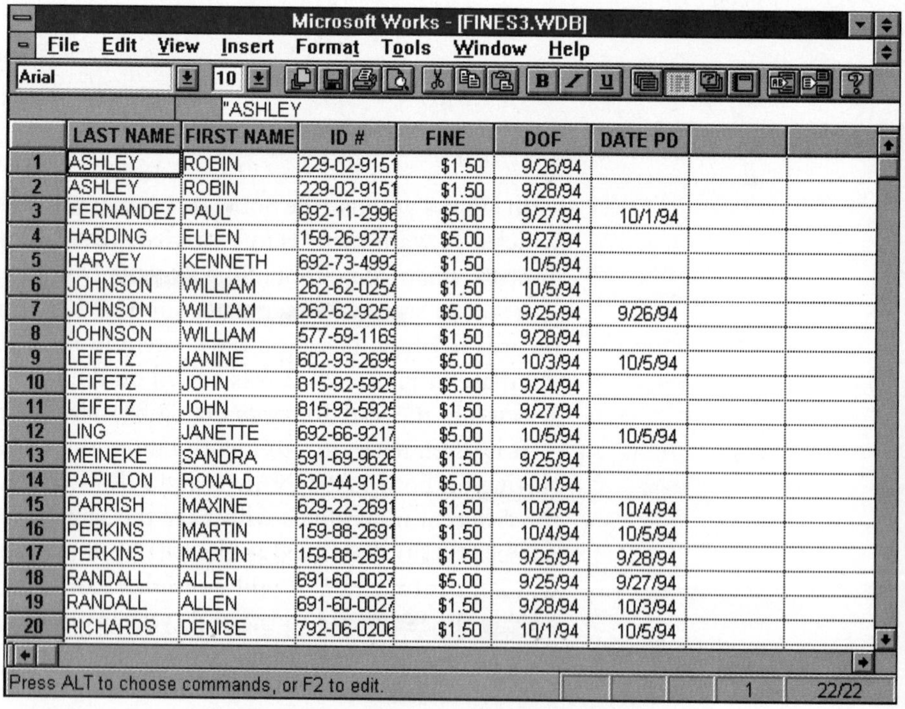

	LAST NAME	FIRST NAME	ID #	FINE	DOF	DATE PD
1	ASHLEY	ROBIN	229-02-9151	$1.50	9/26/94	
2	ASHLEY	ROBIN	229-02-9151	$1.50	9/28/94	
3	FERNANDEZ	PAUL	692-11-2998	$5.00	9/27/94	10/1/94
4	HARDING	ELLEN	159-26-9277	$5.00	9/27/94	
5	HARVEY	KENNETH	692-73-4992	$1.50	10/5/94	
6	JOHNSON	WILLIAM	262-62-0254	$1.50	10/5/94	
7	JOHNSON	WILLIAM	262-62-9254	$5.00	9/25/94	9/26/94
8	JOHNSON	WILLIAM	577-59-1169	$1.50	9/28/94	
9	LEIFETZ	JANINE	602-93-2695	$5.00	10/3/94	10/5/94
10	LEIFETZ	JOHN	815-92-5925	$5.00	9/24/94	
11	LEIFETZ	JOHN	815-92-5925	$1.50	9/27/94	
12	LING	JANETTE	692-66-9217	$5.00	10/5/94	10/5/94
13	MEINEKE	SANDRA	591-69-9628	$1.50	9/25/94	
14	PAPILLON	RONALD	620-44-9151	$5.00	10/1/94	
15	PARRISH	MAXINE	629-22-2691	$1.50	10/2/94	10/4/94
16	PERKINS	MARTIN	159-88-2691	$1.50	10/4/94	10/5/94
17	PERKINS	MARTIN	159-88-2692	$1.50	9/25/94	9/28/94
18	RANDALL	ALLEN	691-60-0027	$5.00	9/25/94	9/27/94
19	RANDALL	ALLEN	691-60-0027	$1.50	9/28/94	10/3/94
20	RICHARDS	DENISE	792-06-0208	$1.50	10/1/94	10/5/94

FIGURE 21-4
The FINES3.WDB database has been sorted according to LAST NAME, FIRST NAME, and ID #.

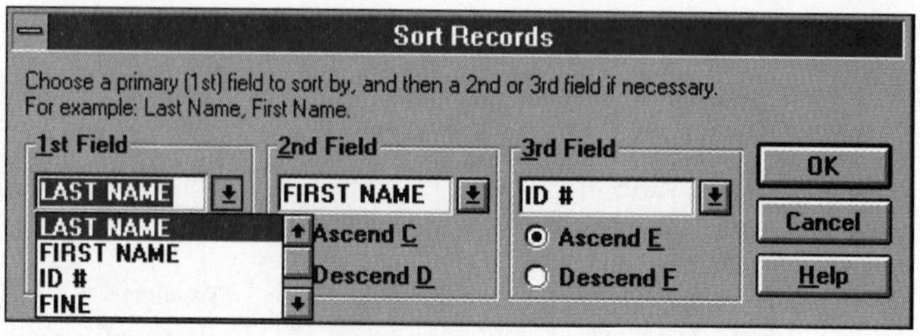

FIGURE 21-5
All database fields are listed in the Sort Records field list boxes.

values are sorted from 0 to 9. A **descending sort** reverses the order of the sort—Z to A and 9 to 0.

To produce the sort shown in Figure 21-4, the ascending, or default, sort order was used for all three sort fields, as shown in Figure 21-5. As a result, the record for JANINE LEIFETZ comes before the records for JOHN LEIFETZ. Also, the records for WILLIAM JOHNSON with ID #262-62-0254 appear before the record for WILLIAM JOHNSON with ID #577-59-1169.

SAVING THE RESULTS OF A SORT

When you sort a database, Works overwrites the current records stored in memory with the newly ordered records. If you save a sorted database to disk under the same file name that existed when you opened the database file, Works replaces the original version with the sorted version. If you want to keep the original order of records in the database, close the file without saving it. If you want to keep both the original and the sorted versions, save the sorted database to disk under a new name.

GUIDED PRACTICE

SORTING A DATABASE

In this exercise you will sort records on the FINES3.WDB database in several arrangements. You will save the different arrangements in different files. First you will sort records in ascending order by LAST NAME and by FIRST NAME. Next you will sort records in descending order by the FINE field. The lab manager wants you to organize records in this way so that all $5.00 fines appear together, followed by all $1.50 fines.

1. Start Works, insert your Student Data Disk in the floppy-disk drive, and display the FINES3.WDB database file in list view.

2. Choose Sort Records from the Tools menu to display the Sort Records dialog box.

3. Select ID # from the 1st Field list box.

4. Make sure that the Ascend radio button is turned on. Compare your Sort Records dialog box with the one shown in Figure 21-6.

5. Click on the OK button to sort the database records on the 1st Field (ID #) in ascending order. Compare your screen with the one shown in Figure 21-7.

FIGURE 21-6

The Sort Records dialog box just before the OK button is clicked to sort the FINES3.WDB database records based on information in the ID # field.

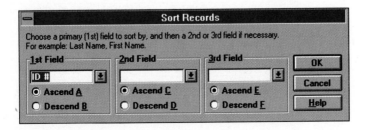

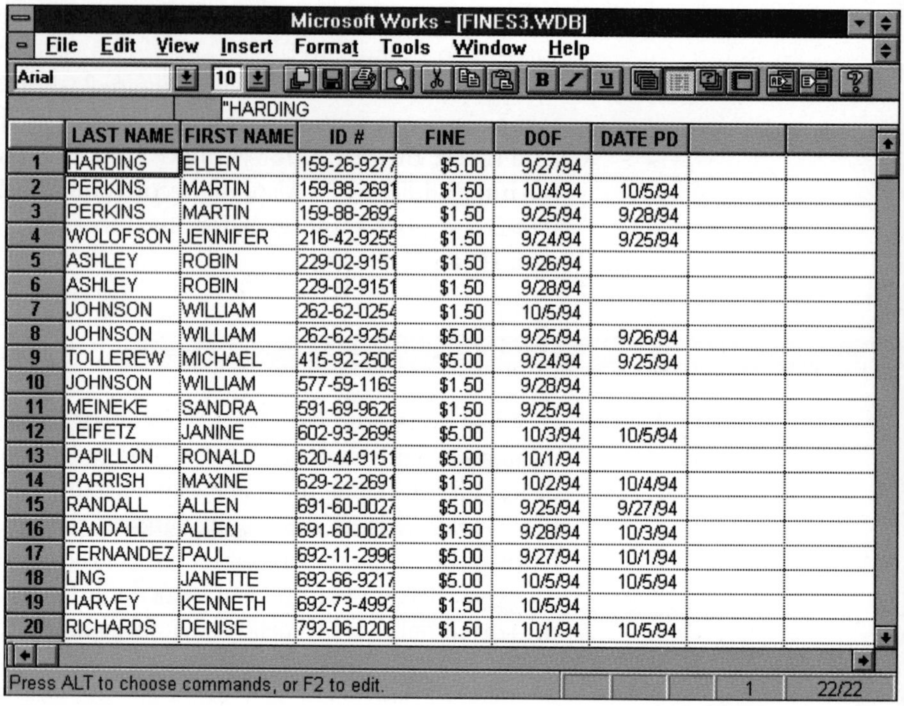

FIGURE 21-7

The FINES3.WDB database after records are sorted based on information in the 1st Field sort box. Notice that numbers in the ID # field are arranged from smallest to largest.

FIGURE 21-7

The FINES3.WDB database after records are sorted based on information in the 1st Field sort box. Notice that numbers in the ID # field are arranged from smallest to largest.

6. Open the Sort Records dialog box again by choosing Sort Records from the Tools menu.

7. Select **FIRST NAME** from the 1st Field list box, then click on the OK button to perform an ascending sort.

8. Open the Sort Records dialog box again and select **LAST NAME** from the 1st Field list box. Click on the OK button to perform an ascending sort. Compare your first 20 records with the ones shown in Figure 21-8.

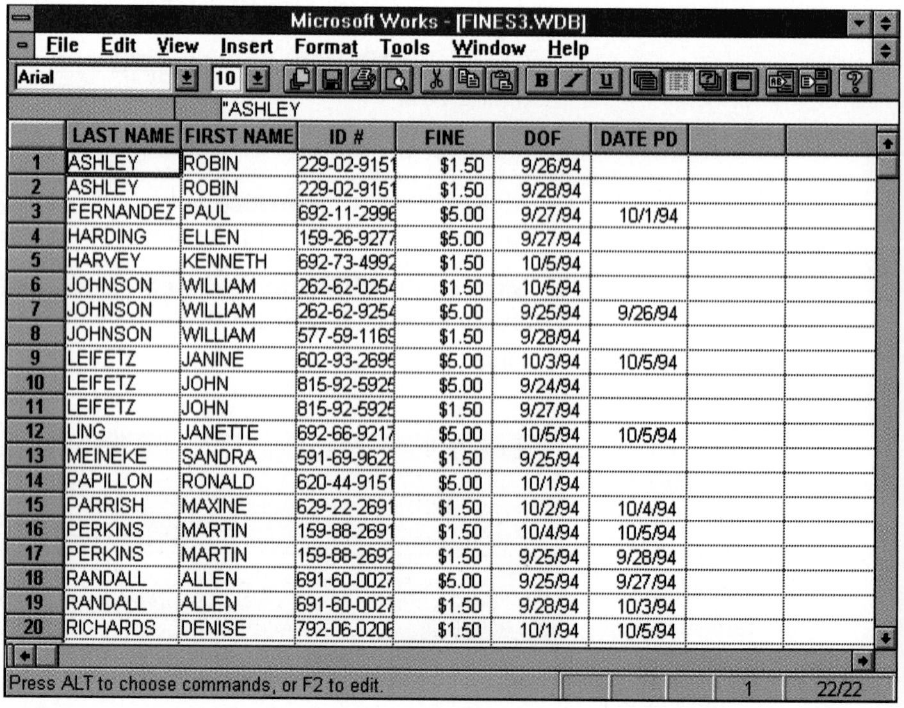

FIGURE 21-8

After you complete step 8, your screen display should look similar to this one.

9. Scroll through the database to examine the result of the sort.

10. Save the sorted database as FINES4.WDB, then close the FINES4.WDB database.

In the following steps you will use the FINES3.WDB database to sort information in the FINE field in descending order.

11. Open the FINES3.WDB file again.

12. Choose Sort Records from the Tools menu, then select FINE from the 1st Field list box.

13. Click on the Descend radio button to turn it on, then click on the OK button to carry out the sort. Examine the information in the FINE field. Notice that all the $5.00 amounts appear together and are listed before the $1.50 fines, as shown in Figure 21-9.

14. Save this version of the file as FINES5.WDB.

SEARCHING FOR SELECTED DATABASE RECORDS

In a database that contains fewer than 20 records, it is relatively easy to search for a particular record or a group of records by scrolling through the database. When databases increase in size, however, it becomes more difficult to search for records visually. In business it is common for a database to contain thousands of records. With these large databases, some other technique must be used to automate the selection of particular records. Works provides three techniques for searching for one or more records in a database. These techniques are described next.

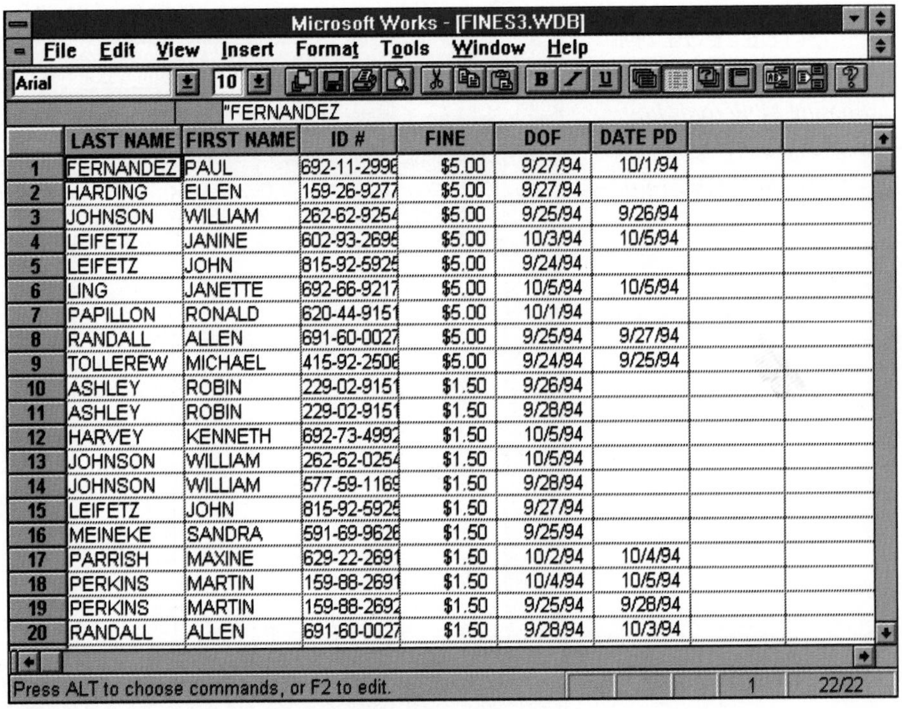

FIGURE 21-9

This screen display shows the FINES3.WDB database after you have chosen the FINE field and sorted it in descending order.

	LAST NAME	FIRST NAME	ID #	FINE	DOF	DATE PD		
1	FERNANDEZ	PAUL	692-11-2998	$5.00	9/27/94	10/1/94		
2	HARDING	ELLEN	159-26-9277	$5.00	9/27/94			
3	JOHNSON	WILLIAM	262-62-9254	$5.00	9/25/94	9/26/94		
4	LEIFETZ	JANINE	602-93-2698	$5.00	10/3/94	10/5/94		
5	LEIFETZ	JOHN	815-92-5925	$5.00	9/24/94			
6	LING	JANETTE	692-66-9217	$5.00	10/5/94	10/5/94		
7	PAPILLON	RONALD	620-44-9151	$5.00	10/1/94			
8	RANDALL	ALLEN	691-60-0027	$5.00	9/25/94	9/27/94		
9	TOLLEREW	MICHAEL	415-92-2508	$5.00	9/24/94	9/25/94		
10	ASHLEY	ROBIN	229-02-9151	$1.50	9/26/94			
11	ASHLEY	ROBIN	229-02-9151	$1.50	9/28/94			
12	HARVEY	KENNETH	692-73-4992	$1.50	10/5/94			
13	JOHNSON	WILLIAM	262-62-0254	$1.50	10/5/94			
14	JOHNSON	WILLIAM	577-59-1169	$1.50	9/28/94			
15	LEIFETZ	JOHN	815-92-5925	$1.50	9/27/94			
16	MEINEKE	SANDRA	591-69-9628	$1.50	9/25/94			
17	PARRISH	MAXINE	629-22-2691	$1.50	10/2/94	10/4/94		
18	PERKINS	MARTIN	159-88-2691	$1.50	10/4/94	10/5/94		
19	PERKINS	MARTIN	159-88-2692	$1.50	9/25/94	9/28/94		
20	RANDALL	ALLEN	691-60-0027	$1.50	9/28/94	10/3/94		

USING THE FIND DIALOG BOX

You use the Find command to look for a single record or to locate records one at a time. When you choose Find from the Edit menu, Works displays the Find dialog box shown in Figure 21-10. Use the Find What text box to enter the string of characters, called the **search string,** that you want Works to use to locate records. When you click on the Next Record radio button, Works searches the database for the next occurrence of the search string and highlights the first field that contains it.

Works does not, however, search beyond the first occurrence. If you want to search for every occurrence of your text string, select the All Records radio button before you begin your search. Works will display a list of the records that contains the search string. After a find-all-records search, you can display all records again by choosing Show All Records from the View menu. Figure 21-10 shows the Find dialog box with william entered as a search string and All records selected as an option. The list shown in Figure 21-11 is the result of this search.

FIGURE 21-10

The Find dialog box is set to find all occurrences of the search string shown in the Find What text box. Notice that the search string does not need to be capitalized.

Find
Find What: william
OK
Cancel
Help
Match
○ Next record   ● All records

FIGURE 21-11

This list results from choosing All Records from the Find dialog box, as shown in Figure 21-10.

Microsoft Works - [FINES3.WDB]

File   Edit   View   Insert   Format   Tools   Window   Help

Arial   10

"WILLIAM

	LAST NAME	FIRST NAME	ID #	FINE	DOF	DATE PD		
3	JOHNSON	WILLIAM	262-62-9254	$5.00	9/25/94	9/26/94		
13	JOHNSON	WILLIAM	262-62-0254	$1.50	10/5/94			
14	JOHNSON	WILLIAM	577-59-1169	$1.50	9/28/94			
23								
24								
25								
26								
27								
28								
29								
30								
31								
32								
33								
34								
35								
36								
37								
38								
39								

Press ALT to choose commands, or F2 to edit.   3   3/22

You can specify a search string that contains all or part of the characters in a field, and you can use either upper- or lowercase letters. For example, typing the search string **Tollerew** will result in Works finding **TOLLEREW**, as will the string **rew**.

Works also searches for wildcards. **Wildcards** are characters that take the place of other characters, allowing you to search for several combinations at once. One wildcard, the asterisk (*), substitutes for any number of characters in a specific position. For example, to search for records, requests, and requisitions, you could enter **re*s** in the search string.

GUIDED PRACTICE

SEARCHING FOR AND DISPLAYING DATABASE RECORDS

In this exercise you will search records according to lab user ID # and the amounts of fines. First you will search for all records that have the ID #815-92-5925. This number is for John Leifetz, who has come to the lab to pay his outstanding fines. Then you will search for and display all records that contain the string 5.00.

1. Start Works, if necessary, and display the FINES3.WDB database in list view.

2. Choose Find from the Edit menu to display the Find dialog box.

3. In the Find What text box, type **815-92-5925** to specify a search string that will locate the first record of a fine assessed against John Leifetz. Leave The Next Record radio button selected. Compare your screen display with the one shown in Figure 21-12.

4. Click on the OK button to begin the search. Notice that Works highlights the field that contains this string in record 2.

5. Tab to the DATE PD field, and enter the date **10/17/94** to show that John Leifetz has paid a $5.00 fine assessed on **September 24, 1994**. Press Enter.

6. Choose Find from the Edit menu to display the Find dialog box again. Since the search string is already displayed in the text box, click the OK button to find the next occurrence of 815-92-5925.

7. When the next occurrence is highlighted, tab to the DATE PD field and enter the date 10/17/94.

8. Repeat step 6. Works takes you back to record 2, where the search string first occurred.

FIGURE 21-12

After you have completed step 3, your Find dialog box should look like this one.

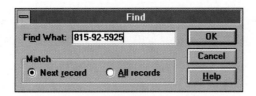

In the next steps you will perform a search to display all records that match the specified search string $5.00.

9. Choose Find from the Edit menu to display the Find dialog box. Notice that the last search string you typed still appears highlighted in the text box.

10. Type **5.00** in the Find What box. This deletes the last string, and specifies a new search string.

11. Select the All Records option by clicking on its radio button. Compare your Find dialog box with the one shown in Figure 21-13.

12. Click on the OK button to display a list of all records that contain 5.00, as shown in Figure 21-14.

13. Choose Show All Records from the View menu to display all records again.

14. Save the database file under the current name FINES3.WDB.

FIGURE 21-13

After you have completed step 11, your Find dialog box should look like the one shown in this illustration.

FIGURE 21-14

The FINES3.WDB list view window after finding records that contain the string 5.00. Notice that the record numbers are no longer consecutive.

	LAST NAME	FIRST NAME	ID #	FINE	DOF	DATE PD		
1	TOLLEREW	MICHAEL	415-92-2506	$5.00	9/24/94	9/25/94		
2	LEIFETZ	JOHN	815-92-5925	$5.00	9/24/94	10/17/94		
5	JOHNSON	WILLIAM	262-62-9254	$5.00	9/25/94	9/26/94		
7	RANDALL	ALLEN	691-60-0027	$5.00	9/25/94	9/27/94		
9	HARDING	ELLEN	159-26-9277	$5.00	9/27/94			
10	FERNANDEZ	PAUL	692-11-2996	$5.00	9/27/94	10/1/94		
15	PAPILLON	RONALD	620-44-9151	$5.00	10/1/94			
18	LEIFETZ	JANINE	602-93-2695	$5.00	10/3/94	10/5/94		
20	LING	JANETTE	692-66-9217	$5.00	10/5/94	10/5/94		
23								
24								
25								
26								
27								
28								
29								
30								

Press ALT to choose commands, or F2 to edit.

PRACTICE APPLICATIONS

Complete the following exercises. Some exercises ask you to answer one or more questions. Write a brief answer to these questions on a sheet of paper.

1. Open the FINES3.WDB file, if necessary. Sort the database in ascending order by ID #, then save the sorted database under the name FINES-ID. Close the database without saving it.

2. Open the EQUIPME2.WDB file in list view. Display as a group only those records that contain the string SOFTWARE. How many records are *11* displayed? Click on the first three or four records. Notice that they have retained their original record numbers. Try to scroll back to Record 1. Show all the records again. Now try to scroll to Record 1.

3. The computer lab manager wants to examine the price of the lab's most expensive software. Sort the EQUIPME2.WDB database in descending order by CATEGORY and descending order by PRICE. Do the records in *NO* a sorted database retain their original record numbers? Save this sorted version as EQUIPSOF.WDB, then close the file.

4. The computer lab manager asks you to create a student profile database using a WorksWizard. Select Use A Works Wizard from the Startup dialog box. Choose Student Profile from the Choose A Works Wizard list box. Follow the directions on the screen to create the database. Provide information for 10 students. Name and save the database when you have finished creating it.

ADD AT LEAST TWO FIELDS FROM ONE OF THE OTHER CHOICES IN THE STUDENT PROFILE.

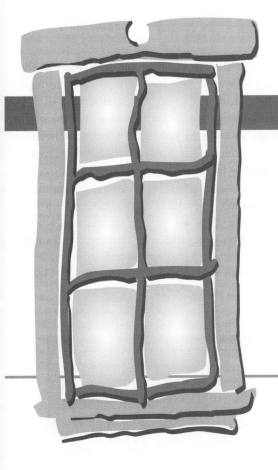

CREATING AND USING QUERIES

OBJECTIVES

After completing this lesson you will be able to do the following:

- *Create and name a query.*
- *Delete a query.*
- *Use And and Or connectors to create a query with multiple record-selection rules.*
- *Use Query view to edit current queries.*

KEY WORDS

In this lesson you will learn the meaning of the following terms:

comparison words   connector
  and phrases   query sentences

CREATING A QUERY

A query is used to tell Works to display only those database records that match certain conditions. When you want to create a new query, choose Create New Query from the Tools menu to display the New Query dialog box, shown in Figure 22-1. You use this dialog box to name the new query and to specify the **query sentences,** or criteria, you want Works to specify to select records for display when the query is used. After you have created and named a query, the query name is listed in the Queries dialog box, displayed by selecting Query from the View menu (if you have not created a query, the Query command is dimmed). The Queries dialog box is shown in Figure 22-2. You can create and name up to eight different queries, which will be listed on the Queries dialog box of a particular database and saved along with the database. When a query is no longer needed, it can be deleted by choosing Delete Query from the Tools menu. The Delete Query dialog box is then displayed, as shown in Figure 22-3.

FIGURE 22-1
The New Query dialog box that is displayed when you choose Create New Query from the Tools menu.

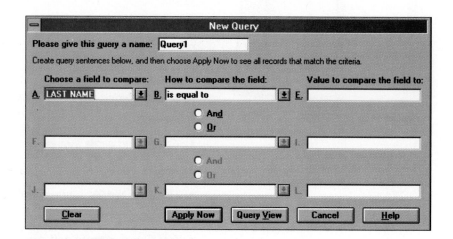

FIGURE 22-2
The Queries dialog box, displayed by selecting Query from the View menu.

FIGURE 22-3
The Delete Query dialog box from the Tools menu.

When you choose the Create New Query command, Works displays the dialog box shown in Figure 22-1 with the first field name in the database highlighted in the Choose A Field To Compare list box. Notice that Works has named the query. You can choose this default name or provide a more descriptive name, based on the database field you want to specify.

Each query can contain up to three query sentences. Each sentence consists of three parts: a field name, a comparison phrase, and comparison information. These three parts are described next.

CHOOSE A FIELD TO COMPARE

The first part of a query sentence is specified when you select a field name from the Choose A Field To Compare list box. Figure 22-4 shows the list box for fields of the FINES3.WDB database. After you select the highlighted field FINE, the word FINE replaces the LAST NAME (the name of the first field in the database) in the Choose A Field To Compare list box.

HOW TO COMPARE THE FIELD

The second part of a query sentence is specified when you select a **comparison** word or phrase from the How To Compare The Field list box. The comparison phrase Is Equal To is the default selection. Other options available on the list box are shown in Figure 22-5. The selected phrase or word indicates the type of comparison that will be made between the selected field and the information you will type in the Value To Compare The Field To text box, described next.

VALUE TO COMPARE THE FIELD TO

The third part of a query sentence consists of information you type in the Value To Compare The Field To text box. When Is Equal To is selected on the How To Compare The Field list box, the Value To Compare The Field To information must be the same as the information in the selected field in order to display the record. For example, you can create a query sentence that will search the FINES3.WDB database for the records of students with a

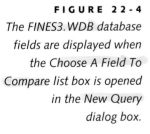

FIGURE 22-4

The FINES3.WDB database fields are displayed when the Choose A Field To Compare list box is opened in the New Query dialog box.

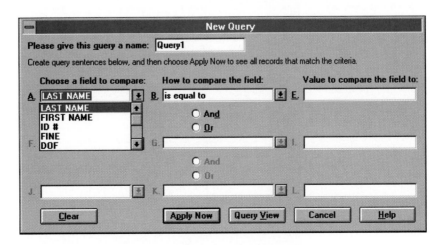

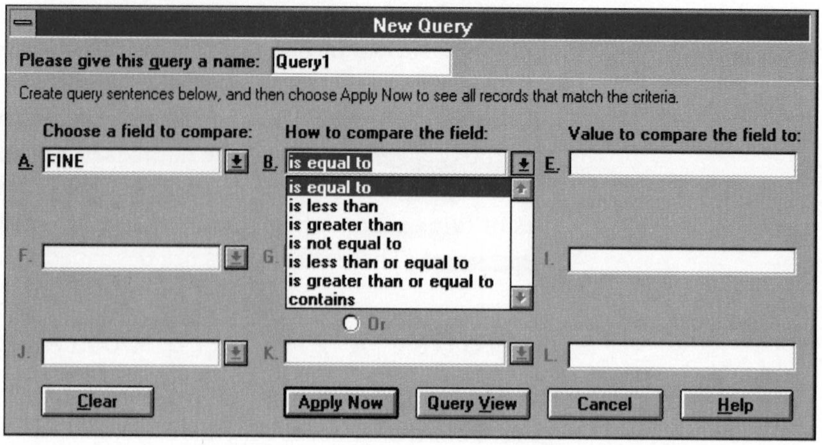

FIGURE 22-5
A display of comparison phrases and words on the How To Compare The Field list box.

fine (Choose A Field To Compare) that is equal to (How To Compare The Field) $5.00 (Value To Compare The Field To). When you type **$5.00** in the Value To Compare The Field To text box, Works displays only those records that contain an amount equal to $5.00 in the FINE field. When Is Greater Than Or Equal To is selected from the How To Compare The Field list box, a Value To Compare The Field To amount of $1 selects records that include amounts of $1, $1.50, and so on. Figure 22-6 shows a list of records that meet the query sentence's criteria: those with $5.00 in the FINES field. Works displays the selected records in ascending order of their record number.

OR JUST 5

If you want to select all of the records that do not meet the criteria specified in the Choose A Field To Compare list box and the Value To Compare The Field To text box, you can select the Is Not Equal To phrase in the How To Compare The Field list box. In the previous example, if Is Not Equal To is selected as part of the query sentence, all records that do not contain $5.00 in the FINE field will be displayed.

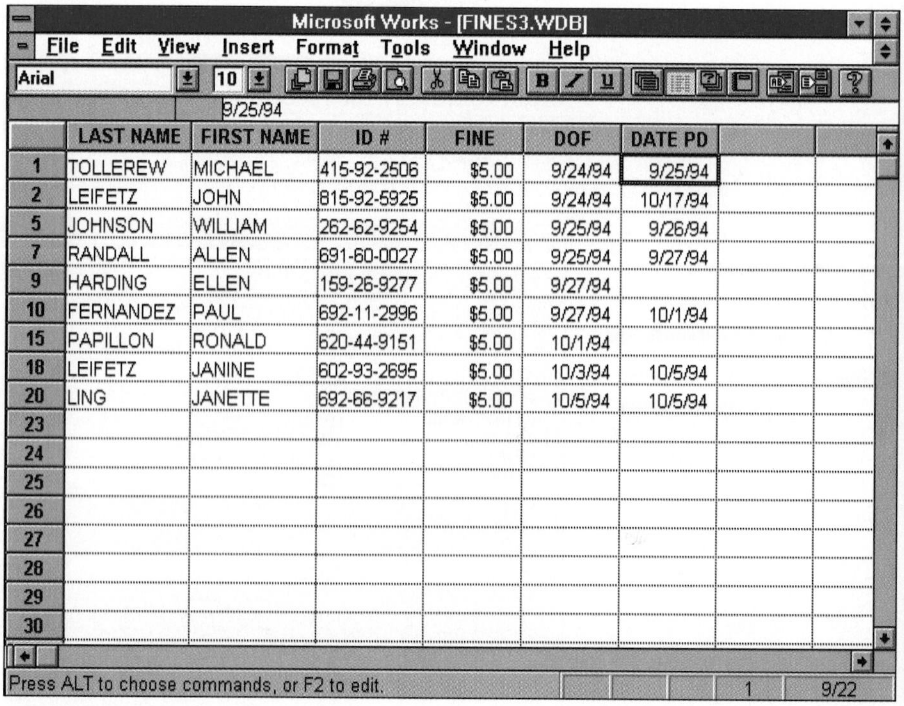

	LAST NAME	FIRST NAME	ID #	FINE	DOF	DATE PD
1	TOLLEREW	MICHAEL	415-92-2506	$5.00	9/24/94	9/25/94
2	LEIFETZ	JOHN	815-92-5925	$5.00	9/24/94	10/17/94
5	JOHNSON	WILLIAM	262-62-9254	$5.00	9/25/94	9/26/94
7	RANDALL	ALLEN	691-60-0027	$5.00	9/25/94	9/27/94
9	HARDING	ELLEN	159-26-9277	$5.00	9/27/94	
10	FERNANDEZ	PAUL	692-11-2996	$5.00	9/27/94	10/1/94
15	PAPILLON	RONALD	620-44-9151	$5.00	10/1/94	
18	LEIFETZ	JANINE	602-93-2695	$5.00	10/3/94	10/5/94
20	LING	JANETTE	692-66-9217	$5.00	10/5/94	10/5/94
23						
24						
25						
26						
27						
28						
29						
30						

FIGURE 22-6
When a query sentence is applied to the FINES3.WDB database, Works displays all records that meet its criteria—in this case, all records for students with lab fines equal to $5.00.

CHANGING, DELETING, AND DUPLICATING A QUERY

When a query has been named and listed on the Queries dialog box, you can use it whenever you need to select records based on the query sentences contained in the query. Figure 22-7a shows how a Tools menu appears before a query is created. Figure 22-7b shows the same Tools menu after a query has been created. Options that were not available before—Name Query, Delete Query, and Duplicate Query—are now available.

Choosing the Create New Query option displays the New Query dialog box, shown in Figure 22-4, in which you can make changes to the query's current name or record query sentences. Choosing Name Query opens the Name Query dialog box. This box allows you to rename a previously named query. Choosing Delete Query displays the Delete Query dialog box shown in Figure 22-3. Choosing Duplicate Query displays a dialog box like the one shown in Figure 22-8, which allows you to duplicate an existing query under another name.

FIGURE 22-7
(a) The Tool menu that is displayed for a database before a query has been created. (b) The Tools menu after a query has been created.

FIGURE 22-8
This dialog box is used to duplicate a query and save it under a different name.

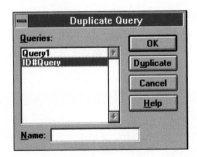

GUIDED PRACTICE

CREATING, DELETING, AND USING QUERIES

In this exercise you will create two queries for the database records in FINES3.WDB. You will then delete the two queries before closing the database.

1. Start Works and display the FINES3.WDB database.

2. Choose Create New Query from the Tools menu to display the New Query dialog box.

3. Highlight Query1, the default name, in the Please Give This Query A Name text box and type **Leifetz**.

4. Accept the default field (LAST NAME) for the Choose A Field To Compare list box.

5. Because you want the query sentence to select all records that are the same as LEIFETZ, you will use the default is equal to phrase for the How To Compare The Field list box.

6. Click an insertion point in the Value To Compare The Field To list box and type **Leifetz**. Compare your New Query dialog box with the one shown in Figure 22-9.

UPPER OR LOWER CASE

7. Click Apply Now or press the Enter key to display a list of three records (shown in Figure 22-10) that fit the query sentence specified in the Leifetz query.

In the next steps you will create another query to locate all records that contain $5.00 in the FINE field.

8. Choose Create New Query from the Tools menu to display the New Query dialog box.

9. Type **FINE** in the Please Give This Query A Name text box.

10. Select FINE from the Choose A Field To Compare list box, use the Is Equal To phrase in the How To Compare The Field list box, and type $5.00 in the Value To Compare The Field To list box.

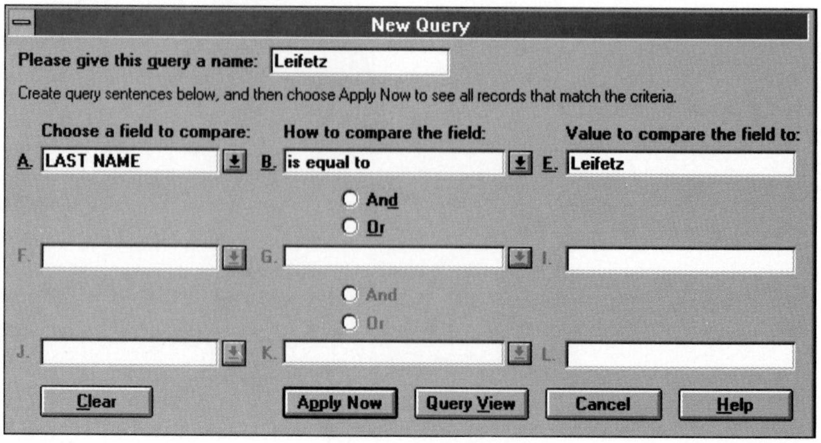

FIGURE 22-9

After you complete step 6, your New Query dialog box should look like this one.

FIGURE 22-10
After you have applied the LEIFETZ query, your database window should display these three records.

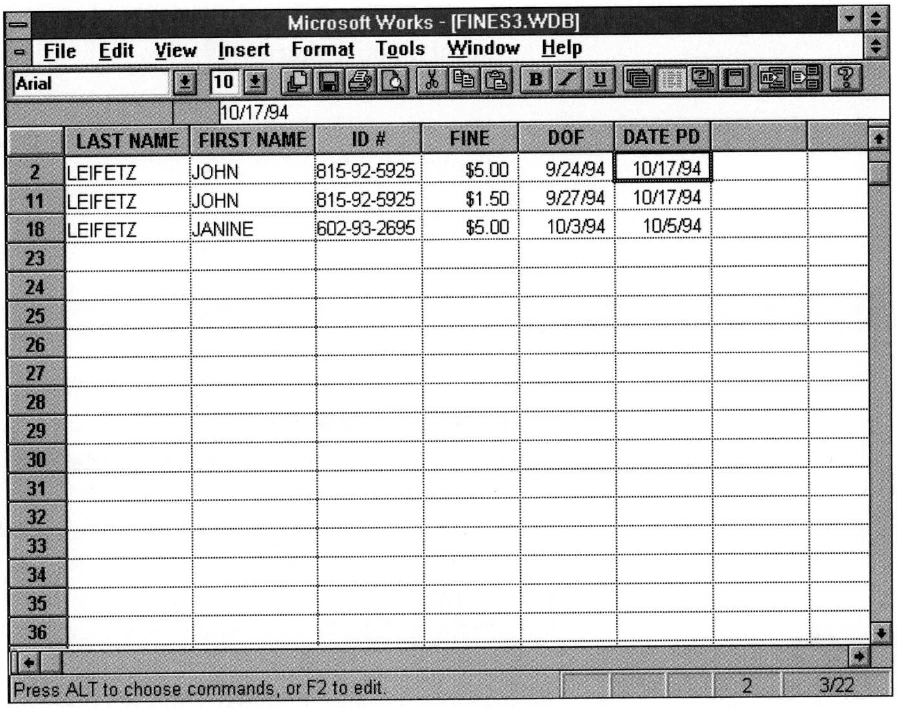
Microsoft Works - [FINES3.WDB]
File Edit View Insert Format Tools Window Help
Arial 10
10/17/94
LAST NAME FIRST NAME ID # FINE DOF DATE PD
2 LEIFETZ JOHN 815-92-5925 $5.00 9/24/94 10/17/94
11 LEIFETZ JOHN 815-92-5925 $1.50 9/27/94 10/17/94
18 LEIFETZ JANINE 602-93-2695 $5.00 10/3/94 10/5/94
23
24
25
26
27
28
29
30
31
32
33
34
35
36
Press ALT to choose commands, or F2 to edit.
2 3/22

11. Click Apply Now or press the Enter key to display the list of records shown in Figure 22-11 that fit the query sentence specified in the FINE query.

In the next steps you will delete the two queries you created.

FIGURE 22-11
After you have applied the FINE query, your database window should display these records.

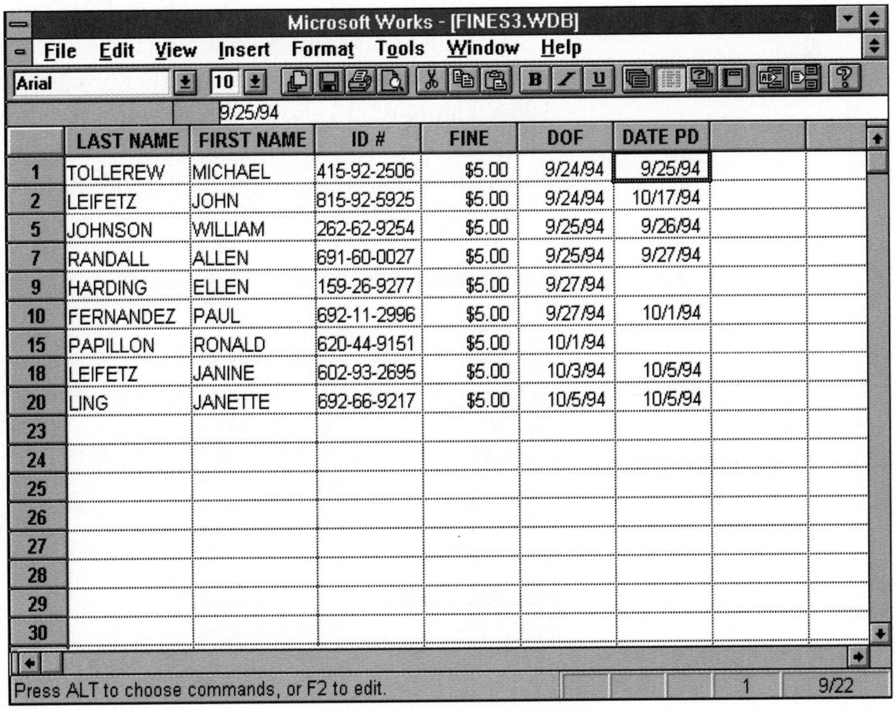
Microsoft Works - [FINES3.WDB]
File Edit View Insert Format Tools Window Help
Arial 10
9/25/94
LAST NAME FIRST NAME ID # FINE DOF DATE PD
1 TOLLEREW MICHAEL 415-92-2506 $5.00 9/24/94 9/25/94
2 LEIFETZ JOHN 815-92-5925 $5.00 9/24/94 10/17/94
5 JOHNSON WILLIAM 262-62-9254 $5.00 9/25/94 9/26/94
7 RANDALL ALLEN 691-60-0027 $5.00 9/25/94 9/27/94
9 HARDING ELLEN 159-26-9277 $5.00 9/27/94
10 FERNANDEZ PAUL 692-11-2996 $5.00 9/27/94 10/1/94
15 PAPILLON RONALD 620-44-9151 $5.00 10/1/94
18 LEIFETZ JANINE 602-93-2695 $5.00 10/3/94 10/5/94
20 LING JANETTE 692-66-9217 $5.00 10/5/94 10/5/94
23
24
25
26
27
28
29
30
Press ALT to choose commands, or F2 to edit.
1 9/22

12. Choose Delete Query from the Tools menu. When the Delete Query box appears, notice that FINE is highlighted. Click on Delete. The FINE query disappears from the list.

13. LEIFETZ is now highlighted. Choose Delete again to delete the LEIFETZ query.

14. Close the FINES3.WDB file without saving any changes.

USING MULTIPLE-QUERY SENTENCES IN A QUERY

You can narrow the information that Works displays even further by using more than one query sentence in a query. To include more than one query sentence, you need to specify a **connector**: And or Or. The And connector is used to select only those records that satisfy both (or all) rules. Each additional query sentence further eliminates records by narrowing the selection criteria. The Or connector is used to select all records that satisfy either rule. When you use Or, you are providing selection alternatives to include more records than would be selected without the Or connector.

For example, if you want to find records with fines of $5.00, you need to specify only one query sentence in the New Query dialog box. To find records with fines of $5.00 assessed on September 24, 1993, you need to specify two query sentences connected by the word **And,** as shown in Figure 22-12. When you make a connector selection (And or Or) for the second query sentence, Works opens the list and text boxes that have been dimmed, allowing you to enter information there. By choosing the Is Equal To phrase in the How To Compare The Field list box and typing **9/24/94** in the Value To Compare The Field To list box of the second query sentence, you are eliminating records that have $5.00 fines assessed on other dates.

By using a third query sentence connected by Or, you can display records with fines of $5.00 assessed on either September 14, 1994, or September 26, 1994. Figure 22-13 shows Query1 with the three query sentences just described. When you use the Or connector, you are providing Works with alternatives that increase the likelihood that more records will be selected.

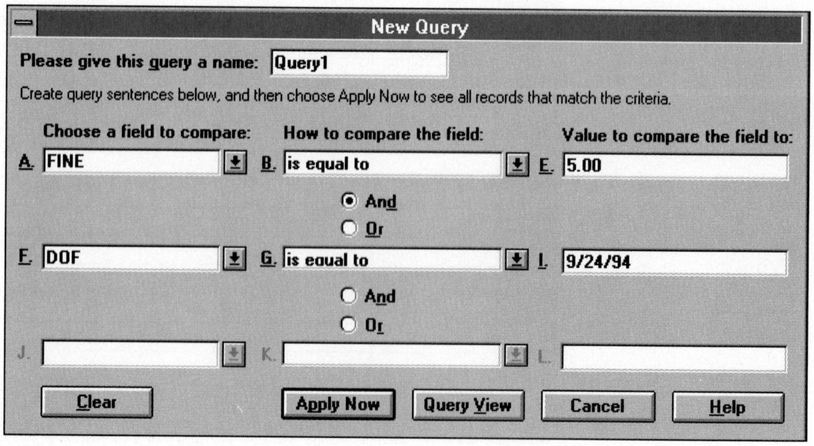

FIGURE 22-12

The New Query dialog box for Query1 after you have specified a second query sentence to select records with fines (equal to $5.00) that were incurred on September 24, 1994.

FIGURE 22-13

The Query1 New Query
dialog box after you have
specified a third query
sentence to select records
with fines of $5.00 that
were incurred on either
September 24, 1994 or
September 26, 1994.

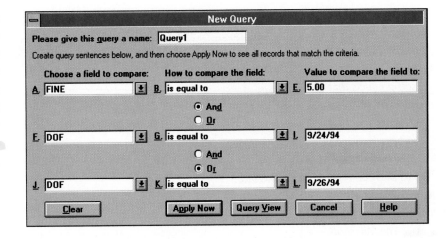

AN ALTER IN
QUERY VIEW

Although Works will not allow you to edit queries by returning to the
Create New Query dialog box, you can edit queries by selecting Query from
the View menu or clicking on the Query view toolbar button. The Queries
dialog box appears, as shown in Figure 22-2, allowing you to select a query.
Selecting Query1 displays Query1 in Query view, as shown in Figure 22-14.
The formula bar displays the query sentences you have already asked Works
to search for, except that query view displays them as mathematical
symbols.

Query view allows you to see all the fields in the database, but does not
display the information. When you want to use more than three query sentences in a query, query view gives you that power. Query view also allows
you to use mathematical symbols or Works functions (equations or functions built into the Works database and spreadsheet applications).

FIGURE 22-14

*Query1 displayed in query
view.*

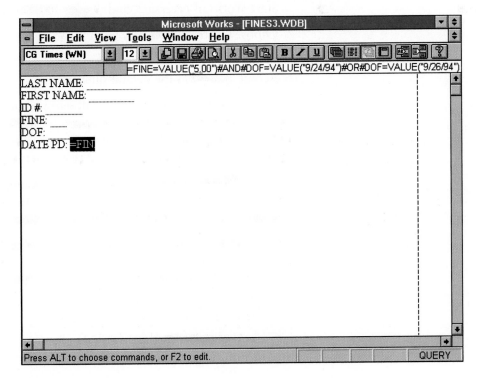

FIGURE 22-15

This query searches the BRAND field for Microsoft products, the PRICE field for Microsoft products that are more than $100, and the CATEGORY field for Microsoft products over $100 that are software. Works uses common mathematical symbols for queries in query view (<, >, =, <>). The Microsoft Works User's Guide offers an extensive list of functions.

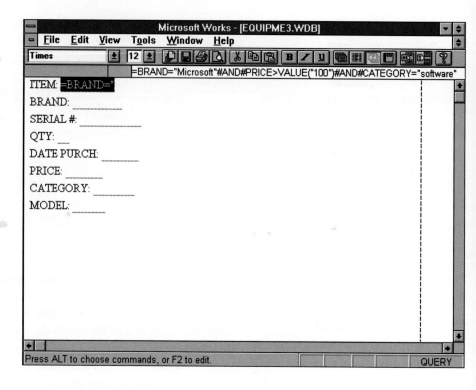

GUIDED PRACTICE

USING MULTIPLE-QUERY SENTENCES IN A QUERY

In this exercise you will use the EQUIPME3.WDB database file to create a query that includes multiple-query sentences.

1. Start Works, if necessary, and display EQUIPME3.WDB in list view.

2. Choose Create New Query from the Tools menu to display the New Query dialog box.

3. Accept Query1 as the default query name.

The following query sentences will select records that have a value in the PRICE field that is greater than or equal to $150 and less than or equal to $500. You must select the default connector (And or Or) before you can enter information in the second and third query sentences.

4. Select PRICE from the Choose A Field To Compare list box. From the How To Compare The Field list box, select the phrase Is Greater Than Or Equal To and type **150** in the Value To Compare The Field To list box.

5. Select And as a connector, and then select PRICE from the Choose A Field To Compare on the second line, select Less Than Or Equal To from the How To Compare The Field, and type **500** in the Value To Compare The Field To list box. Your New Query dialog box should look the same as the one in Figure 22-16.

6. Click Apply Now to close the dialog box and display the records selected when the query is applied, as shown in Figure 22-17.

FIGURE 22-16

After you have completed step 5, your New Query dialog box should look the same as this one.

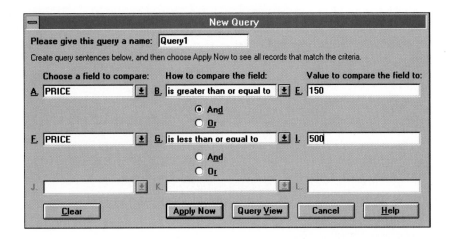

FIGURE 22-17

After you have applied the query you created, the records shown here are selected for display.

	ITEM	BRAND	SERIAL #	QTY	DATE PURCH	PRICE	CATE
12	PRINTER	EPSON	E92602T843	1	8/29/92	329.85	HARI
13	PRINTER	EPSON	E92702T844	1	8/29/92	329.85	HARI
14	MS-WORKS	MICROSOFT	M69266-86-26	1	8/27/92	178.25	SOFT
15	MS-WORKS	MICROSOFT	M69266-92-45	1	8/27/92	178.25	SOFT
16	MS-WORKS	MICROSOFT	M69266-62-83	1	8/27/92	178.25	SOFT
17	MS-WORKS	MICROSOFT	M69266-92-47	1	8/27/92	178.25	SOFT
18	MS-WORKS	MICROSOFT	M69266-26-46	1	8/27/92	178.25	SOFT
19	WORDPERFECT	WORDPERF	J-6926-2025	1	8/30/92	385.5	SOFT
20	WORDPERFECT	WORDPERF	J-6926-2028	1	8/30/92	385.5	SOFT
21	WORDPERFECT	WORDPERF	J-6926-2057	1	8/30/92	385.5	SOFT
22	WORDPERFECT	WORDPERF	J-6926-2061	1	8/30/92	385.5	SOFT
23	WORDPERFECT	WORDPERF	J-6926-2075	1	8/30/92	385.5	SOFT
24	LOTUS 1-2-3	LOTUS	E-245-26269-1	1	9/2/92	349.85	SOFT
25							
26							
27							
28							

Press ALT to choose commands, or F2 to edit.   20   13/24

7. Scroll through the database to examine the PRICE field of the records that fit the query sentences you used for Query1.

In the next steps you will open the Create New Query box and create a new query, reproducing the query sentences from Query1 and adding one more query sentence that specifies a brand name.

8. Choose Create New Query from the Tools menu and enter the criteria shown in Figure 22-16. Name the new query Query2.

9. Select BRAND from the Choose A Field To Compare for the third query sentence. Use the default connector And, and select Is Equal To from the How To Compare The Field list box. Type **Microsoft** in the Value To Compare To list box. The new Query2 is shown in Figure 22-18.

FIGURE 22-18

After you have completed step 9, your Create New Query dialog box should look the same as this one.

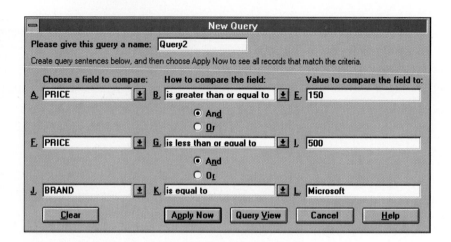

10. Click Apply Now to return to list view. Examine the records that are now displayed, as shown in Figure 22-19.

11. Save the file under its current name.

12. If you are not continuing with the Practice Applications, quit Works and eject your Student Data Disk from the floppy-disk drive.

FIGURE 22-19

These records are selected by applying Query2's query sentences.

	ITEM	BRAND	SERIAL #	QTY	DATE PURCH	PRICE	CATE
14	MS-WORKS	MICROSOFT	M69266-86-26	1	8/27/92	178.25	SOFT
15	MS-WORKS	MICROSOFT	M69266-92-45	1	8/27/92	178.25	SOFT
16	MS-WORKS	MICROSOFT	M69266-62-83	1	8/27/92	178.25	SOFT
17	MS-WORKS	MICROSOFT	M69266-92-47	1	8/27/92	178.25	SOFT
18	MS-WORKS	MICROSOFT	M69266-26-46	1	8/27/92	178.25	SOFT
25							
26							
27							
28							
29							
30							
31							
32							
33							
34							
35							
36							

Press ALT to choose commands, or F2 to edit.   14   5/24

PRACTICE APPLICATIONS

1. Start Works, if necessary, and open the EQUIPME3.WDB database. Create a Query3 to select all records that have a price between $65 and $300 and that have Hayes in the BRAND field? How many records match the query sentences you have specified?

2. Create a Query4 to select records in the EQUIPME3.WDB database that fall into the HARDWARE category, that have a price more than $1,000, and that were purchased before 8/25/92. How many records have your query sentences selected?

3. Save the database as EQUIPHAR.WDB.

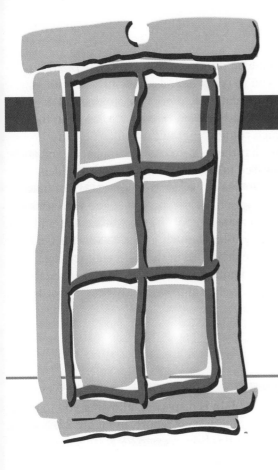

CREATING DATABASE REPORTS

OBJECTIVES

After completing this lesson you will be able to do the following:

- *Create a report to include only desired fields.*
- *Add a header and footer to a report.*
- *Apply statistics to a report.*
- *Calculate a total and count for a column (field) of a report.*
- *Adjust fields to allow for the length of formulas.*

KEY WORDS

In this lesson you will learn the meaning of the following terms:

field-entry instruction

DATABASE REPORTS

In Works reports provide an added dimension for making database content usable. Reports allow you to compile and print only the data you need to examine at that moment. A database report can contain all or selected database records in a row-and-column format. Each row in the report contains a record and each column contains a field. You can rearrange the database fields so that the report columns appear in any order you want. Fields that are not needed in a printed report can be hidden.

You can apply different field formats to change the appearance of fields, and apply character formats to change the fonts, type size, and type style of selected text. In addition, you can create a report header and footer, and add a **field-entry instruction** to calculate column totals and subtotals for fields in the report. These report features are described in the following sections.

After creating and formatting a report, you can print the entire database, sorted or unsorted, or use a query to select and print only those records that meet the query record-selection rules.

CREATING A REPORT

When you choose Create New Report from the Tools menu, the New Report dialog box shown in Figure 23-1a is displayed, allowing you to name the report and select the fields you want in your report. In Figure 23-1b four fields have been added and the report has been named Fines (this name will be displayed on the first page of the report).

FIGURE 23-1

(a) The New Report dialog box, and (b) the New Report dialog box after naming the report and adding fields.

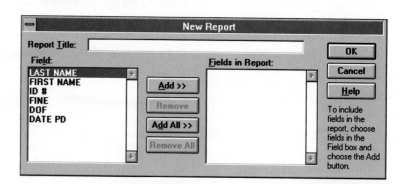

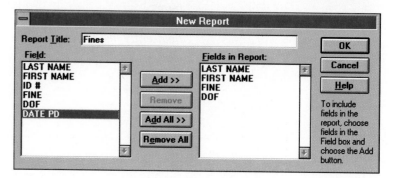

Once all the fields you need have been added to the New Report dialog box, clicking OK displays the Report Statistics dialog box. This is where you tell Works what statistical calculations you want performed when Works creates your report. You do not need to request statistics as part of your report, but statistics are another tool you can use to extract information from your database. Figure 23-2 shows a Report Statistics dialog box in which Count has been selected and the default for positioning the statistics, Together In Rows, has been accepted.

When you click OK in the Report Statistics dialog box, Works creates a report definition, a screen showing you the calculations, fields, and titles you have selected. Figure 23-3 shows the report definition created by the New Report and Report Statistics dialog boxes shown in Figures 23-1 and 23-2. Notice that the row labels displayed down the left side of the report definition explain the purpose of each row.

For example, the Title row label displays the text that Works will print on the first page, in this case Fines. The Headings row label displays the heading that Works will print on every page. The Record row label displays

FIGURE 23-2

The Report Statistics dialog box allows you to perform calculations on the information choosen for your report.

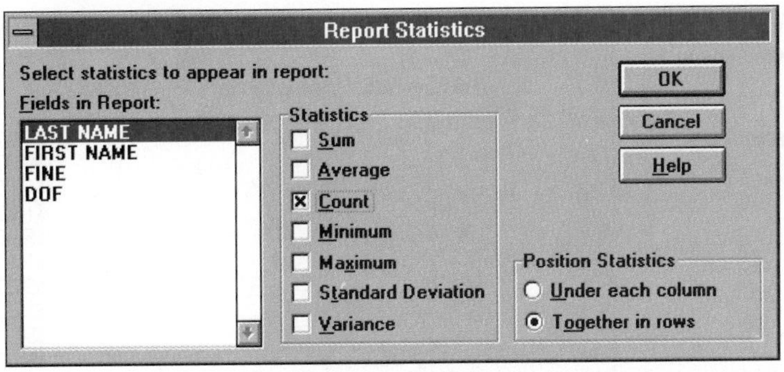

FIGURE 23-3

A report definition displays the choices that will be used to create your report.

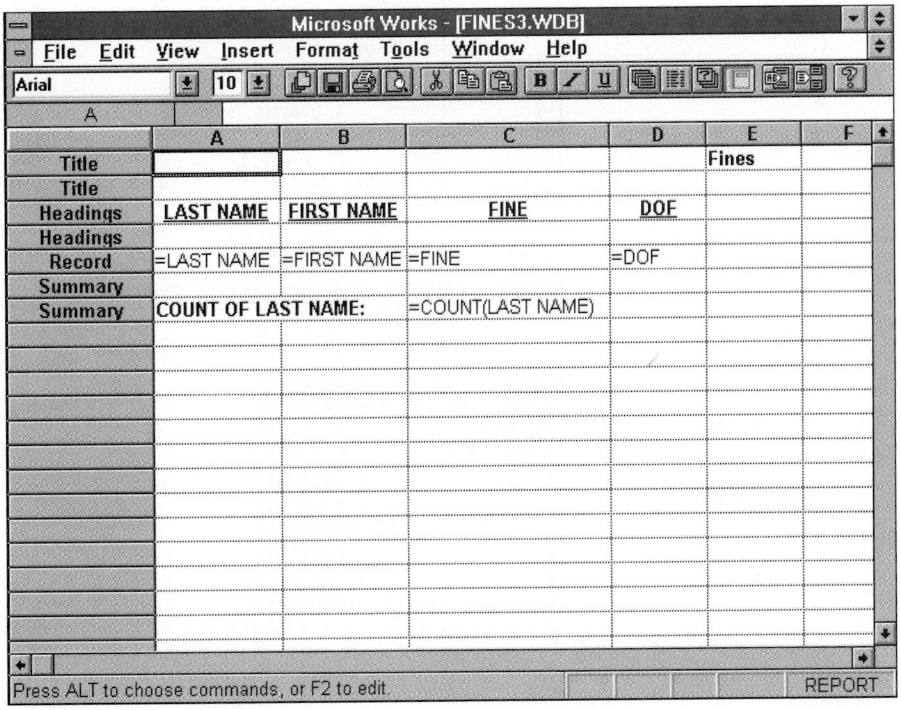

which fields are to be printed and what criteria you have selected. For this record, Works will use the LAST NAME, FIRST NAME, FINE, and DOF fields. The Summary row label shows that a statistical summary will be printed at the end of the report and displays what that summary will be. In this case, Works will count each last name to arrive at a record count. You can add as many rows of titles, headings, and records as you need. You can also delete rows.

Printing the report definition reveals the completed report you asked Works to create. A print preview of this report is shown in Figure 23-4. The Print Preview toolbar button is especially useful when working with database reports.

Once you have generated a report, you can use the View menu (or the Record View toolbar button) to switch to a report from form, list, and query views of your database. If you switch from another view to report view, Works takes you to the last report you opened. To see a list of reports associated with your database, select Report from the View menu. Works opens the Reports dialog box, shown in Figure 23-5.

FIGURE 23-4
A print preview display of the report created from the report definition in Figure 23-3.

Microsoft Works - [FINES3.WDB]			
LAST NAME	**FIRST NAME**	**FINE**	**DOF**
TOLLEREW	MICHAEL	$5.00	9/24/94
LEIFETZ	JOHN	$5.00	9/24/94
WOLOFSON	JENNIFER	$1.50	9/24/94
MEINEKE	SANDRA	$1.50	9/25/94
JOHNSON	WILLIAM	$5.00	9/25/94
PERKINS	MARTIN	$1.50	9/25/94
RANDALL	ALLEN	$5.00	9/25/94
ASHLEY	ROBIN	$1.50	9/26/94
HARDING	ELLEN	$5.00	9/27/94
FERNANDEZ	PAUL	$5.00	9/27/94
LEIFETZ	JOHN	$1.50	9/27/94
ASHLEY	ROBIN	$1.50	9/28/94
RANDALL	ALLEN	$1.50	9/28/94
JOHNSON	WILLIAM	$1.50	9/28/94
PAPILLON	RONALD	$5.00	10/1/94
RICHARDS	DENISE	$1.50	10/1/94
PARRISH	MAXINE	$1.50	10/2/94
LEIFETZ	JANINE	$5.00	10/3/94
PERKINS	MARTIN	$1.50	10/4/94
LING	JANETTE	$5.00	10/5/94
JOHNSON	WILLIAM	$1.50	10/5/94
HARVEY	KENNETH	$1.50	10/5/94
COUNT OF LAST NAME:		22	

Page 1 · Previous · Next · Zoom In · Zoom Out · Print · Cancel

FIGURE 23-5
Selecting Report from the View menu displays a list of the reports associated with your database.

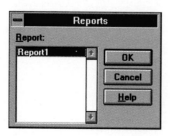

CHANGING REPORT MARGINS, PAGE SIZE, AND ORIENTATION

You can change the margins, paper size, and orientation of your report by selecting the Page Setup command from the File menu. As with a word-processing document, use the Margins tab dialog box to change the report's margins. If you want to include more columns (fields) in a report than will fit on an 8 1/2-by 11-inch sheet of paper in portrait orientation, you can select Landscape (horizontal) orientation to increase the number of columns that can be printed across the page. You can also use the Paper Size list box to choose another size paper. Figure 23-6a, b, and c show the three tab dialog boxes that make up the Page Setup dialog box. You can examine the paper-size and page-orientation changes that you make in the Page Setup dialog box by choosing Print Preview from the File menu.

FIGURE 23-6

(a) The Margins tab dialog box controls margins, including header and footer margins. (b) The Source, Size And Orientation tab dialog box. (c) The Other Options tab dialog box.

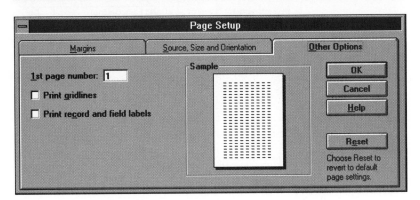

CHANGING THE APPEARANCE OF A REPORT

The information or entries in the columns and rows of a report have the same character formats that are currently applied to the information in list view of the database. You can, however, use the Font And Style dialog box or the toolbar buttons to add character formatting to any part of your report.

Characters in the fields of a new database are formatted in the font and size currently selected in the Font And Style dialog box. By changing font or style in this dialog box and clicking the Set Default button, those changes will be applied to all future database documents, but not to existing documents. For example, if you click on the LAST NAME field in the report definition shown in Figure 23-3 and then open the Font And Style dialog box, the dialog box will show the font and style for that field, as shown in Figure 23-7. If you click the Set Default button, Works displays the message box shown in Figure 23-8. Remember, you can change the formatting of your database without changing Works' default settings.

REPORT HEADERS AND FOOTERS

You can choose the Headers And Footers command from the View menu to print the date, or time, page number, or file name on each page of a report. The header and footer windows that appear in the database application are like the ones for adding headers and footers to a word-processing document.

FIGURE 23-7

The Font And Style dialog box reflects the settings of the LAST NAME field.

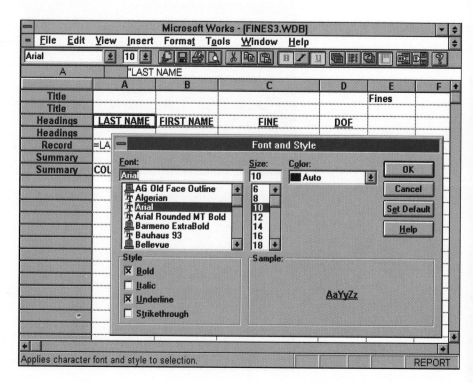

FIGURE 23-8

Works displays this message box when you try to change the database font and style settings.

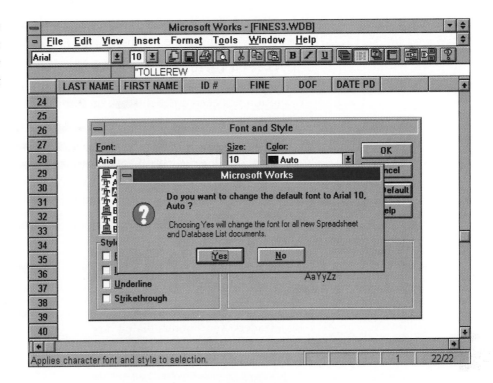

GUIDED PRACTICE

CREATING AND PRINTING A REPORT

In this exercise you will create and print a report that includes selected fields. The lab manager knows that not all of the fields for each record in the EQUIPME3.WDB database file will fit on one report line. In other words, the number of fields in the database creates more columns than can fit across a printed page, even in landscape (horizontal) orientation. The manager wants you to create a report form that limits the fields to be printed to ITEM, QTY, and PRICE.

1. Start Works, if necessary, and display the EQUIPME3.WDB database in list view.

2. Choose Create New Report from the Tools menu to display the New Report dialog box.

3. Type **Report1** in the Report Title text box. Notice that the field names that were displayed in list view are now listed in the field window.

    In the next steps you will select fields so that the report contains the information previewed in Figure 23-10.

4. With the ITEM field highlighted, click on the Add button to add the ITEM field to the Fields In Report window. Click on the QTY field and add it to the Fields In Report window, and do the same with the PRICE field.

5. Click OK to display the Report Statistics dialog box.

6. Click on the PRICE field and select the Sum option. This means that Works will total the numbers in the PRICE field.

7. Click on OK to open the Report Definition window. Works displays a message box, shown in Figure 23-9, to inform you that your report definition has been created. Click on OK to close the message box.

8. Widen the column containing the QTY and PRICE fields so that the entire formula is visible. Select the Print Preview command from the File menu or click the Print Preview toolbar button to preview your report. Click on the magnifying glass on the previewed page. Your report should resemble the report in Figure 23-10.

9. Return to report view by clicking on the Cancel button and closing the Preview window.

In the next steps you will format the column headings, add a footer in the Headings And Footers dialog box, and print the report.

10. Choose Headers And Footers from the View menu to display the Headers And Footers dialog box.

FIGURE 23-9

This message box appears when a new report definition has been created.

FIGURE 23-10

Report1 of the EQUIPME3.WDB database. Notice that the PRICE field has been totaled.

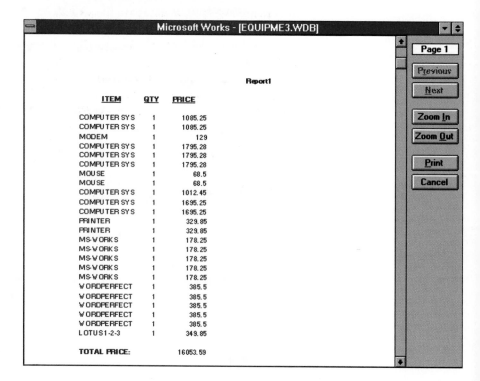

11. In the Footer text box, type **SUMMARY REPORT OF PURCHASES** then click on OK. Works automatically centers headers and footers on the report page.

12. Select Print Preview to check that the new footer will print at the bottom of your report. Click on the Cancel button to exit Print Preview.

13. Select the ITEM heading. Remove its bold and underline formatting by clicking on the Bold and Underline toolbar buttons. Change the ITEM heading font size to 14. Do the same for the QTY and PRICE headings.

14. Highlight the first three fields of the TITLE row by clicking on the A column and dragging the highlight to the C column.

15. Type **Report1**. Clear the original Report1 title by clicking on its field and pressing the Delete key.

16. Although the Report1 heading is now aligned across the A, B, and C columns, it is formatted by highlighting the A column of the Title row. Format the Report1 title in italic by using the Font And Style dialog box. *OR TOOLBAR*

17. Choose Print Preview again to make sure the report looks the way you want it to look. Make sure that all the other columns are wide enough to contain the formulas. After examining the report in actual-size view, return to report view and make any adjustments that are needed.

18. Save the database as EQUIPME4.WDB.

19. Choose Print (Ctrl+P) from the File menu, and print one copy of Report1.

20. Display the EQUIPME4.WDB database in list view.

Sometimes your reports will be longer or wider than one page. Inserting a page break gives you one more tool to use in formatting your report. You can add a page break to a row in report definition by highlighting the row you want to be first on a new page. Choose Page Break from the Insert menu. Works inserts a dashed line across the report definition screen. You can then switch to print preview to see the change in your report. You can also add a page break to a column by highlighting the column you want to be the first column on a new page. To remove a page break, choose Delete Page Break from the Insert menu —this command is only available after a page break has been inserted.

FORMATTING AND PRINTING A REPORT WITH STATISTICS

In this exercise you will begin by creating a new report from the EQUIPME4.WDB file. Then you will create a report definition for the new report with a total calculated for the PRICE field and a total count for the ITEM field.

1. Start Works, if necessary, and open the EQUIPME4.WDB database in list view.

2. Choose Create New Report from the Tools menu to display the New Report dialog box.

3. Add CATEGORY as the first field in the Fields In Report box.

4. Add ITEM to the list in the Fields In Report box.

5. Add MODEL to the Fields In Report box, then add DATE PURCH and PRICE to the list.

6. Name this new report Price Report.

7. Click on OK.

8. In the Report Statistics dialog box, highlight PRICE in Fields In Report. Select Sum from the Statistics list. Also select Minimum and Maximum.

9. Select Under Each Column from the Position Statistics list. Click on ITEM. Notice that Under Each Column has become the default for Position Statistics for all the fields. With ITEM selected, click on Count from the Statistics list.

10. Click OK. Then click OK on the message box. Scroll through the report definition screen. Notice that there are now seven summary rows, including the three statistic fields you have added in the PRICE column.

11. Choose Print Preview from the File menu to examine the report before printing. Click on the Zoom In button twice to enlarge your view.

12. If the number after the SUM field has been replaced by #s, return to the report definition screen and widen the PRICE column until all formulas are visible.

13. In the report definition screen widen the DATE PURCH column to accommodate its heading.

14. Widen the ITEM column so that there is more space between it and the MODEL column. Widen any other column you feel are too narrow. Your reduced-size preview screen should look similar to the one shown in Figure 23-11.

In the next steps you will increase the top margin of the report. This will not affect the title line since it is a part of the header, but it will cause the report to print lower on the page.

FIGURE 23-11

After you have completed step 14, your Print Preview screen should look similar to this one.

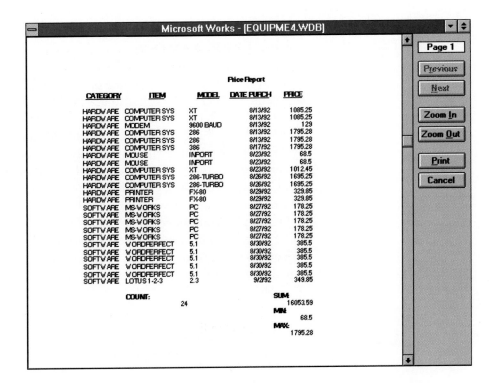

15. Close the Print Preview window to return to the report definition screen. Then choose Page Setup from the File menu and, if necessary, click on the Margins tab to adjust the margins of your report.

16. Change the top margin to 2 inches, then return to report view.

17. Examine the report again in print preview, then return to report view.

18. Save the changes under the current name EQUIPME4.WDB.

19. Print one copy of Price Report.

20. Close the document window.

PRACTICE APPLICATIONS

1. Start Works and open the EQUIPME3.WDB file. Sort the database on the BRAND field in ascending order and save the database as EQUIPME5.WDB.

2. Create a new report for the EQUIPME5.WDB database. The new report will be used to print the entire database with a total for amounts in the PRICE field and a count based on brand names. Give the report an appropriate title. Format the title using the Arial font, 14-point type size, and bold italic type style. If necessary, use the Number command to format the PRICE column for Currency, and accept the 2 decimal default. When you are satisfied with the appearance of the report, print one copy, then save and close the EQUIPME5.WDB database.

CHAPTER REVIEW

You can sort a database on one or more fields. The first field used in a sort is the key field. You can also use the Find command to search a database to find each occurrence of a specified string. Alternatively, you can tell Works to find all occurrences and display them in the database window. You can create a simple query with only one record query sentence, or you can create a query with multiple record query sentences by using the And and Or connectors. A query can be named and saved for later use.

Works provides a great deal of flexibility in formatting a database report to be printed. You can create up to eight reports attached to a database, using different organizational schemes. When creating a report, you can use a query to select fields that will be included and format selected fields. You can also calculate statistics for selected fields.

REVIEW QUESTIONS

TRUE-FALSE

Write your answer on a sheet of paper.

1. When you create records in a database, Works organizes the records in the same order in which they were entered.

2. Works can perform a sort on only one field per database.

3. An ascending sort organizes records based on the highest letter (Z) or number in a field down to the lowest letter (A) or number in a field.

4. You can save the results of a database sort operation to disk.

5. And and Or are comparison words on the Comparison pop-up menu that can be used in creating record-selection rules.

6. After performing a search using the Find command, you can choose Show All Records to deselect the Find command and to display all records in the database.

7. You can specify up to six record query sentences when using the New Query dialog box.

8. When printing a report, you must switch to list view.

9. A page break cannot be inserted in a database document.

10. You can format the font and style of report entries without changing the Works default font and style settings.

SHORT-ANSWER QUESTIONS

Write a brief answer to these questions on a sheet of paper.

1. You want to locate all database records that come before LESTERMAN alphabetically in the LAST NAME field of a database, what record query sentence would you specify in a query?

2. In specifying record query sentences, what is the difference between using And and using Or?

3. To locate all database records that have a DATE field value between (and including) 10/18/94 and 10/30/94, what query sentence would you specify in a query?

4. What is the purpose of the Together In Rows radio button on the Reports Statistics dialog box?

5. How can you increase the length of a line so that more fields can fit on a single line in a report?

LESSON APPLICATIONS

1. Sort the INVENTOR.WDB file so that information in the BRAND field is sorted in ascending order and information in the PRICE field is sorted in descending order. Save the sorted file as INVENSOR.WDB.

2. Create Query1 for the INVENSOR.WDB database that will locate and display records that contain HARDWARE in the CATEGORY field that is more than $500 and less than $1700 in the PRICE field.

3. Create a report for the INVENSOR.WDB database. Rearrange the fields in the following order: DATE PURCH, SERIAL #, BRAND, and PRICE. Create and format an appropriate title for the report. Change the left and right margins so that the report is framed within equal left and right 1 1/2-inch margins. Adjust the top margin so that the first line of the report begins printing 2 inches from the top edge of the paper. Print one copy of the report. Apply the filter you created in Exercise 2 to the INVEN-SOR.WDB database, and print another copy of the report with records selected after you applied the filter.

C HAPTER APPLICATIONS

1. Open the EQUIPME1.WDB database on your Student Data Disk. Perform the following steps:

   a. Use a query to select all items with a purchase price of $200 or less. Create a header, EQUIPMENT $200 OR LESS. Change the font of the entries to CG Times. Use the Gridlines command in the View menu to print this query without gridlines.

   b. Display all records in the EQUIPME1.WDB database. Use the Find command to search for the record that has the SERIAL #J-6926-2025.

   c. Use the All Records option to display all records that contain the string 1,695.25.

   d. Use a query to display all items with a purchase date after 8/22/92 and a purchase price greater than $400. After displaying the records that meet these query sentences, display all the records of the database.

   e. Close the database without saving your changes.

2. Open the FINES.WDB database on your Student Data Disk. Perform the following steps:

   a. Sort the records on ID # in ascending order. Save the file under the new name FINEPRAC.WDB.

   b. Create and name a new report for the FINEPRAC.WDB database that will print only the ID #, FINE, and DOF fields.

   c. Create a new title for your report displayed in the report definition window. Make any column width adjustments. Use the Alignment command to center it over the three fields with formulas.

   d. Highlight each formula and use the Alignment command to center the formula under its column heading.

   e. Print the report you created in steps a and b.

   f. Save the changes under the current name and close the FINEPRAC.WDB database.

CHALLENGE EXERCISES

1. For the following exercises, use the file CONTACTS.WDB on your Student Data Disk.

   a. Some of the column widths in CONTACTS.WDB are incorrect. Determine appropriate column widths and make the necessary corrections.

   b. After adding two new fields, FIRST NAME and ZIP, use the following data to add first names and ZIP codes for each record:

LAST NAME	FIRST NAME	ZIP
BALLSTER	KIMBERLY	83141
BONEUS	BERNARD	92073
CLOSE	CONSTANCE	35004
FRECKMAN	ALICE	95139
GOULDEN	JENNIFER	98301
JOHNSEN	CLARK	85872
KERNSEY	CARY	97213
MILLER	ARNOLD	10154
ROLLEY	WILLIAM	60607
SILVERSMITH	ANTHONY	89503
WILLIAMS	JAMES	53711

2. Use the following instructions to create a report that prints a mailing label for each individual in the CONTACTS.WDB. Use the Microsoft *Works User's Guide* manual or on-screen Help system to look up information on printing mailing labels, placeholders, creating a mailing label document, or the Envelopes And Labels command on the Tools menu in the word processor.

   Print the labels in descending ZIP-code order. (You can use standard 8½- by 11-inch paper to print the labels.)

   Name and save the file when you are done.

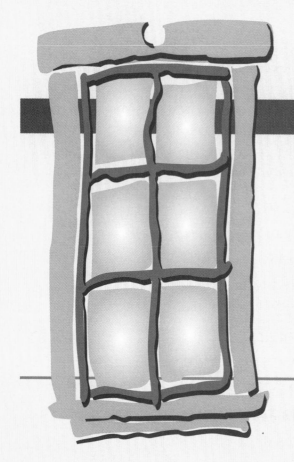

CHAPTER 9

SPREADSHEET STRUCTURES AND COMMANDS

OVERVIEW

This chapter introduces the basic spreadsheet features that are available when you use the Works spreadsheet tool. You will learn about the Works spreadsheet document window and how to navigate through an existing spreadsheet. In addition, you will examine spreadsheet features for creating and formatting labels and values, and you will learn about formulas that are used for calculating data. This chapter also introduces a special feature that allows you to create charts to represent spreadsheet data. Finally, you will use print controls and commands to print all or selected parts of a spreadsheet.

CONTENTS

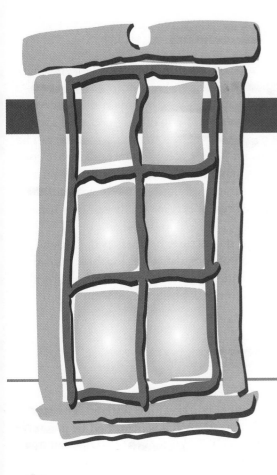

GETTING STARTED WITH THE WORKS SPREADSHEET PROGRAM

OBJECTIVES

After completing this lesson you will be able to do the following:

- *Explain the purpose and benefits of electronic spreadsheets.*
- *Explain the differences between a spreadsheet label, value, and formula.*
- *Describe basic spreadsheet formatting capabilities.*
- *Navigate through a spreadsheet.*

KEY WORDS

In this lesson you will learn the meaning of the following terms:

active cell	*label*
cell reference	*recalculation*
column labels	*row labels*
formula	*value*
freeze (titles)	

WHAT IS SPREADSHEET PROCESSING?

Before the personal computer came into use, business people kept track of financial information by recording figures by hand onto paper spreadsheets that were organized into rows and columns. Many of the numbers in a spreadsheet are the result of calculations. In a manually prepared spreadsheet, each calculation must be made individually, and human error can be introduced at any step along the way. What's more, financial data are constantly changing. To stay current, a manually prepared spreadsheet must either be recreated frequently from scratch or else be littered with erased and handwritten changes. Revising spreadsheets manually can be a messy and annoying job.

When personal computers entered the picture, business people found an alternative to the manual preparation of spreadsheets. Electronic spreadsheet programs provide a means to enter financial data, then change and recalculate data automatically whenever new business situations call for revisions.

ELECTRONIC SPREADSHEET COMPONENTS

The screen displays of computer-driven spreadsheet programs use the same row-and-column format as manual bookkeeping systems. The intersection of a row and column is called a **cell**. A cell is identified by a **cell reference**, which is a combination of the cell's column letter and row number. For example, the cell reference B5 refers to a data item stored at the intersection of column B and row 5. A Works spreadsheet can contain 16,384 rows and 256 columns.

An electronic spreadsheet is created by entering text, values, and formulas into cells. These three basic components are described in the following sections.

TEXT

Text includes headings, labels, and titles that explain part of the spreadsheet. The most common **labels** are the column and row labels used to mark the columns and rows that make up the spreadsheet. However, text can also be noncalculated data within the spreadsheet itself. Figure 24-1 shows a spreadsheet of budget information for the computer lab. The letters across the columns are **column labels;** the numbers down the left side of the spreadsheet are **row labels.**

Text is also placed in the first few rows along the top of most spreadsheets, serving as titles for the entire spreadsheet or as column headings for individual columns of data entries. In Figure 24-2, COMPUTER LAB BUDGET October 1994 is the spreadsheet title entered as a label in row 1. The entries Actual, Budgeted, and Over/Under are column headings entered in row 5 to describe information in the column cells below each label.

Microsoft Works - [BUDGET1.WKS]

File Edit View Insert Format Tools Window Help

Arial   10

B1   "October 1994

	A	B	C	D	E	F	G
1	COMPUTER LAB BUDGET	October 1994					
2							
3							
4							
5		Actual	Budgeted	Over/Under			
6	INCOME						
7	Budget Allocation	7000.00	7000.00	0.00			
8	Fines	265.91	300.00	-34.09			
9	Disk Sales	482.50	450.00	32.50			
10							
11	Total Income	7748.41	7750.00	-1.59			
12							
13	EXPENSES						
14							
15	Fixed Expenses						
16	Service Contract	475.00	475.00	0.00			
17	Equipment Insurance	368.50	368.50	0.00			
18	Salaries	4080.00	4080.00	0.00			
19							
20	Total Fixed	4923.50	4923.50	0.00			

Press ALT to choose commands, or F2 to edit.

A number can also be used as a label to describe information in cells in an adjoining row or column. For example, in a spreadsheet created to show projected purchases for the years 1994, 1995, and 1996, these numbers could be used as column headings at the top of columns where values representing projected purchase amounts will be entered.

VALUES

A spreadsheet **value** is a number, date, or time that can be used for making calculations. In Figure 24-2, the numbers in the columns containing the headings Actual, Budgeted, and Over/Under are values that can be used in calculations. However, not every number in a spreadsheet will be treated as a value. For example, 1994 in row 1 is a number that will not be used in calculations; it is part of the title of the spreadsheet and Works will treat it as text.

FORMULAS

In spreadsheet processing, the value that is displayed in a cell is often the result of calculations performed on values from other cells within the same spreadsheet. A **formula** is used to calculate new values from existing values. In Figure 24-1, for example, the Actual Total Income amount stored in cell B11, 7748.41, was calculated from information in cells B7, B8, and B9. Notice that the formula =SUM(B7:B9) appears on the spreadsheet formula bar just below the menu bar. This formula tells Works to insert into cell B11, the active cell, the sum of the values in cells B7 through B9.

If you change the Budget Allocation amount in cell B7, Works automatically recalculates the Actual Total Income amount stored in cell B11. Calculated values, such as totals, are recalculated automatically when changes are made to one or more cell values included in the formula. One of the most important features of an electronic spreadsheet is the ability to adjust calculated values in cells whenever the contents of related cells change.

SPREADSHEET FORMATTING CAPABILITIES

Recall that text in word-processing and database documents can be formatted to improve their appearance. Electronic spreadsheet programs also provide formatting capabilities that permit you to change the appearance of information in spreadsheet documents.

You can insert or delete columns and rows, as well as change the width of one or more columns or rows. As with databases, you can also format columns and rows so that cell values have a consistent appearance, even when they are not typed in that format. This is accomplished by using the Format menu. For example, if a column is formatted for a number that uses a dollar sign and two decimal places for example, $7,000.00, you can type the value as 7000 and it will automatically appear in the formatted cell as $7,000.00. Columns and rows that contain date and time values can also be formatted in several ways.

By default, a number value is right-aligned in a general number format without commas (for example, 7000); a date value is right-aligned in a short date format (for example, 10/30/93), and a time value is right-aligned in a time format that includes hours, minutes, seconds, and am or pm (for example, 12:00:00 am). By default, labels are left-aligned. Changing the cell format of a value does not change the way the value appears on the **formula bar**—the formula bar displays the value exactly as it was entered.

Figure 24-2 shows the computer lab budget after it has been reformatted. Notice that the title line, COMPUTER LAB BUDGET October 1994, appears in boldface and that the column headings in cells B5, C5, and D5 are bold and underlined. For emphasis, the label in cell A11, Total Income, appears in bold and the spreadsheet gridlines have been hidden.

NAVIGATING THROUGH A SPREADSHEET

It's easy to move through a Works spreadsheet, especially if you are familiar with other Works tools like the word processor and the database. In fact, many of the techniques used to move from one cell to another in the spreadsheet are the same as those used to move from one field to another in a database.

When you click on a cell or use one of the keys listed here to move from one cell to another, the highlighted cell's reference is displayed on the **cell reference bar** below the font list box. This highlighted cell is called the **active cell**. To go quickly to the last cell in the spreadsheet that contains information, press [Ctrl] + [End]. To go quickly to the first cell, press [Ctrl] + [Home].

The following keys are used to move the highlight through a Works spreadsheet one cell at a time:

KEY(S)	MOVES THE HIGHLIGHT (ACTIVE CELL)
Tab or →	Right one cell
Shift + Tab or ←	Left one cell
↓	Down one cell
↑	Up one cell
Home	To the first cell in a row
End	To the last cell with information in a row
Page Up	Up one window
Page Down	Down one window

The scroll bars are used to display any part of the spreadsheet quickly; however, the highlight does not advance when you scroll a spreadsheet. On the vertical scroll bar, you can click the gray area below the scroll box to scroll down one window at a time. Follow the same procedure to scroll up again.

You can also use the spreadsheet window's split bars to display separate portions of a large spreadsheet in the same window. You use the split bars to split a spreadsheet window vertically or horizontally into panes, just as you did when working with a database in list view. Using the Split command in a spreadsheet, allows you to create four panes at once, controlling horizontal and vertical adjustments at the same time. Figure 24-3 shows a spreadsheet divided into four panes.

FIGURE 24-3

A spreadsheet divided into four panes. Notice the four sets of scroll bars.

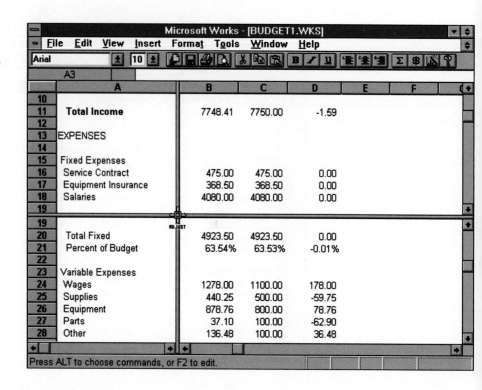

In addition to splitting the window, you can **freeze** the column and row titles, keeping them on screen no matter where you are in the spreadsheet. When you use the Freeze Titles command from the Format menu, Works will freeze the rows above and columns to the left of the highlighted cell. When Freeze Titles is selected, the command is indicated with a checkmark.

GUIDED PRACTICE

MOVING THROUGH A SPREADSHEET

In this exercise you will practice moving through a spreadsheet. To build your skills in the use of spreadsheets, you will practice moving through the BUDGET1.WKS file on your Student Data Disk. This spreadsheet contains the computer lab budget information for the month of October.

1. Start Works and insert your Student Data Disk in the floppy-disk drive.

2. Click on the Spreadsheet tool, and select the Open command to display the Open dialog box.

3. Double-click on the file name BUDGET1.WKS to open the spreadsheet document. Notice that the spreadsheet pointer is in the form of a plus sign(+).

4. Press Ctrl + Home then press the ↓ five times to position the cursor on the label in cell A6. Notice that cell A6 is displayed in the cell reference box, below the Font Name list box. This information tells you the cell reference (the row and column) of the highlighted cell.

5. Press the ↓ once, and then press the → once to move the highlight to the value 7000.00 in cell B7. Notice that the formula bar below the menu

bar displays 7000. Works displays an entry in the format in which it was entered. The amount displayed in cell B7 includes a decimal point and two zeroes because this cell was formatted to include these characteristics.

6. Press ⌃Ctrl + End. Notice that Ctrl + End takes you to the last cell in the database that contains information (Cell D36 in the BUDGET1.WKS spreadsheet).

7. Experiment with other navigation keys and techniques to move the highlight from one cell to another and to scroll through the spreadsheet. When you are finished, click on the first cell in the spreadsheet (cell A1) to highlight it.

8. Close the BUDGET1.WKS spreadsheet without saving your changes.

PRACTICE APPLICATIONS

Complete the following exercises. Some exercises ask you to answer one or more questions. Write a brief answer to these questions on a sheet of paper.

1. Start Works, if necessary, and open the file BUDGET3.WKS on your Student Data Disk. Use the ⬇ key to move to the last entry in the first column (column A). Use the Tab key to move to the last column that contains information. Use Shift + Tab to move to the first column of the spreadsheet. Use the ⬆ key to move to the first cell of the spreadsheet. Display the cell reference in the cell reference bar for the first cell in the spreadsheet that contains a value (7000.00). Display the cell reference in the cell reference bar for the last cell in the spreadsheet that contains a value (-172.18).

2. Explain the navigation technique you used to move to the last cell in the spreadsheet. Do you believe you could have performed the exercise more quickly using different techniques? If so, explain what you could have done differently. Close the BUDGET3.WKS spreadsheet without saving your changes, and quit Works when you have completed this exercise.

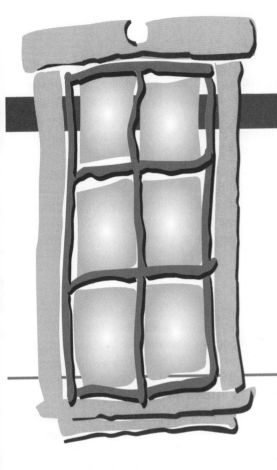

LESSON 25

VIEWING CHARTS

After completing this lesson you will be able to do the following:

- *Explain the relationship between a chart and a spreadsheet.*

- *Describe the appearance of a bar chart, line graph, and pie chart.*

- *Switch between spreadsheet view and chart view.*

KEY WORDS

In this lesson you will learn the meaning of the following terms:

area chart

bar chart

chart

combination
  (bar-and-line) chart

line graph

pie chart

radar

stacked line chart

3-D effects

(X-Y) scatter chart

*T*YPES OF CHARTS IN WORKS

In Works, a **chart** provides a way to view the labels and values for all or part of a spreadsheet in picture format. Basically, a spreadsheet chart is a graph that shows the relationships among values in a spreadsheet. You will learn how to create charts in Chapter 14. At this point, however, you can use the spreadsheet menu bar to view charts that have already been prepared to represent data in the BUDGET1.WKS spreadsheet.

All of the examples that follow, including those in the Guided Practice, illustrate charts that represent a portion of the BUDGET1.WKS spreadsheet. Figure 25-1 shows the cells that were highlighted (cells A24 through D28 or A24: D28) when the three basic chart types shown in Figures 25-2, 25-3, and 25-4 were created. These three basic chart types are described in the following sections.

BAR CHARTS

A **bar chart** represents values as a series of vertical bars. The relative heights (or lengths) of different bars portray the relationship among values that appear in the spreadsheet. The bar chart is the default chart type used when you create a new chart. Figure 25-2 shows a bar chart that represents the selected cells A24 through D28 in BUDGET1.WKS.

A bar chart is an appropriate chart type to use for comparing different values in a category. In Figure 25-2, each item in the variable expenses section of the spreadsheet is represented as a bar with a distinct pattern so that Actual, Budgeted, and Over/under amounts can be compared in a graphic format.

FIGURE 25-1

The BUDGET1.WKS spreadsheet with cells A24 through D28 highlighted.

	A	B	C	D	E	F	G
15	Fixed Expenses						
16	Service Contract	475.00	475.00	0.00			
17	Equipment Insurance	368.50	368.50	0.00			
18	Salaries	4080.00	4080.00	0.00			
19							
20	Total Fixed	4923.50	4923.50	0.00			
21	Percent of Budget	63.54%	63.53%	-0.01%			
22							
23	Variable Expenses						
24	Wages	1278.00	1100.00	178.00			
25	Supplies	440.25	500.00	-59.75			
26	Equipment	878.76	800.00	78.76			
27	Parts	37.10	100.00	-62.90			
28	Other	136.48	100.00	36.48			
29	Total Variable	2770.59	2600.00	170.59			
30	Percent of Budget	35.75%	33.55%	2.20%			
31							
32	Summary						
33		Actual	Budgeted	Over/Under			
34	Total Income	7748.41	7750.00	7748.41			

Press ALT to choose commands, or F2 to edit.

FIGURE 25-2

This bar chart represents values in the Variable Expenses section of the BUDGET1.WKS spreadsheet.

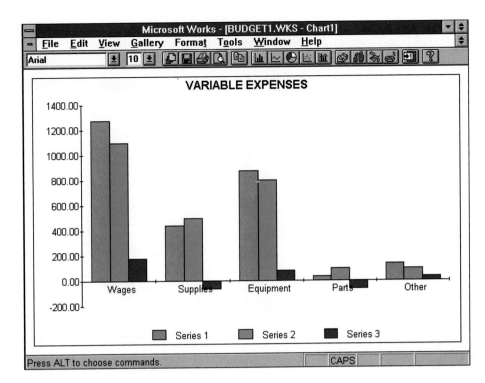

LINE GRAPHS

A **line graph** plots changes from one value to another in a spreadsheet by using lines to connect markers positioned at relative heights in the graph. Figure 25-3 shows a line graph that represents the selected cells A24 through D28 in BUDGET1.WKS.

In Figure 25-3, variable expense items are compared on the basis of their value. Frequently, however, line graphs are used to compare item values as they rise or decline over a period of time.

PIE CHARTS

A **pie chart** is one of the easiest ways to see the relationships among different values in a spreadsheet. As its name suggests, a pie chart displays values as wedges of a circle or "pie." Each pie wedge represents a value that is a proportion of the sum of all the values represented in the pie. Figure 25-4 shows the pie chart that Works created when cells A24 through D28 in BUDGET1.WKS were highlighted. However, since a pie chart is based on a single column of values, Works used the first column of highlighted values (B24 through B28) to create the pie chart.

A pie chart is useful when you want to compare items in a category as a proportion of the total of the items in the category. In Figure 25-4, the pie represents the total variable expenses and the wedges of the pie represent items that make up the total.

FIGURE 25-3
This line graph represents values in the Variable Expenses section of the BUDGET1.WKS spreadsheet.

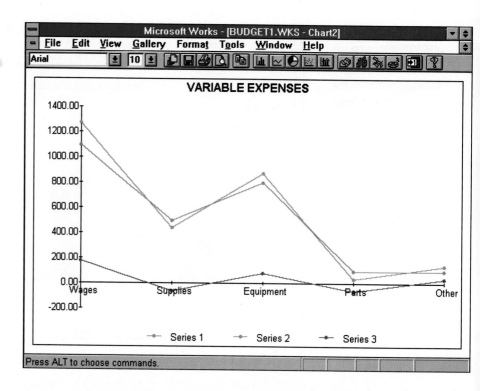

FIGURE 25-4
This pie chart represents the actual variable expenses (values in column B) of running the computer lab for one month. Notice the three-dimensional effect Works created.

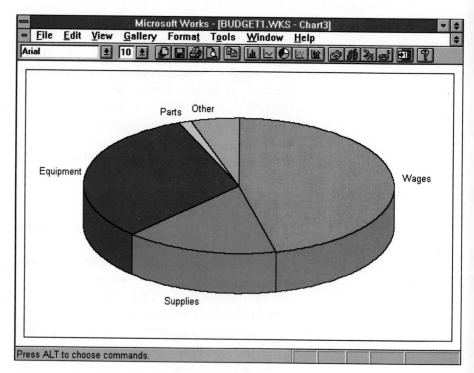

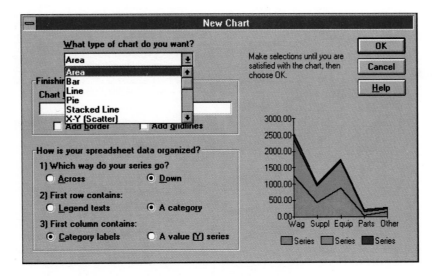

OTHER CHARTS

In addition to these three chart types and their variations (including **3-D effects,** a technique that makes the chart seem to stand out from the page), you can create an **area chart,** an **X-Y (scatter) chart,** a **radar chart,** a **stacked line,** or a **combination (bar-and-line) chart.** Figure 25-5 shows some of the chart types available for selection on the New Chart dialog box, displayed by selecting Create New Chart from the Tools menu or by clicking on the New Chart toolbar button.

V IEWING A CHART

When you create a chart based on values in the spreadsheet, Works automatically gives it a name (Chart1, Chart2, and so on). Works then adds the name to the Charts dialog box, displayed by choosing Chart from the View menu. You can view an existing chart by selecting its name from the Charts dialog box. The Charts dialog box is shown in Figure 25-7.

As you have seen, when Works creates a chart, it displays the chart in a new document window. This window usually obscures the spreadsheet. However, you can always return to the spreadsheet by selecting the Spreadsheet command from the View menu. Similarly, you can switch back to the chart by choosing the Chart command from the View menu. This restores the chart and displays it over the spreadsheet. Even if the chart is in a maximized document window, completely hiding the spreadsheet, you can use the minimize icon to minimize the chart document window. Then you can resize it by dragging the window borders to whatever size you want. Figure 25-6 shows the BUDGET3.WKS spreadsheet with the Chart1 displayed in a resized document window.

To display the information in a different type of chart, choose Create New Chart from the Tools menu (or click on the New Chart toolbar button), and then select another type from the What Type Of Chart Do You Want? list box shown in Figure 25-5.

FIGURE 25-6
*The BUDGET3.WKS
spreadsheet with the
resized Chart1 document
window.*

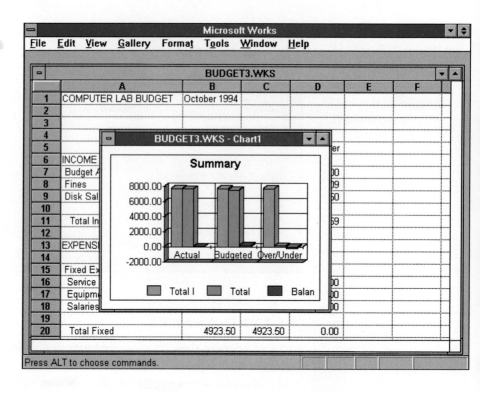

To rename a previously created chart, select Name Chart from the Tools menu. Works displays the Name Chart dialog box, shown in Figure 25-8a. Highlight the chart you want to rename and click on the Rename button. Works displays a message box, shown in Figure 25-8b, prompting you to enter the new chart name. If you think you will have several charts attached to a spreadsheet, it may save time to give them descriptive names consistent with the chart's contents.

FIGURE 25-7
*The Charts dialog box is
displayed when you select
Chart from the View menu.*

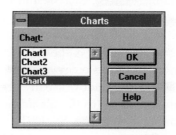

FIGURE 25-8
*(a) The Name Chart dialog
box. (b) Clicking on
Rename opens this message
box.*

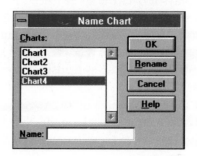

GUIDED PRACTICE

VIEWING A CHART

In this exercise you will create Chart1, based on information in BUDGET1.WKS. Then you will display the chart in different formats and rename it.

1. If necessary, start Works and open the BUDGET1.WKS spreadsheet.

2. Highlight cells A24 through D28, as shown in Figure 25-1. Select Create New Chart from the Tools menu. The untitled chart will be displayed in bar chart format (the Works default chart), as indicated in the What Type Of Chart Do You Want? list box. If your default has been changed, use the What Type Of Chart Do You Want? list box to select Bar chart.

[handwritten: BUDGET1.WKS - CHART1]

3. Click on the Chart title text box and type **VARIABLE EXPENSES**.

4. Click on the Add border check box. Click on the OK button. Your screen display should look similar to the one in Figure 25-2.

[handwritten: CASCADE WILL SHOW WINDOWS CASCADED]

6. Click on the Window menu. Notice that the BUDGET1.WKS spreadsheet and the VARIABLE EXPENSES chart are both displayed, allowing you to switch between them. Close the Window menu.

[handwritten: SWITCH TO BUDGET1.WKS]

6. Open the Window menu as shown in Figure 25-9, and select BUDGET1.WKS to return to the spreadsheet.

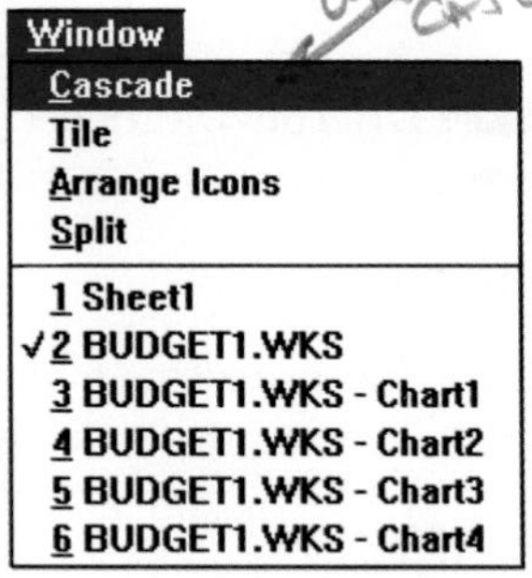

[handwritten: SELECT CHART FROM VIEW MENU]

7. Select Chart1 from the Chart dialog box. Click on the OK button.

8. Select Create New Chart from the Tools menu. Select Radar from the What Type Of Chart Do You Want? list box.

9. Type **Radar Chart** in the Chart Title text box. If necessary, click on the Add Border check box to remove the border around the chart. Click on the Add Gridlines check box to format the radar chart with gridlines.

10. Under Which Way Do Your Series Go? click on the first radio button, Across. Works has stopped displaying the categories of values and is only displaying the values on the radar chart. Click on OK to display the information in Radar Chart, as shown in Figure 25-10. The Which Way Do Your Series Go? options are used to control how the data you have highlighted in the spreadsheet will be displayed. By selecting Across, the data is charted as a series that moves in rows from left to right. By clicking Down, you tell Works to chart the series from top to bottom in columns.

11. Close BUDGET1.WKS without saving your changes.

12. Open the BUDGET1.WKS spreadsheet. Highlight cells A24 through D28, as you have done before. Choose Create New Chart from the Tools menu again.

Window
<u>Cascade</u>
<u>T</u>ile
<u>A</u>rrange Icons
<u>S</u>plit
1 Sheet1
✓**2** BUDGET1.WKS
3 BUDGET1.WKS - Chart1
4 BUDGET1.WKS - Chart2
5 BUDGET1.WKS - Chart3
6 BUDGET1.WKS - Chart4

FIGURE 25-9

By selecting a chart or spreadsheet title on the Window menu, you can switch quickly between the chart or spreadsheet.

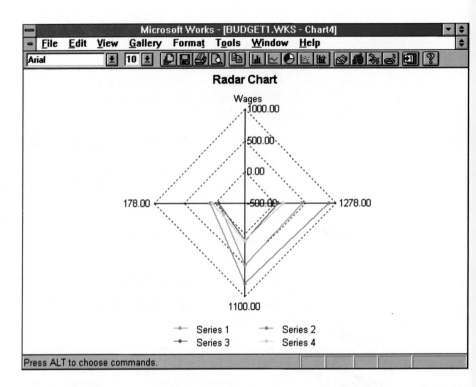

13. Choose Combination from the What Type Of Chart Do You Want? list box. Select Add Gridlines and deselect Add Borders.

14. Click on the OK button to create the combination chart.

15. Save BUDGET1.WKS under its current name. Close the spreadsheet.

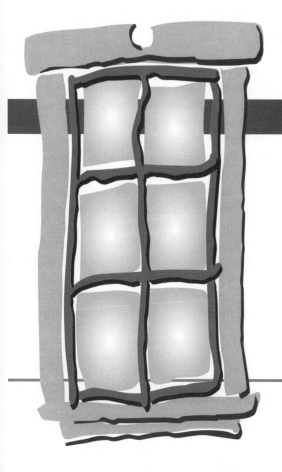

LESSON 26

PRINTING

SPREADSHEETS

AND CHARTS

OBJECTIVES

After completing this lesson you will be able to do the following:

- *Identify horizontal and vertical page breaks in a spreadsheet.*
- *Print an entire spreadsheet.*
- *Print selected cells in a spreadsheet.*
- *Print a chart.*

KEY WORDS

autosum

PRINTING A SPREADSHEET

In Works you can print an entire spreadsheet, including charts, or you can print highlighted cells only. In either case, you use print preview to make sure you have specified margins and print areas the way you want them to appear when the spreadsheet is printed. You can then use the Print toolbar button, the Print button in Print Preview, or the Print command on the File menu to select options in the Print dialog box before printing. To print an entire spreadsheet, make sure that no more than one cell is highlighted when you initiate a print command.

To print a portion of a spreadsheet, highlight the cells that you want to print, then select the Set Print Area from the Format menu. Works displays a message box, shown in Figure 26-1. If you click on OK, Works closes the message box and gives the print area a name. The print-area name is added to the Range Name dialog box, as shown in Figure 26-2, and displayed when you select the Range Name command from the Insert menu. When you print the spreadsheet, only the cells in the print area will print. You can use

FIGURE 26-1

This message box appears after selecting Set Print Area from the Format menu.

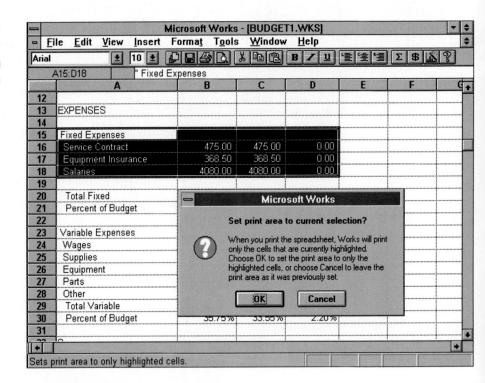

FIGURE 26-2

The name of the cell range you want to print appears in the Range Name dialog box.

print preview to examine the area that will print. Only the cells in the print area will be displayed. To tell Works that you want to resume printing the entire spreadsheet, choose Select All from the Edit menu. Then choose Set Print Area again. Works will print every row and column that has data in it.

To print a chart, display the chart by selecting its name from the Window menu or by selecting its name from the Charts dialog box, displayed by choosing Chart from the View menu (if you have not created a chart, this command will be dimmed). You can then preview the chart before you begin printing.

SPREADSHEET MARGINS AND PAGE BREAKS

Page size, orientation, and margin settings determine the page area that Works uses to print spreadsheet information. You make margin, paper size, and page orientation selections in the Page Setup tab dialog boxes. Works does not display automatic page breaks. To see the effects of automatic page breaks you must select Print Preview. You can, however, set manual page breaks, which are displayed in the spreadsheet as dashed horizontal and vertical lines. In Figure 26-3, the dashed lines under row 12 and to the right of column C result from horizontal and vertical page breaks. Set horizontal page breaks by highlighting the row under where you want to add a page break (an easy way to do this is to click the mouse pointer on the row label number) and selecting Page Break from the Insert menu. Set the vertical page break by highlighting the column to the right of where you want the page break to fall (highlight the column quickly by clicking the mouse pointer on the column label number). To remove a page break, highlight the row below or to the right of the page break you want to delete. Select Delete Page Break from the Insert menu.

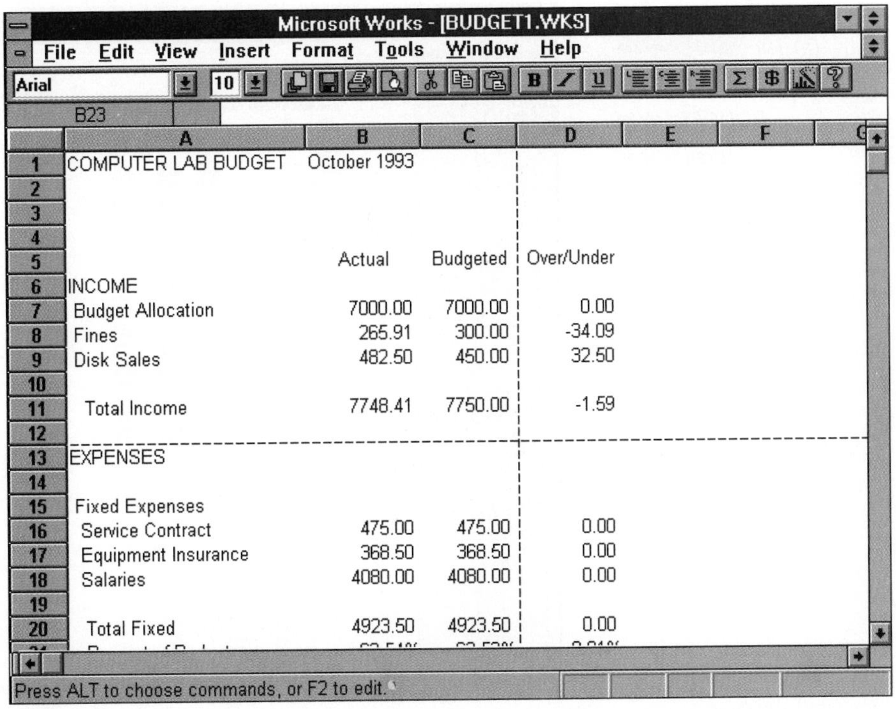

FIGURE 26-3
Works uses dashed horizontal and vertical lines to define manual page breaks inserted in a spreadsheet.

PRINTING SPREADSHEET DATA

In this exercise you will first print the entire BUDGET1.WKS spreadsheet, and then you will select parts of the spreadsheet for printing.

1. Start Works, if necessary, and open the BUDGET1.WKS spreadsheet file.

2. Select Print Preview from the File menu or click on the Print Preview button on the toolbar. The first page of the spreadsheet appears in the print preview display, as shown in Figure 26-4a. Click on the Print button and print the spreadsheet.

3. Using the Chart command on the View menu, open the Chart dialog box. Double-click on Chart1, the combination chart you created in the previous lesson. Display Chart1 in Print Preview, as shown in Figure 26-4b. Click on the Print button and print one copy of the chart.

4. Select cells A5 through D9 (or A5:D9) by positioning the spreadsheet pointer on cell A5 and dragging diagonally to cell D9. Your screen should look similar to the one shown in Figure 26-5.

5. Choose Set Print Area from the Format menu. Click on OK in the Set Print Area message box. Select the Print Preview command. Your screen should resemble the screen in Figure 26-6.

In the next steps you will deselect the Set Print Area command.

6. Exit Print Preview. Click on the Select All command from the Edit menu. Works has now highlighted the entire spreadsheet. Click on the Set Print Area command on the Format menu. Press (Enter) when the Set Print Area message box appears.

FIGURE 26-4
(a) The print preview display of the BUDGET1.WKS spreadsheet.

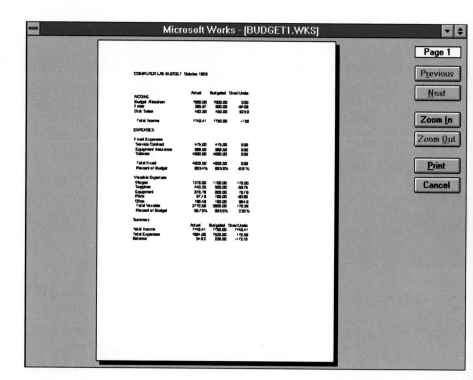

FIGURE 26-4
*(b) The print preview
display of Chart1.*

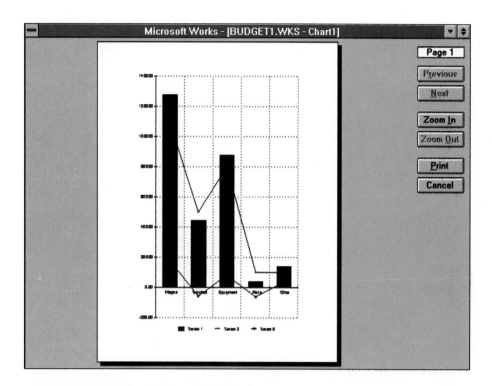

FIGURE 26-4
*(b) The print preview
display of Chart1.*

FIGURE 26-5
*After you select cells A5
through D9, your screen
should resemble this one.*

	A	B	C	D	E	F	G
1	COMPUTER LAB BUDGET	October 1994					
2							
3							
4							
5		Actual	Budgeted	Over/Under			
6	INCOME						
7	Budget Allocation	7000.00	7000.00	0.00			
8	Fines	265.91	300.00	-34.09			
9	Disk Sales	482.50	450.00	32.50			
10							
11	Total Income	7748.41	7750.00	-1.59			
12							
13	EXPENSES						
14							
15	Fixed Expenses						
16	Service Contract	475.00	475.00	0.00			
17	Equipment Insurance	368.50	368.50	0.00			
18	Salaries	4080.00	4080.00	0.00			
19							
20	Total Fixed	4923.50	4923.50	0.00			

Press ALT to choose commands, or F2 to edit.

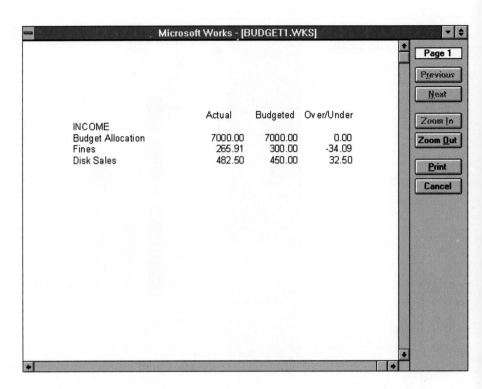

	Actual	Budgeted	Over/Under
INCOME			
Budget Allocation	7000.00	7000.00	0.00
Fines	265.91	300.00	-34.09
Disk Sales	482.50	450.00	32.50

7. Display the spreadsheet in Print Preview. Works now displays the entire spreadsheet.

8. Close the BUDGET1.WKS spreadsheet without saving your changes and quit Works.

PRACTICE APPLICATIONS

1. Start Works, then open the BUDGET3.WKS spreadsheet. Print the entire spreadsheet, then print only cells A1 through D11.

2. Print Chart1 (a 3-D bar graph) for BUDGET3.WKS, and then close the spreadsheet without saving your changes.

CHAPTER REVIEW

Electronic spreadsheets allow you to create financial or other numeric data in a row-and-column format, and then make changes to the spreadsheet without the need for erasures or manual recalculations. Spreadsheets typically contain text, formulas, and values. The most common use of text is in labels, used to create a spreadsheet title or column and row headings. Values are numbers that can be used in making calculations. Formulas are used to automatically calculate cell values, based on values in other cells that are specified in the formula. Charts can be created based on information in a spreadsheet, and can be displayed and printed along with the spreadsheet. Selected parts of a spreadsheet can be printed and a chart can be selected and printed without printing the entire spreadsheet.

REVIEW QUESTIONS

TRUE-FALSE

Write your answers on a sheet of paper.

1. In a spreadsheet, the intersection of a row and column is called a label.

2. A spreadsheet label is a numeric value that can be used to make calculations.

3. A formula can include cell references and arithmetic operators.

4. The formula bar contains a list of formulas available for entry into a spreadsheet.

5. It is possible to change the appearance of labels and values in a spreadsheet.

6. You can use the scroll bars to move to other parts of the spreadsheet.

7. Works identifies columns in the spreadsheet with one or more letters that cannot be deleted.

8. The formula bar of a spreadsheet displays the cell reference of the cell that is highlighted.

9. A bar chart portrays spreadsheet values as a series of dots that are connected by lines.

10. If no chart currently exists for a spreadsheet and you create a new chart, Works assigns the name Chart1 to the chart.

SHORT-ANSWER QUESTIONS

Write a brief answer to these questions on a sheet of paper.

1. In a spreadsheet, what is the difference between a formula and a value?

2. What is a chart?

3. Identify two formatting capabilities that Works can apply to information in spreadsheet cells.

4. How do you use Works to print the information in selected cells of a spreadsheet?

5. How do you use Works to print a chart by itself?

LESSON APPLICATIONS

1. Open MYBUDGET.WKS on your Student Data Disk. Perform the following navigation steps, using the most efficient method:

   a. Display one window to the right of the current screen. Click on the first cell containing text, and read the first note. Notice that although the note is displayed across several cells, the text was actually entered in one cell.

   b. Display one window down from the position in step 1a. Adjust your screen display, if necessary, so that you can read the other note.

   c. Use the vertical scroll bar to return to the top of the spreadsheet.

   d. Position the highlight on the last cell that contains information in the spreadsheet.

   e. From the cell position in step 1d, move the highlight to the first cell in this row.

   f. Position the highlight on the first cell in the first row of the spreadsheet.

2. View Chart1, a bar chart, for MYBUDGET.WKS. Then select Chart2, a 3-D pie chart.

3. Print the entire MYBUDGET.WKS spreadsheet. Close the spreadsheet without saving your changes.

HAPTER APPLICATIONS

1. Open MYBUDGET.WKS on your Student Data Disk. Perform the following steps:

   a. Display Chart2.

   b. View the chart in Print Preview.

   c. Print the chart only.

   d. Close the MYBUDGET.WKS spreadsheet without saving your changes.

2. Open the BUDGET2.WKS spreadsheet, then select and print three different parts of the spreadsheet of your own choosing. Include cells with column and/or row labels in two of your selections. Leave the database open for the next exercise.

3. The computer lab manager wants you to brush up on the **autosum** feature of the spreadsheet—a tool that automatically totals a range of numbers. You decide to use Cue Cards. After clicking on the Learning Works toolbar button to open the Learning Works dialog box, you click on the Cue Cards button. Click on the Show Cue Cards radio button. Click on OK to exit the dialog box and display the Using Cue Cards box. In this box click on the button belonging to I want help from Cue Cards. When the Spreadsheet Menu box appears, click on the Typing Or Revising A Spreadsheet button. When the What Do You Want To Do? box opens, select Have Works Do Calculations For You. A new What Do You Want To Do? window opens. Click on Add numbers. When you understand the autosum feature, close the Cue Cards window, and select the Close Cue Cards button.

4. Close the spreadsheet without saving it.

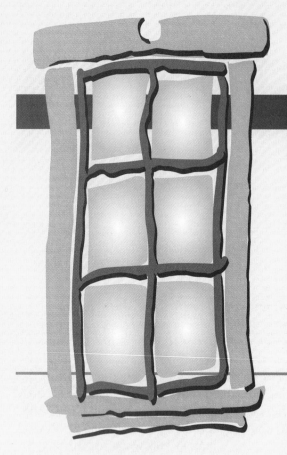

CHAPTER 10

CREATING A

SPREADSHEET

OVERVIEW

In this chapter you will learn how to create a spreadsheet. To create a spreadsheet, you type labels that identify the content of columns and rows, and you enter values and formulas that are used to make calculations. You will learn how to change the appearance of values in cells so that the numbers, dates, and times you enter appear in a consistent format. You will also learn how to apply character formats to change fonts, type sizes, and type styles for labels or values. In addition, you will learn how to insert and delete columns and rows, change the width of columns, create formulas, use functions, and search a spreadsheet.

CONTENTS

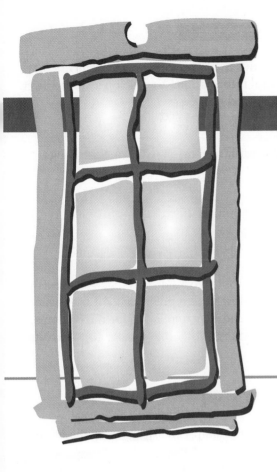

ENTERING LABELS AND VALUES INTO A NEW SPREADSHEET

OBJECTIVES

After completing this lesson you will be able to do the following:

- *Create, name, and save a new spreadsheet.*
- *Enter and format labels in a spreadsheet.*
- *Enter and format values in a spreadsheet.*

THE SPREADSHEET CREATION PROCESS

A completed spreadsheet contains a number of separate elements that must fit together to provide useful information. To develop a spreadsheet, therefore, it is best to follow an orderly process:

1. Open a new spreadsheet document window.

2. Enter labels for the spreadsheet title and column and row headings.

3. Enter values in cells.

4. Format cells.

5. Enter formulas.

6. Process the finished spreadsheet.

When you select the Spreadsheet tool, Works displays Sheet1, the as yet untitled spreadsheet document window shown in Figure 27-1. At this point, you need to create a title for the spreadsheet and labels for the columns and rows. These designations provide an organizational scheme for entering values and formulas.

ENTERING AND FORMATTING LABELS

In most cases, a label can be created simply by highlighting the desired cell and typing the text. The text you type appears on the formula bar at the top of the spreadsheet until you click on the Enter button, press the Enter key, or press one of the other keys used to navigate the spreadsheet. The

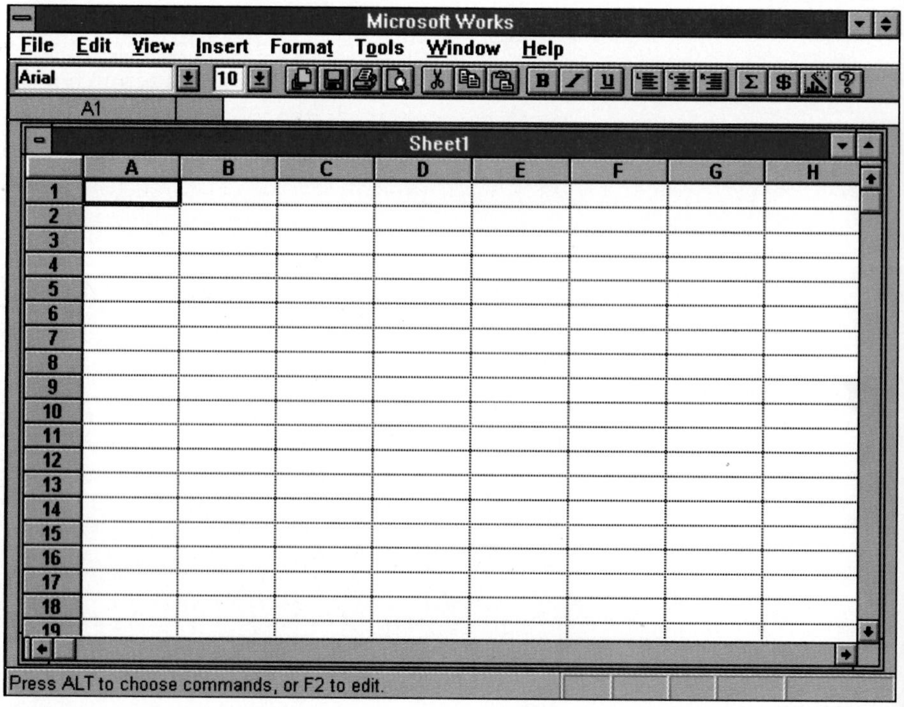

FIGURE 27-1
An untitled spreadsheet document window used to create a new spreadsheet.

Enter button is the square with the check mark in it that appears to the left of the formula bar as soon as you click your insertion point on it. By default, labels are entered into the active cell aligned to the left. If you type a label that is too long to fit in the active cell, Works automatically scrolls the text in the cell, allowing you to see the last characters you typed. When you press Enter, click on the Enter button, or use a navigation key, Works uses as many adjacent, empty cells as necessary to display the new label.

If a label consists of numbers only, you should begin typing the label with a quotation mark ("). For example, you may want to label columns with years: 1994, 1995, and so on. Typing the quotation mark before the year ("1994) tells Works that the entry is a label and not a value and will not be used in a formula. When you click the Enter button, 1994 appears left-aligned in the active cell.

If you forget to type the quotation mark before a number that is being used as a label, Works treats the entry as a value, aligning it on the right in the active cell. If an entry consists of both letters and numbers, Works treats the entry as a label. For example, all of the following entries would be recognized as labels, and all should be typed without the beginning quotation mark: 2nd Shipment, 2 Shipment, Shipment 2.

You can apply character formatting to label cells before or after typing the entry. For example, choose Font and Style from the Format menu to display the Font and Style dialog box shown in Figure 27-2; make font, type size, type style, and type color selections; and then type the label (you can also use the Font Name box and the Font Size box on the toolbar). Alternatively, you can type the label first, highlight the cell that contains the entire label or the beginning of the label, and then make formatting selections in the Font And Style dialog box.

ENTERING AND FORMATTING VALUES

After you have entered labels for the spreadsheet title and row-and-column headings, you can begin entering numbers, dates, or times. Works displays numbers, dates, and times on the formula bar exactly the way you type them. When you click on the Enter button or use an entry key to display the value in the active cell, the entry is displayed the way it was

FIGURE 27-2

The Font And Style dialog box is used to apply character formats to labels and values.

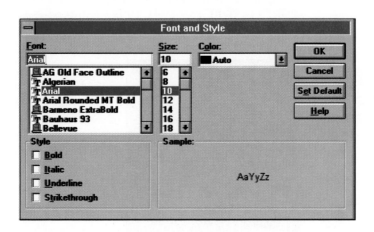

typed, unless you have applied a different format to the cell. For example, if you type the value 8700.5 into a cell that has not been formatted, Works displays 8700.5, which is the default number format. If you first apply a currency format to one or more cells in a column, Works automatically displays the value with a dollar sign and two decimal places. The value typed as 8700.5 is then displayed in the formatted cell according to the currency format you selected—$8,700.50.

Usually all of the values in a single column of a spreadsheet are formatted to have a consistent appearance. For example, if the cells in a column will contain dates, you could format the column so that all entries appear in a consistent date format, regardless of how they are typed. If a column is formatted with the long date format—October 14, 1994—you type 10/14/94 on the formula bar and Works will enter October 14, 1994 in the active cell when you click the Enter button.

Works has an internal calendar that begins with January 1, 1900, and ends with June 3, 2079. If you enter a date outside this range or enter a date or time that Works does not recognize (for example, 23 August), Works treats the entry as text.

To format cells, you must first highlight them. You can drag the mouse pointer to highlight some of the cells in a column or row or click on a column label letter or a row label number to select the entire column or row. Click on the unlabeled cell button to the left of column A and above row 1 and you highlight the entire spreadsheet. For example, after highlighting cells, you can format them by selecting options in the Alignment dialog box, which is displayed when you choose Alignment from the Format menu.

The Alignment dialog box in Figure 27-3 shows some of the formats available. The first format listed, General, is the default format. You select a different format by clicking on its radio button. Clicking the Wrap Text check box tells Works to treat text as a word processor would, wrapping text in lines rather than extending it across several cells.

Formats for dates, time, and other values are shown in the Number dialog box, which is displayed when you choose Number from the Format menu. Figure 27-4 shows the Number dialog box and its default settings. Clicking on a Format radio button either displays an explanation or displays further options in the Options area.

Figure 27-5 shows a sample spreadsheet with a title line (EQUIPMENT PURCHASE PLAN: 1995-1998), column headings (1995, 1996, 1997, and

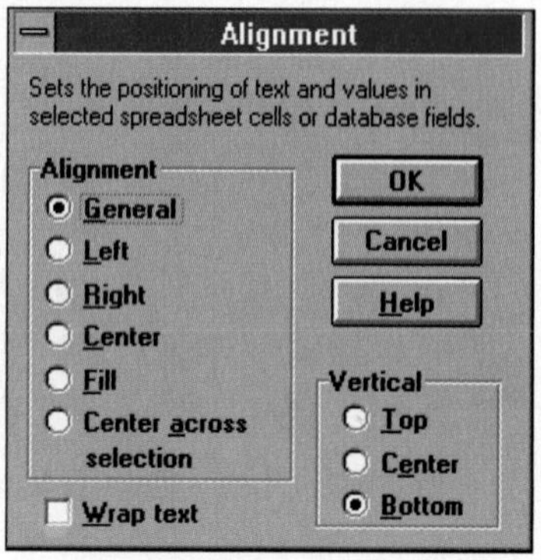

FIGURE 27-3

The Alignment dialog box with the default General format highlighted.

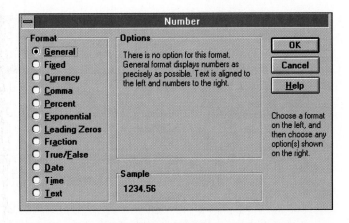

1998), and row headings (the entries in column A). The figure also shows values entered in column B that are displayed in a number format. The format includes the dollar sign, commas, and two decimal places. You will use this illustration as a guide in completing the following exercises.

GUIDED PRACTICE

ENTERING LABELS AND VALUES IN A NEW SPREADSHEET

The lab manager wants you to develop a four-year plan for purchasing equipment for the computer lab in your school. Money for purchasing hardware and software will come from the lab's annual budget and from lab rental fees charged to other departments that use the lab to conduct classes or do research. Sales of computer supplies and fines provide additional income.

In this exercise you will type a title for the spreadsheet, type headings for columns and rows, and specify a different number format for some of the columns in the spreadsheet.

1. Start Works, if necessary, and insert your Student Data Disk in the disk drive.

2. Click on the Spreadsheet tool in the Startup dialog box.

3. Choose Save ([Ctrl] +S) from the File menu and save the new spreadsheet using the name PLAN1.WKS.

4. Click on cell B1 to highlight it.

5. Type **EQUIPMENT PURCHASE PLAN: 1995-1998**. Notice that the text you type appears in the formula bar.

6. Click on the Enter button. The title now appears in the spreadsheet cells in row 1, beginning with cell B1.

7. Using Figure 27-5 as a guide, create labels for row-and-column headings to identify information that will be entered later. Use the double-headed arrow to widen column A, as you did when working with databases. This is one of the functions that the database and spreadsheet applications share. Enter the labels in cells B4, C4, D4, E4, A5 through A9, A11, and A13 through A15. Remember to designate the years as labels by beginning each entry with a quotation mark.

8. Save the spreadsheet under the current name PLAN1.WKS.

9. Click on cell B6 to highlight it, then enter **2000** in cell B6.

In the next steps you will format cells in columns B through E in a number format that includes the dollar sign, two decimal places, and commas.

10. Position the pointer on cell B5, and drag the highlight over to cell E16 in column E to highlight all cells in the four columns (drag by holding down the left mouse button—the mouse pointer should be a white cross—and moving the mouse pointer until the entire range of cells is highlighted). Release the mouse button.

11. Choose Number from the Format menu to open the Number dialog box. Click on the Currency button and notice the default of 2 in the Number Of Decimals text box. Notice that Works displays a sample based on your choices at the bottom of the dialog box.

12. When your Number dialog box looks the same as the one in Figure 27-6, click on OK to return to the spreadsheet. Notice that the number 2000 you entered in cell B6 now appears as $2,000.00. Also notice that, even though the cells containing 1995, 1996, 1997, and 1998 were highlighted when you changed cell formats, their appearance does not change because you designated them as labels by preceding each entry with a quotation mark.

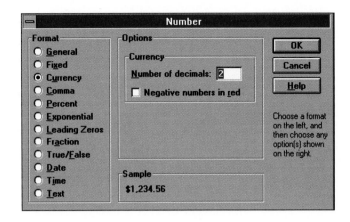

13. Highlight cell B7, type **4000,** and enter the value. Works formats the number and places $4,000.00 in cell B7.

14. Use Figure 27-5 as a guide to enter values for cells B8, B9, B14, and B15.

15. Save the changes to the PLAN1.WKS spreadsheet.

PRACTICE APPLICATIONS

1. If necessary, open the PLAN1.WKS spreadsheet, and save it as PLAN-PRAC.WKS. Add the label **1999** in cell F4. Highlight cells F6, F7, and F8, then select the Fixed number format. Enter sample values into cells F6, F7, and F8 to see the results of your formatting. Select the cells with the values you just entered, and apply other number formats by using the options on the Number dialog box.

   Note: If you use all of the number formats, you may see a number replaced with number signs (#######). This simply means that there is not enough space in the cell to display the entire number in the format you have chosen. You will learn how to make adjustments to avoid this in a later lesson.

2. Enter the labels 2000 in cell G4 and **2001** in cell H4. Enter dates in cells G6, G7, and G8, and times in H6, H7, and H8. Using the Options list box in the Number dialog box, experiment by applying other date and time formats to the dates and times entered in these cells. Did you remember to enter quotation marks before you entered the remainder of the year labels? If you did not, enter the quotation marks now. How will they change the alignment of the labels?

3. Save your changes and close the PLANPRAC.WKS spreadsheet.

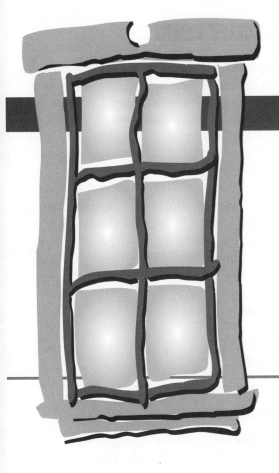

LESSON 28

USING FORMULAS AND FUNCTIONS

After completing this lesson you will be able to do the following:

- Create formulas.
- Use Fill commands to copy values and formulas.

KEY WORDS

In this lesson you will learn the meaning of the following terms:

arithmetic operators	function
Fill Down	range of cells
Fill Right	relative reference

SPREADSHEET FORMULAS AND FUNCTIONS

After setting up the spreadsheet and entering text and values, you are ready to create formulas. As you learned in Lesson 24, a formula is an expression used to calculate values and to display a result. The result of a formula appears in the cell in which you created the formula. The cells used in the calculation are specified within the formula itself.

WRITING FORMULAS

In Works, you use formulas to create new values from existing ones. For example, if the formula =B14+B15 is written in cell B16, the values in cells B14 and B15 will be added and the sum will be placed in cell B16. You can use one or more of the following **arithmetic operators** to perform addition, subtraction, multiplication, and division in a formula:

OPERATOR	OPERATION
+	Addition
−	Subtraction
*	Multiplication
/	Division

A spreadsheet formula must begin with an equal sign (=). You can then type a cell reference you want to include in the formula or you can simply click on the cell and Works will automatically place the cell reference number in the formula. You can continue clicking on cells and adding the operator before each cell reference until each cell you want included in the formula is listed. For example, to construct the formula =D6+D7+D8+D9+ D10+D11+D12 in cell D14, you would first highlight cell D14, type the equal sign (=), and then click on cell D6, add a plus sign (+), and then highlight D7, D8, and so on, adding a plus sign before each new cell reference. Each time you click on a cell, its cell reference is added to the formula. You can also type in each cell reference and arithmetic operator in the formula.

IDENTIFYING AND USING A RANGE OF CELLS IN A FORMULA

The formula D6+D7+D8+D9+D10+D11+D12 represents a range of cells from D6 through D12. A **range of cells** is any rectangular group of cells. A range of cells can be as small as two cells or as large as an entire spreadsheet.

When referring to ranges in a formula, you do not have to type each cell reference or click on each cell in the range. In a column or row, you simply indicate the first cell and last cell in the range and separate them by a colon (:). The range of cells from D6 through D12 is written as D6:D12. If the range of cells is a block of cells, you indicate the cell reference of the upper-left corner cell and the lower-right corner cell. The range notation D6:F9, for instance, identifies a block of cells that is three columns wide and four rows deep.

USING FUNCTIONS IN FORMULAS

Instead of typing in each element of a complex formula, you can use one of the basic functions provided by Works to help construct formulas for mathematical, statistical, financial, and other kinds of calculations. A function is a built-in calculation that performs an arithmetic operation. Each function consists of its name and a set of parentheses that encloses the values (or cell references) the function will use to produce a result. For example, =SUM(D6,D7,D8,D9) is a built-in function that adds the values in cells D6, D7, D8, and D9.

You can type the name of the function you want to use or you can select a function name from the list in the Insert Function dialog box. This dialog box, shown in Figure 28-1, appears when you choose Function from the Insert menu. Notice that the Insert Function dialog box displays the functions for each category selected, in this case the All category. When you select a function, it appears on the spreadsheet formula bar. In Figure 28-2, the statistical function SUM, which was selected in the Insert Function dialog box, has been placed on the spreadsheet's formula bar. The highlighted text (RangeRef0, RangeRef1,...) between the parentheses must be replaced with values or cell references for the cells that contain the values you want to sum.

Instead of typing each cell reference in the formula, you can use a range reference. Thus the formula =SUM(D6,D7,D8,D9) appears as =SUM(D6:D9). If you highlight the cells you want included, Works places the range reference in the formula for you. Figure 28-3 shows how cells D6 through D9 look when you highlight them after pasting the SUM function on the formula bar. The highlighted cells are outlined, and the notation D6:D9 automatically replaces the highlighted text in the formula on the formula bar. When you click on the entry, the sum of the cells D6:D9 appears in the active cell D11. You must delete the unused function placeholder (RangeRef1) before you click on the Enter button.

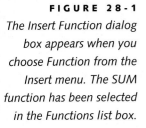

FIGURE 28-1

The Insert Function dialog box appears when you choose Function from the Insert menu. The SUM function has been selected in the Functions list box.

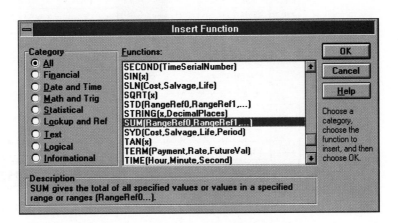

FIGURE 28-2

The spreadsheet formula bar after you have selected the SUM function from the Functions list in the Insert Function dialog box.

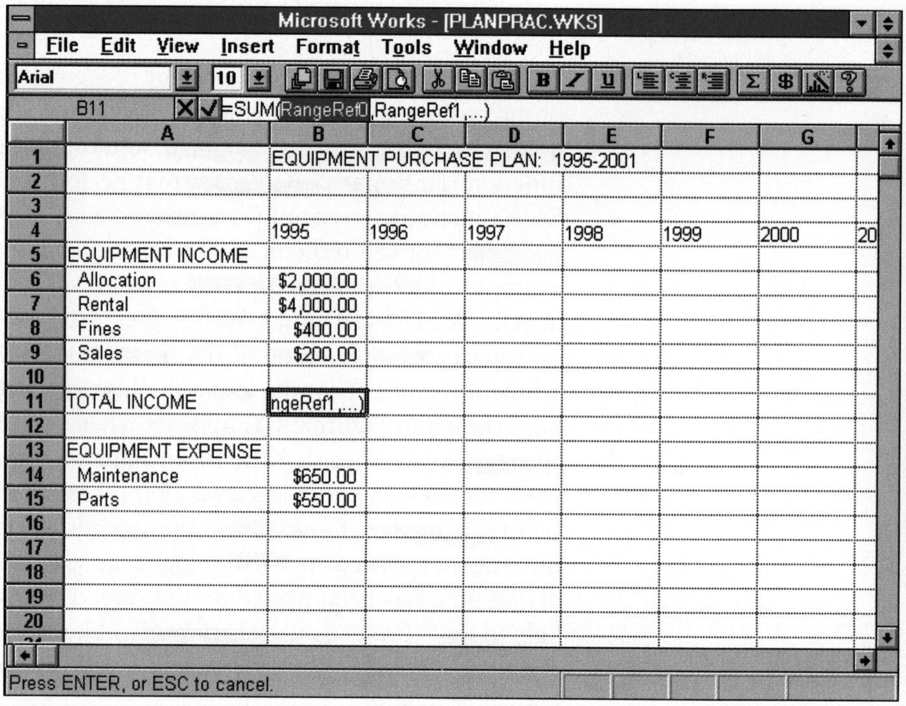

FIGURE 28-3

After you highlight cells B6 through B9, the range reference B6:B9 is placed automatically in the formula on the formula bar. Notice the unused function placeholder (RangeRef1).

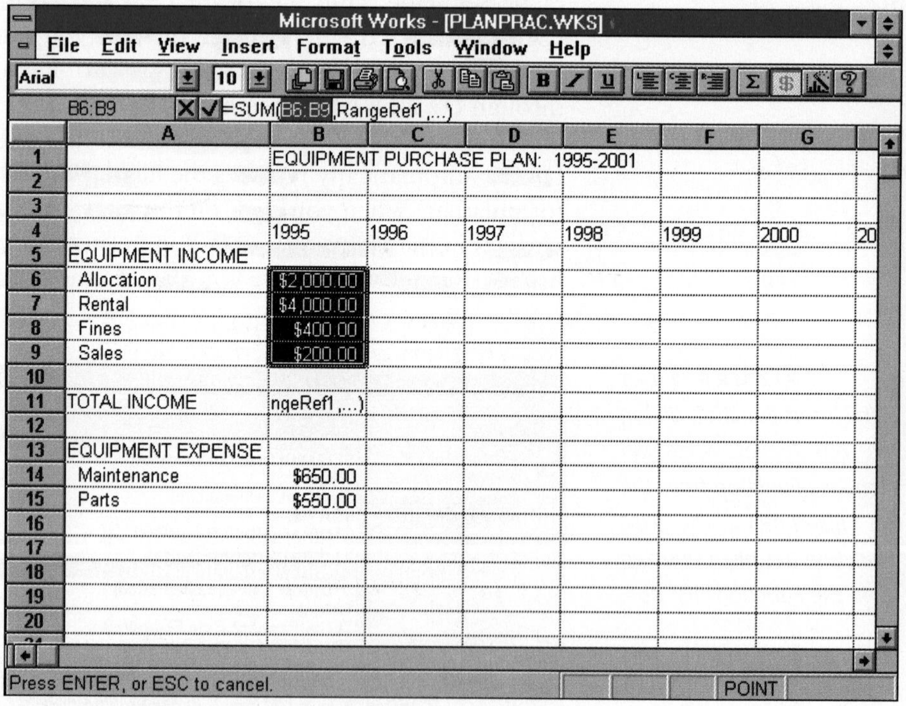

USING FILL COMMANDS

A value or formula that you enter in one cell can often be used in one or more adjacent cells. For example, if the budgeted allocation for the computer lab is $2000 for the years 1995, 1996, 1997, and 1998, you can type the amount once and fill the adjacent cells with the same value automatically. Use the **Fill Right** option on the Edit menu to copy the information in the first cell (the active cell) and fill that information into all the highlighted cells to the right. You use the **Fill Down** option to copy the information in the first cell and fill that information into all the highlighted cells below it.

To use a fill option, first highlight the cell that contains the value you want to copy (either by dragging the highlight using the mouse or pressing Shift +an arrow key), then highlight adjacent cells in the column or row to be filled with this value. Then you choose the appropriate fill option (Fill Right to fill a row; Fill Down to fill a column). The fill option creates entries in the highlighted cells to match the value or formula in the initial cell.

When you specify that a formula is to fill new cells, Works recognizes that you are entering the formula into a cell (or range of cells) that is in a different location than the one used in the original formula and makes automatic adjustments to the formula's cell references. For example, if the formula =SUM(D6:D9) is in cell D11 and you use the Fill Right command to copy the formula into cells E11, F11, and G11, Works automatically adjusts the formula so that =SUM(D6:D9) becomes:

=SUM(E6:E9) in cell E11

=SUM(F6:F9) in cell F11

=SUM(G6:G9) in cell G11

When a cell reference is used in this way, it is referred to as a **relative reference.** A relative reference gives Works general directions on how to locate a cell. Instead of providing directions for locating one or more specific cells, a relative reference provides directions such as "sum the values in the three adjacent cells above." The cells referred to change when a relative reference is copied.

GUIDED PRACTICE

CREATING FORMULAS AND USING FILL OPTIONS

In this exercise you will enter formulas for two cells in the PLAN1.WKS spreadsheet. Specifically, you will increase the value in cell B7 by 4 percent (multiply by 1.04) and place the result in cell C7. This formula assumes that rental income for 1995 will increase by 4 percent in 1996. You will also enter a formula to sum the values in cells B6 through B9, which represent all equipment income for 1995. Then you will use fill options to enter the information into adjacent cells.

1. Start Works and open the PLAN1.WKS spreadsheet.

2. Highlight cell C7 and type **=B7*1.04**. Press the (Tab) key, which will calculate the formula, place the result into cell C7, and move the cell pointer to cell D7.

3. Highlight cell B11 and type **=SUM(B6:B9)**. Click the Enter button to calculate the formula and place the result in cell B11. Your screen display should look similar to the one shown in Figure 28-4.

4. Save the file under the existing name PLAN1.WKS.

The budget allocation amount in the PLAN1.WKS spreadsheet does not change from year to year. Therefore, you can fill the budget allocation columns for the years 1996, 1997, and 1998 with the same amount allocated for 1995. Also, the formula created for cell C7 can be used to fill cells D7 and E7, since the amount charged to other departments to rent lab equipment is expected to increase by the same amount each year (4 percent).

5. Highlight cell B6, the cell that contains the value $2,000.00, then drag the highlighting to select cells C6, D6, and E6, as well.

6. Choose Fill Right from the Edit menu. Works fills cells C6, D6, and E6 with the value $2,000,00.

7. Highlight cell C7, which contains the formula =B7*1.04. Drag the highlighting to select cells D7 and E7, as well.

8. Choose Fill Right from the Edit menu to fill cells D7 and E7 with the formula stored in cell C7. Your screen display should look similar to the one shown in Figure 28-5.

9. Save the changes to the PLAN1.WKS spreadsheet under the existing name.

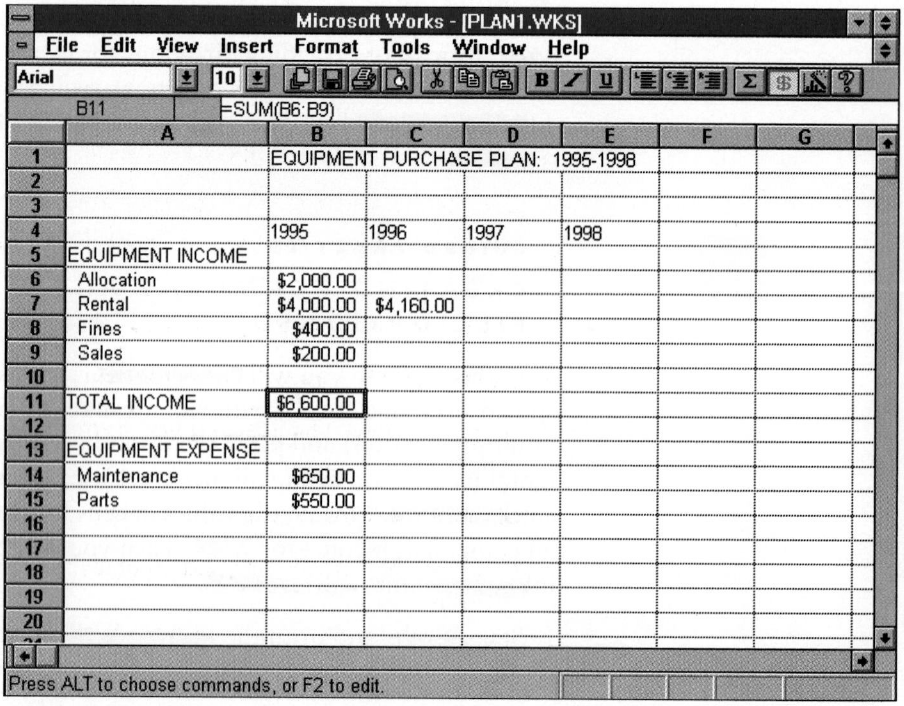

FIGURE 28-4

After you have completed step 3, your screen display should look similar to this one.

FIGURE 28-5

After you have completed the fill operation in step 8, your screen display should look similar to this one.

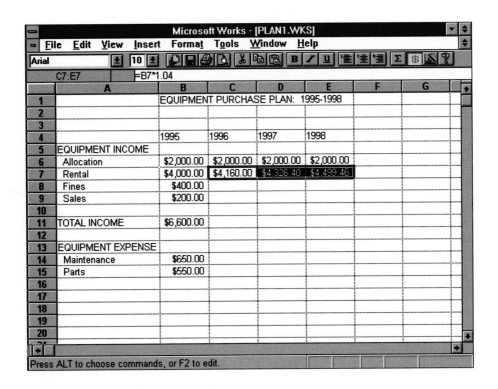

PRACTICE APPLICATIONS

1. Open the PLAN1.WKS spreadsheet, if necessary, and save it as PLANPRA2.WKS.

2. Using the PLANPRA2.WKS spreadsheet, create a formula in cell C8 to subtract $20.00 from the Fines amount in cell B8. Then fill cells D8 and E8 with the formula in C8.

3. Create a formula in cell C9 to add $30.00 to the Sales amount in cell B9. Then fill cells D9 and E9 with the formula.

4. Use the SUM function to add the values in cells C6 through C9 and place the results in cell C11. Then fill cells D11 and E11 with the formula.

5. Save your changes and close the PLANPRA2 spreadsheet.

6. Click on the Learning Works toolbar button.

7. Select the Start The Tutorial text button to display the Works Tutorial screen.

8. Choose the Spreadsheet tab.

9. Click on the Introducing The Spreadsheet button and complete the tutorial.

10. Return to Works.

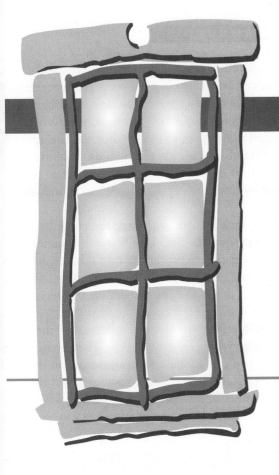

LESSON 29

EDITING AND FORMATTING A SPREADSHEET

OBJECTIVES

After completing this lesson you will be able to do the following:

- *Edit the contents of a cell.*

- *Insert a row or column in a spreadsheet.*

- *Delete a row or column from a spreadsheet.*

- *Change the width of a column.*

- *Place borders on selected cells.*

EDITING VALUES, LABELS, AND FORMULAS

The contents of a spreadsheet document, like the contents of database and word-processing documents, can be easily changed whenever necessary. In fact, this is one of the chief benefits of using an electronic spreadsheet. You can enter new values or formulas into an existing spreadsheet to make new calculations based on changed plans or business conditions. The automatic recalculation feature of a spreadsheet means that you do not have to create the spreadsheet all over again if one or two values or formulas change. Works automatically recalculates the entire spreadsheet to incorporate the new entries.

The simplest spreadsheet editing task involves changing the contents of a cell. The technique used to delete text, values, and formulas is the same. You can delete the entire contents of a cell and enter the new data or delete and replace only a few characters. For example, if the cell references in a formula need to be changed, you can delete the entire formula and retype it or you can delete and retype only the cell references in the formula.

In Works you edit a cell by highlighting it to place its contents on the formula bar. Then you can delete everything by pressing the [Del] key or simply by typing the new data; or you can click an insertion point on the formula bar and use the [Del] or [Backspace] key to delete some or all of the entry. The changed data on the formula bar is entered into the cell when you click on the Enter button or press one of the navigation keys.

DELETING AND INSERTING ROWS AND COLUMNS

You will often find it necessary to delete existing columns and rows or add new columns or rows to a spreadsheet. If information in a column or row is no longer needed, you can delete it. Works will automatically adjust spacing, renumber subsequent rows and columns, and adjust cell references in formulas. You can also add a column or row to an existing spreadsheet when a new category of information needs to be inserted or when you want to add space between columns or rows to enhance the appearance of the spreadsheet.

You insert a row or column by clicking on the column letter or the row number where you want to make the insertion. If a row is highlighted, a new row is inserted above the highlighted row when you choose Row/Column from the Insert menu. If a column is highlighted, a new column is inserted to the left of the highlighted column when you choose Insert.

You delete a row or column by first clicking on the row or column label to highlight all the cells. Then choose Cut from the Edit menu to delete the entire row or column, including any information in the cells. You can also use the Delete Row/Column command from the Insert menu. If there is information in the cells, it is placed temporarily in the Clipboard when the Cut command is used. Information is not stored on the Clipboard when you use the Delete Row/Column command. If you want to delete the information in the cells without placing it in the Clipboard and without deleting the column or row, choose Clear from the Edit menu.

CHANGING THE COLUMN WIDTH

When you create a new spreadsheet, all columns are automatically the same width. If the default width of a column is too narrow or too wide for the information that will be entered, you can change the column width.

Works provides two ways of increasing and decreasing the width of columns. You can change one or more columns by first highlighting the column(s) and then choosing Column Width from the Format menu. A Column Width dialog box, such as the one shown in Figure 29-1a, allows you to increase or decrease width. The Row Height dialog box, shown in Figure 29-1b, functions similarly.

You can also change the width of a column by positioning the mouse pointer on the vertical line between column headings. In this position, the pointer changes to the two-headed adjust arrow that can be dragged to the left or right to change the width of the column to the left of the pointer.

The Best Fit check box on the Column Width and Row Height dialog boxes offers a valuable option for widening a column or row. Select the row or column you want to change and open the pertinent dialog box. Select Best Fit and click on the OK button. Works will examine the longest or tallest line and adjust the row or column to accommodate it.

CHANGING THE APPEARANCE OF CELLS

Works provides several features to change the appearance of a spreadsheet. In Lesson 27, you learned that the Alignment and Number dialog boxes are used to change the alignment and appearance of number, date, and time values. The Alignment dialog box, which is displayed by choosing Alignment from the Format menu, is also used to change the alignment of text.

The procedure for changing the alignment of a label is the same as the procedure for changing the alignment of a number, date, or time value. First select the cell or cells that contain the information, then open the Alignment dialog box and select the appropriate alignment button.

The Border dialog box shown in Figure 29-2 is used to add cell borders to a cell or a group of cells. To surround one or more selected cells with a

FIGURE 29-1

(a) Use the Column Width dialog box to change the width of one or more selected columns in a spreadsheet. (b) The Row Height dialog box adjusts the height of rows. Notice the Best Fit check box in each.

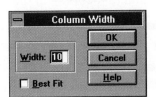

FIGURE 29-2

Based on the options chosen in the Border dialog box, the selected cells will have double-line cell borders on four sides.

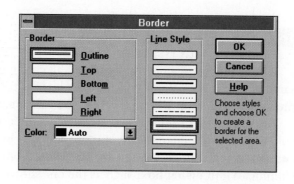

border, use the Border check boxes and Line Style buttons. The seven line-style choices (the first choice—an empty box—removes line style choices) may be used with any combination of Border check boxes. Selected cells might have double lines on the left and right, for example, and single, heavy lines on the top and bottom.

Border lines are difficult to see when they are placed around cells in a spreadsheet with displayed gridlines. To better distinguish the border lines you have added to a spreadsheet, turn off the gridlines by choosing Gridlines from the View menu. The Gridlines command is turned on when it appears on the menu with a checkmark; it is turned off when it appears without the checkmark.

Change the appearance of characters in one or more cells by first selecting the cells and then selecting a different font, size, or style in the Font And Style dialog box, the Font Name and Font Size list boxes on the toolbar, or one of the Font-Style tool buttons.

GUIDED PRACTICE

EDITING AND FORMATTING

In this exercise you will edit information in cells, insert a column and row, increase and decrease the width of columns, and practice making other changes to add emphasis to selected cells.

1. Start Works, if necessary, and open the file PLAN3.WKS on your Student Data Disk. Save the spreadsheet as PLAN4.WKS.

2. Using the PLAN4.WKS spreadsheet, highlight cell B7 to place the cell contents for 1995 Rental ($4000.00) on the formula bar as **4000**.

3. Click an insertion point on the formula bar to the left of the ~~first~~ second O, press the [Del] key once to delete the first O, then type **5**.

4. Click on the entry box to enter $4500.00, replacing $4000.00 in B7. The values in cells C7, D7, and E7, which are based on the amount in B7, are automatically increased when you increase the amount in cell B7.

5. Highlight cell A17 to place the cell contents **TOTAL INCOME** on the formula bar.

6. Double-click on the word **INCOME** on the Formula Bar , then press the [Del] key to delete the word. Type **EXPENSE** and click on the Entry button to enter the corrected label.

In the next steps, you will correct a cell reference in the formula in cell B17. Notice that the value in cell B17 is $650.00. This amount will change when you enter the corrected formula.

7. Highlight cell B17 to place the formula **=B14+B16** on the formula bar.

8. Click an insertion point at the end of the entry and press the [Backspace] key once. Type **5** to change the cell reference B16 to B15, then enter the new formula. Notice that the amount in cell B17 has changed to $1200.00. Your screen display of the PLAN4.WKS spreadsheet should appear similar to the one in Figure 29-3.

9. Save your changes to the PLAN4.WKS spreadsheet.

10. Click on the column label B to highlight the column, then choose Row/Column from the Insert menu to insert a column between the current column B and column A. Notice that the information that was previously in columns B and E has automatically been moved to columns C through F, and that column B is now empty.

In the next step you will insert a row between rows 19 and 20.

11. Click on row heading 20 to highlight the cells in row 20, then choose Row/Column from the Insert menu. Notice that Works inserts a blank row of cells between the row labels ADJUSTED INCOME and PUR-CHASES. Your screen display should look similar to the one shown in Figure 29-4.

12. Highlight columns A through F.

13. Choose Column Width from the Format menu to display the Column Width dialog box.

FIGURE 29-3
The PLAN4.WKS spreadsheet after you have completed step 8.

Microsoft Works - [PLAN4.WKS]

File   Edit   View   Insert   Format   Tools   Window   Help

Arial   10   B19

	A	B	C	D	E	F
1		EQUIPMENT PURCHASE PLAN: 1995-1998				
2						
3						
4		1995	1996	1997	1998	
5	EQUIPMENT INCOME					
6	Allocation	$2,000.00	$2,000.00	$2,000.00	$2,000.00	
7	Rental	$4,500.00	$4,680.00	$4,867.20	$5,061.89	
8	Fines	$400.00	$380.00	$360.00	$340.00	
9	Sales	$200.00	$230.00	$260.00	$290.00	
10						
11	TOTAL INCOME	$7,100.00				
12						
13	EQUIPMENT EXPENSE					
14	Maintenance	$650.00				
15	Parts	$550.00				
16						
17	TOTAL EXPENSE	$1,200.00				
18						
19	ADJUSTED INCOME					
20	PURCHASES					

Press ALT to choose commands, or F2 to edit.   CAPS

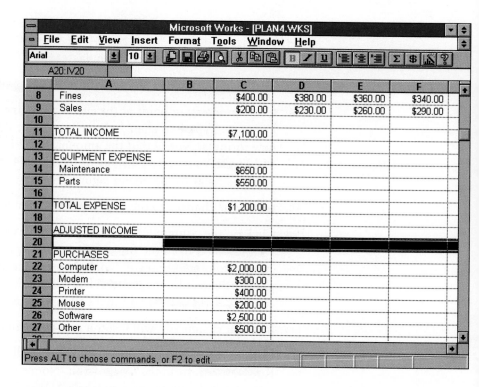

	A	B	C	D	E	F
8	Fines		$400.00	$380.00	$360.00	$340.00
9	Sales		$200.00	$230.00	$260.00	$290.00
10						
11	TOTAL INCOME		$7,100.00			
12						
13	EQUIPMENT EXPENSE					
14	Maintenance		$650.00			
15	Parts		$550.00			
16						
17	TOTAL EXPENSE		$1,200.00			
18						
19	ADJUSTED INCOME					
20						
21	PURCHASES					
22	Computer		$2,000.00			
23	Modem		$300.00			
24	Printer		$400.00			
25	Mouse		$200.00			
26	Software		$2,500.00			
27	Other		$500.00			

Press ALT to choose commands, or F2 to edit.

14. Type **12** in the Column Width text box and click on **OK** or press the
    (Enter) key. Compare the width of column G (which was not highlighted)
    with the width of the columns that were highlighted.

In the following steps you will increase the width of column C by dragging its border, then you will delete the blank column B.

15. Point to the vertical bar between column headings B and C. When the
    pointer changes to the two-headed ADJUST arrow, drag the bar to the
    right approximately ½ inch to increase the width of column B.

16. Click on column label B to highlight the column.

17. Choose Cut ((Ctrl) +X) from the Edit menu to delete column B.

18. Select column label A. Click on the Column Width command on the
    Format menu. When the Column Width dialog box appears, click on
    Best Fit. Press the (Enter) key or click on OK. How has the width of
    column A changed?

19. Highlight the labels in row 4 (1995, 1996, 1997, and 1998) by clicking
    on the row label.

20. Click on the Center Alignment toolbar button. Notice that the date
    labels are now centered within their cells, as shown in Figure 29-5.

21. Highlight cell B9 and display the Border dialog box from the
    Format menu.

22. Click on the Bottom check box (under Border), then click on OK.

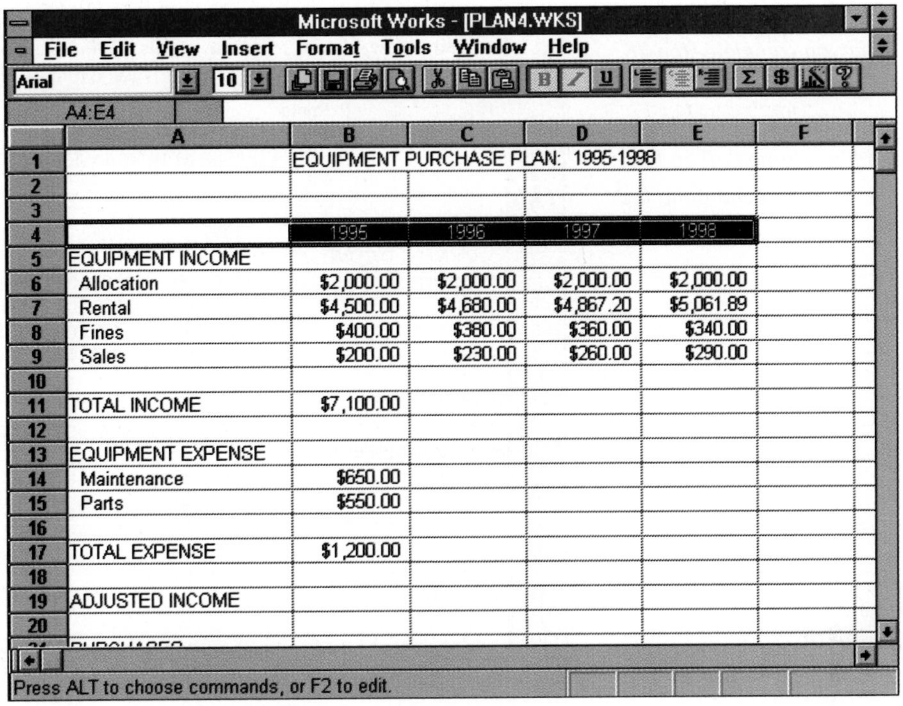

FIGURE 29-5
*The date labels are now
centered in the PLAN4.WKS
spreadsheet.*

23. Choose Gridlines from the View menu to turn off the gridlines, then move the highlight to another cell. The border line at the bottom of cell B9 can now be seen clearly.

24. Choose Gridlines from the View menu to turn on the gridlines.

25. Click on cell B6, hold down the [Shift] key, and click on cell E9 to highlight the block of cells that includes cell B6 in the upper left corner and cell E9 in the lower right corner.

26. Open the Border dialog box, click on the Outline check box, then click on OK. Click to deselect the highlighted cells.

27. Choose Gridlines from the View menu to turn off the gridlines so that you can see the outline border, as shown in Figure 29-6.

28. Highlight the block B6:E9 again.

29. Open the Border dialog box, and click on the first (empty) line style box. Then click on the Top, Bottom, Left, and Right check boxes. Click OK to close the dialog box. Move the highlight to another area of the spreadsheet so you can see that the outline around the block of cells has been removed.

30. Choose Gridlines from the View menu to display the spreadsheet gridlines.

31. Click on row label 4 to highlight cells in this row.

32. Choose Font And Style from the Format menu to open the Font And Style dialog box.

33. Click on the Bold style check box, then click on OK.

FIGURE 29-6

After you complete step 26, your spreadsheet should look like this one, with the gridlines turned off and the outline border around the block of cells.

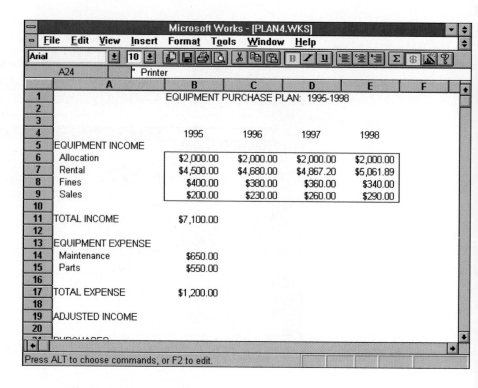

34. Click on the Italic toolbar button.

35. Click on column label A to highlight the column.

36. Click on the Bold toolbar button. Move the highlight to another cell. Your screen display should look similar to the one shown in Figure 29-7.

37. Save your changes to the PLAN4.WKS spreadsheet.

FIGURE 29-7

After you have completed step 36, your screen display should look similar to this one.

	Microsoft Works - [PLAN4.WKS]					
	File Edit View Insert Format Tools Window Help					
Arial	10			B *I* U	Σ $	
A1						
	A	B	C	D	E	F
1		EQUIPMENT PURCHASE PLAN: 1995-1998				
2						
3						
4		*1995*	*1996*	*1997*	*1998*	
5	**EQUIPMENT INCOME**					
6	**Allocation**	$2,000.00	$2,000.00	$2,000.00	$2,000.00	
7	**Rental**	$4,500.00	$4,680.00	$4,867.20	$5,061.89	
8	**Fines**	$400.00	$380.00	$360.00	$340.00	
9	**Sales**	$200.00	$230.00	$260.00	$290.00	
10						
11	**TOTAL INCOME**	$7,100.00				
12						
13	**EQUIPMENT EXPENSE**					
14	**Maintenance**	$650.00				
15	**Parts**	$550.00				
16						
17	**TOTAL EXPENSE**	$1,200.00				
18						
19	**ADJUSTED INCOME**					
20						

Press ALT to choose commands, or F2 to edit.

PRACTICE APPLICATIONS

1. Open the BUDGET1.WKS spreadsheet and save it as BUDPRAC.WKS. Using the BUDPRAC.WKS spreadsheet, delete row 14.

2. Decrease the width of columns B, C, and D to nine characters. Then decrease the width of column A by dragging its border.

3. Apply the bold style to the title in row 1, COMPUTER LAB BUDGET.

4. Select the two sets of three cells with values representing percent of budget in rows 20 and 29, and place an outline border around each set of three cells. Turn off the spreadsheet gridlines. Save your changes to the BUDPRAC.WKS spreadsheet, then close the spreadsheet.

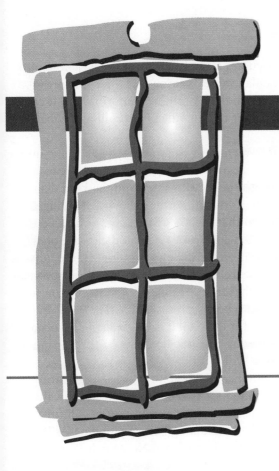

LESSON 30

OTHER SPREADSHEET FEATURES

OBJECTIVES

After completing this lesson you will be able to do the following:

- Use the Find command to find a specific cell reference, value, or text.
- Use the Replace command to replace a specific cell reference, value, or text.
- Explain how cell formulas are displayed and printed.
- Explain the difference between a relative reference and an absolute reference.
- Explain the purpose of the Paste command.

KEY WORDS

In this lesson you will learn the meaning of the following term:

absolute reference
pasting

SEARCHING A SPREADSHEET

In a small spreadsheet that occupies a single screen, it is easy enough to scan the spreadsheet for a particular value or formula. However, spreadsheets often require several screens to display all their information. It can be time-consuming to locate a particular text or value by scrolling through a large spreadsheet.

The Find command on the Edit menu lets you quickly find specific information in a cell or formula. Works searches through the entire spreadsheet, or part of the spreadsheet, to match the string you type in the Find dialog box, as shown in Figure 30-1. When you enter a string, Works highlights the first cell containing information that matches the string. You can continue the search by choosing the Find command again and clicking on OK.

The Look By and Look In options on the dialog box allow you to adjust how Works searches and where it searches. The default setting for Look By is Rows, meaning that Works searches from left to right by row. If you select Columns, then Works searches top to bottom by columns. The Look In option controls whether Works looks for the search string in formulas or in the values inside cells (Works treats text as a value). If you highlight a group of cells before you begin your search, Works will only search those cells.

For example, if you type the number 75.986 on the formula bar for display in cell D21, which is formatted for two decimal places, the value will be displayed as 75.99. When performing a search, Works will find cell D21 only if you specify 75.99 in the Find dialog box. If you type 75.986 in the Find What box, Works will display the message No Match Found. However, if you search for 475, Works will find 475 and 475.00, even if the .00 has only been added by a number currency format. You can also replace a formula, value, or text by using the Replace command from the Edit menu. Figure 30-2 shows the Replace dialog box.

FIGURE 30-1

The Find dialog box is used to find specified information in a formula, value, or text.

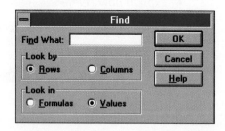

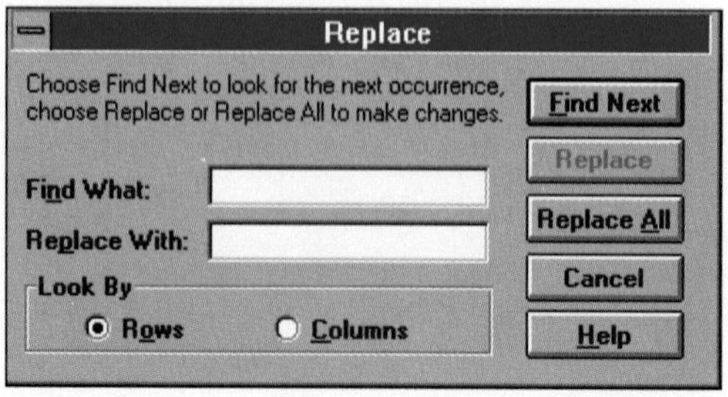

FIGURE 30-2

The Replace dialog box.

When using the Find or Replace command, remember that not all the values displayed on a spreadsheet can be searched for as values. If you are searching for the value 950 and that value was created by a formula, Works will find the formula, not the value, and will report that no match is found.

DISPLAYING AND PRINTING SPREADSHEET FORMULAS

Normally you are interested in the value that results from calculating a formula displayed in a cell, not in the formula itself. However, you may occasionally want to review the formulas used in a spreadsheet. When you choose Formulas from the View menu, Works displays formulas instead of values in the spreadsheet cells. If a formula is too long to fit completely in a cell, Works expands the cell to fit, as shown in Figure 30-3. By stretching cells to fit their formulas, Works may create extra pages. Fortunately, you can see the expanded cells, formulas, and any extra pages in print preview.

You can print the spreadsheet formulas by choosing the Print command from the File menu or the print preview screen, or by choosing the Print toolbar button. When the Formulas option is selected, Works displays a checkmark beside the command. To display the spreadsheet values again, choose Formulas from the View menu again. The checkmark will disappear and the Formulas option will be turned off.

FIGURE 30-3

The BUDGET1.WKS spreadsheet with the Formulas options turned on. Notice that Works has automatically widened the spreadsheet columns.

	A	B	
1	COMPUTER LAB BUDGET	October 1994	
2			
3			
4			
5		Actual	Budgeted
6	INCOME		
7	Budget Allocation	7000	7000
8	Fines	265.91	300
9	Disk Sales	482.5	450
10			
11	Total Income	=SUM(B7:B9)	=SUM(C7:
12			
13	EXPENSES		
14			
15	Fixed Expenses		
16	Service Contract	475	475
17	Equipment Insurance	368.5	368.5
18	Salaries	4080	4080
19			
20	Total Fixed	=SUM(B16:B18)	=SUM(C16

Microsoft Works - [BUDGET1.WKS]

File   Edit   View   Insert   Format   Tools   Window   Help

Arial   10

A16   " Service Contract

Press ALT to choose commands, or F2 to edit.

COPYING AND PASTING CELLS, ROWS, AND COLUMNS

The contents of cells, rows, and columns can be copied and **pasted** into different areas of the same spreadsheet, into a different spreadsheet, or into any other Works document. After highlighting the cell or block of cells with the information you want to copy or cut to the Clipboard, highlight a cell in the new location where the information will be pasted. If you are pasting information from a block of cells, the cell you click on in the new location represents the upper left corner of the block of cells that will contain the pasted information.

You can use the Paste command on the Edit menu (or press Ctrl +V or click on the Paste toolbar button) to paste cell values and their formulas (if any) to other locations. When you copy a cell value calculated with a formula containing relative cell references, Works automatically will adjust the cell references in the formula to reflect the new location where the formula is pasted.

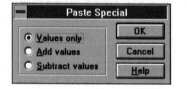

FIGURE 30-4

The Paste Special dialog box is used to specify how cells that are copied or cut to the Clipboard should be pasted into a new location.

If you want to paste cell values and their formats only, without the formulas used to calculate the values, highlight the cell where you want to begin pasting the copied information, and then choose the Paste Special command (instead of the Paste command) from the Edit menu. The Paste Special dialog box, shown in Figure 30-4, appears with the default Values Only button selected. When you click on OK, the information in the Clipboard is pasted into the new location.

If you select the Add Values option, Works adds the values you are pasting to the value in the cell (or range of cells) you are pasting to. If you select the Subtract Values option, Works subtracts the values you are pasting from the cells you are pasting to.

RELATIVE AND ABSOLUTE REFERENCES

As you learned in Lesson 28, a relative reference to a cell in a formula provides Works with directions that are relative to the location of the active cell. If the formula is copied to a different location, the cell referred to by the relative cell reference also changes. A cell reference in a formula is relative unless you change it to an absolute reference. An absolute reference refers to a cell in one location, regardless of where the formula containing the reference is moved or copied.

The dollar sign ($) is used before a cell's column name and row number to indicate an absolute reference. For example, the **absolute reference** BA tells Works always to use the value in cell B1, even when the formula that contains the cell reference is moved to another part of the spreadsheet.

To make a relative reference absolute, highlight the cell containing the formula. On the formula bar, type a dollar sign before the cell's column name and row number. You can change an absolute reference to a relative reference by deleting the dollar sign.

GUIDED PRACTICE

FINDING INFORMATION AND USING ABSOLUTE CELL REFERENCES

In this exercise you will use the Find command to search for a cell reference and a cell value. Then you will create a formula that contains an absolute cell reference.

1. Start Works, if necessary, and open the PLAN5.WKS file. Save the spreadsheet as PLAN6.WKS.

2. Using the PLAN6.WKS spreadsheet, choose Find from the Edit menu to display the Find dialog box.

3. Type **$5,123.02** in the Find What text box, and press the [Enter] key to find the value in cell E30.

4. Open the Find dialog box again, and type **340** in the text box to locate the first occurrence of the number 340. Works locates and highlights the cell containing $340.00 (cell E8).

5. Open the Replace dialog box by selecting the Replace command from the Edit menu, and type **2000** in the Find What text box. Type **3000** in the Replace With text box. Press the Find Next button. Press the Replace button each time Works finds the next occurrence of 2000. When Works has found all occurrences of **2000**, the Replace button will dim. Click on the Find Next button. Works displays the No Match Found message box. Press [Enter] to exit the message box. Then click the Close button to exit the Replace dialog box.

USE REPLACE ALL →

6. Choose Formulas from the View menu. Open the Find dialog box, and type **=B23*1.08**. Click on the OK button. Open the Find dialog box and type **=SUM**. *→ C23* *(EDIT MENU)*

7. Search the spreadsheet until Works highlights cell C11.

8. Click on the Print Preview toolbar button. Click on the magnifying glass twice. Notice the width of columns B, C, and D.

9. Press Cancel to exit Print Preview.

10. Select the Formulas command to end the display of formulas. *(VIEW)*

In the next steps you will use the Paste Special dialog box to copy cells. You will also use the Add Values and Subtract Values options.

11. Highlight cell B23. Press the [Shift] key and highlight cell E28. Click on the Copy toolbar button. Highlight cell G23 and then click on the Paste toolbar button.

12. Select the Paste Special command from the Edit menu. When the Paste Special dialog box appears, click on the Add Values radio button.

13. Press [Enter] to paste the cells from the Clipboard. Notice the new values in the highlighted cells.

14. Display the Paste Special dialog box again, this time selecting Subtract Values. Click on the OK button. Notice that the cell values have returned to their original amounts.

15. Delete the highlighted cells by clicking on the Cut toolbar button or by pressing the Del key.

16. Close the PLAN6.WKS spreadsheet without saving your changes.

In the following steps you will format a block of blank cells, then enter formulas to compare the results of using a formula with absolute references with the results of using the same formula with relative references only.

17. Open the PLAN6.WKS spreadsheet. Format the block of empty cells with F1 in the upper left corner and H3 in the lower right corner by highlighting the block and applying the Currency option in the Number dialog box.

17. Highlight cell J1. Enter **1.04** in cell J1.

19. Highlight cell F1. Enter the formula **=E6*J1** in cell F1.

20. Select cell F1 and drag the highlighting to select cells F2 and F3.

21. Choose Fill Down from the Edit menu.

22. Highlight cell G1. Enter the formula **=E6*J1** in cell G1.

23. Select cell G1 and drag the highlighting to select cells G2 and G3.

24. Choose Fill Down from the Edit menu.

25. Highlight cell H1. Enter the formula **=E6*J1** in cell H1.

26. Select cell H1 and drag the highlighting to select cells H2 and H3.

27. Choose Fill Down from the Edit menu. When you have completed steps 16 through 26, cells F1 through H3 in the PLAN6.WKS spreadsheet should look like those shown in Figure 30-5.

28. Save the changes to spreadsheet PLAN6.WKS.

FIGURE 30-5

After you have completed the practice using absolute and relative references in a formula, cells F1 through H3 will appear like the ones shown here.

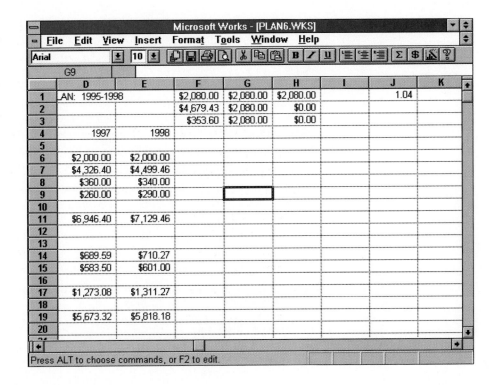

	D	E	F	G	H	I	J	K
1	AN: 1995-1998		$2,080.00	$2,080.00	$2,080.00		1.04	
2			$4,679.43	$2,080.00	$0.00			
3			$353.60	$2,080.00	$0.00			
4	1997	1998						
5								
6	$2,000.00	$2,000.00						
7	$4,326.40	$4,499.46						
8	$360.00	$340.00						
9	$260.00	$290.00						
10								
11	$6,946.40	$7,129.46						
12								
13								
14	$689.59	$710.27						
15	$583.50	$601.00						
16								
17	$1,273.08	$1,311.27						
18								
19	$5,673.32	$5,818.18						
20								

PRACTICE APPLICATIONS

1. Open BUDGET1.WKS. Use the Find command to search for all occurrences of $100 and replace them with $200. Close the BUDGET1.WKS spreadsheet without saving any changes.

2. Open the PLAN6.WKS spreadsheet. Analyze the formulas used to produce the values in the first three cells of columns F, G, and H, and explain how the values in these cells were calculated. You may want to use the Formulas command on the View menu to display the formulas in the cells. Close the spreadsheet without saving your changes.

CHAPTER REVIEW

You create a spreadsheet by entering text, values, and formulas. Use functions, such as SUM, to make writing complex formulas easier. Edit a spreadsheet by changing cell contents, deleting and inserting columns and rows, and changing the width of selected columns. You can also specify one or more borders for a single cell or for a block of cells.

The Find command is used to search a spreadsheet for text, values, or formulas. The Replace command can search and replace text, values, or formulas. An absolute reference is used in a formula when you want Works to use a value in a particular cell, regardless of where the formula is moved or pasted in the spreadsheet.

REVIEW QUESTIONS

TRUE-FALSE

Write your answers on a sheet of paper.

1. If you want Works to treat a number entry list as text, you must precede the entry with a quotation mark (").

2. If you want a number to appear in a cell with a dollar sign ($), you must type the dollar sign ($) on the entry bar along with the number.

3. Works displays cell contents in General format unless you specify a different format.

4. In a formula, the asterisk (*) is the operator used for division.

5. The Fill Right option copies the value or formula in the initial cell into other cells highlighted in the same row.

6. A relative cell reference in a formula tells Works to adjust the references whenever the formula is copied or moved.

7. The range of cells referred to in the notation F1:H3 includes cell F3.

8. After you create a heading for a column, you cannot change the width of the column.

9. The Border dialog box provides a way to format a cell with a single line at the bottom.

10. You can use the Find command to go to a particular formula in Works.

SHORT-ANSWER QUESTIONS

Write a brief answer to these questions on a sheet of paper.

1. In a spreadsheet what is the difference between a value and a formula?

2. How do you print a spreadsheet showing formulas instead of values?

3. How can the SUM function save you time in entering formulas?

4. How is the range reference of a block of cells determined?

5. Explain why you might need to change the default width for a spreadsheet column.

LESSON APPLICATIONS

1. Create a spreadsheet that shows anticipated purchase information for computer lab supplies for two quarters. Develop totals for all purchases for each quarter and total purchases for both quarters. Use the following information to create the spreadsheet. Use appropriate labels and column formats. Save the spreadsheet as SUPPLIES.WKS.

SUPPLY ITEM	UNIT PRICE	QTY/QUARTER 1	QTY/QUARTER 2
3.5" Disks	.79	300	220
5.25" Disks	.59	500	425
Printer Paper	.005	100,000	120,000
Printer Ribbons	4.25	60	70

2. In the SUPPLIES.WKS spreadsheet, insert the following row as the third supply item. Be sure to widen the first column so that the new label fits.

Software Reference Books   15.95   20   25

Next insert a column after each QTY column. The new columns will contain the actual quantities purchased for each quarter. Develop totals for each ACTUAL column. Save the modified spreadsheet under the current name.

ITEM	ACTUAL/QUARTER 1	ACTUAL/QUARTER 2
3.5" Disks	279	222
5.25" Disks	402	445
Software Reference Books	18	27
Printer Paper	120,000	134,000
Printer Ribbons	70	72

3. In the SUPPLIES.WKS spreadsheet, use the Find option to search for cells that contain a value of 70. Display any formulas used in the spreadsheet. Display the values again and readjust the width of columns, if necessary. Save the changes to the SUPPLIES.WKS spreadsheet.

CHAPTER APPLICATIONS

1. Open the PLAN4.WKS spreadsheet, and save it as PLANPRA3.WKS. Using the PLANPRA3.WKS spreadsheet, create formulas and use the Fill option to increase the maintenance expense by 3 percent (1.03) each year and the parts expense by 2 percent (1.02) each year.

2. Use the Fill option to enter appropriate formulas for the empty TOTAL INCOME and TOTAL EXPENSE cells.

3. Enter a formula in cell B19 that will subtract total expense from total income (remember to enter = before your formula).

4. Use the Fill option to enter this formula in cells C19:E190.

5. Format the cells A19:E19 so that the values in the cells will have a dollar sign and two decimal places.

6. Extend amounts for PURCHASES (B22 through B27) so that the values for all the purchase categories except Software increase by 8 percent each year (1996, 1997, and 1998). Extend the amount for software purchases to include an increase of 0.5 percent (1.005) each year.

7. Format cells C22:E27 so that the values in the cells will have a dollar sign and two decimal places.

8. Apply boldface to the title EQUIPMENT PURCHASE PLAN: 1995-1998.

9. Insert two rows after the last row (with values) in the PURCHASES section of the spreadsheet.

10. Leaving an empty row after the PURCHASES section and before the ROLLOVER label, add a new label in cell A29. Type TOTAL PURCHASES.

11. Create a formula to total the computer lab purchases for the years 1995 to 1998. Use the Fill option to place this formula in each appropriate column of the TOTAL PURCHASES row.

12. Format the resulting values with the Currency format.

13. Place an outline border around the cells that contain the total income amounts for 1995, 1996, 1997, and 1998.

14. Place a double outline border around the cells that contain the ADJUSTED INCOME amounts for 1995, 1996, 1997, and 1998.

15. Remove gridlines from the spreadsheet, and examine the outlined cells. Turn the gridlines back on.

16. Save the changes to PLANPRA3.WKS and quit Works.

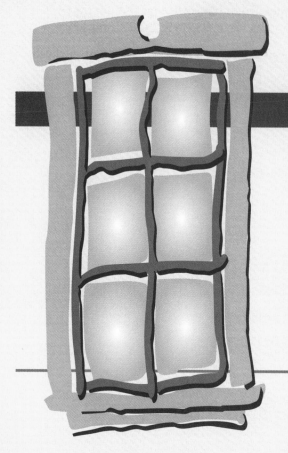

CHAPTER 11

CHARTING

SPREADSHEET

INFORMATION

OVERVIEW

In Chapter 12 you learned about the different types of charts that can be created to represent spreadsheet information. In this chapter you will learn how to create charts in a variety of formats by highlighting a range of cells. You will also learn how to create a chart to include multiple ranges when the information you want to chart is not in adjacent rows or columns. In addition, you will be introduced to some draw features that can be used to enhance a chart linked to a spreadsheet.

CONTENTS

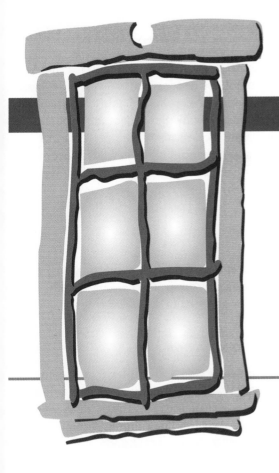

LESSON 31

MODIFYING CHARTS

After completing this lesson you will be able to do the following:

- Explain the use of the vertical (Y) axis and the horizontal (X) axis in a chart or graph.
- Explain how Works creates a legend.
- Delete a chart.
- Vary the size of a new chart.
- Create a legend for an existing chart.
- Display a chart that will be printed in black and white.
- Create a duplicate of an existing chart.

KEY WORDS

In this lesson you will learn the meaning of the following terms:

fill pattern   legend
horizontal (X) axis   vertical (Y) axis

USING CHARTS TO INTERPRET SPREADSHEET INFORMATION

You've probably heard the old expression "A picture is worth a thousand words." What's true for words also holds true for numbers. A spreadsheet may contain hundreds or even thousands of numbers, making it difficult to identify trends and other information simply by glancing at all or part of the spreadsheet. However, when you create a chart, or picture, to represent spreadsheet values, trends and relationships among those values become readily apparent. In Lesson 26, you learned how to create, display, and print a chart. In this lesson you will learn how to modify charts.

THE COMPONENTS OF A CHART

In a chart, spreadsheet values are represented by bars, lines, points, and wedges. A spreadsheet value becomes a single bar in a bar chart, a line in a radar chart, a point in a line graph, or a wedge in a pie chart.

VERTICAL AND HORIZONTAL AXES

Except for pie charts, all of the types of charts in Works organize information along two axes. The **vertical (Y) axis** is a line running along the left edge of the chart that usually provides a scale for measuring values represented in the chart. The **horizontal (X) axis** is a line running along the bottom of the chart that generally shows categories of values represented.

Figure 31-1 is a bar chart that graphically represents the highlighted cells in the BUDGET1.WKS spreadsheet, shown in Figure 31-2. The scale on the vertical axis in Figure 31-1 ranges from -200 to 1400 in increments of 200.

FIGURE 31-1

This chart was created by Works from the range of cells highlighted in Figure 31-2.

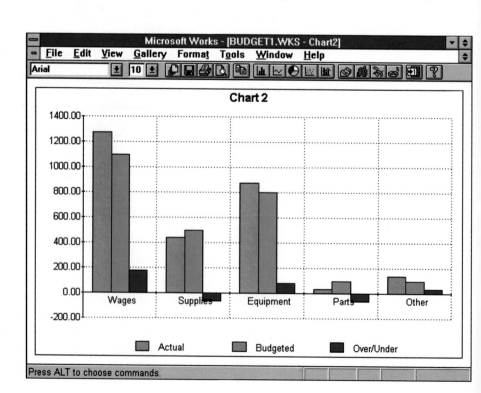

	Microsoft Works - [BUDGET1.WKS]						
File	Edit	View	Insert	Format	Tools	Window	Help

Arial   10

A24:D29

	A	B	C	D	E	F	G
19							
20	Total Fixed	4923.50	4923.50	0.00			
21	Percent of Budget	63.54%	63.53%	-0.01%			
22							
23	Variable Expenses						
24		Actual	Budgeted	Over/Under			
25	Wages	1278.00	1100.00	178.00			
26	Supplies	440.25	500.00	-59.75			
27	Equipment	878.76	800.00	78.76			
28	Parts	37.10	100.00	-62.90			
29	Other	136.48	100.00	36.48			
30	Total Variable	2770.59	2600.00	170.59			
31	Percent of Budget	35.75%	33.55%	2.20%			
32							
33	Summary						
34		Actual	Budgeted	Over/Under			
35	Total Income	7748.41	7750.00	7748.41			
36	Total Expenses	7694.09	7523.50	170.59			
37	Balance	54.32	226.50	-172.18			
38							

Press ALT to choose commands, or F2 to edit.

This increment is based on the range of values (from the lowest to the highest) in the spreadsheet cells that are highlighted in Figure 31-2. The category labels on the horizontal axis of this chart are the same as the spreadsheet labels in cells A24 through A29.

LEGENDS

A **legend** identifies the **fill patterns** used in the bars or wedges of a chart. A fill pattern is the style of lines used to fill in the shapes on a chart. If you have a color printer, Works will fill in these shapes with different colors. The chart in Figure 31-1 shows a legend with three different fill patterns used to identify the bars as Actual, Budgeted, and Over/Under. This information (in row 24) was included in the highlighted range of cells used to create the bars in the chart, so Works created the legend automatically when the chart was created. The information in the first highlighted column (usually text) is used to create and label the chart's horizontal axis. The information in the other highlighted columns is used to create the value scale on the vertical axis and the bars shown in the chart.

DELETING A CHART

Because Works limits you to eight charts for each spreadsheet, you may have to delete charts as well as create them. Delete a chart by selecting the Delete Chart command from the Tools menu. Works displays the Delete Chart dialog box, shown in Figure 31-3. Highlight the name of the chart you want to delete, and click on the Delete button. Works removes the chart title from the list box. When you are finished selecting charts, click on the OK button, and Works will delete the charts. Notice that Works displays no

FIGURE 31-3
*The Delete Chart
dialog box.*

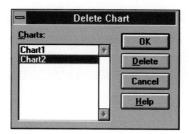

message box when you delete a chart. Also, the Edit menu's Undo command cannot restore a deleted chart. (You can exit the document without saving your changes; then, when you reopen the document, the deleted chart will be restored.)

ADJUSTING THE SIZE OF A NEW CHART

Through the use of the Page Setup command on the File menu, Works allows you to control how your chart is printed by specifying the margins, source, size, and orientation of your chart on the page. When you have a chart displayed on your screen, Works also adds new options to the Other Options tab dialog box, as shown in Figure 31-4. The default choice, Full Page, adjusts the chart to fill the page, changing the chart's width-to-height relationship, if necessary. The Screen Size option prints the chart the same size as it appears on your screen. The Full Page, Keep Proportions option adjusts the chart to fill the page, but maintains its width-to-height relationship.

CREATING A LEGEND FOR AN EXISTING CHART

The information you need to create a legend is not always adjacent to the range of cells used to create the chart. In this case, you will not be able to include the legend information in the highlighted range. When any of the information you want in a chart cannot be selected with a range, you can use the Legends/Series Labels dialog box, shown in Figure 31-5, to tell Works where to find the additional information. This dialog box is displayed when you select Legends/Series Labels from the Edit menu.

The information in Figure 31-5 is based on the BUDGET1.WKS worksheet. The cell references in the first three text boxes describe where Works found the text to describe the fill patterns on the legend.

FIGURE 31-4
*The Other Options tab box
offers three size options for
printing a chart.*

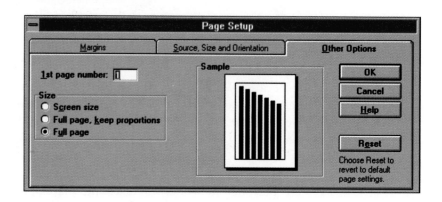

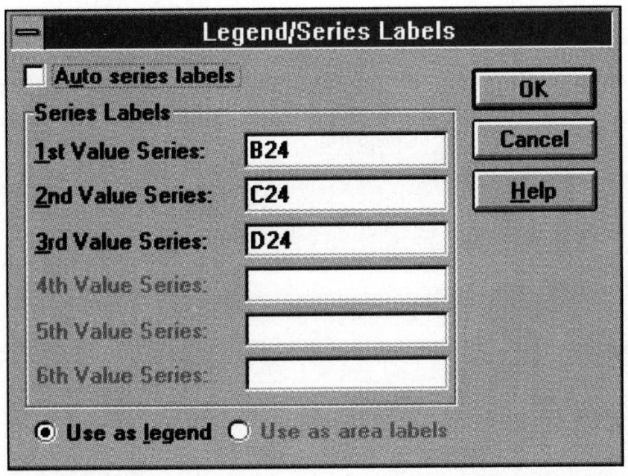

FIGURE 31-5

The information in this Legends/Series Labels dialog box was entered automatically when Works created Chart1 from the highlighted information in BUDGET1.WKS.

Legend/Series Labels

☐ Auto series labels

Series Labels

1st Value Series: B24

2nd Value Series: C24

3rd Value Series: D24

4th Value Series:

5th Value Series:

6th Value Series:

● Use as legend   ○ Use as area labels

OK

Cancel

Help

DISPLAYING A CHART THAT WILL BE PRINTED IN BLACK AND WHITE

After you have created a chart, Works displays the chart in color, using different colors as fill patterns for different sets of values. If you use a printer that prints in black and white, however, your printout will vary. Fortunately, Works offers the opportunity to see the fill patterns used for black-and-white charts. Select Display As Printed from the View menu, and Works will show you the chart as it will print on your black-and-white printer. To return to a color chart on your screen, select the Display As Printed command again.

GUIDED PRACTICE

MODIFYING A CHART

In this exercise you will use the Legends/Series Labels dialog box to edit a legend and the Other Options tab dialog box to adjust the way a chart appears on a page.

1. Start Works and open the PLAN5.WKS spreadsheet, if necessary. Save the file as PLAN7.WKS.

2. Highlight the range of cells A23:E28.

3. Select Create New Chart from the Tools menu or click on the New Chart toolbar button.

4. In the Chart title box, type **PLANNED PURCHASES** to name the chart.

5. Select 3-D Bar from the What Type Of Chart Do You Want? list box.

6. Turn on the Add Gridlines check box.

7. When your dialog box looks like the one in Figure 31-6, click on OK to display the chart.

8. Compare your chart with the cells highlighted in Figure 31-7.

9. The column headings for the four columns of cells you selected are 1995, 1996, 1997, and 1998. Works, however, created a legend using basic legend titles: Series1, Series2, and so on.

FIGURE 31-6

After you have completed step 6, your New Chart dialog box should look like this one.

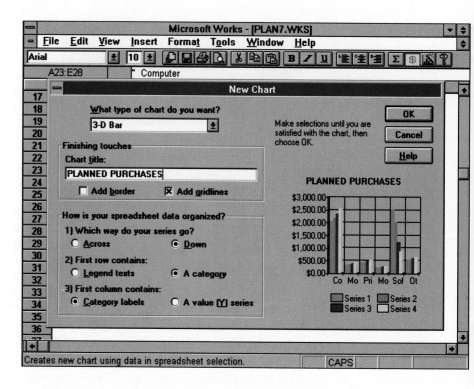

FIGURE 31-6

After you have completed step 6, your New Chart dialog box should look like this one.

10. To change your legend open the Legends/Series Labels dialog box from the Edit menu. Notice that the Auto Series Labels check box is selected. Deselect it.

11. Type **1995** in the 1st Value Series text box. Press the Tab key and type **1996** in the 2nd Value Series text box. Enter **1997** in the third text box and **1998** in the fourth.

12. Click on the OK button. Select the ~~Border~~ command from the Format menu. *✓ ADD*

13. Print the PLANNED PURCHASES chart, and then compare the printout with Figure 31-7.

14. Select the Display As Printed command from the View menu. Compare the screen display of the PLANNED PURCHASES chart with Figure 31-7.

15. Save the spreadsheet under the existing name PLAN7.WKS.

DUPLICATING A CHART

As you discovered in Lesson 25, you can change the chart type of an existing chart by making selections from the New Chart dialog box. For example, you can create a bar chart, then display it in any of the 13 chart types on the What Type Of Chart Do You Want? list box. You may want to highlight a group of cells and create several different charts based on those cells, saving the chart that best displays the information.

To duplicate a chart, first select the Duplicate Chart command on the Tools menu. Works opens the Duplicate Chart dialog box, shown in Figure 31-8. Select a chart from the list box and click on the Duplicate button.

FIGURE 31-7
The PLANNED PURCHASES chart with its new legend.

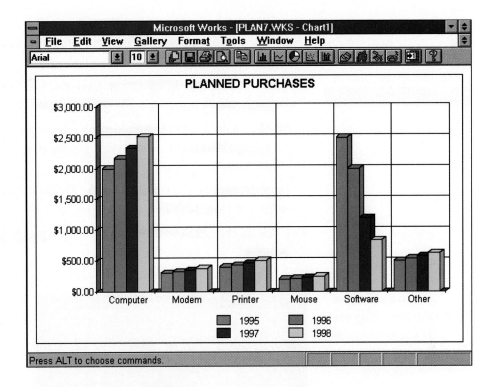

FIGURE 31-8
The Duplicate Chart dialog box.

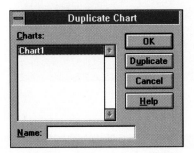

Works creates a new chart and gives it a new name (if you already have Chart1, Works gives the new chart the name Chart2). Now you will have another chart listed on the Chart menu that can be edited and saved with the spreadsheet.

GUIDED PRACTICE

DUPLICATING A CHART AND DISPLAYING DIFFERENT CHART TYPES

In this exercise you will duplicate the chart PLANNED PURCHASES, which you created and saved with the PLAN7.WKS spreadsheet. You will then use the duplicate chart to practice displaying different chart types.

1. Start Works and open the PLAN7.WKS spreadsheet, if necessary. Select chart 1, PLANNED PURCHASES, from the Chart dialog box.   *VIEW — CHAR*

2. Choose Duplicate Chart from the Tools menu. Type **PLANNED PUR-CHASE** in the Name text box.

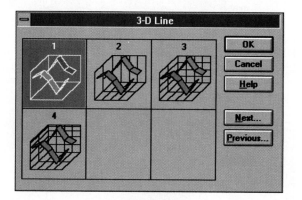

3. Click on the Duplicate button. Works creates a duplicate chart and names it PLANNED PURCHAS (Works limits chart names to 15 characters). Click the OK button.

4. Choose PLANNED PURCHAS from the Chart dialog box. Pull down the Gallery menu to display a list of chart styles. Click on 3-D Line.

5. Works opens a 3-D Line dialog box, shown in Figure 31-9, offering you four 3-D chart styles. One style is highlighted. That is the style Works recommends.

6. Double-click on the suggested style. Works creates a 3-D line chart, as shown in Figure 31-10.

7. Click on the Scatter Chart toolbar icon. Double-click on the highlighted sample.

FIGURE 31-9

The 3-D Line dialog box offers you various chart styles and highlights its recommended selection.

FIGURE 31-10

After step 6, Works creates this 3-D Line chart version of the PLANNED PURCHASES chart.

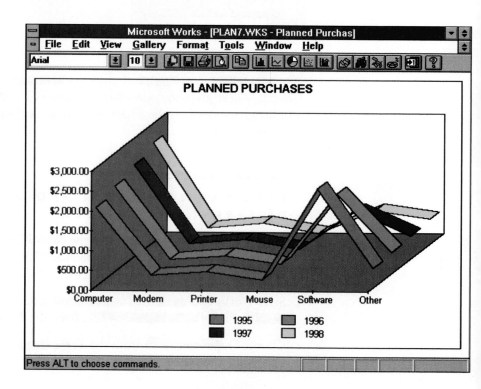

8. Click on the Mixed Chart toolbar icon. Click the OK button to accept the highlighted sample.

9. Select the 3-D Bar Chart toolbar button and click on the OK button.

10. Reformat the chart so that it is once again a 3-D line chart.

11. Save your changes to the PLAN7.WKS spreadsheet.

PRACTICE APPLICATIONS

Complete the following exercises. Some exercises ask you to answer one or more questions. Write a brief answer to these questions on a sheet of paper.

1. Open PLAN5.WKS and save the spreadsheet as CHARTPRA.WKS. Create a bar chart for the range B6:E9. Explain the limitations of this chart. Delete the chart.

2. Create a chart for EQUIPMENT INCOME Amounts. Use the Page Setup dialog box to ensure that the chart prints on a full page.

3. Give the chart an appropriate name, and create an appropriate legend for the chart that you created in Exercise 2. Make a duplicate copy of the chart and save it as PIE 1995. Use the information in the 1995 column to create the pie chart.

4. Save your changes to the CHARTPRA.WKS spreadsheet.

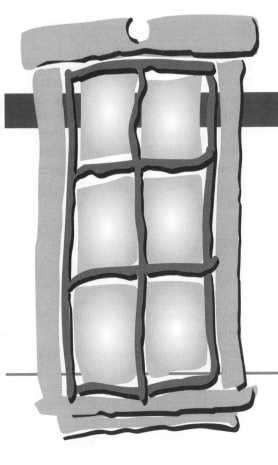

REFORMING A LINKED CHART

OBJECTIVES

After completing this lesson you will be able to do the following:

- *Explain the purpose of linking a chart.*
- *Make changes to a chart that is linked to a spreadsheet.*

KEY WORDS

In this lesson you will learn the meaning of the following terms:

linked (chart)
Y series

LINKED AND EMBEDDED CHARTS

When you create a spreadsheet chart, it is linked to the information that was used to create it. When a chart is linked to a spreadsheet, the charted information is updated automatically when changes are made to the spreadsheet information used to create the chart. When a copy of a chart is linked with another document (a special way of pasting a part of one document into another), it is also updated whenever the original or **source document** is updated. There are times, however, when you would not want to paste a chart into another document and have it updated automatically. In this case, you can embed the chart in the document.

CHANGING THE APPEARANCE OF A LINKED CHART

When a chart is linked to a spreadsheet, you cannot modify the appearance of chart elements that are affected by changes to spreadsheet information. For example, although you cannot change the height of a bar or the size of a wedge, you can change the fill patterns of bars and wedges.

Make fill pattern changes by selecting the Patterns And Colors command from the Format menu. This command is available when you have a chart open in the Works spreadsheet tool. The Patterns And Colors command, like the Legends/Series Labels command, illustrates how Works changes the spreadsheet tool menus when a chart is open. The Patterns And Colors dialog box, shown in Figure 32-1, offers 16 colors for use as fill patterns. By changing fill patterns, you will be altering how the **Y series**—the categories along the vertical axis of your spreadsheet—is represented in the chart. When you open the dialog box, the Series 1st radio button is selected and the Auto option is selected in both the Colors and Patterns list boxes. If you click on the Series 2nd and Series 3rd buttons, you will find that they are also set for the default Auto setting for both colors and patterns.

Change colors by clicking on a Series button and selecting a color. After you select a color, you can choose a pattern. Choose Sparse, for example, if you want a barely colored fill pattern. Choose None and Works supplies no color at all, resulting in a transparent fill pattern. After you have decided on a color and pattern, you can click on the Format button to have Works make changes in the Y series you have chosen. Click on Format All and Works changes all the fill patterns on the chart to reflect your choices. Figure 32-2 shows a chart formatted with the None option from the Patterns list box and the Format All button. Using the Patterns And Colors dialog box is slightly different when reformatting a pie chart. In pie charts you change the fill patterns for slices, instead of fill patterns for series. Otherwise, using the dialog box is the same.

FIGURE 32-1

The Patterns And Colors dialog box offers a variety of fill patterns for formatting areas, bars, and wedges of charts.

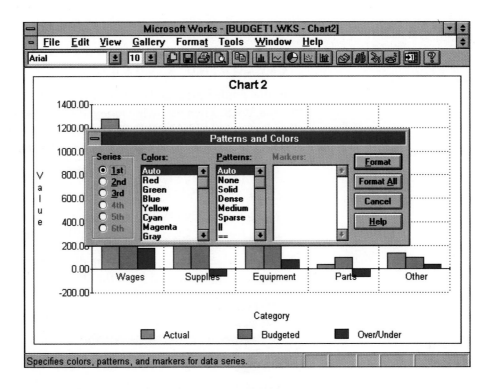

FIGURE 32-2

This chart was formatted with the None option and the Format All button of the Patterns and Colors dialog box.

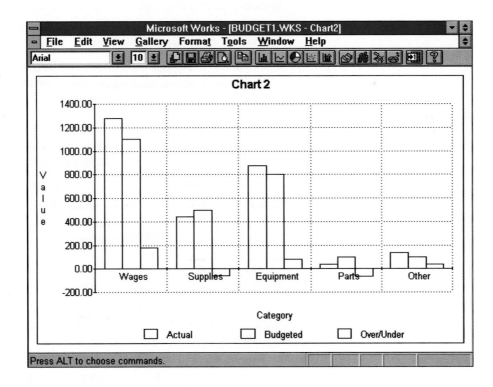

CHANGING FILL PATTERNS AND EXPLODING A CHART

In this guided practice you will save the PLAN7.WKS spreadsheet as PLAN8.WKS. Then you will change the fill patterns used for the bars in the chart you named PLANNED PURCHAS. You will also **explode** a pie chart—a technique that emphasizes the individual slices of a pie chart.

1. Start Works and open the PLAN7.WKS spreadsheet, if necessary. Save the spreadsheet as PLAN8.WKS.

2. Using the PLAN8.WKS spreadsheet, select the PLANNED PURCHAS chart from the Chart command in the View menu.

3. Display the Patterns And Colors dialog box by selecting the Patterns And Colors command from the Format menu.

4. Select Series 1st and change it to the color of your choice. Click on the Format button. Notice that Works changes the chart while it continues to display the Patterns And Colors dialog box.

5. Change the color for Series 2nd and 3rd.

6. Select the Series 4th. On the Patterns list box, select Medium. Click on Format. (Remember that you can move the Patterns And Colors dialog box—by clicking on its title bar and dragging it to a new location—if it obscures the chart.)

7. Click on the Series 1st button and select Cyan on the Colors list box. Click on the Format All button. All the bars are now filled with shades of cyan.

8. Select Series 3rd and click on the Auto option of the Colors list box. Make sure Auto is also selected on the Patterns list box. Click on the Format All button. The PLANNED PURCHAS chart has returned to its original formatting.

9. Close the Patterns And Colors dialog box. Return to the PLAN8.WKS spreadsheet. Highlight cells A23:B28, if necessary, and create a 3-D pie chart. Title the chart 1995 PURCHASES. Your chart should resemble the chart shown in Figure 32-3.

10. Click on the 3-D Chart toolbar button to open the 3-D Pie dialog box. Double-click on option 6, as shown in Figure 32-4. Notice that Works has added percentages to the data labels it copied from the A column of the spreadsheet.

11. Select 3-D Pie from the Gallery menu to reopen the 3-D Pie dialog box. This time double-click on option 2. Your pie chart should resemble the chart shown in Figure 32-5.

12. Close the PLAN8.WKS spreadsheet and save your changes.

FIGURE 32-3

After step 9, your 3-D pie chart should look like this one.

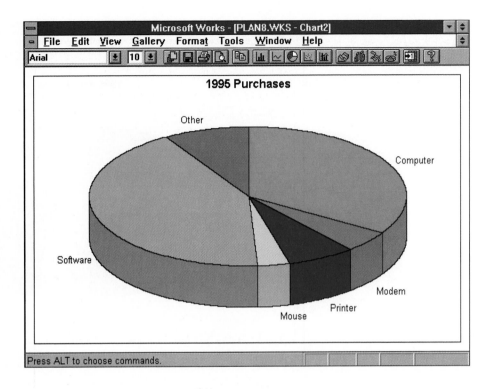

FIGURE 32-4

Option 6 of the 3-D Pie dialog box adds percentages to the data labels.

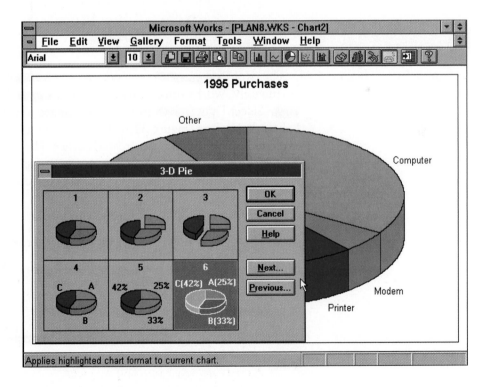

FIGURE 32-5

An exploded 3-D pie chart.

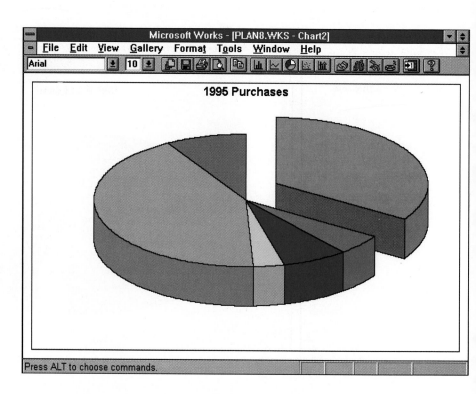

WORKING WITH DATA LABELS

MUST BE OPEN TO PERFORM ACTIVITY →

The exploded pie chart you created has no labels to identify its slices. Fortunately, Works offers a way to add up to two sets of data labels to a pie chart. Select Data Labels from the Edit menu and Works opens the Data Labels dialog box. Figure 32-6 shows the Data Labels dialog box for the exploded 3-D pie chart you created earlier. The exploded pie chart has the default setting of None selected in the 1st Label and 2nd Label lists. The Data Label options produce the following effects:

LABEL OPTION	PRODUCES THIS EFFECT
Values	Adds the value used to plot the slice
Percentages	Adds the percentage each slice represents of the whole
Cell Contents	Adds cell contents
1, 2, 3	Adds sequential numbers to each pie slice
None	Does not add a label

Choosing Cell Contents, for example, requires you to enter a range of cells or accept the default—the cells Works used to plot the chart. You can choose one option from the 1st Label list and one from the 2nd Label list. Figure 32-7, for example, shows an exploded 3-D pie chart with Cell Contents selected from the 1st Label list and Percentages selected from the 2nd Label list.

FIGURE 32-6
The Data Labels dialog box for an exploded 3-D pie chart.

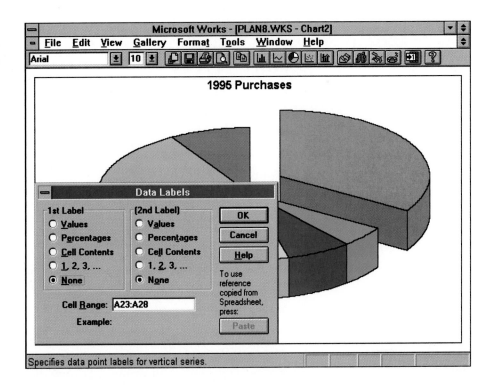

FIGURE 32-7
Cell Contents and Percentages labels added to the pie chart first shown in Figure 32-5.

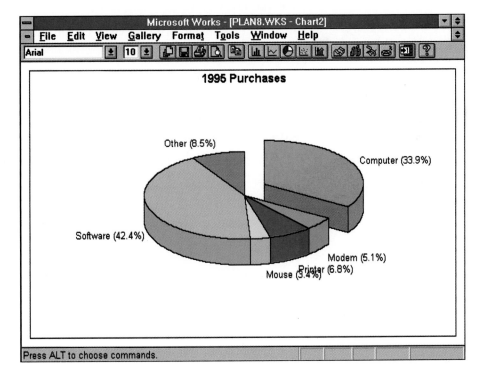

MODIFYING DATA LABELS AND CHANGING FONT STYLES

In this guided practice you will add several data labels to the pie chart first shown in Figure 32-5. Then you will format the chart's title and data labels.

1. Open the PLAN8.WKS spreadsheet, if necessary, and display the exploded 3-D pie chart, Chart2.

2. Select Data Labels from the Edit menu.

3. Select 1,2,3 from the 1st Label list on the Data Labels dialog box. Click OK. Notice the numbered wedges.

4. Display the Data Labels dialog box again. Select Cell Contents from the 1st Label list and Values from the 2nd Label list. Click on the OK button.

5. Print Chart2.

6. Click the title of Chart2, 1995 Purchases, to highlight it. Open the Font And Style dialog box and change the font of the title to CG Times 20 (if it is available with your printer). Format the title in italic and remove the bold. Press (Enter).

7. Inspect Chart2 in print preview. Because several of the slices are thin, the data labels may print on top of each other. Close Print Preview.

8. Deselect the chart title. Open the Font And Style dialog box.

9. With the title deselected, any changes you make in the Font And Style dialog box will affect any text except the title. Format the remaining chart text as 8 point CG Times. Press (Enter).

10. View the chart in Print Preview. If the data labels still look too close together, change the orientation of the page to landscape.

11. When you are satisfied with the changes you have made, save the changes to the PLAN8.WKS spreadsheet.

PRACTICE APPLICATIONS

1. Open the PLAN8.WKS spreadsheet, if necessary, and save it as CHARPRA2.WKS.

2. Using the CHARPRA2.WKS spreadsheet, select Chart1. Reformat the chart as a stacked line chart. Change the colors of the lines so the third data series is black. Reformat the chart so that it has horizontal gridlines. Use the Horizontal (X) Axis command from the Format menu to add the gridlines. Select the title and edit it so that it reads PLANNED EXPENDITURES. To accomplish this, select the Title command from the Edit menu. Edit the legend so that the legend contains the years the purchases will be made.

3. View the chart changes in Print Preview.

4. Save the changes to the CHARPRA2.WKS spreadsheet and close.

CHAPTER REVIEW

The charting features of the Works spreadsheet allow you to create a wide variety of charts by highlighting all or part of the information in the spreadsheet. Line and bar charts contain a horizontal axis and a vertical axis. The horizontal axis typically represents categories and the vertical axis typically represents values. A pie chart is used to represent values proportionally.

Information in a linked chart is updated automatically when changes are made to charted information in the spreadsheet. A linked chart can be changed by reformatting titles, labels, gridlines, and borders. Even colors and fill patterns can be changed. Wedges in a pie chart can be exploded to emphasize the slices in the chart. Data labels can be added to a pie chart, providing up to two kinds of information for each slice.

REVIEW QUESTIONS

TRUE-FALSE

Write your answers on a sheet of paper.

1. A range of cells is basically the same thing as a horizontal axis.

2. Categories are usually represented on the horizontal axis of a bar chart.

3. You can specify the type of chart you want to create in the Create New Chart dialog box.

4. When charting more than one column of values, you must define the range of cells in the Create New Chart dialog box.

5. You can only edit the legends of pie charts.

6. The Display As Printed command is valuable for people with black-and-white printers.

7. The Patterns And Colors command box allows you to view changes without closing the dialog box.

8. To duplicate a chart, use the Copy command on the Edit menu.

9. A legend is a numeric scale that appears on the horizontal axis of a chart.

10. You can delete a chart from a spreadsheet by selecting it and pressing the Del key.

SHORT-ANSWER QUESTIONS

Write a brief answer to these questions on a sheet of paper.

1. How can you create a legend for a chart when the information needed for the legend is not within the range of highlighted cells that are represented in the chart?

2. How can you switch between charts and the spreadsheet they are based on?

3. What are two ways you can use to open the chart-type dialog boxes?

4. How can you change the fill patterns for bars in a bar chart?

5. Which elements of a linked chart can be changed by using the Font And Style dialog box?

LESSON APPLICATIONS

1. Open the PLAN5.WKS spreadsheet, and save it as CHARPRA3.WKS. Use CHARPRA3.WKS to create a bar chart for equipment income for 1995, 1996, and 1997. Title the chart EQUIPMENT INCOME. Make two duplicate copies of Chart1. Change both copies to 3-D pie charts. One pie chart should chart data for 1996; the other should chart data for 1997. Change the chart names to Equipment 96 and Equipment 97. Each chart should have its slices labeled with percentages. One chart should also be labeled with the values used to create them. Format the charts so that they will print in the landscape orientation. Save the spreadsheet under the existing name CHARPRA3.WKS.

2. Reformat the Equipment 97 chart, which you created in Exercise 1, so that it is a 3-D line chart. Select a chart with gridlines. Change the fill patterns used in the ribbons. Change the color of Series 1st to Blue and the pattern to Sparse. View the Equipment 97 chart in Print Preview. Print one copy of the Equipment 97 chart. Save the changes under the existing name CHARPRA3.WKS.

C HAPTER APPLICATIONS

1. Open the BUDGET3.WKS spreadsheet. Create a combination chart that shows the total variable expenses for the three categories (Actual, Budgeted, and Over/Under)/vertical (Y) axis . Add gridlines to the chart. Add an appropriate title and legends to the charts. Change the fill pattern for Series 2nd to the dashed lines(– –). Save the spreadsheet under the existing name BUDGET3.WKS.

C HALLENGE EXERCISES

1. Create a spreadsheet, including appropriate labels and column formats, that contains quarterly sales information for each sales representative in a computer software company. The following table supplies the names of the sales representatives, along with their minimum quotas (total dollar amount of products that each representative must sell during a given period). Create formulas that calculate the total quota amount for all representatives for each quarter, and create formulas that calculate the total quota amount for all representatives for all four quarters. Name the spreadsheet QUOTAS.WKS and save it on your Student Data Disk.

QUOTAS.WKS				
SALES REP	QTR 1	QTR 2	QTR 3	QTR 4
Mitchell, R	80,000	84,000	88,000	93,000
Suzuki, T.	72,000	74,000	77,000	80,000
Harrison, W.	44,000	47,000	51,000	55,000
Ellsburg, M.	63,000	69,000	72,000	77,000
Zunski, H.	91,000	94,000	95,000	100,000

Format the values in the spreadsheet with the Comma format option.

2. Each sales representative earns a 20 percent bonus for every dollar he or she sells over the minimum quota. Use the amounts in the following table to enter actual sales for each representative, and then calculate the bonus for each representative for each quarter. Also, create formulas to calculate the total bonuses for all representatives for each quarter and to calculate the total bonuses for all representatives for all four quarters. You will need to modify the original spreadsheet you created to include new columns and rows.

SALES				
SALES REP	**QTR 1**	**QTR 2**	**QTR 3**	**QTR 4**
Mitchell, R	84,286	85,755	92,015	95,400
Suzuki, T.	78,670	84,926	85,250	86,159
Harrison, W.	44,238	48,802	53,095	57,900
Ellsburg, M.	67,498	68,750	72,506	79,150
Zunski, H.	94,025	98,251	101,254	111,945

3. Create a bar chart that portrays quarterly bonuses for all sales representatives and a pie chart that shows total yearly bonuses, segmented to show proportional earnings for all sales representatives. Change the chart names. Change the fill patterns used in the pie chart.

4. Click on the Create New Chart command to open the New Chart dialog box. Click on the Help text button. Read the resulting help screen. Click on the Category Labels colored text. Read the description of category labels. Click on Category Labels again to close the description. Click on Creating A Chart to read that help screen. Select Exit from the File menu to quit the Help program. Click on Cancel to close the New Chart dialog box.

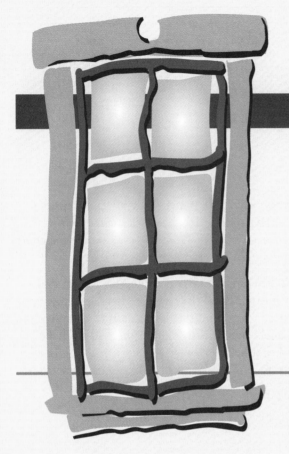

CHAPTER 12

INTEGRATING DATA

OVERVIEW

In this chapter you will learn how to integrate data created from different Works applications. Works allows you to copy information from one type of Works document (word processing, spreadsheet, database, or draw) and paste it into another Works document. You will have an opportunity to practice your data-integration skills, and you will learn how to use additional draw tools to enhance an embedded chart.

CONTENTS

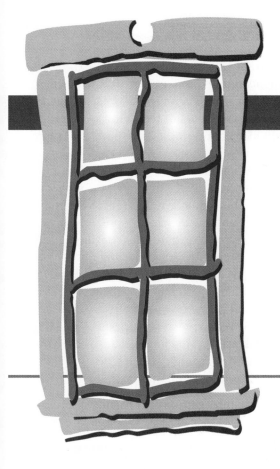

LESSON 33

INTEGRATING DATABASE, SPREAD-SHEET, AND WORD-PROCESSING DATA

OBJECTIVES

After completing this lesson you will be able to do the following:

- Copy data from a document created in one Works application and paste it into a document created in another Works application.

- Adjust and reformat integrated data to conform to the alignment and formats of data in the existing document.

KEY WORDS

In this lesson you will learn the meaning of the following terms:

embedded object   object
linked object

COMBINING DATA FROM MULTIPLE APPLICATIONS

Data compatibility is an important feature in Works because it allows data entered into one Works application to be pasted into a document created in a different application. For instance, a report on the financial status of a company might contain a great deal of text. However, for the report to be meaningful, it might also contain values or charts that represent financial status.

If you are creating such a report using the Works word processor and you need to add a table of financial information, you could type the table directly into the word-processor document. This requires you to set tab stops to separate and align the values in the table and then enter the spreadsheet values by typing them into the table. This approach can be time-consuming, since you must first enter the values and then proofread them carefully.

If the financial values that you want to include in the report already exist in a spreadsheet, you do not have to type the values into the report. Instead, you can copy the spreadsheet cells and paste the values directly into the word-processed document. When the data are pasted into the new document, the pasted data is called an **object**. Pasting an object can save you a great deal of time when entering and formatting data.

Works supports the following data-integration options:

- Copying spreadsheet and database information and pasting it into a word-processed document.

- Copying spreadsheet information and pasting it into a database.

- Copying database information and pasting it into a spreadsheet.

- Copying a spreadsheet chart and pasting it into a word-processed document.

- Copying draw objects from one application document and pasting them into another application document.

Although you can copy text from a word-processed document into a spreadsheet or a database file, this approach is rarely used. Text created by the word processor is usually not in a format that can be used in a spreadsheet or database without a great deal of reformatting and manipulation.

BASIC PROCEDURES FOR INTEGRATING DATA

One of the simplest ways to integrate data is to copy and paste information from one document to another. This can be done within the same application tool or between two application tools. The basic procedures for integrating data are simple:

1. Highlight (or select) the text, object, or other data you want to copy. Then choose the Copy command from the Edit menu. (You can also use the Cut command, but the data will be removed from your original

document.) Works places a copy of the selected information into the Clipboard.

2. Open the document into which you want to paste the information. If the document is already open, select the document's name on the Window menu to display the document in the active window.

3. Position the insertion point or highlight the cell or field where you want to begin pasting the information. Then choose the Paste command form the Edit menu.

INTEGRATING DATA INTO A WORD-PROCESSED DOCUMENT

One valuable use of data integration involves copying data from a spreadsheet or database file into a word-processed document. To integrate information from spreadsheet cells into a word-processed document, first highlight and copy the range of cells in the spreadsheet document. Then open the word-processed document and click on an insertion point where you want the information to appear. When you choose the Paste command, the spreadsheet information is inserted into the word-processed document.

To integrate database information into a word-processed document, change to the database list view and highlight and copy the information in the fields and records. Then open the word-processed document and click on an insertion point where you want the information to appear. When you choose the Paste command, the database information is inserted into the word-processed document.

LINKED VERSUS EMBEDDED DATA

The previous paragraphs describe how to copy embedded data. As mentioned in Chapter 14, however, there is another option for copying data from one document to another. Embedding a spreadsheet object into a word-processed document, for example, means that the object then belongs to the word-processed document. It is an **embedded object**. Its connection to the spreadsheet tool is broken. Works will add some of the spreadsheet tool commands to the word-processor menus, allowing you to adjust the spreadsheet with familiar commands. Works will also allow you to scroll through an embedded spreadsheet and make adjustments in row and column dimensions or switch between an embedded spreadsheet and its attached charts.

One thing Works will not do with an embedded object is update it when its source application is updated. For that, you must insert the data as a **linked object**. Fortunately, the linking process is similar to the steps for embedding an object. The only difference is the command you use to paste the data. Instead of selecting the Paste command, choose the Paste Special command. Works opens the Paste Special dialog box, as shown in Figure 33-1a. When the dialog box opens, Paste is the default option. Click on Paste Link, as shown in Figure 33-1b, to keep the object linked to its source document.

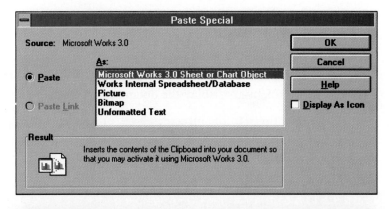

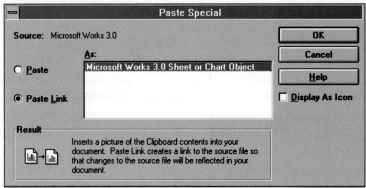

GUIDED PRACTICE

COPYING SPREADSHEET DATA INTO A WORD-PROCESSED DOCUMENT

In this exercise you will copy (embed) a portion of a spreadsheet into a word-processed document—a brief memo that informs the vice president about projected purchase amounts.

1. If necessary, start Works and open the word-processed document PURCHASE.WPS. Save the document as PURCHAS2.WPS.

2. Open the spreadsheet document PLAN8.WKS.

3. Highlight cells A23 through D30 in the PLAN8.WKS spreadsheet.

4. Choose Copy (Ctrl +C) from the Edit menu.

5. Select PURCHAS2.WPS from the Window menu to display the word-processed document.

6. Click an insertion point at the start of the blank line between the word **PURCHASES** (one of the headings line for the incomplete table) line that begins **I have also created**. Add three extra lines before the insertion point.

7. Choose Paste (Ctrl +V) from the Edit menu to copy the spreadsheet data into the PURCHAS2.WPS document. Double click the inserted table.

Notice that it resembles a spreadsheet. Click the Gridlines command on the View menu to remove the gridlines from the table. Click outside the table.

After you have completed step 7, your document should resemble the one shown in Figure 33-2.

In the next steps, you will make alignment and other formatting changes to display the information in the same way it is shown in Figure 33-4.

8. Double-click on the spreadsheet information you have inserted in PURCHAS2.WPS. Works surrounds the spreadsheet with row and column headings, just as in a full-size spreadsheet, and with scroll bars, as shown in Figure 33-3. If you hadn't added the extra blank lines before double-clicking on the spreadsheet, Works would have displayed the spreadsheet tool over the word-processed document headings, making it difficult to align the columns with the headings.

9. Use the ADJUST pointer to widen the first column until the 1995 heading appears centered over the first column of values.

10. Click outside the Spreadsheet tool to check the alignment of the spreadsheet columns. Notice that the resize handles reappear.

11. Click once on the spreadsheet to display the resize handles. Although Works will display the Move pointer, you cannot move an embedded (or linked) object with the mouse. You can, however, resize an object. Click on the center-right handle and pull it to just short of the document's right margin. Release the handle. Works displays another column of values, the values for the year 1998. When works inserts a spread-

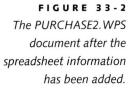

FIGURE 33-2

The PURCHASE2.WPS document after the spreadsheet information has been added.

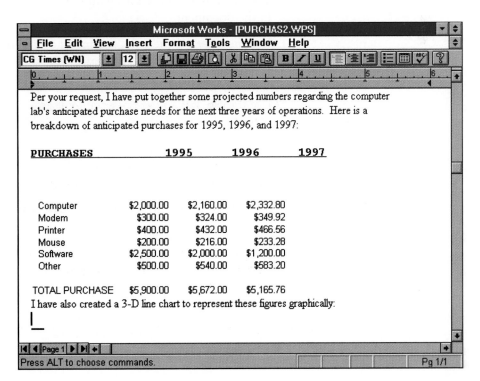

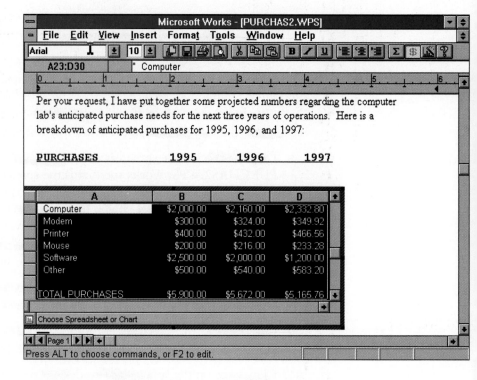

sheet in another document, it inserts the entire spreadsheet, even though it displays only those cells you have selected. You can display other cells if you wish.

12. Reduce the spreadsheet to its former size. Select the All Characters command from the View menu to display the tabs and paragraph marks in the document.

13. Use the ruler (or the Tabs command on the Format menu) to change the tabs used to align the 1996 and 1997 headings. Center those headings above the column of values for each year.

14. Use the ⌈Tab⌋ key to lengthen the underline under the headings so that it extends over every value in the last column.

15. Delete the three blank lines you added in step 6. Add a blank line after the TOTAL PURCHASES line in the spreadsheet. When you finish, your spreadsheet should resemble the one shown in Figure 33-4.

16. Save your changes to the PURCHAS2.WPS document.

FIGURE 33-4.

The embedded spreadsheet after adjustments.

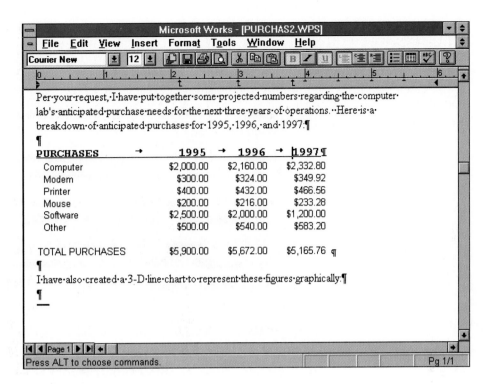

COPYING A SPREADSHEET CHART

A chart is a graphic object that can be selected, copied, and pasted into documents created with other Works applications. The first step in copying a spreadsheet chart is displaying it by selecting its name from the Chart dialog box. A displayed chart can be copied and pasted into another document by using the Copy And Paste commands on the Edit menu in the same way that you copied and pasted data in the previous Guided Practice. After a chart is pasted into another document, it can be resized by dragging on one of its resize handles.

GUIDED PRACTICE

COPYING A CHART INTO A WORD-PROCESSED DOCUMENT

In this exercise you will insert a 3-D line chart into a memo. This chart graphically portrays the spreadsheet data that you copied into a memo in the previous Guided Practice.

1. Start Works and open the PURCHAS2.WPS memo, if necessary. Save the memo as PURCHAS3.WPS.

2. Open the PLAN8.WKS spreadsheet, if necessary.

3. Select the PLANNED PURCHAS 3-D Line Chart from the Chart dialog box.

4. Choose Copy (Ctrl +C) from the Edit menu to copy the selected chart to the Clipboard.

5. Make the PURCHASE3.WPS window active by selecting it from the Windows menu.

6. Scroll to the end of the PURCHASE3.WPS document so that the last line of the memo is at the top of the screen.

7. Click on an insertion point at the beginning of the blank line above the end-of-file marker. Add an extra blank line.

8. If necessary to limit PURCHAS2.WPS to one page, reduce the top and bottom margins to .75" (use the Page Setup dialog box).

9. Choose Paste (Ctrl +V) from the Edit menu. Your screen should look similar to the one shown in Figure 33-5.

10. Click on the chart. Notice that like the spreadsheet in PURCHAS3.WKS, the embedded chart also has resize handles. Click and drag on the lower-right handle until the chart is 6.5 inches wide.

11. Preview the PURCHAS3.WPS document in the Print Preview window. Compare your print preview display with the one shown in Figure 33-6. Print one copy of PURCHAS3.WPS.

12. Save the changes and close the PURCHAS3.WPS document.

13. Close the PLAN8.WKS spreadsheet without saving your changes.

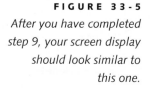

FIGURE 33-5

After you have completed step 9, your screen display should look similar to this one.

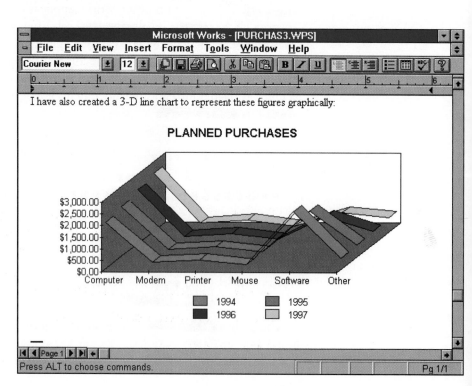

FIGURE 33-6
After you have made adjustments to the chart size in the memo, your Print Preview screen should look similar to this one.

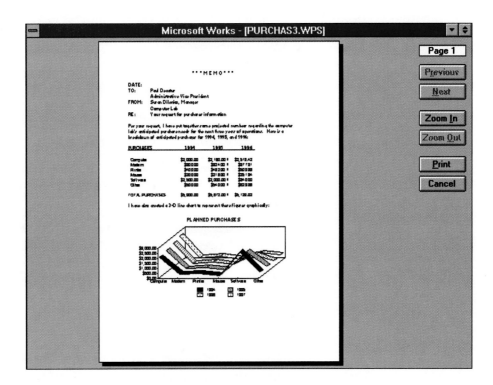

INTEGRATING SPREADSHEET AND DATABASE DATA

You can copy a range of spreadsheet cells into a database or you can copy selected database records and fields into a spreadsheet. Spreadsheet data and database data displayed in list view are organized and displayed in a row-and-column format. When you copy information from a spreadsheet to a database, columns are converted into fields and rows are converted into records. When you copy from a database to a spreadsheet, each field becomes a column and each record becomes a row.

GUIDED PRACTICE

COPYING DATABASE DATA INTO A SPREADSHEET

In this exercise you will copy purchase amounts from the EQUIPME3.WDB database into a spreadsheet, where you will calculate the totals for actual purchase amounts and the differences between projected purchase amounts and actual purchase amounts.

1. Start Works, if necessary, and open the AUGUSTPU.WKS spreadsheet. Save the spreadsheet as AUGUSTP2.WKS.

2. Open the EQUIPME3.WDB database.

Before you copy data from the database into the spreadsheet, you will sort the database so that records in the ITEM field are grouped together by category. You will perform two sorts: first by the CATEGORY field and second by the ITEM field.

3. Choose Sort Records from the Tools menu to display the Sort Records dialog box. Select CATEGORY from the 1st Field list box.

4. Accept the default Ascend A to sort in ascending order.

5. Choose ITEM from the 2nd Field list box.

6. Accept the default Ascend A to sort in ascending order. Press (Enter). You will notice that the first eight records contain COMPUTER SYS in the ITEM field.

7. In the PRICE field, drag to select the amounts for the records that contain COMPUTER SYS in the ITEM field, as shown in Figure 33-7.

8. Choose Copy ((Ctrl) +C) from the Edit menu to copy the highlighted information.

9. Select the AUGUSTP2.WKS spreadsheet document from the Window menu to display the spreadsheet.

10. Highlight cell D18, then choose Paste ((Ctrl) +V) from the Edit menu to paste the selected amounts.

11. Highlight cell D28 and type **=SUM(D18:D25)**. Click on the Enter box to enter the formula and place the calculated amount (11,959.29) in cell D28.

12. Highlight cells D18:D25 and format them with the Currency Format (2 decimal places) by using the Number command from the Format menu. Do the same for cell D28.

FIGURE 33-7
After you have sorted the EQUIPME3.WDB database, the first eight records contain COMPUTER SYS in the ITEM field. The PRICE field for each of these eight records is highlighted in this screen display.

#	ITEM	BRAND	SERIAL #	QTY	DATE PURCH	PRICE	CATEGORY
1	COMPUTER SYS	IBM	XT-1024-5T2	1	8/13/92	1085.25	HARDWARE
2	COMPUTER SYS	IBM	XT-1206-5T3	1	8/13/92	1085.25	HARDWARE
3	COMPUTER SYS	COMPAQ	C9664-Q54	1	8/13/92	1795.28	HARDWARE
4	COMPUTER SYS	COMPAQ	C9675-Q4	1	8/13/92	1795.28	HARDWARE
5	COMPUTER SYS	COMPAQ	C9676-Q9	1	8/17/92	1795.28	HARDWARE
6	COMPUTER SYS	IBM	XT-1047-5T2	1	8/23/92	1012.45	HARDWARE
7	COMPUTER SYS	BELL	B67269UT09	1	8/26/92	1695.25	HARDWARE
8	COMPUTER SYS	BELL	B67269UT911	1	8/26/92	1695.25	HARDWARE
9	MODEM	HAYES	H4775-84S	1	8/13/92	129	HARDWARE
10	MOUSE	MICROSOFT	C3K699926PN682	1	8/23/92	68.5	HARDWARE
11	MOUSE	MICROSOFT	C3K9626PN9261	1	8/23/92	68.5	HARDWARE
12	PRINTER	EPSON	E92602T843	1	8/29/92	329.85	HARDWARE
13	PRINTER	EPSON	E92702T844	1	8/29/92	329.85	HARDWARE
14	LOTUS 1-2-3	LOTUS	E-245-26269-1	1	9/2/92	349.85	SOFTWARE
15	MS-WORKS	MICROSOFT	M69266-86-26	1	8/27/92	178.25	SOFTWARE
16	MS-WORKS	MICROSOFT	M69266-92-45	1	8/27/92	178.25	SOFTWARE
17	MS-WORKS	MICROSOFT	M69266-62-83	1	8/27/92	178.25	SOFTWARE
18	MS-WORKS	MICROSOFT	M69266-92-47	1	8/27/92	178.25	SOFTWARE
19	MS-WORKS	MICROSOFT	M69266-26-46	1	8/27/92	178.25	SOFTWARE
20	WORDPERFECT	WORDPERF	J-6926-2025	1	8/30/92	385.5	SOFTWARE

Press ALT to choose commands, or F2 to edit. 1 24/24

13. Highlight cell D28 and choose Copy ([Ctrl] +C) from the Edit menu to copy the amount in this cell to the Clipboard.

14. Highlight cell C7, then choose Paste Special from the Edit menu. Because the Values Only default button is already selected, click on OK to copy the value $11,959.29 into cell C7 without copying the formula used to calculate the value.

15. Highlight cells D18 through D28, then choose Clear from the Edit menu (or press the [Del] key) to delete all the information in the highlighted cells.

16. Make EQUIPME3.WDB the active window, then use steps 7 through 14 as a guide to copy amounts for modem, printer, mouse, and software purchases from the EQUIPMEN3.WDB database to the AUGUSTP2.WKS spreadsheet and to calculate the totals. Paste each total value (without the formula used to calculate the value) into the appropriate cell in the AUGUSTP2.WKS spreadsheet (two hints: 1. use data in the category field if you are unsure which records can be combined and totaled, 2. one cell in column C of the AUGUSTPU.WKS spreadsheet will be zero). After you have completed these steps, your spreadsheet screen should appear similar to the one shown in Figure 33-8.

17. Format cells C8:C12 with the Currency Format (2 decimal places) by using the Number command from the format menu.

18. Save your changes to the AUGUSTP2.WKS spreadsheet, but close the EQUIPME3.WDB database without saving your changes.

FIGURE 33-8

After you have completed step 15, your AUGUSTP2.WKS spreadsheet screen should look similar to this one.

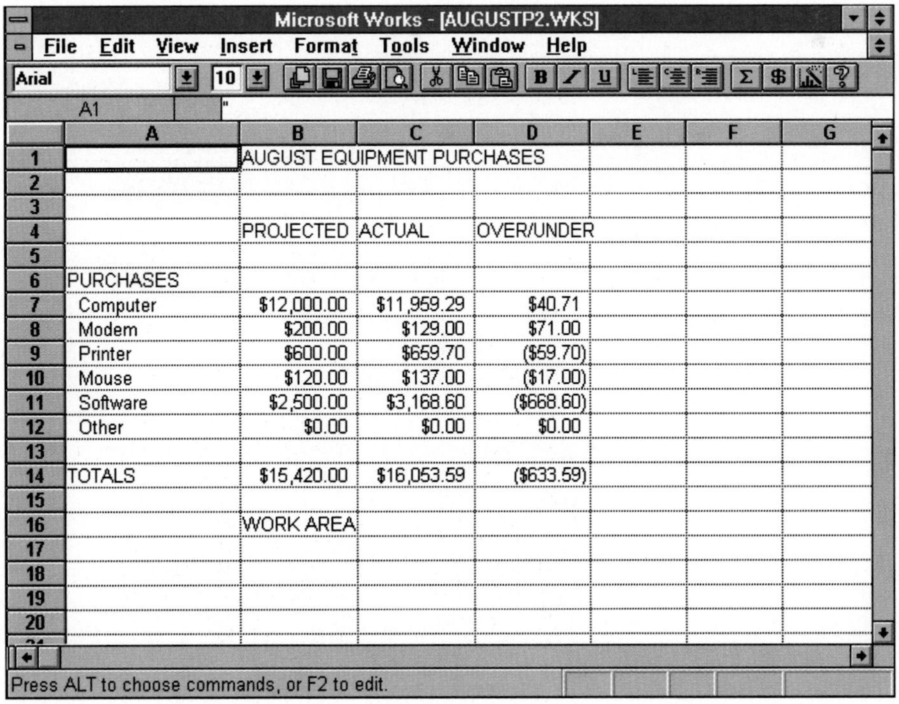

	A	B	C	D	E	F	G
1		AUGUST EQUIPMENT PURCHASES					
2							
3							
4		PROJECTED	ACTUAL	OVER/UNDER			
5							
6	PURCHASES						
7	Computer	$12,000.00	$11,959.29	$40.71			
8	Modem	$200.00	$129.00	$71.00			
9	Printer	$600.00	$659.70	($59.70)			
10	Mouse	$120.00	$137.00	($17.00)			
11	Software	$2,500.00	$3,168.60	($668.60)			
12	Other	$0.00	$0.00	$0.00			
13							
14	TOTALS	$15,420.00	$16,053.59	($633.59)			
15							
16		WORK AREA					
17							
18							
19							
20							

PRACTICE APPLICATIONS

1. Open the PURCHAS3.WPS document. Click on the spreadsheet to display the resize handles. Drag the right edge of the spreadsheet until a fourth column of values appears. Create a new heading for the new column: 1998. Reformat the document until the last heading is centered above the last column. Examine the letter and add 1998 to wherever the other three years are mentioned. Save the document under its present name.

2. Create a new word-processed document, and name it CONTPRAC.WPS. Open and copy the entire CONTACTS.WDB database, and paste it into the CONTPRAC.WPS document. Adjust the left and right margins using the Page Setup dialog box. Adjust the tab stops for the five columns, if necessary. (The tab stops are shown on the ruler. Working with tabs is easier if you select the All Characters command from the View menu)

3. Type and center the title **LIST OF CONTACTS** at the top of the CONTPRAC.WPS document window. Double-space the list of names, and apply boldface to the title. Save your changes to CONTPRAC.WPS and close the document. Close the CONTACTS.WDB database without saving your changes.

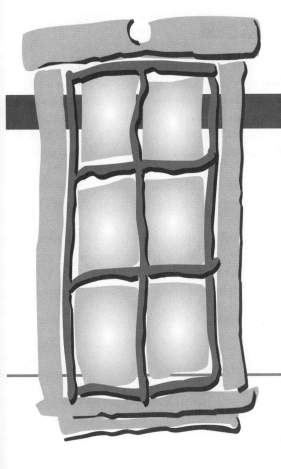

LESSON 34

USING THE DRAW TOOL TO INTEGRATE DATA

Microsoft Draw is available to insert drawings and **clip art** (complete, scalable graphic images) into word-processed documents, as well as into the form view of a database document. You can also edit drawings or clip art already inserted into a document or use Microsoft Draw to import and edit drawings created in other Works applications.

To display the Microsoft Draw window shown in Figure 34-1, you must first open a database file. Then select the Drawing command from the Insert menu—the process is the same whether you are working in a word-processed document or a database form. Works opens the Microsoft Draw window, featuring nine tools down the left border of the Draw window (maximize the window to display all nine tools) and Line and Fill color palettes across the bottom of the screen. When Works opens Microsoft Draw, it inserts a shaded box into your document, describing where the drawing will be placed. Works also highlights the first tool, the Arrow tool. The following table briefly describes the purpose of each draw tool.

TOOL	USED TO
	Select an object; drag to create a rectangle, drag to move objects
	Zoom in or zoom out using seven levels of magnification: 25% through 800%
	Draw straight lines
	Draw ellipses and circles
	Draw rounded rectangles or squares
	Draw rectangles or squares
	Draw an arc
	Draw free-form (open or closed) shapes
	Insert text (up to 255 characters) where you click an insertion point

All the draw tools are turned on in the same way. Click on the tool button to turn on that tool. Clicking on one tool turns off any other tool selected. For example, if you click on the Ellipse/Circle tool and move the mouse pointer over the Drawing window, Works changes the mouse pointer to a cross. Click the cross where you want the top of the ellipse (an egg-shaped form) or circle to be located. By dragging the ellipse or circle once it is created, you can change its shape and size.

The Line color palette allows you to change the color of the outline of any object. The Fill color palette allows you to fill an object with any of the

FIGURE 34-1

When the Microsoft Draw window opens, the last three of the nine draw tools are hidden. Maximize the window to reveal all nine tools. Notice that the Arrow tool is highlighted.

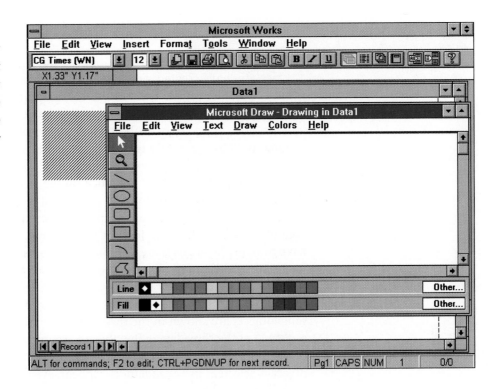

colors shown on the palette. When you select a color, a checkmark appears in that color, reminding you what color you have chosen. If you prefer to fill objects with patterns rather than colors, select the Pattern command from the Draw menu. This command allows you to choose a variety of patterns, as shown in Figure 34-2. The arrow on the menu to the right of the Pattern command indicates that Works will show you a sample of choices.

FIGURE 34-2

The Pattern command allows you to fill an object with any one of seven patterns.

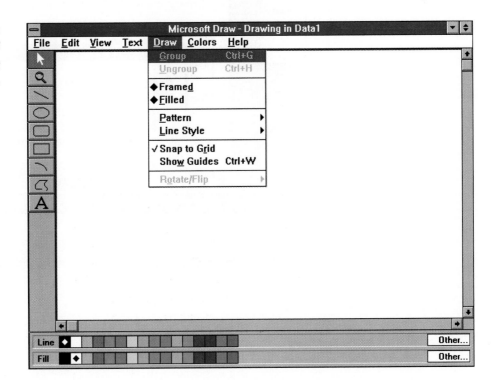

NSERTING DRAWINGS

Once you have created a drawing that you want to insert into a document, choose the Exit And Return to command from the File menu. Works displays the **destination document** name—the document you were working in when you opened Microsoft Draw—as part of the Exit And Return to command. Before it inserts the drawing in the destination document, Works displays a message box, shown in Figure 34-3, asking if you want to update the destination document. If you click on the Yes button, Works will insert the drawing into your document.

The elements of a drawing occupy different **layers**, although these layers are not apparent when you look at the drawing. A document window can have as many layers as there are objects. Because each object occupies a different layer, you can move one object on top of another. You can also rearrange the sequence of the layers by selecting an object and choosing Bring To Front or Send To Back from the Microsoft Draw Edit menu. The same objects are shown in the three displays in Figure 34-4a, b, and c. The sequence of the three layers the objects occupy was changed by selecting one of the objects and using the Bring To Front command. Notice that when an object is selected, its resize handles appear, even if some of the handles are actually covered by another object.

FIGURE 34-3
Works displays this message box before it allows you to update your destination document.

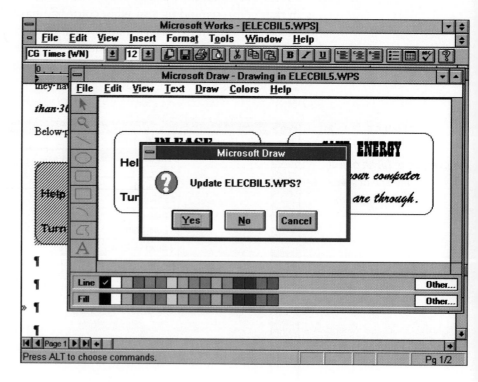

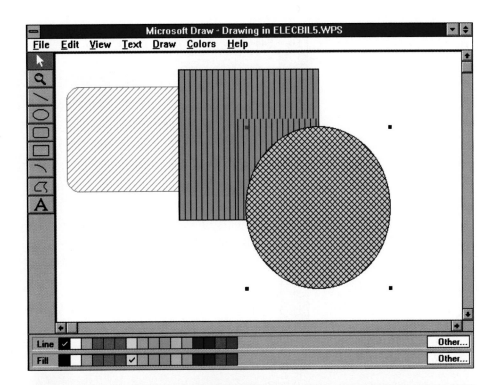

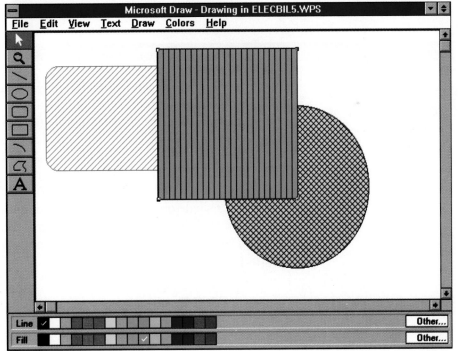

FIGURE 34-4C

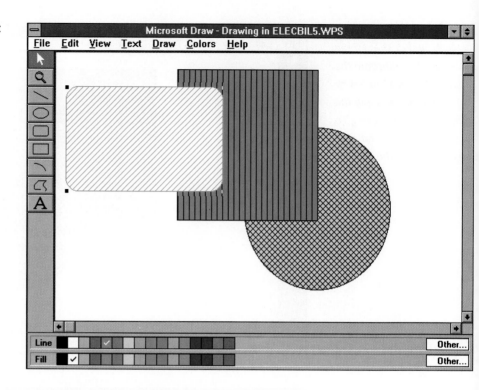

GROUPING AND UNGROUPING OBJECTS

A **graphic**, a visual, nontext image, may contain many individual objects, each occupying a different layer in the window. To combine separate objects so that changes made to one object will apply to all, you can **group** the separate objects into a single object. Selected objects can be combined into a single object by using the Group command ([Ctrl] +G) on the Draw menu. In Figure 34-5, the three objects first shown in Figure 34-4 are combined into a single object after selecting the Group command. Once objects are combined into a single object, you can move, duplicate, resize, and change the fill pattern as if they were one object. To make changes to only part of the graphic, you use the Ungroup ([Ctrl] +H) option on the Draw menu to **ungroup** the combined object.

INSERTING CLIP ART

In Lesson 17 you saw how a database form could be made more interesting by adding graphic elements to it. By opening the database's Insert menu, shown in Figure 34-6, you can see the variety of objects Works offers for insertion. For example, by selecting ClipArt from the Insert menu, you can use a collection of predrawn objects to enliven your document.

When you select the ClipArt command, Works inserts a shaded square into your document, showing where the clip art will be inserted. Then Works displays the ClipArt Gallery dialog box, shown in Figure 34-7. The clip art is arranged by category. The Category list box displays them, allow-

FIGURE 34-5

After you choose the Group command, the three objects are surrounded by a single set of graphic handles.

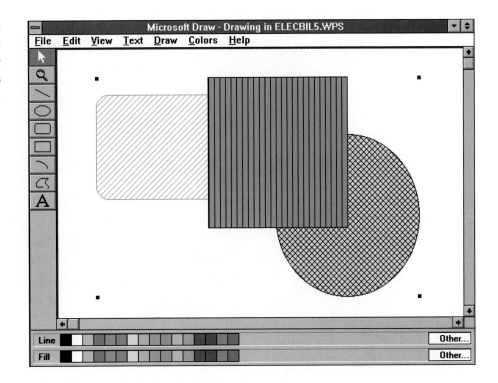

ing you to view only the clip art in specific categories. The default setting is All Categories, allowing you to see all the clip art available. Click on the scroll bars to scroll through the clip art. When you select a piece of clip art, Works highlights that selection with a thick border. Click on the OK button, and Works will insert that piece of clip art into your document. You can resize a clip-art object by clicking on it once to display the resize handles and then dragging the resize handles.

FIGURE 34-6

Works offers a variety of objects that can be inserted into a word-processed document or a database form.

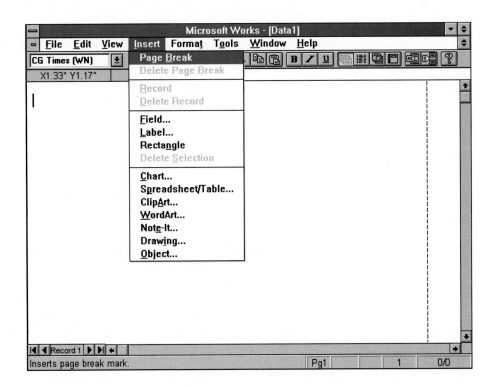

FIGURE 34-7

The ClipArt Gallery dialog box shows the clip art available for insertion into your document. Notice that at the top of the ClipArt Gallery dialog box Works displays the name of the destination file.

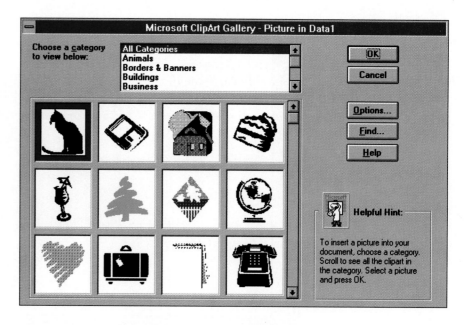

Microsoft Draw has many other features that are not covered here. Experiment on your own by creating a draw document and using each of the draw tools on the tool palette. If you need more information about these tools, refer to the Microsoft Works *User's Guide* that comes with Works, or read about the draw tool in the on-screen Help system.

GUIDED PRACTICE

MAKING CHANGES TO AN UNLINKED CHART

In the following steps you will open a word-processed document, create two drawings, add text to the drawings, and paste them into the word-processed document.

1. If necessary, start Works. Open the ELECBIL4.WPS file you saved in Lesson 11.

2. Save the file as ELECBIL5.WPS. Add a blank line at the end of the document and then type the following:

   Below please find two posters that will be placed throughout the computer lab.

3. Add another blank line and then select Drawing from the Insert menu.

4. Click on the Rounded Rectangle/Square tool button. Move the cross to where you want the top left corner of your graphic in the Microsoft Draw window. Create a rectangle approximately 2½ inches long and 1½ inches deep. Figure 34-8 offers an approximate size.

5. Select Copy ([Ctrl] +C) from the Edit menu.

6. Select Paste ([Ctrl] +V). Adjust the position of the second rectangle so that it aligns with the first rectangle by clicking on it and dragging it.

7. Enlarge the Microsoft Draw window until the Text tool button is visible. Click on the Text tool, and then place the Text pointer in the upper left corner of the first rectangle. Enter the following text. When you finish a line of text, click on the Text tool button again. Then click an insertion point where you want the next line to begin. Continue this process until all the text has been entered.

> PLEASE
> Help your computer lab
> save energy.
> Turn off your computer.

8. In the second rectangle, enter the following text:

> SAVE ENERGY
> Turn off your computer
> when you are through.

9. Now center all the text. To do this click on the text you want to center. Resize handles will appear. A dashed line will appear around the text when you click on it. Drag it left or right until it is centered. If the lines are too close together, click on the line and adjust the line vertically.

10. Click on the first line of text in the first rectangle to select it. From the Text menu, select Font. You must hold down the left mouse button to keep the list of font names open. You will select a font by moving the highlight to the font name you want. Change the first line to the font of your choice. Then choose the Size command from the Text menu. You can open the Size list box by simply clicking on the Size command. Make this line of text 18 points. Select the rest of the text and make it 12 points, formatting it in the font of your choice.

11. Select the first line of text in the second rectangle. Format it in 24 points in the font of your choice. Format the rest of the text in 18 points in the font of your choice. Some fonts may require that you choose a smaller point size before you can fit the text in the rectangle or you might want to enlarge the rectangle.

12. When you are satisfied with the text, open the File menu and click on the Exit And Return To command. Select the Yes button. Your drawings should resemble those shown in Figure 34-8.

13. Click on the drawings to display the sizing handles. Resize the width of the drawings so that they reach the right margin. What happened to the text within the drawings? Use the resize handles to return the drawings to their original size.

14. Use Print Preview to examine your document.

15. Close ELECBIL5.WPS and save your changes.

Now you will create a new database form and select five fields. Next you will create three shapes and experiment with colors, patterns, and placement of graphics. Then you will use the Zoom In/Zoom Out tool to

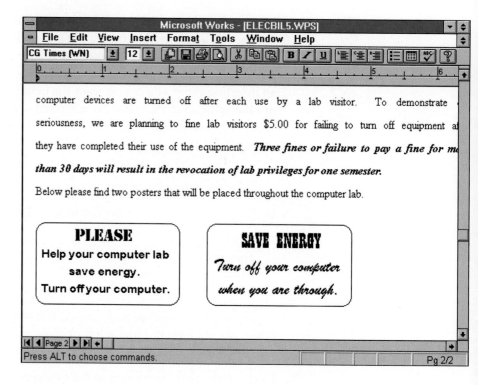

examine the shapes before you insert them. After that you will insert one of
them into a database form.

16. If necessary, start Works. Open a new database file.

17. In Form view create the following fields in the following order: LAST
NAME, FIRST NAME, MIDDLE INITIAL, PREFERRED SHIFT, and
TUTORING. If you wish, add blank lines before each field. Title the
form Computer Lab Personnel Profile. Drag the title until it is centered
over the form. You can drag fields by using the resize handles.

18. Choose Drawing from the Insert menu.

19. Next you will create three shapes, making sure the shapes overlay each
other, as shown in Figure 34-4a, b, and c. Use the Rounded
Rectangle/Square tool to create a rounded rectangle in the Microsoft
Draw window. Next use the Rectangle/Square tool to create a square.
Finally, use the Ellipse/Circle tool to create a circle.

20. Using the arrow tool, click on the circle to select it, then give the circle a
blue fill color by using the Fill color palette.

21. Select the rectangle and give it a red outline by using the Line color
palette.

22. Select the square and then choose the Bring To Front command from
the Edit menu. Practice the same command with the rectangle and
circle.

23. Select the square. Click on the Pattern command from the Draw menu.
Choose a pattern. With the square still selected, choose green from the

Fill color palette. Select the circle and choose a pattern for it. Reformat the circle to a yellow fill.

24. Click on the square and change its outline to black by using the Line color palette. Give the square a pattern.

25. Holding down the Shift key, click on the rectangle, square, and circle. Chose the Group ([Ctrl] +G) command from the Draw menu. Move the shapes to the center of the screen. Click on the red box from the Line color palette. Then click on the black line box. Select the Ungroup command and use the Cut command from the Edit menu to delete the circle.

26. Delete the rectangle.

27. Select the square to display its resize handles. Drag the square's resize handles so that it shrinks to a rectangle. The rectangle should resemble the rectangle shown in Figure 34-9.

28. Select the Pattern command and choose the first option, the no-pattern sample box. Click on the white Fill pattern box.

29. Click on the Text tool button, and click on an insertion point in the rectangle. Type **Important**. Format the text in the font of your choice. Resize it to 14 points. Widen the rectangle if you need to.

30. Select the Exit And Return To command from the File menu. When the Microsoft Draw message box appears, click Yes.

31. Drag the drawing until it is just to the right of the PREFERRED SHIFT field.

FIGURE 34-9
After step 28, your Microsoft Draw screen should resemble this one.

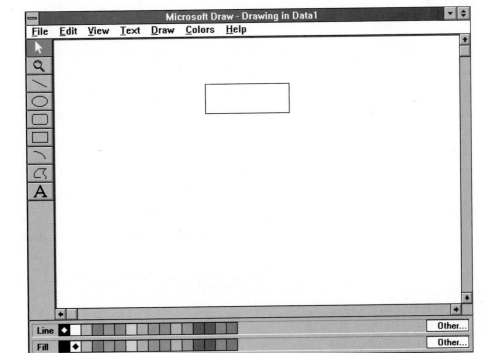

FIGURE 34-10

*After you have completed
step 32, your database form
view should look similar
to this one.*

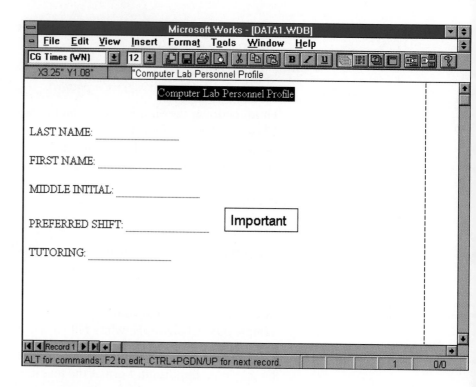

33. Double-click on the drawing to return to Microsoft Draw. Reform the rectangle so that it has a red outline. Return to the database file. Your form should resemble the form shown in Figure 34-10.

34. Examine the new form in Print Preview. Print the document.

35. Save the document as PERSPRO.WDB. Close the file.

PRACTICE APPLICATION

Open ELECBIL5.WPS and add two more posters to the bottom of the memo. The posters should be square. The first poster will contain the text in the first column below; the second poster will use the text in the second column:

DO YOUR PART	BE ENERGY SMART
TURN OFF	TURN OFF
YOUR COMPUTER	YOUR COMPUTER

Use the font and size of your choice, but fill the drawings with text. If the memo wraps to a second page, reduce the margins until the entire memo fits onto one page. Save the file as ELECBIL6.WPS. Print one copy of the file and then close it. Remember to change the reference in the memo's last line of text from **two posters** to **four poster**.

CHAPTER REVIEW

Works allows you to integrate data in several ways. You can copy and paste both text and objects from one Works tool to another. After copying data to another application, you may need to reformat the data to accommodate format differences between the two files. Objects embedded in a document do not change when the source document changes. Linked documents do change when their source documents change, allowing linked documents to be updated automatically.

You can use the draw tool in the word-processor and database applications. Objects occupy separate transparent layers in a document window, but they can be grouped and treated as a single object. You can create objects in Microsoft Draw and add text to those objects.

REVIEW QUESTIONS

TRUE-FALSE

Write your answers on a sheet of paper.

1. You can copy spreadsheet information into a word-processed document, but text from a word-processed document cannot be copied into a spreadsheet document.

2. You can copy one or more columns from a database into a spreadsheet, but you cannot copy rows from a database into a spreadsheet.

3. To copy information from a spreadsheet into a word-processed document, use the Copy command with a spreadsheet window active and the Paste command with a word-processed document window active.

4. After you have copied information created in one application and pasted it into a document created in a different application, you may have to reformat and realign the copied data.

5. To switch between open documents, use the Window menu.

6. You can have multiple documents created with the same application open at a time, but you cannot have documents created with two different applications open at the same time.

7. When you copy text from one document into another, the information is pasted starting at the insertion point or highlight.

8. When a spreadsheet chart is pasted into another document, it can only be embedded.

9. A chart that has been unlinked from its spreadsheet can be linked again by using the Group command on the Microsoft Draw Edit menu.

10. Text can be added to drawings, but that text cannot be formatted.

SHORT-ANSWER QUESTIONS

Write a brief answer to these questions on a sheet of paper.

1. What does the term data compatibility mean in terms of Works' data-integration capabilities?

2. What importance does the row-and-column format of data have in copying information between spreadsheet and database files?

3. How do data-integration capabilities save you time in creating documents?

4. Briefly explain how a graphic object like a chart is positioned in a document.

5. Why might you sometimes have to adjust column widths after you have copied information between a spreadsheet file and a database file?

LESSON APPLICATIONS

1. Open the word-processed document SUPPLIES.WPS, and save the document as SUPPLIE2.WPS. Read through this document carefully. Add today's date to the memo. Notice that spreadsheet information and two charts are to be inserted into the memo. The information to be integrated is contained in the SUPPLIES.WKS spreadsheet that you worked on in previous lesson applications. Use your knowledge of Works and your judgment to create the charts based on the spreadsheet information, then copy the information and charts to SUPPLIE2.WPS. Save your changes and close SUPPLIE2.WPS.

2. Open the PERSPRO.WDB file. Add a rectangle beside the MIDDLE INITIAL field. Inside the rectangle type **OPTIONAL**. Format the text in 24 point Arial. Find a piece of clip art depicting a floppy disk and insert it in the lower right corner of the form, just below the last field. Inspect the form in Print Preview. Save the document under its name.

3. Open an untitled word-processed document. Click on the Drawing command to open the Draw tool. Open the Help menu. Click on the Tools command to open the Using MS Draw's Toolbox help screen. Click on each of the underlined topics and read the resulting screen. Once you are in one screen, you can use the browse buttons ([<<] [>>]) to move from one Help screen to another. What is the advantage of holding down the Shift key as you drag a line?

CHAPTER APPLICATIONS

1. Open the word-processed document INCOMEME.WPS and save it as INCOMEM2.WPS. Find the location in the document where income values are to be inserted from a spreadsheet and position the cursor there. Then open PLAN3.WKS and copy the equipment income labels and amounts into the INCOMEM2.WPS document. Change the character size of the pasted information to match the character size used in the memo. Format the document so that all columns and headings align correctly.

2. Using the information you have pasted into INCOMEM2.WPS, create a 3-D bar chart from that information and insert it below the last sentence in the memo.

CHALLENGE EXERCISES

1. Your Student Data Disk contains a spreadsheet named SALES.WKS. The first four columns of this spreadsheet need to be converted to a database. Create a new database with four fields, using the labels ITEM, UNIT COST, PRICE, and QTY SOLD. Save the new database file as HARD-SALE.WDB. Use your integration skills to copy the four columns of spreadsheet information into the new database file. Use your judgment to format the information in the fields.

2. After you have finished formatting the new information in the HARD-SALE.WDB database, perform the following sorts and create the following reports. Use your judgment to determine whether the instruction calls for a sort or a report.

   a. Print all records in which the QTY SOLD field is greater than 50 and in which the UNIT COST field is greater than $1000.

   b. Print a listing of all records in the HARDSALE.WDB database. The printout must include the net profit earned from all sales. Hint: Create a field called NET PROFIT. Then create a formula for the field. Your formula will need to multiply the results of PRICE less UNIT COST by QTY SOLD. Be sure to total the NEW PROFIT field.

   c. Except for the cells in the ITEM field, format the other cells so that their values are displayed as currency.

   d. Print a listing that shows only the ITEM and the NET PROFIT for each item in the database.

3. Open the word-processed document REQUEST.WPS and save it as REQUEST2.WPS. Copy the records you produced in Exercise 2a into the REQUEST2.WPS document. Use your judgment to determine where to paste the records in the REQUEST2.WPS document. Make any necessary formatting changes, then save your changes and close the REQUEST2.WPS document. Save the changes and close the HARD-SALE.WDB database. Close the SALES.WKS spreadsheet without saving any changes.

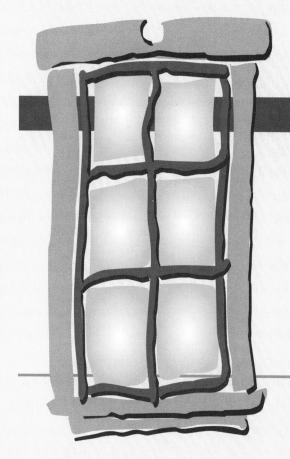

CHAPTER 13

DATA

COMMUNICATIONS

OVERVIEW

In this chapter you will learn how to use the Works communications tool to send and receive data over the telephone lines between computers that are equipped with modems. Even if you do not have a modem or access to a remote computer, you can still examine the Works communications features and review the procedures that are normally used to set up a Works communication document.

CONTENTS

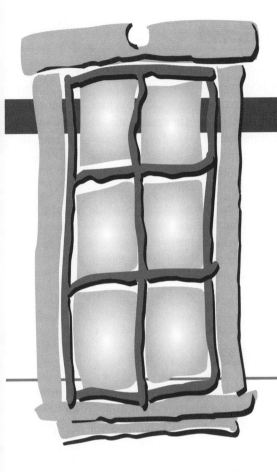

LESSON 35

DATA COMMUNICATIONS BETWEEN COMPUTERS

OBJECTIVES

After completing this lesson you will be able to do the following:

- Explain the difference between a commercial information service and a bulletin board service.

- List the equipment needed and general procedures that must be followed to access an information service or a bulletin board service.

KEY WORDS

In this lesson you will learn the meaning of the following terms:

bulletin board service (BBS) logging off
electronic mail (e-mail) on-line
information services off-line
logging on sysops

OMMUNICATING WITH COMPUTERS

The Works communications application, a modem, and a computer are all you need to send and receive information over telephone lines with another computer with similar equipment. Text messages can be typed and sent simultaneously while you are connected to another computer, or you can create a text or document file first, then transfer the file. You can even transfer applications and graphic files. You can use your computer to send or receive information across town, across the country, or around the world.

Your communications needs may be as simple as connecting to the computer of a friend who lives across town. For example, you may want to transmit some of your Works files over the telephone lines. This type of connection can be accomplished if the computer you want to access is turned on and set to answer when you dial the computer's telephone number. You can even access your home computer when you are at work (or your work computer when you are at home), by leaving the computer turned on and set to answer the call.

NFORMATION AND BULLETIN BOARD SERVICES

Several large companies have established **information services** that take advantage of the growing popularity of computer communications. These information services use large computer networks that provide access to vast amounts of data on almost any subject. For example, you can use an information service to get the latest news and weather reports, do research, go shopping, play games, plan trips, and send **electronic mail** (**e-mail**) messages to business colleagues and personal friends. E-mail can be used to send simple text files (without formatting code) that were created **off-line** (not connected) or to type messages that are sent while you are **on-line** (connected).

Services such as CompuServe and GEnie provide access to many popular computer utility and desk-accessory program files. To receive these kinds of files, you must use the special file-transfer procedures provided in the Works communications tool. These procedures help to prevent the loss of data during the communication transfer process.

A **bulletin board service** (**BBS**) is another type of information service that provides a forum for users to exchange information about topics of common interest. Often a BBS is operated on a personal computer in a person's home, although some bulletin boards are driven by large computers and can support hundreds of calls at a time. Bulletin boards—covering topics from airplanes to computers to zoology—exist around the world, and many provide file-transfer capabilities for sending and receiving formatted documents or program files. Some also allow you to exchange e-mail messages with other members of the BBS.

Most information services charge a subscription fee, as well as an hourly rate, for the time you spend connected to the service. When you subscribe, the service sends you a packet with directions for **logging on** and **logging off** (beginning and ending communications sessions), along with instructions on how to find specific information in the computer's databases.

Some bulletin board services also charge a fee to join or a monthly service fee, but you can probably find several bulletin boards in your local dialing area that provide services without charge. The people responsible for managing BBSs are called **sysops** (system operators). The sysop has access to all the information sent to and received from other computers, including e-mail messages you send to BBS members. Departments of schools and colleges often have student volunteer sysops, who set up and manage a BBS to provide students with information about academic and extracurricular programs and events. If your school or community provides a public-access BBS, you may be able to use your computer to connect to the system, access information, and send and receive e-mail, at little or no cost to you.

PRACTICE APPLICATION

The research for Exercise 1 was part of a Challenge Exercise at the end of Chapter 4. If you have already done the research, review your notes and complete the written report of findings.

At a computer store, get information on a computer information service, such as America Online, Prodigy, or The WELL. Find out what the service costs and what benefits are offered. Also find out what equipment and software are needed to connect a personal computer to a service. Write a brief report about the potential value of database information services for computer users.

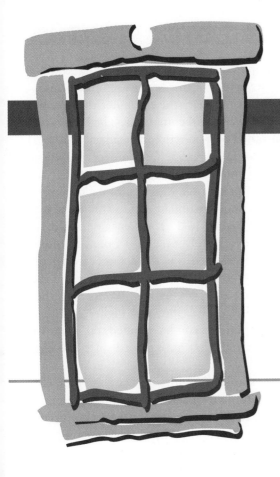

USING WORKS TO COMMUNICATE

OBJECTIVES

After completing this lesson you will be able to do the following:

- *Specify communications settings and default changes for sending and receiving data.*

- *Explain how to log on to an information or bulletin board service.*

KEY WORDS

In this lesson you will learn the meaning of the following terms:

baud rate	*handshake*	*protocol*
buffer	*log-off*	*script*
capture	*log-on*	*stop bit*
data bit	*parity*	*upload*
download	*port*	

ESTABLISHING AND ENDING A COMMUNICATIONS SESSION

Modems, phone lines, and computers are the hardware required to support data communications. However, for this hardware to be of use, communications software must be installed on the computer to control the way communications take place between two computers. The Works communications tool, which was installed on your computer when you installed the other Works applications, will create a document that allows you to communicate with another computer.

When you select the communications tool in the Startup dialog box, Works displays a blank communications document window and opens the Easy Connect dialog box, shown in Figure 36-1. The Easy Connect dialog box (also available on the Phone menu by selecting Easy Connect) offers a quick way to go on-line (make connections) using the default settings of the Works Communications tool. After you enter the phone number you are calling in the Phone Number text box and click on OK, Works dials the number and opens the Dial Status dialog box, shown in Figure 36-2. The Dial Status dialog box displays the number you have called, the name of the service (this is optional), and the seconds that have passed since you began the communication.

To end a connection you have established with another computer, click on the Dial/Hangup button on the toolbar or select the Hang Up command from the Phone menu (only available if you have established a connection). If you have a connection, clicking on the toolbar button or selecting the command will display the OK To Disconnect? message box, shown in Figure 36-3. Click on OK and Works will break the connection.

FIGURE 36-1

The Easy Connect dialog box allows you to quickly establish communications with another computer.

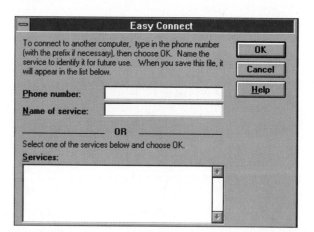

FIGURE 36-2

After you begin your communication, the Dial Status dialog box displays the status of your call.

FIGURE 36-3

Works prompts you for approval before it disconnects a communication.

Working with services such as bulletin boards (BBSs) requires additional steps:

1. When you have reached the service, type the **log-on** information required to establish a connection with the computer's database. Information services generally require an account name and a password that the service provides when you subscribe.

2. When you have finished a session, type the **log-off** information that tells the remote computer you want to end a session. Directions for logging off are provided with the packet of information you receive when you subscribe to a service.

3. After you have finished a session, be sure to log off properly. You can end a session at any time. **However, the disconnect signal may not be immediately detected by the remote computer and your on-line charges may continue to mount, even after you have hung up.** Using the correct log-off procedures helps to ensure that the on-line time charge is limited to the time you are actually connected.

4. After you have ended a session, you can scroll the communications document window to read the transmitted information. If you saved the captured information according to the instructions described below, you can locate that file on your disk and open it into a word-processor window for reading, reformatting, editing, and printing.

Although entering the service you are calling in the Easy Connect dialog box is optional, it is a good idea to do so. When you save the communications document you have created, Works will add the name of the service to the list box at the bottom of the Easy Connect dialog box. It will also add the name of the last service you called to the bottom of the Phone menu box, allowing you to reconnect to that service simply by selecting the service name.

FIGURE 36-4

The Settings menu displayed.

Usually a different communications document is created and saved for each remote computer that you contact regularly. You can create and save as many communications documents as you wish. Then, when you want to communicate with a particular computer, you use the communications document created specifically for that computer.

Before naming and saving a new communications document, you need to make sure that the Phone, Communication, Terminal, and Transfer tab dialog boxes are set up in a way that will make it possible for you to make a connection and exchange data with a remote computer. These dialog boxes are listed on the Settings menu, shown in Figure 36-4, and can also be opened by clicking on Communication, Terminal, Phone, or Transfer Settings toolbar buttons. These settings are discussed in the following sections.

MAKING CHANGES TO THE SETTINGS DIALOG BOX

The Phone tab dialog box, shown with default settings in Figure 36-5, is displayed when you choose Phone from the Settings menu. The following paragraphs discuss the various sections of the tab dialog boxes. Not all these settings will change and some you will change only rarely.

THE PHONE TAB DIALOG BOX

CONNECT OPTION
This section has three options: Dial Once, Redial, and Auto answer. The first setting tells Works to dial a number once. The second tells Works to redial if the number called is busy. Selecting Redial makes the Redial Attempts and Redial Delay text boxes active. The number you enter in the Redial Attempts text box determines how many times Works will retry a number. The Redial Delay number determines how many seconds Works will delay before it redials. Choosing the third connect option, Auto Answer, prepares Works for answering a call from another computer.

DIAL TYPE
If you have a touch-tone phone, choose Tone. If you have a pulse or rotary phone, select Pulse. Tone is the default option.

THE COMMUNICATION TAB DIALOG BOX

You will probably change the settings on the Communication tab dialog box, shown in Figure 36-6, more than any other Settings dialog box.

PORT
A **port** is a connector that links your computer by cable with another device. You modem is connected to a port. The Port list box contains those ports Works discovered when it was installed on your computer. Works selects the most likely port and lists it in this box.

FIGURE 36-5

The Phone tab dialog box and its default settings.

Settings
Phone	Communication	Terminal	Transfer

To connect to another computer, enter the phone number (and prefix if necessary) and press the OK button. If there is a problem, Works will explain what it is and help you try to solve it.

OK

Cancel

Phone number: 555-5555

Help

Name of service:

Connect option
- ● Dial once
- ○ Redial
- ○ Auto answer

Redial attempts: 6
Redial delay: 50

Dial type
- ● Tone
- ○ Pulse

PARITY

Parity is a simple error-checking procedure that some data communications programs use to make sure characters are not corrupted (altered) during transmission. The default setting is None; the other options can be used to meet the requirements of the remote computer (the computer you are communicating with).

DATA BITS

A **data bit** is a binary digit (1 or 0) that is used to make up characters. Some computers and some software packages use seven bits to represent each character of data; other computers use eight bits to represent each character. Eight data bits is the default setting. Seven data bits can be chosen to meet the requirements of the remote computer.

STOP BITS

A **stop bit** signals the end of each character transmitted from one computer to another. Some software packages require that one stop bit be sent at the end of each transmitted character, while other packages require two stop bits. One stop bit is the default setting. Two stop bits can be chosen to meet the requirements of the remote computer.

BAUD RATE

The **baud rate** is the speed at which information is sent across telephone lines. The term is derived from the name of the Frenchman, J.M.E. Baudot, who invented the automatic telegraph late in the nineteenth century. One baud is equal to a transmission rate of approximately one bit per second (bps). Common baud rates are 1200 (1200 bits transmitted per second), 2400, 9600, and 14,400 bps. The higher the baud rate, the more rapidly data can be sent and received. The baud rate you select must be one that both the sending and receiving computer modems can support. For example, if you have a 2400-baud modem but the remote computer has a 1200-baud modem, you will need to change the Baud Rate list box selection to 1200.

HANDSHAKE

In data communications, **handshake** is the term used to describe the **protocol**, or rules, the two communicating computers follow to establish, regulate and control the flow of data. Data are transmitted in blocks of a set number of characters, or **bytes**. Handshaking occurs when the sending computer transmits a block of data with a character that tells the receiving computer, "This is the end of the block; I'm waiting for your signal that you are ready for me to send the next block." When the receiving computer is ready, it sends back a character that says, "I'm ready for the next block."

The default setting on the Handshake pop-up menu is Xon/Xoff, a setting designed to help prevent the loss of transmitted data. Xon is a signal to continue sending data; Xoff is a signal to stop sending data. If the remote computer does not support Xon/Xoff, select the None setting. The Hardware setting is used only if the computers are connected directly by a cable rather than by telephone lines.

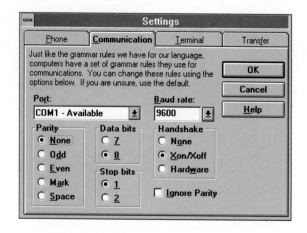

IGNORE PARITY

Check this box if you want no parity setting.

THE TERMINAL TAB DIALOG BOX

A terminal is a computer specifically engineered to communicate with another computer. TTY is a generic emulation (or simulation) tool that is used to communicate with all computers and information services that do not require a specific terminal. Works will emulate five terminals, all displayed on the Terminal list box, shown in Figure 36-7, so you can match the terminal of the computer you are communicating with. The other settings on the Terminal tab dialog box specify how Works displays characters on your screen and how your computer sends and receives information with another computer.

The ISO Translation list box allows Works to automatically translate special international characters when you select the country you will be communicating with. The End Of Lines options control how lines of text appear on your screen as you receive data from a remote computer. Select Add CR (carriage return) if text is not beginning at the left margin. Select Add LF (line feed) if incoming lines are printing over each other. You may need to experiment to determine whether the Local echo check box should be turned on or off. If you are connected with a remote computer and characters are not "echoed" on the screen as you type them, turn on Local echo;

if double characters are echoed on the screen, turn off Local echo. Deselect the Wrap Around check box if you do not want incoming text to wrap to the next line when it reaches the edge of the document window.

THE TRANSFER TAB DIALOG BOX

The Transfer tab dialog box, shown with default settings in Figure 36-8, is used to select the **protocol** that the computers will follow when data are **uploaded** (sent) or **downloaded** (received). Unless both computers use the proper **protocol**, they do not speak the same language. Some information and bulletin board services provide a choice of protocols, and almost all provide for either Kermit or XMODEM, which are supported by Works. Before beginning the file-transfer operation, you need to select one of these protocols to match the one used by the remote computer. The Line Delay text box determines how long Works should delay before sending another line of text. This setting, displayed in tenths of a second, is used if the remote computer cannot process your text as quickly as you send it. The Directory button allows you to select the default directory where the files you download will be saved. Clicking on the Directory button opens the Choose A Directory dialog box, shown in Figure 36-9, which resembles the Open dialog box.

FIGURE 36-8

The Transfer tab dialog box and its default settings.

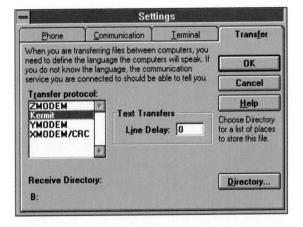

FIGURE 36-9

The Choose A Directory dialog box allows you to select a directory for your downloaded files.

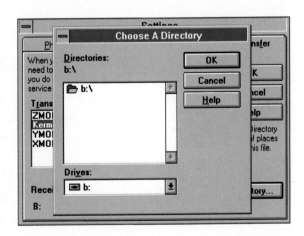

THE MODEM COMMAND

The final command on the Settings menu does not immediately feature settings, but it is still valuable. The Modem Setup dialog box, shown in Figure 36-10, lists the likely communication ports on your computer. If you click on the Test button, Works will examine your computer and tell you which port is connected to your modem. Works will draw the universal sign for No (Ø) across any of the four COM buttons not attached to your modem. The Advanced button displays a sophisticated Modem Settings dialog box, shown in Figure 36-11, that allows you to tailor your modem's interaction with Works. Consult the Microsoft Works *User's Guide* for a discussion of this dialog box.

CAPTURING TRANSMITTED DATA

When you download a file, Works automatically saves it to disk and gives you the opportunity to rename and move it. The data that scroll onto the communications document window during an on-line transmission, however, are saved by Works in a **buffer**, a special part of memory used for temporary data. If you exit the communications tool, the text is lost. Saving the communications document will not save the text, either—communications files only save settings.

If you want to save the information displayed on the screen, you must **capture** it. Choose Capture Text from the Tools menu (or click on the

FIGURE 36-10

The Modem Setup dialog box offers an automated examination of your computer's COM ports.

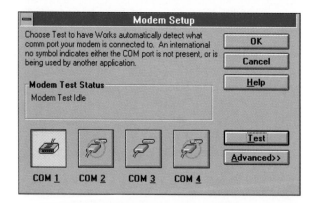

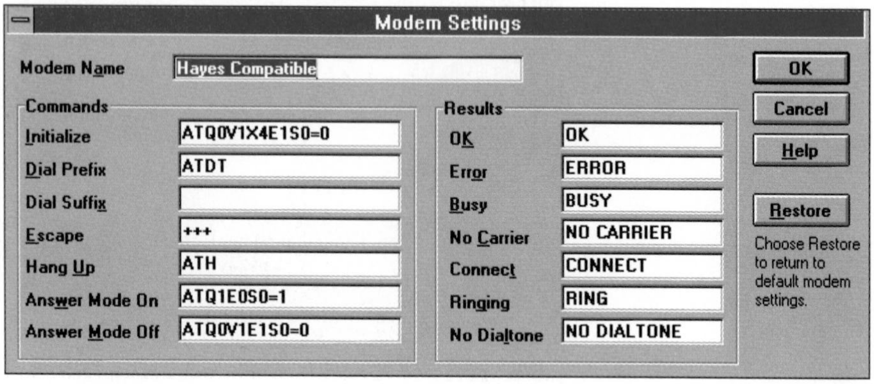

FIGURE 36-11

The Modem Settings dialog box offers ways to customize how Works interacts with your modem.

Capture Text toolbar button) and Works opens the Capture Text dialog box, shown in Figure 36-12, which is similar to the Choose A Directory box shown in Figure 36-9. Works asks you to choose a name for the new file and a directory where it will be saved. In Figure 36-12, Works suggests the file name capture.txt. You can give a different name to the text to be captured or you can accept this name by clicking on the OK button. Using the capture features makes it possible to save and review transmitted information at your leisure.

CREATING AND EDITING SCRIPTS

A **script** is a record of commands that can automate repetitive or time-consuming communications tasks. For example, if you sign on to a stock-quote reporting service every day, you can record a sign-on script. When you play the script back, it will sign on to the stock-quote reporting service automatically. Scripts are attached to communications documents and saved with them. You can edit a script, delete a script, and rename a script. You can, however, only have one sign-on script per communications document.

To create a sign-on script, you must first be connected to a remote computer. Select Record Script from the Tools menu. Works opens the Record Script dialog box, shown in Figure 36-13. If you choose the default in the Type Of Script section, Sign-On, Works will automatically name script 1 Sign-On. If you choose Other, Works will let you type in a script name. Works will display the REC message in the lower right corner of your screen to tell you that a script is being recorded. Works will record both your entries and the responses of the remote computer. You can choose Cancel Recording from the Tools menu at any time (or press the Esc key). If you choose Cancel Recording while playing back a script, Works will display the Stop Script Playback? message box, shown in Figure 36-14. You can also stop recording by selecting End Recording, from the Tools menu. The End Recording command only appears on the Tools menu once you have begun recording a script. Edit a script by selecting Edit Script from the Tools menu. Works will open the Edit Script dialog box, as shown in Figure 36-15.

FIGURE 36-12

The Capture Text dialog box displaying its default document name.

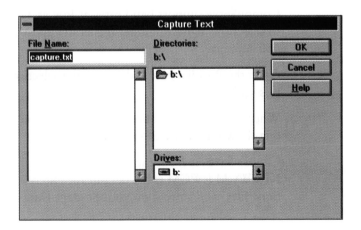

SHORT-ANSWER QUESTIONS

Write a brief answer to these questions on a sheet of paper.

1. Why is it often necessary to modify the Works default communications settings before you connect to a remote computer?

2. What is the difference between the communications settings for data bits and stop bits?

3. Why is a handshaking setting sometimes required to support the transmission of information between computers?

4. How do you tell Works to capture text that is transmitted and displayed on your screen?

5. How do you let Works know that you want to end an on-line session?

LESSON APPLICATIONS

1. Ask the computer lab manager, the librarian, or a computer store sales person for names of computer periodicals with local advertising. Read the classified ad section to locate telephone numbers and information about bulletin board systems in your area. If a voice telephone number is listed, call several BBS sysops for information about joining and using the system.

2. If you have a friend who has a modem-equipped computer, ask what communications settings he or she uses for data communications. Set these options in a Works communications document. Save the document under an appropriate name. If you do not have a friend who uses a modem, use the default settings in a Works communications document; then name and save the document.

3. If you and a friend have equipment and software for communicating, arrange to have the friend's computer set to answer your call at a pre-arranged time. When the call goes through, type brief messages to each other; then disconnect from the on-line session. Close the communications document.

CHAPTER APPLICATIONS

1. Call or visit your local university library and ask whether the university has an on-line database that you can connect with through your modem. Find out what communications settings are required, along with the phone number to use. Then use the Works communications tool to phone the database. Use the database to search for a particular book or collection of books on a particular subject or published by a single author.

2. Use one of the local BBS phone numbers you found in Exercise 2 of the Lesson Applications. Find out which communications settings the service requires, and create a communications document that can be used to dial the BBS. Set the Works capture feature to capture the data that will be transmitted. Follow the instructions provided by the remote computer to log on to the service. Examine some of the menus and features of the service, then log off.

CHALLENGE EXERCISES

1. Refer to the *Works User's Guide* to find additional information about the communications tool. The following topics are listed in the index of the *User's Guide*. Write a brief description of the purpose of the following communications options:

   Modifying scripts

   Comma (pausing dialing with)

   Sending Text and files

   Using Cue Cards, review the following procedures:

   Connecting to another computer

   Hanging up (disconnecting)

2. Refer to the *Works User's Guide* to find out additional information about ways to transmit text. Specifically, describe how text can be sent by typing on-line, by copying and pasting, and by uploading a text file.

3-D effects   Spreadsheet chart features that make the chart appear to stand out from the page.

A

absolute reference   A cell reference in a spreadsheet formula that gives Works exact information about which cell contains the value to be used. If the formula is copied to another cell, the absolute reference still refers to the same cell.

active cell   The highlighted cell in a spreadsheet.

alignment   The position of the left and right edges of text lines in a paragraph or cell. In Works, lines can be aligned left, right, center, or justified.

append   In a database program, to add a record to the end of the database.

application   A job, such as word processing or database management, that is performed using a computer.

application software   Software used to perform a specific task, such as word processing, database management, and so on.

area chart   A representation of information in the shaded area between a line graph and the X axis.

arithmetic operators   The symbols (+, –, *, /) used in formulas to denote the arithmetic operations of addition, subtraction, multiplication, and division.

ascending order   Alphabetized order from A to Z.

ascending sort   An A-to-Z alphabetized organization of records based on information in a field.

automatic page break   In Works, a chevron symbol (») that is automatically set to indicate the end of one page and the beginning of a new page, based on the document's top and bottom margins.

B

bar chart   A representation of information in a series of vertical bars.

baud rate   A measure of how fast digital information is sent across telephone lines. One baud is approximately equal to one bit per second.

bitmapped graphic   A type of digital image in which information is stored about every dot that makes up the image.

boldface   Refers to text that appears darker or heavier than normal text.

buffer   A special part of memory used for temporary data.

bulletin board service (BBS)   A type of information service that provides a forum for users to exchange information about topics of common interest.

bullets   Special display characters used to mark the beginning of the first line of each item in a list.

C

calculating field   A database field that contains information that is created as a result of calculations made on values in other fields.

capture   Placing information that is transmitted during an on-line session into a file for permanent storage.

cell   In a spreadsheet, the intersection of one row and one column.

cell reference   The location of a cell, described by the column letter followed by the row number.

cell reference bar   The area of the screen in the Works spreadsheet tool that displays the cell reference of the active cell.

character formatting   Attributes that can be applied to specific characters.

chart   A representation of spreadsheet labels and values in a picture format.

check box   A dialog box feature that lets you activate or deactivate a software feature by clicking on a small square box. When a check box is activated, an X appears in the box.